LETRAN
AN UNTOLD HISTORY

Volume I: 1620-1872

by FRANCISCO R. LIONGSON IV

2017
Gold Coast, Australia

The top front cover features a portrait ensemble of the Child Jesus in the arms of Our Lady of the Most Holy Rosary with the kneeling Letran founders, H. Fr Diego de Santa Maria OP on the left and H. Juan Geronimo Guerrero OP on the right, together with their respective patrons and wards. (Artist unknown ca. 1900, courtesy of © Colegio de San Juan de Letran). The bottom shows portraits of the school's outstanding alumni of the period (l-r): P. Fr. Juan Feng Shiming OP, St. Vicente Liem de La Paz OP, D.D. Jose Apolonio Burgos, and B.D. Jacinto Zamora.
The *colegial de letran* in the back cover is by Carl Johann Karuth, 1858. (From the Karuth Album courtesy of © Georgina Padilla Zobel de MacCrohon)

Designed by Dominique Louise Liongson

ISBN-13: 978-0-6482132-0-8
Copyright © 2017 by Francisco R. Liongson IV

International Edition

This publication is in copyright with all rights reserved. Subject to statutory exceptions and to provisions of relevant collective licensing agreements, no reproduction of any part may take place without the written permission of the copyright holder.

The author has no responsibility for the persistence and accuracy of URLs for external or third-party Internet Web sites referred to in this publication and does not guarantee that any content on such websites is, or will remain, accurate or appropriate.

Gold Coast, Australia, 2017
Email: inquiries@liongson.com
Website: www.liongson.com

 A catalogue record for this book is available from the National Library of Australia

*To all the alumni of Letran
specially to the graduating classes of
1965, 1969 and 1974
with whom I have shared
many fond memories.*

Alma Mater Hymn

Alma Mater! Letran, esplendente!
Como el sol es tu gloria sin fin!
Y perfuman los lauros tu ambiente,
como exhala su aroma el jasmin.

Orgullosos de ti y de tu historia,
nuestras almas desde hoy juraran;
conquistar por tu honor nuevas glorias!
Y jamas olvidarte, Letran!

Jesus Balmori

Contents

PREFACE	xiii
INTRODUCTION	xix
CHAPTER I - The Beginnings	1
Birth of a Military Order	1
Initiation into the Order	2
Evolution of the Cross of St. John	8
The Decline	10
The Order in the Philippines	10
CHAPTER II - Hermano Juan Geronimo Guerrero	13
Guerrero's Profile	13
The Early Supporters	14
The First Petition	17
San Juan de Letran	21
The Second Petition	22
Financial Affairs	24
Letran's Vice Patrons	25
Hermano Juan's Final Days	28
CHAPTER III - Hermano Fray Diego de Santa Maria OP	31
Ordo Praedicatorum	31
Province of the Most Holy Rosary	35
Kindred Souls	38
A Merger of Two Institutions	39
The Orphan	40
Alumni Profile	41
A Leveled Playing Field	44

Becas	45
A Disaster's Agony and Triumph	45
A Tradition Adopted	46
Fray Diego's Final Days	48
CHAPTER IV - For God and King	**51**
Patronato Real	51
The Mendicant Orders	54
Vanguard of Spanish Hegemony	56
Frailocracy	58
Letran under the Patronato Real	61
A Permanent Home	66
CHAPTER V - From Obras Pias to Friar Estates	**69**
Cost of Evangelization	69
Price of Salvation	72
Rise of Landed Estates	80
Legalizing Spurious Titles	80
Tagalog Agrarian Revolts of 1745	82
Agrarian Unrest of 1822	86
Seeds of Discontent	101
CHAPTER VI - Ecclesial Ties	**103**
The Dominican Family	103
The Third Order	104
Founding the Beaterio	108
The Trials Begin	109
A Passage Way to Letran	112
Our Lady of Aranzazu	113
Iglesia de San Juan de Letran	115
The Ascent of the Filipino Beata	118

CHAPTER VII - The Spanish Colonial Education — 121
- Education under the Habsburgs — 121
- 17th Century Education — 123
- Grammar School — 129
- 18th Century Education — 132
- 19th Century Education — 136
- Educational Reforms — 143
- Compromises to Reforms — 146
- Reaching the Limits of Forbearance — 148

CHAPTER VIII - Of Rogues and Martyrs — 153
- Quickest Way to Heaven — 153
- First Chinese Alumnus Bishop — 156
- Christianity Banned in China — 157
- The King's First Oriental Scholars — 157
- Dominican Martyrs of Fuzhou — 160
- Arrival of More Dominicans — 161
- Martyrdom of Feng Shiming — 162
- Schism of Fuan — 162
- The New Vicar Apostolic — 164
- The Accused's Version of the Schism — 165
- The Aftermath — 168

CHAPTER IX - San Vicente Liem de la Paz OP — 169
- A Mystical Encounter — 169
- Vietnamese Missions — 170
- Years in Letran — 173
- Return to Vietnam — 174
- New Champions of the Cross — 176
- Failed Social Experiment — 178

Forgotten Martyrs	179
An Epiphany	180
CHAPTER X - Purity of Blood	**183**
Origins of Racism	183
Legacy of Slavery	184
Roots of Religious Intolerance	187
Impact of Citizenship	188
1492-1519	191
Fundamental Laws of Indio Slavery	193
The Mexican Experience	197
Sistema de Castas	198
Consequences on Education	205
Impact on Filipinas	207
CHAPTER XI - Metamorphosis of a Slave Society	**209**
The Western Isles	209
Slavery in Filipinas	212
Slave Markets	220
An Abbreviated Caste System	223
Seeds of an Emerging Identity	226
CHAPTER XII - Rise of the Native Cleric	**227**
Educating the Indio	227
Enforcing the Patronato Real	235
Letran's First Non-Spanish Secular Clerics	238
The Conciliar Seminary	240
Secularization	247
End of the Religious Conspiracy	250
First Mestizo Sangley Dominicans	252
Victims of Propaganda	254

CHAPTER XIII - A New World Order 259
 Fall of Ancien Regime 259
 Rise of Spanish Liberalism 262
 Impact on the Spanish Church and Filipinas 265
 The Fall of Secular Parishes 270

CHAPTER XIV - Doctor Don Jose Apolonio Burgos 273
 Colegial de Letran 273
 Priest and Nationalist 278
 The Cavite Mutiny 285
 The Execution 296
 An Epilogue 298

SOURCES AND REFERENCES 305
NOTES 331
INDEX 377

ILLUSTRATIONS

I	Four Generations of Letran Alumni	xii
II	Letran Anda St. Portal Built in 1952	xviii
III	The Dominican Block Circa 1920s	xxiv
IV	The Kneeling Knight Hospitaller of St John	3
V	Philippe de Villiers l'Isle-Adam	9
VI	Grand Prior of Spain	12
VII	Letran's First and Second Home Sites	15
VIII	Guerrero's Letter to Felipe IV, 22 July 1622	19
IX	Letran's Vice Royal Patrons	27
X	Santa Maria's Letter to Felipe IV, 6 July 1644	32-33
XI	St Martin de Porres OP	37
XII	City Map of Manila, 1671	42-43
XIII	Founders Memorial and Letran's Parian Site	47

XIV	Legazpi-Urdaneta Monument	53
XV	Frailocracy	57
XVI	Letran's Royal Patrons	63
XVII	Leran Main Portal Built in 1887	67
XVIII	Felipe II, El Prudente	71
XIX	Different Locations Occupied by Letran	76
XX	Lot Acquisitions Forming the Letran Block	77
XXI	El Tulisan	87
XXII	Mother Francisca del Espiritu Santo OP	105
XXIII	Pasadiso Linking Santa Catalina and Letran	111
XXIV	Beata, Colegial and the Capilla de San Juan de Letran	117
XXV	Cover of First Philippine Printed Book, 1593	125
XXVI	Colegiales de Manila, 1847	135
XXVII	The Presidential Table	145
XXVIII	Letran Internos and UST Physics Laboratory, 1887	149
XXIX	Bishop Gregorio Luo Wenzao OP	155
XXX	Juan Feng Shiming OP	159
XXXI	Dominican Martyrs of China	167
XXXII	San Vicente Liem de la Paz OP	171
XXXIII	San Jacinto Castañeda OP	175
XXXIV	Lady of Aranzazu with St Vincent Liem's Bone Relics	177
XXXV	20th Century Letran Martyrs	181
XXXVI	Dominican Movers of the Spanish Golden Age	189
XXXVII	Isabel la Catolica, Reina de España	195
XXXVIII	Las Castas Mejicanas	203
XXXIX	Indio Genocide	208
XL	San Jacinto de China	219
XLI	La China Poblana	221

XLII	Fathers of the Native Secular Clergy	233
XLIII	Education Dispelling Ignorance	237
XLIV	The Native Secular Priest	245
XLV	Patrons of the Native Secular Clergy	249
XLVI	Carlos III	258
XLVII	The French Revolution	261
XLVIII	Promulgating the Spanish Constitution of 1812	263
XLIX	Doctor Don Jose Apolonio Burgos	272
L	Guardians of the Secular Clergy	275
LI	Controversial Governor Generals	281
LII	Alumni Casualty and Survivor of the Cavite Mutiny	289
LIII	GomBurZa	299
LIV	Letran Grand Cross	304

TABLES

I	Evolution of the Cross of St. John	6-7
II	Land Grants, 1612	79
III	Survey Summary of Philippine Friar Estates 1901-02	85
IV	Dominican Province General State of Affairs, 1893	97
V	Letran Higher Studies Curriculum, 1785	131
VI	Letran Primary Instruction Curriculum, 1886	138
VIIa	Letran Secondary Curriculum: General Studies, 1865	139
VIIb	Letran Secondary Curriculum: Applications, 1865	140
VIII	Other Courses Offered by Letran, 1865	141
IX	J. J. Virey's Sistema de Casta	201
X	Spiritual Care of the Souls in Filipinas, 1751-1761	241
XI	Manila Archdiocese Secular Clergy Composition	243
XII	Manila Archdiocese Secular Clergy Ethnic Profile	253

Plate I
Four Generations of Letran Alumni

Francisco Liongson y Tongio
1869-1919

Francisco Liongson y Alonso
1896-1965

Francisco Liongson y Ocampo
1921-1991

Francisco Liongson y Rodriguez
1951

Preface

I spent fifteen memorable years as a student at the *Colegio de San Juan de Letran Manila*. Like all its alumni, I am proud of Letran's cherished traditions and monumental history. I wrote this book to pay tribute to the school on its 400th foundation anniversary so that others may come to know and appreciate its extraordinary legacy to the Filipino nation. It is a history of an ancient institution of learning that played a significant role in the birth and continuing development of a young independent republic in Asia. It is an old story invigorated by new insights from recently uncovered documented facts. It is a history that shuns the characteristic halo effect of institutional renditions while presenting a fresh perspective from its alumni with all its blemishes intact.

My involvement in Letran began in 1954. During its annual alumni homecoming in November that year, the president of the *Ex-alumnos de Letran* (Letran Alumni Association) lamented the deteriorating standing of the *Colegio* in the country's educational system from the glory days of his youth some forty years hence. With a heavy heart, he declared that Letran was not the same institution of yesteryears. He focused on the failure of the alumni to impart the Letran spirit and love for the institution to the next generation as one of the critical causes. Many alumni children found their way to other centers of learning; withdrawing the very life force away from the *Alma Mater*. He challenged everyone present that day to be true *Letranenses* and not allow this situation to continue any further; thereby assuring the school's continuing pivotal role in the country's contemporary history. That alumni association president was my grandfather, Francisco Alonso Liongson, and his speech sealed my fate.

I was to enter Letran's portals upon reaching the required age much to the chagrin of our closest relatives and friends who argued that Letran was an anachronism overshadowed by more progressive elitist schools. They claimed further that the school's location was not safe considering that Intramuros was still ravaged by Manila's bloody and devastating liberation towards the end of the Second World War. Back then, the squalor of informal settlers filled the walled city and surrounded the school. In spite of all the resistance, my father, Francisco Ocampo Liongson, was obstinate in his declaration that for as long as I carried their name, *I was to study in Letran as he did; like his father and his grandfather did before him*. I would spend 15 years as a student in Letran and I had come to cherish the school as much as my forefathers did. Our values were molded by the school and made us into what we have become. It is in this sense of awe and gratitude that I pay tribute to my dear *Alma Mater*.

I completed kindergarten in 1958 at St Theresa's College Manila under Mother Redempta, the unforgettable Belgian sister of the Missionary Sisters of the Immaculate Heart of Mary (ICM). My awareness of Letran began just before I was enrolled there for grade one. On my first day in school, I was immediately immersed in Letran's many symbols. Their meanings would eventually attain more clarity as the years passed by.

Among these icons were the Letran Cross of St John, the Letran Knight, and the school's red and blue colors.

The cross of St John was always a part of our uniform. Contained in a patch, I learned to stitch it in the left breast pocket of our white short-sleeved shirts in grade school. By high school, a pin on our left collar replaced the patch. The ancient statues of Our Lady of Aranzazu and St John the Baptist, the school's patron saint, were enshrined in the college chapel. The monuments of Saint Vincent Liem de la Paz OP, martyr of the faith and a *Letranense*, towered over us in the grade school stairwell and the rectangular garden along the high school building. The monument of Manuel L. Quezon, Philippine president and alumnus, dominated the other garden plot along the collegiate building. The school's simple motto: "Deus Patria Letran" had a ubiquitous presence throughout the campus. Questions about the origins of these icons emerged when I began my research into the school's history.

Considering that the school is close to 400 years old at this writing, I wondered if there were any ancient, mysterious stories behind them all. Questions like: why is the Letran cross the way it is? Why is the Knight the school's symbol and mascot? How were the red and blue school colors chosen? How was Letran's motto formulated? The challenging aspects of this research centered on the founders of the school because of the limited and sketchy information about them. Who were Hermano Juan Geronimo Guerrero and Hermano Fray Diego de Santa Maria OP? Why did they found the school? Why were many churchmen and soldiers associated with the school? How did the school manage to nurture martyrs of the church and of the state? I uncovered fresh and exciting insights in my search for answers to these questions.

In developing the book, I discarded the standard traditional history about Letran and its founders. I ventured deeper into the original manuscripts and attempted to resolve conflicting accounts that tended to embellish the *wherefore and withal* of the school's journey through time, and most importantly to discern how the milieu affected the students.

Throughout its four centuries of existence, Letran had only two official history books. The first, written by Padre Fray Jose Valdes OP in 1691, was entitled *Relacion verdadera de la fundacion del colegio de los niños huerfanos de los Santos Apostoles San Pedro y San Pablo, de San Juan de Letran, de la ciudad de Manila en las Islas Philippinas, sacada fielmente de diversos papeles y escrituras autenticas, que se halla en el Archivo del dicho Collegio* (True account of the founding of the college of orphan boys of Saints Peter and Paul, of Saint John Lateran of the city of Manila in the Philippine Islands, taken faithfully from diverse authentic papers and manuscripts found in the College Archive). The second, entitled *Historia Documentada del Real Colegio de San Juan de Letran* (Documented History of the Royal College of Saint John Lateran), was written by P. Fr. Evergisto Bazaco OP in 1933.

Valdes' history was faithfully transcribed mainly from the *Libro de Asiento de Los Colegiales* (Boarders Journal), and two other documents. There was the Patent dated 29 May 1644 issued by the Dominican Master General, Most Rev. Master Fray Tomas Turco, confirming the college and erecting it as a College and House of the Order of Preachers. The other was the Acts of the 1652 Provincial Chapter of the Dominican Province of the Holy Rosary accepting and receiving the same college of orphans as a College and House of the Province.

The manuscripts and documents found in the Letran Section of the *Archivo de la Provincia del Santisimo Rosario de Filipinas* (APSR - Archive of the Province of the Most Holy Rosary of the Philippines), kept at the Santo Domingo Convent then, served as the principal source of Bazaco's history. In its latest index, the original collection consisting of eight volumes are presently stored at the Province's archives in Avila, Spain together with the rest of the APSR. Excluding Volumes III and IV, microfilm copies of the other six volumes consisting of 42 documents are available at the *Archives of the University of Santo Tomas, Manila* (AUST).

After conducting a fact-check on the information contained in both books, I uncovered certain inaccuracies which continue to appear in more recent renditions of Letran's history as running errors. Corresponding footnotes found in this book highlighted these errors. The Acts of the Provincial Chapters of the Province of the Holy Rosary contained most of the primary source of information concerning Letran before 1930. Unfortunately, these documents are not accessible to the public. The published *Historia* (history) series of the said Dominican Province were effectively secondary sources considering that the Acts constituted the primary source. The set included the following written accounts: P. Fr. Diego Aduarte OP (1693), P. Fr. Baltasar de Santa Cruz OP (1693), P. Fr. Vicente de Salazar OP (1742), P. Fr. Domingo Collantes (1783), P. Fr. Juan Ferrando OP (1870), P. Fr. Pablo Fernandez OP (1958), and P. Fr. Eladio Neira OP (2008).

Another essential secondary source culled mainly from the "necrological section" of the Acts is the *Catalogo* (catalog) containing the biographies of all the members of the Spanish Dominican Province until 1895 written by P. Fr Hilario Ocio y Viana OP (1895) and updated until 1940 by P. Fr Eladio Neira OP (2000). It was not surprising that every time a new writer updated the history, the same primary sources revealed fresh perspectives; filtered however by the writer's prejudices and his editor's censorship policies. Unable to gain access to the Acts, my research was limited to secondary sources like these.

The Letran News (TLN) and The Letran Mirror (TLM) are valuable sources of primary information for events after 1930.

Beginning as a page in the Varsitarian, the official school publication of the University of Santo Tomas, the TLN spun-off as an independent monthly bi-lingual magazine with the Spanish section known as *Letranense*. The newspaper format was eventually adopted recording all the events that transpired in the *Colegio* and providing literary and artistic outlets for the students. Just before the declaration of martial law in 1972, the TLN ceased to exist until 21 August 1976 when school publications were allowed to operate once again. Since then, the Lance (college students publication), Scroll (high school students publication), and Pages (grade school students publication) filled the vacuum once occupied by the TLN. It will not be until 1990 that the TLN was revived in a magazine format as the school's institutional bulletin catering to all its publics. In 2012, the TLN ceased to exist once again and was reborn as The Knight Life.

The TLM was the annual catalog of the College which featured a pictorial gallery of all the graduates, groups of undergraduates, and the school activities during the year. Now known as *Letranense,* the original name of the Spanish section of the TLN, the date of the annual's initial publication cannot be precisely determined as it appeared intermittently through the years. The earliest extant copy that I have come across was dated 1926.

I struggled miserably through the initial phases of my research. I was nevertheless relentless in looking for primary sources and books that were no longer in circulation. My commitment resulted in discoveries beyond my wildest expectations. I became an appreciative beneficiary of three principal formidable resources.

First, the archives of the Colegio de San Juan de Letran Manila, University of Santo Tomas, and the Dominican Province of the Philippines provided a wealth of information yet to be disclosed to the general public. The Philippine National Library, Rizal Library of the Ateneo de Manila University, and Ortigas Foundation Library are among the main Philippine resources that I have used extensively. I wish to express my gratitude to Br. Gerard Francisco Timoner III OP for granting access to the Archive of the Dominican Province of the Philippines. Br. Clarence Marquez OP and Br. Orlando Aceron OP for obtaining information from the Archive of Colegio de San Juan de Letran. Br. Raymond Mi for articles collected by the Archive of the Vicariate of Our Lady of the Rosary Province, and Mr. Regalado Trota Jose for the use of the UST Archives. I wish to acknowledge the contributions of Br. Pompeyo de Mesa OP for his guidance and counsel, Sr. Maria Jesusa Engingco OP for her insights into the history of the Beaterio de Santa Catalina, Mmes. Jhennie Caldito Villar, Ofelia Legaspi, Angelita de los Reyes and Mr. Randy Castillo for their assistance. I am indebted to many generous copyright owners of graphics used in the book. Their names are all adequately acknowledged herein.

Second, the internet world of digital libraries contained unbelievable volumes of digitized ancient and out-of-circulation books, journals and other information and graphic materials based in different parts of the globe. The Notes, Reference, and Source Sections duly noted all the specific contributors. I wish to however especially acknowledge the *Biblioteca Digital Hispanica* of the *Biblioteca Nacional de España* and the *Portal de Archivos*

Españoles of the *Ministerio de Educacion, Cultura y Deporte, Gobierno de España*. The former is for the digital rare books and graphics and the latter for the extensive online records involving Letran. I am most grateful to *España, Ministerio de Cultura, Archivo General de Indias* for making the digital facsimiles of the Guerrero and Santa Maria letters available to the public.

Third, the Interlibrary Loan System of Australia provided me access to virtually all the rare Filipiniana hard copy collections of libraries throughout Australia. I wish to acknowledge the Southport branch of the Gold Coast City Libraries which assumed the cost and served as my network gateway to the System. I have also extensively used the electronic resources of the National Library of Australia and the State Library of Queensland for which I am very appreciative.

I would like to especially acknowledge and thank two members of my family who have worked closely and patiently with me in the details, administrative and logistical aspects of completing this book. My beloved wife, Marilette, has been my principal source of inspiration for this undertaking and the sole motivating factor to complete it. She provided the necessary software applications to make writing and publishing an easier and a more professional experience. For the excellent front and back cover designs, I have my daughter Dominique to thank for. Her exceptional creative and digital skills, and faithful execution of the set directions and parameters produced the wonderful results for which I am truly grateful.

The book faced some problems and difficulties. Nevertheless, its completion had been a profound, rewarding and humbling experience. From the information collected, many new exciting facts had been uncovered and disclosed for the first time; providing fresh insights into a historical legacy all Filipinos, and especially the Letran alumni and families can truly appreciate. It is an honor and a privilege to have undertaken this challenging task.

Francisco R. Liongson IV

Plate II

Letran Portal Facing Anda St Built in 1952

- Artist unknown, 1952. © Colegio de San Juan de Letran

Introduction

The historical journey of *Colegio de San Juan de Letran* cannot be separated from the history of the Filipino nation as it played an essential role in its birth and continuing development. In this journey, the founding fathers and the alumni figured prominently in defining and shaping the Filipino identity and the nation's destiny as an independent republic either by their compliance or defiance of the policies and objectives of the contemporary authorities then. This narrative of Letran's four centuries of existence is divided into two parts consisting of three periods each. Certain personages of the Colegio who characterized and influenced each era symbolically represented each stage. The lives and times of these figures are dealt with greater depth to fully appreciate their impact and significance.

Historians agree that Philippine history could be divided into two annals with 1872 as the pivotal year. It is in this year that the Philippines embarked on a complete transformation. The dynamics before and after this year are entirely different. As such, we divided the history of Letran into two volumes. The first volume ends on the events that transpired in the 1872 Cavite Mutiny. The second volume begins after that. Each volume contains three periods each.

The First Period between 1620 and 1700 involved the contributions and continuing influence of the founding fathers, Hermano Juan Geronimo Guerrero and Hermano Fray Diego de Santa Maria. It is during this period that the Colegio first established its evolving culture and traditions and defined the qualities that constituted the unique character of the students. The Catholic influence and Dominican spiritual charism founded then would continue to mold the students' attitudes and values to this very day. Towards the end of this period, higher education admitted the *naturales de Filipinas* (natives of Filipinas) for the first time.

The Second Period between 1700 and 1826 was the time when the *Colegio's* students were directed essentially to serve God as ministers and missionaries of the Church. It was during this period that Letran alumni counted among the country's first native secular priests and the first non-Spanish Dominican priests. The glorious martyrdom of Saint Vincent Liem de la Paz OP was representative of this era with the saint serving as an apt symbol. While scanning through the Dominican archives, I discovered that the Vietnamese saint was not the first and only alumnus martyr. There was a forgotten Chinese Dominican alumnus by the name of Feng Shiming who died a martyr in China. Other outstanding Chinese alumni who became Dominican priests filled the period. This book recounts their forgotten stories and highlights the first native *mestizo de sangley* Dominican priests. It further provides the circumstances and reasons why *indio* Dominican priests were unaccounted for during this period of the school's official history.

The Third Period between 1820 and 1872 was characterized by the declining significance of the native secular priests and the awakening of a national identity brought about by the rise and struggle of the *Hijos del Pais* (Philippine-born) priests under a racist regime. The racial conflicts led to the awakening awareness of a Filipino identity. The life, works, and death of alumnus Dr. D. Jose Apolonio Burgos and companions consequently precipitated events that moved a nation towards the revolution of 1896 and the continuing struggle for independence after that. Burgos served as the period's defining icon but was not given the proper recognition and accolade in Letran's official annals.

The road to the Philippine Revolution and Independence aptly describes the Fourth Period between 1873 and 1920. The unstoppable entry of new ideas and commerce from foreign lands would open the eyes of a new generation of Filipinos. Under a new educational system, Letran alumni's educational options were broadened. Opportunities to study abroad would lead to the birth of an *ilustrado* (enlightened) elite. These sons of Burgos would lead a campaign for reforms and when left unheeded would lead a revolution towards achieving independence. Many alumni patriots would shed their blood during this period, but it would be Emilio Aguinaldo who would take the leadership of the armed struggle against great odds.

The Fifth Period between 1920 and 1970 found the country immersed in the task of nation building; struggling through cyclic periods of progress and destabilization. Three alumni presidents would lead the nation during this time, but it was Manuel L. Quezon's vision and tenacity that gained the recognition of Philippine independence from the United States of America. Quezon's national preeminence symbolized a time considered to be the apex of Letran's history when a distinguished alumnus of the Colegio occupied practically every vital government position. Ostracized by his own elitist class, alumnus Pedro Abad Santos advocated the cause of the peasant masses; planting the seeds of an alternative political order. However, the vicissitudes of a world war, communist insurgency, cacique politics and student unrest that followed led to the spiraling decline of the country towards conditions bordering anarchy; taunting the imposition of martial law.

The Sixth Period between 1970 and 2020 witnessed a series of constitutional changes spawned by the interests of a virtual dictatorship and later discarded due to its excesses. It was a time when the spirit of nationalism reached new heights and filipinization spurred changes in the country's educational institutions among others. An alumnus, Jose Maria Sison, would crystallize the impact of neocolonialism and champion a national democratic alternative. Amidst the turbulence of the times, the Philippine Dominican Province was established in 1971 and assumed most of the former Spanish Province's jurisdiction. Letran's future would hence be under the tutelage of Filipino Dominicans symbolized by their first Prior Provincial, Letran alumnus Br. Rogelio Alarcon OP. The Filipino Dominicans would hence be addressed as Brothers (Br) departing from the traditional Fray associated closely with their Spanish mentors. Working largely without the benefit of administrative skills and experience in the initial stages, the Filipino Dominicans gradually began to measure up to the challenge; heralding Letran's transformation into a university.

Writing about the six periods of Letran's history entailed many issues and challenges. The segment on the founding fathers, for instance, was constrained by the dearth of information regarding Hermano Juan Geronimo Guerrero. The period of the martyr alumni, on the other hand, demanded an explanation for the Colegio's focus on religious vocations and the glaring absence of native religious among the Dominicans. The word Filipino appeared for the first time during the third period of Letran's history and its awareness as an identity distinct from the Iberian Spaniard required an explanation of the racist concept of *Limpieza de Sangre* (Purity of Blood). Considering that among the Propaganda Movement's principal proponents were Letran alumni, the hatred for the friars fostered by the *La Solidaridad* required information to explain the underlying causes emanating from the *Patronato Real* (Royal Patronage) and the Friar Estate controversies. The period of nation building demanded an explanation of the dynamics involved in the politics of independence and the emergence of neocolonialism to appreciate the nationalist issues that gave rise to the student unrest and the imposition of martial law. These and other questions had to be dealt with to understand and appreciate better how they influenced the behavior of the *Colegio's* students.

Juan Geronimo Guerrero will forever be an enigma. What little we know about him are incomplete pieces of a puzzle. There are only two extant documents attributed to him and signed by him as *Hermano Juan Geronimo Guerrero*. In honor of the founder's name preference, he will be referred to as Hermano Juan henceforth *sans* the illusory titles of *Don* or *Capitan* which latter-day historians customarily used. His name will likewise be spelled out in the same manner he wrote it. These two documents provided enough insights to question specific information contained in the Valdes' history. Unlike Hermano Juan, the Dominican Province of the Most Holy Rosary better documented the life of his co-founder H. Fray Diego de Santa Maria.

What historians would normally do is to gather available reliable data and begin to draw plausible inferences from the information. The tale that is the most credible and generally accepted becomes the dominant record of history until a tale that is better documented comes along. I have therefore ventured to write a better-documented story of Letran. Stories of Hermano Juan being a Knight of Malta were, at best, feeble attempts to explain the military iconographies and traditions embedded in the school's psyche. It had always been a subject of acrimonious debate. What intrigued me about the Knight of Malta tale, however, was that if Hermano Juan actually *talked the talk and walked the walk* of such a Knight, then there is a high probability that he was one. There was therefore a need to explore the world of the Knights Hospitaller of the Order of Saint John. My journey following the footsteps of the Order recounted in this book reinforced my conviction that Hermano Juan was indeed a member of the Order of Saint John.

H. Juan and H. Fr. Diego were the school's cornerstones and symbols of 17th century Letran. The passing of the school to the care of the Dominican friars in 1640 shifted emphasis from His Majesty the King's military service to a religious one. The school's student archetypes in the 18th century assumed the forms of the venerable alumni martyrs of the church in China and Vietnam headed by Saint Vincent Liem de La Paz OP. Stories of their glorious deaths filled the halls of the Colegio with pride and gave credence to the educational and spiritual formation they received from the Dominicans. Amid the cheers and pomp however, there was a sense of disappointment among the *naturales* of the studentry since they could not avail of similar opportunities to die for Christ. We have to point out that the Filipino identity was still an evolving concept then and did not come to maturity until the Propaganda Movement in the late nineteenth century. Until such time, anyone born on Philippine soil would be referred to in this book as *indios*, *criollos*, *mestizos de español* or *mestizos de sangley* and collectively as *naturales* or *hijos del pais*. How this racial caste system evolved into the Filipino nation is discussed in this book.

I was surprised to discover that Letran was the first *Colegio* to accept *Indios* and *Mestizo de Sangleys* to study latin grammar and humanities at the end of the 17th century. Among these students were the first *naturales* of non-Spanish blood to be ordained as secular priests after completing their higher theological studies at the *Universidad de Santo Tomas*. There were also *mestizo sangley* Letran alumni who became the first ordained native Dominican priests during the second period of the school's history. The racial conflicts and social dynamics involved in these changes led to the awareness of a national identity that was viewed as uniquely different if not menacing to the national interests of Mother Spain. The most learned *naturales* in the 19th century were the secular priests and Letran alumni formed the vanguard in defense of the Filipino identity. At the height of this struggle, three Filipino secular priests were found guilty and executed for their alleged involvement in the Cavite Mutiny of 1872. Their suspicious deaths precipitated an unstoppable popular movement articulating the Filipino identity, the need for reforms, and the expulsion of the friars that culminated in the Philippine revolution of 1896 after remaining unheeded. Headed by Letran alumnus D. Jose A. Burgos, the martyrs of a newly conceived nation became the fitting symbols of Letran in the 19th century. In this book, we deal with the seeds of discontent that catapulted an endless list of Letran alumni patriots to shed their blood in the fight for freedom.

The imposition of American sovereignty over the Philippines in 1899 introduced sweeping changes in all aspects of Philippine life at the turn of the century. Filipinos cloistered in Spanish convents for three hundred years were about to be immersed in fifty years of rapid changes in Hollywood. The Spanish Dominican friars adopted the American educational system and had to learn English. During this period until the proclamation of independence in 1945, the Spanish speaking Letran alumni dominated the country's political landscape if not its economic, social and cultural aspects as well.

Manuel L. Quezon and two other alumni presidents after him led the nation and provided archetypes of the *Letranense* in the 20th century. Letran alumni filled the Supreme Court and the Legislature. It was the golden age of Letran. The hubris was lost with the destruction caused by World War II and with it the diminishing glitter of Spanish influence as well.

An independent nation rose from the ashes of war and the American culture and language emerged well entrenched. As it tried to keep pace with rapid changes, Letran began to lose ground to other more modern and expanding educational institutions. An ominous pattern of behavior began to emerge among the Filipino youth. The schools were producing brown American consumers greatly distanced from the nationalistic aspirations of their Spanish-speaking forefathers. This somber realization began to be more apparent in the Filipino's consciousness towards the 1960s. The country then was in the clutches of a new subtle form of foreign domination called neocolonialism. Not only were the country's leaders under the continued control of a world power, the Filipino mind was still dominated by foreigners. Among the leaders of the emerging struggle against this new form of western imperialism was Jose Maria Sison, a Letran alumnus.

The Spanish Dominicans continued to dictate the policies of Letran. After almost 400 years in the country, Filipinos were just beginning to assume positions of authority in the Dominican Province. With the 1970 student activism and mass actions shadowing it, the Letran administration underwent a silent transition and announced historic changes during the school's austere 350th anniversary celebration – replacement of the Spanish rector with a Filipino and the forthcoming establishment of a new Philippine Dominican province. The following year, Letran alumnus P. Fr Rogelio Alarcon OP became the first prior provincial of the Filipino province. The imposition of martial law in 1972 provided a respite from the turbulence of the times and for changes to be effected within the Philippine Dominican family. I included my memories during this period having witnessed and actively participated in many of Letran's historical milestones as student and as an official of the alumni association.

What happened to Letran after the Philippine Dominican Province took charge? What lies in the future for this cherished institution? It is for you the reader to read on and for me to end this introduction. The book is an honest history of one of the most outstanding educational institutions in the Philippines. It does not attempt to peacock its accomplishments neither does it hide its blemishes with a halo effect. It presents Letran as history recorded it to be and articulates it principally from the perspective of the students themselves. A viewpoint often ignored in official accounts.

The evolving philosophies and social mores of the changing times either guided or misguided the *Colegio's* direction. How the conflicts and struggles ensued and were resolved made the school what it is today. It was not an easy journey but it made the protagonists stronger, wiser and humbler. A school's greatness lies not in its beautiful physical structures. Neither does it rest on the scholastic depth of its professors alone. It emerges from the character, discernment and diligence of students who leave its portals enabled to contribute their share towards the peace, happiness and prosperity of all for God, Country and Community. And so on its 400th-anniversary jubilee celebration in 2020, *Letranenses* everywhere renew their pledge of continuing service to Deus, Patria, and Letran.

Plate III - THE DOMINICAN BLOCK

(1) Santo Domingo Church, (2) Santo Domingo Convent, (3) University of Sanrto Tomas, (4) Plaza de Santo Tomas, (5) Colegio de San Juan de Letran, (6) Beaterio y Colegio de Santa Catalina, (7) Beaterio y Colegio de Santa Rosa.

 - *US Army Air Corps, ca. 1930s*, Colegio de San Juan de Letran

Chapter One

The Beginnings

Colegio de San Juan de Letran is not the product of a rich history that is only four centuries old. The origins of the school's character, values and traditions date back much earlier. To better understand and appreciate the school, one has to go back in time to uncover its roots and to discern how its traditions commenced, developed, and fostered through the centuries. Letran's colorful story did not begin in 1620, the proximate year of its official foundation. It began 500 years earlier.

Birth of a Military Order

In the 11th century, a group of monks from the Benedictine monastery of *Santa Maria ad Latinos* were requested by the merchants from the city of Amalfi, Naples to provide care for the poor, sick or injured Christian pilgrims to the Church of the Holy Sepulchre in the Holy Land.[1] A *xenodochium* (guest house) located in the Muristan district of Jerusalem near the Church of St John the Baptist became the center of their hospice work. The First Crusade conquered the city in 1099. The overwhelming rise in patient numbers from wounded crusaders and the higher influx of pilgrims prompted the reorganization of the former guest house into a hospital. Dedicated to St John the Baptist, a foundation was established and consequently became known as the *Order of Brothers Hospitaller of Saint John of Jerusalem*.

Under the leadership of Blessed Gerard Tongue, the group of brothers vowed to live a life of poverty, chastity and obedience, wore a black habit and mantle with a white cross on the left breast, and lived under the Rule of St Augustine. In 1113, Pope Paschal II confirmed the hospital community as a religious order, put the hospital under his protection, and confirmed the acquisitions and donations of the Order in Europe and Asia in a papal bull.[2]

Large donations from the Christian rulers of Jerusalem, knights and nobles enabled the newly founded order to operate six other *xenodochia* in France and Italy along the pilgrimage road known by the name and style of Jerusalem.[3] In his bull of 1119, Pope Calixtus II confirmed the hospital's privileges and possessions.[4]

The brothers of the order begged for alms in the streets of Jerusalem to support their hospital mission and thereby attracted adherents from the visiting pilgrims. Among them were crusader knights led by Raymond du Puy who succeeded Blessed Gerard and became the Order's first Grand

Master in 1120.[5] Brother Raymond codified the Order's Rule and germinated a military arm that paralleled another monastic military order known as the *Order of the Poor Knights of Christ and the Temple of Jerusalem*.[6]

Also known as the Knight Templars, the latter order adopted the Rule of St Benedict as reformed by the Cistercians at the Council of Troyes in 1128 and wore the white Cistercian habit with a red cross. St Bernard of Clairvaux, the Templar's leading spirit, provided the *raison d'etre* for the warrior-monk when he declared that killing for Christ was *malecide not homicide*.[7] It was the termination of evil not murder. The Islamic concepts of *jihad* and *shahid* evolved into their Christian equivalents of crusade and martyrdom when, according to Pope Urban II, *all who die by the way, whether by land or sea, or in battle against the pagans shall have immediate remission of sins*.[8]

Thus the submissive mendicant hospital brothers consequently evolved into a major fighting force in the Islamic wars.[9] Hence known as the *Order of the Knights Hospitaller of St John of Jerusalem*, Pope Innocent II confirmed the privileges granted to the Order by his predecessors in 1135, issued the Order his protection and additional privileges in 1137, and appealed to the whole Church to support the Order in its task around 1140.[10]

The appeal led to the rapid growth and eventual establishment of the Order's Grand Priories in Provence, Auvergne, France, Italy, Germany, England and Aragon constituting in 1331 the seven divisions called *langues* (languages) of its principal members and supporters.[11] By 1461, Aragon was divided into two parts with the new division constituting the eighth *langue* to be referred to as Castile and Portugal.[12]

In his bull *Christianae fidei religio*, Pope Anastasius IV further granted the Order the right to admit priests and to be independent of the episcopal jurisdiction; making them directly under the Pope.[13] Three classes of members emerged in the Order: the Knights, the Chaplain Priests and the Serving Brothers of Arms.[14] Knights from noble families were known as the Knights of Justice.[15] Sons with fathers of noble birth but mothers of ignoble or plebeian origins were called Knights of Grace. The service of the poor remained the object of the Order, but by the beginning of the 13th century, the defense of the Catholic faith became its second official object.

Initiation into the Order

In the tradition of mendicant orders, they addressed each other in Latin as *Frater* (Brother). In Spain, the word *Frey* instead of *Fray* was used to call members of the military orders distinguishing them from the regular *friales* (friars).[16] The investiture rite of a new Knight Hospitaller of St John described hereafter by Chevalier Louis de Boisgelin's history of the Order published in 1805 capsulized the life the aspirant was about to embark on:

2

Plate IV

The Kneeling Knight Hospitaller of Saint John

- *Westminster Psalter, 1250 or later.* © the British Library Board Royal 2A. XXII, f.220.

Those who are determined to dedicate themselves to the service of the sick, and to the defense of the Catholic religion, in the habit of our Order, are received at their profession in the following manner: - They ought to be perfectly well acquainted that they are about to put off the old man, and to be regenerated; by humbly confessing all their sins; according to the established custom of the church; and, after having received absolution, they are to present themselves in a secular habit, without a girdle, in order to appear perfectly free at the time they enter into so sacred an engagement, with a lighted taper in their hands, representing charity; to hear mass, and to receive the holy communion.

They afterwards presented themselves most respectfully before the person who was to perform the ceremony, and requested to be received into the company of brothers, and into the holy Order of the Hospital of Jerusalem. He then addressed them in a short speech, to confirm them in their pious designs, to explain how salutary and advantageous it was to consecrate themselves to the service of the poor in Christ Jesus, to be constantly employed in works of mercy, and to devote themselves to the defense of the Christian faith - a favor which many had vainly attempted to obtain.

He proceeded to point out the engagement they were to enter into of perfect obedience; the severity of the rules, which would no longer permit them to act for themselves, which obliged them absolutely to renounce their own will and pleasure, and implicitly to comply with that of their superiors; so that if ever they felt an inclination to do one thing, they were, compelled by their vow of obedience to do another.

He next asked the candidate whether he found himself disposed to submit to all these obligations; whether he had ever before taken the vows in any other Order; whether he had ever been married; if his marriage had been consummated; if he owed any considerable sums; and if he were a slave: because, if, after having taken the vows, it were discovered that he had done any of these acts, or had been in the last-mentioned situation; he would be immediately stripped of his habit with disgrace, as a deceiver, and given up to the master to whom he formerly belonged.

If he declared that he had contracted no such engagements, the brother who received him presented him an open missal, on which he placed both his hands, and having answered all the above questions, made his profession in the following terms:

:Io N. faccia voto e prometto a Dio omnipotente, ed alla Beata Maria sempre Vergine, madre di Dio, ed a Sun Giovanni Battista di osservare peretuamente, con Iajuta de Dio, vera obedienza a qualunque superiore che unie sara dato do Dio, e dalla nostra religione, e di piu vivere senza proprio e d'osservar castita."

I N. do vow and promise to Almighty God, to the holy eternal Virgin Mary, mother of God, and to St. John the Baptist; to render, henceforward, by the grace of God, perfect obedience to the superior placed over me by the choice of the Order, to live without personal property, and to preserve my chastity."

Having taken his hands from the book, the brother who received him said as follows: "We acknowledge you as the servant of the poor and sick, and as having consecrated your self to the defense of the Catholic church:" To which he answered: "I acknowledge myself as such." He then kissed the missal, placed it on the altar, which he likewise kissed, and brought it back to the brother who received him, in token of perfect obedience. Upon which, the brother took the mantle, and showing him the white cross upon it, thus addressed him: "Do you believe, my brother, that this is the symbol of that holy cross to which Jesus Christ was fastened, and on which he died for our sins?" To which the new brother replied: "Yes, I do verily believe it." The other he added: "It is also the sign of our Order, which we command you to constantly wear." The new brother then kissed the sign of the cross; and the other threw the mantle over his shoulder in such a manner that the cross was placed on the left breast. The brother who had received him then kissed him, saying,: "Take this sign in the name of the holy Trinity, of the holy Virgin Mary, and of St John the Baptist, for the increase of faith; the defense of the Christian name, and for the service of the poor. We place this cross on your breast, my brother, that you may love it with all your heart; and may your right hand ever fight in its defense, and for its preservation! Should it ever happen that in combating for Jesus Christ against the enemies of the faith, you should retreat, desert the standard of the cross and take to flight in so just a war: you will be stripped of this truly holy sign, according to the statutes and customs of the Order as having broken the vow you have just taken, and cut off from our body as an unsound and corrupt member."

He then put the mantle on the new brother; tied it with strings round his neck, and said: "Receive the yoke of the Lord, for it is easy and light, and you shall find rest for your soul. We promise you nothing but bread and water, a simple habit and of little worth. We give you; your parents and relations a share in the good works performed by our Order, and by our brothers, both now and hereafter; throughout the world." To which the newly professed knight answered Amen, (that is to say) "So be it." After which the brother who had received him, and all who were present on the occasion, embraced and kissed him in token of friendship, peace, and brotherly love.[17]

The Knights of St John distinguished themselves in many battles for the Holy Land preferring death rather than dishonor their vows or take flight.[18] Even if outnumbered, they never withdrew from a confrontation and seldom did they retreat. The hospitallers differentiated themselves from the other military orders by the standard they carried and the surcoats they wore

Table I - EVOLUTION OF THE CROSS OF ST JOHN

Jerusalem Crosses

Fluted Patriarchal — Formee — Formee Patee

figure a — figure b — figure c

Rhodes Crosses

Moline — Formee Branchee — Ancree

figure d — figure e — figure f

a - Great Seal of the Convent of St. John of Jerusalem;[1] b - First Seal of Oxford Hospital circa 1234 and later;[2] c - Second Seal of Oxford Hospital circa 1234 and later;[3] d - Rhodian coin circa 1319-1360;[4] e - Caoursin etching circa 1480;[5] f - Pierre D'Aubisson heraldry 1486.[6]

EVOLUTION OF THE CROSS OF St JOHN

Maltese Cross

Maltese Cross   4 Tari Copper coin 1567 g

Letran Cross

Rhodian Cross   Letran Cross

[a] King 1931- photo-plate opposite page 10; [b] Salter (Revd) H.E. (ed). 1917 Vol III Frontispiece; [c] Ibid; [d] Foster (Revd.), Michael. *History of the Maltese Cross as used by the Order of St John of Jerusalem* 2004 www.orderstjohn.org/osj/cross.htm Accessed: May 30, 2015; [e] Caoursin, Guillaume, Gravures sur bois, *Stabilimenta*, Bibliothèque Nationale, Paris. [f] Velde, François. *Heraldic Tour of Rhodes.* www.heraldica.org/topics/orders/malta/rhodes.htm Accessed: May 30, 2015; [g] Gatt, John as cited in Foster *op. cite.*

over their mail armor. Both of which were black with a white cross.[19] In 1259, however, Pope Alexander IV decreed that the Knights of Justice should wear a different attire from the other brothers within the Order to distinguish them for their hereditary nobility – a strict requirement to earn the title and rank. Henceforth, the Knights of Justice shall *"in campaigns and in battles wear surcoats and other military decorations of a red color on which there shall be a cross of white color sown on it in accordance with that on your standard."*[20]

Evolution of the Cross of St. John

The white cross of St John underwent a gradual metamorphosis over the centuries evolving into one form or another; marking transitions in the Order's history.

The cross on the original Great Seal of the Convent of St John in Jerusalem was a Patriarchal Cross, which added an upper crossbar. The arms of the cross were slightly fluted. As such the Patriarchal Cross was most likely the original Cross of St John in around the year 1100.[21] The Order's military posture soon gave way to the Cross Formée and Pattée Formée with its 8 points more defined. Both early forms of the Cross of St John were Greek Crosses with Fitch and Foot found within the Krak de Chevaliers, a Syrian Castle of the Hospitallers from 1144 to 1271 and the seals of the Oxford Hospital circa 1234 and later.[22]

After the fall of its Acre stronghold to Islamic forces in 1291, the Order moved temporarily to Cyprus until it established sovereignty in the island of Rhodes in 1309.[23] Known hence as the Knights of Rhodes, the Order engaged primarily in naval warfare; patrolling and protecting the Levantine corridor from Islamic pirates.[24] With the eight *langues* established in 1461, an eight-pointed cross became more prominent in the order; evolving into Moliné, Formee Branchee or Ancreé Crosses with its ends splayed into an anchor-like shaped Rhodian Cross. The Knight's sojourn in Rhodes lasted until 1522 when the forces under Sultan Suleiman the Magnificent conducted a successful six-month siege.[25]

Through the intercession of Pope Clement VII who was a Knight of St John, Holy Roman Emperor Charles V granted Malta to the Order in 1530 as its new home where they would stay until 1798.[26] After surviving the Great Siege of 1565, the modern Maltese Cross made its appearance in the 2 Tari and 3 Tari Copper coins of the Grand Master Jean de la Vallete-Parisot in 1567. The cross is made from four straight lined pointed arrowheads, meeting at their points, with the ends of the arms consisting of indented "v's." The Maltese cross was to become the official white cross of the Knights of St John to this day known as the Knights of Malta. The eight languages did not uniformly adopt the Maltese Cross. Variations of the Rhodian Cross persisted until the end of 16th century as in the case of the 1570 Dutch cross used by the Harderwijk Commanderie.[27]

Plate V

Philippe de Villiers l'Isle-Adam
The Last of Grand Master of Rhodes and the First of Malta

- Artist unknown ca.1600s

The Decline

The Maltese phase of the Order's history witnessed the declining support of their eight languages in Europe. The protestant upheavals suppressed the English and German Catholic languages. The disappearance of the Islamic threat to mainland Europe and the unwelcome Papal interventions in the Order's internal affairs in Italy shifted the allegiances of the French and Spanish languages to their respective monarchs. With just three war galleys of their own, the Knights of Malta served as the vanguard of the victorious Holy League's fleet headed by a Knight of St John, Don Juan de Austria, in the 1571 Battle of Lepanto.[28] Far from the Holy Land, its diminished role in naval warfare rendered the Knight Hospitaller an anachronism and gained them the notoriety of being unwanted corsairs of the Mediterranean.[29] Left only with the support of the Italian *langue*, Malta fell to Napoleon Bonaparte in 1798 and eventually became a British possession in 1803.[30]

On 17 April 1802, the Spanish Bourbon King Carlos IV assumed titular leadership of the two Spanish languages as Grand Master and renamed the Iberian branches *Inclito, Sacra y Militar Orden de San Juan de Jerusalen* (Renowned, Sacred, and Military Order of St. John of Jerusalem).[31] Dispersed throughout Europe after the fall of Malta, the Order finally settled in Rome in 1834 under the nomenclature of the Sovereign Military Hospitaller Order of Saint John of Jerusalem, of Rhodes and of Malta. The Order has since focused on activities of its original foundation – the care of the poor and the sick.[32] The Cortes on 29 July 1837 disbanded the Spanish branch together with all other religious orders and dispossessed them of all their lands to address the country's financial problems.[33] It was not until 26 July 1847 that Isabel II revived the Order as a ceremonial one with a limit of 200 knights. Alfonso XII recognized the dignity of the Grand Master of the Maltese Order and returned the authority over the Spanish knights on 4 September 1885.[34]

The Order in the Philippines

The Letran cross is technically a Rhodian Cross of St John that survived and germinated on Philippine soil together with other traditions of the Knights of St John. The question on how these legacies reached the Philippines demand an explanation. Was Hermano Juan Geronimo Guerrero a member of the Order? How did someone like him end up in the Philippines from the other side of the world? My search for answers led me to the following astonishing facts.

The Knights of St John were physically present as early as the discovery of the Philippines. Accompanying Fernão de Magalhães (Ferdinand Magellan) in his attempt to circumnavigate the world was a Venetian adventurer named Antonio Pigafetta. He chronicled the events that occurred on that voyage between 1519 and 1522. After returning on the last remaining ship *Victoria,* he published his journal with the title *Primo viaggio interno al mondo 1519-1522* (The First Voyage Around the World) in 1525. He dedicated this treasure of information to Philippe de Villiers l'Isle-Adam, then the Grand Master of the Knights of St John of Rhodes, because Pigafetta was a Knight of St John.[35]

After the return of *Victoria* in 1522, the King and Queen of Spain issued a document with thirty-three concessions to natives of the kingdom who will fund expeditions to the spice regions to depart from the port in Corunna. In 1525, a fleet of 6 ships left Corunna for the Moluccas under Frey Garcia Jofre de Loaisa as captain-general of the fleet and governor of those islands. A native of Ciudad Real, Loaisa was a Commander of the Order of St John. The voyage ended in disaster with Loaisa and nearly all his officers dead.[36]

In May 1602, a new Spanish governor-general of the Philippines arrived in Manila with a considerable reinforcement of troops from *Nueva España*. The King appointed Don Pedro Bravo de Acuña because of his fearless prowess in warfare and astute administrative skills. A descendant of the first earl of Buendia, Acuña was born to noble families of antiquity and members of the Spanish military orders. A Knight of St. John, he was head of the Order's Salamanca Commanderie.[37] He served the Spanish monarch on land and sea for many years. After his distinguished Mediterranean naval exploits against the Turks in Navarino, Naples and the Levant and his defense of Cadiz from an English invasion, he became captain of the Admiral galley and Vice Admiral of all of His Majesty's Galleys, under his kinsman the *Adelantado* (Lord Lieutenant) of Castile. Given these achievements, the King appointed him governor of Cartagena de Indias in 1593. He fortified Cartegena and decisively repulsed the raids of the English naval commanders, Sir William Hawkins and Sir Francis Drake.[38] While governor there, he elevated someone by the name of Geronimo Guerrero to the office of *Alguacil Mayor* (High Constable) of the city of Cartagena.[39]

Acuña's heralded arrival in the Philippines was considered essential and timely given the threats poised by the raiding Muslims from the south, and the presence of Dutch and British naval and military forces within the territories. Equally needing immediate attention were the abuses and corrupt practices of government bureaucrats, tax and customs duties collectors, colonial traders, the *encomenderos,* and the festering unrest among the Sangleys and the Japanese in the Parian. Throughout its history, the Spanish governor-generals of the Philippines were usually members of the Spanish Military Orders of Santiago, Alcantara, or Calatrava. Acuña was the only Knight from the Order of St. John. His trusted officers and men included his nephew *Capitan* Tomas Bravo de Acuña, *General* Don Diego de Mendoza, *Maestro de Campo* (Master of Camp) Don Geronimo de Silva and others like them of his Order.[40] After personally conducting a successful campaign of conquering the Moluccas, Acuña was fatally poisoned in Manila on 24 June 1606; ending his short-lived tenure at a time when his rein on government was just beginning to show positive results.[41]

Commonly known, his suspected assassins escaped justice, and his only possession disposed of immediately.[42]

In the wake of Acuña's death however, the seeds of the centuries-old history and proud traditions of the Sovereign Military Hospitaller Order of Saint John of Jerusalem, of Rhodes and of Malta germinated and perpetuated in *Filipinas*. That for Hermano Juan Geronimo Guerrero to be instrumental in this event could only be supported by the possibility that he was among Acuña's loyal and trusted retinue of subordinates when they arrived in *Filipinas*. That he was like many of them a hospitaller was also possible as another gathering of their Order in significant numbers would never happen again in Philippine history. Considering further that Acuña appeared to have had powerful enemies, those closely associated with him perhaps sought the refuge of anonymity; being better forgotten in time. Years later, Hermano Juan would, however, resurface again from obscurity to revive the Order's mission of service to the poor and defense of the church because of his compelling compassion and desire to serve his God and King.

Plate VI - Grand Prior

La Inclita y Militar Orden de San Juan de Jerusalem

- *Chromo Litª Heraldica Madrid, 1863. Iñigo y Mier*
Propiedad del Biblioteca Nacional de España

Chapter II

Hermano Juan Geronimo Guerrero

On 1 July 1622, Hermano Juan Geronimo Guerrero filed a petition requesting the King to grant his Royal Patronage and Protection in favor of the *Colegio de Niños Huerfanos de Manila.* Pedro Muñoz de Herrera, the court clerk, duly received it while the presidente and oidores of the Audiencia were in public hearing. Eighteen days later, three *Cabildo Secular* (City Council) officials of the City of Manila, among others, appeared before Juan Saavedra de Valderrama, member of His Majesty's council and *oidor* of the *Audiencia*, to support the petition and to give testimony regarding the said petitioner's character and integrity. The three Manila officials consisted of *Capitan* Justo Claudio Leverastigui, the *Alcalde Ordinario*; *Capitan* Antonio de Arceo, a *Regidor*; and *Capitan* Pedro Sotelo de Morales, the *Depositario General.* They unanimously declared Guerrero to be a virtuous man and good Christian who cared for the orphan boys with much probity and charity and endorsed the petition because of the *Colegio's* great beneficial service to the orphans of Spanish soldiers and the community at large. On the same day, a writ containing the petition, supporting information and testimonies was issued and later dispatched for the disposition of the King and his council.[43] Except for his unquestioned integrity, piety, and works of charity, information about the founder of the home for orphan boys was scant.

Guerrero's Profile

Hermano Juan's two letters to the King of Spain petitioning for His Royal Majesty's support and protection contained the only clues into his personal profile.

He humbly signed his 1626 letter to the King as Hermano Juan Geronimo Guerrero. His name alone was cryptic and yet revealing. His choice of being addressed as Hermano meant that he was not of noble birth and hence could not possibly be a knight but perhaps a serving brother of arms of the Order of St. John.[44] Juan is the name of the hospitaller's patron saint, St John the Baptist. Geronimo is Spanish for the Greek word *Hieronymus* meaning sacred. Guerrero is the Spanish word for warrior. His name, Brother John Sacred Warrior, was serendipitously appropriate for a soldier-monk.

In Letran's first official history, Padre Fray Jose Valdes OP described him as *a poor, old and unlettered Spaniard named Juan Alonso Geronimo Guerrero. In retirement from worldly vanities, the man wore a brown robe like a hermit and in his poor house he dedicated himself with Christian zeal and piety to bring together the poor, orphaned and abandoned boys.*[45] P. Fr. Evergisto Bazaco OP added that *he was neither a man of great riches nor educated in higher sciences.*[46] Described as *a secular, poor in assets of fortune but rich in virtues* by P. Fr. Juan Peguero OP, Guerrero devoted whatever little fortune he had for the care of the orphans.[47]

Official government records, however, drew a different portrait of Guerrero. Being once the *Alguacil Mayor* of the City of Cartagena revealed some things about his background.[48] First, it indicated that he was a man of means as one had to pay the crown for such honorific positions in the colonies.[49] Second, someone from the most prominent families or the most capable individual occupied such positions.[50] Third, the position required some knowledge of the law and legal processes and documentation indicating that he was not just a simple literate man. Fourth, as the choice of the governor over other candidates of the same background hinted a degree of familiarity and trust. Furthermore, his ability to impart primary education to his wards and to write moving letters to the king indicated a magnanimous persona. His celibacy, austere lifestyle, compassion for the poor, and military orientation fitted the profile of a professed member of a military order. This psychological pattern becomes more evident as this narrative progresses.

Orphan boys whose soldier fathers died in the King's service littered the streets of Manila during the early 17th century. Deprived of any education or trade that will assure them of a better future, these street urchins survived on their wits end from the alms they collected. Unlike orphan girls and widows who had the support of the *Obras Pias* (Pious Trusts) because of their gender's vulnerability, abandoned orphan boys had to fend for themselves.[51] Hermano Juan began to collect these poor orphans and abandoned boys; providing food and shelter in his humble dwelling.[52] His compassionate heart reached out to any boy who needed help including young soldiers from *Nueva España*.[53] He taught the boys the rudiments of reading, writing, and Christian doctrine, and prepared them for a trade he knew best - soldiers in the service of God and King.[54] When his resources were no longer adequate to support a growing number of orphans, he resorted to begging. Just like the original Hospitallers of Jerusalem, Hermano Juan and his wards clothed in tawny colored tunics collected alms around the city with a sense of dignity that caught the public's attention.[55] It came to pass that the *vecinos* (citizens) of Manila began to discern how useful Guerrero's charity work was to the orphans and to the city.[56] His efforts attracted many supporters.

<u>The Early Supporters</u>

Among the principal benefactors were the *Hermandad de la Santa Misericordia* (Brotherhood of the Holy Mercy), the *Tercer Orden de San Francisco* (Third Order of St. Francis) and the officers of the Spanish military.

Plate VII

Letran's Original Site corner Real and Muralla Streets

Letran's Second Home Site corner Beaterio and Solana Streets
- © Dominique Liongson, 2015

On 16 April 1594, the *Hermandad de la Santa Misericordia de Manila* was founded for the spiritual and temporal welfare of the Spanish residents in times of greatest calamities and miseries patterned after the premier brotherhood of the same name in Lisbon. The financial board of the confraternity would come to be known as the *Santa Mesa* (Holy Board) because of the sacred services it rendered to the colony. The *Santa Mesa* was composed of the principal secular and ecclesiastical officials of the city with the captain-general usually as its *proveedor* (purveyor). Funded initially by substantial assets, encomiendas, and concessions, the *Misericordia* went on to establish a hospital which provided care, relief, assistance and aid to sick Spaniards. During natural and financial disasters, such as earthquakes, fires or the losses from galleon trade, the *Misericordia* would distribute medicine, food, provisions, and financial relief while gathering and burying the dead.[57] The brotherhood's historian and Letran benefactor, Juan Bautista Uriarte, recounted their many beneficial works:

> *Many alms have been given to the religious orders that they might pursue their work, especially between the years 1600-1650, such alms being used for edifices of worship and other pious purposes. The prisons have been a special object of care to the brotherhood, for the prisoners of the two prisons in Manila have been looked after daily in regard to clothing and other matters; and an attorney has been paid to conduct their cases, in order that they might be concluded at the earliest possible moment. For this more than one thousand pesos had been spent annually. Alms have been given to widows to the amount of four, eight, twelve, sixteen, twenty, and twenty-four reals weekly; and the same is true of poor soldiers disabled in the royal service in the Philippines and vicinity, to whom alms are distributed weekly. The noble families who have been overtaken by adversity have been aided, and that so tactfully that the asking of alms by them has cost no embarrassment. To them the weekly distribution has amounted to twenty, thirty, fifty, one hundred and more pesos. The brotherhood has always been careful to inquire into the morals of those among whom its alms have been distributed, and evil morals have meant suspension from the alms-list, to which they have been readmitted on reforming. Brothers of the confraternity found to be leading an evil life have been expelled from membership until they have given assurances of reform. Especial care has been taken in relieving members who have fallen into misfortunes. Orphan girls whose fathers have died in the royal service in the wars have been sheltered, taught, supported, and, at marriage, given a dowry. From the organization of the brotherhood until 1634, more than three thousand orphan girls have been so aided.*[58]

The *Seminario de Santa Potenciana* and the *Colegio de Santa Isabel* were the *Misericordia*'s principal educational beneficiaries. *Santa Potenciana* was a convent for the shelter of Spanish orphan girls founded as per instructions of Felipe II dated 9 August 1589. The *Misericordia*, which supported the poor Spanish orphan girls in Santa Potenciana and other private homes financially, gathered and housed them all in a school they founded on 24 October 1632 named the *Colegio de Santa Isabel*. The latter was put under the administration of the Daughters of Charity of St Vincent de Paul on 22 July 1862. The 1863 earthquake destroyed many government offices moving these offices to occupy the premises of *Santa Potenciana*. The resulting decline of students forced *Santa Potenciana*'s remaining students to transfer to *Santa Isabel*. The two institutions were merged in 1866 with *Santa Isabel* as the surviving entity.[59] The *Santa Mesa* regularly granted *becas* (scholarship grants) of 3 pesos each annually to five of Hermano Juan's orphan boys who became known as *Hijos de la Mesa de la Santa Misericordia* (Sons of the Board of the Holy Mercy).[60] The brothers of the Third Order would extend similar support but in a much-diminished scale. In as much as alms to support orphan boys were not always readily available, Hermano Juan had to beg from his former brothers at arms and Pedro de Navarrete was one among them.

Capitan Pedro de Navarrete served the King as a soldier in the company of Don Tomas Bravo de Acuña since he came to the islands with Governor Pedro Bravo de Acuña. He rose through the ranks distinguishing himself in the armed expeditions to Zibu, Mindanao, Caraga, Sanguiles and Sincapura. Navarrete fought the Japanese and Sangleys in their rebellions outside the city walls and held the vigil in the Cavite garrison during the Dutch blockade. He married Doña Augustina de Morales, granddaughter of Captain Ruis de Morales, one of the first conquerors of the islands and patriarch of a prominent family of rank in the walled city's social circles. The *Capitan* was a friend and regular benefactor of Hermano Juan and would soon be of even greater assistance.[61]

From the alms given by the city's supportive *vecinos*, Guerrero was able to purchase stone dwellings to house the orphans and to generate an annual income of 50 pesos for the boys' subsistence.[62] By 1622, eight orphans inclined to serve His Majesty left to occupy positions as soldiers while two professed in the Augustinian and Recollect orders. Those who wished to continue further studies moved to the *Colegios of San Jose* or *Santo Tomas*. Those aspiring to the priesthood were selected to serve as acolytes in the city's Cathedral.[63] The alms, however, were not enough to sustain this meritorious service to God and the King. Two principal supporters urged Hermano Juan to petition for His Majesty's *Patronazgo Real* (Royal Patronage). They were the Archbishop of Manila and the Governor-General.

The First Petition

Guerrero's *superior eclesiastico* (ecclesiastical superior) was Archbishop Miguel Garcia Serrano OSA. The archbishop supported Hermano Juan from the beginning. He gave alms for a prayer room to serve as the orphans' chapel.[64] On 5 June 1622, the Manila *Cabildo Eclesiastico* (Cathedral Chapter) under Archbishop Garcia issued a notice to *His Majesty of the foundation of a Colegio de Niños Huerfanos in that city of Manila by the piety and solicitude of*

Hermano Juan Geronimo Guerrero, a person long known to indulge in works of charity... The boys do not have to this day their own means of sustenance, if your Majesty does not grant any act of mercy to the said college.[65] Officially constituted, the *Cabildo Eclesiastico* further encouraged Guerrero to petition for the King's patronage and protection similar to that granted to the *Colegio de San Juan de Letran de Mexico*, a school founded by the Franciscans in 1529.[66] With the help of Licenciado Don Juan Cevicos, treasurer of the Manila Cathedral and Vicar General of the archdiocese, Hermano Juan wrote and submitted a petition on 1 July 1622. He authorized Cevicos, who was about to depart for Spain, to act in his name together with Gonzalo Romero, agent of the court.[67] The *Cabildo Eclesiastico* further authorized Cevicos to advocate for the needs of the Church and to inform the authorities about the state of the Islands in a letter dated 5 August 1622.[68] Among the other matters of concern was their request for the protection of the *colegio de niños huerfanos*.[69] Guerrero's *superior secular* (secular superior), the Governor-General Alonso Fajardo de Tenza, on the other hand, was the *proveedor* (purveyor) of the *Misericordia* which extended alms to the *Colegio*.[70] Being aware of the commendable work undertaken for the orphans, he was said to have written to the King and his *Consejo de Indias* to grant royal protection.[71] Although there was no documentary evidence to support this, the petition was nevertheless favorably acted on by the *Real Audiencia* of which he was the *presidente*.

Guerrero wrote the following letter to the king summarizing the content of his petition:

Sire:

The great shame of witnessing vast numbers of stray and abandoned lads and orphan boys without fathers in this city within the whole kingdom moved me to ponder on its remedy and to appeal to my ecclesiastical and secular superiors. Advocating in God's name and soliciting for alms, found be a college or retreat patterned after His Majesty's San Juan de Letran in the city of Mexico in New Spain as a work of God for its end. Even after much resistance, His Divine Majesty moved the spirit of the residents of this city to give alms making the purchase of a house for the said school a reality. And for the last three years, a few boys who have departed from the school were acknowledged for their usefulness. Now you see among them religious, others as clerics and those benefiting from select positions in the military owing to the doctrine and teachings of the said school where they go to study and continue to do so. Even if this work is in utter poverty, Sire, it would have done more with [the help of] your Majesty. They deserve to partake of your Royal Patronage especially in consideration of these orphans' fathers. They died in Your Majesty's service: a number conquering these islands and others defending them. Years of naval wars with the Dutch demonstrated the fidelity of Your Majesty's loyal vassals in lands so remote and disorderly would be a matter nobly deserving of Your Majesty's munificence. Behold the boys as being recompensed for the services of their fathers and grant

Plate VIII

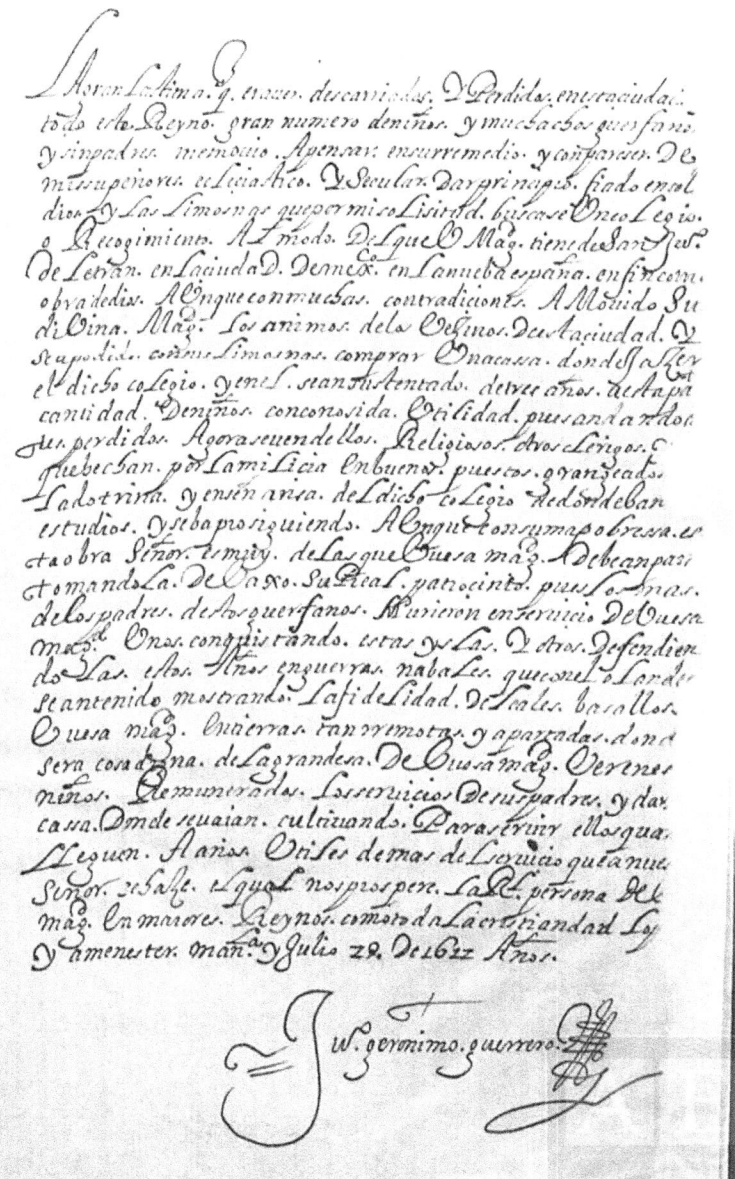

Letter to Felipe IV, 22 July 1622

- ESPAÑA. MINISTERIO DE EDUCACIÓN, CULTURA Y DEPORTE. Archivo General de Indias, ES.41091.AGI/23.6.11//FILIPINAS,5,N.452

them a home where their continued care will enable them to serve others. And when they reach the useful age, their expected service to our Lord and prosperity to the Royal Person of His Majesty throughout the significant kingdoms like the whole of Christendom will be exceeded [illegible] and welcomed. Manila, July 29 in the year 1622.

Juº Geronimo Guerrero (rubric) [72]

The letter was significant not only because of it being the orphanage's first petition for Royal Patronage. It noted that the orphans who left school during the *past three years* had been of beneficial value to the colony. This statement could only mean that the first "graduates" departed from Hermano Juan's school as early as 1619 and that Letran could have existed for some time before the official inauguration of Colegio de Santo Tomas.

Petitions usually underwent a long and tedious process. The Governor-General endorsed the petition's approval to the Viceroy of *Nueva España* whose jurisdiction then encompassed much of North and Central America including what is now known as Mexico, the Philippines and other Pacific possessions. If approved, the Viceroy forwarded it to the *Consejo de Indias* (Supreme Council of the Indies). Based in Castile, Spain, the Council administered the colonies in the America's and the Pacific and determined the merits of the petition. If deemed meritorious, the Council endorsed it for the King's final consideration and decision. This process would, at the longest, take approximately two years. Once approved, the enacting *Real Cedula* (Royal Decree) underwent the reverse of the process; lasting another two years before the decree became operative in Manila under, more likely, another Governor-General.[73] In order not to delay the enjoyment of certain concessions by grantees, the Governor-General enjoyed discretionary authority to approve a concession in the King's name for the immediate interim enjoyment of the grantee subject to the receipt of a confirmation decree from the King within four years, extendable for another two years.[74]

With the availability of digital archives, we can now access more accurate information. It would appear that the process was quicker than expected possibly because of an agent in the court and no one raised any objections or questions. The processing time shortened considerably with Cevicos and Romero expediting the petition. The King issued Real Cedula dated 16 July 1623 ordering Governor-General Alonso Fajardo de Tensa to extend help to the *Colegio* with certain discretions and to take care and educate the boys to be inclined to positions that are beneficial for that republic.[75] Unfortunately, the royal decree arrived in Manila after Fajardo died, and appeared to had been lost or forgotten.

Hermano Juan once again appeared at the Manila *Cabildo Secular* reiterating his petition which was referred back to the King on 3 August 1625.[76] By this time, the *ad interim* governor, Fernando de Silva, was already in Manila scurrying to implement the order. His Majesty promptly replied with *Real Cedula* dated 19 June 1626 ordering the newly appointed Governor, Juan

Niño de Tavora to *help the Colegio in everything that he can*.[77] In the meantime, Hermano Juan decided to officially name his school *Seminario de Niños Huerfanos de San Juan de Letran*. Primary schools then were called *seminarios*.[78] Mission schools in the Philippines were known as *seminarios de indios*.[79]

San Juan de Letran

San Juan de Letran is the Spanish name for the major basilica of Saint John Lateran, the oldest and first-ranked among the four great patriarchal basilicas of Rome. Initially the residential palace of the *Laterani* family, the manor was given to the Church by Emperor Constantine in 311 CE and had since become the residence of the Pope until the papal seat's departure to Avignon in 1348. The Lateran ceased to be the official papal residence when the Popes returned to Rome but it continues to be the official cathedral and seat of the Bishop of the City of Rome to this present day. Initially dedicated to the Most Holy Savior around 324, Saint John the Baptist and Saint John the Evangelist assumed the patronage of the Basilica Salvatoris after the 6th century and had been known by those names since.[80] Given the frequent use of its magnificent baptistry by the ordinary people of Rome, the basilica became more associated with Saint John the Baptist. The Church liturgy celebrates the dedication of the Basilica on November 9 each year since the year 324. Initially confined to the city of Rome until 1565, all the Churches of the Roman Rite have since celebrated it.[81]

Hermano Juan neither doubted nor hesitated in naming his school after the Church of Saint John the Baptist. The name not only served to remind the King that his school deserved His Majesty's Royal Patronage as much as the Mexican college with the same name. It also bore his name and his Order's patron saint. It further symbolized the Mother Church he had vowed to defend. Pope Benedict XVI in his Angelus Address on 9 November 2008 succinctly explained the theology behind the reverence of the basilica:

> *The honoring of this sacred edifice was a way of expressing love and veneration for the Roman Church, which, as St Ignatius of Antioch says, "presides in charity" over the whole Catholic communion (Letter to the Romans, 1:1).*
>
> *On this solemnity the Word of God recalls an essential truth: temple of stones is a symbol of the living Church, the Christian community, which in their letters the Apostles Peter and Paul already understood as a "spiritual edifice," built by God with "living stones," namely, Christians themselves, upon the one foundation of Jesus Christ, who is called the "cornerstone" (cf. 1 Corinthians 3:9-11, 16-17; 1 Peter 2:4-8; Ephesians 2:20-22). "Brothers, you are God's building," St Paul wrote and added: "holy is God's temple, which you are" (1 Corinthians 3:9c, 17).*

The beauty and harmony of the churches, destined to give praise to God, also draws us human beings, limited and sinful, to convert to form a "cosmos," a well-ordered structure, in intimate communion with Jesus, who is the true Saint of saints. This happens in a culminating way in the Eucharistic liturgy, in which the "ecclesia," that is, the community of the baptized, come together in a unified way to listen to the Word of God and nourish themselves with the Body and Blood of Christ. From these two tables, the Church of living stones is built up in truth and charity and is internally formed by the Holy Spirit transforming herself into what she receives, conforming herself more and more to the Lord Jesus Christ. She herself, if she lives in sincere and fraternal unity, in this way becomes the spiritual sacrifice pleasing to God.[82]

The Second Petition

The school's new name first appeared in Guerrero's letter dated 1 August 1626 to Felipe IV. The following contents of the said letter petitioned for a more stable endowment such as an *encomienda* or similar devices and other matters together with the memorial and endorsements. It also provided information on what transpired to his first petition including marginal notes and instructions of the King:

+

Sire:

Since the beginning of the so firm foundation of this seminary of San Juan de Letran, I have made known to your Majesty by faithful relations the great fruit obtained for God our Lord and for the service of your Majesty, in protecting and sheltering in the seminary so many orphan boys, the sons of old Spanish soldiers, who [without it] would evidently be ruined for lack of instruction and good morals. So good results have been achieved in this, as experience has shown by those who have left this seminary - forty for the service of your Majesty, to serve as soldiers, six others as religious, and six who serve in this cathedral church as acolytes. There are now in the seminary more than fifty boys. Your Majesty, having examined the dispatches, was pleased to send me a royal decree, ordering the governors of these islands to protect and favor this seminary with incomes. In these islands revenues are so few, that Governor Fernando de Silva assigned three hundred pesos in chattels - namely, certain small shops, which are suppressed today and opened tomorrow. In order that this enterprise may go on increasing for the service of God and of your Majesty, will you order that an encomienda be given to us. With it and my feeble efforts we could support ourselves, and so great a work as this would not fail.

I beseech your Majesty, for the love of God, that when my life is over, [the Brotherhood of] La Misericordia may take charge of the seminary, with the brothers of the third order; and that a boy who has been very long in this college may remain to shelter them, so that this work, that is so acceptable to God our Lord, may continue to increase and not to diminish. May God preserve your Majesty for many years, as Christendom desires and as is necessary. Manila, August first, one thousand six hundred and twenty-six.

Your Majesty's humble vassal,
+
The Brother Juan geronimo guerrero (rubric)

[Instructions: "Let the governor be again charged to observe what has been ordered him, May 11, 628."]

+
Sire

Brother Juan Geronimo Guerrero, who has charge of the seminary of Sant Juan de Letran for orphan boys in the city of Manila, declares that in consideration of the general welfare of the said children, and their education and teaching, your Majesty was pleased to order Don Fernando de Silva, governor of those islands, by your royal decree of July 16, 623, to aid the said seminary with some taxes, so that the boys in it might be reared and supported. But, as no taxes were found, the said royal decree has had no effect; and to this day not more than the small sum of three hundred pesos has been assigned to the seminary - an amount so small that it does not suffice to provide shoes for the boys who are now there. The number there is daily increasing, and the expenses incurred are very considerable and the alms but little. With what they have they cannot be supported. In order that so pious a work may continue, and so that those orphan boys may be suitably assisted with the necessaries of life, and not be ruined:

He petitions your Majesty that, favoring by your sovereign mercy a work so greatly to the service of our Lord, you will be pleased to order that some encomienda of Indians, or a pension from those that shall be allotted, may set aside for said seminary - or in any other manner which your Majesty pleases, and for the period that your royal will deems best. (I ask this) because from it will follow considerable profit for your royal service; for the boys reared there incline to become soldiers, and up to the present time forty of them have gone out to serve your Majesty in that employ, while five have become friars, and twelve are studying. And, in order that they may learn the art of navigation, will your Majesty be pleased to command an examined pilot to come to the said seminary to teach it to them. Will your Majesty also be pleased to order that, inasmuch as there are many children of Spaniards among the Indian women of these islands, conceived by the latter, these children may be taken from them and brought to be reared in the said seminary, so that they may not become idolaters like the Indian women, when they are grown. Our Lord will be served by that, and will receive especial blessing and favor.

[Endorsed: "The seminary of Sant Juan de Letran for orphan boys in the city of Manila.:]

[Instructions: "Señor Don Fernand Ruiz Contreras: Let a decree be issued for them that, in the same manner as the other three hundred pesos, I set aside for them, from the taxes that I shall possess there, the further sum of three hundred ducados.[83] *As for the other things that he requests, refer them to the governor, so that he may take what measures are advisable in everything, in order that the service of God our Lord and of his Majesty may be attended to. November 18."]*

[In the margin: "In regard to what is asked in this section, his Majesty issued a decree, that the governor of Philipinas shall assign the said seminary three hundred ducados in taxes that do not belong to the treasury, as another three hundred pesos were assigned. All the other things requested are referred to the governor, so that he may provide everything advisable, in order that they may attend to the service of God and that of his Majesty."] [84]

Hermano Juan's 1626 petition highlighted informative facts regarding the orphans and the nature of support the seminary received.

There were over 52 orphans under his care by 1625. Forty left the *Seminario* and became soldiers in His Majesty's service. Six became friars in the service of God and six served as acolytes in the Cathedral. It is interesting to note that the roles of "Knights, Priests and Serving Brothers" observed in the Order of St John were evident in the *Seminario*. There were more than 50 orphans in 1626 and 12 were students. The orphans appeared to be all Spanish children. The care for Spanish mestizo orphans had not been attended to as he inquired about the King's permission and financial support in this regard. There was no mention of *indios*. In the event of his death, Brother Juan indicated an unnamed successor prepared to continue his work and preserve the traditions established in the *Seminario*. The purpose of the *Seminario* was explicitly stated as the education of orphan boys to become useful Christians in the service of *God our Lord, and His Majesty the King*. This purpose would be echoed repeatedly in the school's historical records and consequently evolved into the institution's motto: God, Country and Letran, the only home the orphans ever knew.

Financial Affairs

We now turn our attention to the *Seminario's* financial condition - the reason for the petition in the first place. Traditional historical accounts described the *Seminario's* founder as its principal benefactor. He was reportedly a wealthy, retired military officer with the honorific title of *Don* or *Capitan* occasionally inserted before his name by writers far more removed in time. Except for his stint as *Alguacil Mayor* of Cartagena, there was no evidence to support this during his stay in Manila. If indeed he was one of Manila's wealthy residents, his name would not fail to appear among

Manila's inconsequential rich like the Navarrete's and the Morales' who enjoyed the benefits of encomiendas and the galleon trade, the only principal sources of wealth in 17th-century colonial Philippines. His austere life would seem to be by choice. Begging for alms appeared to be customary to him as was the case in mendicant orders; receiving perhaps a modest pension from the *Misericordia* like disabled soldiers would at that time. He had no family of his own to inherit his purported wealth; not even to perpetuate his legacy. He purchased the stone dwelling he occupied with the boys from alms. Inscribed in the second petition, Hermano Juan willed his only asset, Letran, to the *Misericordia* and the brothers of the third order. How does one make sense of his disciplined, generous, pious and noble behavior in the grips of his apparent poverty and celibacy? It only made sense if he professed the ecumenical vows of obedience, poverty, and chastity and *consecrated himself to the service of the poor in Christ Jesus, to be constantly employed in works of mercy, and to devote himself to the defense of the Christian faith* as a brother hospitaller of St John.[85] Devoid of any support from a mother convent, a solitary dedicated hospitaller of St John living in the western Pacific fringes of the Spanish empire could only explain the paradox that was Hermano Juan Geronimo Guerrero. Under these circumstances, the King's support was in dire need indeed.

Felipe IV's financial support did not come from the colonial government's treasury, but from the King's income. He increased the 300 peso subsidy set in 1625 by an additional 300 ducados in 1628 and left the manner of addressing the other needs to the Governor-General's discretion. It fell into the hands of Governor Fernando de Silva, the Island's interim Governor and Captain General in 1625-1626, to implement the King's first endowment and tax concession to the *Seminario* which proved to be inadequate. It should be noted that the Philippine colonial treasury at that time was consistently operating in a deficit spending mode and relied heavily on a subsidy from *Nueva España* called the *situado* to address the shortfalls.[86] With the *situado* delayed or lost at sea while in transit from Acapulco, the Governor-General had to regularly borrow money from the *Misericordia* and other wealthy *vecinos* of Manila to continue operating. It was therefore extremely difficult for incumbent Governor-Generals to source the necessary financial support petitioned by Hermano Juan. It would take a Governor-General with extraordinary resourcefulness to manage a delicate financial position while still being able to implement essential expenditures for the maintenance and defense of the colony. Silva's successor, Governor Juan Niño de Tavora, possessed such a rare talent and executed Hermano Juan's second endowment while granting additional concessions beneficial to Letran during his term of office.

Letran's Vice Patrons

Juan Niño de Tavora, Knight of the Order of Calatrava and *Commendador* of Puerto Llano, was Spanish Governor and Captain General of the Philippines from 1626 to 1632. He distinguished himself as *Maestro de*

Campo of the Spanish lancers in Flanders. His term of office witnessed engagements against the Dutch in Formosa and Macao, and a punitive expedition against the Muslims in Jolo.[87] Beset with problems with the *Real Audiencia,* he was noted for achieving results using questionable methods. He completed the Manila bridge and the hospital for Sangleys funded by the latter's own coffers.[88] He improved the city's fortifications in spite of the colony's precarious financial condition.[89]

Under his governance, Letran's subsidy from the King increased to 600 pesos annually. Tavora's measures to implement the King's decrees were considered unorthodox and controversial. In 1628, he granted an encomienda to the *Seminario's* benefactor, *Capitan* Pedro de Navarrete, in recognition of his merits and service to the King, and secured the latter's pledge to donate five thousand pesos for the completion of the *Seminario's* building.[90] Unfazed by the ensuing criticisms, he deemed the *completion of the seminary of these boys, without any cost to the royal revenues and any damage to the community* as overriding and justifiable considerations.[91] The *encomienda* and 5000 peso pledge was confirmed by the King on 19 August 1631.[92]

In 1630, Tavora created another controversy by ceding ten rice and ten maize Sangley wine presses to the *Seminario*.[93] The King likewise confirmed the twenty concessions on 27 January 1632.[94] Tavora's obsequious implementation of the *Patronazgo Real* finally relieved the stresses besetting the orphans and allowed Hermano Juan to expand his *Seminario*. Adjacent lots were acquired, and a new edifice began to rise over a bigger area.[95] Located at the corner of Real and Muralla Streets opposite the Parian Gate, the orphans' dwellings gradually morphed into how a school would typically look like with rooms for learning, oratory, a small chapel, a choir, and living spaces to accommodate the increasing numbers.[96] Letran's most resourceful vice patron died on 22 July 1632. The Colegio would miss Tavora sorely. The successor, Governor Corcuera, assumed his appointment officially on 25 June 1635 and terminated Letran's 20 Sangley wine press concessions the following year.

Don Sebastian Hurtado de Corcuera, Knight of the Spanish military Order of Alcantara, was the Island's governor, captain general and president of the *Real Audiencia y Canceleria* from 1635-1644. An able administrator, he was governor of Panama before then and, became governor of the Canary Islands after his term in the Philippines. Considered among the leading military leaders of colonial Philippines, his tenure witnessed expeditions against *Moros* (Muslims), Sangley insurrections, and the loss of *Hermosa* (Taiwan) to the Dutch. He was a man of firm convictions and ruled despotically.[97] His term was marred by conflicts with the ecclesiastics and the Archbishop of Manila, Hernando Guerrero OSA, whom he exiled briefly to Mariveles.[98] In 1640, he founded the *Capilla Real de Nuestra Señora de la Encarnacion* (Royal Chapel of our Lady of the Incarnation) for the military forces in Manila and the *Colegio de San Felipe de Austria* both in charge of the Jesuits.[99]

Plate IX - LETRAN'S VICE ROYAL PATRONS

Juan Niño de Tavora
Knight of Calatrava

- Velasquez, Diego, The Surrender of Breda 1635
Museo del Prado, Madrid

Sebastian Hurtado de Corcuerra
Knight of Alcantara

- Artist Unknown
El Oriente, 22 November 1875

These events caused much consternation among the ecclesiastics. The *Capilla Real* deprived the other churches of the alms from a majority of the city's citizens.[100] *San Felipe*, on the other hand, threatened to diminish an already small student population of the existing colleges. A complicated man to deal with, Corcuera would prove to be troublesome to the Dominicans but a generous benefactor to the Jesuits and Letran during his term of office.

Just before Corcuera's ascendancy, Hermano Juan's agent in Madrid submitted a memorial for the new governor to extend the same support contained in the 1623 decree and to grant a vacated encomienda to augment the subsidy to the *Colegio*.[101] On 10 July 1635, a *Real Cedula* was issued to Corcuera reiterating Letran's *Patronazgo Real* contained in the previous decrees.[102] Heeding His Majesty's decree, he terminated the controversial wine press concessions and finally granted Hermano Juan's original petition for an encomienda on 25 January 1636.[103] The encomienda, rendered vacant by the death of Don Nicolas de Ribera y Guzman, was located in Baratao (Bacnotan), Ylocos consisting of 700 tributes annually.[104] This benefaction, confirmed by *Real Cedulas* dated 8 November 1638 and 9 February 1646, was extended a number of times over 100 years until it was granted *in perpetuum* by the first Bourbon King, Felipe V, on 8 February 1743.[105] Since then, Letran had been referred to as the *Real Colegio de San Juan de Letran* until the end of Spanish sovereignty. Corcuera surprisingly continued being Letran's generous benefactor even after the school's relinquishment to the Dominicans in 1640 notwithstanding his disdain for friars who resolutely undermined his authority.

Hermano Juan's Final Days

In time, Hermano Juan's advancing age became more apparent. His recurring ailments began to take its toll. During his frequent absences to heal, he entrusted the *Colegio* in charge of persons who proved to be unreliable and incapable of administering the school and disciplining the students. Students began to desert the premises and to decline in number.[106] Seeking succor from Archbishop Hernando Guerrero OSA, he was permitted to go to the Santo Domingo Convent for healing and convalescence towards the end of 1638.[107] The Prior, Padre Fray Sebastian de Oquendo OP, extended the use of the convent's infirmary and sent the convent's porter, Hermano Fray Diego de Santa Maria OP, to take temporary charge of Letran while its founder recuperated.[108] Free from any pressing worries, Hermano Juan found peace at last in his old age and made known of his desire to adopt the habit of the Order of Preachers. Cognizant of Hermano Juan's virtuous life of piety and charity, P. Fr. Sebastian allowed him to profess as a Dominican *lego* (cooperator brother) on 16 November 1639 before completing a year as a novice.[109]

Sensing his imminent death, Hermano Juan declared his present state of affairs and renounced his legal rights as founder and administrator of the

Colegio de Niños Huerfanos de San Juan de Letran. He transferred its inventoried assets and encomienda, and bequeathed the care and doctrinal instruction of the orphans in favor of the Prior of the Santo Domingo Convent, P. Fr. Sebastian de Oquendo, in front of a notary public and witnesses on 11 June 1640. He acknowledged the Dominican Order to be the most worthy to assume the task considering the vigilance and care they will accord to this noble mission and service to God and the King. Hermano Juan admonished the Prior to attend to all the legal requirements and documentation that concerned the Governor of the Islands and the Archbishop of Manila to complete the transfer[110]

On 18 June 1640, Governor Corcuera acknowledged the wishes of Hermano Juan and authorized the Dominican Order with the care and catechetical instruction of the orphans after being assured that a religious of the Order who is engaged in a similar undertaking would attend to it. He further granted *a piece of land one hundred brazas long by 50 wide in the Parian - free, and without paying land tax to the city - as help towards its support*.[111] He also granted the use of a *quinta* (country home) along the shore of Parañaque, once occupied by *Alferez* Francisco Muñoz de Echague, as a vacation home for the students.[112] On September that year, he established an annual stipend of 100 pesos for six students to render services at the *Capilla Real*.[113]

In as much as Hermano Juan was under the jurisdiction of the Metropolitan Archbishop of Manila, the parties concerned informed the Most Illustrious Hernando Guerrero OSA of the juridical relinquishment of the *Colegio,* and the approval thereof by the Governor as Royal Vice Patron. On 12 July 1640, the Archbishop noted the precedents and thus ordered the Vicar General to effect the smooth transition to Hermano Fray Diego de Santa Maria OP who was already engaged in a similar undertaking.[114] Two days later on the 14th of July, the prior provincial of the Order of Preachers, P. Fr. Clemente Gant, announced that Hermano Fray Juan Geronimo Guerrero died a friar of the Order. He further officially accepted in the name of his Order to take charge of *Colegio de San Juan de Letran* together with all its temporal and spiritual assets.[115] None of the documents referred to a precise date of death. Considering that the Archbishop's order to effect transition had no reference to his death, Hermano Juan died more likely on 13 July 1640. He was accorded with the sacred ceremonies and privileges extended to the professed religious of the Order and interred at the Santo Domingo church.[116]

On 27 July 1642, H. Fr. Diego de Santa Maria OP wrote to His Majesty informing him of the death of H. Fr. Juan Geronimo Guerrero OP and the transfer of his school and care of the orphan boys to the Order of Preachers. He further requested that the sources of the school's subsistence consisting of 700 tributes from the Baratao encomienda and the 100 brazas of land in the Parian granted by the Governor-General be confirmed. Attached to the letter were two memorials petitioning that these boys acquire the same privileges and mercies enjoyed by the orphan colleges in Spain and that they receive the medicines of the *Hospital Real* (Royal Hospital).[117] The Parian land grant was confirmed by *Real Cedula* on 17 February 1644.[118] The Baratao encomienda was likewise confirmed on 9 February 1646.[119] The King did not confirm all of Corcuera's orders and concessions. On 11 August 1644, his successor, Diego Fajardo, arrested and held him prisoner for five years to answer accusations filed against him during his *residencia*.[120] He was later ordered released by the King and appointed governor of the Canaries in 1659. Letran's most gracious supporter died in Tenerife on 12 August 1660.[121]

Moved by their plight, a serving brother of Saint John's Hospitallers appeared from obscurity and began to gather helpless orphan boys from the streets of Manila. He provided them with refuge, food, and a primary Christian education. The *vecinos* of Manila discerned the importance of the charitable service being rendered and supported it with alms. Encouraged by the Archbishop and Governor-General, Hermano Juan Geronimo Guerrero petitioned and received the King's protection and patronage of his school for orphan sons of Spanish soldiers. The boys turned out to be useful vassals of His Majesty; serving as soldiers, clerics, and other occupations needed by the burgeoning colony. After nurturing the *Colegio* for more than twenty years, the promising future of Hermano Juan's legacy was passed on to the competent and vigilant care of the Dominicans. The *Colegio de San Juan de Letran* was then poised to embark on the next phase of its development.

Chapter III

Fray Diego de Santa Maria OP

Sometime in 1655, Manila's *Alcalde Ordinario, Capitan* Luis de Aduana, ordered an audit of the Dominican institution *Colegio de San Juan de Letran*. Conducting the review was his scribe, *Alferez* (Second Lieutenant) Tomas de Palensuela, in the presence of two *escribanos publicos* (notaries public) Miguel de Moroto and Juan de Torres, and three trusted witnesses. The audit which accounted for all the students since 1640 and their current statuses revealed an impressive array of graduates in the service of God and King in compliance with the objectives of the school's foundation and the expectations of the *Patronazgo Real*. Returning to his home convent in Spain, the school's administrator for the previous 15 years, Dominican Cooperator Brother Diego de Santa Maria, initiated the census.[122]

Ordo Praedicatorum

Letran's official transfer to the Dominicans signaled a shift in its emphasis from a military focus towards a religious one.

St Dominic Guzman founded the *Ordo Praedicatorum* (Order of Preachers) on 17 November 1205. The Order created apostolic preachers to counteract the Albigensian heresy during the Middle Ages by the teaching of the holy gospel. Adopting the Rule of St Augustine, the Order's first Monastery in Prouille, France became the center of the Order's missions and apostolic works. The Order was solemnly confirmed by Pope Honorius III on 22 December 1216 granting it canonical existence and determined its unique vocation to teaching and defending the truths of faith. 2016 marked the 800th anniversary of the Order's official recognition. The following year, the Dominicans established centers in Toulouse, Paris, Madrid, Rome, and Bologna. The first general chapter in Bologna drew the Constitutions regulating the organization and life of the Order in 1220. The end aim of the Order is the salvation of souls principally using preaching as a means. The Dominicans belonged to the first order instituted by the Church with an academic mission. Dominican convents and schools spread rapidly throughout the known world, and its doctors wrote monumental works in all branches of knowledge.[123]

The discovery of the *Islas del Poniente* (Western Isles) by Fernão de Magalhães in 1521 caused tremendous interest among the missionary orders because of the archipelago's proximity to the heart of Asia. Four attempts to establish a Dominican outpost in what was to be known as *Filipinas* were carried out by elements of the Dominican Province of Santiago de Mexico.

Plate X a

El Her.no Jul.º Per.mo quarrero, que en esta Ciudad de manila de las Islas philipinas tenia a su cargo la administracion del Collegio de
S. Ju.o de Letran cuidando en el de la Educacion y Crianza de los niños
guerfanos y desamparados de que ha seguido a V. Mag.d el util q se
ha visto. saliendo del dho Collegio numero dellos para marineros
y soldados, fue dios servido de llevarsele por el mes de Julio de mill
y seis cientos y quarenta. Aviendose recogido en su enfermedad, y ve-
jes. al Convento de mi padre santo Domingo; adonde murio y se
profeso, aviendo antes de su muerte hecho dexacion de la dha administracion, y encargadola a mi Religion con orden q ynterviº
no assi del Governador destas Islas, como del Arzobispo desta Ciudad
La qual mi orden acepto. con mucho gusto por ser obra tan del servicio de Dios. nro señor. y el de V. mag.d; La qual me ha encargado el padre provincial. para que yo cuide de la Educacion y crianza de dhos.
niños: q oy son en mayor numero q xamas han sido, pues son mas de
ochenta, por el cuidado particular conque mi Religion acude a esta
obra, y porque en virtud de cedula que V. mag.d ayembiado a este Govierno, se le hizo merced para ayuda de su sustento y crianza de se-
tecientos tributos, que vacaron por muerte de Don Nicolas de Maura en la encomienda de Baratao, con trecientos pesos de pension q
se sacan primero para obras pias; y assi su procedido no era
considerable para poder passar, se le hizo nueba merced. de cient
brazas de tierra del parian de los sangleyes, para que las casas
que se fabricaren en ellas, paguen los arquileres al dho collegio
para ayuda del sustento de los dhos niños, con cargo de que se pi-
da confirmacion de dha merced a V. mag.d a quien humildemente

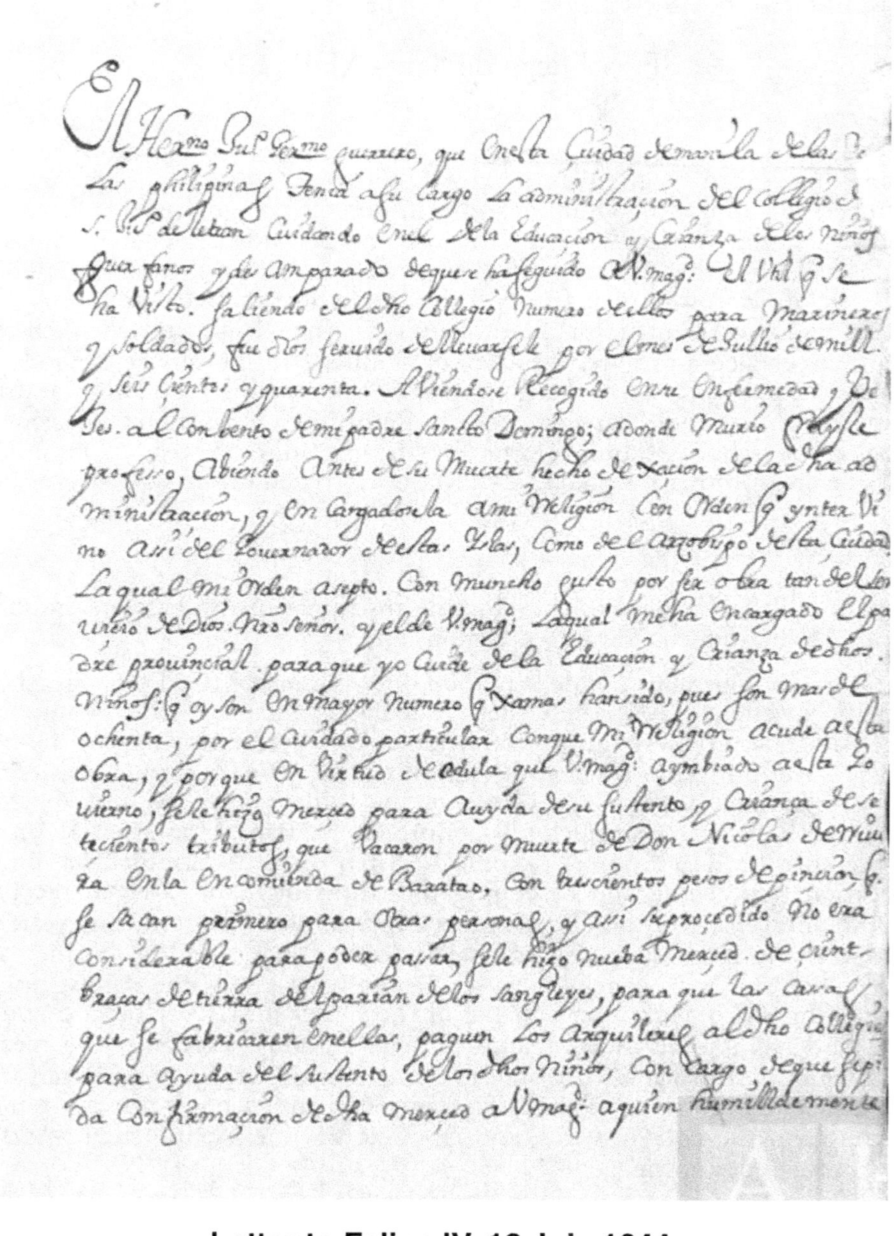

Letter to Felipe IV, 16 July 1644

- ESPAÑA. MINISTERIO DE EDUCACIÓN, CULTURA Y DEPORTE. Archivo General de Indias, ES.41091.AGI/23.6.406//FILIPINAS,85,N.94

Plate X b

Pido q̃ así de la merced como la de la encomienda las mande
confirmar V. Mag.: que para todo Remito los papeles q̃ sobre todo
sean Actuados y Juntamente con ellos Remito a Vmag. y a
Real Consejo. Dos memoriales q̃ di. en el gouierno el vno q̃
para q̃ a los d'hos Niños les Conseda Vmag. los priuilegios y
mercedes q̃ gosan los demas Collegios, q̃ ay en españa de niños, guerfanos, de quien es patron Vmag. = El otro para q̃ del
hospital Real y su botica se den las Medicinas Necessari
as. para la Cura de los d'hos Niños. en sus enfermedades, por te
ner. Como tengo en Cassa enfermeria adonde Cuido de su Cu
ra y Regalo tan a satisfacion de la Republica, como Vmag.
siendo seruido podra ynformarse, y porque fio de la gran
piedad, y selo de Vmag.: que he de Reciuir mayores mercedes
Ruego a dios Nro. señor Conserue a Vmag. muy largos Años.
Con acrecentamiento de mayores Reynos, y amparo de
la Christiandad. Manila y Bullio. 27 de 1642.

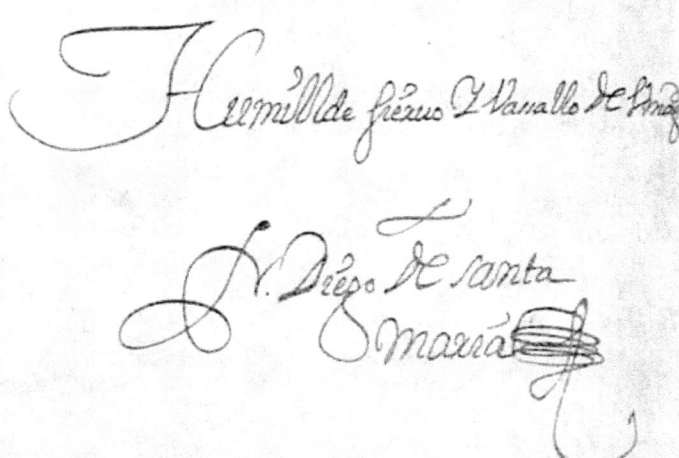

Humillde siervo y Vassallo de Vmag
Diego de santa
maria

P. Fr. Domingo de Betanzos OP, the founder of the Province of Santiago, initiated the first attempt to establish an outpost of the Province between 1540-1545 but failed. Pp. Fr. Fernando de la Paz OP and his brother Domingo de la Anunciacion OP undertook the second venture in 1570 but also failed to materialize. The first Bishop of *Filipinas*, P. Fr. Domingo Salazar OP, organized a group of Dominicans from Spain and Mexico to found an independent province but surrendered when faced with unexpected resistance from the Mexican Province. A member of Salazar's cabal, P. Fray Juan Chrisostomo OP, would undertake a fourth attempt that would overcome numerous barriers and delays to succeed finally.[124]

The Dominican Province of "the Most Holy Rosary of Mary the Mother of God, ever virgin" to which Fray Diego belonged was conceived by a group of friars from the Province of Mexico to establish missions in Asia with the Philippines as its pivotal point. P. Fray Juan Chrisostomo OP was tasked to secure the necessary approvals from Spain and Rome. He obtained from the Master General of the Order, P. Fr. Pablo Constable de Ferrara OP, a charter dated 14 July 1582 giving him authority to establish a province of thirty brethren of the Order for the *Philippinas* Islands and the kingdom of *China* with privileges of the province of Mexico granted to it. The Master General also issued a circular letter to the members of the Order confirming Chrisostomo's authorities. In Rome, P. Fr. Juan obtained a brief dated 15 September 1582 from Pope Gregory XIII which granted to the Dominican province of *Philippinas* and *China* powers of absolution from sins, excommunications, and other sentences, censures and pains, even in cases reserved for the Apostolic See.[125] The Pope also gave him many precious relics for the new province, granting many indulgences to those who visited them.

The Pope's approval required the Spanish King's *pase regio* (royal consent). Chrisostomo encountered unexpected resistance and long delays in Spain. It would appear that the delay was caused by a pending petition of the 8Dominican Province of Santiago to send a group of Dominicans to *Filipinas*.[126] He eventually secured the endorsement of the new province from the King of Spain to the governor of the *Philippinas* Islands dated 20 September 1585. P. Fray Juan de Castro assumed the leadership of 23 missionary volunteers from different Dominican convents throughout Spain and departed for Vera Cruz from Castilla in May 1586.[127]

Unknown to the group, the 1586 General Junta of Manila was held to discuss important matters for the King's consideration. Contained in a Memorandum dated 26 July 1586 was a summary of the requirements of the country, the necessity of the journey to the King's court by the Junta's representative, P. Alfonso Sanchez SJ, and the necessity for convening other assemblies. Among the recommendations of the Junta was a statement indicating the need for more religious of *the three existing orders and no new orders to come*. Bishop Salazar was among the signatories of the Memorandum.[128] By the time the pioneer Dominicans of the new province were about to depart from Mexico, Sanchez had arrived and informed the

Viceroy of Nueva España about the Junta's recommendations to stop the Dominicans from continuing their journey to *Filipinas*.[129] The intervention caused further delays, but would not deter the group's determination. 15 arrived in the port of Cavite on 21 July 1587. Three died in the voyage across the Atlantic, two stayed in Mexico, and three proceeded directly to Macau.[130]

Province of the Most Holy Rosary

By the time H. Fray Diego de Santa Maria arrived in the Philippines, the Dominicans had been in the island of Luzon for 45 years with established missions in the challenging areas of Bataan, Pangasinan, Cagayan, Nueva Vizcaya, Babuyanes and the Parian of the Sangleys. They undertook to build outposts in China, Cambodia, Formosa, and Japan but met with varying degrees of success and failure. Manila's Dominican bishop Domingo Salazar greatly assisted the pioneering Dominicans to overcome the difficulties associated with establishing a new enterprise in a strange land. Inside the walled city, they built an elegant convent and church named after their order's founder, *Santo Domingo*.[131]

In 1587, a *Seminario de Indios* was founded by P. Fray Pedro Bolaños OP in Bataan. It was however closed shortly after because of his deteriorating health. At the age of 62, he was the first among the pioneers to die in the Islands the following year.[132] It will take over 400 years later for P. Fr. Pedro's dream of a regular school to actualize with the 2006 opening of Letran in Abucay, an original centre of the Dominican missions in Bataan.[133] Another pioneer's aspiration that just took nine years to materialize was that of P. Fr. Miguel de Benavides OP. Benavides was the first Bishop of Nueva Segovia in 1597, and Archbishop of Manila in 1602 who initiated the foundation of the province's first college.[134]

The Dominican missions were principally for the conversion of souls, and the missionaries assigned there had varying levels of education and experience. Some did not complete their studies in Spain and required further instruction from the experienced professors of the province. Whenever the need arose, the Santo Domingo Convent organized a make-shift school which closed as soon as the need ceased to exist. This temporary but recurring need crystallized the importance of establishing a regular college with a permanent teaching staff.[135] Benavides thus bequeathed his library and the rest of his estate to *be spent in aiding the foundation and endowment of a college-seminary where the religious of the [Santo Domingo] convent may pursue the study of arts and of theology; and where the religious may instruct the* novices *and other religious who wish to avail themselves of their aid, others who are sons of inhabitants of this city and the islands and any other persons.*[136] The executors of his and others' wills completed the articles of establishment for the *Colegio de Santo Tomas* in 1611. On 15 August 1619, the college officially opened its portals, and twelve lay collegians from noble Spanish families of the city entered into residence.[137]

Letran was closely intertwined and shared a parallel history with Santo Tomas until 1910 when each assumed separate corporate personalities.[138] With very few and rare exceptions, it was thus customary to expect that a student of Letran would continue his secondary and higher studies at Santo Tomas after completing his primary education. After 1768, a Manila student who studied in Santo Tomas was axiomatically presumed to be a graduate of either Letran or San Jose until the return of the Jesuits in 1859.

The Dominicans also established the Church of *Los 'Sanctos' Reyes* and maintained the *Hospital de San Gabriel* in the Parian for the spiritual and temporal care of the *sangleys*. Under their care, the *sangleys* seldom died without receiving the sacraments. A church was constructed for the converted Christians among them in the Binondo settlement. Attempts to establish missions in China, Cambodia, Formosa, and Japan during this period proved precarious with many Dominicans suffering persecution and martyrdom most notably in Japan. It was during the height of this evangelical fever that H. Fray Diego de Santa Maria arrived in Manila with the Dominican mission of 1632.[139]

Fray Diego was born in 1595 in Miajadas, a villa in the province of Caceres, diocese of Plasencia, Spain. He professed as cooperator brother at the Dominican Convent of *San Pablo de Sevilla* on 20 December 1626. Fray Mateo de Villa, who was recruiting for the Province of the Most Holy Rosary, awakened his missionary zeal. Inspired, he joined Villa's mission of 31 Dominican religious and departed from Spain on the feast of Corpus Christi in 1631. After arriving in Vera Cruz, the group rested in Mexico at the *Hospicio de San Jacinto*.

San Jacinto was not just a place of rest for Dominicans in transit to *Filipinas* and the Far East. It was a place to prepare the friars *for their work, which included studying native languages, geography and the like.*[140] On 15 January 1599, the Viceroy of Nueva España granted the Philippine province a license to establish a hospice in Mexico. A conflict over jurisdiction ensued considering that Mexico was under the Dominican Province of Santiago. The Master General P. Fr. Agustin Galamino OP placed the hospice under the jurisdiction of the Province of the Most Holy Rosary in May 1611 with Pope Paul V's approval contained in his 3 January 1612 bull. The *Consejo Real de Indias* confirmed both documents on 24 February 1612.[141] San Jacinto eventually became known as *San Jacinto de China* or *San Jacinto de los Filipinos* because of the many *chino* and *indio* slaves from *Filipinas* residing and working there. They performed an invaluable service as cultural intermediaries. The slaves' knowledge of places and customs aided and prepared the Dominican missionaries for their assigned destinations.[142]

H. Fray Diego and his companions traveled 80 arduous leagues by foot to the port of Acapulco to catch the ship departing for Manila. Six died along the way. The rest departed on 23 February 1632 and arrived at the port of Cavite the following May.[143] Once settled, the superior distributed the members of the group to Santo Domingo, Santo Tomas, and the different missions and parishes.

Plate XI

St Martin de Porres OP
1579 - 1639

- *Artist unknown, 1639.* Monasterio de Santa Rosa de las Monjas de Lima

Kindred Souls

H. Fray Diego became the porter of the Santo Domingo Convent. Among his duties as porter was to attend to the needs of all visitors who came to call. In time, visitors began to recognize and acknowledge him to be a man of example, virtue, and perfection. His compassion reached out to the visiting poor and needy. The orphans and abandoned boys deprived of love, food, and home at a very young age moved him the most. Their plight prompted him to implore the Prior of the convent to provide shelter and care for the boys within the convent. Appreciating his concerns, the Prior allotted an area beside the porter's quarters and allowed H. Fray Diego to care for the boys after fulfilling his duties as a porter. Thus, the tasks of gathering, rearing and educating orphans commenced. He taught them their first letters. He sent those inclined to polish their grammar and learn Latin to the *Colegio de Santo Tomas* nearby.[144]

Fray Diego's busy schedule allowed him brief moments of rest. It was in one of those rare moments that an unexpected holy visitor came to call on him. According to P. Fr. Vicente Salazar OP:

> *It happened that a citizen of Manila made a journey to the city of Lima, where the venerable brother, Martin de Porres, resided in our convent of El Rosario; and as that servant of God was so charitable, he was so very much pleased for others to be so. That citizen of Manila, by name Francisco Ortiz, told him that he knew a lay-brother religious, a laborer of this place of Manila, a man of most holy life, who supported with alms twenty-four orphan boys, whom he gathered, and was teaching them to read and write. And the most special thing which was admired in him was that he never went forth from the convent in search for alms, but that our Lord directed them to him in order that he might carry forward the work of charity, which he was doing with the said poor boys. Appreciating the good news, the servant of God desired greatly to know and to deal with that holy lay-brother, who lived in this city of Manila at a distance of three thousand leagues from the city of Lima. After three days, Francisco Ortiz returned to visit the servant of God, whom he found very cheerful and happy. Smiling the latter informed him that he had already met and talked with the said lay-brother religious of Manila, and had encouraged him to proceed in so pious a work. What most astonished Francisco Ortiz was to hear the servant of God talk the Chinese language, which the Sangleys of this country used.*[145]

Through a mystical phenomenon that is known as bi-location, H. Fray Diego was indeed blessed to meet a fellow cooperator brother from distant Lima. It is because of this holy meeting of kindred souls that Letran became a center for propagating the veneration of Saint Martin de Porres towards his eventual canonization in 1962.[146]

Hermano Juan Geronimo Guerrero was another kindred soul who became Fray Diego's close friend given their shared interests and similar charitable concerns.[147] In as much as Hermano Juan already attended to the needs of poor and orphan Spanish boys under the King's patronage, one cannot help but wonder who Fray Diego's orphans were. The only possible candidates would be legitimate *mestizos de españoles* or non-Spanish slaves.[148] It is reasonable to expect that Spanish mestizos constituted most of Fray Diego's wards considering that the King ignored Hermano Juan's query regarding their care. As the Mexican experience indicated, mestizos were rejected and abandoned by both the Spaniards and *Indios* because they did not belong to either race.[149] Another probable source of orphans could be from the Dominican missions in Japan and among the Parian *sangleys*. Christian refugees from the persecutions in Japan and children of Christian *sangleys* had no other refuge than their missionary patrons. These challenges did not faze H. Fray Diego. Unlike Hermano Juan who had to beg, alms easily found their way to H. Fray Diego as reported.[150]

A Merger of Two Institutions

The city's residents admired H. Fray Diego's boys for their unique familiar demeanor molded by an orderly way of life. They always moved around the city in pairs and never alone. They soon became known as Diego's twins. The increasing numbers led him to form a congregation under the patronage of the Church's twin titans, Saints Peter and Paul and named it *Seminario de Niños Huerfanos de San Pedro y San Pablo*.[151]

When Hermano Juan relinquished Letran to the Dominicans in 1640, the two institutions consolidated but the choice of the surviving entity's name became a problem. The Dominicans retained the appellation of *Seminario de Niños Huerfanos de San Pedro y San Pablo*. The superiors sent a petition to erect the *seminario* into a college of the Province and the Order to the Master General, P. Fray Tomas Turco OP. The Master General issued an official patent erecting the *seminario* as College of the Province and the Order with all the graces and privileges enjoyed by such houses in accordance with the general laws of the same on 29 May 1644.[152] The Province accepted and received the *seminario* as its house and college, and selected the Commissary of the Holy Office, P. Fray Jeronimo de Zamora OP, as its first president in the Acts of the 1652 Provincial Chapter.[153]

Unfortunately, the school that was known as *Colegio de Niños Huerfanos de San Juan de Letran* still officially enjoyed the protection and financial support of His Majesty the King and was the beneficiary of the Bacnotan and the Parian encomiendas. The school adopted a combination of both names to address such unforeseen implications of this oversight. Thus, *Colegio de Niños Huerfanos de los Santos Apostoles San Pedro y San Pablo, de San Juan de Letran* became the school's name unofficially for a period of time. However, the use of the name chosen by Hermano Juan Geronimo Guerrero was still the basis for the continued patronage of the King. Furthermore, the name Letran was more popular and regularly used by the residents of Manila given its longer history with the city. It would not be until 1706 that the Provincial Chapter effected the necessary official changes and the Colegio of the Province and Order was hence officially called *Colegio de San Juan de Letran* to this day. Nevertheless, as Salazar pointed out and stressed, the school ended not only with one but with three patron saints.[154]

The Orphan

17th century Iberians categorized orphans among the marginal members of society which included prostitutes, major and petty criminals, gypsies, and *conversos* (new Christians).[155] They believed that *[orphan] children who were left uneducated and unattended would follow their supposedly natural, 'evil' instincts, become worrisome brats, and then lead depraved, criminal, and even heretical lives.*[156] As such, neglected orphans would eventually become sinful and criminal in their habits. *Having been brought up free and without a 'boss,' they divert themselves and that having been raised in liberty, when adults, they necessarily become destructive of the public good, corruptive of good customs, and disquieting to people and towns.*[157] To overcome such tendencies, children should be placed in schools to become loyal, obedient, pious and industrious subjects. Being an orphan however was never a simple matter.

Although Spanish orphanages were established initially for destitute and parentless children, they did not always strictly adhere to this purpose. A diversity of 'orphan' boarders emerged and would most likely also manifest among Fray Diego's wards. Valentina Tikoff's study of orphanages illustrated the following array of players in 18th century Seville. There were the full orphan, *Huerfano de Padre y Madre*, and the half orphan, *Huerfano de Padre* or *Huerfano de Madre* where the former was preferred over the latter. There was the *de facto* orphan due to poverty and other disadvantages, and the 'entitled' orphan whose admittance was due to an influential or high official's intervention. Occasional day students, boarders and delinquents would emerge. Day students began to manifest among the half orphans. As the reputation of the orphanage became established, a *pensionista noble* (noble pensioner) would occasionally reside there in separate quarters. The effective disciplinary measures practiced by the shelter would earn admirers and lead to the entry of incorrigible boys intended for "correction."[158] Surprisingly, the 1655 audit of Letran would reveal similar patterns highlighted by Tikoff. Considering the divergent backgrounds of the students who would live in the *Colegio*, the predominant culture of the abandoned child interacting with the other players would lead to a new norm of collective behavior that defined the character of the students. Qualities fostered and emulated through the centuries.

In the context of psychology, Dr. Carol Pearson described the orphan as an archetype. *Fearing exploitation, the Orphan seeks to regain comfort of the womb and neonatal safety in the arms of loving parents. To fulfill their quest, they must go through the agonies of developmental stages they have missed. Their strength is the interdependence and pragmatic realism that they had to learn at an early age.*[159] Depending on how the *Orphan* is developed, two ultimate undesirable outcomes may result. In the words of Anna Craycroft, he could become either a *Beguiling Orphan* or a *Piteous Orphan*. The Beguiling Orphan *is a charmer, one who knows how to manipulate his emotional performance for optimal interpersonal results. He is charming, adorable, savvy, manipulative, calculative, and a master of disguise. The Piteous Orphan is one whose social operations take place exclusively in the real, genuine and heartfelt emotional experience. He exhibits true pathos, raw emotional presence, and always almost but never becoming.*[160] Concluding, Pearson points out disappointingly that *they will fall into the victims mentality and so never achieve a heroic position.* However, if appropriately developed, he becomes Craycroft's *Dissident Orphan, the maverick who habitually paves his own path through every circumstance. He is precocious, self-sufficient, an island, courageous, autonomous, jaded and world-weary.* He undergoes a metamorphosis from *Orphan* to *Everyman.*[161] He transforms into a fearless, heroic populist *paragon that can be defined, classified, patterned and emulated by the host.*[162]

The process of molding the character of the Letran alumnus began with Hermano Juan. His tales of the heroic hospitaller knights were embedded in the orphans' psyche to emulate. Dominican spirituality and education would add enriching dimensions to this formation.

Alumni Profile

Letran became the *de facto* primary education department of *Santo Tomas* when integrated into the Dominican community in 1640. The Prior of Santo Domingo, P. Fray Sebastian de Oquendo, assumed responsibility for the *Colegio*, while H. Fray Diego was the administrator known as the *Presidente's Hermano Compañero*.[163] The 1655 auditors examined three journals.[164] The first contained the names of Hermano Juan's remaining 12 students as of 1640.[165] There were no records before that year.[166] The second journal included the names of H. Fray Diego's 23 students. The third listed the names of the students after 1640. Hermano Juan's 12 students joined the 23 already in Santo Domingo where they were all housed. Of these 35 students: 12 were orphans, seven sons of soldiers, seven indigents, 3 abandoned, four from affluent families, and two by 'special' accommodation. As to origin, 18 were from Manila, 6 Japan, 3 China, 2 Spain and the rest from Pampanga, Pangasinan, and Bataan. After leaving Letran, 14 became soldiers, five religious, three seculars, one ordained friar, one school teacher, one music teacher, one laborer, one continued religious studies, and three died.

The Crown Prince of Calonga, Don Juan de Pozaleta, became the most notable alumnus.[167] The most successful among them was Agustin Delgado who became the Receptor of the Royal Audiencia.[168] Other outstanding alumni of the group included: Pablo Mah-jun, a Sangley orphan who grew up as an *escribano* (scribe) due to his proficiency in the Spanish language.[169] *Capitan de Campaña* Hernando Lopez distinguished himself in the pacification of the Pangasinan rebellion and died in the 1661 Ilocos engagement.[170] Diego Alonso, an intrepid mariner from Mexico, earned renown in the 1646 Battle of Mariveles against the Dutch.[171]

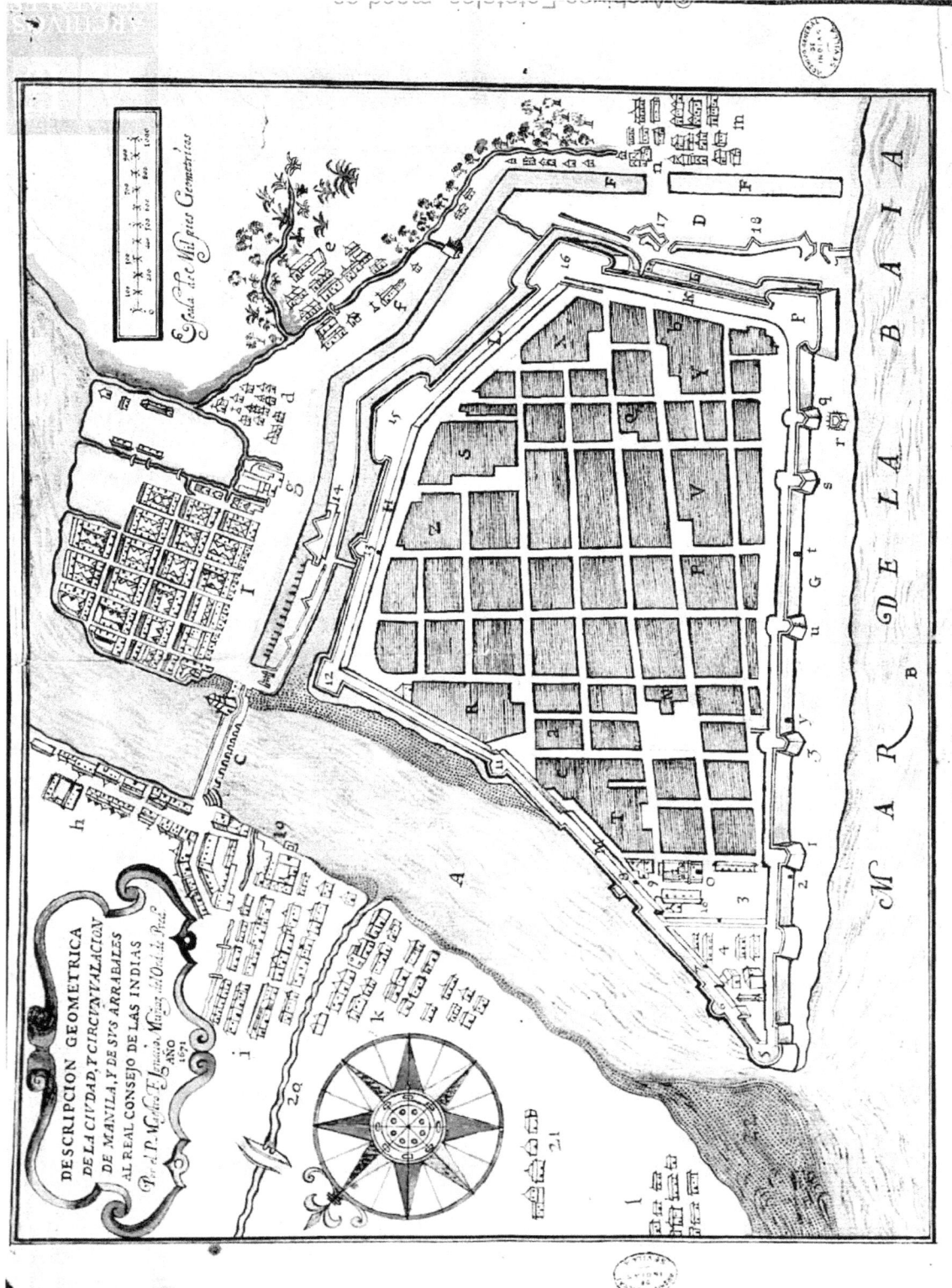

Plate XII

Abecedario, y guia de las partes, y lugares notables de la Planta, y circunvalacion dentro, y fuera de los muros de la ciudad de Manila Metropoli de las Islas Filipinas.

A. Rio de Pasig
B. Mar de la Baia
C. Puente
D. Parte Meridional
E. Fosso
F. Contrafosso
G. Cortina de Santa Luzia
H. Cortina del Parian de los Chinos
I. Pueblo del Parian
K. Cortina de Bagumbaya
L. Cortina de Dilao
M. Cortina del Rio
N. Iglesia Metropolitana
O. Capilla Real
P. Recogimiento de la Misericordia
Q. Recogimiento de Sta Potenciana
R. Convento de Santo Domingo
S. Convento de San Francisco
T. Convento de Monjas de Sta Clara
V. Convento de San Agustin
X. Convento de los Recoletos Agustinos
Y. Colegio de la Compania de Jesus
Z. Convento, y Hospital de S. Juan de Dios
a. Colegio de Sto Tomas, Universidad Real
b. Seminario de la Compania de Jesus
d. Pueblo de San Anton
e. Pueblo de Dilao
f. Hospital de los Naturales
g. Niños huerfanos de S. Juan de Letran
h. Pueblo de Quiapo
i. Pueblo de Binondoc
k. Pueblo de la Estacada
l. Pueblo de Lingon

m. Pueblo de Bagumbaya
n. Convento de S. Juan de Recoletos Agustinos
p. Baluarte de San Diego
q. Reducto, y Fortin San Lorenzo
r. Fortin San Joseph
s. Fortin S. Eugenio
t. Puerta de Santa Luzia
u. Fortin San Pedro
y. Puerta del Pallacio del Governador
z. Fortin San Juan
1. Baluarte San Francisco
2. Puerta al Quartel de Banderas
3. Quartel de Banderas
4. Fuerza de Santiago
5. Plataforma, llave de la Barra del Rio
6. Media naranja, y Revellin
7. Podigo de la fuerza de Santiago
8. Puerta de los Almazenes al Rio
9. Herreria del Rey
10. Almazenes Reales
11. Baluarte de Santo Domingo
12. Baluarte San Gabriel
13. Fortin con Puerta principal al Parian
14. Tenaza Real Santiago
15. Baluarte San Francisco, de Dilao
16. Baluarte San Nicolas, y de Carranza
17. Revellin de la puerta Real de Bagumbaya
18. Sitio de los Arrozeros en el Parian
19. Hospital de los Chinos
20. Estero, que va al pueblo de Tondo
21. Sitio de Pescadores
22. Baxo en la Boca del Rio

Letran-Parian marked "g" in the 1671 City Map of Manila

- Muñoz, Ignacio OP, 1671-11-8. ESPAÑA. MINISTERIO DE EDUCACIÓN, CULTURA Y DEPORTE. Archivo General de Indias, ES.41091.AGI/27.11//MP-FILIPINAS,10

A Leveled Playing Field

The profile of the student population indicated that H. Fray Diego committed an unthinkable act during those days. He mixed the scions of Manila's elite with the marginal boys of the city.

To address the impact of this social experiment, P. Fray Sebastian de Oquendo decided to adopt the Rule of St Augustine for the *Colegio*. All the students followed the school's statutes and the Rule observed by both the Dominicans and the Hospitallers of Saint John. The Rule became the great equalizer among the students. It consisted of 20 observances covering the foundation of communal life, prayer, moderation and self-denial, safeguarding chastity, fraternal correction, the care of community goods and treatment of the sick, asking pardon and forgiving offenses, governance, and obedience.[172] Those from wealthy families were admonished not to look down at the poor ones because they lived together in holy company. No one could claim ownership of anything as all owned everything in common. Anything received was shared equally with everybody. The dynamics developed humility and compassion among the rich and instilled dignity and self-confidence among the poor in a leveled playing field.

In 1742, P. Fr. Vicente Salazar OP expressed astonishment at the imposition of such *very holy and very strict statutes since the boys were not obliged to attain so great perfection, and still being boys, were not able to show so much. After some years, the said statutes were revised in a chapter of this province.*[173] Nevertheless, the earlier students somehow emulated and passed-on the conditioned attitudes and internalized practices. The populist attitude and behavior of the Letran alumni became defining qualities that distinguished them from the elitist orientation of those from *Santo Tomas* and *San Jose*.

Beginning 1640, the students wore a distinctive attire designed by P. Fr. Clemente Gant, the prior provincial, to avoid envy and discord arising from social class distinctions in attire and grooming.[174] Uniforms were provided free with punishment exacted if not kept neat and clean. It consisted of a blue mantle with white collar, long black sleeves, and a black bonnet as headgear to distinguish them from the students of *Santo Tomas* who wore green silk robes.[175] A *beca* (tippet) was later added to identify a scholar from the rest.[176] One who paid the full tuition did not wear a *beca*. Red in color, *the tippet was folded in two parts and crossing over the breast and drawn up behind the shoulders.*[177] The white cross of St John was encrusted on the red tippet as practiced by the Hospitaller Knights of Justice. The white eight-pointed cross on a field of red was a last visible trace of Hermano Juan's diminishing influence in the school. This added vestige from the past, which perhaps the alumni of the *Colegio* clamored to preserve, eventually defined the school's colors of red and blue. After the *Colegio* was declared an ecclesiastic college in 1690, the uniform enjoyed the privilege of being an ecclesiastical habit and students ordained *in sacris* may say mass without having to change into any other required garments.[178] It would remain its official uniform until 1865 when Letran was declared a first class private college of secondary instruction.[179]

Becas

Becas were scholarships from endowments bequeathed by benefactors for specific purposes and beneficiaries. Benefactors who founded *obras pias* (pious trusts) for the particular purpose of providing education established what was known as *becas de fundacion* (foundation scholarships). Endowments from other donors were known as *becas de donacion* (donation scholarships). At the discretion of the rector, the school also granted *becas* for its account known as *becas de gracia* (awards of grace).[180]

Colegio de Santo Tomas was an *obra pia,* and it was founded to provide education for *hijos de españoles* (Spanish sons). On the other hand, Letran was not an *obra pia* as many mistakenly believed it to be. Under its *Patronazgo Real*, Hermano Juan's wards were *becarios de donacion* (donation scholars) of the King of Spain. This *beca de donacion* was explicitly for *huerfanos de españoles* (orphan sons of Spaniards). Non-orphans were beneficiaries of *becas de donacion* of other benefactors while the destitute benefited from *becas de gracia* in exchange for the gratuitous chores and tasks to be performed within the *Colegio*.

All *becarios* (scholars) were known as *colegiales* (boarders) or *internos* (interns). Known as *porcionistas, colegiales* who were not scholars had to pay for their tuition, board, and lodging. Day students were known as *externos* (externs). It would not be until the 1690's that benefactors established the first *becas* for *indios* and *mestizo sangleys* in Letran.

A Disaster's Agony and Triumph

In a matter of months, the number of students surpassed 200. The boisterous boys compromised the solemnity and regularity of the convent. Returning them to the original site of Hermano Juan's school was not an option due to its distant location and decrepit state.[181] The Province decided to sell it and transfer the students to the property donated by Don Pedro Pinel opposite the convent's church and close to *Santo Tomas*.[182] The new site was located along Solana St and bounded by Beaterio and Anda Streets on each side. Occupied by the former residence of *Sargento Mayor* Bartolome Thenorio, the building was renovated to comply with the ordinary, government and city licenses required for school rooms, a church, and belfry to observe the divine offices.[183] The students transferred in 1643 and stayed there until 30 November 1645 when the San Andres earthquake struck the city.[184] The Dominicans lost their convent and church and a significant part of the *Colegio de Santo Tomas, but neither the religious nor the students were injured*.[185] The edifice housing *Colegio de San Juan de Letran* fell to the ground but all the boys, more than one hundred and twenty in number, escaped alive.[186] Not only were lives spared, but the disaster also ushered in blessings for the good friars: forthcoming good news from Rome, and overwhelming support from the city.

Through the intercession of Felipe IV, Pope Innocent X signed a bull dated 20 November 1645 elevating the Colegio de Santo Tomas into an *Academia*. It would be under *perpetual supervision, management and administration of the order of the friars of St Dominic and that of its master general conceding and granting to it power to obtain, employ, and enjoy all and singular, the privileges, indults, liberties, immunities, exemptions, favors, concessions, prerogatives, honors and preeminences*.[187] It rivaled the dominance of the Jesuit academy in Manila, the *Colegio de San Ignacio*.[188] Carlos II granted his patronage to *Santo Tomas* on 11 May 1680. After the Jesuit expulsion from the islands and the closure of their educational institutions on 21 May 1768, the title of royal was granted by Carlos III to *Santo Tomas* on 7 March 1785.[189] The Royal and Pontifical University of Santo Tomas became the only university of its kind in Asia located 3,000 leagues west from the nearest institutions of equal stature in Lima and Mexico.[190]

The porter's quarters in *Santo Domingo* was the least damaged by the San Andres earthquake and thus became Letran's home once again until 1648. A new wooden school edifice funded by the Dominican coffers and the city's *vecinos* began to rise on Governor Corcuera's Parian concession located at the corner of today's Padre Burgos Avenue and Aroceros St, where the Manila Metropolitan Theater now stands. The school's regular benefactors generously donated. *Almirante* Don Pedro Zarrate contributed three thousand pesos.[191] While waiting for the completion of the new site, the Philippines faced the invasion of a Dutch naval fleet.

A Tradition Adopted

As a consequence of the Dutch War of Independence, a series of five naval battles between Spain and the Dutch Republic transpired in 1646 on Philippine waters. Governor Diego Fajardo Chacon had at his disposal three galleons, a galley, and three brigantines for the defense of the Islands. The Dutch fleet, on the other hand, was composed of three squadrons with 18 vessels under the command of Maarten Gerritz Vries. In spite of being greatly outnumbered, the Spanish fleet won decisive victories while the city of Manila was in prayer invoking the intervention of Our Lady of the Most Holy Rosary, the patroness of the Victorious Battle of Lepanto.

The victories defied all expectations, and only a miracle could explain the glorious outcome.[192] On 9 April 1652, the Cathedral Chapter of Manila declared the five sea battle outcomes as miracles after a thorough canonical investigation.[193] *Thanksgiving [for this victory] was celebrated by a solemn fiesta, a procession, divine worship and [a parade of] the squadron, with other demonstrations - in fulfillment of the vow made to the Virgin of the Rosary, the city making a new vow to continue this anniversary every year.*[194] Since then, the city observes the annual celebration of Our Lady of the Most Holy Rosary of La Naval de Manila every second Sunday of October, the month

Plate XIII

Founders Memorial Portrait
-*Unknown Artist, ca. 1900s.* Colegio de San Juan de Letran

Letran's Parian Site now Metropolitan Theater's Home
- *Unknown Artist, 1933.* Bazaco 1933

of the Holy Rosary. A cherished tradition of the school, Letran students have been active participants in the annual observance since inception. Five Letran alumni distinguished themselves heroically in the Dutch wars: Diego Alonso (Navy), Diego de Alcarazo (Navy), Jose del Mercado (Army), Sebastian de Albornoz (Army), and Tomas Lopez (Army).[195] P. Fray Juan de los Angeles, who would become Letran's rector for three terms, was a Dutch captive held as a prisoner in New Batavia (Jakarta).[196]

Fray Diego's Final Days

The boys moved into the Parian campus in 1648 before its completion and stayed there until 1669. The new location proved to be of notable discomfort and detriment to the students' temporal and spiritual well-being. It was far from *Santo Tomas* where the students had to attend classes, and the Manila Cathedral and *Capilla Real* (Royal Chapel) where they had to fulfill altar and choir duties. The constant flow of market effluents also made the area damp and unhealthy. Surrounded by unconverted sangleys, the Dominicans feared the students' exposure to morally scandalous and detestable behavior.[197] In the event of another ethnic uprising, the school was precariously in the crossfire between the *sangleys* and the walled city's canons.

Not long after, Fray Diego yearned to return to his mother convent, the *Convento de San Pablo* in Sevilla, having served almost 25 years in the Islands. His superiors granted permission and the audit ordered by Capitan Luis de Aduana followed. The third of the three journals contained simple records of students after the merger beginning 1640 until 1655. Of the 595 boys, 141 were orphans, 120 sons of soldiers, 100 affluents, 75 indigents, 32 abandoned, 20 scholars, and others marked as unknown or *influencia* (influence). Of the 501 who left school, 306 became soldiers, 70 agriculturists, 44 religious, 29 pursuing higher studies, 13 secular clerics, 13 sailors, 10 bookkeepers, 5 pages, 3 military officers, 2 bachelor degree holders, 1 chemist, 1 tailor, and 1 shopkeeper. As to origin, 232 were from Manila, 73 Mexico, 31 Pampanga, 30 Cavite, 21 Spain, 16 China, 16 Japan, 15 Cebu, 12 Flanders, 11 California, 8 Cagayan, 8 Panay, 8 Parañaque, 7 Bataan, 6 Formosa, 5 Terrenate, 4 Bicol, 3 Pangasinan, 2 Ilocos, 2 Laguna, 2 Nueva Ecija, 2 Tayabas, 1 Bulacan, 1 Mindoro, 1 Taguic with the remaining marked as unknown.[198]

Three notable alumni exemplified the top three career choices and highlighted the diversity of this group - a young Spanish benefactor of the school, an *Indio* agricultural magnate, and a *Sangley* bishop.[199]

Lope Felix de Alcarazo belonged to a family of soldiers. His father was Juan de Alcarazo, general of the Spanish army who died during the *sangley* rebellion of 1639. Letran admitted him in 1641. He completed the humanities and joined the military immediately after. Frail and ailing, he returned in 1650 and died shortly bequeathing his beloved *Alma Mater* with close to 4000 pesos, a fortune during those days. He was among Letran's first benefactors. His endowment is discussed further in a later chapter of this book.[200]

Diego de Aguas was the poor orphan son of Alejo and Maria Linga, *Indios* from San Fernando, Pampanga. He entered Letran in 1649. He was among those students who preferred to till the soil - a career choice favored by students next to soldiery. He returned to his hometown after completing his education and readily found a job as a farmer. He saved enough capital to purchase land. He became a wealthy proprietor making good use of economy and science.[201]

Bishop Luo Wenzao, the first Chinese Dominican priest of the province and the first Chinese bishop of China, arrived in Manila to study and become a Dominican missionary in 1645.[202] He learned his first Spanish letters at Letran at a very advanced age of 30 before taking philosophy at Santo Tomas.[203] Known by his Christian name of Gregorio Lo Lopez, he received the Dominican habit on 1 January 1650. He performed outstanding pastoral work in China during the Christian persecutions of 1665 to 1671. He became Bishop of Basilitano and Vicar Apostolic of Nanjing in 1684.[204] We will delve into this outstanding alumnus further ahead.

The fifteen-year period highlighted significant developments. Letran became widely known throughout the Islands, and its fame moved Spanish officials and soldiers in the provinces to enroll their sons at the *Colegio*. The number of affluent and privileged boys was approaching those of the disadvantaged wards; prompting Letran to collect an annual tuition from those who could afford. The tuition amounted to 50 *piastre* annually by 1755.[205] Using titles of *sacristanes* (sextons), *porteros* (porters), *libreros* (book custodians), and other *oficios mecanicos* (mechanics), some do not pay anything at all.[206] Some beds appeared to be set aside for Chinese and Japanese boys groomed perhaps for future missionary duties in their home countries. Sons of *caciques* or *principales de indio* (native nobility) from Dominican missions and parishes began to appear in the student rolls. New donors increased the number of scholarships. The 1655 audit concluded that Letran exceeded expectations in its purpose of transforming disadvantaged boys into productive Christian members of society in the service of God and King.

At the end of his administration, Fray Diego left the economic and financial foundation of the *Colegio* on sounder and firmer grounds with revenues from rental properties, endowments willed by Spanish families, and tuition fees from paying students.[207] *Through [sheer] diligence, he sustained [an average of] 100 boys to assist with such regularity the community, mass, prayer, choir, refectory, silence, school, chapel singers, and for themselves officiating solemn matins and masses, trips and activities outside a house that acted like an order's novitiate.*[208] Fray Diego personally involved himself in the lives of students from the moment they entered the school to the day they departed. He found positions in the military and the government for boys who displayed no inclination for further studies.[209] Those who excelled were encouraged to continue studying and become teachers or ministers of the church. Having accomplished his mission, H. Fray Diego gradually turned

Diego de Santa Maria

over the administration of the *Colegio* to H. Fray Alonso de Villegas as early as October 1653.[210] He departed Manila in May 1657. Upon arriving in Acapulco however, his frail constitution succumbed to the distressing long voyage. He died later that year and interred in the *Hospital de San Hipolito*.[211]

The only memorials to remember the Dominican Cooperator Brothers Juan Geronimo Guerrero and Diego de Santa Maria are the simple 1941 Philippine Historical Committee's wall plaque beside Letran's front entrance and an obscure monolithic monument built in 1970 by the Fraternal Order of Knights in front of the school gymnasium. Both often ignored and forgotten by the students who continue to benefit from their lasting legacy - the *Colegio de San Juan de Letran*.

Chapter IV

For God and King

There was a time when the graduates of Letran were expected to enter the King's service as soldiers, sailors or public servants. Most of the graduates found themselves among the ranks of the ecclesiastical hierarchy by the end of the 17th century. His Majesty, in fact, encouraged it. As early as September 1640, the school agreed to Governor-General Corcuera's request to provide six students to serve as acolytes and choir at daily masses in the *Capilla Real* with one among them acting as *sacristan menor* (minor sexton).[212] The college choir of *tiples* (boy sopranos) was also to be made available on Sundays, holidays, anniversaries, and funerals of the military.[213] As a customary practice since Hermano Juan's days, 12 students were also required to serve at the Manila Cathedral on Saturdays, Sundays and holidays.[214] The King granted additional subsidies from the Capilla Real to support a seraphic tertiary order which maintained fifty colegiales in education.[215] By 1690, the Archdiocese declared the school an ecclesiastical college. Scholarships for Asian students destined for missionary work in their origins of birth were to follow in the next century. This conscious and deliberate effort to transform the school into a novitiate was an offshoot of the symbiotic relationship between Church and State under the *Patronato Real de Indias* (Royal Patronage of the Indies).

Patronato Real

Under the *Patronato Real, all funds for the support of religion became by a fiction of law government moneys, to be dispensed by the administration of Madrid or by its subordinate viceroys, who gave approval and direction to every major religious activity. All religious corporations looked directly to the court for authorizations, permissions, subventions, or judgment of pleas. The crown held the nomination of bishops, canons, parish priests, the erection of convents, colleges, welfare associations, and the conceding of* pase regio *(royal consent) to all indulgences, privileges, and pontifical bulls. The official backing given this system by the papacy from the first days of the* Reconquista *made its prerogative unquestioned*.[216] The Spanish monarch was the *de facto* head of the Catholic Church of Spain and its empire. Initially a concession from the Pope to Kings, it would evolve into a sovereign right and consequently into a power of the state. This situation would cause much instability and turmoil throughout the empire for many years to come. Understanding the *Patronato Real* and its history deserves serious attention.

Conceptually, patronage was *the protection given by a powerful man over another of modest means*. In Church matters, however, the right of patronage was technically different by the 12th century. In exchange for benefices such as land and church edifices, the donor-patron enjoyed the rights of disposing of the land, proposing and even imposing the minister of his choice on the bishop who gave him the canonical institution. The practice devolved into a personal right clarified by doctrine and legislation over time.[217] The term *Patronato Real* refers to the juridical system that was primarily a series of rights and duties that, under explicit concessions by the Holy See, pertained to the rulers of Spain and Portugal beginning in the fifteenth century.

In Aragon, the Crown claimed a patronage over churches and chapels founded on lands retaken from the Saracens, over ancient mosques converted to churches and over new churches. In 1486, the Catholic kings, Fernando of Aragon and Isabel of Castile obtained from Innocent VII the right of *Patronato Real* for Granada, Canary Islands, and Puerto Real (Cadiz) for the conquest of Granada.[218] In 1493, Alexander VI granted the Iberian monarchs, under the Treaty of Tordesillas, the concession of *patronato* over the churches of the conquered Indies, the *Patronato Real de Indias*. For their part, the sovereigns agreed to build and endow the churches within their territories. By 1523, Pope Adrian VI granted Carlos I *Patronato Real* for the entire of Spain because of the meritorious reconquest of the whole peninsula.[219]

Felipe II gave it a broad interpretation in a document known as the Magna Carta of the Patronato Real in 1574. The Magna Carta assigned broad powers to the Spanish sovereigns, including oversight of ecclesiastical life and punishing and exonerating clergy who did not fulfill their obligations. On this basis, the jurists worked out a theory whereby the sovereign could intervene in the internal affairs of the church of the Indies by virtue of the claim to be the vicar of the Supreme Pontiff - the theory of *Regio Vicariato Indiano*. The *Patronato Real* effectively removed the churches of both Spain and Portugal, as well as their territories in the West and East Indies, from the direct control of the Holy See. It, nevertheless, made it possible *to carry out the vast and intense work of evangelisation that the papacy, at least until the first half of the seventeenth century, would not have had the means to promote*.[220]

The separation of church and state was thus an alien concept in the Spanish empire from the 16th century onwards. What existed was a symbiotic relationship between the two towards attaining the Christian conversion of the heathens – the King's primary justification for the conquest and the establishment of western European hegemony over the New World. The strategy of proselytization involved military subjugation followed by the formation of manageable Christian settlements known as the *reduccion*, and the imposition of the *encomienda* (tributary system), *diezmo* (tithing) and *repartimiento* (forced labor drafts*) bajo la campana* (under the bell of a church).[221] Cowered by military intimidation, the natives severed all pagan links to the past and adopted a new subservient Christian way of life under the close watch of the missionaries.

Plate XIV

PATRONATO REAL - Symbiosis of Church and State
Legazpi-Urdaneta Monument

- Querol, Agustin Subirat, 1893. Filipinas Heritage Library © 1940.

The Mendicant Orders

When the towns first organized under ecclesiastical administration, not enough secular priests acted as curates. To fill the ranks, the King had to turn to the mendicant orders. However, their vows, their obligations to live in convents, and the prohibitions on property disqualified them. Pope Pius V had to grant the religious orders temporary exemption from these impediments until a sufficient number of secular clergy became available. Thus, the Franciscan, Augustinian, Dominican, and Recollect friars, the Jesuits, and other religious institutions assumed the responsibilities of diocesan clerics throughout the new Spanish dominions with the right to obey only the superiors of their respective orders.[222] It was an *ad interim* arrangement whereby the initial missions that developed into regular curacies were to be turned over to secular priests when sufficient numbers were available.

Greed eventually moved the *conquistadores* to enslave and abuse the native *Indios* of America to mine the gold, silver and other riches of the continent. The missionaries assumed the role of protectors of the oppressed and became intermediaries between the natives and the Spanish overlords.

Dominican P. Fray Bartolome de las Casas, known as the Protector of the Indians, witnessed the genocide of indigenes in the colony of *La Española* and *Cuba*.[223] He fought to end slavery and to adopt more humane ways of colonization.[224] The works of de las Casas and other Dominicans like Antonio de Montesino influenced and inspired a seasoned Dominican missionary in Nueva España, P. Fray Domingo Salazar OP, before his appointment as Bishop of Manila.[225] Salazar was initially hesitant to accept the nomination from Felipe II, but his desire to alleviate the enormous sufferings of all newly conquered people had endured and to establish missions in China moved him to do so. 20 Dominicans from the convent of Salamanca were sent to Mexico to accompany him. 12 died crossing the Atlantic, and seven were stricken with illness and remained in Mexico. He arrived in Manila with P. Fray Cristobal de Salvatierra OP as his sole companion in 1572. One can only imagine the joy Salazar felt when 15 from the newly created Philippine province of his Order arrived in 1587 and began the missionary work that he longed for. As the sole bishop in the Philippines, his policy of defending and protecting the native inhabitants from abuses earned him many enemies. He had to sail for Spain to petition the King's support personally in 1594.[226] Accompanying him was the erudite and respected P. Fray Miguel de Benavides OP who acted as the *procurador general* (syndic general) of his province in its petition for more religious.

During deliberations, the King's court and the Supreme Council of the Indies solicited Benavides' opinion on the prevailing doctrine espoused by a Jesuit theologian, Alfonso Sanchez. The Jesuit elucidated that *preaching of the holy gospel in heathen countries should be begun by soldiers, who by force of weapons and musketry should make the country quiet and subject the Indians, in order that the preachers might do their office immediately without resistance.*[227] According to Fray Diego Aduarte in his *Historia*, Benavides responded that:

> *This doctrine is very well suited to human prudence but is contrary to Divine Providence, to that which the Lord has ordained in His gospel, and even to the very nature of the faith, which demands a pious affection in those who hear it. This is not acquired as the result of the violences, murders, and conquests wrought by soldiers. On the contrary, as far as in them lies, they make the faith to be hated and abhorred; hence the Lord commanded that the preachers should be as sheep among the wolves, conquering them with patience and humility, which are the proper arms to overcome hearts. Hence not only the apostles, but all the other apostolic preachers who had followed them, have by these means converted all the nations of the earth. This father saw all this very well; but it seemed to him, as indeed he said, that these were old-fashioned arguments and that the world was now very much changed; and that no conversion of importance could or would be made unless soldiers went before to bring into subjection those who were to listen to the gospel, before the preachers preached it. He painted out this monster with such fair colors of rhetoric and with arguments so well suited to our weakness, our little spirit, and our less readiness to suffer for Christ and His gospel and to the works of saints who acted in conformity therewith...[R]egard it as a great inconsistency to say that our Lord Jesus Christ had acted with so short a view as a legislator that, when He made a law which was to last to the end of the world, He had announced a method which was to be followed at the beginning by the preachers of it who were presented before Him, and not under the same conditions by those who should follow after – just as if His providence was unable to apprehend that which was distant and future. It will be further be seen, if we consider it well, that the gospel received much more opposition at the beginning than it does at the present time; and it was not necessary at that time to subject kingdoms by war, in order to preach the gospel to them, much less will it be so now. Hence grave scandal would arise in the church if, when the Lord commands that gentle sheep shall be the ones to introduce His gospel, the introduction of it should be entrusted now to bloodthirsty wolves.*[228]

Benavides' retort was not an empty exercise of platitudes. The King was aware that the collective experiences of Benavides' brother Dominican missionaries and his own in the missions evangelizing the Sangleys at the Parian together with P. Fray Juan de Cobo OP supported his statement. There he painstakingly learned to speak, read and write their language while ministering to their illnesses in San Gabriel, the hospital he founded.[229] These skills he used well when he undertook missionary work in China together with the prior provincial, P. Fray Juan de Castro OP.[230]

Benavides was to be proven right when Christianity eventually took roots in Asia without the need for military intervention but at the cost of martyrs.

Japanese Christians, for instance, proliferated in number and prompted the Shogun to stem the tide through persecutions, executions and finally expulsion. The Shogun's actions were more political than religious. His eyes saw the subterfuge behind the mask of religion – the subversion of his power over his people by foreigners. The allegiance of his subjects was shifting to the agents of the vicar of the Supreme Pontiff.[231] The monarchs of other Asian kingdoms saw it too and awaited the dreadful coming of the ominous tide to reach their shores – the engorging wave of European imperialism.

Vanguard of Spanish Hegemony

Felipe II was so affected by Benavides that he convened a special council attended by the president of Castilla, the father-confessors of the princes, the auditors of the *Audiencia*, the lords of the *[Consejo de] Indias*, and many distinguished theologians to redefine the roles of soldiers in the task of evangelization.[232] The council determined that *there should be soldiers in the Spanish towns for the defense of the country, but that these soldiers shall not go as escorts to the preachers, and that they should not go in advance of them subjugating or killing indians; for this would be changing into a gospel of war that gospel which Christ our Lord delivered to us – a gospel of peace, love, and grace.*[233]

These policies involved logistical implications. Should it be proven that the religious can efficiently subjugate and control colonial vassals without the need of substantial military force, the cost of supplying soldiers and other military resources to distant colonies, such as *Filipinas*, could be significantly reduced and re-channeled towards the development, training, and support of religious personnel instead. Thus, the missionaries gradually became the King's vanguard whose ranks were quickly filled by the best and the brightest because martyrdom provided the shortest path to sainthood.[234] The effectiveness of the friars to control the *indios* (indigenes) had led a Viceroy of Mexico to remark that *in every friar, the king had in the Philippines a captain general and an entire army.*[235] At a time when Spanish military presence was no more than 5,000 men. There were 1,194 friars ministering to 6.5 million Catholic souls just before the 1896 Philippine Revolution.[236] The resulting heavy dependence on the friars, however, had its negative consequences.

The transition from the religious orders to the secular clergy was implemented in the American colonies thereby consolidating the crown's control over the ecclesiastical estates there. In Mexico, for instance, a sufficient number of *criollo* and *mestizo* secular priests took over the curacies painstakingly nurtured and developed by the friars and Jesuits for almost a century. Witnessing the losses suffered by their Mexican religious brothers, the Provinces of *Filipinas* conspired to avoid a similar fate by preserving their control over the *indios* and reinforcing their indispensable presence in the islands. Protected by ecclesiastical privileges under the *Fuero Eclesiastico* (Ecclesiastic Privileges and Immunities), the colonial government enforced laws and policies that favored the friars and ignored and violated those

For God and King

Plate XV - FRAILOCRACY

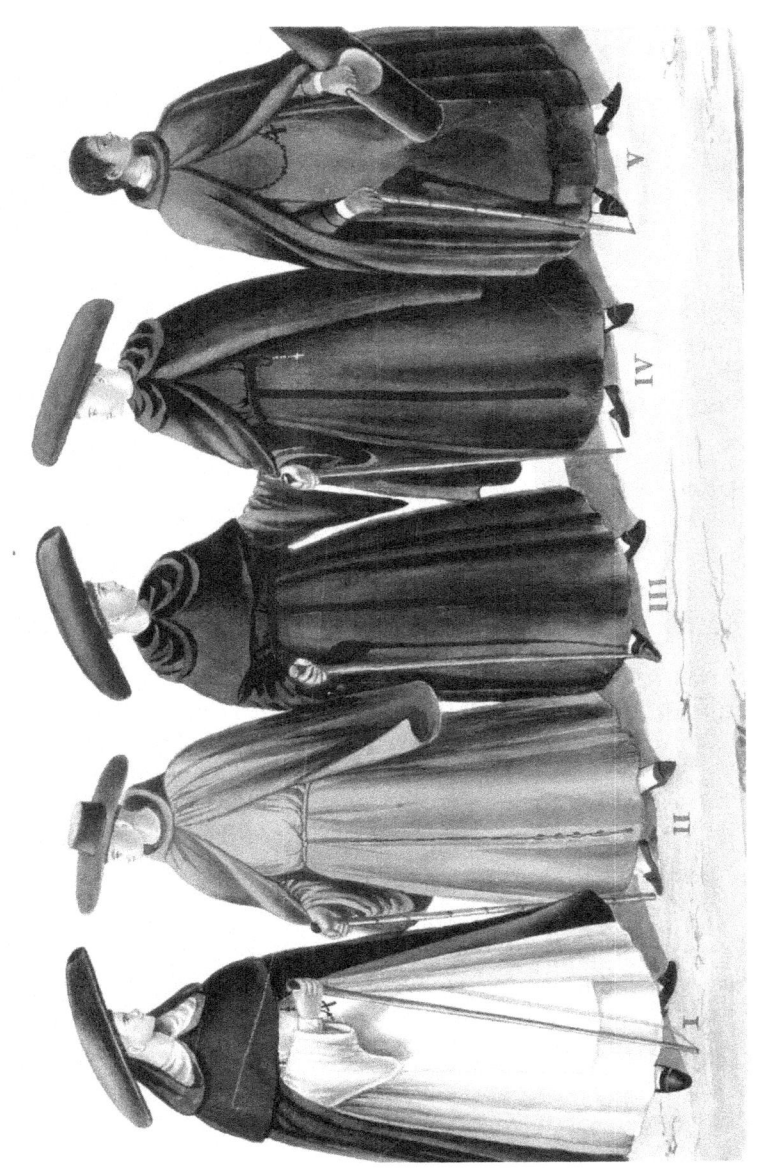

I - Dominican II - Franciscan III - Recollect IV - Augustinian V - San Juan de Dios

- Lozano, Jose Honorato, 1847. © Propiedad de Biblioteca Nacional de España bdh0000025759

detrimental to their designs.237 The Spanish governing principle of *obedezco pero no cumplo* (I obey but do not comply) or simply known as *cumplase* was applied whenever the 'chief executive' deemed the royal order impractical or detrimental to the welfare of the colony.238

Instead of teaching the Spanish language among the *indios* as required by law, the friars mastered and utilized local dialects to foster regional divisiveness and to ensure the government's dependence on them to communicate and to control the countryside.239 They purposely failed to report, refused to submit to diocesan visitations and obstructed the development and growth of native secular priests to impede the transition to episcopal control of the parishes. The crown had no choice but to succumb to the friars' recurring threat of parochial abandonment given the insufficient number of secular priests. Under the Laws of the Indies, the friars virtually became the only Spaniards in the Philippine pueblos by strictly disallowing Spaniards, *mestizos,* and *mulatos* from living with the *indios* in the *reducciones* outside Spanish settlements known as *villas.*240 Without the watchful eyes of other Spaniards, the friars were free to do whatever they wanted in the outlying areas of the archipelago. While acknowledging His Majesty's *Patronato Real* to benefit from his continued financial support, they generated their revenues independently and refused to accede to the controls and audits of the crown's bishops and vice patrons contrary to law.241 The Spanish monarch was effectively a King in name only, while the friars were the *de facto* rulers of *Filipinas.*242

Frailocracy

The Augustinian Provincial P. Fr. Jose Lobo OSA, during a hearing of the Taft Commission on 31 July 1900, compared *the Government of Spain in the Philippines [as] a round table having but one leg, and that leg in the center of the table, the friar here being the leg and the sole support of the main body of the table.*243

The Franciscan Provincial, P. Fr. Juan Villegas OFM, explained the role of the friar in greater detail with the following testimony:

> *[The priests do not have any political or civil functions in the parishes to which they were assigned]* except in so far as duties were entrusted to them, or required of them, by the government, for the reason that the parish priest was the party in whom they had the most confidence.
>
> The following may be mentioned as among the principal duties or powers exercised by the parish priest: He was inspector of primary schools; president of the health board and board of charities; president of the board of urban taxation; previously he was the actual president, but lately honorary president of the board of public works.
>
> He certified to the correctness of the cedulas - seeing that they conformed to the entries in the parish books. They did not have civil registrations here, and so they had to depend upon the books of the parish priest. These

books were sent in for the purpose of this cedula taxation, but were not received by the authorities unless viseed by the priest.

He was president of the board of statistics, because he was the only person who had any education. He was asked to do this work so that better results could be obtained. It was against the will of the parish priest to do this, but he could only do as he was told. If they refused, they were told that they were unpatriotic and not Spaniards. If they had declined, they would have been removed from their charge. He was president of the census taking of the town.

Under the Spanish law every man had to be furnished with a certificate of character. If a man was imprisoned and he was from another town for his antecedents, and the court would examine whether they were good or bad. They would not be received, however, unless the parish priest had his vise on them. The priest also certified as to the civil status of persons.

Every year they drew lots for those who were to serve in the army, every fifth man [quinto] drawn being taken. The parish priest would certify as to that man's condition... Every year they would go to what they call the sacramental books and get the names of all those who were twenty years of age. This list being certified to by the parish priest, the names were placed in an urn and then drawn out. Every fifth man was taken... All the men were brought to Manila and the regiments formed were very much mixed...

By law he had to be present when there were elections for municipal offices. Very often the parish priest did not want to go, but the people would come to him and say: "Come, for there will be disturbances, and you will settle many difficulties."

He was censor of the municipal budgets before they were sent to the provincial governor.

A great many of the duties I am enumerating were given to the priests by the municipal law of Maura.

He was also counselor for the municipal counsel when that body met. They would notify him that they were going to hold a meeting and invite him to be present.

The priests were supervisors of the election of the police force. This also had to be submitted to the provincial governor.

He was examiner of scholars attending the first and second grades in the public schools.

He was censor of the plays, comedies and dramas in the language of the country, deciding whether they were against the public peace or the public morals. These plays were presented at the various fiestas of the people.

He was president of the prison board, and inspector (in turn) of the food provided for the prisoners.

He was a member of the provincial board. Besides the parish priest there were two curates who served on this board. Before the provincial board came all matters relating to public works and other cognate matters. All estimates for public buildings in the municipalities were submitted to this board.

He was also a member of the board of partitioning crown lands. After the land was surveyed and divided, and a person wanted to sell his land, he would present his certificate and the board would pass upon the question whether or not he was the owner. This would be viseed by the board for purposes of taxation. When a private individual wanted to buy government land, he would apply to the proper officer, pay his money, and the board would determine whether the transfer was according to law.

In some cases the parish priests in the capitals of the provinces would act as auditors. In some of these places there would be only the administrator, and then the curate would come in and act as auditor.

Besides the above there were other small things which devolved upon the priest. It might be said that there were times, however, when nothing of moment was done in towns... [V]ery often they interfered in these matters for the benefit of the town itself. Of course, the only thing entrusted was the spiritual welfare of the people, but they had to do this other work because asked to do so by the government.[244]

Villegas' testimony would like us to believe that given the *Patronato Real*, friars were 'compelled' to act as the crown's agents or face censure and removal from their charge. To this day, religious historians would continue to assail the *Patronato Real* to explain and rationalize their role in governance. Villegas, however, failed to highlight the friars' complicity in all affairs of state whether good or bad and the abuse and corruption that broad authorities and discretion ultimately lead to.

The Governor-General yielded absolute power in *Filipinas*. Collectively, the five religious institutes were his equal if not more. The mendicant orders of St Augustin, St Francis, St Dominic and St Augustin Recollects, and the Society of Jesus were the masters of the provinces.[245] The bishop was free to assign missions and parishes with the approval of the vice patron and assigned the territories among the five. Among the laws concerning the conduct of the religious estate in *Filipinas*, Felipe II decreed that *there should be no Franciscans where there were Augustinians, nor religious of the Society where there were Dominicans*.[246] The more prized missions were already administered by the Augustinians (1565), followed by the Franciscans (1577), and the Jesuits (1581). The Dominicans who arrived in 1587 accepted the challenging missions of Bataan, Pangasinan, Cagayan and the Babuyanes.[247] Aside from conflicts with governors and bishops, the Dominicans were not always in agreement with the other Orders. These political and social dynamics would eventually affect the institutions associated with them. The departure of the Jesuits in 1768 gave way to the Dominican's dominance over education in the Philippines.

Letran under the Patronato Real

Being a Dominican institution in Manila sheltered Letran from the realities prevailing in the provinces, and tethered its destiny to the designs, triumphs, and challenges of the Order. The line between the training of a temporal soldier or a spiritual one became thinner and the religious formation more intensive.

The veneration of our Lady of the Most Holy Rosary housed at the Santo Domingo Convent was the principal devotion of the boys. The favored form of prayer was the daily recitation of the rosary. According to the Roman Breviary, *the rosary is a certain form of prayer wherein we say fifteen decades or tens of Hail Mary's with an Our Father between each ten, while at each of these fifteen decades we recall successively in pious meditation one of the mysteries of our Redemption.*[248] In the conflict against the Albigensian heresy in Toulouse, Our Lady instructed St Dominic of Guzman to *preach the Rosary among the people as an antidote to heresy and sin.*[249] It had since been ascribed to St Dominic as the originator of the devotion and actively propagated by the Dominicans. P. Fray Domingo Fernandez Navarrete OP shared the following observations of the *Colegio* during his stay there circa 1650:

> *In my time it had more than two hundred boys, and was of great benefit to those islands. The way in which the boys were managed was inimitable in any other seminary. They were taught reading, writing, grammar, and music there. Those who studied the arts and theology went to our college. They were given two suits of clothes per year, and received religious instructions. In the morning, before breakfast, they recited aloud in chorus one-third of the rosary, at noon another third, and at evening the remaining third, and the salve chanted with the litany of our Lady; and at midnight of important feasts, the matins. While they were eating at dinner and supper one of them read at the table. They confessed and took communion every month, and were punished or rewarded. Some of those boys became soldiers, some secular priests, and some took the habit in the convents of St Francis, St Augustine, and St Dominic, so that the seminary was a general camp of soldiers, both temporal and spiritual. An encomienda was obtained from his Majesty to aid in their support. Alms were obtained from burials and also from the indians. It is certainly a heroic work.*[250]

Under the school statutes, only Spanish orphans and children of poor Spanish parents between the ages of 7 and 16 were admitted gratuitously given the nature of the endowments. Letran also admitted Spaniards, mestizos, indios, and sangleys who could afford the fifty pesos annual matriculation. Considering that *Santo Tomas* and *San Jose* charged one hundred pesos and over annually for a secondary education, Letran's tuition was unquestionably reasonable. Non-Spanish indigents could obtain free education and board by working as *famulos* (domestics) in return for rudimentary knowledge. They were also known as *capistas* given the short black capes they wore. The *Colegio* did not admit illegitimate boys and those who deserted or expelled once before from Letran or other schools.[251]

As ordained, the students allowed at least two hours to prepare for his lessons in the communal study room under the guidance of a president to maximize time and to provide assistance in compositions, problems or difficulties. At the start of classes, they proceeded quietly in orderly rows of two by two with much composure, contemplating or reviewing his lessons most particularly if his levels were at the university. The different professors checked attendance and notified the prelate of the absences, and those who lagged in class or those who did not work on their compositions. The students had an hour of a religious, scientific conversation held everyday, divided into groups and presided by the Honorable or *Padre Presidente*.[252]

According to P. Fr. Fidel Villaroel OP, the *P. Presidente* was assisted by the *Decano* (Dean) chosen among the students. *The Decano exercised the functions of Vice-President and was immediately responsible for the orderly march of the Colegio. He was empowered to reprimand and punish erring students and to designate the individuals for particular jobs. Under the Decano was a Mayor del Colegio who helped the former in his discharge of his duties and substituted for him in his absence. And under them, there were the Mayores de Salon who responded for the cleanliness of the study halls and watched over their companions during the study time.*[253]

The school assessed the students according to their progress and ranking to advance further. If everyone observed a disinterest in the study, the *Decano* or Director intervened immediately to rectify and motivate when appropriate. Disciplinarians used corporal punishment and peer pressure as motivational tools. If a student offends anyone, he is expected to prostrate himself before the offended party until forgiven. If unable to progress given his rudeness or excessive feebleness, a student may be expelled from the *Colegio* so that he would not bother or be a bad example to others. If 'motivation' was ineffectual, other grounds for expulsion after two warnings included: bad habits, disobedience, profanity, obscenity, rudeness, untruthfulness, dishonesty, impropriety, vice, indecency, and maliciousness. The students must be on the school premises before the *Ave Maria*. Otherwise, tardiness without a valid excuse or an apology was a ground for expulsion. The *Colegio* closed at ten in the evening, the hour when everybody retires orderly and silently to their cells. A candle was always kept lit in the dormitories. Unauthorized sleep-out was considered a serious offense with the offender summarily expelled. If no further progress is evident after eight years in the *Colegio*, the *P. Presidente* finds a position for the student as soldier, artillerist, mariner, or other occupations in the service of His Majesty in order to make his cell available to a beginner. Otherwise, the student was expected to continue his studies at the university.[254]

Talking was prohibited in the refectory. A senior student read the rules of the *Colegio* or the lives of saints while the *colegiales* ate their served meals. Eating or drinking outside the reglementary time was utterly prohibited. Recreation during class days was for one hour, and on Thursdays and

Plate XVI
LETRAN'S ROYAL PATRONS

FELIPE IV
House of Habsburg

Velaquez, Diego, 1656. Museo del Prado, Madrid.

FELIPE V
House of Bourbon

Ranc, Jean, 1723. Museo del Prado, Madrid.

Sundays, it was for two and half hours. The smaller boys were separate from the bigger ones, and physical sports prohibited to avoid fights. Two or three assigned trusted students acted as secret official proctors to monitor abusive language and behavior and to report to the *P. Presidente*. Homestays resulted in unwanted changes in behavior. As a policy, students were not allowed to return home during school breaks but sent instead to the Parañaque summer house reclused from the heathens. Living together in a community meant everyone shared communal ownership of all belongings and everything received from outside the school. Students who needed to leave the school premises were always accompanied by seniors to watch over their modesty, courtesy, and humility. The students must still be in pairs outside the school walking with composure and in measured steps with their bonnets on. They must observe utmost courtesy with hats removed with care in the presence of priests, religious, collegians, and other honorable persons. [255]

Aside from the daily rosary, a daily prayer was rendered for the benefit of the Church and the Supreme Pontiff, for all the Bishops and Archbishops especially for the Manila Metropolitan, for the King of Spain, for the Governor of the Philippines, for all the benefactors and relatives. The boys confessed at least once a month and received holy communion at least every two weeks. Mortification practices included fasting every Fridays in honor of the Passion of the Divine Savior and every Saturdays in honor of the Virgin Mother. The boys regularly took turns to go out in the city to beg for alms door-to-door as religious mendicants with permission from Manila Archbishop Hernando Guerrero to all the city and towns along the coast and in the neighboring provinces of Bulacan and Pampanga free from any trouble and exempt from parochial permission.[256]

They also assisted at burials where they received ten pesos each. Everyone dealt death with utmost reverence and solemnity. If a student died, his body clothed in the habit or uniform was presented, accorded with the Mass and rituals, and interred in the Colegio's church. All the boys were required to attend and recite three complete rosaries for the repose of the departed soul. If the *Colegio's Presidente* died, the students, with rosaries and candles at hand, proceeded in columns of two to Santo Domingo where they sang the Responsory for the Dead at the departed's presentation. The students followed the body until its internment in the cemetery. If a former superior official of Letran died, the *colegiales* rendered the three complete rosaries only. When a student's parent, a school benefactor or a Dominican priest died, all the students assisted in the internment by rendering an entire rosary and singing the litanies of the Virgin for the departed. During All Souls Day every year, two High Masses were offered: one for all departed alumni, and another for all the deceased benefactors of the school.[257]

The ritual of death was a community event when a prominent public official dies. Solemn religious processions through the streets of Manila were integral to city life. All the government, ecclesiastical, religious, academic and community organizations attended. Participants observed a standard protocol and decorum in all these festivities defining the respective positions in the political-religious-social order of the city. The following funeral ceremonies and procession in memory of Spain's crown prince Don Balthasar Carlos on 9 November 1648 provide engaging insights into this hierarchy and how Letran fared in it:

> ...At two in the afternoon the bells of all the churches began to ring, in so sad and doleful tones that they filled the air with sorrow, and the hearts of those who heard their plaints with bitterness and grief, learning from the very bronze to grieve for so considerable a loss. At that same time all the religious communities assembled, with their crosses, priests, deacons, and subdeacons, clad in their vestments, in the royal chapel of the garrison... Each community in succession chanted its responsory, with different choirs of musicians, so well trained that they could vie with those of Europa. While those pious action was going on, the ecclesiastical and secular cabildos were assembling, as well as the tribunal of the royal official judges, the superiors of the orders, the rectors of the two colleges – San Jose, which is in charge of the fathers of the Society of Jesus; and San Tomas, which is ruled by the fathers of St. Dominic – and the members of the bureau of the Santa Misericordia in the hall of the royal Audiencia. There the managers assigned them their position, observing toward each one the order of his seniority and precedence. They left that place in the same order to express their condolences to Don Diego Faxardo, the governor and captain-general of these islands who stood in the hall of the royal assembly...and represented very vividly in his majestic appearance the royal person - in whose name he received the condolences for the death of the royal son and heir, Don Balthassar Carlos, the prince of España.
>
> First entered the royal Audiencia...expressing in brief and impressive sentences the universal grief of all the community and special grief of the Audiencia. Having finished their oration, the royal Audiencia gave place successively to the ecclesiastical cabildo, the secular cabildo, the tribunal of the royal official judges, the superiors of the orders, the colleges, and the bureau of the Santa Misericordia – each one taking its proper place as regards precedence... After his Lordship had answered with equally apposite speech what good judgment dictated and sorrow forced out, that act of mourning came to an end.
>
> ...[T]he parade, which commenced at the palace, encircled the entire plaza of arms under the galleries, and ended at the royal chapel... The orphan boys of the Colegio de San Juan de Letran – who number more than one hundred and fifty, and are reared at the expense of his Majesty, in charge of the fathers of St. Dominic – marched first of all, two by two (the universal order that was observed in that act by all the tribunals and communities) holding their candles of pure white wax, which were distributed, that day and the following, with magnificence and liberality by this illustrious city. The alguacils followed and then the ministers of justice, the attorneys, the judges, secretaries, the notaries, public and royal, with their gowns and cloaks trailing behind them. Next to them

came the confraternities with their pennants and banners, and after these the parishes from the suburbs of the city, with their crosses, and their curas clad in black cloaks. Next in line was the college of Santo Tomas, and following it that of San Jose, with their badges (becas) turned back at the collar as a sign and token of grief. Then followed the bureau of the Santa Misericordia (which is composed of the most noble persons of this city) all clad in their black surtouts and hats, with heads covered, bearing their small bells, and the standard with their insignia infront. The holy families also marched: the brethren of St. John of God, the Recollects of St. Augustine, the Society of Jesus, the hermits of St. Augustine, the seraphic family of St. Francis, and that of the Preachers...

The ecclesiastical cabildo followed with their black choir-cloaks, with the skirts extended and their heads covered; and altogether with so grave and majestic a demeanor that they commanded the eyes and also the applause of all the people. The city [cabildo] followed, together with the tribunal of the royal official judges, bearing their maces and insignia. They were accompanied by the nobility of the city with flowing black mourning cloaks, with heads covered... The royal Audiencia with their president, the governor of these islands... were followed by the government and court secretaries, and by the gentlemen and pages of the palace.[258]

A Permanent Home

The colegiales visibly earned the city's respect and recognition. The plight of the students in the Parian did not pass unnoticed by the school authorities and its benefactors. Plans to immediately move them to a better place began a few years after what was considered a transitory sojourn at the Parian. The Dominicans identified and initially negotiated for the properties proximate to Santo Domingo and Santo Tomas. Availability of funds however delayed implementation indeterminately.

It was the death of a lady, Doña Maria Ramirez Pinto, that changed the school's fortune. Doña Maria owned three adjoining lots framed by the *Baluarte de San Gabriel* (Bastion of San Gabriel) just behind the garden of the Santo Domingo Convent. Considering the ideal suitability of the three lots, the Dominicans purchased them from the lady's estate.[259] The property occupied a third of a cluster of lots where Letran's new home would rise. Improvements to accommodate classrooms and offices in what was once a garden were completed together with a stone church and its belfry. By the end of 1668, the school obtained licenses to transfer formally. The new school edifice was officially opened on 8 May 1669 with great pomp and solemnity by its rector and prior, P. Fray Juan de los Angeles OP. The whole city celebrated and rejoiced at this new milestone of the school that had gained everyone's appreciation and respect. Over time, the school purchased adjoining lots and a building built on a block bounded by Beaterio St in the north, Muralla St on the east, Recogidas (Anda) St in the South and Cerrada (San Juan de Letran) St in the west to become Letran's main home until today.

Plate XVII

LETRAN MAIN PORTAL FACING BEATERIO ST. BUILT IN 1887.
Artist unknown, ca. 1920s. Colegio de San Juan de Letran.

The transfer marked a new phase in Letran's history with the successes of its alumni bringing more recognition to the school. Salazar observed:

> *...For that was a matter that all desired, as that college had always merited the general esteem of this city... And in fact, that college is of great use to this community, not only as it shelters and rears therein all the orphan and abandoned boys, but also because any well-raised youth leaves that college, or seminary, for all walks of life in this community. Some adopt a military life, others a sea-faring life, and others the ecclesiastical estate, both monastic and religious, and from them are regularly supplied most of the curacies of these islands, and other employments more noteworthy, both in the ecclesiastical and in the political world. Excellent students leave that college, many of whom graduate not only with the degree of bachelor, but also with higher degrees.*[260]

Letran's motto of *Deus Patria Letran* had its roots in the *Patronato Real de Indias* - a symbiotic relationship between church and state. Although the patronage began originally as a concession made by the Pope to the Iberian monarchs, it evolved into an absolute right of the King and consequently of the state. The King mobilized the Mendicant Orders, and the Society of Jesus to expedite the evangelization of the New World under special papal dispensation to temporarily fill the many curacies left unfilled by the secular clergy. Eventually, the parishes of the regular religious in the Americas transitioned to the secular curates but not in *Filipinas*. The Augustinian, Franciscan, Jesuit, Dominican and Recollect Provinces conspired to impede the development of the local secular clergy and to entrench their power and influence over the outlying provinces. Consequently, they became the archipelago's *de facto* rulers.

We have to view Letran's colonial history in the context of the *Patronato Real* and the conventual oligarchy that defined Spanish sovereignty and culture over the Philippines. In this manner, the nature of education at that time and the students' response to it can be better understood and appreciated. Being teachers and rulers, the Dominicans had free-reign to mold their students in whatever way they want them to be. The Letran alumnus, on the other hand, became either a product of the Spanish colonial designs or its dissident. The ensuing struggles would lead to the awareness and development of a unique national identity.

Chapter V

From Obras Pias to Friar Estates

The availability of financial resources largely dictated the pace of progress in the colonies. Since the sixteenth century, *Filipinas* depended entirely on the King. No one accomplished anything significant without His Majesty's direct financial support and patronage. The Crown established and carefully nurtured the galleon trade between China and Mexico to stimulate early commercial activities and to encourage individual entrepreneurial initiatives in the colony. The Spanish vecinos of Manila made considerable fortunes and, as a consequence of this prosperity, substantial bequests funded charitable activities. The *obras pias* (pious trusts) were established to primarily support religious observances called the *capellanias* (chantry) and other charitable beneficiaries involved in the colonial education, health, and welfare systems. The *patron* (trustee) was usually a religious individual or institute. There were only two primary investment options. The trustees invested these funds either in the galleon trade or in large tracts of lands to be known collectively as the Friar Estates. How the latter eventually evolved in time sowed seeds of discontent in the hearts of the populace. Letran would become a part of this web of activities as a good number of its students came from these estates and its surrounds.

Cost of Evangelization

From the beginning, the King of Spain paid the expenses of every friar and cleric commencing on the day they departed from their convents in Spain to the day they arrived at their final destination in Manila. During their stay in *Filipinas*, the entire ecclesiastic estate received annual stipends, and *fabricas* (honoraria).[261] The state assumed the cost of building the leading cathedrals and the Orders' churches and convents. As contained in a *Real Cedula* dated 10 July 1606, funds were allotted to feed the missionaries and to provide them with habits, breviaries, missals, fares, freight, and lodgings while in transit to the Islands.[262] The estimated average landed cost of each missionary shipped to Manila reached 1,000 pesos by 1766.[263]

Ever since *Adelantado* Miguel Lopez de Legazpi settled in Manila, the Augustinians received an annual *tepuzque* (stipend) of 100 pesos and 50 *fanegas* (about 36.75 cavans) of rice for every five hundred tributes they ministered to.[264] This arrangement was extended to the curates of all the religious orders in 1585 with the rice increased to 100 *fanegas* and ornaments and decorations as were needed for the altars in the churches included.[265] It was customary in Mexico for wine and oil used in celebrating religious rites to be a part of the *fabrica*.[266] The Dominicans began benefitting from these stipends and benefits in 1579 and and by 24 April 1580 all the religious priests enjoyed free wine and oil.[267] All the bishoprics, churches, convents and schools also received their own *fabricas*. Santo Tomas and Letran, for instance, enjoyed their share of Santo Domingo's *wine and oil, and had 400 pesos in money and 800 cavans of rice for the stipend of four priests in active service, who must reside in the said convent in virtue of a royal decree dated 23 July 1639.*[268] The contribution of wine and oil was extended indefinitely by *Real Cedula* dated 15 September 1726.[269]

On 18 August 1608, Pedro Zaldierna de Mariaca submitted a report on the Philippine government's annual receipts and expenditures. *The incomes total 120,561 pesos common gold and 2 granos, and the expenses 255,578 pesos, one tomin, and 8 granos. In conformity to this, the said expenses exceed the said incomes by 135,017 pesos, 1 tomin and 6 granos.*[270] Contributing to this deficit were expenses for the ecclesiastical estate amounting to 34,636 pesos. Burdened with the cost of wars in Europe, it was, therefore, no surprise that this budget deficit in *Filipinas* contributed to Spain's bankruptcies during the reign of Felipe II, ruler of the first global empire. The King was advised to abandon *Filipinas*. Under these difficult circumstances, Felipe II refused to leave the archipelago that bore his honorable name. He was reported to have declared:

> *For the conversion of only one soul of those there, I would give all the treasures of the Indias, and were they not sufficient I would give so willingly whatever España yields. Under no consideration shall I abandon or discontinue to send preachers and ministers to give the light of the holy gospel to all and whatever provinces may be discovered, however poor, rude, and barren they may be, for the holy apostolic see has given to us and to our heirs the duty possessed by the apostles of publishing and preaching the gospel, which must be spread there and to any infinite number of kingdoms, taking them from the power of devils and giving them to know the true God, without any hope of temporal blessings.*[271]

Financial advisers would reintroduce the proposal to abandon the Philippines whenever Spain underwent a financial crisis. In each instance, the successors of Felipe II honored his established policy. In 1742, Don Pablo Francisco Rodriguez de Berdozido, accountant and royal official for his Majesty in the Philippines, reported that *the cash in stipends, contributions, and grants with which the ecclesiastical estate in these islands is aided on his Majesty's account totaled 100,586 pesos, 3 tomins and 6 granos.*[272] *The cash equivalent of the rice, wine and oil honoraria amounted to 162,530 pesos, 1 tomin and 6 granos.*[273] From 34,636 pesos in 1608, the crown's support to the ecclesiastical estate reached a staggering amount of 263,116 pesos in 1742. By 1896, the curate's stipend reached 500 pesos annually in poor remote parishes to a high of 1,200 pesos annually for the more prominent and more prosperous parishes.[274] The Crown's financial support continued even when the friar orders were already independently wealthy enjoying more than adequate revenues from sacramental fees and their vast

Plate XVIII

FELIPE II, EL PRUDENTE
1527-1598

Titian 1549, Museo del Prado, Madrid

estates by the 18th century.[275] Conceptually, these stipends and subsidies were to be sourced from the King's share of the *diezmo* (tithe) but were shouldered by the royal coffers instead because of 'collection difficulties' in *Filipinas*.[276] Thus, Letran's embryonic survival was due to the King's generosity. The royal grants, however were not enough to sustain the school in the long run. Surprisingly, the Catholic Church's doctrine of purgatory primarily assured Letran's future.

Price of Salvation

According to Catholic teaching, *purgatory is a place or condition of temporal punishment of those who, departing life in God's grace, are, not entirely free from venial faults, or have not fully paid the satisfaction due to their transgressions.*[277] Contained in the Decree of Union drawn by the Council of Florence and in the decree of the Council of Trent, this doctrine established *that there is a purgatory, and that the souls therein are helped by the suffrages of the faithful, but principally by the acceptable Sacrifice of the Altar.*[278] The biblical parable of Lazarus and the rich man further reinforced the belief that eliciting the poor's suffrage lessened the sojourn in purgatory even more.[279] Thus, prayers and most especially masses for the departed would hasten the soul's early exit from purgatory and entry into heaven.

The practice of establishing a trust fund to ensure that a certain number of masses were paid and said in the name of the departed known as *capellania* began. *Capellania* is a technical term which refers to an ecclesiastically authorized *obra pia* (pious trust). It involved a gift of a sum of money held in trust whose income is to be used exclusively for the payment of a number of masses by one or more chaplains for the soul of the trustor, or other persons named by him. The trust designates a *patron* (trustee) who disposes the assets held in trust according to the wishes of the trustor. An *obra pia* is a foundation established for some religious or charitable purpose and administered with ecclesiastical approval as ecclesiastical property possessing a distinct juridical personality capable before the canon and the civil law of entering into legal relations with other collective entities and individuals.[280] All *capellania* were *obras pias ecclesiasticos* (ecclesiastical pious trusts) under the bishop.[281] Assets attributed to a *capellania* bore an ecclesiastical lien usually annotated as a *censo* (quit rent or mortgage) on the title and registered in the diocesan records.

The Hermandad de la Santa Misericordia and the Third Order of Saint Francis administered the earliest *obras pias*. Eventually, the friar orders managed bequests under their care as trustees known as *obras pias generales*. The Manila Archbishop's *obras pias ecclesiaticos*, collectively known as the Mitre Fund, were at his sole discretion.[282] The Philippine church and its numerous charitable institutions were critically dependent on the profits of the *obras pias*. *Censos* from real property earned only 5%. During its existence, the galleon trade provided the most lucrative returns. The terms of the legacies usually divided the original endowment into three parts: one-third lent to the Acapulco trade, one-third on ventures to China and India, and one-third retained as reserve funds. A third allocated to commercial purposes had the character of both bank loans and marine insurance. Premiums on advances for the Acapulco trade fluctuated between twenty and fifty percent and were earmarked for pious and charitable works as specified in the endowments.[283] The investments, however, had their inherent risks. The galleon could get lost at sea, and the edifices on a real property could be destroyed by fire and other natural calamities; causing severe losses on the fund's principal. Consequently, the number of masses rendered, as stipulated in the *capellania*, would eventually consume the entire principal in a matter of time; completely discharging the trustee from his obligations.

After the Dominicans assumed responsibility for Letran, they moved the school premises to a property along Solana St donated *inter vivos* (living trust) by Don Pedro Pinel for his future *capellania*. They sold the original school site of Hermano Juan Geronimo Guerrero to Capitan Gabriel Gomez del Castillo for 3,500 pesos in common gold payable by *censo*. The sale proceeds were turned over by P. Fr. Sebastian Orquendo OP, superior and *capellan* (chaplain) of Letran, to the *Mesa* of the *Santa Misericordia* together with 500 pesos from Don Pedro de Augusto Salazar and 620 pesos from General Julio Esguerra. For some years, the combined funds earned over 3 pesos weekly which was adequate for the Letran boys to live on. Hermano Juan's former property alone earned 100 pesos annually for some years. The earthquake of 1645 ruined the improvements on the property, and the income began to decline; reaching 10 pesos and 4 tomines after 1647. By 1693, the fund's principal diminished to just 10% of its original value resulting in contentious legal actions with the *Misericordia's Santa Mesa*. Aside from depriving the students of their home, the 1645 earthquake rendered Don Pedro Pinel's former property of no use to the school and was sold to the Polish general Don Teodoro de Sanlucas. Under these problematic and needy circumstances, the *Colegio* consumed food and clothing sparingly. The school also moved to the Parian and reduced the number of students when circumstances demanded it. The frustrating experience with the *Misericordia* moved the Dominicans to administer their own *obras pias* and to gain direct control over their financial destiny.[284]

Letran, being a refuge of destitute orphans, was more likely a favored beneficiary of donations because of its perceived capacity to deliver potent suffrages due to the Lazarus effect. School benefactors benefited not just from the rendered number of masses but also from their inclusion in the prayers of the students. Letran benefited from the different variations of the *capellania*. The case of Letran alumnus Don Lope Felix de Alcarazo provides an excellent illustrative case of the process as narrated by P. Fr. Evergisto Bazaco OP:

> *Towards the end of May 1650, don Lope Felipe de Alcarazo, an old alumnus scholar, presented himself at the Colegio de Letran, extramuros de Manila; manifesting desires to spend the last days of his life. Near death, he gave some sealed documents to Hermano Fr. Diego de Sta.*

Maria, written by the notary public and signed by the same don Lope. It read like this:

'IN THE NAME OF GOD, AMEN

BE IT KNOWN that many viewed this testament letter, how I, don Lope Felix de Alcarazo, son of General don Juan de Alcarazo and of doña Ursula de Villafama, former citizens of this city, deceased, - being how I am, sick, in bed, of infirmity who served the mandate of Our Lord: and believing with firm faith the mystery of the Most Holy Trinity, God the Father, Son and Holy Spirit, three distinct persons and one true God; and in all that the Holy Mother Roman Church possesses, believes and confesses, in whose faith and creed I declare to live and to die as a catholic and faithful christian; and invoking, like I do through Mother Advocate, the most glorious Virgin Mary, Our Lady, conceived without original sin; and already being fearful of death which is natural throughout creation. - DO AND ORDAIN MY TESTAMENT IN THE FOLLOWING FORM AND MANNER:

ITEM, I ORDER that a *capellania* is constituted of all my assets, complying with this my testament, of high masses every fridays of the year for my soul, in the Capilla de Santo Cristo of the Colegio de San Juan de Letran. And I nominate as its patrons the Father Prior of the Santo Domingo Convent and the Father whom the said Colegio de San Juan de Letran is in charge of (for having been raised therein), in order that the said capellania neither wants nor is removed from the balance of all my assets; and to the Priest and Cleric who says this mass be given his alms, and the rest of the income to be spent in altar adornments, vestments, and cantors of the said chapel and in candles.

AND TO FULFILL and pay this my testament, I nominate as my executors the present Fr. Diego de Sta. Maria, Administrator of the said *colegio*, and Diego de Torres, resident of Manila: each one in *solidum* as such, to take charge of all my assets, and inventory them, even one year after death and for this it is my will to extend one, two or more accordingly.

AND I REVOKE AND ANNUL and abrogate and grant for naught any other testaments, codicils, powers to make a will, which before this was executed, and rendering not one valid, save this which I by my eternal will wish to keep and fulfill.

IN TESTIMONY of which I granted and signed in my name in this Colegio de San Juan de Letran of the Parian of the Sangleys, extramuros of the city of Manila, on 30 May 1650. (Signed) D. Lope Felix de Alcarazo.

WITNESSES, Geronimo Caravallo, Luis de Fuente, Geronimo de Morales, Roque de la Cruz and Francisco Gonsales.

I, THE NOTARY PUBLIC, bear witness that I know the said D. Lope Felix de Alcarazo, who is of sound mind, appeared to me sick in bed.

- Juan de Torres, Notary Public.'

With Don Lope dead and interred with the habit of St. Dominic in the Capilla del Rosario, Fr. Diego de Sta. Maria moved in search of the licenses needed to complete his commission. He first obtained that of the Most Reverend Father Provincial Fr. Carlos Clemente Gant, much later that of the Municipal Magistrate, Sr. General don Lope de Colindres, and lastly the judge for Testamentos, Capellanias y Obras Pias, the Bachelor Pedro Diaz, archdeacon of the Holy Cathedral Church.

Later Fr. Diego de Sta. Maria and the other executor, Diego de Torres, dedicated themselves to document the inventory before the Royal Secretary don Felipe de Soto, and determined a capital of more than 5000 pesos. Debts were collected when possible, funeral expenses were covered, 500 pesos were paid to the boys of Letran for assisting in the funeral (as indicated by the deceased), and still resulted in a surplus balance of 3,869 pesos with 5 tomines invested in some shops of the Parian and in the houses of don Francisco de Larea, Capitan don Pedro Urquico and the Almirantes Pedro de Zarate and Fernando Galindo.

The excess of the principal which produced nearly 200 pesos annually founded the Capellania de Alcarazo which carries with it an obligation to say High Mass (without ministers) every fridays of the year, and precisely in the Capilla del Santo Cristo of the Colegio. … Over time it suffered involuntary losses and diminished the obligations.[285]

The death of Doña Maria Ramirez Pinto in 1668 initiated a string of events that materialized the school's return to Intramuros in 1669 and its eventual expansion to the neighboring properties within the block. The Dominicans purchased three adjoining lots from her estate. They acquired the land of Capitan Nicolas Luzuriaga between Doña Maria's and the garden of the Santo Domingo Convent located on the corner of Beaterio and Cerrada streets in 1687. The Colegio completed the entire block's acquisition over the next forty years with the last lot on the corner of Muralla and Recogidas (Anda) Sts purchased in 1737.[286]

Meanwhile, in 1680, the widow of Alferez Don Juan Gomez, Doña Maria Moreno de Garcia, having no heirs, willed her estate to various beneficiaries with Letran among them. Her late husband highly esteemed Hermano Juan Geronimo Guerrero. In view thereof, she granted the Lolomboy Estate in Bulacan to the Dominican Province of the Most Holy Rosary with

Plate XIX

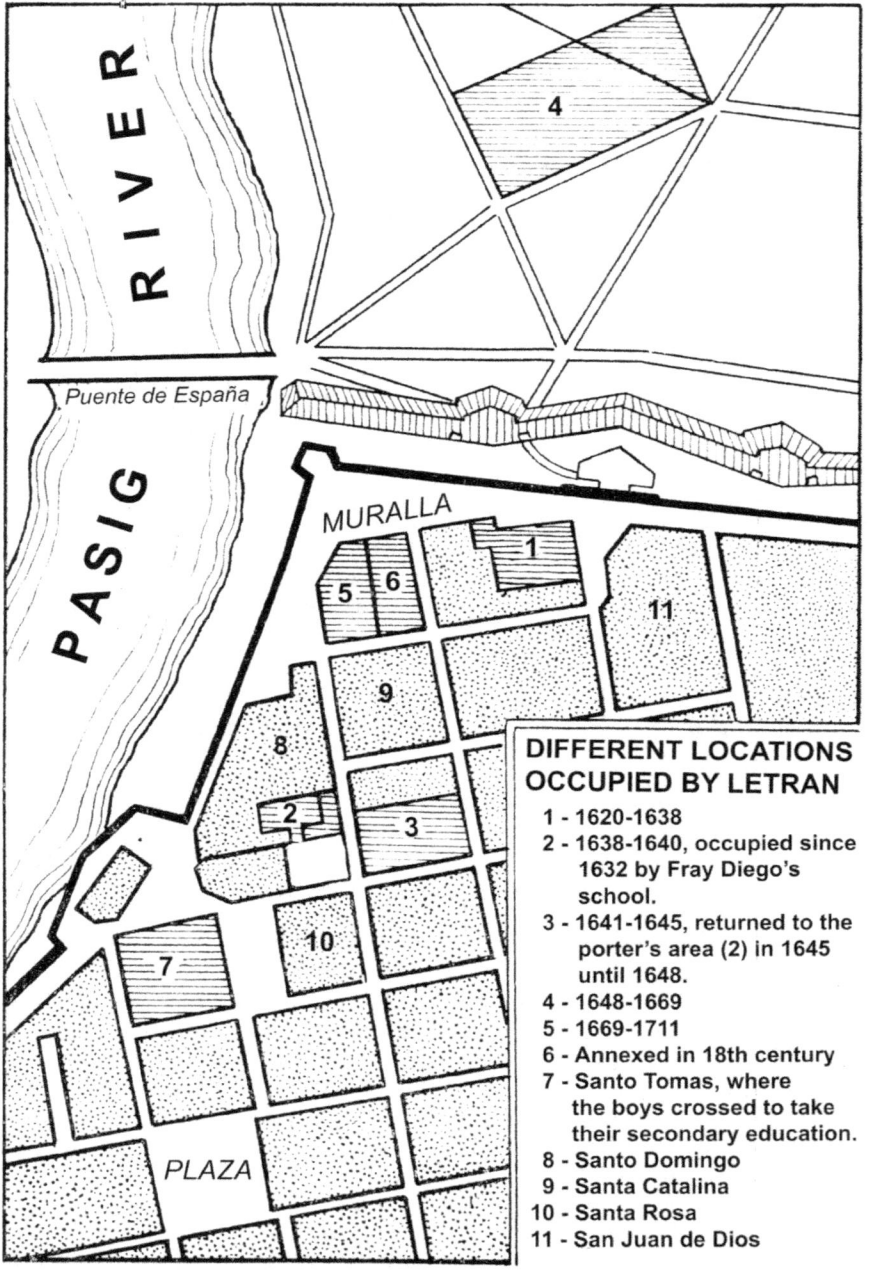

- Bazaco 1933

Plate XX - Lot Acquisitions Forming the Letran Block
1668 -1737

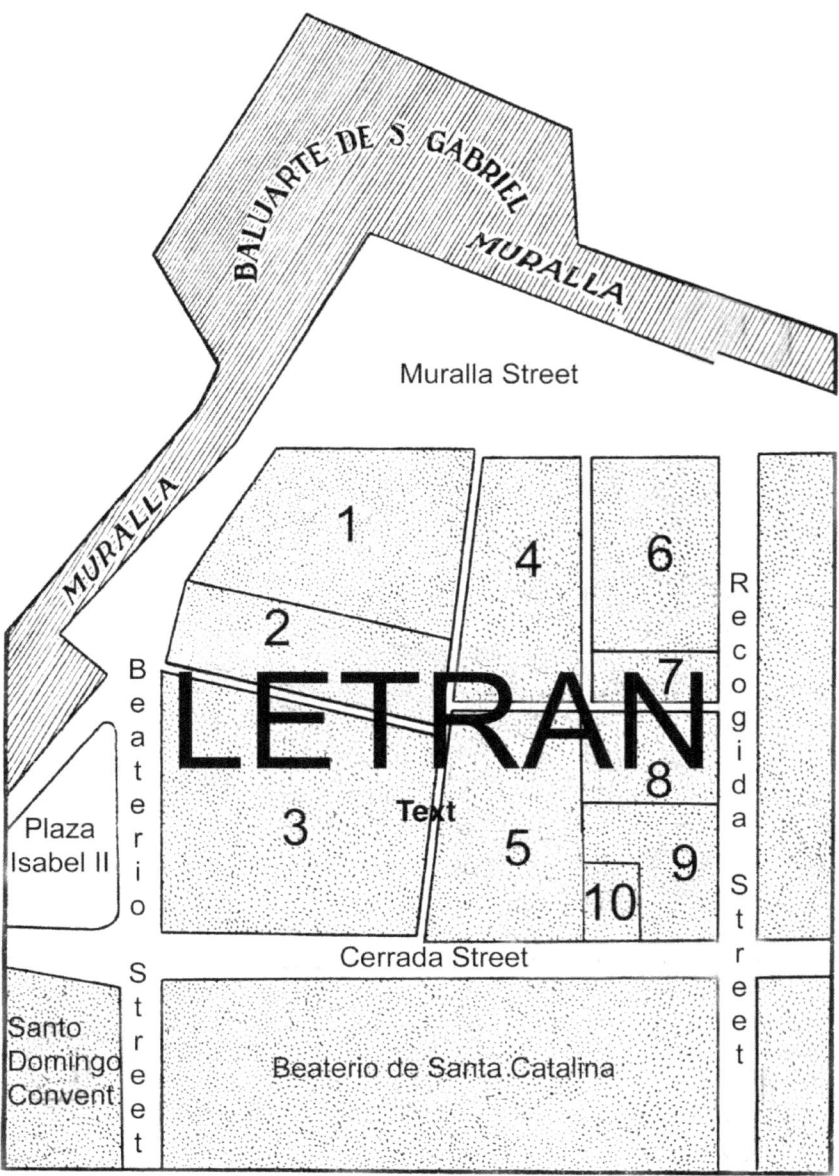

1,2,4 - Maria Pinto Raminrez (1668); 3,5 - Nicolas Luzuriaga (1687); 7 - Poor Dwellers (1711); 9,10 - Santa Catalina (1720); 8 - Maria Arriola (1727); 6 - Hippolita de Aro. - *Bazaco, 1933*

instructions to provide 200 cavans of rice annually for the students of Letran and all the beef the students of Santo Tomas and its younger brother, Letran, can consume. Removing the days of abstinence throughout the year, the annual beef consumption of both schools amounted to 40 heads of cattle. This endowment became known as the *cuarenta vacas de Santo Tomas* (forty cows of Santo Tomas). Her will further founded various *capellanias* with students of Letran as the preferred chaplains, and Letran's rector Fray Juan de los Angeles as the principal chaplain, and in his absence the Father Provincial of the Dominicans as the *patron*.[287]

Over the years, other benefactors continued to grant Letran with generous bequests to fund *capellanias*. Among the notable ones were Don Pedro de la Cruz (1690), Doña Monica de la Cruz (1725), Capitan Don Juan Bautista Uriarte (1737), Don Francisco de Cardenas (1748), Don Juan Infante de Sotomayor (1770), and Doña Petronila de Guzman (1820).[288]

The King's stipends and subsidies were not enough to sustain the Dominican's apostolic mission. As in the case of Letran, the *obras pias* addressed the Order's temporal needs. The first substantial property acquired by the Dominicans was in Orion, Bataan - the smallest of the estates consisting of 2,109.57 hectares.[289] The Dominican missionaries taught the town folks well about the doctrine of purgatory and how a legacy of agricultural land can establish a perpetual *capellania* to hasten their entry into heaven. The pastors were so compelling that on 29 December 1637 Domingo Pasan, Maria Francisco, Benito Manalar, and Ursula Cayanihan bequeathed Balibago and Sagaly-Bantan subject to the obligation of celebrating masses for the repose of their souls after death. The fathers were not allowed to dispose of the said lands except to revert them to the said Domingo Pasan and his co-donors.

The Dominicans received the first large tracts of land reluctantly and moved them to define a set of rules in the purchase and management of estates in 1640:

> *The haciendas will be cultivated and improved in order to transport religious from Spain to the Philippines… These haciendas will be under the custody of the Rector of our College of Santo Tomas who will have the book of receipts of these funds. The Provincial will expend the money only for purpose of transporting religious from Spain, and for no other purpose, because this is the only instance in which our province is permitted to have temporal possessions and incomes. He will not use any of the surplus for anything else, regardless of the benefits to the province, because we do not wish to have properties, but only to assist the Crown in transporting members of our order.*[290]

On 29 August 1673, Nicolas Bagtas, Maria Bagtas, Catalina Mayalanti, Ana Campaning, Juan Cachamines, Tomas Pasana, Agustina Veronica, Maria Josefa, Isabel Clava, Sebastian Clara, Isabel Languay, Magdalena Batol, Ursula Josefa, Luis Titol, and Nicolas Laquindanum bequeathed Balicbalic imposing the obligation of celebrating 12 high masses every year for the

Table II
1612 LAND GRANTS
24 of 34 Estancias Acquired by Religious Orders

HACIENDA	PROVINCE	RELIGIOUS ORDER
Piedad Mariquina	Tondo	Jesuit (17th century)
Meysilo y Payatas	Tondo	Jesuit (17th century)
Macati	Tondo	Jesuit (17th century)
Santa Ana	Tondo	Jesuit (17th century)
Tunasan	Tondo	Jesuit (17th century)
Maysapang	Tondo	Augustinian (17th century)
Malamica	Tondo	Augustinian (17th century)
Tunacilla	Tondo	Dominican (1643) / Recollect (1675)
Biñan	Laguna	Dominican (1644)
Tabuco	Laguna	Dominican (1660)
Calamba Nueva	Laguna	Jesuit (1759) / Dominican (1833)
Calamba Vieja	Laguna	Jesuit (1759) / Dominican (1833)
Los Baños	Laguna	Jesuit (1759) / Dominican (1833)
Lian	Batangas	Jesuit (1666)
Nasugbu	Batangas	Jesuit (ca. 1695)
Santa Cruz	Cavite	Augustinian (1720) / Dominican (1761)
San Nicolas	Cavite	Recollect (1680)
Imus	Cavite	Recollect (1685)
Malabon	Cavite	Augustinian (1866)
Naic	Cavite	Jesuit (ca. 1695) / Dominican (1831)
Maragondon	Cavite	Jesuit (17th century)
Looc	Cavite	Jesuit (17th century)
Indan	Cavite	Augustinian (1720) / Dominican (1761)

Source: APSR, Haciendas, tomo 12, folio 136.

repose of the souls of the donors and their successors.[291] The duty of providing a free grave and burial in the convent was among the conditions. The act ignored the Spanish law protecting the legitimes of the donors' heirs. Towards the end of the 17th century, the restraints initially imposed on land acquisition and management appeared to had been discarded. By 1903, the Dominican Province had 60,461.73.96 hectares of landholdings with an estimated value of $5,473,799.13 in Mexican currency.[292]

The Rise of Landed Estates

Beginning with 2,109 hectares in Orion, Bataan, the Dominicans expanded their landholdings to Laguna, Bulacan, and Cavite.

Between 1653 and 1678, the Estate of San Isidro de Biñan in Laguna was acquired by *Colegio de Santo Tomas* in four tranches. The Dominicans subsequently divided this estate into two: the Biñan Estate consisting of 3,739.10 hectares and the Santa Rosa Estate composed of 4,750.14 hectares.[293] The ecclesiastical liens annotated on the titles were indicative of obligations related to *capellanias*.[294] The Lolomboy Estate in Bulacan consisting of the land inherited from Doña Maria Moreno de Garcia in 1680 and subsequent acquisitions from 1710 onwards of adjacent land parcels in Toro, Pasolo e Isla, Malanday y Lingahan aggregated a total hectarage of 4,329.[295] Also in Bulacan, the Santa Maria de Pandi Estate covering 12,069.57 hectares consisted of various acquisitions with Tomasina Belohani's *capellania* among them.[296]

Had the Society of Jesus not been expelled from the Philippines in 1768, the landholdings of the friar orders would have paled in comparison to those of the Jesuits considering that the Society *placed no barrier in the way of obtaining temporal possession.*[297] Their expulsion resulted in the *desamortizacion* (confiscation and public auction) of all their properties.[298] The Dominican land acquisitions from the late 18th century onwards were former Jesuit estates purchased by parties who were financed by *obras pias*. The Jesuits had extensive land holdings in the province of Cavite. Among them was the Malabon Estate consisting of three areas: Naic, Santa Cruz de Malabon (Tanza) and San Francisco de Malabon (General Trias). The Augustinians acquired San Francisco de Malabon and the Dominicans the other two with the assumption of the respective estate's censos. The Dominicans acquired Tanza consisting of 8,902 hectares in 1761 and Naic with 7,922 hectares in 1831. The single biggest acquisition, however, was the San Juan Bautista Estate in Calamba composed of 16,424 hectares. With the Dominicans holding the censo of this Laguna property, ownership transferred to them via *dacion en pago* (payment in kind) in 1831.[299]

Legalizing Spurious Titles

In the middle of the 16th century, Spain faced pressing difficulties in maintaining the integrity of its dominions and confronting other continental powers. Felipe II had to urgently find ways of raising funds to sustain the Spanish military presence in Europe. The sale of crown lands in the colonies was an area focused on. Many of the properties held by Spanish colonial subjects were subject to cases of erroneous ground measurements, usurpation of native titles, and excessive accumulation of land holdings. The process of correcting and legitimizing these discrepancies called *composicion* presented opportunities to generate revenues while protecting the land rights of the native population.[300] Any land found without a title immediately reverted to the crown.

In 1692, Carlos II enacted the *Superintendencia del Beneficio y Composicion de Tierras* (Supervision of Land Benefits and Settlement) whose activities focused on the fair collection of monetary resources, the indictment of officials remiss in their duties, and the recovery of crown lands usurped by settlers. It aimed to expedite the official decisions concerning the distribution and regularization of property, and the collection of the corresponding adjudicated financial obligations with the Royal Treasury. The Audiencia oidores (judges) in the colonies formed the *Juzgado Primativo de Tierras* (Exclusively Lands Court) to implement the decree. The court examined and determined the quality of titles. If found in order, the titles were confirmed and released. In the event of any irregularities, it verified the ownership, sale history, measurements and monuments of the titles in the archives and in the field. The court marked, valued, ascertained, and recommended any excess crown land for settlement through the *composicion*. The court's jurisdiction included all cases of plunder, invasion, and destruction of monuments involving the towns of indios and did not need to pass through other tribunals. Resolution and settlement of conflicting claims required the delinquent party to indemnify the victim. The juridical process had an imposed deadline of six years.[301]

The authorities in Nueva España constituted such a *Juzgado Primativo de Tierras* for Filipinas composed of a team of four oidores. To serve a term of six years, licentiates Don Alonso Abellafuertes, Don Juan de Sierra y Osorio and Don Jeronimo de Barredo Valdes arrived in Manila in 1688. Licentiate Don Juan de Ozaeta y Oro followed a year later. The *oidores* took their offices in the hall of the *Audiencia* and immediately carried out their commissions. A Knight of Calatrava from Asturias, Sierra assumed responsibility over the religious and clerical estates and issued notices to the respective prelates to submit the titles of their lands for adjudication.[302]

The five religious institutes refused submission on the grounds of immunity from civil prosecution as provided by the *Fuero Ecclesiastico* and filed an appeal with the Real Audiencia. The Audiencia upheld Sierra's ruling that the religious privilege invoked did not apply in this case. Failing to submit to the court over a prolonged period, Sierra ruled that the religious orders did not have any titles whatsoever over lands they claimed to own. The outraged friars pleaded their case with Manila Archbishop Diego Camacho y Avila. The archbishop declared that only the properties of the Monastery of Santa Clara and the Colleges of Santo Tomas and San Jose where secular priests studied were ecclesiastic. All other lands were not. The declaration sparked a contentious debate with the friars who invoked the intervention of the Delegate of His Holiness and Bishop of Nueva Caceres, Senior Don Fray Andres Gonzales OP. Enmeshed in a number of administrative issues, the conflict between the two princes of the church became ugly with each one excommunicating the other. All opposing parties submitted their positions over the controversies to Spain, and the long wait for a final resolution commenced.[303] Meanwhile, Sierra's six-year term expired and Juan de Ozaeta y Oro inherited his pending cases.

A native of Lima, Ozaeta proved to be a pragmatic and practical man. He resorted to resolving the impasse extrajudicially, a protocol recognized by the Crown but not utilized by his fastidious predecessor. It was founded principally on the testimony provided by the owner regarding his land without the need for field verification of the information. By agreement, the parties concerned settled the *composicion* based on trust. This consensual process was rapid, economical and favorable to all parties. The religious orders unanimously agreed to the extrajudicial alternative and Ozaeta concluded the matter in *a few days*.[304] In the case of the Dominican Estates, Ozaeta confirmed all the titles except those of the Orion Estate; collecting in each case a donation of 4000 pesos to His Majesty the King.[305] The Lolomboy Estate was re-monumented according to the citations of all the adjoining landowners with 7 *quiñones* granted to the natives of the *visita* (hamlet) called "Santa Maria" in addition to the existing 3 *quiñones*.[306] In 1699, Ozaeta accomplished his commission and generated substantial revenues for the Royal Treasury to the satisfaction of the title holders before the expiry of his term.

Ozaeta effectively confirmed titles from documents and testimonies presented to him and in the process forever legitimized the ownership of the friar estates based essentially on trust. The integrity of this arrangement, however, was shaken 75 years later by what is referred to in Philippine history as the Tagalog Agrarian Revolts of 1745.

Tagalog Agrarian Revolts of 1745

Towards the end of the 17th century, cattle from the Dominican Biñan Estate began to cross its borders into Silang, Cavite to graze. According to documents attributed to the Jesuit provincial, the people of Silang and San Mateo agreed that the said cattle could pasture in the sitio of Bual in 1704. Fernando Palanco Aguado cited the provincial's account:

> *Some years later, the people intended to revoke that permission, but the Dominicans refused to abandon the use of those lands for grazing. In 1717 the people injured a herdsman and killed some cows. In response, the tenants of the estate burnt several houses in Silang. The Dominicans left the lands under litigation, but in 1741 they occupied them again. The people of Silang went to court, and the decision was in their favor in the first instance. But the Colegio de Santo Tomas appealed and the Real*

> *Audiencia decided in its favor on 1 September 1744. According to the Jesuit provincial, the Audiencia's decision was celebrated in the estate with comedias* (stage plays), *fireworks, and the ringing of the bells, even as the people of Silang seethed with indignation. Furthermore, according to the same source, the other religious orders took advantage of this opportunity to consolidate the expansion of their respective estates.*[307]

The decision recognized the Dominican's ownership over surveyed lands containing an area of 28,782,700 square brazas and 12/8 over what in reality was only 10,663,546 square brazas of 3 varas less one-eighth each.[308] The fraud committed in the said survey caused the uprising of the Silang residents, *which occasioned deaths, damage and losses to the natives and expenditures to the royal treasury.*[309]

Armed disturbances began in Silang after the order of arrest was issued on the town's *principales* on 1 May 1745 for insisting on the rights of the natives and for destroying a warehouse and two dams built on lands usurped from them by the power of the friar's money. After unsuccessful attempts by the *Audiencia* to mediate, instances of land monuments destroyed and cattle dispersed to the mountains occurred in Parañaque. The unrest spread to Taguig and San Mateo shortly after. In Bacoor, the *indios* resorted to killing the friar's horned cattle given similar acts of usurpation in the Recoleto Estate. Cavite Viejo (Kawit), Malabon, Indang and all their *visitas* followed suit. Governor Gaspar de la Torre feared the spread of the discontent to the other Tagalog provinces and appointed a commissioned judge, Don Pedro Calderon y Henriquez, to stem the tide in the areas of Cavite, Tondo (Rizal) and Bulacan, and sent *Sargento* Don Juan Gonzales de Pulgar to Batangas.

Calderon immediately enacted *measures to correct the abuses of the estates. He granted the people of Parañaque their free use of pasture land and access to firewood. He signed the same order in Bacoor and added an arbitrary formula to solve the disputes over land: until a new measurement or higher order is received, the people could sow the land they claimed as theirs and deposit the amount needed for leasing the land in the hands of a neutral person or entity.*[310] The same decrees applied to the earlier affected areas with the leaders of Silang pardoned.

By June, rebellion unleashed in San Mateo but quickly subdued. Its church was the only structure left standing after the combined Spanish and Pampango forces put the town to the torch. The insurgency reached the villages of Angat, Baliwag, Bigaa, Bocaue, Casay (Norzagaray), Quingua (Plaridel), and Santa Maria all belonging to the friar estates in Bulacan. An estimated 5000 armed rebels entrenched themselves in Bocaue and the Lolomboy Estate. Calderon offered amnesty to everyone except the leaders. After laying down their arms and accepting the government's offer, they could present their grievances to him, and he would do justice, as he had done in Silang. If they persisted in their revolt, he would treat them in the same way as the people of San Mateo. The *principales* of the said towns all submitted by 23 June 1745 with Calderon pardoning everyone except the leaders.[311]

The unrest in Batangas centered in the towns of Balayan, Taal and Rosario. Rebel *indios* led by a native cleric, Francisco Matienza, occupied the Jesuit Estates of Lian and Calatagan, subdivided the land and rented them out to the people. Like San Mateo, the Spanish forces crushed the armed resistance and exacted severe retribution with 30 men condemned to death and 18 to public flogging. Ecclesiastical justice condemned Matienza to eight years imprisonment in Zamboanga.[312] By 2 October 1745, the Tagalog revolt ended. Sentenced in absentia, many of the condemned became fugitives of the law and joined the ranks of *tulisanes* (bandits).[313]

On 9 November 1745, Commissioner Pedro Calderon y Enriquez adjudicated that a grave mistake or fraud had been committed in the survey of the Biñan Estate made two years before. He considered the said survey as a significant influence in the court decision rendered on 1 September 1744. Notwithstanding the protest entered by the Dominicans against the commissioner's verdict, the latter ordered the estate of Biñan resurveyed and re-monumented at once in January 1746. In March 1746, the commissioner rendered two final judgments declaring that the area of the property be reduced to 10,663,546 square brazas and ordered the estate re-monumented per this decision.[314] *Real Cedula* dated 7 November 1751 approved the commissioner's order in its entirety, and overruled the protest of the Dominicans.[315]

Three years later the procurator of the Dominican corporation, in the name of the Santo Tomas College, offered to present witnesses to prove that the 3,727,423 square brazas that appeared to be in excess in the estate of Biñan over the just area of the same as previously declared had been peacefully possessed by the said college for so long that prescription lied, and prayed that after establishing these facts he might be granted a *composicion*. The said Commissioner Calderon Enriquez granted the request and admitted the *composicion* referred to subject to the payment of $700. Thus, the total area of the estate came to be 14,390,969 square brazas of 3 varas less one-eighth. To avoid all doubts and litigation in the future, the commissioner set the boundaries to the estate of Biñan in his order. The decision involved the statute of limitation of the contested area.[316] Unfortunately, after the ten-year prescription period provided by Spanish law, the title to ownership became incontestable and rendered any claims after that moot.

The revolt of the Tagalogs was not due solely to the issue of land seizure. It involved other issues of oppression and abuse. The people of Silang complained about the friars renting out lands to *sangleys* and *sangley mestizos* rather than to them. They denied access to woods, pasturelands, wild fruits, hunting and fishing. The natives of Parañaque complained about the exaction of twelve thousand cavans of lime every year without any kind of allowances. Those of Binacayan felt defenseless because in order to obtain justice they had to pay notaries, procurators, and lawyers, for which they had no money. The issues for Batangas included the tribute and the *polo* (draft labor). The people of Bulacan cited six grievances other than the land usurpation issue. They included: (1) Lifting prohibition to gather forest

Table III - SUMMARY OF PHILIPPINE FRIAR ESTATES SURVEY 1901-1902

Estate	Province	Hectares
AUGUSTINIAN		
Banilad	Cebu	1,538.43.00
Barascoain	Bulacan	54.29.57
Binagbag	Bulacan	294.00.00
Dampol, Quincua	Bulacan	962.00.00
Calumpit	Bulacan	74.82.95
Guiguinto	Bulacan	
- Alang-ilang		241.42.94
- Malapat		7.20.08
- Recoleto		456.95.16
Isabela	Isabela	23,000.00.00
Mandaloya	Rizal	4,033.00.00
Muntinlupa	Rizal	5,397.84.00
Malinta	Bulacan	3,432.00.00
Piedad	Rizal	3,604.00.00
Quingua	Bulacan	
San Francisco de Malabon	Cavite	13,000.00.00
Santa Isabel	Bulacan	
- Daquila		38.83.49
- Anibon		65.33.52
Tala	Rizal	5,197.00.00
Talisay and Minganilla	Cebu	7,362.90.00
	Total	68,770.26.04

Estate	Province	Hectares
DOMINICAN		
Biñan	Laguna	3,739.10.15
Calamba	Laguna	16,424.14.00
Lolomboy	Bulacan	106.53.00
- Malanday	- Polo	65.19.50
- Pasolo	- Polo	4,158.09.66
- Bocaue	- Bocaue	7,922.29.00
Naic	Cavite	2,109.57.24
Orion	Bataan	8,902.37.50
Santa Cruz De Malabon	Cavite	12,069.57.02
Santa Maria de Pandi	Bulacan	4,750.14.24
Santa Rosa	Laguna	156.49.35
San Juan del Monte	Rizal	58.23.30
Toro	Bulacan	
	Total	60,461.73.96
RECOLETO		
San Juan and San Nicolas	Cavite	18,419.56.12
San Jose	Mindoro	23,266.00.00
	Total	41,685.56.12

SUMMARY

Augustinian Estates	68,770.26.04
Dominican Estates	60,461.73.96
Recoleto Estates	41,685.56.12
TOTAL	170,917.56.12

Source: Survey conducted by Juan Villegas, 4th Annual Report of the Philippine Commission 1903 Part 1. pp. 202-203..

firewood with the penalty of flogging and confiscation of *bolos* (native machete). (2) Ceasing the payment of tribute in places contrary to law. (3) Differentiating the exaction of the *vandala* (compulsory sale of produce to the government) according to the financial capacity of the people. (4) Stopping the maltreatment and providing adequate food to men drafted for timber cutting. (5) Moderating the excessive taxes on the beetle nut and wine. (6) Granting equal treatment of *mestizo sangleys* and *indios* concerning *polo* and tribute, and disallowance of non-Christian *sangleys* to reside in their towns. Calderon addressed all the concerns except those already regulated by law.[317] The furor eventually settled down in the troubled areas but the sanguinary relationship between the friars and the people festered.

Agrarian Unrest of 1822

The British invasion of 1762 would spark uprisings throughout Luzon which occupied Simon de Anda's attention more than battling the British. In early January 1763, disgruntled farmers in Cavite and Bulacan destroyed the haciendas and cattle ranches owned by the Dominicans.[318] It was during this dark period that *tulisanes* murdered H. Fr Felipe Valin OP, administrator of the Santa Cruz de Malabon Estate, and H. Fr. Benito Alaguero OP, the administrator of the Santa Maria de Pandi Estate.[319] The sad fact was that displaced farmers from friar estates joined the swelling number of *tulisanes*. Sixty years later peasant unrest would reach critical proportions.

In 1822, 48 farmers marked a sanguine trail through the rice and sugar producing provinces of Cavite, Batangas, Laguna, Tondo, Bulacan, Pampanga, and Bataan - the locations and surrounds of the vast friar estates. Led by Luis de los Santos (aka Luis Parang), this *reunion de malhechores* (gathering of criminals) committed *robberies, cruelties, violence and assassinations.*[320] They were former peasants of the Cavite friar estates in Imus, Bacoor, San Francisco de Malabon, Santa Cruz de Malabon and Silang who were rebelling against excessive irrigation charges, *talacsan* (firewood) exactions and forced labor. During this period, the administrator of the Dominican Malabon Estate, P. Fr. Pedro de la Iglesia y España OP, was found barely alive after an attempt to end his life.[321] Cavite became known as the *Madre de Los Ladrones* (Mother of Thieves), and the Recollect hacienda in Imus was the hotbed of agrarian unrest.[322]

With his base in Imus, Parang earned the title of *El Tulisan* (The Bandit) for his unparalleled notoriety.[323] The rebellion lasted for six years. Through the mediation of Cavite's Vicar Forane, B.D. Mariano Gomes de los Angeles, Parang and his band surrendered and were granted amnesty by Governor-General Mariano Ricafort Palacin y Abarca on 21 May 1828.[324] Although there were still other insurgent groups who refused to surrender, the peace and order situation improved significantly.[325]

Luis Parang and his colleague Juan Silvestre (aka Juan Upay) were subsequently elected as *capitan* and *teniente* respectively of the Imus

Plate XXI

EL TULISAN

- Andrews, C.W., 1860, Propiedad del Biblioteca Nacional de España bdh00188343

cuadrilleros (municipal militia) in 1832.[326] Two years later, he was elected the town's *gobernadorcillo*.[327] He was closely associated with the controversial P. Fr. Nicolas Becerra OAR, the parish priest of Imus. By March 1835, Parang and his band were back spreading terror in all parts. He was captured a month later in his Sambong forest hideout in Imus and condemned to death on 4 August 1835.[328] Becerra died of poison on 2 September 1840, after losing a court case for unjust taxation filed by the *caciques* of Imus.[329]

The number of peasants dispossessed of their lands in Cavite increased dramatically in the latter half of the 1860s. A new peasant rebel leader by the name of Casimiro Camerino emerged. A native of Imus, his band of *tulisanes* operated out of the forests of Dasmariñas. At the peak of the unrest, H. Fr. Claudio Diaz del Rosario OAR was murdered in the *Hacienda de Imus* on 24 February 1868. Upon due consultations, Governor-General Carlos Maria de la Torre granted Camerino amnesty on 15 August 1869 and commissioned him as head of the *Batallon de Guias* (Scouts Battalion) to complement the existing police infrastructure of the Spanish military forces.[330] The new contingent proved to be a capable force in reducing the brigandage problem.[331] However, its conspiratorial role in the 1872 Cavite Mutiny resulted in the execution of Camerino and the imprisonment of 11 of his men.[332] The battalion disbanded and an additional regiment of the Guardia Civil established in its place.

Peasant discontent would continue to be a festering issue culminating in the 1896 Philippine Revolution. The history of Imus provides significant insights towards a better understanding of the agrarian situation and the farmer's hostility towards the friar landlord and the status quo. Felipe Calderon submitted the following narrative about Imus to the Taft Commission in 1900:

> *The pueblo of Imus was a barrio of Old Cavite prior to this century, whose chapel was erected in the place known as Toclon, still a barrio of the same name within the limits of Imus, and since that time a large amount of land has been cultivated by the natives in the places known as Medicion, Toclon, Alapan, Bucandala, Balangon and Anabu, and in different places within the boundaries of Imus, the land for the most part being devoted to the sowing of palay (paddy). At that time there was no dam or means of retaining water; but after many years had elapsed, when the barrio had a sufficient number of inhabitants and sufficient means to support a pueblo, on the petition of the natives, the Spanish Government declared the pueblo civilly independent of the town of Old Cavite. The spiritual administration continued pertaining to the curacy of Old Cavite for many years, the natives constructed a provisional church and a court in the place known as the barrio of Pueblo Viejo (old town), where was established the pueblo of Imus. The production of palay having rapidly extended, it being raised up to the vicinity of Tampus, now the pueblo of Perez Dasmariñas, still there was no dam or means of retaining water in the entire territory of Imus. During this time a Peninsular Spaniard, whose name and surname I do not recall,*

with his wife, named Doña Augustina, who were said to be punished by the government of Spain, arrived from Spain. But it was evident from his kindly and amiable treatment of the natives and his manner of living that he was a person of high rank. He selected for his residence the site near Tampus, now known as Perez Dasmariñas. It is supposed that he had preferred this place on account of its temperate climate.

He lived a very peaceful life during the entire period of his life in this pueblo, was very fond of riding horseback, and so he bought a large number of horses. He sowed grass for their feed, but there came a time when from the month of January it did not rain, and therefore caused the grass to die. The Spaniard decided to register that place if he had any means of irrigating his grass, and he found a suitable place, where he then constructed a dam composed of stone and wood, and although this dam is not now in existence, there still remain traces of it. There in the months of October and November of the year in which the construction of the dam was completed, the time in which the palay was beginning to be formed, there was a scarcity of rain, on account of which the farmers of the place known as Malagasang, now barrio of Malagasang, appealed to the Spaniard and asked for water to irrigate their crops. He, seeing that he had more than enough water for his grass, furnished water to the farmers, charging $1 per cavan of seed sown, which they irrigated and maintained with the water from the dam; and in time this water was not only used by the inhabitants of Malagasan, but also by those of Bucandala. Doña Augustina died in the year 1795 or 1796, according to estimates, Friar Francisco de Santiago being the first friar curate of Imus, recently appointed, to whom the Spaniard entrusted the administration of the dam on leaving for Spain. This father administered and collected the dues for the use of the water from the dam for a period of two or three years without changing the amount which they had formerly paid to the Spaniard. This practice was continued until Fr. Alonso Jubera de la Concepcion came to occupy the curacy, who likewise undertook the administration and collection of the dues for the use of water from the dam. And this curate, observing that the collection of the dues for the use of water was being delayed by the low price of palay, admonished the farmers to pay in grain and just equivalent to $1 which they formerly paid to his predecessor, and as the price of palay was only from 3 to 4 reals per cavan, the farmers, in accordance with the indication of the friar curate, paid in the following year two cavans of the palay for each cavan of seed which they irrigated or maintained with the water from the dam, this being the equivalent value of $1. This curate was much esteemed by his parishioners through his frank and agreeable character. Being talking one day with some leading men of the pueblo at a wedding, one of them, it is not known why, had the curiosity to ask the curate when the Spaniard, the owner of the dam, was going to return to Imus. The curate answered that perhaps he would not return to the Philippines, as he was a member of a rich family in Spain, and owned estates. The same leading person again asked *if any member of the family was coming to collect the product of the dues of the dam. The curate said that no one would come of the family for the product of the dam, as its owner had dedicated the earnings to the sustaining of the Church of Nuestra Señora del Pilar de Imus, and therefore, you the farmers, who pay your portions for the use of water of the dam, should always be punctual in the payment of two cavans of palay for each cavan of seed which you irrigate or maintain by that water, as this amount you do not pay to the Spaniard, or to the curate, but to the Virgin of Pilar herself. After a lapse of two or three years Friar Manuel de San Miguel took the place of Father Alonso in the curacy as well as in the management of the dam, and in the following year, as is handed down, he constructed the dam in Salitran, upon the completion of which the farmers of Anabu received water therefrom for their crops. The curate collected three cavans of palay for each cavan of seed; he likewise collected the same quantity of palay from those of Malagasan, Bucandala, and the other places where water was obtained from the dam. At the expiration of three or five years another came to fill the curacy of Imus, named Friar Mariano de San Miguel. This curate respected the above custom regarding the payment for the water, neither raising nor diminishing the figure during the ten or twelve years that he occupied the curacy.*

It is supposed that he is the one who ordered the construction of the dam of Julian, and upon its completion the inhabitants of Medicion, Balangon, and Toclon likewise paid an amount of palay equal to that paid by the others; but after some years he caused four cavans to be paid for each cavan of seed which was irrigated from the water of the first dam and that of Julian. And it is to be noted that this friar curate remained many years in the curacy, when he was replaced by another, who did not alter the charge for water and remained incumbent but for a short time. Then Padre Nicolas Becerra de V. de la Montaña took his place in the curacy, and it is stated that he was at the same time provincial of the corporation, known as Santiago, who assisted him in the administration and collection of the charges for the use of water. After this provincial curate had been in charge of the curacy some months, he called all the leaders of the pueblo together to treat upon the moving of the pueblo to the place where it is situated today. At the meeting he stated the idea to them, showing the convenience of the change, and the benefits and advantages to be derived therefrom by the pueblo. After the leading men had been thoroughly informed on the matter, and in being in accord with him the government did not delay in ordering the change of the site of the pueblo to where it is situated today. On his account the friar curate convoked the leaders again and informed them in a body according to their resources to the speedy construction of a church and parish house.

That is to say, that the males over the age of 12 years should take their turns in working a week at a time, in accordance with their number, and according to the division of the work that should be made, and the *headmen of Barangay were obliged to present the individuals to work each week. In addition to this, all those possessing lands were to contribute a talacsan (firewood) of wood for each cavan of seed, having to make the payment along with that for the use of water. Anyone who could not pay with that article would do it in equivalent in cash at the ordinary value, which is $1 per talacsan, besides increasing the pay for use of water to five cavans of palay for every cavan seed. The head men agreeing to all the propositions of the friar curate, they immediately began to bring in and pay the talacsans when they paid for the water. By this act there was immediately erected a temporary church and house for the curate, of light materials.*

It would be noted the talacsan of wood was used in the manufacture of brick and lime necessary for the construction of the church and parish residence of masonry. The work on the church was commenced in the year 1820 or 1821, according to estimates, but upon the completion of the church and the parish house, and after the period of one or two years, they still continued demanding the payment of the talacsan of wood. The chiefs demanded of the very same curate himself that they be exempted from the payment of the talacsan, *who not only did not pay any attention to their complaints, but threatened them with the stocks and other punishments if they ceased bringing in or paying the talacsan until the termination of the construction of a private house of the faithful, the house now called the hacienda of San Juan de Imus. And the chiefs having noticed the hard nature of the bishop, did not complain again, but continued to pay their* talacsans. *But becoming tired of so many sacrifices, the chiefs had a secret meeting, and appointed six of them to present their complaint in the court of first instance of Cavite against the abuses of the friar curate. Upon the filing of the complaint and preparation of the record, some of the poor chiefs were put in jail, and the others who had been prevented by some reason or other from appearing on the day fixed by the judge, were persecuted by the curate. But although they continued to hide themselves, the other chiefs continued with the case, assisted by an influential woman of Manila, and it is known that there was a favorable decision on the complaints of the chiefs by the royal audiencia of Manila after some years of litigation. The litigants remained absent from their pueblos until the curate died, and it is said that the death of this curate was occasioned by the decision of the royal audiencia in favor of the chiefs, as he died suddenly, foaming at the mouth, on the very day on which he was notified of the decision of the royal audiencia, and on this account the opinion prevailed that the death was a suicide by means of poison.*

Upon the death of the curate disappeared the payment of the talacsan; from this time the proprietors of the land ceased to pay the talacsan on that account. This curate allowed the pueblo to see his real influence with the government, for as soon as a criminal could reach him and seek his protection, that was enough to make him free from all responsibility. So he was the close friend of the most celebrated pardoned criminals of the district; and when he went to Manila his carriage was drawn by two pairs of horses, and he was generally escorted by these people. On his return he was escorted by two or three pairs of cavalry. Therefore he was very greatly feared by the residents of the vicinity.

Returning now to the assistant administrator, named Santiago, a lay brother, who collected and administered the charge for the water, he did not make a single change during his occupancy except to increase the charge by one cavan of palay, which was done at the will of the parish curate Becerra. There afterwards came another layman named Matias Carbonel to take his place, Father Becerra still being the friar curate; and in time he built the dam of San Agustin and Lancaan in order to increase the force of the water of the first above-mentioned dam; and so they continued constructing dams down to that of the landing place. Lastly, this lay brother seems to have carried on the business as an administrator appointed by the provincial curate; therefore he disposed freely in all matters concerning the use of water. In time the collections of $1 for each house-site was commenced, and it is stated that they have the right to collect, as they were using the water for the dams; and afterwards they went on to collect from the house-sites in the barrios at the rate of two reals each. Although the neighbors were surprised by this new tax, they did not protest through the fear entertained by them of suffering the same experience as was meted out to the leading men when they complained against the talacsan, some of whom, in addition to being impoverished, were placed in jail, and the others concealed themselves for a long time. This same lay brother was the one who invented the contract documents for the watering of the crops, with the house-site included, after the time of the collection of the new tax. They accepted the contracts because they believed that by this means they would avoid in the future the continuous increase of the pay for the watering of the crops. The contrary resulted, however, because each administrator demanded an increase and a new contract, the most expensive of all being the one who introduced reforms in his administration, and the charges ascending according to the reforms introduced, as will be seen later.

On the death of the lay brother Matias Carbonel, his assistant succeeded him, another layman named Joaquin [Arellano], who reformed the documents of contract regarding water for crops and house-sites, by abolishing the manuscripts and substituting printed ones. He increased the cost of the water one cavan, so that the five cavans for each cavan of seed was made six. Then he measured the meadows and the house-sites, and after this measurement he collected according to the number of balitas or quiñones in each parcel possessed by the farmers, abolishing then the custom of collecting according to the number of cavans of seeds, there resulting thereby a considerable increase of the charge for the use of water and house-sites. The entire population became alarmed at this, but after many deliberations they changed their ideas to only protesting against the proceeding of the administrator, because they saw that the influence of the friars was more powerful than theirs with the authorities. Because they saw from these reasons that any complaint would be useless which could be made against the friars, and the natives were right in their calculations, because Father Becerra, still being curate, avoided any attempt to complain, on account of the experiences of the chiefs when they protested on the talacsan of wood, for the old men had warned the young and their successors that they should never have any trouble with the friars, and much more when they are curates, and, therefore, they paid according to the demands of the lay administrator, both for the house-sites and the meadows.

The provincial curate died in the year 1839 or 1840, and was succeeded by friar Manuel Zubiri; but before this time there was a substitute, whose name I do not recall, who managed the affairs for a short time. Nevertheless, the lay administrator continued the same, and Curate Zubiri did not give any reason for complaint to the natives during the time he was curate. Besides, he became friendly with his parishioners, even having many compadres, because he was accustomed to be godfather at the baptism of the sons of leading men, which multiplied the names of Manuel and Manuela, because he gave his own name to god-children. After this curate, according to the statement of the natives, the administration of the water was entirely separated from the parish, and the lay brother, Joaquin, freely carried out his task after that time, as did his successor. In the year 1849 Father Guillermo Royo occupied the curacy, the same layman, Joaquin, being administrator, and the curate did not intervene in any way in the administration and collection for the use of water.

In the year 1864 Father Jose Varela occupied the parish - an upright priest who carried out his duties with entire justice, and was very greatly beloved by his parishioners, who likewise didn't meddle in matters pertaining to the administration of the water or in the affairs of the municipal captain; for he often refused to place his O.K. on documents and accounts of the tribunal, giving as a reason that he was a curate of souls, and that his intervention in civil matters was not just, because this demand for his signature was only on account of the lack of confidence in the local chiefs of the government, and lack of confidence is the mother of distrust and makes thieves. All his acts are worthy of mention, and the pueblo in mass bless him every time that they think of him. He showed the people the uselessness of the money spent in the fiestas, as it produced nothing more than the misery of the pueblo. On various occasions he showed the vanity of pompous burials. He became indignant at the exorbitant price of the water for the fields, and exclaiming, said: "Where will the infernal souls of the administrators of the water go?" May God take the soul of this holy man to his bosom!

It was about the year 1865 or 1866 when the provincial of the uncalced Augustinians ordered a tax on mangas (mangos) and cane, Father [Francisco] Villa[s] being the administrator of the water. He was the faithful executor of the acts of the provincial, the said Curate Varela, who defended the pueblo, so that that new tax of two reales for each manga tree and one real for each mata of cane, should not be carried into effect, and the result was a very great disgust on the part of the blessed father; and the pueblo had to carry the weight of the new tax, although the residents already were aware of the illegality of the said tax, through the simple reason that, if they protested, the tax might disappear; yes; but on the other hand they might increase the cost of water for the fields, and it would be worse for them. On account of these considerations, they crossed their arms and paid, cursing the author of the idea. It is likewise supposed that the same priest who was administrator reduced two very honorable families of the pueblo to misery, despoiling them of their fields. These families continued to implore clemency of the authorities and of the same provincial, but accomplished nothing. From this fact the more intelligent of the pueblo suspected and figured that the pay for the use of the water is not directly for the water, but for the land, and that this was the cause of the despoiling. These intelligent men of the pueblo sought a means to set aside the unjust proceeding of the administrator, because they know that all the land of Imus is the property of the cultivators, and if they pay a portion to the administrator, it is for the use of the water from the dams, and nothing more. Thereupon they appealed to the persons of influence in Manila, and only obtained traditional advice from the old men to not interfere with the friars, because, as they say, the very governors themselves of the Philippines tremble before the gold and influence of the friars. That great influence is demonstrated by the friars of Imus daily, for the hacienda of San Juan, the house of the friars, is very much frequented by the highest authorities of Manila and their families. There they take their vacations in the hot season. Therefore these intelligent men ceased to use their rights, as was counseled by experience.

During this same time of the Curate Varela and the Father Villas, the administrator, was Don Bernardino Abad, formerly copyist of the hacienda, showed when Señor Escosura arrived at Manila with the title of royal commissioner, and with the special commission of requiring friars to show their title documents concerning the titles to the haciendas, and as the provincial did not find in the convent of the Recoletos any document to justify the title to the territory of Imus, he answered that there did not exist any. "In that case what do you know about our possession of those lands." "If your reverence will have the kindness to pay attention I will explain it to you," answered Don Bernardino, and thereupon he related the history from the time of the Spaniard, owner of the dam, up to that time, in the manner stated in the preceding paragraphs. Upon the provincial's being informed thereof, he again asked: "*How do you know the history which you have just related?" Don Bernardino answered that he knew through his father, Don Casimiro Abad, formerly scribe of the parish and of the hacienda at the same time, who had told it to him one day when he was in a good humor.* "In order to satisfy the royal commission which Señor Escasura brought to Manila, sent by the government of Spain to require all the religious corporations to produce the documents of title to our haciendas, do you think there is any remedy?" "Yes, father." "And what is it?" "Father, give large amounts, and in gold, which can rule this high official." *In fact, the father provincial ordered this, and Don Bernardino is one of the men that arranged the matter, and it is calculated that 20,000 pesos was the amount of the gift, and Señor Escasura did not delay long in disappearing from Manila.*

The history heretofore stated was given on various occasions by Don Bernardino Abad when he was alive, as well as that of the Spaniard who was the owner of the dam.

In the year 1873 Curate Varela died, and Fr. Andres Galdeano substituted him in the same year, and the administrator, Fr. Villa[s], was relieved by Fr. Gaudencio Marquez much before the death of the curate Varela. Fr. Andres was a great worker; he was the one who increased the height of the steeple, altered the interior of the church, and did not give any cause for complaint to his parishioners. It is also thought that Fr. Gaudencio is the one who ordered the construction of the country house in Salitran, where the friars generally take their vacations. After the construction of that house he also collected a percentage in cash for the crops in the mountains, such as palay and sugar cane, the time in which the civil guard invaded the entire province of Cavite, doing great damage, as faithful followers of the friars and executors of their acts. By this new tax on crops raised in the mountains, it was confirmed more and more that the collection for the use of water was not made in that conception, but for the land, because the places where they sow the sugar cane and palay are impossible to be watered; and although the natives desired to exercise their rights, it was now too late, because the civil guard on one side and the influence of the friars on the other are two axioms which prevent the public from exercising their real rights. Nevertheless, a resident of Perez Dasmariñas, formerly captain there, protested against the collections of tax on mountain products before the provincial of the Recoletos and the authorities. He did not obtain a single favorable decision but, on the contrary, was robbed of his fields with danger to himself. So that every day they continued to tighten the reins on the farmers, and the despoiling takes place every year.

On the completion of the estimate of Father Andres upon the alteration of the interior of the church, the parish house and the elevation of the steeple, the father provincial of the Recoletos took up the expense to be occasioned by the projected work, to the end that the funds of the hacienda should pay for the expense demanded by the estimate, the total of which reached the sum of $25,000. In the beginning the provincial inferred that the funds of the hacienda were under the control of the father in charge of the hacienda, and that therefore he could not dispose of them. In view of this answer, he appealed to the father in charge of the *hacienda, who also told the curate that under no conception could he make any expenditure without express authority of the four definers of the said corporation. Therefore Father Andres, as one of the definers, convoked his companions to a meeting, they unanimously resolved to authorize the expenditure solicited by Father Andres, but there were debates when treating of the matter, and Father Andres relied on the argument that the entire hacienda belonged to the pueblo; that the church and the parish house also belonged to the pueblo, and that therefore the expense of the church should be borne by property of the pueblo, and so he was successful in his purpose. He also asked of the archbishop another sum for other expenses, which was granted; and two wealthy men of the pueblo, on their part in response to the worthy actions of the curate, paid for the acquisition of the chandeliers of the church, and the bells and hand-bells which are now in the belfry.*

Father Gaudencio, the administrator, went out of office and was succeeded by Father Valentin Apellaniz, his assistant being the lay brother Roman Caballero. This priest had good principles, although young; he treated the farmers well, and permitted claims with the consent of the provincial. But his assistant was a miserable person, who only possessed the idea of charging for all the taxes. If any resident asked for the reduction for some manga trees which had died through old age or other reasons, he did not allow it, but compelled him to plant others to take their place without giving any reduction for the dead ones, and he also did the same with cane. The plundering went on every year through some caprice of the layman. In the course of time there was a great increase in the taxes upon house sites and the hill lands, crops on the mountains, and land sown. This same layman directed the work on the dam of Pasong castila, as the people recollect, the only one with license from superior authority, because in the archives of the court no other license is registered for the many dams in the territory of Imus, and upon the completion of the work he considerably increased the pay for water for the crops of Alapan.

In the year 1880 Father Andres Galdeano died, and was succeeded by Father Jose M. [Le]arte, the same Father Valentin Apellaniz being administrator, and his aide being the layman Roman Caballero. The blessed curate died without beginning the work on the floor of the church, because when he set out to commence the work he fell sick, was unable to recover from the illness, and expired. Father Valentin went to the parish the day succeeding his death and took out of the convent all the money which was in the chest of Father Andres, the sum reaching $38,000. According to persons close to the curate, of that sum only $32,000 belonged to him, $5,000 was for the expense of the tarima, and $1000 funds of the church. Fr. Valentin took all to the hacienda house, and it is not known what was afterwards done with the money. According to statements, Father Learte, the curate of Santa Cruz of Manila, learning of the death of Father Andres, endeavored to occupy the parish of Imus, while others say that they expelled him from Santa

Table IV
DOMINICAN PROVINCE OF THE MOST HOLY ROSARY
1893 General State of Affairs Summary

Provinces	Ministries			Religious			Souls
	Parishes	Missions	Total	Male	Female	Total	
Filipinas							
Bataan	7		7	10		10	44,419
Batanes		5	5	6		6	9,166
Cagayan	17	1	18	26	7	33	100,802
Cavite	2		2	5		5	18,415
Isabela	6	6	12	17		17	52,804
Laguna	4		4	8		8	49,915
Manila	1		1	82	31	113	50,961
Nueva Vizcaya		9	9	11		11	22,615
Pangasinan	27		27	44	7	51	250,303
Tarlac	5		5	6		6	51,677
Vigan				3	6	9	
China							
Emuy		8	8	8	13	21	3,700
Fo-Cheu		22	22	21	5	26	35,276
Formosa		7	7	6		6	1,195
Hong-kong				3		3	
Tung-king							
Oriental		21	21	12		12	40,017
Central		33	33	17		17	173,733
Septentrional		15	15	11		11	25,102
España							
Avila				148		148	
Ocaña				127		127	
Madrid				5	13	18	
Others				2	4	6	
Total	69	127	196	578	86	664	927,898

Source: Provincia del Santisimo Rosario, Estado General 1893. Manila, 1894

Cruz because they did not like his methods. However, no matter why he took his departure, the fact is that he was likewise not well suited to Imus, for after he had occupied the curacy one week he learned that the pueblo was not congenial to him nor he to the pueblo.

The active hostility between the pueblo and the curate lasted for a long time, it being terminated by the revolution of 1896. The friar endeavored to retard progress. He compelled school teachers to educate the children in Tagalo, and if any father of a family sent his children to Manila to study, that was enough to make him his enemy, and every resident who spoke a little Spanish, in his opinion, the filibusters increased, because they progressed in the Spanish language. In the year 1883 the custom of kissing the hand of the curate disappeared entirely, and was a fatal blow to him. From that year he began to recruit filibusters, believing, perhaps, that by this means he would bring about the people's return to their primitive condition of submission to the friars, and, not content with this, he likewise founded lodges of Masonry (sic), slightly known to the people, and, as he did not tire of preaching against Masonry, making it appear abominable, as he said, because it did not recognize any other God than their own criminal acts; then the ignorant people, anxious to know the facts thoroughly found someone to seek the truth in the capital, Manila in the Orient lodge of the same. It was found to be entirely opposite to what the curate had stated, and that in the heart of Masonry reigned peace and concord, and its doctrine is to love God before all things and your neighbors as yourself, teaching and inculcating in the hearts of men equality and brotherhood, the doctrine which our Lord Jesus Christ taught his disciples. By virtue of this Masonic lodges soon appeared in different parts of the province of Cavite. He became terrified at the shadow of the name Mason as he learned that there were Masons on every corner. From that time he could not rest easy; he sought a means of impeding the march of progress of Masonry and went out, always laughed at, with all his civil guard.

Masonry was still unknown in this pueblo when the pueblos nearest to Manila celebrated the fiesta of General Despujol, and one of these was Imus. All of its head men appeared at Malacañang with the proper obsequiousness, presided over by the local chief of the same, and on their return they were threatened by the father in charge of the hacienda with a total confiscation of their lands, which was not carried out for reasons unknown. But all were branded filibusters by Curate Learte and the father in charge of the hacienda, Juan Herrero. From that time they sought means to eject or expel from the pueblo some of these head men, and meanly descended to a deceitful piece of work; that is, pretending an uprising. They gave good money to some low people who were to be the actors in the drama that to take place in this pueblo. But their diabolical intentions miscarried, because the pueblo became aware of the trick. The most active men took a great interest in discovering who were the persons hired to be actors in the said function, and encountering them they told the truth. They said that they were actually paid by the friars, and although they had received a certain sum, it was not with the intention of carrying out the agreement made with them, but only to take advantage of their liberality. That is, they would procure for them as much money as they could and never would do what they were ordered, because they knew that the entire public in mass would be upon them and that therefore they would derive no benefit from the money received; so that on two occasions when the pretended uprising was announced, nothing particular happened, notwithstanding that some head men of the pueblo, advised by a Spaniard, absented themselves and changed their residence to the province of Tarlac in order to avoid trouble with the curate and the friar in charge of the hacienda, and these were threatened with confiscation by the friar in charge of the hacienda.

In order not to break the succession of those in charge of the hacienda, let us here state the names of those who preceded Father Juan Herrero and their deeds. Father Exequiel Moreno took the place of Father Valentin Apellanis, because the latter went to Bacoor as temporary curate of the same, and Father Moreno, although elected manager, in no wise interfered in the matters of the hacienda and left everything to the will of the lay brother, Roman Caballero, because the managing friar can not witness collections with a tranquil conscience; so that one day at the feast of St John the Baptist, the head men being at the house of the hacienda, the manager invited one of the head men, in who he had confidence, to a private conversation, and when they were alone and after having concluded the necessary ceremonious formalities, they seated themselves, and the manager began: "I want to tell you that within a few days I leave here for the Recoleto Convent." "Father, I am sorry, and I shall deeply feel the departure of a manager as good as your reverence," *replied the head man,* "and why do you have to go so soon? Is not this work as peaceful as a priest can hope for?" *The manager replied:* "You can speak well of this position and wish it as well as you may, for you do not understand it at bottom; this aside from the fact that men differ in feature the same as they do in character, and my character is not one to discharge curacies nor managerships of haciendas, for my conscience will not allow it. A corner in the convent of the Recoletos is more agreeable to me than all the haciendas and curacies of the corporation." *The head man could not utter a sound, because the reasons advanced seemed to him very strange, and he began to suspect that he was talking to a saint. The priest, noticing that his interlocutor had ceased to speak, arose from his seat and said that perhaps his companions would be impatient, and the two bade each other good-bye very courteously, the friar conducting him to the last step of the stairs and immediately moving off toward the Recoleto convent; but he did not last there either, for it is said that he was elected rector of a college in Monte Agudo, which place he left for another locality as bishop. Well did he deserve this last charge, for he was the true pastor!*

When this priest left the hacienda Father Victor, whose surname it is said was Ruiz, took his place, the same lay brother Roman remaining as assistant. The latter priest left the management and direction of things on the hacienda to the discretion of the assistant; nevertheless, he is a strong defender of its interests, as is shown by a case, which is as follows: The public treasury of Cavite, suspecting that the haciendas of San Juan, San Nicolas, and Muntinlupa, suppressed the truth in the sworn statements presented in that year as to net profits yielded by the said haciendas - at a time when the government charged a certain percentage on the land tithe - the local chief of Imus ordered an immediate inquiry to be made in order to arrive at the truth, and without raising a hand the said chief in compliance with his duty enters upon the said inquiry as follows: He published a notice in and outside of the town for all the residents who paid anything in money or in products to the hacienda of San Juan to present themselves, requesting at the same time of the fair manager, through a courteous communication, a certified copy of the schedule or list of those paying tithes for a certain number of years, pursuant to the provisions of the said order, for the purpose of comparing them with the depositions appearing in the record. The friar manager becoming apprised of the communication and notice published for three consecutive nights, he appeared in the parish and begged the parish priest, Learte, to kindly summon the local chief. The parish priest did this; and Don Bernardino Paredino Paredes, for the chief was so named, without saying a word to him, the parish priest goes into his room, leaving him alone with the manager, who, after a moment's wait, spoke and said, "Captain, if you don't change your mind it will cost you dearly." *The poor captain was dumbfounded and somewhat perplexed over the first remark of the manager, but coming to himself he replied:* "Father, be kind enough to elucidate and repeat what you have said, for in truth I do not understand what you wish to say to me." "Well, this," *said the manger,* "have you not published a notice for three nights calling upon the residents to appear in the court and make depositions about _____?" "Yes, father, pursuant to an order from the government." "Well, you are very much mistaken about your carrying out the order, and I repeat to you that it will cost you dearly if you do not change your mind. I will despoil you of your lands and will substitute the badge you carry with iron. If the government has placed it on our chest, I will put it on your ankles," *and he said a thousand other things to the poor captain which prudence will not allow to be repeated;* "tomorrow morning at the first hour, I want to hear your answer from your own lips and at the house of the hacienda," *and he departed immediately, leaving the captain alone, without being able to articulate a word.*

Soon afterwards the parish priest, Learte, emerges from his room and found him half stunned, and as soon as he saw the priest come out he excused himself and left with his baton of office, dishonored by the despot manager, making his way to his house and locking himself in his room alone, preoccupied with the drama he had just witnessed. About 10 o'clock at night the crestfallen captain left his room, calling upon one of his agents to summon at once an ex-captain in whom he had full trust. The agent did so, and the ex-captain was much astonished at so untimely an invitation; nevertheless he dressed himself quickly and followed the agent, for he presupposed that a case of much importance must have arisen to be called upon at such an hour, and when he had reached the house the local chief came out to meet him, and after an exchange of courtesies conducted him to his office, causing him to take a seat at his side and afterwards addressing him, saying that he had made bold to summon him at that hour because he could not himself reach a decision upon a case which had occurred a short time ago, and told him all that had occurred with the manager as is set forth above, and consulting him as to what he should do in the premises. The ex-captain becoming apprised of what had occurred, sighing: "So you have stood all these insults addressed to your authority with your baton of office in hand, when others would have broken the skull of the manager with the baton itself before suffering such insults to the prejudice of all authorities; but since it all happened thus, may God grant you reward in His holy resignation, and I now counsel you not to pass the doors nor the threshold of the hacienda, so as not to suffer other insults, worse, perhaps, than the last, and very early tomorrow morning go to the governor and tell him everything that has occurred to you with the manager, showing him the order of the government, and in view of it, request him to kindly solve the problem of the friar manager. At the same time ask him if there will be no objection to his acting as your second in a duel you desire to have with the manager, because your honor and your conscience cannot allow an offense to pass without satisfaction, and that you will inevitably call out the manager." *On the following morning the captain went to Cavite, as did also the manager, and it was subsequently learned that a settlement was reached and the record pigeonholed. This manager a few days later departed for the Visayas as a curate, as rumor has it, and he was replaced by Father Juan Herrero, whose deeds we have already recorded herein before.*[333]

Whether the preceding tale was consistent with documented facts or not was irrelevant. It was a tale passed on from one generation to another close to a hundred years. To the people of Imus, it was nothing but the truth.

Seeds of Discontent

The pace of Letran's growth and development depended on the financial resources available to it. The Spanish crown and the *vecinos* of Manila provided the initial support, but it was the Dominicans who assured its long term survival. *Capellanias* addressed the cash short falls. Over a period of time, the collective resources generated by the *obras pias* were invested in landed estates that generated revenues to support the Dominican province's apostolic mission.

By 1893, the Dominican Province's missionary, educational and parochial activities stretched the breadth of four countries, 16 provinces, 69 parishes, and 127 missions with 578 friars and 86 sisters ministering to 927,898 souls.[334] The amount of resources needed to sustain the required logistics would appear to be staggering. By the same year however, the Dominicans owned 9 Friar Estates in five provinces with aggregate landholdings of 60,461.74 hectares of agricultural land; producing enough revenues to sustain their operational requirements.[335] However, greed and corruption followed the accumulation of wealth and power. Using the friars' wealth, knowledge of the law and their ecclesiastical immunities, large tracts of land were usurped from helpless natives who could not afford the cost of litigation against the influential transgressors. Armed rebellion spread throughout the Tagalog provinces in areas where the friar estates were located. Law and order was subsequently restored, and the aggrieved parties vindicated.

Tainted by recurring accusations of usurpation, illegal machinations, abusive and unjust estate administration, the accumulated hectarage sowed seeds of discontent in the social landscape.

During these agrarian controversies, many baptized *sangleys* were working on the Dominican estates. Among them was Domingo Lamco who worked in Barrio Tubigan of the San Isidro de Biñan Estate.[336] Lamco witnessed the agrarian unrest of 1745 and his son, Francisco Mercado, experienced the uprising in the haciendas during the British invasion of 1762 when the consequent retribution found expression. What appeared as isolated incidents were portents of far graver consequences in the future. By 1887 Francisco's grandson, Francisco Mercado Rizal, was an *inquilino* (tenant) on the Dominican estate of San Juan Bautista de Calamba with a lease covering 500 hectares of what were claimed to be the best lands of the hacienda.[337] Together with other *inquilinos,* the family would become embroiled with litigious land disputes that engendered an anticlerical attitude on Mercado's son, Jose Rizal. Like Rizal, many Letran alumni belonged to families involved in one way or the other with the friar estates, and their shared experiences of abuse would precipitate a dissident movement to expel the friars from their homeland.

Chapter VI

Ecclesial Ties

When I was a primary school student in Letran, one of our favorite games was swords play. We used our forearms as swords, and the clenched fist had the second node of the index finger protruding to simulate the sword's tip. We would cross, thrust and parry with our imaginary swords and end up with our arms and other body parts, where the "sword" found its mark, bruised black and blue at the end of the day. During our breaks, we formed groups and galloped through the playground like knights mounted on their steeds similar to the horseless knights of the Monty Python film *Holy Grail*. The older boys would assume leadership of a pack and lead it against the others. Like the knights of old, we would gallop around the campus like a herd of mustangs clashing in the middle of the field to engage in a melee. Occasionally, a lone wolf would stand tall and taunt anyone to challenge him in single combat. Sometimes the challenge was accepted by a brave soul, but a pack usually attacked the lone wolf instead to teach him a lesson on humility - *pinagtutulungan* (a concerted group bashing). Buttressing the northern perimeter walls of the campus along Beaterio St, was a row of ancient sandstones less than a meter high and about 50 centimeters thick. In our juvenile fantasy, this was a castle to be either attacked or defended. So packs would take turns of either fortifying it or invading it. It was great fun. As children, we were not aware that the stump of adobe wall and traces of what were once granite and ceramic tile floorings on our playground were remnants of an ancient school for women ran by Dominican sisters, the *Beaterio y Colegio de Santa Catalina de Sena* (Residence and College of Saint Catherine of Siena). Like Santo Tomas, this venerable institution for women was a part of Letran's history for over two hundred years because of a relationship involving a church.

The Dominican Family

The Order of Preachers underwent many changes over the centuries. In 1992, the Acts of the Mexico General Chapter of Friars declared:

> *The Dominican Family consisted of friars, nuns, sisters of apostolic life, members of secular institutes, priestly fraternities and laity who belong to fraternities or new groups accepted by the order…Thus as if arising from a tree planted beside living fountains, the branches of the Dominican Family are numerous. Each one has its own character, its special status, its autonomy. However, since all participate in the charism of Saint Dominic, they share the very same vocation to be preachers in the Church.*[338]

Traditionally, the Order of Preachers consists of the First Order, the Second Order and the Third Order. Fray Thomas McGonigle OP explains:

> *The First Order, the Friars, is composed of clerical brothers and lay brothers. Clerical brothers are friars who are either priests engaged in ministry or students preparing for priesthood. Cooperator brothers (formerly called lay brothers) are friars who once cared for the temporal needs of the community but who now also serve in a variety of other ministries including the diaconate.*
>
> *The Second Order is composed of contemplative nuns living in cloistered monasteries, usually under the jurisdiction of the local bishop. The Master of the Order also provides oversight and support for the nuns in their contemplative life.*
>
> *The Third Order, which came into existence at the end of the thirteenth century, is divided into the Third Order Regular and the Third Order Secular. The Third Order Regular was initially composed of women who chose to live Dominican religious life without the strict rules of a cloistered monastery. In the nineteenth century the Third Order Regular also came to include Papal and Diocesan Congregations of Dominican Sisters established to engage in active ministries of service such as education and health care. Members of the Third Order Secular, originally called Tertiaries and now called the Dominican Laity are lay men and women living in the world. Their Rule states that "As members of the Order, they participate in its apostolic mission through prayer, study, and preaching according to the state of the laity."* [339]

The Congregation of Dominican Sisters of St. Catherine of Siena is a member of the growing Dominican Family with its distinctive character and status because of its unique history. It began as a group of Lay Dominicans of the Third Order of St. Dominic in 1696 under the Province of the Holy Rosary and evolved into a congregation of apostolic sisters of diocesan and pontifical right by 1970.[340] The following narrative is about the first Philippine Dominican apostolic sisters' early history as a *beaterio* characterized by a special relationship with Letran.

<u>The Third Order</u>

On 5 August 1621 at the instance of Felipe II, a group of nine *monjas* (cloistered nuns) of the Second Order of Saint Francis headed by Madre Geronima de la Asuncion arrived in Manila to found the *Monasterio de Santa Clara de Manila* (Monastery of Saint Claire of Manila).[341] The cloister known as the *Convento de la Concepcion Purisima* (Convent of the Immaculate Conception) was the first of its kind in the Far East and would be the only one in the Philippines until towards the end of Spanish sovereignty. Manila residents petitioned for the monastery. The generous piety of *Maestro de Campo* Pedro de Chaves and his wife Doña Ana de Vera initially funded the new foundation of religious women. The nuns began to receive daughters of the noblest and wealthiest men of Manila, but the

Plate XXII

Mother Francisca del Espiritu Santo OP

- © Chioa, Davy OP, 2011. Plasuela de Madre Francisca, Intramuros.

majority of the noble postulants were poor. Dowries and inheritance from some of the affluent women gave rise to the humble cloister.[342] His Majesty granted an annual stipend of 2000 pesos from the Royal Treasury and 500 pesos from an *encomienda* to support 40 Spanish nuns and 26 *oblatas* (oblates).[343] In a short time, the monastery housed 56 nuns.

By 1633, the Dominicans began the initial steps to found its own monastery of *monjas* of the Second Order of St. Dominic. Substantial bequests willed by Doña Agustina de Morales, the widow of Hermano Juan Geronimo Guerrero's friend and benefactor Pedro de Navarrete, and her cousin, Sor Maria de Jesus of the Third Order of St Dominic occasioned the move.[344] *Santa Catalina de Sena* was to be the patroness of the proposed monastery. The *Procurador General* (Syndic General) of Manila raised his objections in as much as public alms were not enough to support two convents for women in the city considering that Santa Clara by then already had 65 nuns; leaving single males with slim prospects of finding brides.[345] Informed about this plea, His Majesty issued a *real cedula* dated 16 February 1635 prohibiting the creation of the new foundation and instructing the viceroy of Nueva España to stop the passage of Dominican nuns from Mexico to this effect.[346] The Dominicans hence withdrew their intentions after an appeal was rejected and used the funds to construct a church in Guadalupe along the Pasig River instead.[347] Without a Second Order, the Third Order of St. Dominic flourished in the archipelago.[348]

Known today as the Lay Fraternities of St. Dominic, the Third Order in the 17th century was composed of Lay Dominicans of both genders who were deemed not fit to enter the first two orders but may nevertheless enjoy the advantages and privileges of the Dominican Order. Diocesan priests who adopted Dominican spirituality as a way of life also became members of the Third Order. This group of clerics evolved into what is currently known as the Priestly Fraternities of St. Dominic. As a rule, non-Spaniards were not allowed into the first and second orders.[349] The Lay Dominicans, then known as *tercieros* and *tercieras,* professed simple vows and lived either individually on their own as *seglares* (seculars), or in a community as *regulares* (regulars). A *seglar* lived and interacted more actively in the temporal world with a lighter prayer regimen compared to a *regular*. They were permitted to wear the habit of the order under certain circumstances, but without the scapular customarily worn by *regulares*.[350] Upon temporary profession, the Lay Dominican wore a small, blessed white cloth scapular day and night under their regular clothing instead and addressed as *hermano* (brother).[351] *Donados* were lay members of the Third Order who offered services to a convent and lived there permanently, receiving food and lodging as compensation for their work.[352] Saint Martin de Porres was a *donado* before becoming a *lego*.[353] A *terciera*'s title was *hermana* or *soror* (sister), and *madre* (mother) for superiors and seniors.

As early as the mid-fifteenth century, the term *beata* was used to describe a woman who withdraws from the world to live in prayer while subsisting on alms. In the beginning, they involved women who could not proffer the dowry required by the convent and simply emulated a nun's life in the privacy of their homes. The advent of tertiaries provided more spiritual alternatives for women and broadened the *beata* concept to include women who joined the third order.[354] When beatas lived together as a community, the residence they occupied was known as a beaterio. There were no beaterios for men in the Hispanic world.[355] Given historical circumstances, the Dominicans in the Philippines did not follow the original concept of the *beata* strictly and modified it with elements of the second order and other practices unique to the province. According to Dominican historian, P. Fr. Fidel Villaroel:

> *Properly speaking, the ancient foundation was not strictly a monastery of nuns, in the canonical sense of the term, as the Poor Clares were. The Beaterio did not make public solemn vows. But neither were they an Institute of active life as the Daughters of Charity, founded a little earlier (1655) by St. Vincent de Paul, were.*
>
> *Those of Manila, like other counterparts in Spain and South America, were Dominican Tertiaries, living in community under a rule, with less rigid enclosure and with simple private vows, dedicated to both contemplation and to the work of educating some girls inside the Beaterio; they shared from both kinds of consecrated life, the contemplative and active. Not nuns but Sisters; not a monastery, neither just a residence; they were beatas in a Beaterio.*[356]

Religious women in the 17th century followed the *camino de perfeccion* (path of perfection) which involved a life of prayer and contemplation, and strict observance of fasting, abstinence, and penance under the guidance of a confessor.[357] Acts of mortification were not only practiced to pay for their sins and those of others, but for achieving a divine intimacy that occasioned raptures, revelations and other mystical experiences. Santa Catalina de Sena, a Dominican *beata terciera*, modeled this life of strict asceticism in the imitation of saints and in pursuit of a closer relationship with the divine for other laywomen to emulate.[358] Beginning in Europe, this mystic-ascetic tradition of holy women spread to the Spanish colonies and enjoyed the approval and praise of contemporary ecclesiastical authorities. Spanish mysticism involved the spiritual uses of pain and suffering exemplified by religious saints such as San Pedro de Alcantara, Santa Teresa de Ávila, and San Juan de la Cruz.[359]

Self-inflicted torture was not unusual in the practice of traditional Christianity. Fasting, pilgrimage, flagellation, and *cilicia* (cilice) or the wearing of hair shirts and spiked chains accompanied the devotion of countless holy men and women.[360] Practices that would shock us today were yesterday's conventions.[361] In 1671, Pope Clement X canonized Santa Rosa de Lima, a Dominican *beata terciera,* and proclaimed the first saint of the New World as the Patroness of Peru, all of America, the Indies, and Filipinas.[362] Her sainthood further popularized the mystic-ascetic form of spirituality in the colonies.[363] Immersed in this religious environment, pious lay women in the Philippines aspired and became *beatas tercieras* of the Dominican habit.

Founding the Beaterio

By 1686, Manila recognized a *beata india* and three *beatas españolas* for their individual religious sanctity, severe austerities, and mystical gifts.[364] Sebastiana de Santa Maria OP was a maiden *ladina* (Spanish-speaking *India*) from Pasig whose asceticism since childhood gained for her the gift of revelation. In the last fifteen years of her life, she subsisted purely from the Holy Eucharist and prayed intensely for four hours at a time in a kneeling position. She foresaw the foundation of the *Beaterio,* its future location in front of the Santo Domingo Convent, the initial number of 15 *beatas,* and the trials that awaited the community when the number exceeded 15.[365] Two of the Spanish ladies, Francisca del Espiritu Santo de Fuentes and Antonia de Jesus Maria y Esguerra, were widowed sisters-in-law who shunned their past worldly lives, while the third, Mariana de Salzedo, was an angelic young maiden. Like Sebastiana, they all led lives of contemplative prayer, excessive austerities and mystical experiences resulting in constant states of illness. Together, they shared the desire to found a *beaterio* where Lay Dominicans lived as a community perpetually praising and serving God as all *beatas* with high levels of perfection did. The four sought the help of their communal confessor, P. Fr. Juan de Santa Maria OP to establish a *beaterio.*

In 1686, the provincial chapter approved the founding of the *beaterio* with license issued on 11 January 1688. They were not able to secure a permanent site until a new confessor, P. Fr. Juan de Santo Domingo OP, began to minister the tertiaries. Santo Domingo relates a moment of extraordinary grace:

It was on one of these days that Doña Clemencia de Naveda died, leaving me as her last will's executor, as Prior of Santo Domingo. Then the Beatas, specially Mother Francisca del Espiritu Santo started to urge me about the Beaterio in as much as the house of Mrs. Clemency could serve the purpose. But since I was of the contrary opinion, I told her no, as always. One day, after hearing her confession, she returned to press me again. Somewhat angry I told her that she was impertinent and would not give weight to my reasons. Then, with a courageous tone, Mother Francisca told me:

"Fr. Prior, the Beaterio will be constructed and Your Reverence will see [to] it."

I confess that suddenly I got confused and I could not manage to say anything or question her about it until the following day, when, having heard her confession, I asked her:

> *"Mother, what was your basis in telling me with much determination what you told me yesterday? Was it revelation or a dictate of the Holy Spirit?"*
>
> *She was embarrassed and I did not go any further. But everything happened as she has said it would, and I saw so much of it that I actually did everything.*[366]

Meanwhile, the four *beatas* dealt on the matter of founding the *Beaterio* with more frequency. Salazar relates the *Beaterio*'s first bequest:

> *With the communication Mother Antonia had with Mother Sebastiana de Santa Maria ... and with the other two Beatas of great perfection, this matter was dealt on with more frequency. And one time the Mother Sebastiana told her: "Mother Antonia, the Beaterio will be founded, but neither your mercy nor I will ever see it happen." With what was confided the Mother Antonia, she disposed certain matters for the foundation, and firstly she raised in her house some maidens in holy fear of God and admirable deportment, with encouragement that they become beatas and as agreed it came to pass... And she also bequeathed the house she lived in so that the Beaterio is founded in it in view of its early beginnings there even if it was necessary after to expand to other neighboring houses which were purchased. And in order to sustain themselves, she left the beatas certain shops which she owned in the Parian of the Sangleys, which the said Beaterio possesses up to now. And with death very near, she had the Father Provincial called, who was the same P. Fr. Juan de Santo Domingo, and she earnestly beseeched him for the love of God, to grant the Beata habit to two maidens, who were educated by her in her house because she wanted to set a precedent for the foundation of the new Beaterio with this act; and for this purpose she bequeathed her house and hacienda.*[367]

Leaving behind for the *Beaterio* her estate and home located far from Santo Domingo, Sor Antonia de Jesus Maria y Esguerra OP died after receiving the sacraments in 1694 and was interred in the Santo Domingo Convent beside the tomb of Sor Sebastiana de Santa Maria OP who died on 20 March 1692.[368] Neither witnessed the founding of the *Beaterio*. Mariana de Salzedo OP died in 1693.[369] Supported further by the estate of the late Doña Clemencia de Naveda and other benefactors, P. Fr. Juan de Santo Domingo OP inaugurated the *Beaterio de Santa Catalina de Sena de las Hermanas de Penitencia de la Tercera Orden* (Residence of the Sisters of Penitence of the Third Order of St Catherine of Siena) on 26 July 1696 with Madre Soror Francisca del Espiritu Santo as its founding prioress. The site was not the former home of Sor Antonia but a property in front of the Santo Domingo Convent in fulfillment of the prophesy.

<u>The Trials Begin</u>

As the Provincial, P. Fr. Juan de Santo Domingo OP established the Rule of the Beaterio based largely on the Rule of the Third Order including certain items from the Second Order and the general ordinances of the province. The ambiguous character of the original rule would become a source of confusion and conflict during the *Beaterio*'s formative years.[370] He further set a limit of fifteen choir sisters of Spanish blood in honor of the fifteen mysteries of the rosary.[371] They were to take the perpetual solemn vows of obedience, chastity, and poverty.[372] The *Beaterio* attracted many postulants and benefactors. When the number of sisters exceeded fifteen, the problems prophesied by Sor Sebastiana began.

P. Fr. Juan appeared to have overlooked the need to secure the King's approval of the new community as provided by the Law of the Indies.[373] The process entailed the prior approval and endorsement of Manila's Archbishop Diego Camacho y Avila, the same tormentor of the Dominicans in the friar estates litigations. A jurisdictional conflict ensued and the sisters were excommunicated, stripped of their habits, and banished from the *Beaterio* for obeying their Dominican prelates instead of the Archbishop. After a period of exile at the *Colegio de Santa Potenciana* as secular women, the Archbishop relented and recognized the *Beaterio* under Dominican supervision when the sisters agreed to his condition of enclosure in 1706.[374] An essential element that distinguished the *Terciaria* from the cloistered nuns of the Second Order was removed.

During this trying period of banishment, the *beatas* continued to enjoy unrequited support from benefactors. The most notable among them was General Juan de Escaño y Cordoba OP, a *terciero* who designated the *Beaterio* as his universal heir. He provided assets valued at over 60,000 pesos for the establishment of a school for Spanish and native girls after his death on 14 February 1710.[375] His controversial bequest triggered Santa Clara's belligerent opposition by invoking the Royal Patronage and Protection they enjoyed to influence the King's consequent actions concerning the *Beaterio*.

Over a period of time, the King issued a series of decrees to placate Santa Clara's concerns. On 24 August 1714, the *Beaterio* was finally granted its license but was not permitted to be a "sacred place," have a bell or practice enclosure.[376] On 2 February 1716, the King issued a number of decrees. He reiterated his previous decree and directed the governor to implement Escaño's will provided that the *Beaterio* was maintained as a school exclusively for teaching pure secular native girls until they reached the proper state and was prohibited from begging alms that would appropriately be for Santa Clara's benefit.[377] He further advised the Archbishop and Dominican Provincial that the *Beaterio* would subsist without any support from the Royal Treasury and that its financial records were to be regularly examined by an auditor and by the Provincial.[378] In the event these conditions were unacceptable to the Dominicans, the *indias* would be distributed to the houses of Santa Potenciana, Misericordia and the Jesuits. On 17 February 1716, enclosure was again imposed provided that it was not by virtue of a vow.[379] The Dominicans accepted the King's conditions in order to insure the continued existence of the *Beaterio* on 9 July 1718.[380] On 16 February 1731, the king affirmed his *Real Cedula* of 17 February 1716

Ecclesial Ties

Plate XXIII

Pasadiso Linking Santa Catalina and Letran
- *Artist unknown, ca.1890*. Sienna College Retreat House, Bulacan

and ordered its compliance and execution.

With the decree finally silencing Santa Clara, the Dominicans persisted in their petition for the *Beaterio*'s own public church and belfry. On 10 September 1732, the King finally allowed the *Beaterio* to have its own public church and bell but reiterated that it should not be a "convent" of religious women.[381] What originally started as a simple residence for contemplative lay Dominican sisters, the *Beaterio* became a cloister by the intervention of an archbishop, and later transformed into a school subject to close scrutiny by royal decree. This pattern of harassment would continue until 1779.[382] The sisters would quietly bear more similar challenges during the next hundred fifty years; severely testing their faith while strengthening their fortitude.

A Passage Way to Letran

The first prioress, Madre Soror Francisca del Espiritu Santo OP, together with her sister-in-law, Sor Antonia de Jesus Maria OP, joined the Dominican *Tercieria* in 1682. She chose the Dominican habit over the Franciscan one because she saw a vision of herself bowing to St Dominic instead of St Francis when the two saints appeared beckoning before her.[383] Her faithfulness to heeding the whisperings of the soul led to what would become an ecclesial union between the *Beaterio* and Letran.

Upon the imposition of enclosure in 1706, approval of the *Beaterio*'s petition to house the Blessed Sacrament in their own church was met with considerable delays. Acquiring a regular private access to the Blessed Sacrament occupied Madre Francisca's mind and moved her to look for temporary alternatives. In a meditative state, she heard a sound on the wall behind her bed's headboard. Fully awake, she realized that the occurrence was not a dream but a message, because behind the wall across Cerrada St was the newly constructed *Iglesia de San Juan de Letran* (Church of San Juan de Letran). The church was the fourth for Letran having moved from its last site on Muralla St in 1706. The choir of the Church was exactly across the *Beaterio*.

M. Sor. Francisca asked Letran's rector if a *pasadiso* (passage way) bridging the *Beaterio* and the church could be built to provide a private access for the sisters. While the approval for the *Beaterio*'s own church continued to flounder, the necessary permissions for the Letran *pasadiso* and other church enhancements for the sisters' exclusive use were quickly expedited.[384] P. Fr. Juan de Santo Domingo OP related the story:

> ...she started more urgently to tell me that she heard sounds near the head-board of her bed, which was in front of the choir of San Juan de Letran. But I, who do not pay attention to revelations because I thought that those noises were products of her imagination and her desire to have the Blessed Sacrament, was not moved in the least...

> *...the fact was, that the passage would have to lead to some balcony as it is in Sta. Potenciana, in the main chapel, and there I found no small inconvenience, for the narrowness of the space, and for the dependence on the College of those boys who are usually noisy.*
>
> *... I carried out the plans...The choir of the boys was made below and was capable and decent and there was placed the communion rail of the Sisters with its well-built door and facade. Above, immediately by the choir of the Beatas, was left a spacious room with key in which there were two confessional boxes with iron gates and corresponding small door on the side of the choir; and everything came out quite pretty, which I should not be the one to say.*[385]

The passage way was completed in 1710 and the renovated Church was inaugurated on the feast day of *Santo Tomas* in 1711. On Ash Wednesday that year, the statue of *Nuestra Señora* (Our Lady) was installed on the main altar, and M. Sor Francisca and her community happily crossed the *pasadiso* and descended into their special choir. The church was closed to the public for their exclusive use. M. Sor Francisca del Espiritu Santo died on 24 August 1711 at the age of 63. She was the first to be interred in the *Iglesia* over the steps of the Major Altar, on the side of the gospel.[386]

Our Lady of Aranzazu

During the Chapter of 21 April 1714, P. Fr. Juan de Santo Domingo, Commissary of the Holy Office, was elected *Presidente* of *Colegio de San Juan de Letran* for the second time. In May 1716, he was elected the superior of both Letran and the Vicarate of the *Beaterio y Colegio de Santa Catalina*. Since then until 1863, it became customary that Letran's President was concurrently the Vicar of Santa Catalina.[387]

Whenever the liturgical calendar of both schools ran parallel to each other, they were observed jointly at the church of Letran with its rector officiating. One particular *novenario* celebrated by the two schools was in honor of *Nuestra Señora de Aranzazu* (Our Lady of Aranzazu) from the 16th of December until the 24th. For nine days, *misa cantada de aguinaldo* (high mass of the aguinaldo kind) was observed culminating on Christmas eve with the *noche buena* (holy night). Aguinaldo masses were high masses during which Christmas carols called *villancico* were sang instead of the regular choir music. The spirit of giving and receiving guided this festive liturgical observance. The novena began in 1732 during the term of Letran's Venezuelan Rector, P. Fr. Juan Arechederra OP, who may have introduced some of that country's traditional practices.[388] In Venezuela, native folk music was sang by the community led by a group called *parranderos* using indigenous musical instruments.[389] After the mass, the gaiety continued outside the church with dancing and the sharing of christmas tokens, native delicacies, and hot chocolate. This popular annual event would become a Philippine national observance called the *Simbang Gabi* (Dawn Masses).[390]

The devotion to Our Lady of Aranzazu began in 1468 in the town of Oñati, Gipuzkoa, Spain. A year earlier the Basque country in northern Spain was experiencing severe drought that caused so much suffering. The rains returned after the discovery of a madonna on a thorn-bush by a pastoralist named Rodrigo de Balanzategui. Bazaco relates the story:

> *One afternoon in the month of June, Rodrigo while descending the Aloña hill with his herd noted after a short distance the presence of a majestic person over a thorn-bush and heard the echo of a distant bell which compelled him to draw nearer. Overcoming difficulties, he managed to open a passage between the virgin hawthorn which covered the mound, reached the wonderful hawthorn like Moses, and was amazed to see that the person lodged on it was the august semblance of the Virgin Mary. The pastoralist exclaimed: Arantzan zu?! (Thou, among the thorns?!); later he concealed the discovery between the branches and ran home to relate what happened. Another day later he returned to that site in the company of his own parents passing through the villa of Oñati which offered a better way. They saw the town folks leaving in a prayerful procession so that the Lord may show compassion for the fields; and in the middle of the procession, Rodrigo began to shout with a divinely inspired impulse: "Countrymen, I have found the remedy to our misfortune. Come with me to see a little image over a thorn-bush, farther on from Guezalsa." They assumed him to be mad and did not mind him. Articulating more forcefully, he said: "I assure you, that if you do not go to visit her, it will not rain." But the 'ancho chapel' - the nickname they called him - had no more proof than his own affirmation and no one was convinced. There were many who longed for rain at that time, and the simple herder was able to heed the longing. Finally, he concluded: "The strong and the young come, and if what I say is not true, throw me over the cliff of the same hills where the image is." Confronted with this protest - finally beholding Rodrigo as a sincere and humble youth - the town council carefully considered the matter of much importance and named some commissaries to follow the herder. They went there on June 5, they were convinced by the veracity, and it is traditional that at returning home a torrential rain came over those parched lands. Faced with the sudden and unexpected rain, the neighboring towns agreed to raise a chapel where to transfer the miraculous image adjacent to the parish church of Oñati. Implementing what they conceived proved very useless, because another day later they discovered that the Lady had disappeared, only to find her back at the hawthorn place. With the deed repeating several times without a knowledgeable explanation, it was determined to build a road through the rough track and to raise a spacious and beautiful sanctuary on the site where it appears.*[391]

Our Lady of Aranzazu's fame spread throughout Spain. By the 18th century, it reached every corner of the Spanish empire. Her presence in the Philippines was attributed to Don Francisco Echeveste, a pious devotee who was a Basque general of His Majesty's galleons in Mexico.[392] Through communication with his friend, P. Fr. Arechederra, he learned about *San Juan de Letran* which he discerned to be the vehicle to propagate the devotion. He donated 2,000 pesos to establish an *obra pia* in 1732 that would principally fund a *novenario de misas cantadas* for our Our Lady and support the Colegio's orphans. He would spend another 12,000 pesos for the founding of a Confraternity dedicated to Our Lady.

Pope Benedict XIV approved on 20 September 1749 the foundation of a Confraternity for both genders under the name of Aranzazu to pay perpetual homage at the holy image and to promote Christian piety in the populace through good works. King Fernando VI granted his *pase regio* and placed the Confraternity under his royal protection. He ordered that the statutes be formulated and sent to his Royal Council to receive the seal and character that so dignified an association deserved. Basilio Sancho de Santa Justa, Archbishop of Manila, belatedly approved the first statutes of the Confraternity on 23 November 1772 with the confirmation of Carlos III.[393]

The Royal and Pontifical Confraternity of Our Lady of Aranzazu was finally inaugurated on 16 December 1772 with the image of Our Lady installed in the Confraternity's chapel inside the *Iglesia de Letran*.[394] The event was celebrated in the city for three days. The first president was Letran's Rector, P. Fr. Cristobal Rodriguez OP, with Basque Governor General Simon de Anda y Salazar as the first Hermano Mayor. Under the direct patronage of the Pope, the Confraternity became very popular with Manila's nobles and dignitaries joining because of the many indulgences, privileges and favors attached to the membership. It was not until the end of the term of Letran's rector, P. Fr. Antonio Robles OP, in 1798 that interest in the Confraternity waned. The students of Letran and Santa Catalina nevertheless continued the annual observance of the *novenario de misas cantadas de aguinaldo* which became a national tradition.

Today, the devotion to *Nuestra Señora de Aranzazu* continues to be observed at its Diocesan Shrine in the town of San Mateo, Rizal and is no longer observed in Letran. The image of Our Lady of the Holy Rosary had since assumed the former's presence on the side altar of the college chapel. However, her ancient image is displayed together with the sacred relic of St. Vincent Liem de la Paz OP during special occasions celebrated by the school.[395] The historical ties continue to be acknowledged and remembered. Every year during the feast of the Immaculate Conception, the San Mateo image of Our Lady is housed at the Letran chapel prior to the Annual Grand Marian Procession.

Iglesia de San Juan de Letran

The *Iglesia de San Juan de Letran* has its own notable history. It began as a prayer room in Hermano Juan Geronimo Guerrero's dwelling. With the helpful alms of Manila Archbishop Miguel Garcia Serrano OSA, the oratory became a chapel. In 1640, Archbishop Hernando Guerrero OSA granted license to build a church opened to the public.396 Letran had a church and a belfry in all the sites it occupied thereafter.

After the Parian, the church was relocated on the corner of Muralla St facing the Baluarte de San Gabriel in 1669. Letran rector P. Fr. Juan de Santo Domingo OP started the construction of its new site on the corner of Cerrada St. (San Juan de Letran St) with its main entrance facing the *Plaza de Isabel II* (site of present Boy Scout monument) in 1700. The completion of the new Church was delayed by his subsequent election as prior of Santo Domingo Convent in 1702. His successor P. Fr. Sebastian Castillo OP saw to its completion and the Church was finally inaugurated in 1706. The Church had a high and majestic facade with a towering belfry. It was spacious inside with three naves and had an adjacent Chapel of the Santo Cristo.

After Santa Catalina was granted permission to have its own public church on 10 September 1732, the *Beaterio* purchased the Church from Letran for 5,000 pesos on 30 December 1733 as witnessed by public notary Francisco de Maldonado. The *Beaterio* took possession of the Church with great solemnity on 10 January 1734 as witnessed by the royal notary Miguel Allanigue.397 There could be no conceivable reason why such a sale of a part of Letran's heritage could transpire without any significant dissension. Unless, it was done as a preemptive measure to safeguard the *Beaterio* from Santa Clara's belligerence and the crown's vacillating attitude towards her. There were well-founded fears that the *Beaterio*'s license to have a public church could easily be withdrawn at a whim. The unusually careful documentation of the purchase and possession would further support this assertion.

The Letran church became famous by the middle of the 18th century with the establishment of the Confraternity of Our Lady of Aranzazu occupying the Chapel of Santo Cristo within its premises. The Chapel's altar enjoyed a papal privileged status which grants the release of a deceased member's soul from purgatory whenever a mass for Our Lady was celebrated at certain prescribed times. Later, the Holy Pontiffs bestowed the Letran Church with all the graces and indulgences enjoyed by the Basilica of the same name in Rome.398 The Church, which became commonly known as the *Iglesia de San Juan de Letran y del Beaterio de Santa Catalina*, was used indistinctly by Letran and Santa Catalina under the direction of the Rector of Letran who was normally the concurrent Vicar of Santa Catalina until 1863.

On 3 June 1863 at 7:35 in the evening, a massive earthquake hit Manila with two to three violent shocks killing *hundreds of people including five of the most notable in the population, four clergymen, and eight collegians. The Cathedral, Government House, the churches of St Dominic, St Thomas, Parian, Binondo, and St Francisco, hospitals and other buildings, were thrown into a mass of ruins. The church of St Augustine escaped, as it has on this occasion.*399 The Dominicans experienced tremendous losses. The Santo Domingo Church was totally destroyed with a religious found dead under the ruins. A part of the convent was spared with its walls bared open. The community of

Plate XXIV

A Beata of Santa Catalina and a Colegial of Letran
- *Karuth, Carl Johann, 1858.* Karuth Album © Georgina Padilla Zobel de MacCrohon

Capilla de San Juan de Letran - A Shared Legacy
- *Artist unknown, ca. 1890.* Bazaco 1933.

Santo Domingo moved temporarily to the Lolomboy Estate. The Binondo church was in ruins as were Santo Tomas, San Juan de Letran and Santa Catalina de Sena. The Santa Catalina sisters took refuge in a Navotas shelter owned by Santo Tomas. The Church of San Juan de Letran and Beaterio de Santa Catalina was rendered inaccessible and became the least in the reconstruction priorities.

At that time, the Dominicans were expecting a forthcoming release of a royal decree elevating Letran into a First Class College and was mindful of its eventual independence from any other institution in whatever future plans. It was therefore deemed expedient to have the Vicarate of Santa Catalina separate and distant from Letran. The Chapter of 1864 therefore established a separate and independent residence for the Vicar and disallowed all priests from Letran to serve in concurrent capacity. The joint use of the church however was to continue. The questions of ownership, reconstruction, upkeep and control of the church hence became focal issues when faced with limited financial resources. The *Beaterio*'s ownership of the Church was somehow obscured by the virtually non-existent lines that separated institutions within the Order specially after 130 years of peaceful coexistence between Letran and Santa Catalina. Amidst Letran's counterclaims of historical rights to ownership, the impasse was resolved by the Father Commissary, P. Fr. Antonio Orge OP, by declaring the Church to be the radical property of the Dominican Province and hence under its jurisdiction; while recognizing the *Beaterio*'s right to pursue whatever legal action it may have in the event it secedes from the Order. He further ordered that the expenses for rehabilitating the Church would be shared equally by the two institutions. Once rebuilt, a protocol defining the separate responsibilities of both parties and the equitable use of the Church was to be established and followed.[400]

The Church was reconstructed with a sturdier structure albeit of humbler countenance after 1865. It had lost its own grand facade and was incorporated as part of Letran's general facade. The main entrance that faced the plaza was closed and the lateral accesses with Cerrada St on one side and the interior galleries of the school on the other were opened. The Chapel of Our Lady of Aranzazu was not rebuilt and the image was set on the lectern side of the main altar facing the altar of Santo Cristo. Considering its newfound simplicity, the famous church would hence be appropriately known as the *Capilla de San Juan de Letran* (Chapel of San Juan de Letran).[401] It would not be until 1924 that Letran assumed exclusive ownership and use of its own chapel and the *pasadiso* that linked the two institutions for 214 years was torn down.[402]

The Ascent of the Filipino Beata

Since its foundation, the choir sisters of the *Beaterio* were women of Spanish blood. The non-Spanish *tercieras* could only aspire to be a sister of obedience or *lega* assisting their Spanish counterparts, and attending to the education of native girls. Their role drastically changed in 1858 when the Dominicans began to send *legas de mestiza sangley* to China to undertake apostolic work.

Sor Ana del Sagrado Corazon de Jesus OP of Sampaloc and Sor Pascuala Biron del Sagrado Corazon de Jesus OP of Binondo became the first Filipino missionary sisters. Posing as Chinese women, they worked in the *Asilo de la Santa Infancia* (Asylum of the Holy Childhood) in Fuzhou, Fujian Province for over 50 years.[403] More Filipino *tercieras* followed and by the early 20th century they were working in three orphanages with schools, seven asylums, and five colleges for girls in China, Taiwan and Japan.[404] In the Philippines, the sisters of the *Beaterio* were entrusted with the following mission schools: *Colegio del Santisimo Rosario* (1890) in Ligayen, Pangsinan; *Colegio de San Jacinto* (1892) in Tuguegarao, Cagayan; and *Colegio-Asilo de la Sagrada Familia* (1911) in Sta. Rita, Pampanga.[405] The growing demand for more missionary sisters could not be filled by the Philippine *Beaterio*; prompting the Dominican Province to source them from Spain. The *Beaterio y Colegio del Santisimo Rosario de Madrid* was eventually founded in 1892.[406] Considering the preceding circumstances, the historic first visit of the Dominican Master General in 1917 would radically alter the future of the Filipino *beatas*.

P. Fr. Ludwig Theisling OP was the 77th Master General of the Order of Friars Preachers whose term of office was between 1916 and 1925. Born in the Netherlands, he was the Order's first Master General to visit houses of the Dominican family worldwide. During his canonical visit to the Philippines in 1917, he was surprised to discover that none of the Filipino *tercieras indias* in the *Beaterio* were choir sisters and that they were still treated as *legas*. The Filipino *beatas*, led by Madres Filomena de la Soledad OP and Catalina de la Visitacion OP, petitioned the order's highest official to grant full membership to native aspirants who were at least secondary school graduates regardless of their racial background.[407] Noting the racial disparity between the Spanish and Filipino Lay Dominicans, the Master General granted their request.[408] The ascendancy of the Filipina apostolic sisters polarized the Spanish elements of the community. The conflict reached its height in 1933 when the Spanish sisters officially disclosed a new separate community, the *Congregacion de Religiosas de la Tercer Orden de Santo Domingo* (Congregation of the Religious of the Third Order of St Dominic).

The Dominican province allowed the Filipinas to retain one of the Intramuros edifices but granted the new Spanish congregation with all the rest including 17 other houses.[409] Deprived of their apostolic missions, Madre Filomena became the *Beaterio*'s first Filipino prioress under such trying circumstances. On 14 March 1933, the Sacred Congregation for Religious decreed that the *Beaterio de Santa Catalina de Manila* should form an independent community under the jurisdiction of the Ordinary. The decree was agreed by all parties concerned and signed on 15 October 1933. During the next seven years, the newly formed autonomous religious community known as Congregation of Dominican Sisters of St. Catherine of Siena established three more houses in Calbayog, Palawan and La Union. In 1937, Madre Catalina became the second prioress of the new Congregation and from her own funds remodeled and reconstructed the only building alloted to the Filipina sisters in Intramuros. After her death in 1940, the building was destroyed by the Japanese aerial bombardment of Manila on 27 December 1941; leaving the Congregation without a permanent home until June 1953. On that occasion, their own four storey school building in Sampaloc was inaugurated; signaling their unparalleled growth and metamorphosis into a congregation of apostolic sisters of diocesan and pontifical right by 1970 .

From the time it was first conceived by four lay Dominican sisters in 1686, it took the *Beaterio* ten years before it was finally inaugurated in 1696. The community of sisters had to endure many more trials and to surmount successive obstacles thereafter before it could finally enjoy the life of prayer and service in relative peace. The *Beaterio*'s continued existence under such trying circumstances led a Dominican Provincial to remark: *[The Beaterio] appears to be God's design, and (no matter how much we try) we cannot resist the power of His Divine Decrees; with us closely seeing to it that His Divine Will is fulfilled.*[410] It was through the leadership and example of Mother Francisca del Espiritu Santo OP that fortified the sisters to withstand the many attempts to end the *Beaterio*. With each challenge faced, the sisters emerged stronger and more dedicated to their religious convictions and apostolic zeal.

Letran played a role in overcoming those obstacles and developed a special relationship with the *Beaterio*. Memorials of those historical ties are preserved around the premises of Letran. Behind the Baluarte de San Gabriel on Muralla St in Intramuros, one would find the *Plasuela de Madre Francisca* where her full body bronze statue stands facing the *Colegio*'s main facade as a constant reminder of her vigilant presence. Inside the school campus, one would likewise come across the National Historical Institute wall plaque marking the burial site of Mother Francisca del Espiritu Santo. Her lasting memorial and legacy however is the *Beaterio* she founded; whose daughters figured in the formation of the Congregation of Dominican Sisters of St. Catherine of Siena, the Dominican Sisters of the Most Holy Rosary of the Philippines, the Monastery of Our Lady of the Rosary, and the Queen of Angels Monastery to name a few. They have all become living testimonies to verses 38 and 39 of the Acts of the Apostles chapter 5: *For if this endeavor or this activity is of human origin, it will destroy itself, but if it comes from God, you will not be able to destroy them; you may even find yourselves fighting against God.*

Chapter VII

The Spanish Colonial Education

The educational system of 17th century colonial Philippines was essentially patterned after Habsburg Spain. By the 18th century, Spain together with her colonies lagged behind the rest of Europe prompting the Bourbons to intervene. The social, political and economic upheavals throughout the 19th century introduced major reforms in education; bringing with them liberal ideas that shook the empire's conservative religious foundation. To shelter the Philippines from the influence of what were considered as radical and subversive ideas, the friars introduced a diluted version of these educational reforms at a staggeringly slow pace. The constantly changing governments in the peninsular capital somehow contributed to the somewhat retarded development of the Philippine educational system. Nevertheless, the *indios de filipinas* under Spain were comparatively far better educated than any other western colonial natives in the world. It was under these "protective" circumstances that the students of Letran were educated often in silent frustration of its shortcomings.

Education under the Habsburgs

Education in Habsburg Spain was extensive. At the beginning of the 17th century, there were 32 institutions of higher learning and at least 4,000 grammar schools. Many of them were founded in the 16th century and largely supported by the Church. In 1590, there were 7,000 students attending the universities and 20,000 in higher education as a whole. Proportionately, it was the largest student body in Europe.[411] Schooling was organized primarily on a local or independent basis, and only began to be centrally administered and directed toward the end of the 18th century.

Early education was performed by four distinct but overlapping and often complementary agencies: the family, the private tutor, the *Escuela de Primeras Letras* (School of Primary Letters) or *Seminario*, and the *Escuela de Gramatica* (Latin Grammar School) or *Colegio*.[412] Upon completion of Latin grammar, a student may continue to what was commonly known as *Estudios Generales* (General Studies) later to be known as *Universidades* (Universities). Universities were distinguished from grammar schools by their teaching chairs in the advanced faculties of law, medicine and theology, and the right to grant licenses or degrees of scholastic attainment - the *bachillerato* (baccalaureate), *licenciatura* (master's license) and *doctorado* (doctorate). *Estudios Particulares* (Specialized Studies) or simply *estudios* rivaled universities but lacked the complete faculties or the right to grant degrees. Many *colegios* taught liberal arts and theology in addition to latin grammar, but had no power to grant degrees; only certificates of study.[413] However, certain *colegios* known as *academias* (academies), were given special authorities from the Pope and King to grant university degrees even if they do not have the required faculties for *estudios generales*.[414]

Spaniards believed that children who were left uneducated and unattended would follow their supposed natural "evil" instincts, become worrisome brats, and then lead depraved, criminal and even heretical lives.[415] To overcome such tendencies, it was understood that children should be placed in schools to become loyal, obedient, pious and industrious subjects. To improve indoctrination, the three Rs were included.

Primary education began when a child reached the age of six which was considered the age of discretion.[416] Strict obedience and discipline became a fundamental rule of thumb. The whip was a tool used regularly to force the child to submit to the family's as well as the schoolmaster's will.[417] It is at this stage that the father or guardian determines much of the child's adult life.[418] Tutors and schools were selected and the type of education chosen often dictated to the child his later vocation and career. Formal, rigorous instruction in literacy and religion now began, and apprenticeship contracts were arranged.[419] A decision regarding holy orders was frequently determined before the age of nine as well, this being the youngest age at which a youth could take the religious vows and become eligible for ecclesiastical rents.[420]

Sixteenth century Spaniards, particularly those connected with schools, foundling homes, orphanages, and the like, regarded the years after six as a stage in life during which the children had to be moulded in order to prepare them for adult responsibilities.[421] This transitional stage ended only with the coming of puberty, which contemporaries officially pegged at twelve for girls and fourteen for boys.[422] The first responsibility which six-year-olds had to face was the completion of their primary education. It involved learning how to read and write in the vernacular, to perform simple arithmetic calculations, and to recite parts of the catechism and a few simple prayers under the guidance of someone in the family or a paid tutor in more affluent homes.[423] Aided by the free use of the cane, pedagogical techniques included: memorization, endless repetition and review, constant practice and copying.

Secondary education in Habsburg Spain was represented by the *colegio* where the seven liberal arts consisting of the *trivium* (grammar, logic, and rhetoric) and the *quadrivium* (arithmetic, geometry, music and astronomy) were taught. Here *latinidad* (latin grammar) was the key subject as all the arts were taught in that language, and Antonio de Nebrija's text book was the only one used after 1598.[424] Reading was largely confined to Latin literature and instruction included Christian doctrine. Philosophy and Natural Sciences were taught in Church schools largely due to the pioneering efforts of Dominicans in the 13th century and became required courses in preparation for the university faculties of theology, law and medicine. The adoption of Aristotelian philosophy was attributed to the pioneering works of St. Albert the Great OP while that of Platonic Philosophy to Meister Echart OP.[425] The works of St. Thomas Aquinas OP led to the integration of the natural sciences and the revitalization of the church's theological teachings. The pedagogical practices did not differ much from primary instruction, but the scholastic system of *disputatio* (disputation) became an accepted Dominican educational practice in the higher studies.[426]

In 1581, the Society of Jesus was contracted by the University of Valladolid to teach grammar within its premises. Five other universities followed soon after.[427] Beginning 1631, the Jesuits began to take charge of troubled municipal colleges augmenting 118 of their own colleges throughout Spain by the end of the 17th century.[428] With a well organized four to six-year course of graduated study and superior pedagogical program, the Jesuit colleges proved to be highly successful with the Society becoming the leading organizer of secondary education in Hapsburg Spain.[429] By mid-18th century, the Augustinians, Dominicans and Franciscans belatedly began to challenge if not supplant the popularity of Jesuit schools, managing to siphon off part of what would have previously been the Society's exclusive clientele.[430]

17th Century Education

However rudimentary, education in colonial Philippines somewhat paralleled the Iberian model wherever plausible. The first *real cedula* regarding education in the Indies was issued by Carlos I on 7 June 1550 containing the following:

> *Having made particular examination over [the issue], even among the most perfect indio languages that can explain well and appropriately the Mysteries of our Holy Catholic Faith, it has been recognized that it is impossible not to commit great dissonances and imperfections, and even if there were established faculties where priests were taught to indoctrinate the indios, it was insufficient remedy in view of the many varieties of languages. And having come to the conclusion that it is suitable to introduce the Spanish language, we ordain that instructors be assigned to the Indios who voluntarily desire to learn it, in such manner as to be the least troublesome and at no cost. It seems that the task described could well be done by the parish church sacristans, similar to the hamlets in our realm where they teach reading, writing, and christian doctrine.*[431]

On 2 December 1578, Felipe II ordained that clerics and religious were not to be admitted in *doctrinas* without knowing the general language of the *indios*.[432] Felipe III reinforced the implementation of this decree in 1619.[433] On 8 March 1634 and again on 4 November 1636, Felipe IV ordered the teaching of the Spanish language to all residents of the *Indias*.[434] It was not until Carlos III convened the Provincial Council of Manila on 21 August 1769 that uniform educational policies throughout the archipelago, including the teaching of Spanish, were instituted and adopted by all the religious.[435]

From the moment the first Augustinian missionaries arrived in the Philippines in 1565, the task of education immediately began. The conversion of *indios* to a new religion was impeded by the use of a foreign language. The *doctrineros* (pastors) found it more expedient to learn and use the native languages to spread the gospel.[436] The task of producing a grammar and vocabulary manual of indigenous dialects became an ongoing concern of the *doctrineros*. Tagalog became a priority because it was the dialect most commonly used in the archipelago's main trading center - Manila and its surrounds.[437]

The Augustinian P. Fr. Juan de Quiñones OSA and the Franciscan P. Fr. Juan de Plasencia OFM were given credit for the first Tagalog grammar manuscripts which were mainly the collective effort of members of their respective orders.[438] It was Plasencia's *Arte, Vocabulario y Doctrina Cristiana del Idioma Tagalog* (Art, Vocabulary, and Christian Doctrine of the Tagalog Idiom), however, that was approved by Manila Bishop Domingo de Salazar OP and adopted by the prelates of the religious orders in 1581.[439] The primer/catechism manuscript would pass the hands of the different religious orders and undergo a number of revisions and refinement until the first xylographic printed book of the *Doctrina Cristiana* was published by the Dominicans in 1593.[440] The book contained Tagalog texts printed in the indigenous *Baybayin* characters and their Latin equivalents together with Spanish translations.[441] The book had many contributors but the Dominicans credited it principally to P. Fr. Juan de Cobo OP who died before its publication.[442] By the time Letran was founded, a primary educational system was already in place largely influenced by the early mission schools of the Franciscan missionaries.

When P. Fr. Juan Plasencia OFM became the *Custodio* (Custodian) of the Franciscan Province of San Gregorio on 1 July 1583, he ordained the establishment of primary schools called *escuelas de niños* (schools for children) in all of the order's missions and parishes to teach not only christian doctrine, reading and writing, but including arts and trades for the formation of good useful Christian citizens.[443]

Franciscan historian Fr. Juan Francisco San Antonio OFM described a typical day in an *escuela de niños*:

> *Whatever school activity or knowledge explored was called a "juego" (game) in those days, and since it was a "juego", San Geronimo would have viewed it as a child's expression of intelligence: which an astute teacher could tap by balancing severity with love. With this prudent diligence, our Custodian intends [that]…these poor primitives of God could inhabit his house like co-workers of those who evangelize his divine law, become serving ministers of the altar and sing the divine praises from the puerile age, and positioned as such in the Lord's atrium, they are enabled to become teachers of the rest until their matured age.*

Plate XXV

Cover of First Philippine Printed Book, 1593
- Lessing J. Rosenwald Collection. Library of Congress, Washington

> *In this manner, the objective of the 'escuelas de niños' is achieved.*[444]
>
> *...Everyday, without fail, at the signal of the church bell, the children of the 'escuela' promptly congregate in the church: the choir boys sing reverentially and devotionally the "Te Deum" with their teacher which is concluded with the verse and prayer of the Holy Trinity, singing the prime 'Oficio Parvo de la Madre de Dios' (while) leaving the conventual mass; after this the boys pray the rosary together with other devotees who wished to remain, and leave orderly with a small crucifix while praying; the classes to the designated place to learn and the children's choir with their teacher for singing practice. The bell is rang twice at the designated dismissal time, and each one returns to his house to eat.*
>
> *For vespers, the bell rings at two o'clock and they meet at the church to sing the 'Oficio de Parvo.' On conclusion, they leave in the same manner, each one to his assignment until five 5 o'clock when at the sound of the bell they form a devotional procession from the church that turns through all the streets singing and praying the rosary, ending in the church with the litany, the antiphon of the Immaculate Conception of the Mother of God, and a response blessing souls of purgatory...*[445]

Elementary reading was traditionally taught using as a *cartilla* (primer) the common prayers, ten commandments, and catechism. The boys memorized the alphabet with simple phonic exercises and then proceeded directly to reading aloud from the primer. Accurate recitation was more important than understanding what was being read.[446] The order of learning could be inferred from the sequence found in the *Doctrina Cristiana*. The lessons began with the memorization and oral recitation of the alphabet, the vowels and consonant-vowel syllabaries such as *ba be bi bo bu* with occasional three-letter syllabaries namely *ban ben bin bon bun*. The exercises progressed to reading the four Sunday prayers: *Paternoster*, *Ave Maria*, *Credo*, and the *Salve Regina*. Catechism followed starting with reading the Fourteen Articles of Faith, the Ten Commandments, the Five Precepts of the Church, the Seven Sacraments, the Seven Mortal Sins, the Fourteen Works of Mercy, the Act of Contrition, and a Set of 33 Questions and Answers which Plasencia called *Toksohan* (banter).[447]

Training in writing involved repeated exercises of script lettering, and technicalities in penmanship. The following learning techniques developed by Plasencia was described by Vicente Barrantes:

> *For every two boys, a case filled with the finest white sand placed in front of them had been traced with letters and words by the more experienced finger between the pair. They have other extensive leaves of banana, like turgid and whitish pieces of a dawning sky, where with a bamboo splinter the boys engrave the same words they hear their reading partners pronounce. Other boys, who already know that lesson, roam seriously between both rows approaching one and then the other correcting and scolding them. At the bottom of this scene, under a rustic crucifix, on a crudely woven cane chair, an aged friar with a fretful and*

melancholy countenance leans his elbows on a table where the young directors placed those banana leaves etched by the crude stylus. In their own dialect, as resonant and affectionate as can be discerned, the Padre delivers his observations in a grave tone which would otherwise cause tremors or irritation and contempt to the boys if received from the lips of their peers; but inspires them with utmost reverence instead when the Padre transmits it himself. At this juncture, the bells of the church nearby ring twice prompting the religious to bless the boys as they come to kiss the hand and the cord, and leave the school processionally singing the "Veni creator" or the "Sinite parvulos"…[448]

The Franciscans shared their pedagogical practices with the other religious institutes freely. The Jesuits, who arrived in the Philippines together with Bishop Salazar in 1581, took special interest in Plasencia's works in the Tagalog language and contributed to the improvement of the *Doctrina Cristiana*.[449] The Tagalog *Arte y Vocabulario* and *Doctrina Cristiana* proved useful when their first mission schools, which they called *seminario de indios,* were established.[450] By 1595, the Jesuits had established an *escuela de niños* for Spanish boys attached to a college of higher studies, the *Colegio de Manila* (San Ignacio).[451]

According to P. Horacio de la Costa SJ, the following pedagogical system was practiced by the Jesuits:

"They begin class by reciting a cadenced prayer on their knees. Thus by eight o'clock those who are learning to read are reading, and those who are learning to write are writing their copy and this shall be until nine o'clock. From nine to ten the written copies are corrected; first the copies of those who write large, who shall have finished first, then the copies of those who write medium, and after that the copies of those who write in small letters. While the copies are being corrected they are to chant the catechism beginning with 'Todo fiel cristiano' [Every faithful Christian].

Nothing else is scheduled for the morning. In those days Manila lunched at eleven, because this enabled everyone to take a siesta and still have enough daylight left to wind up the affairs of the day. The pens that had to be sharpened were, of course, quill pens; pencils had not yet come into use. Apparently all the boys in the reading and writing class occupied one large classroom, but were divided into several sections. There was a lowest section of those who were just learning to read. Then three writing sections, composed respectively of beginners ('those who write large'), boys who have progressed sufficiently to form medium-sized letters, and the proficient who could write a small, probably a cursive hand. There was, as we shall see presently, a fifth section composed of those who were learning sums. The following was the afternoon order.

"The boys come to school at two o'clock. Pens are sharpened from two to two-thirty. At two-thirty class begins with a prayer as in the morning. Then those who are learning to write are given lessons in continuous or letter writing; first, those who write small in order that they may have

> *more time to do their copies, then those who write large; and these latter shall be assigned the model that they are ready for. From two-thirty to three-thirty those who are learning to read do their reading assignments; at three-thirty they begin to recite in order and without confusion. Those in writing are to work on their copies until they finish, which shall be until four-thirty. From four o'clock to five, as in the morning, while correction is going on, they chant the table [of prayers] and recite the catechism. At five o'clock they say the holy rosary on their knees for the space of a quarter of an hour... During the morning and afternoon sessions attention shall be paid to those who do sums at the time most convenient."*[452]

Immediately after the Dominican's arrival in 1587, P. Fr. Pedro Bolaños founded their first *escuela de niños* in Abucay, Bataan. During its short period of existence, everybody in the *doctrina* was taught to pray. The children were taught how to read and write catechism, while the adults learned to sing devotional music.[453] Considering that Bataan was inhabited by Tagalogs, Plasencia's works on the vernacular was of prime importance to the Dominicans. The first typographical press was transferred by the Order to Abucay in 1610 where the *Arte y Reglas de la Lengua Tagála* (Art and Rules of the Tagalog Language) written by P. Fr. Francisco Blancas de San Jose OP was printed.[454]

Being under the watchful eye of the Archbishop, Hermano Juan Geronimo Guerrero's curriculum and pedagogy would more likely approximate those practiced by the preceding religious institutes. The orphans learned their first Spanish letters and catechism through the customary memorization, endless repetition and review, constant copying under the proverbial whip. Military training was integral to their education. Apprenticeship as pages to military and church officials was practiced. The more promising students were assigned to the Governor General or the Archbishop.[455] At school days end, it was basically a choice between *armas* (arms) or *letras* (letters). Writing was a prized skill as it assured the student of a position in the government as in the case of alumni Felipe de Mendoza who became an *escribano publico* (notary public) and Pablo Mah-jun who became an *escribano* (scribe).[456] Having completed their first Spanish letters, those who wished to pursue further studies found themselves in either *Santo Tomas* or *San Jose* to study Latin grammar.[457] After the Dominicans took over Letran in 1640, H. Fray Diego de Santa Maria OP introduced lessons in *urbanidad* (rules of deportment) and cleanliness not documented in other schools.[458]

The completion of the *escuela de primeras letras* was sufficient to engage in a trade or vocation. Generally speaking, Spanish students who were interested in pursuing priesthood continued on to the *escuela de gramatica* to learn Latin and the Liberal Arts in preparation for future studies in Theology. Sons of the Spanish nobility likewise attended grammar school as part of their formation without having to continue on to Theology. *Indios*, *mestizo de español* and *mestizo de sangley* did not go farther than catechism in the vernacular and rudimentary Spanish literacy.

Grammar School

Secondary education was the Jesuits' primary concern and as such the foundation of their *colegios* quickly followed. Though the Augustinians and Franciscans had their *estudios* in grammar, arts, and theology, they did not have any authorization to grant degrees.[459] The Jesuits, on the other hand, had been empowered by Pope Julius III to confer degrees on its own members and this privilege was extended by Pius IV in 1561 to include day students in Jesuit colleges who fulfilled the requirements for graduation.[460] By 1601, The Jesuits had three *colegios*: *Colegio de San Ildefonso* (1595) in Cebu, and in Manila the *Colegio de San Ignacio* (1595) for externs and the *Colegio de San Jose* (1601) for interns. It was in San Ignacio that the scholars of San Jose who were candidates for degrees attended lectures in philosophy, theology and law along with the Jesuit scholastics who were studying for the priesthood. On 9 July 1621, Pope Gregory XV specifically authorized Jesuit colleges in the Spanish Indies to confer university degrees in his brief *In supereminenti* published in Manila with the royal *exequatur* on 30 July 1623.[461] De la Costa described the curriculum:

> ...*grammar was taught in three graded classes, lower, middle and upper, in each of which the scholar ordinarily spent a year. The master was a resident Jesuit priest and sometimes, though rarely, a scholastic. Grammar, of course, meant Latin grammar, the objective of these classes being the mastery of Latin required to take the next two courses: Humanity or Poetry, and Rhetoric. These were also a year in duration and taught at San Jose by a resident master. Their objective was the formation of habits of logical thought, balanced judgment and clear, persuasive speech through the study of selected classical Latin authors. None of the so-called social sciences were taught formally, but from the 'prelections' or explanations of the classical text given by the instructor, and the 'erudition' demanded by him during the recitation and disputation periods, the student picked up informally a fairly broad acquaintance with history and some insight into the workings of human nature, both individual and collective.*
>
> *The five-year plan of studies just described (variously called 'grammar,' 'estudios de gramatica,' the humanistic curriculum) was looked upon as a unified whole, preparatory to the higher or university studies which immediately followed, but at the same time complete in itself. Those who did not intend to take a degree left San Jose at the end of Rhetoric; those who did, or planned to study for the priesthood, continued to reside at San Jose but attended lectures at the College of Manila...*
>
> *...The philosophical or arts curriculum in Jesuit colleges as prescribed by the Ratio Studiorum of 1599 took three years. Completion by the student of the humanities curriculum (one year of Poetry and one of Rhetoric) was a prerequisite. The first-year subjects were Logic and Introduction to Physics, the professor basing his lectures on Aristotle's*

logical treatises. The second-year subjects were Cosmology, Physics, Psychology and Mathematics. Aristotle's Physics, 'De Coelo' and 'De Generatione' (Book I) were the texts on which the lectures were based. Mathematics was studied from Euclid. The third-year subjects were Psychology, Metaphysics and Moral Philosophy, expounded from Aristotle's 'De Generatione' (Book II), "De Anima', Metaphysica and Ethics.

The theological curriculum took four years, with courses in Scholastic Theology, Moral Theology, Sacred Scriptures and Hebrew. In the Moral Theology course a weekly discussion of practical moral cases was prescribed. Canon law was treated in this course before it was taught as a separate subject. The 'Summa Theologica' of St. Thomas Aquinas formed the basis of the course in Scholastic Theology.[462]

In 1595, the Dominicans began their *estudios* in the arts, philosophy and theology at the Santo Domingo Convent for the members of their religious community.[463] Their first grammar school for Spanish boys, the *Colegio de Santo Tomas,* officially opened its doors in 1619 offering the primary letters as well. With its cession to the Dominican family, Letran assumed the primary education function in 1640 under the supervision of the *Hermano Legos*.

Like the Jesuits, the Dominicans were also authorized to grant degrees in the Philippines by Popes Paul V, Urban VIII and Innocent X who erected *Santo Tomas* into an *academia* with the faculties of Theology and Philosophy in 20 November 1645.[464] In 1734, Pope Clement XII included Canon and Civil Law and other faculties to be established over time elevating Santo Tomas into a public university of general studies.[465] The competition between the two religious institutes assured the Manila students of the latest pedagogical practices.[466] The expulsion of the Jesuits in 1768 would leave Santo Tomas as the sole university to grant degrees in the Philippines until the end of Spanish sovereignty.

It should be noted that Santo Tomas the *Colegio and* Santo Tomas the *Universidad* were two distinct entities under the same rector. The *Colegio* existed basically on funds provided by *obras pias* and thus covered by special laws.[467] It also owned substantial assets acquired from these funds. The *Universidad*, on the other hand, was dependent and subsisted on the *Colegio* for its financial needs. While it did not have its own assets, the university had the authority to establish faculties and to confer degrees subject to a different set of laws and jurisdiction.[468] This fine distinction was generally overlooked until the Spanish government attempted to takeover the university in the 19th century. Without its own physical assets, a university, whose only value was to confer degrees, became disinteresting to any institutional takeover.[469]

Letran's relationship with Santo Tomas would be dictated by this fine legal distinction when circumstances required it. Due to its statutes, Colegio de Santo Tomas was exclusively for Spanish students because of the nature of

Table V
1785 LETRAN HIGHER STUDIES CURRICULUM

I. GRAMMAR		- Reading in Spanish - Etymology in Spanish - Ortography in Spanish - Prosody in Spanish - Principles of Rhetoric - Poetry - Latin Grammar - Principles of Arithmetic - Urbanity - Music - Religion
II. PHILOSOPHY	**Logic**	- Argumentation - Arithmetic - Algebra - Geometry - Logarithms - History
	Physics	- General Physics - Elements of Mechanics - Optics - Hydrostatics - Hydraulics - Elementary Particle Physics - Elementary Cosmogony - Geography - Natural History - Astronomy
	Metaphysics	- Metaphysics - Ontology - Cosmology - Natural Theology - Ethics
III. THEOLOGY		- St. Thomas' Summa - Sacred Scriptures - Canons - Moral Theology

- Bazaco 1933

its endowments. This restriction did not however apply to Letran making it more flexible to accept students of any race.[470] As such, Santo Tomas and Letran were treated as separate colleges under the umbrella of the university. Students attending the university were identified as either a *colegial de Santo Tomas* or a *colegial de Letran* by the uniform of the school where the scholar's tuition, board and lodging were in charge of. Consequently, the school of primary letters was centralized in Letran, latin grammar at *Colegio de Santo Tomas,* and philosophy and theology degree courses at the *Universidad de Santo Tomas.* Letran would gradually carry more grammar courses until its elevation to a first class college in 1867 introduced a more comprehensive curriculum.

In the 17th century, secondary education taught at the *Colegio de Santo Tomas* was known as *Humanidades* (Humanities) which included Latin and Spanish Grammar, Rhetoric and Poetry. The Faculty of Theology was housed at the *Universidad de Santo Tomas* whose tertiary education curriculum centered on *Filosofia* (Philosophy) and *Teologia* (Theology) which was limited to the study of Dogmatic and Moral Theology and the works of St. Thomas Aquinas.[471] For the rest of the century, Letran students would study at Santo Tomas a curriculum consisting of the three courses: Humanities, Philosophy and, if the student wished to pursue priesthood, Theology. P. Fr. Evaristo Fernandez Arias OP elucidates the mission of education at that time:

> *In the beginning the only courses were dogmatic and moral theology, philosophy and the humanities; Latin and Spanish grammar, rhetoric, and poetry were included in the humanities, and the study of all the branches comprised in the works of Santo Tomas de Aquino formed a part of the courses in theology and philosophy. This was the custom in most of the universities existing at that time, a custom that responded perfectly to the necessities of that century, and more particularly to the special requirements of this country at that period. In the first stage of their civilization, education in the Philippines was based exclusively on religion; and the local necessities and the aspirations of the first Spaniards, echoing faithfully the sentiments expressed many times concerning this subject by the Catholic monarchs, demanded a literary center where the bishops and missionaries might find a solution for the many and varied doubts which arose in the exercise of their ministry; where the governors-general might receive ideas of profound and consistent methods of government for the direction of towns and for their relations with neighboring nations, and where the alcaldes and encomenderos might learn the lessons of Christian charity and justice, which they not infrequently failed to observe.[472]*

<u>18th Century Education</u>

Spanish education under the Habsburgs stagnated and was left behind by the rest of Europe towards the end of the 17th century. The ascendancy of the French Bourbons to the Spanish throne signaled the gradual shift to an enlightened autocratic monarchy, introduced major changes in all aspects of Spanish life, and enabled education to catch up momentarily before lapsing back to inertia.

During the reign of Felipe V, Spain transformed from a collection of kingdoms into a better administered nation under one sovereign.[473] Under Carlos III, ideas of secularism and progress prevailed in education in contrast to the 17th century's religious and rationalistic character. The expulsion of the Jesuits from Portuguese, French and Spanish dominions, and their subsequent papal suppression caused a significant vacuum in education and presented opportunities to introduce secular alternatives.⁴⁷⁴ The 18th century was marked by five reforms: modernizing the university system by direct intervention; developing secondary schools and institutes; using the mother language over Latin in teaching; including the exact sciences into the curriculum; and encouraging critical and empirical forms of pedagogy over superstitious practices.⁴⁷⁵ These reforms resulted in restructuring the Humanities, Philosophy and Theology curricula and the creation of new professorial chairs in Jurisprudence, Canon Law, Roman Law, Civil Law, Medicine, Pharmacy, Mathematics and Fine Arts commencing 1785.⁴⁷⁶ By 1875, all these new faculties were established and Letran students were no longer limited to priesthood or the military as a choice of profession.

In 1754, the curriculum appeared to be more robust with two courses of *Humanidades* being shifted to and taught in Letran.⁴⁷⁷ Grammar consisted of Reading, Etymology, Ortography and Prosody of the Spanish language; Principles of Rhetoric; Poetry; Latin Grammar; Principles of Arithmetic; Deportment; Music and Religion. These subjects were not designed to be completed within a specific period of time. Depending on the mental capacity and diligence of the student, they could be completed within one to four years to earn a Certificate of Proficiency and progress to the Philosophy courses. *Filosofia* was divided into three courses: *Logica* (Logic), *Fisica* (Physics) and *Metafisica* (Metaphysics) and each course took about a year and must be successfully completed before progressing to the next one. The last course of *Filosofia* was taken at Santo Tomas and the student earned a *Bachillerato en Filosofia* (Bachelor of Philosophy). Those who were interested in becoming priests continued studying *Teologia* at Santo Tomas and earned a *Bachillerato en Teologia* (Bachelor of Theology). The medium of instruction was Spanish except for advanced Latin Grammar and certain subjects in *Filosofia* and *Teologia*. The students were accordingly called *Gramaticos*, *Artistas* and *Teologos*. ⁴⁷⁸ During most of the 18th century, neither formal matriculation nor specific number of courses were observed.⁴⁷⁹

By 1785, the three *Filosofia* courses were more defined.⁴⁸⁰ *Logica* subjects consisted of Argumentation, Arithmetic, Algebra, Geometry, Logarithms, and History. *Fisica* included General Physics, Elements of Mechanics, Optics, Hydrostatics, Hydraulics, Elementary Particular Physics, Elementary Cosmogony, Geography, Natural History and Astronomy. *Metafisica* covered Metaphysics, Ontology, Cosmology, Natural Theology and Ethics. Upon completion of the three years, the student earned a Bachelor of Philosophy degree from Santo Tomas which qualified him to pursue further university studies. By this time, the faculties of Jurisprudence, Canon Law, Roman Law with degrees in *Teologia* was structured for four years consisting of *Summa Theologiae* of Saint Thomas Aquinas, Sacred Scriptures, Canon Law and Moral Theology with a four-year *pasantia* (apprenticeship) to earn a Bachelor of Theology degree.

The teachers guided the students simultaneously so that exercises were executed uniformly. When certain students straggled behind, they were assigned individually to an advanced student for personalized instruction in order to catch up. In the higher classes, the professor conducted his lectures or conferences for the regular students to take notes. The subject matter was reviewed afterwards in another session with the students correcting each other until their perfect understanding was achieved through the guidance of the professor. The same process was observed in thesis writing or other original works that were occasionally assigned.[481] The Dominican *disputatio* was explained by P. Fr J. B. O'Connor OP:

> *The pedagogical method adopted by St. Dominic involved the following. 'The master lectured daily on the subject-matter of the class. The following Friday one of the students was called upon to give a substantial summary of all the lectures of the current week. Every two weeks the students were called upon to take part in 'circles,' formal disputations, the theme of which was selected by the master, who presided at these academic exercises. The subjects of these discussions were taken from matter under consideration in the class. This was the simple method by which the greatest lights of the Order, including St. Thomas of Aquinas, were formed.'*[482]

Other aspects of the pedagogy was memorialized by Letran Rector P. Fr. Jose Gonzalez OP in 1861:

> *In matters of higher education, including the Latinidad, this Colegio is dependent and subordinated to Santo Tomas, being the University that it is, where daily classes in their respective faculties were attended to together with day students. The Province decided that the grammar courses be transferred to [Letran] in charge of advanced students from the major faculties in view of: the high increase in the number of Latinidad students from past levels, insufficient space to accommodate all, and the dearth of religious instructors entrusted to teach Latinidad in view of the Province's more urgent engagements in the ministry of the missions. In this way, they simultaneously master their respective faculties while pursuing their occupation as students, or smooth transition into ready qualified day teachers in the event a vacancy occurs in the Colegio. In either case, their works need always to be appreciated. In actuality, of the three current professors of Latinidad, two are boarding students teaching the rudiments of Grammar; each assisting two hours a day in class, and the other a salaried day teacher who teaches the rest until Syntax included; assisting four hours a day in class. And to study the final part in Latin or its completion and perfection, the students attend the major faculties at Santo Tomas.*

> *Furthermore with few exceptions, in all the days of the year including breaks in the University, all boarders divide themselves into groups or sections according to their faculties and have their daily review hours or lesson repetitions presided and directed by authorized tutors in the faculty of philosophy, and by bachelors in the respective higher faculties. The sessions were effectively reviews of what were previously taken in class and in reviews during certain days and hours designated for the explanation of christian doctrine served as a preparation, a necessary*

Spanish Colonial Education

Plate XXVI - COLEGIALES DE MANILA

1 - de Santo Tomas.   2 - de San Juan de Letran.   3 - de San Jose

- *Lozano, Jose Honorato, 1847.* Propiedad del Biblioteca Nacional de España bdh0000025754

requisite, to obtain superior grades if they do so opt for it. With respect to everything concerning these literary exercises include those of piety, spirituality and devotion in the public church of the Colegio and its internal chapel, also in the respective bedchambers, and attendance in Royal celebrations and public processions, and in particular all the known traditional functions of the Church, conserving the primary religious and moral education they received inside and outside the Colegio...[483]

The movement for a universal primary education in Europe began its initial stirring in Spain under the Bourbons. Public funding for this purpose became available for the first time in the Philippines on 19 October 1752 when Governor General Jose de Ovando directed that salaries of town teachers should be paid from the public treasury.[484] The 1771 Provincial Council of Manila convened and issued a decree containing eight recommendations on local primary education among other matters. The following were the more significant ones:

Art. 1. Mindful that some negligence has crept into the country's elementary level instruction the Council requests the civil authorities to provide schooling for boys and girls in every parish where this is not already done.

Art. 2. The teacher should be mature, of unblemished morals, and skilled in Spanish. The vernacular should be prohibited in studies other than religion.

Art. 3. Religion is to be taught in both the vernacular and in Spanish.

Art. 5. The pastor should visit the school twice weekly.

Art. 6. In their deanery conferences let the pastors often discuss how the school curriculum, the teachers, and the equipment can best advance the spiritual and civic development of the pupils.

Art. 8. A class day should have two sessions, - the morning one beginning at half past ten and the afternoon one commencing at three o'clock and lasting to five.[485]

The recommendations of the 1771 Provincial Council of Manila underlined two main problems afflicting the primary educational system that continued to fester into the next century: the lack of adequate funding for a sustainable system, and the availability of properly trained teachers. The changes in the economic landscape over the next 50 years would likewise highlight the need for technical skills that had to be addressed by the educational system. While religion dominated the first two centuries of Philippine education, the following two centuries would be significantly influenced by science and business.

<u>19th Century Education</u>

In 1776, Governor General Jose Basco y Vargas ventured to reduce the archipelago's dependence on Mexico by implementing an ambitious economic development plan. The two institutions that would play critical roles in the growth of commerce, agriculture, industry and the arts were the *Tribunal de Comercio* (Chamber of Commerce) established in 1772, and the *Real Sociedad Economica Filipina de Amigos del Pais* (Royal Philippine Economic Society of Friends of the Nation) created in 1780.[486] The *Sociedad* articulated the need for a beneficial partnership between industry and education when it declared that:

> *Public welfare depends on good industry and popular education. For the Filipino people to be effective, they specially need the light of practical arts and sciences, and among the most important [considerations] develop the method of establishing a public school ... and providing the faculties.*[487]

The *Tribunal* instigated the establishment of the *Academia Nautica* (Nautical Academy) on 1 January 1820 and the *Escuela de Comercio* (School of Commerce) on 1 October 1839. The nautical school was prompted by the demise of the galleon trade due to the ongoing Mexican War of Independence, and the unavailability of higher mathematics in existing schools. The commerce school was intended to teach the English and French languages, business correspondence, and double entry accounting demanded by English and other European mercantile firms proliferating Manila after it opened to free trade in 1834.[488] The *Sociedad* founded the *Escuela de Dibujo* (School of Drawing) on 8 October 1823 and supervised the *Escuela de Botanica y Agricultura* (School of Botany and Agriculture) created by royal decree on 29 May 1861.[489] The drawing school aimed to address the needed skills in technical drawing, artistic design, and color rendering needed by a budding manufacturing industry such as textile and paper, while the agricultural school was to develop skilled farmers for the expanding production of commercial crops.

The *Sociedad* likewise promoted the development of manual skills for small manufactures such as embroideries and handicrafts for women, and mechanical skills for men to work in factories.[490] In response to these needs, the Augustinians established eight trade schools called *escuelas patrioticas* (patriotic schools) by 1793 to provide for the agricultural, industrial, and artistic skills required.[491] The growing demand for professional and vocational courses would lead to their eventual adoption into the educational main stream, but the pace of change would only begin to gather momentum with the concerted threat to secularize the existing educational institutions and the return of the Jesuits in 1859.[492]

Meanwhile, the following were Letran's educational practices in 1854 as described by Villaroel:

> *...There were 57 Spanish children as against 203 Filipinos* (pupilos indegenas). *Following the intentions of the founder, only those admitted as orphans had to be sons of Spaniards, or mestizos in whom Spanish blood prevailed. But the orphans were a small minority, a little more than ten per cent of the total student population...*

Table VI
1886 Letran Primary Instruction Curriculum

Clase Elemental
(Elementary Grade)
- Christian Doctrine I-A
- Introduction to Reading
- Introduction to Numeracy
- Introduction to Calligraphy

Clase Media
(Median Grade)
- Christian Doctrine I-B
- Reading Prints
- Reading Manuscripts
- Caligraphy I-A
- Spanish Grammar I-A
- Urbanity I-A
- Religion and Morals I-A
- Arithmetic I-A

Clase Superior
(Superior Grade)
- Christian Doctrine I-C
- Reading in Prose
- Reading in Verse
- Caligraphy I-B
- Spanish Grammar I-B
- Urbanity I-B
- Religion and Morals I-B
- Sacred History
- Arithmetic I-B

Preparatoria
(Preparatory to Secondary Education)
- Basic Geometry
- Basic History
- Basic Physics
- Basic Natural History
- Rudiments of Latin

- Bazaco 1933

Table VII a
1865 Letran Secondary Education Curriculum

GENERAL STUDIES

First Year

- Latin and Spanish Grammar, first course - two lessons/day
- Christian Doctrine and Sacred History - three lessons/week

Second Year

Latin and Spanish Grammar, second course - two lessons/day
- Descriptive Geography - three lessons/week
- Christian Morality - one lesson/week

Third Year

- Latin Analysis and Translation, and rudiments of Greek - one lesson/day
- Universal History and History of Spain - three lessons/week
- Arithmetic and Algebra - one lesson/day

Fourth Year

- Rhetoric and Poetry, Spanish and Latin Composition - one lesson/day
- Geometry and Rectilinear Trigonometry - one lesson/day
- Social Ethics - one lesson/week
- One course of French or English in alternating classes which may be studied during the fourth or fifth year.

Fifth Year

- Psychology, logic and moral philosophy - one lesson/day
- Physics and chemistry - one lesson /day
- Natural History - three lessons/week
- One course of French or English in alternating classes which may be studied during the fourth or fifth year.

At completion of the General Studies, the student earned a Bachelor of Arts degree after successfully passing an oral examination. The degree was officially conferred when the student reached the age of 20

- Arias 1883

Table VII b
1865 Letran Secondary Education Curriculum

STUDIES OF APPLICATION

Profesor en Segundo Enseñanza (Professor in Secondary Education)

- Pass examination to teach subjects in Secondary Education.

Agrimensor y Perito Tasador de Tierras (Land Surveyor and Appraiser)

- Linear drawing, etc. - course of lectures not indicated
- Elements of mathematics - two lesson/day
- Topography and Topographical drawing - one lesson/day
- Physics and natural history - one lesson/day
- Theoretical and practical agriculture - one lesson/ day

Perito Mercantil (Commercial Expert)

- Arithmetic and algebra - one lesson/day
- Mercantile arithmetic - one lesson/day
- Bookkeeping and practical accounting, etc - one course of three lessons/week
- Mercantile correspondence and transactions - one course of three lessons/week
- English - one course of three lessons/week
- French - one course of three lessons/week

Perito Industrial (Industrial Expert)

- Elements of mathematics - two courses of daily lessons
- Physics and chemistry - one course of one lesson/day
- Chemistry as applied to the arts - one course of one lesson/day.
- Drawing, etc. - no courses indicated
- French - one course of three lessons/week.

Perito Quimico (Chemical Expert)

- Elements of mathematics - two courses of one lesson/day
- Physics and chemistry - one course of one lesson/day
- Chemistry as applied to the arts - one course of one lesson/day
- Drawing, etc. - no courses indicated
- French - one course of three lessons/week.

- Arias 1883

Table VIII - OTHER COURSES OFFERED IN LETRAN, 1865

PREPARATORY UNIVERSITY COURSES

Theology and Canon Law	- Ontology - Theodicy
Jurisprudence	- Cosmology - History of Philosophy
Medicine	- Amplification of Physics - Chemistry - Natural History
Pharmacy	- Natural History - General Chemistry

OPTIONAL NON-DEGREE COURSES

Religion, Morals and Urbanity

Literature	**Seccion Inferior** (Inferior Section)	- Grammatical Analysis - Letter Writing
	Seccion Superior (Superior Section)	- Composition in Prose I - Composition in Verse I - Declamation I
	Seccion Academico (Academic Section)	- Composition in Prose II - Composition in Verse II - Declamation II
Fine Arts	**Dibujo Superior** (Advanced Drawing)	- Lineal Drawing - Topographic Drawing - Decorative Drawing - Pencil Landscape - Water Color Landscape - Oil Landscape
	Paisage (Landscape)	- Copy of Laminates - Plaster or Classic - Painting
Music	**Seccion Primera** (First Section)	- Vocal I - Piano I - Violin I
	Seccion Segunda (Second Section)	- Vocal II - Piano II - Violin II
	Seccion Tercera (Third Section)	- Vocal III - Piano III - Violin III
Gymnasium		

- Arias 1889, Bazaco 1933.

...There were the day-students or externos *who resided not only in Intramuros but also in the suburbs of Tondo, Binondo, Santa Cruz, Malate and other neighboring pueblos. The boarding students were called* colegiales, *and of these some were* Pupilos *who were Filipinos, mestizos or Spaniards and paid a modest boarding fee; others were* Huerfanos; *... and others were called* Agraciados, *children of poor families who were given totally or partially free boarding and tuition, and of whom some were called* Capistas *or* Famulos. *The latter paid their boarding and studies by doing some manual service in the college, and for that they were classified as* Sacristanes, Porteros, *etc...*

...Academically, they were called according to the faculty they belonged to at the University of Santo Tomas. Theology students were called Teologos *and* Moralistas, *law students* Legistas, *and philosophy students* Metafisicos, Fisicos, *and* Logicos; *and the younger ones who still handled the humanities were called* Gramaticos, *and in particular, according to their respective year, they were divided into* Quintistas, Cuartistas, Oracionistas, Minimistas, Temporistas *and* Esculapios...

...It was the external attire that brought that disconcertingly heterogeneous group closer to a uniform community. The younger ones up to the fourth year of the humanities, together with the graciados *and the* externos *wore an ordinary suit, except that the jacket had to be a dark blue color showing the college seal in the lapel. The older boys who attended classes at the University, namely, those in the fifth year of high school* (quintistas) *as well as those taking collegiate courses* (filosofos, legistas, canonistas, teologos) *wore a blue gown, red beca or sash over the gown with the college coat of arms, white collar, black sleeves and black cap. This attire was obligatory for community acts, for public acts outside the school and for academic functions at the University, including the daily attendance to class...*

...Study in common covered one hour after breakfast, another from 10:00 to 11:00 and another in the evening. A characteristic exercise of the boarding students was the Paso (Passage), *a period of preparation or review of the class lesson conducted by one student, usually a graduate who was called* Pasante (Assistant Teacher), *and chosen by the Father President. There were separate* Pasos *for the grammarians and for the university students. The assigned lessons were recited, discussions followed, questions and doubts raised, and the* pasante *had to elaborate on the topic until it was clarified. One hour was devoted to the paso on class days; while during vacation days, the exercise was extended to two hours...*

...The college of Letran provided for the teaching of the humanities only up to the fourth year, while the subjects for the fifth or last year (quintista) *were given at the University. The whole course of grammar or latinity comprised the following: Christian Doctrine, Spanish Grammar, Latin Grammar, Elements of Rhetoric, Poetry, Urbanity and Religion.*

> *But these subjects were not strictly classified under fixed academic courses. The only requirement needed to pass on to the study of philosophy was a certificate of approval and sufficiency, it being irrelevant whether* Latinidad *was studied in two, three or more years…*
>
> Latinidad *was an accepted name for the pre-university education, until the reforms of 1865 changed the latinity schools into a more organized and up to date system of* Escuelas de Segunda Enseñanza *(high schools).*[493]

Educational Reforms

It would not be until 20 December 1863 that Isabel II established an obligatory and gratuitous public system of primary instruction, a normal school for teachers in charge of the Jesuits, and provided funding from the central treasury in the Philippines.[494] The comprehensive implementing regulations defined a standard curriculum, the penalties incurred by heads of family for neglecting their children's instruction, and the qualifications, compensation, privileges required and granted for both male and female teachers among its salient provisions.

Article one of the implementing regulations defined the curriculum to include the following subjects: (1) Christian doctrine and principles of ethics and sacred history, suitable for children (2) Reading (3) Writing (4) Practical instruction in the Spanish language, principles of Spanish Grammar, and Orthography (5) Principles of Arithmetic, which shall include the four rules for figures, common fractions, decimal fractions, and instruction in the metric system and its equivalents in ordinary weights and measures (6) General Geography and History of Spain (7) Practical Agriculture as applied to the products of the country (8) Rules of Deportment and (9) Vocal Music. The first instruction for girls excluded the 6, 7 and included work appropriate to their gender. The curriculum consisted of three grades known as *de entrada* (entry), *de ascenso* (advanced), and *de termino* (completion). In 1880, Elements of Drawing was added to the curriculum because of its perceived importance.[495]

Letran complied with the regulations and was categorized a first class primary school.[496] By 1886, Letran's primary instruction curriculum was upgraded by then rector Archbishop Bernardino Nozaleda OP, and included an intermediate course preparatory to secondary education as practiced in Europe. On that same year, the school uniform was changed to conform with the times. The new uniform consisted of a navy blue *americana* (high-buttoned south american suit) with red pin stripes, white vest and pants, and a cap emblazoned with the school's *escudo* (coat of arms). Worn in all academic activities, the use of the uniform was gradually limited to official functions, and eventually discarded at the turn of the century.[497]

Changes in higher education were just as comprehensive. In 1865, educational reforms were introduced in Philippine secondary education with degrees in bachelor of arts, commercial expert, chemical and industrial expert, land surveyor as in the universities in the Peninsula.498 This program was given the supreme approval in 1867 and Letran was declared a first class college of secondary instruction.499 Published in the *Gaceta de Manila* on 7 April 1867, the implementing regulations of the 28 January 1867 Royal Order designated the Rector of the University as *ex-officio* head of secondary education and inspector of all the private colleges incorporated to the University of Santo Tomas. The Rector was further designated as head of Philippine education with powers to inspect higher and secondary education, both in relation to the content of their courses and the text books used among other broad powers.500

As contained in the new regulations in force, secondary education was composed of General Studies and Studies of Application. General Studies was for five years leading to *bachiller en artes* (bachelor of arts) degree, and Studies of Application were for 2-3 years leading to professional titles. The fifth year together with the studies of application were required to be taken at Santo Tomas.501 Upon completion of these studies, the students may secure the diploma corresponding to the bachelor's degree and to each of the professions indicated by passing an examination, and thereupon enter the exercise of their profession if the age of 20 years had been attained. The course of surveyor or expert appraiser of lands and the commercial course were concluded in three years; and that of mechanical and chemical experts in two years each.502

The decree of the general government of 18 February 1876 provided that the examinations for the degree of bachelor in any faculty consisted of miscellaneous questions on the subjects studied during the course, to be put by the three members of the examining board during the period of one hour - that is to say, twenty minutes each. If the examiners were the professors of the faculty or section, each one put questions upon the subject matter of his class. If an examiner were not the professor himself, he was required to put questions upon the subject taught by the professor whose place he took. After the president of the examining board had declared the exercises mentioned in the preceding article to be closed, the beadle cleared the room, in which there remained only those who composed the examining board and the secretary thereof. The president distributed to each of the judges three big dice, one of which bore the letter S - *Sobresaliente* (Excellent), another an A - *Aprobado* (Passed), and another an R - *Reprobado* (Rejected); thereupon a secret ballot was held. In order for a student to be classified as excellent, it was necessary for all the judges to deposit the letter S; in other cases the candidate was passed or rejected, according to the vote of the majority. Should all the balls not bear an S, the candidate was considered simply to have passed.503

At the end of the school year 1881-82, 6,844 students were matriculated in secondary education subjects at Letran and Santo Tomas; of this number 3,781 passed.504 According to Arias, the low success level was due primarily to the poor mastery of Spanish particularly from provincial students.505 Nevertheless many students still enrolled without any serious intention of

Plate XXVII

The Presidential Table

The Presidential Table was used in the solemn exercise of conferring degrees at the University of Santo Tomas. On the table, one would find two silver vases for the votation; ebony chips with silver letters A, S and R nailed on them; a silver platter where the votes were collected; and an hour sand clock. - *Bazaco 1933*.

completing courses. Having studied in a Manila secondary school was sufficient for a student to gain prestige in his home town. A good example was Emilio Aguinaldo, the president of the First Philippine Republic, who openly admitted his failure to complete his secondary education in Letran.[506]

According to the regulations, it was permissible for some of the branches of studies of the first years to study under the direction of a licentiate in philosophy or in science, or a bachelor of arts who was required first to prove his qualifications in an examination in the studies which he desired to teach. These private schools were obliged to conform to the regulations in force, and the supervisors of public instruction had the power to visit them and recommend their establishment or removal. The Rector of Santo Tomas was the ex-officio principal of all these schools. The pupils were obliged to enroll and be examined in said university, excepting such as were in far away provinces, who could be examined by a board composed of the alcalde mayor, the parish priest, and the respective professor. The result of such examination was required to be sent to the secretary of the university.

During the term of 1886-87, there were 41 private schools of secondary instruction. Of these, 12 were situated in the suburbs of Manila and 2 in Intramuros, the rest being in the provinces of Luzon and Visayas. Of the 41 professors in charge thereof, only 1 had the degree of doctor (in charge of a school in Intramuros), 8 were Licentiates in different faculties; and the rest held only a degree of Bachelor of Arts. Five taught the first three years of general studies and resided in the provinces of Manila, Laguna, Batangas and Pampanga; 28 taught the first two years throughout the provinces of the archipelago, and the rest taught only the first year.[507] Many students were matriculated in Letran while actually under the instruction of these private teachers or school to assure the completion of their qualifications. It was difficult for private schools to offer complete courses because of the difficulty to comply with existing government regulations for the fourth and fifth year of secondary instruction.[46]

Apolinario Mabini, the Brains of the Philippine Revolution, was a product of this system. He studied the first three years of general studies at D. Valerio Malabanan's private school in Tanauan, Batangas.[508] He transferred to Letran on his fourth year and became a classmate of my great grandfather, Francisco Liongson y Tongio. They both completed their fifth year at Santo Tomas earning their *Bachiller en Artes* degrees in 1887.[509] Mabini went on to complete his *Titulo de Maestro en Latinidad* in 1893, his *Licenciado en Jurisprudencia* in 1893 and *Licenciado en Derecho Civil* 1894.[510] My great granduncle, Pedro Liongson y Tongio, was a year ahead of him and both would become closely associated during the revolution.[511] My great grandfather Francisco would finish his *Titulo de Professor en Segundo Enseñansa* in 1888, and *Titulo de Agrimensor y Perito Tasador de Tierras* in 1889 while waiting to receive his Bachelor's certificate when he reached the age of 20. He left for Spain thereafter to complete his *Licenciado y Doctorado en Medicina*.

Compromises to the Reforms

Greatly impeded by constant shifts in the balance of power between the liberal and conservative political factions in Spain, the curricula for higher studies took its final form by 1875 after a series of failed attempts to implement legislative changes since 1837.[512] The reluctance to adopt reforms in education was due primarily to the fear that *any changes were likely to endanger the indios' continued loyalty to Spain, the Monarchy and the Christian religion.*[513] An acceptable curriculum was finally adopted and implemented in 1867 only to be discarded after the fall of the monarchy in Spain's glorious revolution of 1868 and the adoption of a new constitution in 1869. The new liberal regent of the kingdom, Francisco Serrano, and his overseas minister, Segismundo Moret, jointly issued a number of decrees secularizing higher and secondary education by the end of 1870.

A decree dated 6 November 1870 established the *Instituto Filipino* (Philippine Institute) which involved the merger of secondary education institutions which included Letran, Ateneo Municipal, San Jose, *Academia Nautica*, *Academia de Dibujo y Pintura* and the faculties of accounting and languages. In a separate decree, the *Real y Pontificia Universidad del Colegio de Santo Tomas* was to be known as *Universidad de Filipinas* (University of the Philippines) with a rector nominated by the government from among the professors in the university. Santo Tomas was not to be involved in secondary education. The implementation of the reforms was however aborted by a timely reversion to a moderate government - a new king, Amadeo I; a new overseas minister, Adelardo Lopez de Ayala; and a new governor general, Rafael de Izquierdo. Governor Izquierdo reached an acceptable compromise with the *Junta Interina de Instruccion Publica* (Interim Commission of Public Instruction) composed of parties opposed to secularization. Meanwhile, the short-lived First Spanish Republic intervened in 1873 before finally capitulating to the Bourbon restoration in 1874 with Alfonso XII as King. Never implemented, the Moret decrees were finally annulled in 1875 and a new system of higher education was officially implemented in charge of the Dominicans; based on agreements reached with Izquierdo in 1871.[514]

The Royal Order of 29 October 1875 declared that *the Royal and Pontifical University of Santo Tomas of Manila will continue as heretofore under the charge of the religious Order of Saint Dominic and under the protection of the Governor General of the Philippine Islands, the Royal Vice-Patron.*

The following were among the important articles contained in the order: (1) the university was required to conduct studies in Jurisprudence, Theology, Canons, Medicine, Pharmacy, and Notary; (2) the organization and the educational system, the orders, plans, programs, and regulations were obliged to be dictated by the Governor General of the Archipelago; (3) a Rector and a Vice-Rector, who possess the degree of Doctor and are or had been professors, were to be nominated by the Order of St. Dominic, and from these nominations, the Overseas Ministry and the Governor General of the Philippines shall choose and be sworn-in in the established form; (4) the faculties of Theology, Canons and Ecclesiastical Discipline shall be carried out by Religious of the cited Order, nominated for the same; (5) the vacancies of the other faculties shall be filled by the Overseas Ministry, subject to public examination and proposed in a short list of three by a Professorial Tribunal constituted in the University of Manila; (6) the faculties of Medicine and Pharmacy, while being integral parts of the university, shall be installed in the *Colegio de San Jose* whose income, net of pious and charitable charges, shall be channeled for the maintenance of these chairs; (7) the faculty of Medicine will maintain its chairs in Pathology, and Surgical and Medical Clinic at the Civil Hospital of San Juan de Dios, with its rooms and amphitheater at the disposal of the Order of St Dominic; (8) the Order of St. Dominic shall retain the *Colegio de Santo Tomas,* annexed to the University; but will transfer part of its faculties to the *Colegio de San Juan de Letran*.515 These institutions and the *Ateneo Municipal* shall for the present be the only ones who can officially conduct secondary education in Manila; (9) the decrees of 6 November 1870 concerning the secondary and superior education in the Philippines and their implementing orders thereafter were repealed; and (10) the Royal Orders of 21 December 1861, Royal Decrees of 20 December 1863, 15 December 1865 and 26 January 1867 that were not modified by this decree and its complementary resolutions were reinstated.516

The Dominicans did not only preserve the rectorate of the university and its direction, they assumed patronage over the chairs as well as the inspection of higher and secondary education, both in relation to the content of their courses and the text books used.

Reaching the Limits of Forbearance

In place over the next 25 years, the 1875 educational system's inadequacies began to become apparent. The faculty of philosophy had effectively disappeared and its elementary courses integrated into the secondary education. The higher philosophy and science courses which taught students to think were quietly omitted.517 The courses in law, medicine and pharmacy did not go farther than the Licentiate level; compelling students to complete their doctorates in Spain.518 Needless to say that only the rich could afford this option. Being perceived as a source of insurrectional ideas, the subject of political law was excluded from the Law curriculum.519 Twenty-five years after its introduction, the faculty of medicine still had *no library worth considering, and that some text-books in use dated back to 1845, that no female cadaver had ever been dissected and the anatomy course was a farce, that most graduates never had attended even one case of confinement or seen a case of laparotomy…*520 Criticism about the system was suppressed in view of the censorship laws in the Philippines.521 The Filipino students in Spain however exposed these deficiencies in a fortnightly publication called *La Solidaridad*.

A series of articles highlighted the outdated curricula and unscientific teachings. In his outlawed book, *El Filibusterismo*, Jose Rizal mocked the modern physics laboratory which the Dominicans proudly showcased in the following passages:

> *For years and years physics had been taught without laboratory experiments… [although] once in a while, as if descended from Heaven, a little machine might be shown to the class from afar, like the Blessed Sacrament to a congregation in obeisance bidden to gaze but not to touch. From time to time, when the professor was inclined to spoil his class, one day in the school year was set aside for the students to visit the mysterious Laboratory where they might admire at a distance the enigmatic equipment displayed in the cabinets; nobody could have reason for complaint for on such a day there was much brainwork and glass to be seen, many tubes, disks, wheels, bells… But the students were*

Plate XXVIII

Letran Internos 1887

UST Physics Laboratory

- *Album de Vistas de la Universidad y Colegios de Santo Tomás, San Juan de Letran, San José y Santa Catalina: Manila 1887.* © Biblioteca Nacional de España bdh0000038102

> *convinced that the equipment had not been bought for their benefit; the friars were not such simpletons! The laboratory had been set up to be shown to foreigners and high officials from the Peninsula, to make them nod approvingly while their guide smirked as if to say:*

> *'Aha! You thought you were going to deal with a pack of backward monks, didn't you? Well, we are abreast with the age; we have a laboratory!'*

> *And the foreigners and the high officials, having been lavishly entertained would afterwards write in their travel journals and memoirs: "The Royal and Pontifical University of Santo Tomas in Manila, under the direction of the erudite Dominican Order, is equipped with a magnificent physics laboratory for the instruction of the youth. Some two hundred fifty students take this course every year but, either from apathy, laziness, the native's mental deficiencies, or other causes ethnological or beyond comprehension, the Philippine-Malay race has yet to produce a Lavoisier, a Secchi, or a Tyndal, even in miniature!"*[522]

But the biggest drawback of the educational system was neither the outdated curricula nor the unscientific teachings. It was the blatant discrimination that spawned an incendiary situation among the country's educated class. Tomas G. del Rosario elucidates:

> *Although the Spanish Government officially recognized the diplomas of the young men who had long years in study at the university and had graduated with the academic degree or as lawyers, physicians, pharmacists, notaries, etc., nevertheless these graduates did not receive any official aid in their country, where at that time individual initiative was regarded as a symptom of insubordination or the beginning of future conspiracy. For this reason there were but few at that time who were able to pursue their professions in the official position. It appeared that the doors of the public offices were closed to every one who held a university degree. This was the case with those who obtained the title of notary, since for a period of eight years they were not permitted sooner to hold any public office. This was also the case with graduates in law, to whom the promise had been made that they would be permitted to hold half the offices connected with the service of public prosecution; there were, however, very few Filipinos who obtained these positions, and most of them were appointed only temporarily. A similar thing occurred with the Filipino physicians from the University of Manila. It had been ordered that one-half the number of positions of official physicians should be given to Filipinos, but, nevertheless, most of the places were given to Spanish doctors, either from the Peninsula or those residing in the archipelago. Naturally when these professional men noticed how laws enacted especially for the purpose of favoring them were eluded, and observed the anxiety to isolate them and to annul their rights without taking into consideration their academic degrees, they felt humiliated by this unjust governmental procedure. Consequently, the protest came; then the conspiracy came, and, as is logical, each succeeding conspiracy became stronger on account of the tenacious opposition and the cruel*

persecution to which those interested were subjected; and finally, in accordance with the natural laws of history shown in the case of many an oppressed people came the revolution. Sooner or later, if the force of right is not respected, the right of force imposes itself, and when this moment arrives the destinies of a people are in the hands of Providence.

All these conditions tended to make the system pursued in the University of Manila and in the other establishments of instruction under the direction of the friars everyday more disagreeable. Favoritism prevailed, and benefits and privileges of all kinds were granted to the favorites. This protection was not based on justice, nor was it a reward for virtue or merit. It was usually bestowed upon Spaniards or the sons of Spaniards, whom they considered superior to the Filipinos, accentuating these differences for the purpose of maintaining a constant state of division and enmity.[523]

Notwithstanding its shortcomings, the Spanish colonial education in charge of the religious institutes had contributed greatly to uplifting the Filipino people. Through the centuries, history presents no other human institution that is more beneficial, more civilizing and more constant than the great religious families who, maintained, nourished and inspired by the spirit of God, spread the true light throughout the world. There were proportionately *more persons who can read and write than even in Spain, and in some other civilized countries.*[524] *Education in the Philippines, both of the children of the country and of the mestizos and Indians of both sexes, is not so greatly neglected as certain persons pretend, and that the colony has made, on the contrary, from the earliest times the greatest efforts for the instruction of the people.*[525] Compared to colonies of other foreign powers that were principally driven by the temporal needs of trade and profit, the Filipino people benefited more from the civilizing and edifying Catholic formation that made it the virtual Christian oasis in Asia at tremendous cost and endeavor to Spain and its agents.[526] During a most turbulent period in Spanish history, the Philippines was shielded by the friars from the violent 19th century clashes between liberal and conservative forces that destabilized Spain and its former American colonies. Liberal ideas that spawned revolutions in the United States and France were censored in order to maintain peace and tranquility in the archipelago. The Philippines, however, could not remain isolated indefinitely. The opening of the Suez Canal in 1869 and Manila's telegraphic link to the world in 1880 made information and ideas more readily accessible with their consequences more pronounced and immediate.

We conclude this chapter with the prophetic words of Fedor Jagor first published in 1873. A German ethnographer-traveller, Jagor wrote about his observations and insights about the Philippines during his stay there between 1859 and 1860. His conclusions provided an appreciation of Spain's contribution, the current state of affairs, and the future that awaits the archipelago. He wrote:

Credit is certainly due to Spain for having bettered the condition of a people who, though comparatively speaking highly civilized, yet being continually distracted by petty wars, had sunk into a disordered and uncultivated state. The inhabitants of these beautiful islands, upon the whole, may well be considered to have lived as comfortably during the last hundred years, protected from all external enemies and governed by mild laws, as those of any other tropical country under native or European sway, - owing, in some measure, to the frequently discussed peculiar circumstances which protect the interests of the natives.

The monks, also, have certainly had an essential part in the production of the results.

Sprung from the lowest orders, inured to hardship and want, and on terms of the closest intimacy with the natives, they were peculiarly fitted to introduce them to a practical conformity with the new religion and code of morality. Later on, also, when they possessed rich livings, and their devout and zealous interest in the welfare of the masses relaxed in proportion as their incomes increased, they materially assisted in bringing about the circumstances already described, with their favorable and unfavorable aspects. Further, possessing neither family nor good education, they were disposed to associate themselves intimately with the natives and their requirements; and their arrogant opposition to the temporal power generally arose through their connection with the natives. With the altered condition of things, however, all this has disappeared. The colony can no longer be kept secluded from the world. Every facility afforded for commercial intercourse is a blow to the old system, and a great step made in the direction of broad and liberal reforms. The more foreign capital and foreign ideas and customs are introduced, increasing the prosperity, enlightenment, and self-respect of the population, the more impatiently will the existing evils be endured.[527]

Chapter VIII

Of Rogues and Martyrs

In my research into Letran's past, I was surprised to discover that St. Vincent Liem de la Paz OP was not the first alumnus to die a martyr. What is more surprising is that the story of this first alumnus martyr became obscure and virtually forgotten through the years. In my pursuit to uncover the truth behind this apparent oversight, I was able to uncover a dark tale of rogues and martyrs that was perhaps better left lost and forgotten in the Dominican archives. I was however haunted by the long dead alumni involved in this story; beckoning me to set the record straight so that the world may know the truth. This is principally the story of two Letran Chinese classmates who became Dominican missionary priests that disturbed the Dominican mission in China for 30 years.

Quickest Way to Heaven

When I was in Letran grade school, there was an exhibit displayed intermittently over the years in the college library. It showcased the martyrdom heritage of the Dominican Province of the Most Holy Rosary. Using cloth dolls filled with sand or grain, the dolls dressed in Dominican habits depicted the various kinds of torture and execution the missionary friars had to endure in their distant oriental outposts. I became aware of this tradition of dying for the faith and how much it was valued by our spiritual mentors. In the 17th and 18th centuries, Letran's belfry would ring gloriously when news of the martyrdom of a Dominican or an alumnus was received; initiating a series of religious festivities akin perhaps to today's *fiestas*. The Spanish Dominican province had a long, and proud tradition of martyrs among its ranks.

The first Christian saints were martyrs, witnesses of the new religion who gave their lives freely for the faith. The horrific executions in Rome became defining events for Christianity; making martyrdom the highest form of sanctity in most people's eyes. Church legal minds recognized that, in cases of martyrdom, the cumbersome procedures of official canonization need not be followed to the letter and, under these circumstances, everything could be done *more easily and lightly*.[528] Martyrdom was the fastest way to sainthood. It was therefore not surprising that the Asian missions of the Dominican Province of the Most Holy Rosary benefited from numerous volunteers from the other provinces in Spain and Europe.

The first mission outside the Philippines was in Kyushu, Japan which was established in 1602; spreading to Nagasaki, Omura, Kyoto and Osaka. The China missions started in Hermosa (Taiwan) in 1626 and in Fokien (Fujian) province in 1632, while the first Dominicans arrived in Tonkin (North Vietnam) in 1676. Of the 183 martyrs under the Dominican umbrella in Asia: 111 died in Japan, 13 in China, and 60 in Vietnam.[529]

The first Japanese Dominican priests of the province came from the ranks of Christian refugees displaced by Tokugawa Ieyasu's Expulsion Edict of 1614 which virtually halted conversions and forced Japanese Christians to go underground.[530] Defying the Edict, San Alfonso de Navarrete OP was beheaded on 1 June 1617 and became the Dominican protomartyr of Japan.[531] The Japanese Christians who were banished from Japan settled in the parishes of San Miguel and Dilao (Paco).[532] Jesuit-educated catechists were among these refugees. Unlike the Jesuits and Franciscans in the Philippines at that time, only the Dominicans and Augustinians accepted non-European vocations.[533] The Dominicans recruited two of these Jesuit Japanese proteges and vested them in their Order's habits after further studies at Santo Tomas. San Jacob de Santa Maria OP (*Kyusei Gorobioye Tomonaga*) and Santo Tomas de San Jacinto OP (*Hioji Rokusayemon Nishi*) were both tortured and executed by the slow and painful death of the *ana-tsurushi* (hanging in the pit) in Nagasaki.[534] Suffering the same fate, a third martyr priest ordained by the Bishop of Cebu, San Vicente de la Cruz OP (Luis Shiwosuka) received his Dominican habit while on his way to Japan.[535] Missionary activities in Japan completely ceased with the imposition of the Sakoku (Closed Country) Edict of 1636.[536] An early reopening of Japan was hoped for and thus between 1640 and 1655, 16 Japanese students were enrolled in Letran to be groomed more likely as potential Japanese-speaking missionaries.[537] Maintaining such number was however discontinued after the stream of refugees ceased. It will not be until 1858 when Japan opened its doors to the western world once again.[538]

The China missions had a longer turbulent history. Between 1587 and 1631, nine attempts to establish a mission in China proved unsuccessful.[539] It was not until 1632, when Dominican P. Fr. Angelo Cocchi OP successfully founded a mission in Fogan (Fuan) on an invitation from a group of Fujian *literados* (literary degree holders) who were introduced to Christianity by the pioneering Jesuits.[540] The mission blossomed and spread to the neighboring towns in the Mindong region. The presence of a new religion however precipitated intermittent conflicts and persecutions of the new Chinese converts and their pastors. In the midst of the Ming-Qing dynastic clashes of 1648, the Dominican protomartyr of China, San Francisco Fernandez de Capillas OP, was beheaded.[541] A fragile coexistence of Christianity with Confucianism, Buddhism and Taoism eventually emerged due largely to the Jesuit's syncretic accommodation of Chinese thought and customs to the Christian faith and practices while serving in the Qing Emperor's court. The relative harmony's seed of destruction was however sown when Dominican P. Fr. Juan Bautista de Morales OP was scandalized at what became to be known collectively as the Chinese Rites Controversy and advocated for its prohibition in 1645.[542]

Plate XXIX

BISHOP GREGORIO LUO WENZAO OP
First Chinese Bishop of China

- Gonzales, J, 1964, I:529

The issues involved were numerous and complex and are amply discussed in other books.543 For the sake of brevity, three core issues evolved: (1) determination of the Chinese word for God; (2) prohibition for Christians to participate in the season rites to Confucius; and (3) prohibition of Christians to use the ancestral tablets as site of the departed's soul and to follow the Chinese rites of ancestral worship. The Jesuits argued that the folk practices of the Chinese were civil in nature and not in conflict with the Catholic faith. The Dominicans argued that the rites were superstitious acts of idolatry. The Chinese Rites Controversy festered with the *Propaganda Fide* (Sacred Congregation for the Propagation of the Faith) siding with the Dominicans in 1645 and thereafter with the Jesuits in 1656. In 1704, Pope Clement XI officially banned the Chinese Rites. Pope Benedict XIV reaffirmed the ban and forbade any further debate in 1742. The ban infuriated a succession of Chinese Emperors and polarized the Chinese converts resulting in the expulsion of missionaries, and the persecution and martyrdom of countless lives. It is under the preceding setting that a number of Letran alumni lived and worked in; earning either heroic or vilified reputations for their actions.544

First Chinese Alumnus Bishop

During the Calendar Case persecutions of Yang Kuan-sien (Yang Guanxian) in 1665-1671, four of five Dominicans in the Fujian mission were banished to Canton.545 They were PP. Domingo Coronado, Domingo Navarrete, Domingo de San Pedro and Felipe Leonardo OP. The only one left free to carry the burden of the entire mission was the non-Spanish Dominican P. Fr. Gregorio Lo Lopez OP (Luo Wenzao).546 With his intimate knowledge of the language, sentiments and aspirations of the people, the Letran alumnus and first Chinese Dominican of the Province travelled incognito throughout the provinces of the empire to administer the sacraments to the faithful and to comfort them during the great tribulation.547 He was able to earn their respect and veneration; converting 2,565 adults in two years.548 His heroic exploits caught the attention of two French bishops: François Pallu MEP, and Pierre Lambert de la Motte MEP. In view of the expulsion decree, these bishops were unable to enter China to assume their vicariates and led them to endorse Luo's papal appointment as first Chinese bishop of Nanking (Nanjing).

Luo turned down the Pope's appointment.549 Notwithstanding the endorsement of P. Fr. Domingo de Naverette OP, his Dominican brothers in the province opposed Luo's appointment because of his inadequate education and theological training and his sympathy for the Jesuit's position on the Chinese Rites Controversy. At the Pope's command in 1684, he finally accepted the appointment as titular Bishop of Basilitanus, Vicar Apostolic of Nanjing and Administrator of Jiangsu, Anhui, Shandong, Hebei, Shanxi, Shaanxi and Henan provinces.550 His consecration as bishop was however stymied in the Philippines. He had to escape to China where he was finally consecrated in Canton (Guangzhou) on 8 April 1685 by

Franciscan Bishop of Beijing, Bernardino della Chiesa OFM. The Franciscans, instead of the Dominicans, became his theological advisers and he supported the Jesuit's position of accommodation and inculturation.[551] In spite of their disappointments with Bishop Luo, the Dominicans did not forget the effectiveness displayed by a Chinese missionary in concealing himself and still be highly productive in a hostile environment.

Christianity Banned in China

After the Papal ban of the Chinese Rites, the Kangxi Emperor ordered in 1706 that only the Christian missionaries who followed the Jesuit Rites would be given the *piao* (imperial permit) to stay in China. By 1721, the Kangxi Emperor officially disagreed with Pope Clement XI and totally banned Christianity from China.[552] Missionaries were expelled while others defiantly stayed and went underground. Persecutions began and Christian lives were threatened. Under those trying circumstances, the Spanish Dominican missionaries in Fujian had to spend most of their time hiding, dressed in peasant clothes; while constantly transferring from one Christian convert's house to another. The memory of Bishop Luo Wenzao's exploits under similar circumstances resurfaced and the urgent need to cultivate indigenous Chinese missionaries crystallized.

The deeper appreciation and understanding of their countrymen's psyche, inner yearnings, habits and vices made it easier for native missionaries to be easily accepted and sheltered by their own kind.[553] For this purpose, Pope Clement IX approved the *College General* (St. Joseph Seminary), a secular seminary in Siam under the *Societe des Missions Etrangeres de Paris* (MEP) in 1669.[554] The Dominicans, on the other hand, prepared to send sons of worthy Chinese parishioners to Manila for theological studies and missionary training for free. In a petition for financial support sent to the Spanish monarch, the Dominican Procurator, P. Fr. Francisco de Serrano OP, cited the success encountered by the French seminary in Siam and highlighted the relative ease that native missionary priests possessed in disappearing into the population while stealthily performing their apostolic work even under the watchful eye of anti-Christian elements. A feat no European missionary could ever hope to equal.[555] On 7 November 1738, Felipe V granted six scholars each for Letran and Universidad de Santo Tomas to children of Christian Chinese and Tonkinese parents with 100 pesos allocated annually for the maintenance of each to be provided by the Royal Treasury in Mexico City, Nueva España.[556]

The King's First Oriental Scholars

Eight Chinese students were admitted in Letran between 1736 and 1741. Francisco del Rosario (Francisco Ly, 1736) would not complete the course, while Miguel de los Angeles (Miguel Hang, 1741) and Matias de los Santos (Matias Ching, 1741) returned to China and became secular priests. The remaining five would profess their vows and complete their studies at Letran and Santo Tomas. They were Juan Feng Shiming (aka Juan Bautista Fung de Santa Maria, Juan de Santa Maria, Juan Fung, Fung Yo-han, Feng Shiming, 1736), Pedro Yan (Pedro Nien de Santo Domingo, Pedro Nien, Pedro Ngieng, 1737), Simon Luo (Simon Lo del Rosario, Simon de Santa Cruz, Pedro Lo, 1741), Pedro Miao (Pedro Mieu de Santa Rosa, Pedro de San Francisco, Pedro Meu-to, 1741) and Vicente Huy (Vicente Huy de Santo Tomas, Jorge de los Reyes, Jorge Hang, 1741).[557] These five Letran alumni would share common ties and experiences, and their destinies would closely intertwine. The principal protagonists of this narrative are the venerable martyr Feng Shiming and the schismatic Pedro Yan.

Juan Feng Shiming was born in 1719 to Ambrosio Feng and Maria Dien in Sanyang (Shuangfeng), Fujian about three kilometers from the Christian community of Kesen (Qitian) and two leagues from the burgeoning town of Moyang (Muyang).[558] The Feng lineage gained prominence during the Ming dynasty and became an influential Christian family in Fuan county.[559] His parent's home was frequently used by persecuted Spanish missionaries as a place of refuge and concealment. Their honesty and religiousness were duly noted by the missionaries and qualified their son to the coveted Manila scholarship. Impressed by young Juan's good conduct and fine character, San Joaquin Royo Perez OP, one of the five Dominican martyrs of Foochow (Fuzhou), influenced the young man's parents to let him study in Manila in order to receive the Dominican habit and eventually become a priest.[560] He was seventeen years old when he arrived in Manila and enrolled at the Colegio de San Juan de Letran on 8 July 1736.[561]

The following year, Pedro Yan arrived and enrolled at Letran on 18 April 1737.[562] Pedro was born in 1728 in Aupoa, Chanchiu (Zhangzhou) to Antonio Yan Teng-kua (Antonio Ngieng Tien, Anton Nien) and Maria del Rosario.[563] The Yan family was totally devoted to the Christian faith with family members suffering persecution, imprisonment and torture repeatedly.[564] His father was a well-known *literado* and physician with the title of *sei-chai* (*xiucai*) in the imperial civil service.[565] This honor was however revoked by the State in view of his steadfastness to the faith. Humble and charitable, Antonio was a devout Christian highly trusted by the Dominicans. He built tall, hidden chambers in his abode to house missionaries and safe-keep their valuables, confidential records and personal belongings.[566] He and his family were imprisoned and tormented on several occasions. In one such torturous captivity during the reign of Emperor Yung-ching (Yongzheng), he was granted the habit of the Third Order of St Dominic for fear of his impending death in 1733. He survived the ordeal only to be banished to the frontiers of the Chinese empire. Facing this sentence of slow death, he requested that his younger son, Pedro, be a recipient of the Manila scholarship.[567] His petition was granted. The Yongzheng emperor died and his son, Kienlung (Qianlong), granted a general amnesty with Antonio being pardoned and freed in 1735.[568]

Both Juan Feng and Pedro Yan received their Dominican habits at the Santo Domingo Convent on 2 July 1743 between the hours of 2 and 3 in the

Plate XXX

P. Fr. Juan Feng Shiming OP

- *Bazaco 1933*

morning after the matins. Both were approved to profess on 9 May 1744 and made their vows on 3 June 1744 at 2 in the afternoon before P. Fr. Bernabe de Magdalena OP with the prior and master of novices, P. Fr. Santiago Barreda OP, signing the act together with the professed natives of the Empire of China. They assumed the names Juan Feng de Santa Maria OP and Pedro Yan de Santo Domingo OP respectively. Similar to Bishop Luo Wenzao OP, their formation was likewise accelerated because of the urgency of their presence in China. Juan Feng was ordained a priest by the Archbishop of Manila, Pedro de la Santisima Trinidad Martinez de Arizala, and sang his first mass on the feast day of his patron saint, St John the Baptist, at the Colegio de San Juan de Letran in 1747. On the insistence of the Vicar Apostolic, San Pedro Martir Sanz e Jorda OP, Feng departed immediately after for China.[569]

The Dominican Martyrs of Fuzhou

On his arrival in Zhangzhou on 12 November 1747, Feng was informed about the beheading of Bishop Sanz on 26 May 1747 and the woeful state of the Christians in Fuan. Imprisoned in Fuzhou were the four remaining Spanish Dominicans: San Francisco Serrano Frias, San Juan Alcober Figuera, San Joaquin Royo Perez and San Francisco Diaz del Rincon OP. Fearing his capture, the Christians of Zhangzhou dissuaded him from assisting the holy captives in Fuzhou and from helping the Christians in Fuan. On his older brother Vicente's plea, Bishop Serrano and Vicar Provincial Alcober wrote to him to desist from traveling particularly to Fuan because the authorities were alerted of his return to China and were searching for him. Being unable to restrain himself any further, he arrived in Fuzhou on 12 February 1748 but was unable to see any of the missionary prisoners. He visited various Christian settlements where he had to constantly hide and flee from pursuers. His attempt to withdraw to Macao was frustrated by blockades along returning routes and by the imprisonment of his Christian collaborators. Returning to Fuzhou, he learned that the four holy captives were transferred and executed on 28 October 1748.[570]

While stranded in Fuzhou, Feng was able to document the deaths of the five martyrs and to officially notify the authorities concerned. He gathered eyewitness accounts of Sanz's beheading, the horrible tortures and deaths of Serrano and Royo by suffocation, and those of Alcober and Diaz by strangulation. All the bodies were burned to ashes and were thrown in a common grave for criminals. At great risk and danger to himself, Feng recovered the relics of the five martyrs with devotion and kept them in a secure place. The ashes of the martyrs that were retrieved and kept by faithful Christian followers were collected. The remains of Bishop Francisco Serrano OP were kept by Feng in six tin containers divided into the heart, bones, chains and padlock, handcuffs, valise, and two Bishop caps. He moved to Fuan to recover the ring of Bishop Sanz, the pectoral of Bishop Luo and a number of items belonging to the martyrs. The relics of the five martyrs of Fuzhou were sent to Santo Domingo Convent and some to Rome.[571]

For the next five years, Feng was the sole missionary ministering to the Dominican Fujian mission. While reaping abundant fruits from his apostolic work, he bore sufferings, persecutions and danger of all kinds in the midst of many controversies during this period of solitude. Among his notable accomplishments were the conversion of Bishop Serrano's jailer together with his family among the many new Christians he baptized, and the expulsion of Christians who worshipped ancestral tablets contrary to insidious rumors circulating in Manila that he consented to the practice. He pleaded to the Father Provincial to send over his brothers and countrymen P. Fr. Pedro Yan OP and P. Fr. Simon Luo OP to be his companions *to obtain many fruits for God, and it would be so shameful to lose them considering that the venerable fathers drenched this earth with their sweat and blood.*[572]

Arrival of More Dominicans

The province finally sent a group of missionary priests to China in 1753 composed of PP. Domingo Castañedo, Diego Terradillos, Pedro Yan and Simon Luo OP.[573] P. Fr. Domingo Castañedo OP was elected vicar provincial of the mission with Terradillos and surprisingly Yan as the other nominees.[574] Feng who was already working in the missions and more knowledgeable than anyone else was overlooked. Terradillos, who was noted for his distain for indigenous missionary priests and his flagrant criticisms of their shortcomings, would eventually become the vicar provincial at Castañedo's death.[575] Two other Spanish Dominicans followed later: PP. Antonio Loranco OP and Pedro Feliu OP, and, by 1758, PP. Vicente Huy de Santo Tomas OP and Pedro Miao de Santa Rosa OP arrived at the mission.[576]

On 3 September 1753, Pedro Yan visited his hometown in Zhangzhou where Simon Luo was assigned earlier.[577] His mother recounted to him the sad tale of his family. She was imprisoned with her husband, Antonio, for months while the latter was tortured mercilessly. Yan's father was banished once again in 1750 to the frontier town of San-jay-kuang where he would die in 1764.[578] Pedro's Dominican tertiary elder brother Agustin Yan went into hiding but surrendered after his son, Ngieng Fat, was beaten to reveal his whereabouts. Agustin was a trusted courier of the Dominicans who would carry silver and distribute them to the needy Christians. Like his father, Antonio, he was subjected to the painful ankle crushing torture after refusing to reveal where the Dominicans hid their wealth.[579] Another brother, Giam Kiong, surrendered to the authorities after his in-laws were arrested.[580] Fortified by his family's sacrifices for the faith, Yan became more resolute to pursue his apostolic work and proceeded to his assignment at Gu-ting-chieng.

Martyrdom of Feng Shiming

After successfully eluding his captors during his years in solitude, Juan Feng was captured at a time when six other Dominican missionaries were currently working at the mission. In a letter dated 29 October 1754, Simon Luo wrote about Feng's imprisonment:

> *In March [1754], a cruel persecution started against the Catholic religion in Fogan, During this period P. Fr. Juan Fung de Santa Maria was imprisoned. It was on Holy Saturday… The original punishment decreed was three years of exile, which was then extended to perpetual exile in the province of Kiang-si… Before leaving, Juan went to confession to P. Fr. Pedro Nien, his classmate in novitiate, and then received Communion from his hands. In his turn, P. Fr. Pedro Nien also went to confession. On 20 March 1754, Juan left looking like a veritable prisoner with an iron chain around his neck, handcuffs and shackles on his feet. He was escorted by two soldiers and three Christians who wished to accompany him… Before arriving at the place of his exile, Juan had to appear before 36 tribunals.*[581]

In chains and shackles; suffering from hunger, thirst, and the vagaries of extreme weather changes throughout the great distance, Feng arrived in June 1755 at his cramp cell in Kiang-si (Jiangxi) without the benefit of any rest or sleep. The untold difficulties and sufferings did not however break his apostolic dedication. Loyal witnesses who accompanied him on his journey attested to his robust display of joy and contentment; nobly declaring his willingness to suffer in the name of Jesus Christ. With his eyes transfixed on a rustic crucifix hanging on his prison cell wall, he succumbed three days later on 1 July 1755 to an acute fever exacerbated by fatigue and the debilitating physical stresses of the long journey.[582]

The 1757 Acts of the Provincial Chapter contained the following exquisite necrological note concerning Juan Bautista Fung de Santa Maria: *He honored our holy habit in life and in death* and conceded to him the title of *glorious martyr*.[583] In 1761, his uncorrupted body was exhumed and transferred to his native Sanyang.[584] Acknowledging his martyrdom a century later, P. Fr. Hilario Ocio y Viana OP lamented: *It is a great shame that his beatification was not introduced with the other Europeans*.[585] The five martyrs of Fuzhou were beatified by Pope Leo XIII on 14 May 1893 and canonized by Pope John Paul II on 1 October 2000.[586] There was no serious attempt to advocate the Venerable Feng Shiming's cause for sainthood despite Ocio's lamentation being echoed repeatedly by other Dominicans through the years. Why was such an apparently deliberate oversight committed?

The Schism of Fuan

A year after the Venerable Feng Shiming's body was transferred to Sanyang, P. Fr. Pedro Yan OP was excommunicated by the vicar apostolic, Bishop

Francisco Pallas OP, in 1762.[587] His excommunication triggered a schism that would adversely affect the Dominican Fujian missions for the next thirty years. Yan's Letran school mates, Pedro Miao de Santa Rosa OP and Vicente Huy de Santo Tomas OP, and two Spanish Dominicans, Antonio Loranco and Pedro Feliu, joined the schism.[588] The incident emanated from developments that transpired after Simon Luo died receiving the last sacraments from Pedro Yan on 24 February 1761 in Kitung (Qidong).[589] Yan was ordered to assume Luo's position in Zhangzhou. Dominican historian, Juan Ferrando OP, recounted the following official report of this controversy:

> ... in accord with the Vicar Provincial, Pallas nominated Pedro Ngien to take Simon Lo's place for being a native of that place and for enjoying much robustness. It appeared that the position was made specially for him. This disgraced missionary did not openly reject the Prelate's order immediately; Much more, the exaggerated affection that he had and professed [for] the hospitality of the house where he lived for a very long time, he threw away in major disorder at his disgrace.
>
> Presenting themselves before everyone, some christians from Chan Chiu with an extensive memorial to the Vicar Provincial of the mission pleading him to leave P. Ngien in his district. In view of the frivolous reasons and futile motives that supported their position, their demand was not accorded with any importance and his pretensions were not considered. Therefore they declared open rebellion against their superiors, dragging P. Ngien in the lead for his culpable condescension in this part. Convinced that the Vicar Provincial had reached the limits of his authority to impose obedience in that christian community, he appealed to the Vicar Apostolic to be involved and withdraw the license to administer the holy sacraments. This was not enough to cauterize the wound to address his obstinacy, and was therefore excommunicated. Nothing, nevertheless, made a nick in that hardened soul, and each day more obstinate, he became the leader of a rebellious and scandalous faction that intended to combat the jurisdiction of His Grace Pallas in the missions which became the origin of the great schism that will last in the church of Fukien.[590]

Other "official" narratives tended to further discredit the schismatics with matters unrelated to the principal issue of disobedience. In one such narrative, Simon Luo was casually included among the schismatics even if he died long before the incident.[591] Dominican historian, P. Fr. Jose Maria Gonzalez OP, declined to discuss details of the unsavory episode but provided helpful leads and references for the more dedicated investigators.[592] What was perfectly clear among these narratives was that the accused's version of the story was nowhere to be found, and deliberate attempts to distort the issue with conflicting innuendos were apparent. My interest in the pursuit of the truth stemmed from the following considerations: first, that the Yan family was staunchly Catholic and trusted completely by the Spanish Dominican martyrs, and their sacrifices could not be flippantly disregarded by Pedro Yan; second, that two Spanish Dominicans sided and joined Yan and his Chinese compatriots; and third, whether the incident was a result of or the cause for the disinterest in Venerable Feng Shiming's journey to sainthood. I was able to piece the puzzle together, and the following narrative reveals an interesting story of rogues and martyrs.

<u>New Vicar Apostolic</u>

After the martyrdom of Bishop Francisco Serrano OP, Pope Benedict XIV appointed P. Fr. Francisco Pallas OP as Vicar Apostolic of Fujian on 11 July 1753 and as the new titular Bishop of Sinopolis the following day. He was likewise conferred with a special commission and authority to conduct an inquest into the deaths of the recent martyrs. At the time of his appointment, Pallas just completed his term as Provincial of the Province of the Most Holy Rosary and was about to assume the position as the province's procurator general in Spain. He was professor of canons at the University of Santo Tomas from 1739 to 1747 and the Chinese scholars may had been among his students.[593] Unlike Terradillos, he was in favor of indigenous priests. He justified their presence as *aunque corto podra servir* (useful even if inadequate) while complaining about their failure to master Latin and their perceived mental weakness.[594] He arrived at Fuzhou on 12 January 1757 and embarked for the next two decades on *repeated and largely unsuccessful attempts to change local practices that he thought conflicted with Christian values and canonical church law, from marriage customs to moneylending to financial contributions for lineage activities.*[595]

Nearly two years after Feng's death, the Vicar Apostolic began processing the martyrdoms in April 1757. The commission was composed of Pallas as judge, Domingo Castañedo OP as fiscal, Pedro Yan OP as procurator of the cause, and Antonio Loranco OP as notary.[596] Yan's principal role was to gather witnesses and evidences for the cause. The deliberations were delayed by the death of Castañedo on 22 March 1758, the ongoing persecutions and the reported infirmities of Yan and Loranco. Terradillos assumed Castañedo's position as vicar provincial and fiscal of the commission with Yan and Loranco eventually no longer actively involved. The *proceso* (inquest deliberations) was finally ready to be sent to Rome in 1763, two years after the *glorious martyr* Feng's remains were exhumed and a year after the schism began. Regrettably, the venerable Chinese martyr was not included together with the five martyrs of Fuzhou. P. Fr. Pablo Domingo Yan OP, a cousin of Pedro Yan whose acceptance to the Order was endorsed by Feng, was the Dominican entrusted by Pallas to hand carry the *proceso* to the Pope in Rome. The preceding facts could be subject to a number of interpretations and it is because of this that conflicting innuendos were prevalent in official narratives. It is only after discovering the following contents of Pedro Yan's unpublished letter to Antonio Loranco and Pedro Feliu dated 18 October 1762 that a more sensible interpretation of facts could be discerned.[597]

The Accused's Version of the Schism

Recently excommunicated by Pallas, a distraught Yan wrote to Loranco and Feliu to explain his side of the controversy, and in all humility to ask for advice and help. He stressed that he never disobeyed their superiors but was a helpless victim of circumstances. It all began when he was assigned to Zhangzhou. This assignment made him very happy considering that his family was from there. On 3 February 1762, he prepared for his departure while ministering to the mission in Kang Kia (Kanjiaban). The local Chinese Christians became apprehensive about losing their minister in as much as securing a replacement entailed difficulties and delays. They began to meet and inquired from P. Fr. Miao de Santa Rosa in Ky Chian (Qitian) whether it was a sin to detain their priest. He replied that it was a great honor on the part of the priest to be detained. They went to see the Vicar Provincial in Kang Tang (Gantang) the following day to explore various options. Among them were: not to order Yan to leave; write a letter to Macao to send a replacement priest at their cost; or delay departure to a number of possible dates. None of the petitions was granted.

Departing the following day as ordered, Yan asked the blessings of Terradillos on 19 February 1762. That same evening, the local Christians gathered at the river passage determined to stop Yan by any means. More pleadings and representations were made. After delaying his departure for a number of days, they finally relented to the Vicar Provincial who refused to yield his authority to a mob. Yan finally boarded a boat that was previously denied him. As the journey along the river began, a multitude of weeping local Christians appeared to bid farewell at his passing parade.

A few days later he received a letter from Terradillos recalling him and blaming him for the "revolution" that ensued from his departure. Evading gentile pursuers, he returned to Kang Kia after many intervening delays. On 4 March, a formal precept was issued ordering Yan to leave for Zhangzhou within two days. The underlying motive of the precept was to establish that *if the father wanted to depart, the Chinese Christian converts could not impede him. If they are able to impede him, it is because the father wants to disobey.* The precept was suspended when Terradillos intervened citing that *the father is obedient, the Chinese Christian converts are the rebels.* Notwithstanding these official declarations, Yan was unable to secure his passage after a number of attempts. It was like asking for *pears from elm trees.* No one dared to assist him for fear of being *thrashed running through rows of beaters.* Terradillos and Yan realized that it was difficult to deal with the local Christians and that some form of acceptable compromise had to be reached. A number of alternatives were explored but rejected because they undermined Terradillos' authority. The principal issues began to crystalize and they centered on the Vicar Provincial's authority and the local converts' sinful detention of Yan against the expressed order of their prelates.

Interim arrangements that did not undermine Terradillos' authority were agreed on with Yan being able to move around nearby areas. On 30 April,

Yan was ordered to go to Ting Teu (Dingtuo), and as usual a group of local Christians stalked his movements. It was apparent to Terradillos that the converts were determined to make Yan their slave. As such, the Vicar Provincial surmised that they might as well provide sustenance for Yan. By 17 May, final arrangements were nearly reached with the Chinese parishioners agreeing to provide Yan with financial, living and liturgical support such as the purchase of wine for consecration. Yan did not receive any instructions from his superiors with regard to these matters. Rumors began to circulate wildly; dragging P. Fr. Pedro Miao OP into the controversy. Meanwhile, the Vicar Apostolic wrote to Terradillos *not to accept the sustenance under whatsoever circumstances as this idea will enable [the converts] to take [Yan] away from the latter's jurisdiction.* Somehow, letters on these matters were not received by Yan and as such no exchanges could ensue. His three letters to the Vicar Provincial remained unanswered, and he was advised by Terradillos' minions to desist from trying as the Vicar Provincial did not trust him.

Yan finally received a letter from Terradillos containing various false accusations and advising him that the precept was reintroduced and two Chinese Christian *literados* (beholden to Terradillos) who were responsible for transporting him to Zhangzhou declared that *had [Yan] ordered us to bring him to Chang Cheu, they would have done so.* Terradillos did not defend Yan's honor from this lie and used the preceding testimony to officially declare him disobedient. As the controversy unfolded, the Chinese Christians were pardoned from the sin of detaining Yan against the orders of their prelates while Yan was alternatively excommunicated by Pallas for disobedience. All in one day, Yan received news of his suspension, excommunication and condemnation on 11 October 1762. Using his apostolic discretion further, Pallas excommunicated Miao and P. Fr. Vicente Huy de Santo Tomas OP as well with accusations of sins only the Vicar Apostolic was aware of.

Yan referred to himself as *padre no se que* (father I-do-not-know-what), a derisive nickname his Dominican superiors most likely labeled him with. Humbly invoking his nickname in the letter to Loranco and Feliu, he ended it with a plea for help if they believed his version of the controversy.

Disgusted by their superiors' machinations and subterfuge, Loranco and Feliu did believe in Yan's account and joined the three Chinese Dominicans. After their licenses to administer the sacraments were revoked, the rebels continued doing so invoking provisions of the *Bull Omnimoda*.[598] The ensuing Schism of Fuan was supported by the local Christians.[599] A concerted effort to discredit the schismatics with other issues was undertaken by Pallas and Terradillos; rendering possibilities for reconciliation more remote.[600] Between 1766 and 1767, the local Christian Chinese addressed at least five petitions to the *Propaganda Fide* complaining about Pallas's policies and defending the schismatic priests. One document contained 269 signatures from Fuan, Dingtou, Sangyang, Yangzhong, Qidong, Muyang, Kanjiabang, Lianshou, Luojiaxiang and Qitian.[601]

Plate XXXI

DOMINICAN MARTYRS OF CHINA
Feng Shiming and a Tertiary in the Foreground
- *Artist unknown ca 1770.* Convento de Santo Tomas, Avila.

The Aftermath

As investigations by *Propaganda Fide* and the Province progressed, Bishop Pallas made known of his intentions to resign.[602] Terradillos was asked to resign from his position as Vicar Provincial in 1767.[603] Bishop Pallas likewise tendered his resignation but was rejected and stayed on as Vicar Apostolic until he died on 6 March 1778.[604] Before his death, Pallas was able to deploy nine Dominicans in the mission by 1775. Of the five Chinese Dominicans among them, four were Letran alumni.[605] P. Fr. Pedro Feliu OP was recalled to Manila and opted to return to his mother convent in Aragon, Spain arriving there on 31 March 1767.[606] P. Fr. Antonio Loranco OP died in Fuzhou an unheralded martyr on 14 August 1769 during the persecutions of that year.[607] P. Fr. Vicente Huy de Santo Tomas OP and P. Fr. Pedro Miao de Santa Rosa OP committed apostasy during the same persecutions. Huy died as an apostate in 1789 while Miao repented and returned to the bosom of the faith before his death on 6 June 1797.[608] P. Fr. Pedro Yan OP died in 1797 with his wish to reconcile unconsummated. The schism ended with his demise.[609]

The Dominicans did not have any new Chinese martyr since the Schism of Fuan. Considering that a principal candidate for the altar like P. Fr. Juan Feng de Santa Maria OP was overlooked, the chances of other past and prospective Chinese candidates became foregone conclusions.[610] In 1895, Dominican historian P. Fr. Hilario Ocio's lamentation made the introduction of Feng Shiming's cause a possibility.[611] Thirty-eight years later, P. Fr. Evergisto Bazaco OP looked forward to the introduction of the cause and expected it on the altars shortly.[612] In 1958, P. Fr. Pablo Fernandez OP continued to cite Feng with the five Martyrs of Fuzhou.[613] In 1989, Ocio was again quoted in the book edited by P. Fr. Ceferino Puebla Pedrosa OP with the following statement enthusiastically added: *But, it is not too late to still do it and thus have him raised to the honors of the Altar.*[614] When the five martyrs were canonized in the year 2000, P. Fr. Eladio Neira OP reiterated Ocio's lamentation and reminded us of the venerable's title of *glorious martyr*.[615] Notwithstanding these clamors, no action was undertaken to address them. The unrestrained words of praise about the venerable martyr were unfortunately left unmatched with resolute action.

Before completing this chapter, I wrote to P. Fr. Javier Gonzalez Izquierdo OP, then the Prior Provincial of the Province of the Most Holy Rosary, to inquire whether there was any existing work or serious intention to pursue the cause of Feng Shiming. I did not receive any reply. It appears that the martyr's memory is at the moment left ignored in the Dominican archives. It is now a matter for a committed individual or group to take on the challenging cause and hopefully one day soon a Letran Chinese alumnus is finally raised to the honors of the altar.

Chapter IX

San Vicente Liem de La Paz OP

San Vicente Liem de la Paz OP is representative of the Letran alumni of the 18th century and a fitting icon of the school's history of that period. To this day, he serves as an ideal model for all Letran students to emulate. Ever since I can remember, the St Vincent Ferrer Elementary Building was dominated by Liem's towering statue in the main stairwell. As students, we were all familiar with his biography and his heroic martyrdom, and took it for granted that he would become a saint someday. His path to sainthood was however not an easy one. The failure of others along the same path made his accomplishments even more outstanding.

A Mystical Encounter

On 6 January 1969, all Dominican Houses throughout the world were elevated into convents. The Convent of Saint John Lateran was officially established with Letran Rector, P. Fr. Lorenzo Rodriguez OP, as its first prior. Something extraordinary happened to me that year when I was a senior in Letran high school.

It was late afternoon and classes were over for the day. The concrete court facing the monument of then Blessed Vicente Liem de la Paz OP was filled with the sound of noisy students running and playing basketball. I began to be aware of a faint sound of music while strolling along the northern corridor of the St Raymond of Peñafort High School Building, on my way towards the administration offices on the east end. It was the sound of the Dominican fathers singing Latin devotional hymns in the chapel. *Strange*, I thought to myself as I seldom witnessed the fathers praying together and much less singing as a group. *It must be because of the new convent*. The beauty of the music rendered in reverential and deep masculine voices captivated me, and I remember wishing *if only the friars could do this more often*.

With the hymns still audible in the background, a strange new sensation started to take hold of me as I passed St Raymond's stairway; reaching the perimeter of the Beato's monument. The cacophony of sounds around me faded into deep silence. I experienced an awesome stillness followed shortly by a soaring sensation. Ascending rapidly into space, I exploded in ecstatic joy. And just as quickly, the afternoon's dissonant sounds and vivid scenery returned to my awareness. *What was that?*, I wondered in total shock and amazement while still in a state of bliss. I could not explain what happened to me or why it did. I only knew intuitively that I was in God's awesome presence in one brief moment and it happened in Letran. It was not until

1988 that it all began to make sense to me. On June 19 that year, Pope John Paul II canonized our illustrious alumnus martyr, San Vicente Liem de La Paz OP.

Vietnamese Missions

Phạm Hiếu Liêm was born in 1732 in Tra Lu, Xuân Phương, Xuân Trường District, Nam Định Province, Vietnam to Christian noble parents, Antonio and Monica Daeon (Thieu Dao).[616] The family belonged to the Nguyen royal dynasty.[617] The new born was gravely ill and was quickly baptized in their home by P. Fr. Jose Chien de Santo Tomas OP who christened him Vicente.[618]

At the time of his birth, Vietnam as a nation was known as the empire of Dai Viet with the Later Le Dynasty as its nominal emperors. The real rulers of Dai Viet were the Trịnh and Nguyễn families. Thang Long (Hanoi) referred to the seat of power of Dong Ngoai (the northern provinces) ruled by the Trịnh family, while Phú Xuân (Huế) was the capital of Dang Trong (the southern provinces) ruled by the Nguyễn family. The border between the North and South Dai Viet was the Gianh River in Quảng Bình province. With the exception of the southern province of Soc Trang, the empire reached its present size in 1745.[619] Compared to Japan and China, the Christian missions in Vietnam had different historical and political roots and became the ideal model for missions at that time.

The kingdoms of the Asian mainland were under the suzerainty of Portugal and subject to the privileges of Royal Patronage. Thus the Portuguese enjoyed a virtual monopoly over the lucrative trade as well as the apostolic work among the gentiles in the Orient. Even when Felipe II became King of both Spain and Portugal, the *status quo* of Portugal's *padroado real* was respected. The Popes were however not happy at the pace of evangelization and began to gradually remove Portugal's privileges and to assume direct control. The vehicle for this change was the Sacred Congregation for the Propagation of the Faith (*Propaganda Fide*) founded in 1622 by Pope Gregory XV. On 22 February 1633, Pope Urban VIII gave permission to all classes of missionaries, seculars and religious, to evangelize the Orient in whatever way without Portugal's permission. The politics of missiology was radically changed in Japan, China and the Indochina Peninsula since bishops were directly answerable to the Pope and not through an intervening monarch. The resistance to ecclesiastical oversight continued among the religious however and had to be overcome. After initial resistance to the new non-Iberian Vicars Apostolic, acquiescence to papal authority was effected after subjecting dissenters to disciplinary action.[620] To achieve effective control, the *Propaganda Fide* began to send significant numbers of French secular missionaries beginning 1660.

After their banishment from Japan in 1614, the Portuguese Jesuits based in Macao began the evangelization of Dai Viet the following year. Christianity

Plate XXXII

SAN VICENTE LIEM DE LA PAZ OP
First Vietnamese Religious Martyr
- *Garcia Llamas, Antonio, 1952*, photo by *Chiao, Davy OP* © Colegio de San Juan de Letran

became known as *Hao Lang Dao* (Religion of the Portuguese).[621] Between 1619 and 1646, French Jesuit Alexandre de Rhodes SJ worked in the mission, studied the Viet language, translated many books to the vernacular, and developed a romanized writing system called the Quốc Ngữ.[622] After being expelled twice from Vietnam, Rhodes returned to Rome in 1649 and began to appeal for more mission funding while spreading tales of the riches of the Indochina peninsula.[623] His plea generated interest and yielded in 1659 the first secular volunteers of the *Société des Missions étrangères de Paris* (Society of Foreign Missions of Paris, M.E.P.): François Pallu, Pierre Lambert de la Motte and Ignace Cotolendi, who were sent as Vicars Apostolic to the Orient.[624] MEP had the objective of adapting to local customs, establishing a native clergy, and keeping close contacts with Rome. Siam became MEP's first mission; followed by Dai Viet and parts of China.[625] Meanwhile other religious orders established their respective missions. P. Fr. Juan de la Cruz OP and P. Fr. Juan de Arjona OP were the first Dominicans to arrive in Tonkin (Dong Ngoai) on 7 July 1676.[626] The mission was ministering to 20,000 souls by 1701; reaching 60,000 by 1750.[627]

Using the Song Hong (Red River) as boundary, the sole Vicariate of Dong Ngoai was divided into the Western and Eastern Vicariates in 1673. The French MEP occupied the west while the Spanish Dominicans were assigned to the east. The Dominican mission was well-organized and grew into three Vicariates: Eastern (Hai Phong, 1673), Central (Bui Chu, 1849) and Northern (Bac Ninh, 1914).[628] Each one had its own structure, hierarchy and institutions. There was an extraordinary development of native clergy, catechists and auxiliaries. Women were called sisters and dedicated to works of charity, such as in nurseries where they cared for abandoned little girls. Lay Dominicans and members of the Confraternity of the Rosary were numerous and of great help to the missionaries.[629]

Following the French model, recruitment and formation of native clergy, diocesan and religious, were encouraged from the beginning. New clergy were typically formed communally in an institution known as Nhà Đức Chúa Trời (House of God). In the mid-eighteenth century, communal formation was in small groups formed by a single priest or missionary. Formation generally followed a basic outline: missionaries, priests, and notables chose talented youth, usually around the age of nine or ten, to live communally with the parish clergy and catechists, usually in the presbytery, where they began to learn to read and write and to study religion, as well as to serve the clergy and the community. Most continued to the *probatorium*, often linked to a seminary, until they were deemed ready to continue into formal training as priest. The more capable ones were sent to Manila for their studies. Others went to schools for catechists or continued to serve the House of God as auxiliaries.[630] It was in one of these Houses of God in Luc Thuy that Liem had his initial education and formation. Under the watchful eye of Dominican P. Fr. Houy, Liem learned his first lessons in virtues and the sciences.[631]

Years in Letran

Not long after, the good friar noted the boy's aptitude for serious studies and wrote to the Rector of Letran, P. Fr. Juan Canduela OP, endorsing the young Liem's application to the King's scholarship. The Rector approved the application and soon after Liem was bidding his parents farewell as the ship departed for Manila. Five other compatriot scholars were with him in the journey to Manila: Jose Huyen de Santo Tomas, Juan Thi Kong de Santo Domingo, Juan Huy de los Santos, Pablo Huyen de la Santisima Trinidad (Pablo Huyen de la Flor), and Pedro Martir Thieng de Jesus Maria. Another Vietnamese by the name of Juan de Santa Rosa would arrive later. Of these seven royal scholars, only three will ever return to Tonkin. No additional Vietnamese scholars would be admitted thereafter.

Liem and his companions arrived in Manila on 21 May 1747. Since the school opening was still five weeks away, Liem studied the intricacies of the Spanish language and was able to join the beginners course at the start of classes. Within three years, he mastered Spanish perfectly, learned Latin, and completed eight courses of primary and secondary education within a short time. He continued on in Letran as teacher's assistant for the lower courses while studying the higher courses at the *Colegio-Universidad de Santo Tomas.* He completed his studies in 1753. Liem received the Dominican habit; professing the solemn vows on 9 September 1754 together with: Pablo Domingo Nien (Yan), Juan Thi Kong de Santo Domingo, Pedro Martir Thieng de Jesus Maria, and Juan Huy de los Santos. He continued his studies in Philosophy and Theology at Santo Tomas and, on 28 January 1755, he received his first tonsure and the four minor orders in the town of Santa Ana. The three major orders followed in the next three years with license to hear confession in the archdiocese granted.[632] He was since known by his new name of P. Fr. Vicente de la Paz OP.

During his school days at the *Real Colegio de San Juan de Letran*, Liem's intellectual capacity and virtuous demeanor received accolades of praises. He was however not given any official recognition. For his achievements, the title of *decano* (dean of students) would have been appropriate but this privilege was reserved only for those of Spanish blood.[633] Considering his extraordinary talents, we can only surmise that he must had been treated better than his other compatriots.

The royal scholars were all expected to return to their respective homelands whether they completed their courses or not. Of the first eight Chinese scholars, three did not become Dominican priests but all eight returned to China. Of the seven Vietnamese scholars, only three returned as Dominican priests. The remaining four would die in the Philippines under dubious circumstances. P. Fr. Jose Huyen de Santo Tomas died due to unknown causes on 26 November 1756.[634] His presumed replacement, H. Fr. Juan de Santa Rosa, also died an acolyte due to unknown causes on 9 September 1759, a year after receiving his habit.[635] P. Fr. Juan Thi-kong de Santo Domingo's departure for Vietnam was revoked because of a *defect* displayed by him. Like the two before him, he died in the Santo Domingo Convent on 4 August 1977.⁶³⁶ P. Fr. Pedro Martir Thieng de Jesus Maria was surprisingly assigned to Binmaley, Pangasinan instead of Dai Viet and died there in 1770.⁶³⁷ Because of their unexplained deaths and circumstances on foreign soil, one cannot help but wonder how they were treated by their mentors. Perhaps Liem's remaining compatriots who returned to Vietnam could provide some clue to the puzzle.

Return to Vietnam

Together with Liem, P. Fr. Pablo Huyen de la Santisima Trinidad and P. Fr. Juan Huy de los Santos were approved to depart for their land of birth on 3 October 1758. The permission given to Huy was however revoked on 6 November 1758 and again on 26 October 1776. He was finally allowed to return to Vietnam arriving there on 16 January 1781. He was the last living Vietnamese royal scholar by then. Huyen died in the mission in 1768 while Liem was executed in 1773. In the refuge of his Tonkin homeland, Juan Huy published a Latin pamphlet entitled *De perditione Manila* exposing the abuses the scholars were subjected to and denouncing the Dominican Provincial and all the Manila religious for the acts of perdition.⁶³⁸ This bit of information provided by P. Fr. Hilario Ocio OP is the only insight we have to explain the latent anger that the indigenous royal scholars harbored against their Spanish mentors. The repressed anger found its full expression in the Schism of Fuan and in the Tonkin Pamphlet. The revelation however only highlighted further the virtues of the Letran alumni martyrs, Phạm Hiếu Liêm and Feng Shiming. Subjected to the same kind of abuses and intolerance, they humbly remained faithful to God, submitted to their superiors, and excelled in their chosen vocation under pain of death.

P. Fr. Vicente Liem de La Paz OP returned to Dai Viet on 20 January 1759. Arriving at the mission superior's residence in Trung Linh, he was immediately put to task considering his native familiarity with the language. His apostolic work brought him to the Catholic communities in the Red River delta: Phu-tay (*Phú Thai*), Cuat-lam (*Quất Lâm*), Tru-lao (*Trung Lao*), Luc-thuy (*Gia Thuy*), Thu-oug (*Thuong Ti*), Ke-met (*Ke Mat*) and Tai-bau. The threats of persecution, physical harm, and perilous travels could not deter him from bringing the light of truth and help to Christians in the shadow of death wherever and whenever his presence was required. Fearing his capture by enemies, his boldness to take risks caused much concern among his superiors and local Christians. On 2 October 1773, this dreaded anxiety was realized.⁶³⁹

China's suzerainty and influence permeated every aspect of the Dai Viet empire. The Vietnamese social, political, economic and cultural life was patterned after China. The behavior of the Dai Viet court paralleled the imperial court in the Asia mainland including policies on foreign religions. Throughout Vietnam's history, an estimate of over 130,000 Catholics died as martyrs by a variety of execution, torture and suffering.⁶⁴⁰ Of this number, only a few would be documented and a still fewer representative number

Plate XXXIII

SAN JACINTO CASTAÑEDA
- *Artist Unknown.* Catedral de Valencia, España

would be canonized. Harassment and persecution of Christians occurred on an intermittent basis as early as 1663.[641] In 1712, the *chúa* (lord) of the Northern provinces, *Trịnh Cương* the *An Đô Vương*, issued the Edict of Persecution of Christians. During his reign, San Mateo Alonso Liciniana OP and San Francisco Gil de Federich OP became the Dominican protomartyrs of Vietnam on 22 January 1745.[642] The *Vương's* descendants would follow his policies against the Christians. In 1767, *Trịnh Sâm* the *Tĩnh Đô Vương* became *chúa* and would adjudicate the charges brought against Liem in 1773.

New Champions of the Cross

After 14 years of apostolic life, a group of anti-Christian conspirators apprehended Liem in Thai Binh.[643] Pulling him by the hair, they threw him to the ground, dragged him through the mud and beat him mercilessly while cursing and causing other injuries. He was brought to the market in the next town to be publicly humiliated among a great multitude of gentiles and to strike fear among the local Christians. The sub-prefect of the district arrived and ordered Liem thrown into a cage and brought to the prison in Hung Yen where other Christians were imprisoned.[644] Liem was united there with another Dominican P. Fr. Jacinto Castañeda OP. The following day, all the prisoners were sent to Hien Nam where the Sub-prefect could collect his reward for the Christian captives.[645] Reaching their destination on 16 October, the Principal Mandarin did not allow the use of the public jail, neither to molest nor to allow anyone else to molest the captives. The Sub-prefect had to disappointingly look for other confinement space and comply with the conditions set. During this momentary lull, Liem and Castañeda preached the word of God. With their cages containing signs of *Hoa Lang Đạo Sư* (Principal Teacher of Portuguese Religion), they were brought soon after to the capital, Hanoi.

In the rural district of Bac Ha of the northern Lào Cai Province, the Catholic church there preserved memories of an important debate ordered by an official of the Vương (king) during this period. The church's history recorded a debate among the four major religions: Confucianism, Taoism, Buddhism, and Catholicism, in a small book entitled "*Hội Đồng Tứ Giáo*" (The Council of Four Religions). The debate lasted for three days and focused on three topics: the origin of one's life, the purpose of one's existence; and life after death. *During the debate, the Catholic representatives applied the Apologetic method and also used classic references from Chinese literatures to explain their theory so clearly that they earned the officer's admiration.* In his book, *Sử Ký Địa Phận Trung*, historian Gisbert identified Gia (Castañeda) and Liem as the Catholic representatives.[646] The King and the Queen Mother were very pleased with the debate. The Queen Mother went further and asked Liem: *If it is so, as you say those who follow the religion of the Portuguese, all of us who worship the idols will go to hell, and you who follow the Christian religion will go to heaven?* Liem answered *It is exactly as you say it, your majesty.*[647] The Queen Mother's displeasure sealed the two

Plate XXXIV

Our Lady of Aranzazu with Liem's Bone Relics
- *© Chiao, Davy OP*, Colegio de San Juan de Letran.

Dominicans' death sentences.

An official of the king advocated to spare Liem's life by invoking his nationality as a Vietnamese. Concerned for his Dominican brother's life and not mindful of his own, Liem answered as succinctly as he did the queen mother earlier:

> *If Fr. Gia is condemned to death for religious reason, I should deserve the same sentence. He and I are both priests; if the law of the country does not condemn me, neither should it condemn Fr. Gia. Since I am Vietnamese, I should obey the rule of my country more than the foreigners. If Fr. Gia is killed and I am released, the sentence would not be fair. I would like to request that we should have the same sentence. That would be fair.*[648]

Condemned to death for being priests of a banned religion, the two servants of God were led to the execution ground of Đồng Mơ to be decapitated on 7 November 1773. With one blow, Liem's head swiftly parted his body. The executioner had to attempt three times before dispatching Castaneda's. The faithful followers collected the martyrs' bodies and brought them to Trung Linh where they were laid in marked caskets and buried in the rites of the Church.[649] P. Fr. Vicente Liem de la Paz OP became the first recorded religious Vietnamese to die for the faith.[650] The following eulogy was included in the acts of his *proceso*:

> *He understood his ministry as not being limited to a particular place or district, but as any place where he could penetrate. Untiring in the confessional, he would spend throughout the evenings giving commendable counsel to the poor Christians encouraging them to bear the overly unending and terrible persecutions that ruptured there. He preached to christians and gentiles, and exhorted them to keep the Holy Commandments of the Lord: both day and night he would reach out to the sick beds and never ceased in his ministry. Persecuted for the doctrine he preached by those same ones whose birth he witnessed, he yields his own blood for a cause so holy.*[651]

<u>Failed Social Experiment</u>

Notwithstanding the martyrdoms of the Venerables Phạm Hiếu Liêm and Feng Shiming, the Dominicans deemed the royal scholarship for indigenous Oriental priests to be generally a failure. Dominican historian Ferrando explained:

> *Until then the few priests of [China], that assisted in the cultivation of that vineyard, watered by the sweat and blood of the european missionaries, had been educated in Manila; more so the experience had unfortunately taught and made sense of the grave inconveniences of such a system. The interaction and communication with the youth that frequented the rooms of our University and colleges in Manila, had contaminated them with certain bad habits that opposes the spirit and*

religious absorption, that always needs to be a part of the christian priest's sphere of influence.

It is true that in the end many of the young ones intended and took the holy habit in our Manila convent; more so the equality that presides over the religious spirit of our Congregation, which does not admit hierarchies of either race or color, was also to a certain extent detrimental to the established system. The equality before the Corporation and before the law, which were recognized by the Institute, equating them in everything with the european religious, made it difficult to subordinate them to their respective Superiors in their country; whose authority they did not respect when it was desired. This is the reason why many of these young ones serve only to embarrass the missionaries in pursuing the work of God and of his kingdom. The same inconveniences affected the Vietnamese missions, and for the benefit of the same, it was necessary to radically change the system, stopping the youth from being sent to the colleges in Manila, and creating seminaries in the principal centers of religious propagation, where they can be initiated in the duties of the order and the priesthood, without the inconveniences and contamination that we indicated.[652]

In view of the preceding observations, the Spanish Dominicans preferred to train their seminarians in their respective countries thereafter. The Vietnamese were the first to receive their Dominican habits in their own soil following the French mission model. P. Fr. Juan de Santo Domingo OP was the first Vietnamese son of the Dominican Priory in North Dai Viet to profess in 1739.[653] The seven royal scholars from Vietnam would be the last to be sent to Manila. Priests thereafter were all educated in local seminaries.[654] On 12 July 1813, the missionary priests in China were authorized to ordain as practiced in Vietnam.[655] A secret seminary was established in Ki-chin (Qi Tian) by Bishop Roque Carpena Diaz OP in that year. Principally administered by P. Fr. Tomas Sala OP, the *Seminario de Santa Cruz* (Holy Cross Seminary) was approved by the *Propaganda Fide* in 1816.[656] The first Dominican to profess in China was P. Fr. Tomas Ling (Hung) de San Bernardo OP in 1816.[657] The seminary was however closed in 1834. Other seminaries were established in Loyen (Luoyan), and Soe-Uin (Suiyüan). Students from China nevertheless continued to study in Manila occasionally.[658]

Forgotten Martyrs

There appeared to be no activity concerning the *proceso* of the 1773 Dominican martyrs of Vietnam until 1818 when the letter for the compulsory formation of the *proceso* was received. The Vicar Apostolic, P. Fr. Clemente Ignacio Delgado OP, recognized their relics for the first time to initiate the apostolic *proceso* for beatification. After a lapse of 45 years, it was extremely difficult to find living eye witnesses and to collect written testimonies. The *proceso* was nevertheless completed on 19 August 1818. The official documents were dispatched to Spain where it would be buried under the rubbles of the anarchic revolution transpiring in the peninsula at that time.[659] Complicating the situation further, Bishop Delgado himself died a martyr on 12 July 1838 during the onset of the persecutions of the Emperor Minh Mang, Nguyen Phuoc Chi Dam; raising serious concern whether any documents survived at all.[660]

Between 1838 and 1862, 56 Dominicans were martyred in Vietnam.[661] Throughout its history, Vietnam would be drenched with the blood of over 130,000 martyrs; prompting the Popes to recognize representative witnesses of the faith in the Indochina peninsula. On 27 May 1900, Pope Leo XIII beatified 64 martyrs of Vietnam. 27 were Dominicans who died between 1838 and 1851.[662] Our alumnus martyr and three other 18th century Dominican martyrs were not among them. On 14 November 1903, the Vicar Apostolic of Central Tonkin, Bishop Maximo Fernandez OP, conducted a second recognition of the forgotten martyrs' relics and distributed them for public veneration. The Venerable Liem's sacred hip bone and a censer were given to the *Real Colegio de San Juan de Letran*, where he lived for six years before embarking on his religious journey.[663] Pope Pius X beatified 28 Vietnam martyrs on 2 May 1906.[664] 8 Dominicans were beatified with Blessed Liem among them.[665] Pope John Paul II canonized all 117 beatified martyrs of Vietnam on 19 June 1988.[666] 60 were Dominicans.[667] The 24th of November was designated as the feast day of all known and unknown martyr saints of Vietnam in the Liturgical Calendar.

An Epiphany

When I received news of Letran's newly canonized saint in 1988, my juvenile memory of the Divine Presence in Letran was rekindled. I couldn't associate Letran with anything sacred then and was therefore not able to comprehend its significance. San Vicente Liem de La Paz's canonization made sense of it all and precipitated a number of realizations which provided a fitting conclusion to this chapter.

My first epiphany was that the grounds I had been walking on during my student days in Letran were sacred all along. Through the centuries, Letran had been visited by or had been the home of holy people. Among its first saintly visitors was St. Martin de Porres OP who shared H. Fr. Diego de Santa Maria's concern for orphan children. Beside those who were raised to the altars of the Church, alumni martyrs in our country's struggle for independence also passed through the same halls and passageways of the *Colegio*. PP. Jose Burgos, Jacinto Zamora and countless heroes of the Philippine revolution were among them. While in transit to the missions, saintly Dominican friars were guests, teachers or administrators in Letran. The sanctity of the school's grounds was further glorified with the actual presence of three martyrs of the Spanish Civil War: Blessed Eugenio Sanz-Orozco Mortar OFM Cap, a Letran alumnus, and two college administrators: Blessed Jesus Villaverde Andres OP, a former Rector, and Blessed Antonio Varona Ortega OP, a former Athletics Moderator.[668] For having once been the home of a good number of sanctified guests, Letran is

Plate XXXV

20th Century Letran Martyrs

Eugenio Sanz-Orozco Mortar
OFM cap

Antonio Varona Ortega OP

Jesus Villaverde Andres OP

- Artists unknown. Public domain.

indeed on sacred grounds - a true national shrine of saints and heroes.

My second realization involved the racist undercurrent that tainted the relationship between the Spanish mentors and their Oriental proteges. The pronouncements of racial equality within the Dominican Order were not matched by the behavior of some friars; particularly the superiors. Notwithstanding their openly declared admiration for Vicente Liem and Juan Feng, the rest of the students were never good enough and all the orientals were constantly viewed with suspicion. *Aunque corto, podra servir.* Considering the Asian sensitivity to save face, the deplorable abuse was tolerated and dealt with silent forbearance. Their apparent acquiescence was erroneously interpreted as compliant docility; if not innate weakness bordering idiocy. But when they appeared to assert themselves, they were viewed as rebellious, disobedient and a threat. This undesirable behavior was attributed to the contaminating influence of local students in the Manila *colegios*. Was Letran's underground dissident culture a likely cause?

After the Schism of Fuan, China went on to produce 114 more martyr saints in the following two centuries.[669] None of them were Dominicans. Just as the schism swept away Feng Shiming's cause into oblivion, Pham Hieu Liem's dormant cause surged forward by the relentless tide of his fellow countrymen's martyrdom. One can only surmise that sainthood by martyrdom is not only a matter of dying for the faith. No matter how much human intervention is resorted to, the elusive sainthood of a martyr, or any aspirant for that matter, is ultimately in God's hands alone.

Finally, I found Manila's 1773 reception of the news regarding the two Dominican martyrs of Vietnam quite intriguing. As Ferrando related:

> *The news of this martyrdom produced in the capital of Filipinas an enthusiasm never before seen. The ecclesiastical and civil cabildos, the Real Audiencia of the Islands, the secular and religious clergy, and finally all the classes of this very noble city hastened to take part in the grand religious demonstrations that were conducted at that time in Manila to celebrate the triumph of the new champions of the Cross.*[670]

I could not help visualizing the students of Letran participating in these festive and joyful celebrations. In the midst of this revelry, there were probably some native students who were not completely happy; wondering about certain realities that hindered their own capacity to become martyred champions of the Cross. Among the questions that perhaps crossed their minds were: *Aside from the Spaniards, why were the Chinese and Vietnamese students the only ones sent to the missions in the Far East and not a single native from Filipinas among them?* Or *why were these oriental proteges ordained as Dominican priests in the first place, while the natives of Filipinas could not even dare dream of becoming one?*

Why indeed?!

Chapter X

Purity of Blood

In our present times, the world's consciousness commonly views humanity as one race of individuals with equal rights in the eyes of the law. Discriminatory and racist behaviors are generally discouraged. The Universal Declaration of Human Rights, adopted by the United Nations General Assembly on 10 December 1948, contains 30 articles expressing the rights all human beings are inherently entitled to. Although not legally binding, it has become part of customary international law and foundation for a growing number of national laws, international laws and treaties. This was not however the situation throughout most of the previous four centuries.

Used as an instrument of power and control, racial discrimination was prevalent. In societies where slavery flourished, social, political and economic exclusions constituted the prevailing social order. Religious intolerance followed and devolved into vilifying racial dimensions. The previous chapters of this book indicated instances of this racist attitude. Throughout its Spanish colonial history, *Filipinas* was under the shadow of this somber view of humanity. From a Christian colonizer's perspective then, it was the right thing to do in order to civilize pagan savages. Racism festered discontent in the Iberian colonies. Although men of the cloak worked towards their gradual eradication, the uglier aspects of slavery and racial prejudices continue to persist even today under deceptive contemporary labels of human trafficking and racial profiling. Providentially, there were a few enlightened men who relentlessly challenged the system and gradually instigated changes for the benefit of all humanity.

Origins of Racism

Certain historians and anthropologists point to Spain as the origin of European racism. Others dispel this assertion as a legacy of the *Leyenda Negra* (Black Legend), an anglo-saxon conspiracy to disparage Spain's global prestige and influence, and instead highlight what is believed to be a widespread attitude of white supremacy throughout the European continent.[671] Regardless of where racism actually originated and developed, this narrative is focused on its evolutionary history in Spain and its principal colony in the New World, *Nueva España* (New Spain), in view of their consequent impact on the Philippines.

The inhabitants of the Iberian peninsula had been a mixed race throughout its history. Spain was settled by waves of different races crossing the Pyrenees from Europe and the Mediterranean from Africa. Phoenicians, Greeks, Carthaginians, Jews, Celts, Romans, Germans, Arabs and Northern Africans constituted an amalgam of what would become the native peoples of Spain. Miscegenation was more evident in Spain than anywhere else in Europe. Seven hundred years of Islamic presence developed a high level of culture and civilization with Christians, Muslims and Jews learning to live peacefully with one another. After the Battle of Covadonga in 722, the peninsula's domination gradually shifted from the Muslim Caliphates over to the victorious Christian rulers during a period in Iberian history known as the *Reconquista* (Reconquest). Different dynamics of power, privilege and prestige ensued; giving rise to religious and racial intolerance in Spain and eventually spreading to its colonies in the new world.

Five principal factors would define Spanish racial policies: first, the legacy of an ancient system of slavery; second, the religious intolerance that expelled non-christians from Spain and marginalized new converts; third, the evolution of the Castilian concept of citizenship; fourth, the legal framework that spawned a discriminatory caste system; and fifth, the subversion of compassionate Spanish laws of equity and justice by glaring contrasts between intent and reality. These five factors interacted with one another to create Hispanic colonial societies whose social, political, economic and cultural impact and influence continue to this very day.

Legacy of Slavery

Deprived of most rights held by free people, a slave was a property whose owner can use and dispose in virtually any way he wishes. Slaves were principally acquired as spoils of war, as victims of kidnapping and piracy, as punishment for the crime or debt, or as a voluntary act to ensure survival. Slavery existed globally since ancient times. In Europe, Athens and Rome were the first known major slave societies.[672] The Greek philosopher Aristotle described slavery as a natural state. His discourse on natural slavery would greatly influence the western world's attitudes towards slaves. In his book *Politics,* he concluded that:

> *Where then there is such a difference as that between soul and body, or between men and animals (as in the case of those whose business is to use their body, and who can do nothing better), the lower sort are by nature slaves, and it is better for them as for all inferiors that they should be under the rule of a master.*[673]

Slavery in Europe, as anywhere else in the world, could be traced to time immemorial. In Spain, laws on slavery were included in *Las Siete Partidas* (the Seven-Part Code), Castile's ancient legal code compiled by Alfonso X *el Savio* (the Wise) between 1251 and 1265. Effected in 1348, the provisions on slavery were based on legal precepts of the Visigoths and Romans particularly on the Byzantine Justinian Code. Under the code, the owner could do anything he wants to his slave except to kill him or to inflict insufferable cruelty.[674] Slaves were not distinguished by either race or religion. The Catholic Church had however greatly influenced the interpretation and implementation of the laws while not completely prohibiting slavery *per se*. In due time, the Popes prohibited Christians to sell white Christian slaves to Muslims. Eventually, Europeans ceased to maintain white Christian slaves altogether with the latter evolving into serfs or peons. The demand for white Christian slaves among the Muslims continued to be high however; presenting substantial rewards to spawn an illicit trade.

Venice became a principal slave market in the middle ages, and Venetian slave traders would brazenly buy white Christian slaves near the Papal seat in Rome. In 747, Pope Zachary ransomed these Christian slaves from them and eventually prohibited the trade.[675] At the instance of Popes and Emperors, Venice prohibited the trade but failed to enforce it. By 1304, Dominican Pope Benedict XI admonished Venice's subjects to cease the ill-fated sale of white Christian slaves to Muslims and issued a Papal Bull excommunicating and exacting severe penalties on transgressors.[676] The Venetians were unmoved and continued with the illicit trade. Exasperated, Pope Clement V excommunicated Venetian traders for being usurpers of St. Peter's patrimony four years later; depriving them of all their legal rights over their racial assets within the republic and all the merchandisable properties they possess in other countries. He further prohibited all Christians from doing business with them, anathematized them up to the fourth generation, authorized the commencement of hostilities against them, and decreed their enslavement when captured.[677] These harsh measures had not shaken the merchants but most pious Christians heeded the Pope's directives.

The profits from the trade of contraband slaves appeared to have been so attractive that merchants from Florence, Pisa, Genoa and Catalonia competed in satisfying the demand in the Muslim world. By the early 15th century, white Christian slaves were being sourced from the Slavic shores of the Black Sea. On 3 June 1423, Pope Martin V confirmed the papal bulls of his predecessors, excommunicated Christians who sold white Christians to Muslims or to people of other religions, and imposed severe penalties.[678] The decline of Venice and the other slave trading European states eventually put a complete halt on white Christian slavery. A shift of focus gave rise to black African slaves in Spain.

It was when Islam ruled over a significant portion of the Iberian peninsula between 711 and 1492 that the practice of slavery in Spain had fully developed. By the 9th century, the Muslim slave trade began making distinctions between the *mamluks* (white European slaves) and the *abid* (black African slaves). The *mamluks* were highly valued because they commanded substantial Christian ransom and they could be exchanged for Muslim captives. The white slaves were customarily used as household servants. The *abid*, on the other hand, were lower valued and assigned to arduous tasks under the worst conditions. This early association of inferiority to *abid* was eventually extended even to the free blacks. Throughout the Islamic world, blackness equalled slavery and the degradation that slavery implied. Blacks were assumed to be culturally inferior and were therefore naturally suited for slavery. Black Africans were hence held in contempt even if they shared the same Muslim faith.[679]

In Iberia, once the traits of the infidel and the slave became associated with blackness, race became the driving force in the formation of Spanish and Portuguese attitudes toward sub-Saharan Africans. Christians, who already equated color with religious infidelity, were well disposed to adopt the color prejudice of neighboring Muslims. In addition to the religious and cultural differences between Christians and Muslims, Christians now made distinctions based strictly on race that appear with increasing frequency after the beginning of the fourteenth century. Muslim slaves were by then classified by the color of their skin with its attendant aversion to blackness. In the 1450s, the African trade became the principal slave supplier for Spain and Portugal. *After the 1460s, the institution of slavery would be considered the preserve of black Africans. Where blackness always had implied slavery in Castile, slavery now implied blackness.*[680]

During this period of the 15th century, natives originating from the *Islas de Canarias* (Canary Islands) began to appear in the slave markets of Castile. The skin color of the inhabitants of the *Canarias*, known as *Guanches*, was neither white nor black. The *Guanches* were *de color cobrizo* (copper-colored) and became permanent fixtures when Castile annexed the *Canarias* in 1479. But by then, life's possibilities for people of any color but white were severely circumscribed. Even though a fully developed ideology of racial superiority was not yet articulated, fifteenth century white Iberians made distinctions among peoples based on skin color and attributed less worth to human beings who had black or brown skins.[681]

What appeared to be a mutation of Aristotle's thinking, an insidious ideology concerning savages in general began to take root during the reign of Isabel I of Castile. Justifying the enslavement of *Guanches,* Augustinian friar Martin Alfonso de Cordoba OSA in his book *Jardin de nobles doncellas* (Garden of Noble Maidens) argued that:

> ...*the barbarians are those who live without the law; the Latins, those who have law; for it is the law of nations that men who live and are ruled by law shall be lords of those who have none. Wherefore they may seize and enslave them, because they are by nature the slaves of the wise.*[682]

The preceding justification spurred the enslavement of natives of newly conquered gentile lands. Pope Eugene IV promulgated a series of edicts that would greatly influence the laws on enslavement. On 17 December 1434, he promulgated the bull *Creator Omnium* excommunicating anyone who took converted natives from the Canary Islands to sell as slaves; effectively declaring that conversion was the only effective guarantee against slavery. With the enslavement of the *Guanches* unabated, he issued a compromise papal bull *Romanus Pontifex* on 15 September 1436 allowing the Portuguese to conquer all parts of *Canarias* as yet unconverted while protecting the Christian converts from capture and enslavement under a general edict. It was applying the legal notion of just war between Christianity and Islam beyond the boundaries of the Mediterranean. To justify the Portuguese slave raids of West Africa, the just war rationale was again employed in his *Illius qui* on 19 December 1442 granting full remission of sins to all who participated in military expeditions against the Saracens.[683] Ten years later, Pope Nicolas V expanded the coverage of enslavement to include pagans and any other unbelievers in his bull *Dum Diversas*. The unbridled slave trade that ensued casted an ominous shadow over the future of the New World.

Roots of Religious Intolerance

The Islamic rule between the 8th and 11th centuries introduced an advanced culture and civilization influencing and enriching the way of life in the Iberian peninsula known then as *Al-Andalus*. As a practice, vassals were usually given a choice between death or conversion. Christians and Jews were however exempted from this choice being considered as *Ahi al-Kitab* (People of the Book). Muslims believe that the holy scriptures of the three religions are all inspired by God. Although viewed as inferiors, Christians and Jews were nevertheless granted the *Dhimma* (writ of protection). Muslims hence lived peacefully among Christian and Jewish *Dhimmis* notwithstanding the discriminatory laws, exclusionary policies and segregational measures imposed on the latter two.[684] By the time the Christians successfully gained sovereignty over most of the peninsula in the 15th century, racial and religious prejudices were deeply engrained in the Spanish psyche.

Tolerated initially, Spanish Jews began to be persecuted by Christians in 1212. Occuring intermittently thereafter, it became widespread culminating in the massacres of 1366. The persecutions of 1391 beginning in Seville claimed large numbers of victims initiating mass conversions of Jews to Christianity. A new caste of *cristianos nuevos* (new christians) called *maranos* (Jews converted to Christianity) emerged. The appearance of this new caste polarized the *cristianos viejos* (old christians). It will not be until the fall of Granada in 1492 when the remaining Sephardic Jews were expelled from Spain.[685] In 1510, the compulsory conversion of Muslims to Christianity was decreed in the Kingdom of Castile and its territories; adding *moriscos* (Muslims converted to Christianity) to the caste of *conversos* (new Christian converts). In 1526, the same decree was extended to the remaining Christian territories of Spain. Although many Muslims became *conversos*, the motives of their conversion was questioned and viewed as acts of convenience. After almost a century of the *Morisco Problem*, Muslims were expelled from Spain in 1610-1614.[686]

The conflict between the *cristianos viejos* and the *cristianos nuevos* highlighted the need to preserve the purity of the former's lineage from contamination, and to relegate the *conversos* to the despised positions in society. Thus, the concept of *limpieza de sangre* (purity of blood) emerged and became a pervasive and influential thinking. Its initial form was enacted in 1449 in Toledo, Spain.

At that time, Castile was at war with Aragon. The constable of Toledo attempted to raise a million *maravides* from its residents for the defense of the realm. The people resisted and their indignation escalated when they learned that a *marano* merchant by the name of Alonso Cota instigated the levy. Notwithstanding the protests, the collection of the levy was implemented. As the bells of the church of Santa Maria rang, a mob of *cristianos viejos* gathered at the plaza and proceeded to invade, sack and set Cota's home on fire. The homes of other rich *maranos* in the barrio of Magdalena suffered the same fate. The *alcalde mayor*, Pedro Sarmiento, listened to the demands of the rebels and consequently overpowered the resisting *conversos* and hanged them all in the public plaza. In a people's assembly on 5 June 1449, Sarmiento proclaimed the *Sentencia Estatuto* (Statutory Sentence) that allowed the expulsion of all the *conversos* of Jewish origin from important positions in Toledo including councillors, judges, mayors and specially providing for the documentation and the public acts of declaring one's faith.[687]

On 1 November 1478, the *Tribunal del Santo Oficio de la Inquisicion* (Tribunal of the Holy Office of the Inquisition) was founded to combat heresy particularly among *conversos*.[688] It contributed further to the expanding exclusionary list of the *estatuto de limpieza de sangre*. Children and grandchildren of those convicted of heresy were prohibited from being promoted to holy orders and holding any public offices, posts, and honors. Soon after, individual authorities extended prohibition to any family member of those condemned including *conversos* even if not acted on by the Inquisition. The *Estatuto* survived the abolition of the Spanish Inquisition on 15 July 1834.[689]

By 1541, the *Estatuto* was adopted in Badajoz, Sevilla, Jaen, Cordoba, Oviedo, Leon and Siguienza. In 1547, the Archbishop of Toledo required being *cristianos viejos* as one of the prerequisites for any ecclesiastical benefice. Other ecclesiastical and secular institutions quickly followed suit. It became necessary to present a *probanza* (proof) to validate the purity of one's lineage as far back as the 4th generation. During Felipe II's reign, proof dating to time immemorial was required. By the end of the 16th century, genealogical proofs of the purity of one's lineage were a compulsory requirement in the four chief military orders and in all the principal colleges and universities. Racism became irrefutable in a society when a person's ability to secure a career in Church and State was determined by genealogical evidence. It will not be until 16 May 1865 when the last of the proof of purity requirements was abolished in Spain.

Impact of Citizenship

As the Kingdom of Castile's territories expanded, the issue of who could enjoy the benefits of empire arose. The *naturales* (natives) of Castile guarded

Plate XXXVI

Bartolome de las Casas OP
First Protector of the Indians

Tomas de Torquemada OP
First Grand Inquisitor

Dominican Movers of the Spanish Golden Age
- *Artists unknown.* Public Domain.

their rights of exclusivity to positions of power, privilege and prestige particularly on commercial rights and trade monopolies. Although Castile and Aragon were united by the marriage of the Catholic Monarchs in 1469, the emergence of what was referred to as *España* (Spain) had no legal personality. The Kingdom of Castile and the Kingdom of Aragon remained legally separate and distinct with their respective monarchs, laws and institutions. Castile which included the newly conquered Kingdom of Granada, the Canaries, the enclaves of Ceuta and Melilia, and the yet to be discovered lands of the New World were united under the same language, laws and institutions. Aragon, on the other hand, respected the different institutions, cultures and traditions of its vassal states which included Catalonia, Valencia, Majorca and other mediterranean possessions. As such, only the *vecinos* (citizens) of Castilian local communities could enjoy the opportunities that an expanding kingdom could offer *vis a vis* foreigners. It would not be until the ascendancy of the Bourbons to the throne in 1714 that a unified *Reino de España* (Kingdom of Spain) was officially established; dissolving the former Kingdoms of Castile and Aragon. The subjects of the new kingdom would hence be known as *naturales de España* (natives of Spain) and *vecinos* (citizens) of its local communities.[690]

Understanding the legal concepts of *naturaleza* (nativeness) and *vecindad* (citizenship) in the early modern period of Spain's history is essential towards appreciating the social, political, economic and cultural dynamics that moulded Spanish colonial society at that time.

The laws of Castile clearly differentiated *naturales* (natives) and *vasallos* (subjects). One's eligibility to rights in the kingdom depended on nativeness and not vassalage. A *natural* had a relationship with the community while a *vasallo* had a personal relationship with the king. As Prof. Tamar Herzog explained: *While people could be subjects of the King of Castile, Aragon, the Spanish Netherlands, Naples and so forth, they could only be natives of their own kingdom. This meant that royal vassals were divided into many groups of natives: there were natives of Castile, natives of Aragon, natives of Naples, but not natives of Spain.*[691]

Rather than setting rules for nativeness, the laws referred to adopted a much wider legal doctrine. This doctrine set the rule that people who loved the community, complied with their duties and were loyal to it were worthy of recognition as natives. Thus, communities had the ability to grant citizenship in as much as they were established by the collective will of their members. The community further exercised its discretion to disqualify people considered detrimental to its interests and occasionally excluded *converso* Jews and Muslims, Gypsies, individuals of African descent, non-Catholics and non-vassals. This municipal doctrine was extended to the kingdom's realm. Because the kingdom was a conglomerate made of local communities, natives were people tied to local communities. In 1716, all citizens of Spanish kingdoms on the peninsula were formally declared natives of the Kingdom of Spain.[692]

The criteria to distinguish natives of Spain from foreigners were extended to the New World where *Spaniards fought to exclude non-Spaniards from benefiting from the fruits of the colonial enterprise*. While foreigners could easily become citizens and naturalized in Castile, it was not the case in the New World. During the early period of the colonization, the Castilian concepts of *naturaleza* and *vecindad* were observed. This however changed over time. By the late seventeenth and eighteenth century, it was assumed throughout Spanish America that in order to be a citizen, one had to be Spanish. Indios, mestizos and mulatos as well as non-Spanish Europeans were excluded.[693] Where in Castile, *vecinos* could become *naturales de España*. In Spanish America, only *naturales de España* could become *vecinos*, Thus, positions of power, privilege and prestige were given to native Spaniards while the other subjects of Spain assumed inferior statuses. Hence, a child of Spanish parents born outside Spain became a vassal of the King of Spain but not a Spanish citizen. This Spanish child, known as a *criollo*, was therefore a *natural* of the New World but not of Spain, and hence considered inferior.

1492 - 1519

1492 was a quintessential year in Spain's history. It was the year when Granada, the last Islamic Kingdom on the Iberian peninsula, fell to Castile; marking the completion of the *Reconquista*. It was the year when the Sephardic Jews were expelled from the realms; signaling the religious intolerance that would transform Spain into a completely Catholic nation. It was the year when *Cristoforo Colombo*, a Genoese maritime explorer under the royal patronage and protection of *Isabel la Catolica* of Castile, discovered the New World. Spain's Golden Century commenced with its religion, laws, institutions, culture and values spreading throughout what was to become the first global empire.

With the Silk Road rendered impassable at the end of the Mongol empire, it was every European's dream to find a new route to the treasures of the Far East known as *Las Indias* (The Indies). Marco Polo's tales of the rich fabled lands of *Cathay* (China) and *Cipango* (Japan) inspired navigators like Colombo to find a new direct sea route. Colombo departed from Palos de la Frontera with three ships on 3 August 1492 on such a risky venture funded by the Catholic Monarchs of Spain. In as much as Portugal had the exclusive rights to the eastward sea route, he had to reach *Las Indias* traveling westward based on the *absurd* notion that the world was round.

Crossing the unexplored area of the Atlantic Ocean, known as *Mar Oceana* (Ocean Sea), Colombo discovered an island in the *Lucayos* (Bahamas) archipelago and named it *San Salvador* on 12 October 1492. He wrote in his journal describing the people he encountered there as having *the color of Canarians, neither black nor white*. He further noted that the natives *would make good servants*.[694] His ominous observations virtually condemned the *Indios* to the fate of the *Guanches* - slavery.

Driven by the greed for gold, he explored the adjoining islands searching for the elusive source claimed by the *Indios*. In the process, he discovered many islands with *Isla Juana* (Cuba) and *Isla Española* (Haiti) as the principal finds. Convinced that he had reached *Las Indias,* he returned to Spain on 15 March 1493 with specimens of the natives, flora, fauna, and golden artifacts. His triumphant return earned him the titles of *Almirante del Mar Oceana* (Admiral of the Ocean Sea) and *Virrey y Gobernador de las Islas y Tierra Firme de Indias* (Viceroy and Governor of the Islands and Mainland of the Indies). He was to be compensated generously under the terms of the *Capitulacion de Santa Fe* (Santa Fe List) signed by the Catholic monarchs.

Colombo's second voyage departed Cadiz on 24 September 1493 with 17 ships and 1200 men to establish a permanent colony in *Española*, the site of the fabled golden mines. Among the notable people on this journey were his brother Diego, Juan Ponce de Leon, and Pedro de las Casas, the father of Bartolome de las Casas. His other brother Bartolomeo would follow a year later. After failed attempts, a permanent settlement was established in a suitable place named Santo Domingo, today's capital of the Dominican Republic. Extensive explorations were conducted with more islands discovered. It would not be until his fourth voyage that he reached a place with such abundance of flowing fresh water that exhibited signs of a mainland. On 14 August 1502, he sighted Punta Caxinas now known as Puerto Castillo, Honduras.[695] Disembarking on its shores, Colombo finally landed on the continental mainland, known as *Tierra Firme* or the Spanish Main. The immensity of which would gradually be unveiled.

During the next decade, further explorations along the lengthy eastern coastline were conducted by other navigators. Amerigo Vespucci, a respected Florentine navigator and Spain's Chief Pilot, would definitively confirm in his letters that the continent was not the *Indias* but a new and unexplored one.[696] *America* was hence used for the first time by German cartographers, Martin Waldseemüller and Matthias Ringmann, to name the new continent in their 1507 map *Universalis Cosmographia*.[697]

Meanwhile, the *Indios* of *Española* were enslaved and abused under the tyrannical administration of the Colombo brothers. Unable to initially produce the desired quantities of gold through forced labor, tribute was exacted and *indios* were shipped to Seville's slave market for the first time to compensate for the cost of colonial enterprise. The *repartimiento* (distribution) followed soon after; allocating *caciques* (chiefs) and their respective vassals to work in the gold mines, supply food and render personal service to the principal Spanish settlers. By 1499, accusations of brutality, tyranny and gross mismanagement against the Colombo brothers reached the Spanish royal court. Cristoforo Colombo was replaced as governor by Francisco de Bobadilla and his promised rewards substantially withdrawn on 21 May 1499. The abuses on the *Indios* were however not curtailed.

The dwindling native population caused by wanton cruelty had to be replenished. Raiding the neighboring Antillean islands for slaves was resorted to; resulting in the dissipation of those islands' native numbers as well. In 1505, seventeen negro slaves arrived to address *Española*'s alarmingly declining labor supply. By 1511, Fernando V (Fernando II of Aragon) permitted the importation of Negro slaves in great numbers. *Española* became the template of the conquests that followed. Under Colombo's former lieutenants, the same patterns of indignities, robberies, brutalities and killings were carried out in Puerto Rico, Jamaica, Tierra Firme, Cuba and Florida between 1509 and 1519. The already decimated *Indio* population would be reduced to virtual extinction in 1519 by a Spanish spawned epidemic which the natives had no natural immunity to - small pox.

Fundamental Laws of Indio Slavery

On 24 January 1495, Cristoforo Colombo transported the first 500 *indio* slaves to Spain in four ships. Another 300 were dispatched in June of the same year. There were no Crown policies on slaves from the New World then, and as such the human cargo was treated as any other commodity in the slave market of Seville. It was not until the year 1500 that Isabel I expressed her wishes on how the *Indios* of the New World were to be governed and treated in a *Carta Real* (Royal Letter). On that same year, a one state religion policy was instituted expelling Muslims who refused to convert to Catholicism. Consistent with this policy, was the recognition of the gentile *Indios* as being free and not subject to servitude, and the implementation of their conversion to the *Santa Fe Catolica* (Holy Catholic Faith).[698]

A *Real Cedula* was issued on 20 June 1500 manumitting the *Indio* slaves transported by Colombo in 1495 and ordering the return to their places of origin.[699] The recognition of the *Indios* as a free people and the emancipation of Colombo's slaves did not however prohibit slavery. The *Real Provision* (Royal Provision) of 30 October 1503 reiterated the *Carta Real* of 1500. It however contained a provision, petitioned by Colombo, allowing the capture and enslavement of an alleged troublesome cannibalistic tribe known as the *Caribes*.[700] Although the existence of such a belligerent *Indio* tribe was not fully substantiated at the time, the *Caribe* myth provided the legal loophole for an illicit slave trade. Any *Indio* could be indiscriminately enslaved by being simply identified as a *Caribe*.

Isabel I died on 26 November the following year and her Last Will and Testament contained the following clause:

> When we had conceded to us by the holy Apostolic See the islands and the terra firme of the ocean sea, discovered or to be discovered, our principal intention was, at the time that we besought the said concession from Pope Alexander VI, of good memory, to gather and bring together and prevail upon the people of said islands and main land, and convert

> *them to our holy Catholic faith, and to send to them prelates and religious clerics and other persons learned in the faith and possessed of the fear of God, in order that they might instruct the said inhabitants in the holy Catholic faith and indoctrinate and introduce good customs among them and better modes of life, as has been more fully set forth in the text of said concession; therefor I most affectionately beseech my Lord, the King, and I charge and command the princess, my daughter, and the prince, her husband, that they shall make it their principal object to execute and carry out this my will, and that they neither consent nor allow any of the Indians native of or residing in said isles and main land to receive any harm whatever, either in person or property, but that they command them to be well and justly treated; and if they have received any injury, that they remedy it and so provide that in no manner shall the precepts enjoined and commanded in the apostolic letters of said concession be neglected.*[701]

Notwithstanding the good intentions of the gracious queen, the Spanish pioneers in the New World were principally motivated by gold and glory during the initial stages of colonization. On 30 April 1508, the coverage of the 1503 *Caribe* law was expanded to include any rebellious *Indio*; accelerating the illicit slave trade throughout the Spanish Main.[702] This decree further authorized the transfer of *Indios* from islands considered *inutil* (useless) such as Puerto Rico and Jamaica to work as forced laborers in the mines of *Española*.[703] On 14 August the following year, a Real Cedula allowed *Indios* of *inutil* islands to become slaves if they refused to work as domestics in the forced service of Spaniards.[704] The need to address the demand for cheap forced labor to work in the mines, cultivate food and attend to domestic needs of the colonists took precedence. God and His message of love and salvation were evidently ignored if not forgotten. This gross disparity between good intentions and actual reality would become a regular pattern of relationship between future monarchs and colonists. The first missionaries would arrive a year later to alleviate the worsening situation of the *Indios*.

In September 1510, Dominican missionaries led by P. Fr. Pedro de Cordoba OP were sent to *Española* to establish the first mission and to stop the maltreatment of *Indios*. The Spanish settlers were outraged by the stirring sermon of P. Fr. Antonio de Montesinos OP. When the recall of the Dominican was petitioned, Montesinos was sent back to Spain to raise the issues directly to the Spanish monarchs. Fernando II was apparently disturbed to learn of the *Indios*' plight and convoked the *Junta de Burgos* (Burgos Assembly).

Two legal minds principally dominated the deliberations: P. Fr. Matias de Paz OP and Juan Lopez de Palacios Rubios.

Paz argued that there is a great difference between the *Reconquista* of the Peninsula and the conquest of the New World. The former involved Muslims who were aware of Jesus Christ and consciously committed the sin of infidelity. It was therefore holy and justified to fight, capture and enslave

Plate XXXVII

Isabel la Catolica, Reina de España
- Palmaroli, Cayetano 1837-1841. @ Biblioteca Nacional de España 3667655-3001

these perpetual enemies of Christians. The latter *Indios*, on the other hand, were gentiles and not aware of Christianity and therefore had the right to defend themselves unless they were admonished to embrace the faith voluntarily. Conquered under those circumstances, they cannot be enslaved unless they reject obedience to the prince or refuse to surrender to the kindness of the Savior. Captives who become aware of the Redeemer and accept baptism voluntarily should absolutely not be treated as slaves.[705]

Palacios Rubios, on the other hand, affirmed that the *Indios* were naturally and essentially free before and after the conversion to Christianity. Furthermore, it was not legal to enslave them not unless the infidels assault the Christians and thereby obliging the latter to engage in a legal defensive war.[706] Both Palacios Rubios and Paz however agreed that Christian princes have no legal rights either to conquer the lands of American infidels to satisfy their lust for power and riches or to subjugate natives to servitude. However, intervention was considered legal if the purpose was to spread Christianity; including the use of arms if the infidels resist accepting the Christian religion and offend the Europeans. Both do not exclude enslavement of *Indios*, but allow it solely in case of a just war.[707]

As a result of the consultations, the King promulgated the *Leyes de Burgos* (Laws of Burgos) on 27 December 1512. Although the Dominicans found it unworkable and evasive, it was the first major breakthrough. The set of 35 laws governed the behavior of Spaniards towards the *Indios* in *Española*; prohibiting their maltreatment and endorsing their conversion to Catholicism among others. The laws were extended to other colonies but did not however save the *Indios*. The key phrases *native resistance* and *just war* were legal justifications to continue slavery, exploitation and abuse.

The *Leyes de Burgos* moved Spain's rulers to ordain the *Requerimiento* (Requirement) in 1513 establishing the legal possession of new territories, and justifying the subjugation, exploitation and genocide of natives. It was to be read to the *Indios* in Spanish informing them of Spain's rights to conquest. Resistance would be deemed as defying God's plan and thus justifying conquest.[708]

The *Requerimento* invoked five theological principles that guided Spanish hegemony: (1) The sole and final validity to legitimize Spanish sovereignty is the Christianization of the indigenes. (2) The Pope is the vicar of Christ; on him the universal authority, spiritual and temporal, rests. He has authority to cede the rights to Spain. (3) The indigenes, through the guidance of Spaniards, must accept the said supremacy of the Church and the Crown of Castile. (4) If the indigenes do not accept said supremacy, the monarchs are authorized to wage war and subdue them to their authority. (5) Endeavors of conquest have the spiritual and the religious as the principal end.[709] Conquest was thereafter more driven, but often overlooking the purported spiritual ends. In the same year the *Requerimento* was enforced, Bartolome de las Casas was present at the conquest of Cuba where he witnessed the unrestrained massacres and atrocities inflicted on the *Indios*.[710] Haunted by the specter, he began his public advocacy against enslavement and abuse of the *Indios* in 1514 which would earn him the title of *Protector de Indios* (Protector of the Indians) from Cardinal Francisco Jimenez de Cisneros in 1516.

The Mexican Experience

The conquest of *Anahuac* (*Nueva España*) began in April 1519 when Hernan Cortes' army and retinue of *Negro* (black) slaves landed on the Yucatan peninsula now known as *Vera Cruz*. Using successful strategies developed and employed during military campaigns in the Spanish Main, alliances with friendly *caciques* (chiefs) were forged with the objective of jointly vanquishing *Moctezuma II*, the ruler of the dominant Aztec Empire of Central Mexico. The Aztec Empire fell with its capital *Tenochtitlan* (Mexico City) sacked in 1521.

The fall of the Aztecs was attributed in some measure to the first small pox epidemic brought by the *conquistadores* in 1520. The slave trade that marked the trail of new conquered territories was followed by the first measles epidemic of 1531. The process of introducing Spanish social, political, economic and cultural institutions commenced at the cost of a declining population caused by atrocities, famine, exploitation, and diseases that *Indios* had no natural immunities to.[711] By 8 March 1535, the *Virreinato de Nueva España* (Viceroyalty of New Spain) was officially created with a native population of Central Mexico reduced by at least 50% from pre-conquest levels.[712] After the first typhus (1545) and first mumps (1550) epidemics, estimated population figures between 1519 and 1560 extrapolated declines between 76.5% and 85.8%.[713]

The *Requerimiento* was faithfully observed. Natives who surrendered to Spanish sovereignty, paid tribute and accepted Christianity became protected vassals of the Crown. *Indios* who defied the *Requerimiento* were enslaved to provide cheap forced labor for the new colonial economy. The unrestrained abuses prompted *Carlos I* (Emperor Charles V of the Holy Roman Empire) to issue a *Real Cedula* dated 9 November 1526 prohibiting enslavement and servitude of any free *Indio* unless they engage in armed resistance or refuse to receive instructions of the faith, to recognize Spanish sovereignty, or to work in the mines. The inclusion of *non-willingness to work in mines* indicated the increasing need to address commercial interests. The edict did not however stop the illicit slave trade of peaceful, non-delinquent and non-rebellious *Indios*. With the influence exerted by P. Fr. Bartolome de las Casas OP, Carlos I radically prohibited unconditionally the prospective slavery of *Indios* on 2 August 1530. The colonists vehemently raised their displeasure and grievances prompting the Emperor to issue acceptable amendments in his Decree of 20 February 1534. The *just war* and *ransom* provisions were reinstated as legal grounds for enslavement.[714]

In 1537, the papal bull *Sublimis Dei* and its brief of execution *Pastorale officium* were issued. Under these documents, Pope Paul III declared that the

Indios were human beings and they were not to be robbed of their freedom or possessions; forbade unjust kinds of enslavement; and excommunicated violators of the new ruling. This virtual human rights *magna carta* of the *Indios* somehow revoked the *Patronato Real* granted to the Spanish monarchs by Pope Alexander VI. The *Pastorale officium* had to be annulled the following year in view thereof. Nevertheless, the irreversible tide to free the *Indios* from slavery could not be deterred any longer. On 21 May 1542, Carlos I firmly decreed the emancipation of *Indios* from slavery and replaced it with forced labor.[715]

Slaves from other races, together with certain *Indio* exceptions, were not however so fortunate.[716] Slavery of *negros* would continue to be legally recognized in Spain until 7 October 1886 when its last vestige in Cuba was officially abolished.[717] The Vatican would be the last state to officially condemn slavery in 1888.[718] Over and above disguised forms of slavery, the condescending racial prejudice of the European masters towards their former slaves however remained and would prevail much longer than the official end of slavery.

The emancipation of the *Indios* endowed them with a unique status in the colonial society; giving them special privileges and protection. This enhanced the early observance of allowing *caciques* to continue their traditional roles as local rulers; preserving their laws, customs and practices. The segregation of the *Indio* communities from the Spanish settlements led to the emergence of two *republicas* (polities) under one colonial government: the *Republica de Españoles* and the *Republica de Indios*. Each *republica* had its own separate laws and its own courts. Unlike the Spanish *republica*, *Indios* were not subject to the Holy Office of the Inquisition because of their *newness* to the faith. As a recognized vassal of the King, the *Indio* enjoyed privileges and status albeit inferior ones *vis a vis* an *Español*. The brown *Indios* hence became second to the white *Españoles* but above the *Negros* (Africans), *Chinos* (Asians) and the *mestizaje* (mixed races) in what was to become a racial social order known as *Sistema de Castas* (Caste System).

Sistema de Castas

By the early 17th century, *Nueva España* was a multiracial melting pot. The principal cities and surrounding areas were populated by races described principally by the color of their skin. They were the indigene *cobrizos* (copper-brown), the *blancos* (whites), the *negros* (blacks) and the *amarillos* (yellows). Attempts by the Spanish authorities to impose endogamy failed. Miscegenation flourished among the races and led to an increasing diverse blend of *mestisaje* (mixed races). By 1823, Friedrich Wilhem Heinrich Alexander Fresher von Humboldt estimated a Mexican population consisting of 3,700,000 *Indios* and 1,860,000 multiracial's; only to be reversed dramatically a century later.[719] The 1930 Census of Mexico revealed a population of 4,620,886 *Indios* and 9,040,590 *mestizos*.[720] Angel Rosenblat observed that *the history of Mexico is marked by its continuing transformation into a multiracial society that is defining its ideal ethnic identity and national personality.*[721] This ultimate transformation was however at the cost of an oppressive journey.

The aboriginal *cobrizos* were the *Indios* whose existence and destiny would be threatened and changed completely by the arrival of the *blancos*. Principally *Españoles*, the first 12 *blancos* to be shipwrecked on Mexican soil in 1511 had two survivors who adapted to the indigenous way of life. Gonzalo Guerrero married a daughter of the *cacique* and their children became the first Mexican *mestizos*. Jeronimo de Aguilar, on the other hand, became Hernan Cortes interpreter. The successive waves of invading Spanish forces were warmly welcomed by the *Indios* and as tokens of friendship native maidens were offered to *Españoles* as wives or as companions. Many of the single Spanish officers married noble native maidens whose *mestizo* children would inherit their father's official titles and estates. In as much as there were hardly any Spanish women in *Nueva España*, the other virile *Españoles* were readily disposed to cohabit with *Indias*. It was not unusual for an *Español* to maintain a harem of 30 concubines as polygamy was part of the native culture.[722] A proliferation of illegitimate mestizos would become a major social problem in due time.

In 1518, the first *negros* in Mexico were brought by Hernan Cortes from Cuba to tow his artillery.[723] One among them was Juan Garrido who distinguished himself as the first to plant and harvest wheat in Mexico.[724] It was also alleged that the first small pox epidemic of Mexico in 1520 was traced to a black slave carrier on board the punitive fleet of Panfilo Narvaez.[725] By 1523, *Negros* reportedly escaped their masters to live among the *Zapotecas*.[726] As the economic opportunities on the Yucatan mainland became apparent, the Spanish colonists from the Greater Antilles began to migrate bringing with them their black slaves and offsprings.

Offsprings of *blancos* and *negras* were known as *mulatos*. Unlike *mestizos* however, *mulatos* remained as slaves unless manumitted by their fathers. Marriages between *negros* was prohibited until 1527. *Negros* and *Indios* were also prohibited to wed but illicit liaisons could not be effectively curtailed. Offsprings between *Indios* and *Negros* were known as *zambos*. The slave status of a child is determined by the mother. A free *india* mother meant a free *zambo* offspring, while a *negra* slave mother meant the *zambo* offspring was a slave. The increasing percentage of Spanish blood among the *mestizos* improved the status of the following generations. A third generation offspring between an *Español* and a *mestizo* was called a *castizo* and as a *cuarteron* (1/4 *indio*) he was considered technically an *Español*.[727] This privilege was not however extended to a *morisco* (1/4 negro). Having the blood of a black slave condemned one to among the lowest ranks of society. The only chance for redemption was to mask one's genealogy by lightening the skin color of generations that followed.

The Galleon Trade introduced Mexico to the *amarillos* from the slave markets of Manila. The first *nao de manila* (Manila ship) arrived in Acapulco in 1565 with the first *Chinos* (Asians) to land on American soil. Aside from native *indio* slaves, the Manila market traded in *chino* slaves brought in by

Portuguese ships from all over Asia. The diverse origins included India, Bengal, Ambon, Borneo, Java, Makassar, Maluku Islands (Indonesia), Melaka, Malay (Malaysia), Ceylon (Sri Lanka), Japan, Macau (China) and Timor.[728] Although the *indios de nueva españa* had been emancipated since 1542, the status of the *indios de filipinas* remained ambiguous and were classified as *chinos* in the ships' manifests. It was not until the reign of *Carlos II* that Real Cedula of 12 June 1679, as amended on 1 May 1686, was issued phasing out slavery over a given period of time. After 8 August 1692, new slaves were totally forbidden, and children, grandchildren and descendants of slave parents born thereafter were considered free.[729] In view of these decrees, the free *indios de filipinas* among the *chinos* would come to be assimilated into the native population of Mexico. Unless they could prove to be an *indio*, *chino* slaves could only marry another *chino* or *negro* slave. The word *chino* would henceforth become associated with the *casta de negros* and used to describe any person with kinky hair. Its Asian roots would eventually be discarded and forgotten.

As a complex population of mixed races began to grow and develop, discontent gave rise to rebellions and conflicts which prompted the authorities to take steps to assert Spanish supremacy and to maintain the *limpieza de sangre*. The *sistema de castas* (castes system) crossed the Atlantic and adapted to the realities of the New World. Under the old social order of medieval Spain, purity of bloodline signified an ancestry that was free from jews, moors and inquisitorial convicts. In Spain's colonial world, the *sistema's* notions of purity revolved around Spanish ancestry. Thus, the power, privilege and prestige of the *cristianos viejos* (old christians) were assumed by those whose ancestries were *españoles puros* (undiluted spaniards). The *sistema de castas* became the product of evolving ideas on racial identity developed in the colony over time.[730] It was a process that would not be completed until the 18th century and by then an elaborate array of phenotypical categories had been formulated.

The hierarchy was based on a rigid division of one society into groups of castes to insure the domination of the conquered territory. The superior caste who assumed positions of authority and responsibility in the colony were the *españoles de procedencia europea* (European Spaniards) otherwise known as *gachupines* in Mexico. The next caste was constituted by the *españoles americanos* (American Spaniards) more commonly known as *criollos,* children of Spanish parents born in *Nueva España*. The *indios*, who enjoyed a unique legal status, formed the next caste. Despised for their blood, the *negros* finally constituted the lowest caste. The carnal exchanges among these main races presented vexing problems in classifying their offsprings within the confines of the *blanco, cobrizo* and *negro* niches.[731]

By the early 19th century, the *sistema de castas* that evolved in Mexico contained some 24 racial nomenclatures. J. J. Virey's Table is just one of a number of classifications that is indicative of the society's fastidiousness over purity of blood and skin color. Considering that these factors generally decided social position in Nueva España, a mere rumor was enough to

Table IX
J. J. VIREY'S SISTEMA DE CASTA

1er. Grado	1. Blanco X negro	*mulato*
	2. Blanco X indio	*mestizo*
	3. Negro X indio	*zambo, lobo o chino (en Mejico)*
2do. Grado	4. Negro X mulata	*zambo, grifo o cabro*
	5. Negro X china	*zambo*
	6. Blanco X mulata	*terceron o morisco (a veces llamado cuarterón)*
	7. Blanco X mestizo	*cuatralbo, castizo*
	8. Indio X zambo	*zambaigo*
	9. Indio X mestizo	*tresalbo*
	10. Indio X mulato	*mulato prieto*
	11. Negro X zambo	*zambo prieto*
3er. Grado	12. Blanco X terceros	*cuarteron, albino*
	13. Blanco X castizo	*postizo u octavo*
	Blanco X cuatralbo	
4to. Grado	14. Mulato X terceron	*salta atras**
	15. Mestizo X cuarteron	*coyote*
	16. Grifo X zambo	*jibaro*
	17. Mulato X zambaigo	*cambujo*
	18. Blanco X cuarteron	*quinteron*
	19. Blanco X octavon indio	*puebuelas*
	20. Blanco X coyote	*harnizos*
	21. Blanco X cambujo	*albarrasado*
	22. Blanco X albarrasado	*barzinos*
	23. Negro X terceron	*cuarteron salta atras*
	24. Negro X cuarteron	*quinteron salta atras*

Notes:

* *Although seldom used, certain nomenclatures appeared from time to time with ambiguous meanings in other classifications. They include the following:*
- *salta atras or torna atras (a turn backwards): a child darker than the mother e.g. mulato x terceron*
- *tente en el aire (have in the air): neither progress or retrogression in color e.g. cambujo x India;*
- *no te entiendo (i do not understand you) : tente en el aire x mulata*
- *ahi te estas (there you are) : no te entiendo x india*

- Rosenblat 2:175-176

dishonor a family. The rights and duties of each *casta* in the resulting racial hierarchy were defined precisely by the Laws of the Indies. The legislation assigned persons distinct positions according to the ethnic composition. Even more severe than the legislation and the authorities, certain sectors of society assumed the role of zealous guardians of racial distinctions. Privilege and status were determined by how white one's skin was and by how pure one's Spanish ancestry was.

With the preponderance of mixed races, the colonial regime evolved into a regime of castes.[732] The *castas* could be differentiated into five main ethnic categories ranked as to their diminishing whiteness: (1) *españoles puros* (pure white Spaniards); (2) *euro-mestizos* (a preponderance of Spanish blood); (3) *afro-mestizos* and *indo-mestizos;* (4) *indios;* and (5) *negros*. In order to improve ones social, economic and legal status, one had to undergo the progressive genetic process of *blanqueamiento* (skin whitening).[733] Among the mixed races, *mestizos* and *mulatos* of good economic or social standing could easily be treated as if they were white. Otherwise, they had to face the dreaded laws of segregation, prohibition, and discrimination.

A sample of these laws could give one a taste of the iniquities suffered by the underprivileged *castas* in the Spanish colonies.[734]

Segregation was among the first measures to be implemented. Slaves were branded on their faces or backs to distinguish them from free people and to certify them as legally licensed. This inhumane practice was stopped in 1784. *Españoles, negros, mestizos and zambos* were prohibited from residing with *indios*.[735] Even if they owned properties in *indio* villages, they were likewise prohibited from living there.[736] There were separate designated churches and curates for *castas*. The *españoles* attended the cathedral, the *negros* a hermitage, and the mixed races in separate churches.[737] Church registry records were also segregated.[738] The *castas* had their respective *gremios* (trade guilds).[739] In official functions, the viceroy received *españoles* in one reception area, and the other *castas* in another.[740]

The *castas* were subject to numerous prohibitions and restrictions. Marriage of persons belonging to different categories was prohibited. This prohibition was however difficult to enforce and was hence often ignored. *Indios* and *Negros* were likewise prohibited from dressing in the Spanish manner, or from wearing certain types of fabrics and jewelry commonly used by Spaniards.[741] *Indios*, *mulatos* and *zambos* were prohibited to carry arms.[742] Learning certain trades, especially the making of arms was restricted. *Mestizos* were prohibited from becoming *protectores de indios* (Indio Protectors).[743] The religious orders of Mexico repeatedly opposed *indios*, *mestizos* or *criollos* from receiving sacred orders in spite of laws enacted to the contrary.[744]

Caste discrimination manifested in privileges, distinct possibilities of access to public office, distinct functions in the military, different occupations, different possibilities of admittance to the schools and universities, and different penalties and severity of corporal punishments for crimes.[745]

Plate XXXVIII
LAS CASTAS MEJICANAS

- *Barreda, Ignacio Maria, 1777.* Pubic Domain.

Españoles exercised political, economic and social hegemony. They are distinguished by their apparel, access to education and culture, use of public office and exemption from servile labor. Military service was required of them unless a paid substitute was opted for. All were exempted from tribute and forced labor. Only *españoles europeos* or the *gachupines* however were considered *vecinos* (citizens) and occupied the higher civil, ecclesiastical and military positions.

Españoles born in *Nueva España*, otherwise known as *americanos or criollos*, could not aspire for high government positions and honors, enjoy military commissions of high rank, and occupy high ecclesiastical positions or become regular religious. Until the end of the 17th century, only *españoles* could aspire for higher education. *Indios* could advance no further than the first letters, while the *negros* had access to catechism only. Among the *indios*, only the *caciques* or *principales* were allowed to occupy local government positions and were exempt from tribute and *corvee*. *Mestizos* and *mulatos* could be conscripted to the military under the command of an *español europeo*. *Indios* were exempted from military service but were used as auxiliary troops.[746] By early 19th century, they were incorporated in the regiments of *pardos* and *morenos* with white officers. Manual occupations were considered below the dignity of the *españoles* and reserved for *indios* and *negros*. Legitimacy of birth determined the treatment of *mestizos* and *mulatos*. Since most were illegitimate, they were treated as social pariahs. Rejected by their parental races, they ended up as troublesome vagabonds living in the fringes of *indio* villages. The few of legitimate birth among them could easily pass for white.

The *negros, mulatos* and *zambos* suffered the most. *Negro* revolts against their inhumane treatment initiated the imposition of even more restrictive laws on them. They were forbidden to carry arms, to assemble, or to be out at night. No more than three *negros* and *mulatos* could congregate in any place and at any time. Slaves who ran away, who were absent from service, or who concealed fugitive slaves were meted with lashes or death. Punishment for most offenses were not uniform. There was a double standard of penalties - a light one for Spaniards and a severe one for persons in the "low" castes. Corporal punishment anywhere between 50 to 200 lashes of the whip were meted out for offenses. Punishments were so severe for any normal human being to survive and live another day.

These laws underwent many changes until the Mexican War of Independence. Some were lifted and then reimposed; only to be abrogated once again. Others were never implemented in view of enforcement problems. More often, laws were interpreted to conform to the social tolerance or official discretion of the times. There were, of course, exceptional cases that defied the colonial society's expectations and restraints. The *sistema de castas* and its abuses precipitated the eventual severance from mother Spain in the 19th century.

Consequences on Education

The influence of *limpieza de sangre* was significantly manifested in the way education was dispensed with. The practice of submitting a *probanza de limpieza de sangre* was faithfully practiced to determine ones qualification for the higher levels of education. To go beyond a basic education, it was assumed that a student intended to join the ranks of the clergy. Higher studies in theology would require completion of a secondary education consisting of latin grammar and humanities. The *españoles* had the privilege of accessing all levels of education. In the beginning, *indios* had the same privilege until it was curtailed and limited to the first letters by mid-16th century. *Negros,* on the other hand, were limited to catechism only. The fate of *mestizos* were subject to the arbitrary assessment of their perceived *suficiencia* (sufficiency) and worthiness.

Although theoretically equal, *españoles americanos* were discriminated from the *españoles europeos*. In the eyes of the *peninsulares,* the *criollos* were inferior because the latter's loyalty and attitudes were tainted by the negative influences and attachments to a foreign soil. Originally used to label *negros* born in the New World, the term *criollo* was used to disparage the *americanos* until it gained respectability through the intervention of the Jesuits. Sporadic *criollo* rebellions further reinforced the growing suspicions of their misplaced loyalties. In view of these reservations, the social status of *criollos* became subordinated to that of *peninsulares* over time. The religious regulars banned *criollos* from joining their orders and limited the latter's clerical pursuits as seculars until the end of Spanish sovereignty. During their Coban Chapter of 1570, the Dominican Province of St. Vincent of Chiapa and Guatemala not only prohibited the granting of the Dominican habit to *criollos,* it also redefined the meaning of *criollo* to include those born in Spain but raised in the *Indias* during the first 10 years of their lives.[747]

Mestizos had a more checkered history of education. Cohabitation of *españoles* with native women was fostered by the dire lack of Spanish women. These relationships inevitably resulted in the proliferation of illegitimate *indio* half-breeds. This situation caused a number of problems. *Mestizos* were not accepted by either their parent's races and were mercilessly abandoned. Infanticide was not uncommon. In view of the worsening situation, the Franciscans founded the *Colegio de San Juan de Letran de Mexico* under the royal patronage in 1529 to address the *mestizo* problem.[748] The school accepted only legitimate boys in order to encourage parents to legalize their espousal arrangements.[749] It was observed that the bad traits of both races were more pronounced in the troublesome *mestizos*. As children of *españoles*, legitimate *mestizos* had the right to access education. Beginning in 1575 however, Felipe II issued a series of *cedulas* to the principal archbishops and bishops of the New World and forbade the ordination of *mestizos*.

Children of the *caciques* initially had access to higher education. Under the royal patronage, the Franciscans founded in 1533 the historic *Colegio de*

Santa Cruz at Tlatelolco in the hope of developing an indigenous clergy. However, the initial *indio* graduates of the latin grammar and humanities school proved to be disappointing. They were willfully independent and averse to celibacy. The embarrassment of a failed experiment moved the Franciscans to limit the school to teaching only the first letters thereafter. Other colleges of the regular clergy followed suit and barred *indios* from further clerical formation.[750]

The most definitive acts to influence education emanated from the ecclesiastical authorities of Nueva España and were sanctioned in the *Junta Apostolica* of 1539, the First Mexican Provincial Council of 1555 and the Third Mexican Provincial Council of 1585.[751]

The *Junta Apostolica* of 1539 permitted the ordination of *indios* and *castas* to the four minor orders for the service of the parishes and the help of their priest shepherds.[752] The legislation was a definite and cautious move toward allowing *indios* and *mestizos* to enter priesthood. This was however revoked by the First Mexican Council of 1555. Ordinations of *indios, mestizos* and *mulatos* were prohibited. By the 1570's, the shortage of priests who knew the native languages moved the Pope and King to relax the policies.[753]

On 25 January 1577, Pope Gregory XIII issued the brief *Nuper ad Nos* which stated that

> ... *the illegitimate sons of Spaniards and Indian women, as also of Spaniards who live in the Indies, [can] receive all the orders, hear confessions and preach the word of God, provided that they master the native language and have the qualities that the Council of Trent prescribes for ordination, notwithstanding the defect of birth or any other defect whatever, provided that they are not bigamists or guilty of voluntary homicide.*[754]

By 1578, Felipe II modified his stance by instructing the Archbishop of Mexico not to desist the admittance of *mestizos* suitable to the orders but rather to proceed with the greatest caution.[755] This *cedula* brought the laws of the indies within the scope of *Nuper ad Nos*. The papacy continued to oppose the royal policy on the ordination ban of *mestizos* and in 1588 secured a revocation and amendment to the royal cedulas.[756]

It would not be until the decisions of the Third Mexican Provincial Council of 1585 became the law of the Archdiocese of Mexico City that far-reaching racial consequences would affect the archdiocese until 1896 and spread its influence to the rest of Nueva España including the Philippines until 1918.[757] Book I, title IV, paragraph 3 contains the decree on the ordination of *indios, mestizos* and *mulatos*. The last sentence states: *Whence also neither those of mixed blood, whether from Indians or Moors, nor mulattoes in the first degree are to be admitted to orders 'without the great caution.'*[758] This sentence, contained in the 1622 first printing, did not strictly prohibit the ordination of *indios* and *castas* and apparently removed the absolute exclusion imposed by the First Council. The arbitrary interpretation of this clause however determined the capacity of *indios* and *castas* to actually access higher education. Since old attitudes and behavior lingered on, the status quo remained until the end of the 17th century. It was during the reign of the last Habsburg King, Carlos II, that a series of enlightened legislation began to finally open the doors for the *indios* and *castas*.[759]

On 30 May 1691, Carlos II ordered the establishment of schools in every city, villa and places in Peru and Nueva España to teach *indios* the Spanish language over a period of four years in order to enable them to assume official government duties.[760] To serve as a model to be replicated throughout the *Indias*, the King mandated on 11 July 1691 the foundation of a *Seminario Conciliar* (Council of Trent Seminary) in the city of Mexico with a fourth of the scholarship funds allocated to sons of *caciques*.[761] These two decrees were received acrimoniously by the Spanish colonial authorities as *indios* and *castas* were generally considered as *linaje maculado* (tainted or blemished lineage) under the *limpieza de sangre*.[762] As such, they cannot outrightly comply with the *probanza* required for state and ecclesiastical positions. The reluctance and resistance to implement the decrees moved Carlos II to issue two additional *cedulas* to resolve the matter. Citing the precedents of his progenitors, he declared on 22 March 1697 that the *indios naturales de america* should be equal to other vassals of Spain and should enjoy the same privileges and prerogatives.[763] Four days later, the crown favorably declared the general elevation of the *indio-mestizo* nobility to institutions that were exclusively for *españoles* transcending their historic educational limitations to catechism and spanish literacy.[764]

As early as 1592, Felipe II ordered the foundation of seminaries throughout all the vice kingdoms of Spain. It would not be until 1 October 1689 that the first its kind, the *Seminario Conciliar de Mexico* (Conciliar Seminary of Mexico), was finally founded by Archbishop Francisco Aguiar y Seixas.[765] The seminary commenced and became functional only on 18 October 1697 after the enabling decrees of Carlos II were issued.[766] The lifting of the seminary, the colleges and the university from racial restrictions greatly motivated the *indio* nobility to pursue university degrees thereafter and consequently facilitated their sacerdotal ordination.[767]

Impact on Filipinas

Being under the jurisdiction of *Nueva España*, *Filipinas* would become subject to the Laws of the Indies and the administrative and judicial rulings of the vice kingdom and its ecclesiastical authorities. As such, the five principal factors that shaped Spanish racial policies would be implanted into the archipelago commencing 1565 after Miguel Lopez de Legazpi took possession of the islands in the name of the Spanish crown.

Spanish concepts and laws on slavery would redefine a pre-existing slave society among the natives. Those of *limpieza de sangre* and *vecindad* would cast the natives among the *linaje maculado* and relegate them to an inferior subordinated role and status within a *sistema de castas*. The compassionate Spanish laws of equity and justice would be ignored whenever suitable to the colonial authorities and consequently subverting royal intent to the perceived needs of the settlers. Comparatively, *Filipinas* would be spared from the scale of violence and sanguinary history of Spanish American conquest. Its distance from Spain and Mexico would buffer her from the rippling consequences of the turbulent events occurring there. Lulled in a protective cocoon, the *naturales* de *filipinas* were groomed in child-like innocence to accept their exploitation and abuse in a state of cultivated superstitious ignorance. Although painstakingly slow in coming, the tides of change were inevitable. Gradually, intent would approximate reality in the waning course of time.

Plate XXXIX

Indio Genocide

A scene witnessed by Bartolome de las Casas OP during the invasion of Cuba in 1513.

- Van Winge, Joos (designer) and De Bry, Theodor (engraver) 1664. **Heidelbergae**

Chapter XI

Metamorphosis of a Slave Society

The first Europeans to arrive in *Las Islas Filipinas* discovered a slave society among the natives. It was a society essentially divided into three classes: the rulers, the free men and the slaves. The islander's concept of the slave was however different from how Europeans defined and treated slaves. The differences would eventually disappear as Spanish laws civilized indigenous slavery into what was considered the proper Christian way. The Philippines was subjected to the laws, policies and practices of Nueva España being under its administrative jurisdiction. Thus, the Mexican experience was transplanted and began to transform all aspects of *indio* society accordingly. The dynamics of these intercultural exchanges would bring about the metamorphosis of the native's psyche and initial stirrings of a unique identity as a nation - a process Letran had been involved with from its beginnings.

The Western Isles

After *Fernão de Magalhães* discovered the *Islas de Ladrones* (Archipelago of Thieves), and *Las Islas de San Lazaro* (Archipelago of Saint Lazarus) in 1521, three succeeding attempts to take possession of the Philippines proved unsuccessful.

Leaving Coruña Spain in 1525, *Garcia Jofre de Loaísa* led the second expedition to the *Mar del Sur* (South Seas) by which name the Pacific Ocean was known then. The expedition led to the discovery of San Bartolome, an outlying island of the Marshals, but ended in disaster with Loaisa and most of his crew losing their lives marooned in Tidore. The third expedition headed by *Álvaro de Saavedra Cerón* departed from *Zihuatanejo* on the Pacific coast of *Nueva España* in 1527. After sighting the north coast of Mindanao, the expedition established a base in Tidore. The expedition discovered a number of islands in the Pacific Ocean which formed part of New Guinea, the Admiralty Islands and the Carolines among others in its failed attempts to return to *Nueva España*. The remaining crew members were captured by the Portuguese and returned to Spain. The last failed attempt was carried out by *Ruy López de Villalobos*. Departing from *Jalisco, Nueva España* in 1542, the expedition arrived at the eastern coast of Mindanao on 29 February 1543. Villalobos named the islands of Leyte and Samar as *Las Islas de Filipinas* in honor of the then Prince of Asturias, Felipe II. Unable to successfully settle there, the remaining crew sought refuge from the Portuguese in the Moluccas where they were held captives.[768]

All the islands discovered in the *Mar del Sur* became known as *Las Islas del Poniente* (Western Isles) in the Spanish empire; and the name would become more closely associated with *Filipinas*. The demarcation line agreed upon between Spain and Portugal in the 1494 Treaty of Tordesillas defined their territorial rights of exploration and colonization in the Atlantic hemisphere but not on the other side of the world. The Spanish intrusions into the Moluccas discovered earlier by the Portuguese precipitated diplomatic and military conflicts. In urgent need for funds to finance his wars in Europe, *Carlos I* signed the 1529 Treaty of Zaragoza with *João III* conceding a larger Pacific territory to Portugal in exchange for 350,000 ducats in gold. The treaty defined the anti-meridian as 297.5 leagues or 17º to the east of the Moluccas which placed the Philippines within the Portuguese jurisdiction. Villalobos' incursion in 1543 was a blatant violation of the treaty in spite of his 'feigned' insistence of being in Spanish territory.

Sometime 1559, preparations began for an expedition of discovery to the *Islas del Poniente* located within the Spanish side of the Zaragoza demarcation line.[769] Miguel Lopez de Legazpi was appointed Governor and General for the discovery by the King and the Viceroy of Nueva España and received his secret orders from the *Real Audiencia de Nueva España*.[770] With a fleet of four sea vessels and 350 men, the expedition departed from the port of Navidad on 21 November 1564.[771] Accompanying Legazpi were P. Fr. Andres Urdaneta OSA, a survivor of the 1525 Loaisa Expedition and Guido de Lavezaris, a survivor of the 1542 Villalobos Expedition.[772] 100 leagues from the port of departure, Legazpi revealed the sealed orders to his crew and set sails directly for *Las Islas de Filipinas*. The crew was aware of the Treaty's violation but did not question the King's instructions and construed it as a temporary and exploratory mission before arriving at a final strategic decision.[773] All future plans were dependent on achieving a most critical objective - the discovery of a still unknown return route to Nueva España, the source of all the necessary logistics and support to sustain the survival of any colony in the Pacific.

The mission orders were quite specific. The principal goal of the expedition as declared by the King was

> *...to bring to the inhabitants of those places our Holy Catholic Faith and to discover the return route to this New Spain to the credit of the patrimony of the Royal Crown of Castile, through trade and barter and through other legitimate ways, which with a clear conscience should be carried on to bring back some spices and some of the wealth found in those places.*[774]

As regards the natives of the islands,

> *... be careful that nobody vex and offend them; rather, treat them with great prudence as a people of great dignity, as it is being told they are people of reason and pride and white like ourselves, because the higher their culture the better they become.*

… You shall get information on the customs, the standard and manner of living, and the attitude of the natives. You shall also investigate their religion and sect, what they worship, what rites and sacrifices they perform and how they are governed. Find out if they have kings; if these are elected or if they rule by right of succession; if they govern as Republics or as hereditary monarchs, and what tributes or taxes they give to which persons and in what manner. Find out also what things on earth they value most and what things you have they like best.

… You will offer them friendship and brotherly relations so that there maybe intercommunication and trade between their subjects and vassals. You will offer them friendship in the name of His Majesty, giving them some of the best presents, those that please them most. In all this, you are instructed to exercise great prudence, as expected of your person. You shall not seek vengeance for any indiscretion; nor shall you and your men bear any ill feeling towards them. Above all, there must be peace and friendship as is to be expected from our treatment and intercourse.

… According to information, in those parts of the West, the inhabitants have the custom to trade, sell, and barter slaves from one place to another. As you will have need of some of the slaves to learn their language and also to have information about those islands, you shall order the purchase or barter of some from different places for this purpose, treating them well so that they will like you and tell you always the truth. You shall not allow a native in any place to be captured or taken by force; rather, as has already been said, he shall be obtained through barter or as present to you from some prominent man. Neither shall any soldier buy or barter a slave during the voyage in order not to increase those to be fed. But when, God willing, you land, and settle in a certain place, you will permit the captains and the rest of the men to buy or barter slaves to serve them; however, they shall not be permitted to sell or bring said slaves to New Spain until His Majesty so provides and orders. Nevertheless, it would do good if two or three of the slaves are taken to New Spain so that the people here can see them and learn from them things about their lands.[775]

The orders contained military, security, intelligence, trade, logistics administrative, accounting and contingency instructions. Among them pertained to the completion and manning of the fleet. The fleet was composed of two galleons, the San Pedro and the San Pablo, and two *pataches*, the San Lucas and the San Juan de Letran.[776] Used as a tender for the bigger vessels, a *patache* was used principally for maritime surveillance and inspection. Under the command of *Capitan Juan de la Isla,* the *San Juan de Letran* was the second vessel by that name to reach *Filipinas*. The first was a carrack in the Villalobos fleet which failed in its task to find a return route under the command of *Bernardo de la Torre*.[777] These vessels would somehow introduce the venerable name to the archipelago's memory and to remain there throughout its history.

Except for the *patache* San Lucas which lost its way, the Legazpi expedition sighted *Las Islas de Filipinas* on 14 February 1565 and anchored off Cebu on 27 April of the same year.778 Four months later on 1 June 1565, the San Pedro departed Cebu in search of a return route to Nueva España with P. Fr. Andres de Urdaneta OSA, possessions taken in His Majesty's name, and the first native slaves from *Filipinas* to be transported to Nueva España on board.779 It would not be until 15 October 1566 when the *patache* San Geronimo arrived in Cebu bringing news that the return route to Nueva España was successfully discovered with the San Pedro arriving in Acapulco on 8 October 1565.780 San Geronimo however did not bring either provisions or reinforcements to enliven an already distressed camp beleaguered by the belligerent Portuguese and hostile natives.

Slavery in Filipinas

Before the arrival of Legazpi, a slave society existed in *Filipinas*. Slavery as observed then did not however conform to European concepts and practices. It would however gradually be immersed and transformed into the Spanish model and system of economic utility and value.

P. Fr. Martin de Rada OSA described his observations on native slavery to Marquis de Falces:

> ...*This race is the most arrogant that was ever seen and the slaves are the freest that can be imagined, for they do only what they wish; and besides this [it is seen] by the lack of loyalty which they preserve toward one another. For although they be relatives or brothers if they meet one another in the open, he who is strongest lays hands upon the other and sells him...*781

Native tribes conducted regular raids on neighboring villages and islands and the Visayans were notorious for slave raiding. The Visayan word for raid is *mangayaw*. After the Spanish authorities prohibited slave raiding and disarmed the Christian *Indios,* the Visayans would become vulnerable preys for the Muslim *Moros* who became the uncontested players of the traditional *mangayaw*. The *Moros* would raid coastal towns as far as Luzon coming from Jolo, Mindanao, Borneo, Ternate and Sanguir. They would sack coastal towns and leave them severely depopulated.782

In view of the existing Laws of the Indies and the instructions contained in the orders, the forced enslavement of natives was restrained until permission from the King was secured. The lack of provisions, ammunitions and reinforcements further discouraged any acts to unduly antagonize natives into armed conflicts. In recognition for the work carried out in His Majesty's service, Legazpi's officers petitioned for 15 royal favors contained in a memorial to Felipe II. Two articles in the petition involving slavery were as follows:

> ... *in as much as in these your kingdoms and dominions deal with moros [who] bring the gold which abounds in these islands and other*

fruits such as wax cinnamon and other items that until now [thou] has not come to be aware, and in as much they disrupt and attempt to disrupt the trade between the natives and ourselves and they preach the bahometanga (mohammedan) *sect and do not provide space wherein the holy gospel could be cultivated that the said moros be made slaves and dispossessed of their property which they attentively take that they commit the above stated harm and are prejudicial to the holy catholic faith and gain of the royal crown and this is advisable that your majesty provides.*[783]

… that they are permitted to purchase and buy slaves sold in the land in order that they may be served by them according and in the manner they serve the nobles and natives hereabout like in mines and in other such things that they offer.[784]

Five years after arriving in *Filipinas*, a letter from Felipe II dated 16 November 1568 together with dispatches and royal favors arrived at Legazpi's camp in Panay. The King was very pleased with Legazpi's accomplishments and how the latter conducted himself particularly with regard to the good treatment and conversion of the natives. Authority to implement *repartimiento* and *reduccion* was officially given signaling the commencement of conquest and the establishment of permanent settlements. With regard to slavery, Felipe II ordained the following:

We have also been petitioned in your name that, in consideration of the fact that there are islands inhabited by Moros in that land, and that they come to trade and traffic, thus hindering the preaching of the gospel, disturbing you, we grant you permission to enslave such Moros, and to seize their possessions. You must take note that if such Moros are Moros by birth and nation and come for the purpose of spreading their cursed Mahometan worship, or to make war on you or on the Indians subject to us and to our royal service, then you can enslave them. But you shall under no consideration whatever enslave those who were indians who may have adopted the worship of Mahomet; but you shall endeavor to convert them and to persuade them to accept our holy Catholic faith by good and legitimate means.

Report has been made me on behalf of the conquistadors of that country that many slaves have been made there by the natives of those islands. I have been entreated to grant permission to those conquistadors to purchase them and hold them as slaves in the same manner as the said natives hold them. Inasmuch as I desire to be informed of the custom in this matter and of what is advisable to do, I order you to submit a report of the causes why slaves are made in that country - whether slaves are made mutually among the natives themselves; whether the Moros who wage war upon the said native's are made slaves; or whether there are various sects among them, so that they wage and maintain mutual warfare among themselves and make slaves mutually of one another. You shall report on the other characteristics of that race in so far as they touch this matter; and when the said report is ready you shall send it to our

Council of the Indies, so that, after they have examined it, the most advisable measures may be taken in accordance with justice.[785]

The King's letter would initiate significant changes in the attitudes and behavior of the conquistadores. Notwithstanding the violation of the Zaragoza treaty, the Spanish presence became permanent; conscious that a war with Portugal was at risk.[786] Plans would revolve around establishing settlements, reducing the natives into Christian communities and distributing them as *encomiendas* granted as just rewards to the conquistadores. The *caciques* would remain in power and used in the Crown's name to collect excessive tributes, source scarce food supplies and exact forced labor. Only numbering 100 *cristianos nuevos* then, conversion of the natives would hence be actively pursued.[787] The existing military detachment was strengthened with fresh reinforcements, ample provisions and sufficient ordnance. The use of military force would be resorted to more often. The instructions on slavery provided loop holes. Until unlawful slavery was clearly defined, the Spaniards freely purchased slaves from among the natives. Furthermore, the ambiguous nature of what constitutes a legal Moro slave gave license to indiscriminate slave raiding activities.

The emerging abuses prompted P. Fr. Diego de Herrera OSA to inform Felipe II of the situation:

…the people promise better than those of Nueva España. But since your majesty does not provide anyone permanently and prescribe the manner of living, and protect and defend the natives, and keep justice for them, and power to punish whoever injures them, all will be lost in a very short time, for the policy employed with the natives could last but one year here if there is much greater violence. That consists in robbing them, burning the villages, and enslaving them. If this is not done it is affirmed that it is impossible to find support. This is false, for on the contrary, it is impossible to find support in this manner, for everything is being destroyed [by this manner of acting] and the natives are becoming so exhausted because they are not left for an instant. However, they all desire peace in an extraordinary manner and to live under the protection of your Majesty and to pay tribute. They would give the sum asked of them, if they thought that no evil was to be done them. But today they are made friends and on the morrow they are robbed. Many of them have been killed and many villages burned.

…They sent from here to petition your Majesty to concede to them the favor to allow them to rob and enslave the Moros throughout these districts. The reason that they gave for it was to say that they were Moros and that they were preventing and opposing the preaching of the gospel. The statement that they were preventing the preaching of the gospel was false, for they have never prevented it nor do so at present. On the contrary, there is an increase to be observed in families where the husband is a Moro and the wife a pagan, who come in order to beg the religious to baptize their son and make him a Christian; for they do not at all object to each one living according to the belief that he likes best.

For all the Moros who live in these islands have been Moros for but few years back. Many of them, such as those of Luçon have nothing except the name, and the fact that they do not eat pork; for they have no mosque or cacique [sic] (who are their priests). This worship is only a trifle more firmly established among those of the island of Burney than in the other, although they are also of recent date there. Not all the island is Moro, but only certain villages along the coast, for the inhabitants of the interior are heathens. None of them possess the lands of the Christians or wage war on them, or do them any injury; although we do to them, and much, for four or five ships of Burneo have been pillaged and many people killed, while many more from Luçon have been killed, although excellent friends to us. As to the chiefs, they made the land friendly to us, or at least exerted a great influence in that direction. They supplied us with food in abundance and stuffs very suitable for clothing, and gold for our silver, in order that we might barter for our necessities. Now, however, conditions are such that no one dares come [to trade]. I do not believe that any other reason can be given for authority to rob them, except that they are Moros; and that is no legitimate reason and cannot be done.[788]

In response to Herrera's letter, Real Cedula dated 4 July 1570 clarifying the enslavement of Moros was issued containing the following:

To the district of the islas Filipinas and its confines are adjacent to those of Mindanao whose natives have rebelled, taking the sect of Mahoma and confederating with the enemies of this Crown and inflicting major suffering to our vassals, and to facilitate their punishment it appeared to be an effective remedy to declare as slaves those who were captured in war. We order that it be done as such, proceeding with the distinction that, if the Mindanaos were purely gentiles [they] are not to be dealt as slaves, and if they were of the nation and natural born moros and arriving to other islands to preach and teach their mohametan sect or to make war to the españoles or indios who are My subjects or at our Royal service, in this case they can be enslaved; further more those who were indios and converted to the sect are not to be enslaved and are to be proselytize through licit and benevolent means [so] that they be converted to our Holy Catholic Faith.[789]

The pattern of abuse that accompanied Spanish conquest in the New World would be replicated in *Filipinas* albeit on a diminished scale. The prevailing laws and the watchful eyes of the friars restrained the colonists in no small measure. The economic necessity for slaves however led to the development of a slave market in Manila, a city founded by Legazpi on 19 May 1571 and confirmed by Felipe II on 19 June 1572. The city was already a center of trade with China and Japan before the coming of the Spaniards. When Felipe II ascended the throne of Portugal in 1581, the Portuguese traded freely in Manila and slaves from all over their Asian possessions were among their principal commodities. With the 1565 discovery of the Manila-Acapulco return route, the Manila Galleon Trade officially commenced with *slaves* from *Filipinas* among its first cargo. In as much as the *indios de filipinas* were not yet officially declared as vassals of the King, the ship manifests would register them as *chinos* to avoid any legal complications the term *indio* could imply. To confuse the authorities, *indios* were mixed with other legal Asian slaves collectively known as *chinos*. There was a time when the Pacific Slave Trade competed with the Atlantic Slave Trade before bowing out to the latter's dominance by 1690.[790]

Legazpi died on 20 August 1572 as the first Governor and Captain General of the Spanish East Indies. Among the King's orders that he failed to render was the report on the system of slavery in the Philippines. The non-submission of the report delayed the official recognition of the *indios de filipinas* as the King's vassals and their coverage under the Laws of the Indies particularly with regard to the issue of slavery. Guido de Lavezaris, Legazpi's successor, submitted the following report as ordered:

Sacred Royal Catholic Majesty:

By one of your royal decrees, dated Madrid, May 18, 1572, your Majesty commands me to send you an account of the slaves that exist in these parts; and how, and with what justification, they are slaves. What has been ascertained about them, to the present time, in this island is as follows:

Some are slaves from their birth. Their origin is not known, because their fathers, grandfathers, and ancestors were also slaves. But although the reason for slavery is not known, we may believe that it was for some one of the causes here named. Some are captives in wars that different villages wage against each other, for certain injuries and acts of injustice, committed either recently or in ancient times.

Some are made captives in wars by villages that have neither treaty or commerce with them, but go only to rob, without any cause. This is because a chief of any village, when he dies, imposes upon it a sort of mourning or grief; all his near relatives promise to eat no bread (which is rice), millet, or borona, and wear no gold or any holiday dress, until they take some booty, or kill or capture men. They would go to do this, wherever they could, and where there were no friends or powerful towns who could easily avenge themselves. Some, especially those who pride themselves on valor, have a custom, after gathering their harvests, of going to rob, without any cause, towns with which they have no commerce or relationship; or whomsoever they meet on the sea, where - a thing that causes wonder - they exempt not even their relatives, if the latter are less powerful than they. Some are enslaved by those who rob them for a very small matter - as, for instance, a knife, a few sugar-canes, or a little rice. Some are slaves because they bore testimony, or made statements about some one, which they could not prove. Some are thus punished for committing some crime; or transgressing rules regarding their rites or ceremonies, or things forbidden among them, or not coming quickly enough at the summons of some chief, or any other like thing; and if they do not have the wherewithal to pay, they are made slaves for it.

If any one is guilty of a grave crime - that is, has committed murder or adultery, or given poison, or any other like serious matter - although there may be no proof of it beyond the suspicion of the principal person against whom the hurt was done, they take for their slaves, or kill, not only the culprit but his sons, brothers, parents, relatives, and slaves.

If anyone who is left an orphan come to the house of another, even of a kinsman (unless it be his uncle paternal or maternal), for food only, its inmates enslave him. Likewise in time of famine and distress, during which they may have given relatives food only a few times, they have sold the latter for their slaves.

Many also become slaves on account of loans, because these loans continue to increase steadily every three or four months; and so, however little may be the sum loaned to them, at the end of little more or less than two years they become slaves. And now, sacred Majesty, if it be forbidden, in those places where the Spanish live, to acquire slaves in any shape or manner - those who were made slaves and were slaves before we came here and are slaves now, and whom the natives buy and sell among each other, as merchandise or other profitable wares that they possess - without them this land cannot be preserved. This, your Majesty, is all known here of the slaves that I have been able to find out, having diligently sought and made the acquaintance of persons who know their language and customs.[791]

Consequently, Felipe II prohibited all *españoles* from owning *indio* slaves in a Real Cedula dated 7 November 1574 containing the following:

We order that not one español can have indio slave for whatever cause in Filipinas, even if the indio had been enslaved by other indios or españoles and obtained in just war. And because in those islands and other parts it has been understood that they are beyond their liberty many indios who were tyrannically enslaved by other principales, claiming that they had them in their possession for many years, and that they sell and trade fathers and sons, in Our desiring their liberty we order the Viceroys, Presidents of all the Royal Audiencias appoint a Minister or other satisfactory person of good conscience to visit and acquaint himself of these causes in every Province, in order not to permit these slaveries by virtue of the right and laws of this book, those thereby voided, and instate the indios in their natural liberty, without the constraints of any kind of possession.[792]

The law prohibited enslavement of *indios* but did not prohibit slavery. Technically speaking, the *indios* including *moros* were henceforth protected by the Laws of the Indies and *españoles* could only own non-native slaves. However, *caciques* and other rich *indios* could legally own both *indio* and foreign slaves.[793]

The decree reached Manila on 17 September 1581 on a galleon with the new bishop of *Filipinas*, P. Fr. Domingo de Salazar OP, on board. The decree officially recognized the *indios de filipinas* as the King's vassals; prohibited all Spaniards from owning *indio* slaves; but allowed the existing native system of slavery. Among Bishop Salazar's first acts was to call the *Junta de Tondo* (Tondo Assembly) of all church leaders to discuss the decree and to issue an ecclesiastical position on the matter.794 A resolution was issued on 16 October 1581 declaring that: (1) there was nothing new about the law considering laws against *indio* slavery already existed, and as such no reasons could justify the non-observance of the King's wishes; (2) the governor cannot neglect to implement the law notwithstanding the clamor of the slave masters; and (3) the liberty of the *indios* should be expedited immediately but a deferment of no more than 30 days could be adopted if circumstances required it.795

A period of hostile confrontation between the clerics and the colonists ensued. After a delay of two years, the Governor-General finally ordered the implementation of the law amidst strong opposition. To ensure the compliance of the law, the clerics imposed sacramental bans on slave owners particularly the refusal to grant confessional absolution among others. The emancipation of *indio* slaves began to hold ground among the Spaniards and a clamor to completely phase-out slavery among the *indios* gathered momentum. The 1586 Junta General de Manila (General Assembly of Manila) recommended stricter legal enforcement of the law among erring Spaniards and that *now and henceforth ... children born to those who are now slaves, or appear to be slaves, should be born free; that those held at present may not be sold to pagans, or to Indians not subject to his Majesty.*796 The Junta's *examinadora* (examiner) further proposed that any *indio* could no longer be enslaved; that those born of slaves should be considered free; that those ten years of age should serve up to 20, and those over 20 until 25; and that they could be ransomed at the price that the governor and the bishop indicated.797

During this period of uncertainty, Felipe II ascended the throne of Portugal. The ensuing friendly relations between Spain and Portugal prompted Bishop Salazar to seek clarification whether the Portuguese would be allowed to trade slaves in Manila.798 The King did not reply. It was assumed to be disallowed because of an existing law recognizing *indios* within the Portuguese domain as free.799 Notwithstanding this law, the Portuguese slave traders unloaded the first 100 *chino* slaves in the port of Manila in 1588.800 The legality of this trade was never challenged and consequently the *vecinos* of Manila viewed *chinos* as legal slaves in as much as they were not *indios de filipinas*. By 1620, the *moros viejos* enslavement law was reinstated.801 *Chinos* and *Moros* would hence be considered as legal slaves to Spaniards providing convenient loopholes to casually identify any slave under those labels.

The arrival of Governor Gomez Perez Dasmariñas in 1591 would make the 1574 slavery law even more untenable. In his possession was Felipe II's instructions in reply to the recommendations of 1586 General Assembly of

Plate XL

SAN JACINTO DE CHINA
- Artist unknown. Centro evangelizador y cultural, Rosademaria 2013-7-13.

Manila. In his instructions to the incoming governor dated 9 August 1589, Felipe II reiterated the strict enforcement of the existing prohibition on Spaniards but did not act on the recommendations phasing out slavery among the *indios*.[802] Law abiding Spaniards would thereafter comply with the law by freeing their *indio* slaves and maintaining *chino* slaves. Although illegal, *encomenderos* would surreptitiously use *caciques* to order the latters' slaves to do their bidding.[803] Most *vecinos* would however simply ignore the law.

The pre-hispanic traditional slave raids between *indio* villages was disrupted by the coming of the Spanish colonizers. The *nuevos conversos* were disarmed and became vulnerable victims to the raids of non-christian natives particularly the *Moros*. The *españoles* with their Christian native cacique allies however would continue the traditional raids but "only" against the *moros viejos*. What became known as the *moro-moro wars* in traditional Philippine history were initially raids conducted mutually to supply lucrative slave markets. Manila became the principal Spanish slave market shipping about 300 slaves a year to Nueva España and receiving unrecorded numbers from Portuguese slave ports.[804] The Sultanate of Sulu became a major player after 1768 and Jolo became its principal slave market place receiving captives throughout Southeast Asia.

Slave Markets

The King's inaction on the Portuguese slave trade query and the recommendations to completely phase out *indio* slavery would apparently be perceived by colonists as an opened door to bend the rules. By 1621, slavery was generally accepted and became ubiquitous in every aspect of colonial life in *Filipinas*.[805] Even the poorest Spanish soldier would have one to three slaves.[806] A third of Manila's population then were slaves.[807] The cathedral had an assigned secular priest to minister to both *indios* and slaves.[808] The clergy who initially implemented the abolition of Spanish slavery adopted the colony's *modus vivendi*.

The Augustinians who freed all their slaves in 1574, for instance, set a limit of one slave per priest in 1627 and raised the maximum to four by 1650.[809] The convent slaves were known either as *donados* (donated) or *rescatados* (ransomed). The *donados* were either child slaves donated to the clergy by pious benefactors or older individuals who voluntarily surrendered themselves as slaves to either escape poverty or take refuge from life's harsher realities. The *rescatados* were slaves who were ransomed for the remaining term of their indentured bondage under the clergy's charge. These slaves were considered essentially free and were *given everything they needed* to live comfortably by their clergy masters in exchange for their uncompensated service as domestics.[810] The term *capista* would eventually apply to these slaves to remove whatever allusions to their past status. Soon after, the term would apply to all students whose free education was exchanged for their uncompensated service. Although the laws were not strictly complied with, *españoles* and *indios* alike circumscribed their choice of slaves to natural

LA CHINA POBLANA DE MEXICO
- *Iriarte, Hesiquio 1854. Litª de M. Murgia y Compañia.*
Frias y Soto 1854.

---

slaves (by birth, war, theft, etc.), the "old" Muslims, natives who attack Spaniards or natives protected by them, and slaves sold by the Portuguese.[811] The number of slaves gradually decreased over time.

Indio slaves from Manila together with other Portuguese slaves were shipped to the slave markets of Nueva España. They would come to be collectively known as *chinos*. The institution with a large number of *chino* slaves was the Dominican Holy Rosary Province's *Hospicio de San Jacinto* located in the outskirts of Mexico city.[812] Chino slaves were employed as servants to attend to the traveling friars, to upkeep the rest home and to act as cultural intermediaries providing information on the places, customs and languages where the Dominicans would be assigned.[813] *Hospicio de San Jacinto* would also come to be known as *San Jacinto de China* or *San Jacinto de los Filipinos*.[814]

By 1676, Carlos II became aware that *indios de filipinas* were being sold as *chino* slaves in Nueva España; prompting him to issue Real Cedula dated 13 March 1676 liberating the *indios de filipinas* from slavery and providing them with land to live outside the capital.[815] Since it was difficult to distinguish an *indio* from a *chino,* all *chino* slaves were thereafter considered as *indios* with the courts in Nueva España consequently setting them all free.[816] A remaining influence of the *chinos* continues to live in Mexico's cultural icon the China Poblana.

It is ironic that the *indios de filipinas* slaves in Mexico were set free ahead of those in their own homeland. It would not be until 1681 when the Manila slave society would be shaken from the doldrums of its comfortable lifestyle. Arriving in Manila with the royal fiscal was a Real Cedula dated 12 June 1679 issued by Carlos II stating among others that: *Those who are now living in slavery and their children and descendants, shall be free in fact.*[817] Both *español* and *indio* slave owners, including the clergy this time, protested vehemently. Faced with this unexpected resistance, Carlos II prudently advised the Viceroy of Nueva España and the Audiencia de Mexico on 1 May 1686 to expedite the decree's implementation considering the reported concerns and prevailing circumstances.[818] The resulting implementing Ordinance of the Real Audiencia de Manila effectively adopted the recommendations of the 1586 Manila General Assembly to wit: *In as much as Indian slavery is forbidden; and since the transfer of those slaves by custom is also forbidden; as is also that their descendants born after August 18, 1692 (the date of the publication in Manila of the act of the royal Audiencia of Mexico, in accordance with the royal decree of Buen Retiro, May 1, 1686), would be slaves: the officials are to carefully carry this law into effect, and prevent such slavery.*[819]

With these limitations implemented, former slave owners shifted to the practice of "voluntary" uncompensated domestic servants and became accustomed to paid forced labor known as *polo*. As the Manila Slave Market faded away, the Sultanate of Sulu became the principal trade entrepôt towards the end of 18th century collecting custom duties, maintaining banking houses and issuing slave trading licenses to non-Spaniards.

From 1768 onwards, the demand for slaves peaked with the increase in the demand for traditional Tausog export commodities of *tripang* (sea cucumber), sulu pearls, mother of pearl oysters, tortoise shell, and bird's nest. British traders and other independents bartered them with arms, gunpowder, war stores, opium and textile. To meet demand, more slave workers were needed to source and produce the goods; transforming Jolo into a major slave market place. Relying on available data, James Warren, estimated that between 200,000 to 300,000 slaves were delivered to Sulu between 1770 and 1870 and were supplied largely by Iranun and Balangingi Samal raiders.[820] The trade dwindled with the active intervention of the Spanish navy in the 19th century. The arrival of steam gunboats and the improvement of coastal defenses virtually curbed slave raiding after 1860.[821]

A number of treaties were entered into between the Sultanate and the Spanish authorities but they were as good as the value of the paper written on. Slave trading continued but in a greatly diminished scale. *Small scale Samal marauding and slavery were only abolished when the Americans closed the slave markets on Sulu and Tawi-tawi in the first decade of the 20th century.*[822]

Although slavery in Spanish Philippines virtually vanished by the middle of the 18th century, the attitudes and behavior of former masters towards an inferior race of former slaves would remain much longer as a *sistema de castas* defined the privileged and non-privileged classes of the colonial social order.

An Abbreviated Caste System

Manila was a thriving city in 1621. Goods from all over Asia found its way to the city. Aside from its European residents and transients, it was filled with a multitude of races. Archbishop Miguel Garcia Serrano OSA described the city's population that year:

> *Within the walls of Manila there is no more than one parish of Spaniards, which is the Cathedral… in which two thousand and four hundred communicant Spaniards are ministered to, men and women, among whom some mestizos are included: one thousand are male residents and transients, and eight hundred and sixteen are on the payroll; the other five hundred and eighty-four are women, and this number does not include the religious, priests or children…There is also one curate in whose charge are the native indios of this city, and the slaves and freedmen who live within it who ministers to one thousand seven hundred and forty communicant indios, and one thousand nine hundred and seventy slaves, who include a few freedmen.*[823]

The preceding population of 6,000 within the walls of Manila consisted mainly of resident and transient *españoles*, *mestizos de español*, *chino* and *moro* slaves, with a larger teeming population of *indios* and *sangleys* outside its walls. Outside the city's east wall, some 15,000 to 20,000 *sangleys* lived around an *alcaiceria* (silk market) known as the *Parian*.[824] Surrounding the Spanish and Sangley settlements were 201,600 Christian *indios* living in the Archdiocese of Manila.[825] The small Spanish population and the limited economic activities in *Filipinas* would alter the *sistema de castas* that characterized Nueva España. Taxation would effectively define one's position in the social ladder.

Exempted from rendering any tribute or forced labor, the *españoles* would continue to occupy the seats of power, privilege and prestige. Between 1624 and 1656, the lay *españoles* resided principally in five *villas*: Manila, Cebu, Caceres, Nueva Segovia and Arevalo. At its peak, Manila would have 400 *vecinos* and the rest of the other *villas* would account for nearly 200.[826] At its lowest level, there would be just 60 lay *españoles* residing outside Manila and Cebu.[827] It was the lone religious parish priest who represented the Spanish crown in most of the provincial towns, and the total ministries throughout the archipelago then required at least 400 religious priests.[828] In view of their small number, *criollos* and *mestizos de españoles* were treated almost but not quite as equals. Marriages between poor *españoles* and *indio* women were even encouraged by providing dowries no matter how small.[829] This somewhat unique status would however change towards the 19th century.

Below the *españoles* were the *indios* with their own social hierarchy. The *caciques* or *principales* were known as the *maharlikas*. Only the *cacique* and his first born son were exempted from tribute and forced labor. The plebeian freemen were known as the *timawas*, and below them were the slaves known as *alipins*. There were two classes of *alipins*: *alipin sa namamahay* and *alipin sa gigilir*. Living in their own homes, the *alipin sa namamahays* were effectively indentured peons who paid off their familial, financial or penal obligations with either currency or personal service to the slave owner over a determined period of time. The *alipin sa gigilirs* were what Europeans would consider as the traditional resident slaves who were owned and traded as chattels by their owners. The number of slaves owned by the master was a measure of wealth and status in his community. The *alipin sa gigilir* belonged to the lowest caste together with the *chino* and *moro* slaves. As more and more *caciques* were Christianized, pressure to free their slaves was exerted by their pastors. The services of *alipin sa namamahay* would be supplanted by the mandatory *corvée* known as the *polo* which all non-Spanish vassals were subjected to. The *alipin sa gigilir* would transition into the *alila* (servant) rendering free domestic services in exchange for food, shelter and clothing. Thus by the 18th century, the *indio* slave was transformed into the uncompensated servant or assistant. The system of subservience would effectively continue under different names while the same prejudices, attitudes and behavior between former masters and slaves persisted.[830]

De nacion china (Chinese national) followed the *indios* in the social ladder. The *indios* referred to Chinese nationals as *sangleys* from the Hokkien *siong lay* meaning frequent visitor.[831] The word *sangley* was readily adopted by the *españoles* to informally denote *de nacion china* considering that the word *chino* in the Spanish lexicon of Nueva España at that time was generally understood to mean: Asian slave. Despised by the *españoles* for their barbarous heathen ways, the *sangleys* were tolerated in view of their indispensable role in the colony's economy and everyday comfort. The *sangleys* supplied food, merchandise, crafts, trade and personal services sorely needed by the Spanish *vecinos* and their families. A number of statutory attempts to limit their numbers failed. The *sangley* population would rise and fall depending on the galleon trade season and the genocides and banishments that followed recurring racial clashes.[832] Practically an all-male lot, the *sangleys* paid the highest taxes and were subject to many prohibitions.[833]

There was already a community of 40 *sangleys* living in Manila by the time Legazpi arrived and about 150 in the surrounding areas.[834] Early attempts to convert the heathens met limited success until the arrival of the Dominicans in 1587. The Dominicans earned their trust after establishing a hospital to care for *sangleys* while learning to speak and write in their language. Consequently, conversions increased dramatically.[835] Land known as Binondo was donated by Governor Luis Perez de Dasmariñas for married converts to settle across the Pasig River. The Christian *sangleys* intermarried with *indio* women and soon after a new *mestizo de sangley* race began to emerge. This new race inherited the benefits enjoyed by their *indio* mothers and the skills and commercial cunning of their fathers. They could own land, paid lesser taxes, and became preferred *inquilinos* (tenants) and business associates of the friars. Known simply as *mestizos,* the *indio-sangley* mixed race would occupy a higher caste position over the *sangleys*. They would eventually join the ranks of the *principales* as intermarriages with landed *cacique* spouses were frequently resorted to.

Slaves constituted the bottom of the *sistema de casta de filipinas*. This caste was essentially comprised of the *chino* and *moro* slaves. It should be noted however that these were merely labels used to hide the contraband nature of the slaves' origins. *Indio* or any other kind of slave could indiscriminately be labeled as either *chino* or *moro*. The *chinos* were actually sourced from the different ports where the Portuguese slave ships docked. Japanese slaves would normally come from the port of Nagasaki while Chinese slaves from Macao.[836] From the Indian sub-continent, slaves were sourced from Chite, Cochin, Corumbi, Goa, Lumbini, Malabar and Mogo.[837] Other Pacific sources included Ambon, Borneo, Java, Makassar, Maluku Islands, Alternate, Bregui, Chati, Pali, Papua and Vuica.[838] Known as *cafres, negro* slaves from Mozambique, Guinea and Cape Verde found their way to Acapulco via Manila recorded as *chinos* in the ship manifests.[839] Documents in Mexico would record *chino* slaves originating from Cagayan, Calamianes, Calubian, Camarines, Cavite, Lubao, Manila, Pampanga, Panay, Pasiculas, Jolo, Mindanao and Zamboanga - all from *Filipinas*.[840]

Although all the slaves in *Filipinas* would theoretically had been freed by mid-18th century, slavery would continue in the form of *tanores* (uncompensated involuntary servitude), peonage, human trafficking and other offenses against liberty. When the United States of America assumed sovereignty over the Philippines, the colonial authorities were surprised to discover that slavery continued to exist in both the Christian and non-Christian territories which included Agusan, both Camarines, Ifugao, Isabela, Kalinga, Misamis, Moro, Nueva Vizcaya, Occidental Negros, Palawan, Pampanga, Romblon, Tarlac, and Zambales.[841] They were amazed to discover that there was no law in either the Philippine Islands or the United States prohibiting the sale of human beings, and were therefor unable to legally address and remedy slavery, involuntary servitude, peonage and the trade in human beings.[842] It would not be until the implementation of the Revised Penal Code on 1 January 1932 that slavery and its disguised forms were finally criminalized.[843]

In 1810, Tomas de Comyn estimated the population of *Filipinas* to be 2,526,406. Catholic *indios* totalled 2,395,687; Catholic *mestizo de sangleys* -

119,719, *sangleys* - 7,000 and *blancos* - 4,000. By the later half of the 19th century, the *sistema de castas de filipinas* would have been transformed by economic and cultural realities while still following the tax system. Although Spanish supremacy would remain paramount, wealth and education would result in the rise of new elites among the *naturales de filipinas* then known as the *hijos del pais* (sons of the country).

The *españoles europeo* would remain at the apex of the hierarchy, followed by a clearly distinct and separate class of *criollos,* by then already known as *filipinos,* and *mestizos de español* immediately after. The *principales* came after the Spanish-blooded *castas*. Originally limited to the *indio* nobility, this *casta* by then included landed, wealthy, educated and enterprising *sangley mestizos* and *indios* who essentially intermarried within the same socio-economic circle. Those educated overseas would earn the distinctive nomenclature of *ilustrado* (enlightened). Among the crown's vassals, the *indio* masses and residual slaves would constitute the bottom of the social ladder.

Although not vassals of the king, *forasteros* (foreigners) constituted an important class of its own in the colony considering that most of them were involved in trade and industry, and paid the highest taxes. Neither recognized nor accepted, the *sangleys* constituted the largest number of *forasteros* in *Filipinas*. Although still classified as *sangleys* in the tax rolls, they had since been appropriately referred to as *chinos*. They competed with the *mestizos* in domestic trade and eventually dominated it. They also closely collaborated with other European and American trading firms acting as their *compradores* (purchasing agents). Many among them would establish permanent residency but would still be considered as society's outsiders. Their influence would nevertheless be significantly felt in the background.

<u>Seeds of an Emerging Identity</u>

The 19th century was a turbulent period in Spain's history. It was a period when the seat of power was constantly contested between liberal and conservative forces and often decided by war. It was a time when Spanish religious, political and economic institutions were radically challenged and incessantly changed through parliamentary or armed struggle. It was when Spain lost most of its American empire. The wars of independence in Spanish America were led by either *criollo* or *mestizo americanos*. Their *filipino* counterparts would hence be treated with suspicion and contempt. Discrimination consequently followed. The segregation would become pronounced as more and more Spaniards displaced from the former American colonies in the 19th century resettled in *Filipinas* spirited with the rising fervor of Spanish patriotism. Discriminated by the *españoles europeo*, the *criollos* and the *mestizos de español* developed attachments to their land of birth and espoused causes affecting them. They would unwittingly plant and nurture seeds of discontent shared by other *hijos del pais*.

Chapter XII

Rise of the Native Cleric

Much had been said about the significant role Spanish missionaries played in educating the *indios de filipinas*. For almost a century, *indio* education was however essentially vernacular literacy using catechism and prayers as the primer. The immediate objective of the friar was to train catechists and servers to spread the word of God more extensively and more productively. He was successful in producing many workers to evangelize the countryside and to serve the parishioners, but it stopped there. In as much as it was decided in Mexico that the *indio* was incapable of becoming a priest, his education did not go farther than the first letters as only those who intended to become priests could pursue higher education. The crown needed to enforce its royal prerogatives under the *patronato real* and to alleviate the huge financial burden of subsidizing Spanish religious clerics. Secularization was deemed to be the answer with the King opening higher education to Spanish mestizos and the sons of indigenous nobility, and establishing conciliar seminaries to develop an adequate number of secular clergy among the *naturales*.

Educating the Indio

In 1595, Capitan Esteban Rodriguez de Figueroa entered into an agreement with the Jesuit Vice-Provincial Ramon Prat to complete at his expense the church and residence which the Jesuits had under construction and to establish a financial endowment of 21,000 pesos for the living expenses of the fathers. In return, *Figueroa was to be acknowledged as the founder and patron in perpetuity of a College of Manila with all the rights, privileges and graces which the Society was accustomed to impart to the founders of its colleges according to its constitution.*[844] The Figueroa endowment was large enough to cover the maintenance of the Jesuits, the *Colegio de Manila* (San Ignacio) and even the *Colegio de San Jose*. In view thereof, the civil authorities transferred the King's *San Jose* subsidy to the *Colegio de Indios,* a college conceived and founded by the Jesuits in 1589.[845] Although essentially for the training of *indio* catechists and missionaries, it was nevertheless an institution whose germinal mission could readily be upgraded sometime in the future. Its existence was however short-lived when the subsidy was discontinued in 1599.[846] The *indio*'s chances for higher education would consequently be delayed by nearly a hundred years.

In the meantime, *indio* education was limited to vernacular catechism. This was what the non-Spanish wards of Fray Diego de Santa Maria OP learned in Letran. Among Fray Diego's wards were Spanish mestizos, and possibly cacique sons of the Dominican missions. Considering the slave culture at that time, it was also not unlikely that *chino* and *moro* slaves counted among the *colegio's* student population as indicated by their presence at the *Hospicio de San Jacinto* in Mexico. The *colegio's* student profile between 1640 and 1655 included origins that paralleled those of a number of *chino* and *moro* slaves documented in Nueva España.[847] The more gifted students among them would be taught Spanish literacy and other lessons that the Spanish boys were normally taught.

Secondary education was however taught at the *Colegio de Santo Tomas* where only students of legitimate pure Spanish blood were accepted subject to the statute of *limpieza de sangre*. Illegitimate Spanish boys together with Spanish mestizos and other non-Spanish students did not advance to grammar school. There were exceptional cases, of course, as virtue and intelligence could not be ignored indefinitely. *Indios* wearing black or purple cotton tunics were reportedly studying latin grammar and the arts at the Dominican and Jesuit colleges as early as 1677.[848] *Indio sacerdotes* (native clerics) were likewise noted to be in the service of P. Fr. Juan Lopez OP, Dominican Bishop of Cebu.[849] It was during the reign of Carlos II and the term of P. Fr. Felipe Fernandez de Pardo OP as Archbishop of Manila, that higher education was officially opened to *indios de filipinas*.[850]

In the Real Cedula dated 22 August 1677 addressed to the Archbishop of Manila, Carlos II expressed his desire for educating *indios* who were inclined to the priesthood and his intention of founding seminaries in the absence thereof. In the interim, he authorized the colleges of St. Dominic and the Society of Jesus to initiate the instruction of *indios* in the Holy Orders.[851] The decree was ambivalently received. The Archbishop convoked a *junta* of religious prelates to discuss the matter. Predictably, the *junta* echoed the established perceptions of the *indio's* incapacity for the higher studies entailed in priesthood. The following minute of Pardo's letter dated 6 June 1680 conveyed the sentiments of the *junta*:

> *The archbishop stated the little inclination that the Indians have for theological and moral studies, and that there was the additional difficulty of their evil customs, their vices, and their preconceived ideas - which made it necessary to treat them as children, even when they were fifty or sixty years old. He considered even the sons of Spaniards, born in the islands, unsuitable for priests, since they were reared by Indian or slave women, because of their defective training and education in youth. Finally, on account of the sloth produced by the climate, and of effeminacy and levity of disposition, it was evident that if they were ordained priests and made ministers to the Indians when they were not sufficiently qualified therefor, through the necessity there was for them, they did not again open a book, and with their vicious habits set a very bad example to their parishioners. That which should be done was to send from España those religious who were most zealous for the conversion of souls.*[852]

Pardo had been singularly maligned for the preceding racist views by critics who failed to discern the fact that the letter represented the junta's views and not necessarily his own alone. His personal views were finally articulated seven years later when he wrote to the King on 15 June 1687 regarding a *colegio de indios* among other proposals to wit:

Sire

> *Considering that it is impossible for the churches of these islands to found seminaries in the form required by the Holy Council of Trent and ordained by Your Majesty in the Laws of the Indies, and that it is of major necessity in all the other parts of Christianity due to the lack of europeans raised in governance, being able to be easily replaced with natives who discover sufficient capacity for all sciences and faculties as is experimented in the University and College of Santo Tomas of the Order of Preachers, which actually has pure* indios *in the final course of Arts more outstanding than the rest of their Spanish classmates, and have obtained in other times the title of sextons, even if always fewer, in view of restrictions in whatever other title [due] to its foundation and statutes which requires those who receive their scholarships to be pure and legitimate Spaniards. And considering likewise that the major cause of many idolatries, as they are being discovered, are the darkness of the natives' ignorance and the greed of the Spanish ecclesiastics and seculars, each one on its own path and that all will be rectified if natives indoctrinated in the sciences and liberal Arts apply themselves in some office in the Republic nurtured from nine to ten years until twenty-five in virtue, prayer, doctrine and withdrawal sans communication from the rest [of the]* indios, *not even dealing with the Spanish boys ...*[853]

His letter admitted the presence of pure *indios* studying the arts on an experimental basis at *Santo Tomas* and fairing better than their Spanish counterparts. He further highlighted that the *indios* were few and restricted in number because the foundation and statutes of *Santo Tomas* restricts scholarships to pure and legitimate Spaniards. He expressed alarm by the prevalence of idolatry among the converted *indios* and believed that education in complete isolation from both Spaniards and other *indios* could address the problem. He continued further by proposing a solution to the problem.

> *... many times to find [a] way to remedy great harm, and did find neither other feasible nor more convenient [solution] than to reduce all those of Spanish blood in the said college, founding other scholarships of distinct color, with which entry in it is enabled whoever person has a part or all of Spanish blood without having to cede rigorous information that is now made [regarding] purity of blood and legitimacy because in this way the founded [beneficiaries] do not lose their esteem and the orphans of the college of saint john lateran, which is of the same order, remain improved, and [from] this disengagement to place in it*

> *considerable number of indio boarders, who with the spaniards suffice to make a sufficient competition for all sciences and faculties...*[854]

He proposed to transfer Spanish orphans of the *Colegio de San Juan de Letran* to *Santo Tomas* so that Letran would be able to accommodate more *indios* in their place. He indicated that a special *beca* would have to be founded in order to accommodate those who could not pass the requirements of *limpieza de sangre* and legitimacy. Furthermore, he volunteered to provide 10,000 pesos of his own funds to support the transferees and to free the existing endowments of Letran to be used primarily for the *indios*. His personal bequest was not however sufficient. He therefor petitioned the King to grant the encomienda of Tabuco with 2,000 tributes from within the surrounding areas to *Santo Tomas* to support the Spanish *becarios* and three professorial chairs for jurisprudence and two for medicine to address the need for legal and medical expertise in the islands.[855]

While carefully avoiding the issue of training future priests, Pardo's letter shared not only his insights and motives concerning the constraints and promise of educating *indio* students in the arts. He also revealed a number of interesting facts about Letran. He established that at that time Letran admitted Spanish and Spanish mestizo orphans whether legitimate or illegitimate. He however failed to explain how *indio* students managed to study arts at *Santo Tomas* when the college was restricted to only pure and legitimate Spanish boys. It is possible that there were already *indio porcionistas* or *manteistas* studying there as *colegiales de letran*. As such, the practice was perhaps carried out on the basis of an untested legal loop hole and was better left ambiguous.

By 1689, Pardo's ideas were clearer and more defined. He wrote about his proposed bequest to the superiors of the Dominican Province of the Holy Rosary on 12 March 1689 containing the following key elements:

> ... *I am minded to place thirteen thousand pesos with the Monetary Fund of the Board of Guardians so that from the interest (which will be three thousand, five hundred) five hundred shall be paid to those holding the Chairs of Law and Medicine that I wish to establish in the University of Santo Tomas. [Two hundred and fifty pesos are to be given, during his lifetime, to Bachiller don Francisco Espinosa de Monteros.] The remaining two thousand five hundred are to be used for the upkeep of as many Spaniards as possible in the aforesaid College, so that the College of St John Lateran may be left free to maintain as many indios as possible who may have from their tenderest years be brought up in virtue and learning. To this end they are to be given a Master, books for their lessons, and time for meditation; nor is the recitation of the Rosary of the Blessed Virgin to be omitted, for by such means they draw close to our Order and obtain every blessing from God our Lord. But after the death of the aforesaid Bachiller don Francisco Espinosa it is my wish that the said two hundred fifty pesos be applied to clothing and maintaining the above mentioned Collegians of St. Thomas university.*

> *I recognize clearly that the most fitting course of action in this matter will always be that chosen by your Reverence, but, in order to contribute to the best of my ability, it seems right to put before your Reverences the ways and means which appear to me to be most proper. That is to say: that all the scholarships in the College of our holy Father Saint Thomas shall continue to be of the standard demanded by the statutes; that six Collegians are to be given an emblem, a sun made of gold or silver gilt, to be worn on the breast of their academic tippets; moreover none shall enter this group except there be a vacancy; and then only those students who have already spent three years as ordinary scholarship holders shall be eligible. Let there also be admitted, with academic gown, but without the tippet, all the remaining Spaniards who can be maintained, provided that they be at least mestizos on the father's side, excluding all the* manteistas.
>
> *In the College of St John Lateran let there be admitted such Indios and Sangley, Chinese and Japanese mestizos as may appear most capable of studies in the humanities and sciences. Thus this Commonwealth may begin to have men of status the lack of whom keeps the temporal state in confusion and disorder. Thus also there may be produced, not only from among the Spaniards, but also from the other races here, good apothecaries, surgeons, trained doctors who shall cure with some degree of accuracy and skill, thus preventing the tragedies that follow when ignorant men without even the rudiments of technical knowledge set themselves up to cure. There may also be remedied the lack of attorneys, notaries, and lawyers; and many acts of injustice may be avoided by the removal of those who, though themselves never pupils, yet play the Domine. The door will thus be opened and the way made straight so that many other natives may leave off their pusillanimity and may raise their hearts to the service of God and the Commonwealth, serving it in many other employments.*[856]

The Dominican Province declined Pardo's offer.[857] Their letter of 24 April 1689 contained the following observations and recommendations:[858]

> First, the transfer of orphans to *Santo Tomas* and their replacement by *indios* alters the foundation of *Colegio de San Juan de Letran* whose objective was the care of Spanish orphan boys and for which purpose an encomienda was conceded by the King and certain incomes bequeathed by others having witnessed the harvest of creditable clerics, religious and seculars from among the *colegio's* ranks.
>
> Second, the special tippet with an encrusted sun to be used by the transferees appeared to be a great inconvenience and an affront to the rest of the students for not wearing the same emblem.
>
> Third, the collection of the *obra pia's correspondencia* (corresponding income) from the *Mesa de la Santa Misericordia* was fraught with great contingency that an unforeseen disaster may compromise the

Province's ability to sustain the transferees considering that the Province was founded and maintained in extreme poverty and would not be able to withstand collection difficulties.

Fourth, having students, the religious of the same Order are able to lector Canon Law with the sole approval of the Province just as they do for Theology and Arts, and in view of the lack of students, the chairs for Canon Law, as well as those of Civil Law and Medicine, are being opposed. Ultimately, it would be more convenient to found a *colegio de indios* with the *obra pia* income used to sustain it instead.

Fifth, the *obra pia's* principal amount could alternatively be used to purchase a livestock station that can generate a more secure income. For this purpose, the Province offered to set aside a place for the new college within the premises of Letran, provide the school's physical facilities and assign religious staff to raise the *indios* in virtue and letters similar to the arrangements enjoyed by Letran.

Archbishop Felipe Fernandez de Pardo OP died on 31 December 1689 at the age of 78. Before he died, he saw to it that his plans would be looked after through his last will and testament signed at San Gabriel on 5 August 1689.[859] The last will provided funds for the establishment of the professorial chairs and scholarship for six *becarios,* but included contingencies. Contained in Pardo's will was a clause authorizing the Dominican Father Provincial to dispose the bequest for the chairs for another *obra pia* that the Provincial deemed to be worthy and that such act would be considered in accordance to Pardo's will in the event the original intent was not feasible.[860] The agreement entered earlier with the *Mesa de la Santa Misericordia* on 20 March 1689 for the management of the *obra pia's* funds provided an option for the withdrawal of the full amount of 13,000 pesos and corresponding income subject to a stated protocol. The Rector of Santo Tomas could withdraw the full amount with the concurrence of the Father Regent and Lectors and the permission of the Father Provincial.[861]

Pardo's death would signal the forthcoming changes in the educational landscape. There was much excitement at how his bequest would finally affect Letran and Santo Tomas. Towards his final years, Pardo elicited the active involvement of Letran students in the cathedral performing altar duties and choir services.[862] It was already widely anticipated that Letran was being groomed for added responsibilities. It was therefor not a surprise when Letran was declared an ecclesiastical college on 11 December 1690 by Mtro. D. Geronimo Fernandez Carvallo, Lord Judge Provisor and Vicar General of the Vacant Archdiocesan Seat of Manila contained in the following order:

> *...Having seen the petition of the Rev. P. Fr. Jose Valdes of the Order of Preachers, Secretary of the Holy Office and President of the Colegio de Los Santos Apostles San Pedro y San Pablo de San Juan de Letran of this said City, regarding the request to declare said College as ecclesiastical, and its collegians as ecclesiastical persons: and that in gatherings*

Plate XLII
Fathers of the Native Secular Clergy

Abp Felipe Fernandez de Pardo OP
1680-1689

- Artist unknown 1680-1689.
The Manila Cathedral

Abp Diego Camacho y Avila
1695-1704

- Artist unknown 1707-1712. Galería de
Obispos y Arzobispos, Guadalajara.

involving burials, processions and other public functions preference should be given them over whichever confraternity and brotherhoods, such as the Santo Cristo de Burgos, and Las Animas; sighting the documentations presented by the said Reverend Father regarding the erection of the said College as Religious of his Order and being accepted as a house and college of his Province of the Most Holy Rosary by Apostolic authority, and considering all the special laws and privileges and immunities that are enjoyed by all the Churches, Convents and Colleges of the said Order; and likewise approved with authority of the Ordinary, and having been instituted, and conserved until this day today, where poor lads, orphan students dedicated to the service and devotion of God and of the Church are maintained and sustained. - Be it so declared as I declare said College as ecclesiastical, and its collegians as ecclesiastical persons during the period that they observe the form of their statutes, that as it is they should be preferred in or out of community in gatherings for burials, processions and other public functions to whichever congregations or persons of said lay brotherhoods and confraternities. And in conformity with this, I order and mandate that from here onwards none of the said brotherhoods and confraternities presume to be preferred in place and order over the said Colegio de San Juan de Letran in the said public functions or be penalized with Excomunion Mayor latae sententiae, uno pro trina canonical monitione premissa; and fifty pesos applied equally between the Holy Cathedral Church and the Holy Crusade for their support. And so that all will be notified of the petition of the said R. P. Fr. Jose Valdes, be it so published and posted in the form of an edict in the customary locations and places. And by this edict, be it so provided, ordered and signed by said Lord Judge Provisor, which I do attest. (Sgd.) Mtro. D. Germo. Fernandez Carvallo.[863]

On 3 July 1691, the *Cabildo Eclesiastico* of the Archdiocese of Manila contested Pardo's last will and testament and filed a counterclaim. P. Fr. Raimundo Berart OP, the Catalan Procurator General of the Dominican Province, filed a petition on 14 July 1694 to execute Pardo's intent to found a *colegio de indios* under the care of the Dominicans.[864] The petition was not a simple one. It entailed addressing the opposition of the *Cabildo Eclesiastico,* and harmonizing the Archbishop's original intent with the concerns of the Dominican Province. An outstanding and respected legal mind, Berart was Pardo's close *confidant* and legal advisor during his incumbency as Archbishop and was considered the most appropriate authority to resolve the issues. There were no documents found containing the decision on the petition. We can only surmise the outcome from the events that followed.

The Chairs of Canon Law, Civil Law and Medicine were approved by Pope Innocent XI and Carlos II. The Tabuco encomienda was awarded to Antonio Nieto on 18 May 1690.[865] The curacy of Tabuco, on the otherhand, was retained by the archdiocese as a secular parish which would be divided on 9 December 1702 into two as originally proposed by Abp. Pardo - Tabuco and San Pedro de Tunazan.[866]

In view of the lack of students and adequate funding, the three chairs remained virtually inoperative and were consequently withdrawn until circumstances made them more viable.[867]

The scholarships which originally entailed the transfer of Spanish students of Letran to Santo Tomas to accommodate *indio* students as their replacements were not implemented as proposed. What transpired was the legal articulation of the institutional difference between *Santo Tomas* the College and *Santo Tomas* the University. The statute limiting students to pure blooded and legitimate sons of *españoles* only applied to the College and not the University. Ineligible students of Spanish and non-Spanish blood could still study at the University but through *Colegio de San Juan de Letran* which was not impeded by any racial statutory limitations. Thus, the six scholars at the University and the corresponding number in Letran became the template for future clerical *becas* involving non-Spanish *becarios*. This resolution also officially opened University admission to non-Spanish paying students known as *manteistas* or *porcionistas*. Furthermore, the practice of students remaining as *colegiales de letran* while studying at *Santo Tomas* would persist in modified forms until the end of Spanish sovereignty.

The Dominicans would likewise go on to acquire an *estancia* in Tabuco; indicating that Pardo's bequest may had been used for that acquisition as a more secure investment to fund a *colegio de indios*. The series of *indio* decrees issued by Carlos II during the last decade of the 17th century made legal obstacles to higher education for natives moot and academic. A separate *colegio de indios* was hence no longer deemed necessary.

By 1700, the first non-Spanish Letran alumnus became a secular priest and was assigned as acting parish priest of Balayan, Batangas.[868] He earned his licentiate and magistral degrees in arts at the *Universidad de Santo Tomas* in 1699 and 1700 respectively.[869] His name was Joseph Kengsun de Ocampo, a *mestizo de sangley* and the first of his race to earn the said university degrees.

<u>Enforcing the Patronato Real</u>

The conflicts that ensued from implementing the decrees of the Council of Trent and the *Patronato Real de las Indias* were the more significant factors that facilitated the increase in native clerics in the Philippines. The Council of Trent introduced many Church reforms strengthening the diocesan prelate's authority over every aspect of religious life and activity within his territory. The implementation of the Tridentine decrees in the Spanish empire was advantageous to the King as he could easily impose his *pase regio* and oath of obedience over all levels of episcopal authority and the secular clergy. However, episcopal visitation and the royal patron's choice of curacy appointments could not be observed among the parishes controlled by the regular religious orders in *Filipinas*.

The maintenance of the regular religious clergy involved tremendous financial cost and was an economic and political strain to the crown. The secular clergy, on the other hand, presented more advantages. The Mexican experience validated the following benefits gained from the seculars: (1) the *diezmo* (tithes) were collected and the king's share was surrendered to the royal treasury; (2) seculars paid for their *mesada eclesiastica* (application fee for a benefice) which regulars were exempted; (3) unlike regulars, seculars do not enjoy subsidies of wine and oil; (4) seculars assisted the crown in collecting alms for the construction of cathedrals; (5) seculars maintained accessible records of parishioners which regulars refused to disclose; (6) parishes replaced with seculars experienced considerable return of *indios* who departed to avoid the personal services and economic exploitation exacted by the regulars and thus improving administration and control; and finally, (7) unlike regulars, seculars who were guilty of any transgression could be penalized monetarily or sent to the holy crusade.[870]

To address the crown's concerns, the solution was simply to replace the friars with secular curates. In 1640, Juan de Palafox y Mendoza, Bishop of Puebla de los Angeles in Nueva España, subjected all the clerics of his diocese to an examination to determine their ability to preach in the native tongue of their curacies as required by various royal decrees.[871] The regulars could not comply with the requisites and were replaced by Palafox with seculars within three days.[872] This was easily done in Puebla because the diocese had 700 qualified seculars who were unable to occupy parish positions filled by regulars.[873] The situation in *Filipinas* was not the same.

Learning from the Mexican debacle, the religious institutes in *Filipinas* studied and learned the indigenous languages. Conversion of the natives was accomplished at a systematic and rapid pace. Hospitals, colleges, orphanages and other social service institutions developed in Mexico were easily replicated. There were fewer criollo secular priests because of the small Spanish population. Hence the colonial government was highly dependent on the friars not only to minister to the Christian native souls but also to politically administer and keep the population under the control of the Spanish crown. Considering the tremendous work accomplished in a distant and isolated colony, the friars were not about to yield to either the visiting authority of any bishop or to the appointive powers of any governor under the *patronato real*. Attempts to impose the Ordinary's oversight was countered with threats of parochial abandonment. In as much as there was not enough Spanish secular clerics to replace the friars, Archbishops and Governors General would eventually capitulate and resign themselves to the *status quo*.[874]

Since the time of Abp. Domingo Salazar OP, archbishops would attempt to impose their authority and implement *visitas* (episcopal visitation) but failed.[875] The only way to neutralize the friars' threatening leverage was to produce more secular priests. Considering the perennial lack of Spanish secular priests, the only viable option left was to develop more non-Spanish curates. It was however an option no Archbishop wanted to pursue until the

The Native Cleric

Plate XLIII

Education Dispelling Ignorance with the Cup of Knowledge

- *Monti, Francesco Riccardo, 1952.* © Colegio de San Juan de Letran

appointments of Abp. Diego Camacho y Avila and Abp. Basilio Sancho de Santa Justa y Rufina SP.

Letran's First Non-Spanish Secular Clerics

Aware of the urgent need to increase the number of secular priests, Abp. Diego Camacho y Avila wrote to Carlos II in 1697 about the need to found a conciliar seminary in Manila before departing from Acapulco enroute to Manila.[876] In the meantime, he had to rely on the resources available to him. Camacho took possession of the vacant seat of Manila on 15 September 1697 and was enmeshed immediately after in various conflicts with the religious institutes. Exhausting his existing criollo secular priests to fill vacated curacies, Camacho resorted to ordaining the first non-Spanish secular priests. Bachiller Don Francisco Baluyut became the first known *indio priest*.[877]

Between 1698 and 1703, Camacho and his suffragan bishops ordained a good number of non-Spanish secular priests. The racial identification process was extremely difficult considering that most of the parties involved used Spanish names and surnames. Non-Spanish priests were principally determined by their documented racial profiles or by their indigenous and Chinese surnames. There were other less reliable criteria used. In his book *The Hidden Light*, historian Luciano P. R. Santiago identified what he considered as the first 12 *clerigos naturales* (native clerics).[878] This book is of special interest as it contains reliable facts concerning the first *mestizo sangley* and *indio* secular priests of *Universidad de Santo Tomas*.[879] As we have indicated earlier, *Colegio de Santo Tomas* accepted only pure and legitimate Spanish boys at that time. Students of other races entered the *Colegio de San Juan de Letran* to access higher education at the *Universidad de Santo Tomas*. The first determinable *mestizo sangley* and *indio* secular priests of the university were therefor *colegiales de letran*.

Camacho ordained three non-Spanish secular priests who earned their university degrees at *Santo Tomas*: Joseph Kengsun de Ocampo - the first *mestizo de sangley* secular priest, Blas de Santa Rosa - the first *indio* pastor, and Juan Mañago - the first *indio* military and hospital chaplain.

Maestro Don Joseph Kengsun de Ocampo was the first determinable *mestizo de sangley* secular priest and chaplain.[880] He was born in Binondo to a wealthy *sangley* father named Kengsun and an *india* mother, Doña Melchora de los Reyes. He was the first *mestizo de sangley* to earn his *Licenciado en Artes* in 1699 and his *Maestro en Artes* in 1700 from the university. Using his inheritance while still a cleric in the minor orders, he founded a 2000 pesos *capellania de misas* of 40 masses a year for his soul, and that of his parents and relatives on 23 March 1699 to which he was installed as chaplain on 30 May by Abp. Camacho. Ordained shortly after, he was the first *mestizo de sangley* to found a *capellania* and the first to serve as *capellan*. He was assigned as assistant parish priest of Balayan, Batangas in 1700, as acting pastor of Malabon, Cavite for a brief period, as assistant parish priest of

Ermita in 1702 and Quiapo in 1706. In 1707, he was granted the title of preacher and general confessor of both men and women by Abp. Francisco de la Cuesta OSH. In 1709, he moved to the vacant see of Nueva Caceres more likely to have better chances of becoming a curate. After serving in Malinao, he became a proprietor pastor of Virac, Catanduanes in 1712. It was a position he would hold for the next 40 years.[881]

Bachiller Don Blas de Santa Rosa earned his Bachelor of Arts degree from UST in 1692. Abp. Camacho ordained him in early 1703. He became the first *indio* curate of *Filipinas* when he was appointed proprietary parish priest of San Policarpio de Tabuco on 7 September of the same year. Being the first *indio* pastor, he was closely monitored and was subjected to an investigation by Abp. Cuesta because of groundless accusations of being negligent in his duties by neighboring friars. On 24 June 1708, he was exonerated by the Vicar Forane, Mro. D. Protacio Cabezas, who vouched for his integrity and diligence supported by written accounts of reliable witnesses to Cuesta. After being housed in a temporary structure since the town transferred to a higher ground in 1665, Santa Rosa built a permanent church edifice for the parish of Tabuco in 1716. He was however regularly incapacitated by illnesses during his lifetime and died in 1733. The parish would remain under the custody of the native clergy until the end of Spanish sovereignty.[882]

Bachiller Don Juan Mañago was the first *indio* military and hospital chaplain. The first graduate of the university with an indigenous surname, he earned his *Bachiller en Artes* in 1700. Archbishop Camacho ordained him in 1705 and appointed him to the dual position of *teniente del cura* (assistant to the parish priest) of Santiago Extramuros and chaplain in the Chapel of the Royal Regiment. He was granted the license to serve his "first and other masses" for a duration of time at the will of his prelate. In 1709, Mañago was licensed as a confessor "except of ministers and merchants" by Cuesta. The following year, he was summoned by Cuesta to be the only *indio* among the extra confessors at the Manila Cathedral for the Lenten season. He was transferred to the Royal Hospital in 1715 as *teniente del capellan* (assistant chaplain). In 1718, he was licensed as general confessor "except for ministers of justice and traders" for a period of a year and six months. He applied for vacant curacies but would not gain an appointment. Like most non-Spanish clerics, the position of *teniente* was the best he could aspire for.[883]

During Camacho's term as Archbishop of Manila, 12 non-criollo *clerigos naturales* were ordained priests. This number would grow to 47 by the end of his successor's term in 1723.[884] In his book published in 1738, Franciscan historian P. Fr. Juan de San Antonio OFM wrote the following statement about Letran:

> *Their principal rule was the education of the said orphans, so that they might go thence as soldiers, and to occupy other posts in the community. Now most of them become priests, studying the branches of philosophy and theology; and almost all the seculars of the bishopric of Camarines*

[Nueva Caceres], and many others in the other bishoprics of the islands, come from that seminary.[885]

By 1760, Abp. Antonio Rojo reported that there were 155 secular clerics in the Archdiocese of Manila consisting of 67 *español*, 41 *indio tagalo*, 12 *indio pampango*, 18 *mestizo sangley*, 8 *mestizo español*, 5 *portugués*, 2 *mestizo portugués*, 1 *mestizo japon* and 1 *indio yloco*.[886] The diocese of Nueva Segovia reported 16 secular clerics consisting of 7 *indios*, 6 *mestizo sangleys* and 3 *mestizo españoles*.[887] In 1761, Bp. Miguel de Ezpeleta reported 17 secular clerics in the Diocese of Cebu.[888] The latest report from the Diocese of Nueva Caceres was dated 2 June 1751 and Bishop Isidoro de Arevalo reported 18 secular clerics then.[889] Before the 1762 British invasion, the total secular clergy population reached 155 clerics in the Archdiocese of Manila. The arrival of Abp. Basilio Sancho de Santa Justa y Rufina SP in 1767 would accelerate the secularization of parishes. Towards the end of his term, the secular clergy population of the Archdiocese of Manila totaled 232 in 1786, representing a 49.7% increase from the 1760 level.[890] Of this number, 23 were *colegiales de letran* studying at the university.

The Conciliar Seminary

Having no heir of his own, Carlos II died on 1 November 1700 bequeathing the Spanish crown to his grand nephew Philippe of Anjou. The succession was contested by Archduke Charles of Austria with the support of the Habsburg's and their allies. The acceptance and enthronement of the Bourbon heir to the Spanish crown precipitated the War of the Spanish Succession in 1702. The war ended 13 years later with the Austrians gaining most of Spain's European domains while the Duke of Anjou retaining the Spanish mainland and its empire in the Indies on the condition he renounced his claim to the French crown. Action on the conciliar seminary Abp. Camacho petitioned for in 1697 would be delayed by the preceding events. Philippe of Anjou became Felipe V of Spain and the establishment of the conciliar seminary of Manila with 8 Spanish *becarios* was approved by him on 28 April 1702.[891]

Governor Domingo Zabalburu received the Real Cedula sometime in 1704 but did not give Camacho a copy of the decree. On 22 June 1704, Camacho wrote the King that he did not have the means to erect the seminary and complained that the governor refused to give him a copy of the decree.[892] Two days later, the governor informed the King that he did not have the resources to implement the project.[893] It was about this time that the titular Patriarch of Antioch Charles Thomas Maillard de Tournon, accompanied by Abbe Gianbattista Sidoti, arrived in Manila on his way to the court of Beijing as Legate of the Holy See.[894] Impressed by the infrastructure of the Metropolitan Archdiocese of Manila, a plan was drawn with Camacho to make Manila the seat of a regional Tridentine Seminary which would train candidates for priesthood from all the Catholic missions in East Asia. Satisfied with the performance of the first native priests, Camacho consulted Letran's Dominican rector with regard to organizing a conciliar seminary

Table X
Spiritual Care of the Souls in Filipinas
1751-1761

Bishopry	Tributos Naturales	Tributos Mestizos	Pueblos	Clerigo	OP	OSA	OAR	OFM	SJ
Manila[a]	53,063	7,155.5	130	14	7	43	15	33	18
Tondo	10,480.5	3,270.0	27	4	2	7	1	4	9
Bulacan	9,099.5	1,381.0	16	1	-	10	-	5	-
Pampanga	11,389.0	1,949.0	26	-	5	19	2	-	-
Cavite	2,380.0	368.5	8	3	-	-	2	-	3
Bay	7,847.5	124.0	27	3	-	-	-	24	-
Balayan	6,181.5	39.0	12	2	-	7	-	-	3
Mindoro	3,217.0	-	8	1	-	-	4	-	3
Mariveles	553.5	-	2	-	-	-	2	-	-
Sambales	1,914.5	24.0	4	-	-	-	4	-	-
Nueva Segovia[b]	42,278	293	65	3	40	22			
Cagayan	8,268.5	-	25	1	24	-			
Ylocos	17,936.0	293	21	2	-	19			
Pangasinan	16,073.5	-	19	-	16	3			
Nueva Caceres[c]	28,417.5		56	18		1	2	35	
N. Caceres	12,990.5		32	6		-	-	26	
Tayabas	845.0		13	3		1	-	9	
Albay	14,582.0		11	9		-	2	-	
Cebu[d]	53,272.0	3,000	120	14		30	17		65
Cebu	13,765.0	3,000		4		6	1		11
Panay	5,827.0			4		4	-		4
Leyte	500.0			1		-	-		30
Negros	4,451.0			4		-	-		3
Yloylo	21,600.0			1		20	-		-
Caraga	5,285.0			-		-	12		-
Calamianes	1,844.0			-		-	4		-
Mindanao	-			-		-	-		11
Marianas	-			-		-	-		6
Total	177,030.5	10,448.5	371	49	47	143	34	68	83

- Cl. *Expediente sobre provisión y visita de doctrinas, 1748.* ES.41091.AGI/23.6.388//FILIPINAS, 303,N.5
[a] Carta de Manuel Antonio Rojo. Manila, 15 julio 1760. Fols. 524r-525v
[b] Estado general de las provincias que comprenden el obispado de Nueva Segovia. Manila, 27 julio 1760. Fols. 526r-526v.
[c] Carta de Isidoro [de Arevalo], obispo de Nueva Caceres. Nueva Caceres, 2 junio 1751 Fols. 64r-72v.
[d] Carta de Miguel de Ezpeleta, obispo de Cebu. Manila, 5 julio 1761. Fols.631r-642v.

while Abbe Sidoti mobilized resources to house some 80 students consisting mostly of *indios* from *Filipinas* and other non-vassals of the King from Asian missions.[895] The seminary was named San Clemente, the patron saint of the reigning Pope.

On 22 June 1707, Zabalburu informed the King that, from the donations solicited by Sidoti, construction of the seminary was initiated adhering to the statutes drawn by Camacho before departing for the seat of Guadalajara.[896] Unfortunately, the new Bourbon King of Spain, was not informed of the changes made to his original patronage of 8 *becarios* before receiving Pope Clement XI's congratulatory brief dated 15 October 1707 through the papal nuncio in Spain.[897] Conscious of his royal prerogatives under the *Patronato Real*, Felipe V was upset by being informed after the fact and reacted accordingly after due investigation.

Real decreto dated 15 August 1708 to the *Consejo de Indias* was issued to expedite the orders to severely reprimand Governor Zabalburu, the *Audiencia* and the former Archbishop of Manila Camacho for their acts regarding the seminary and the revocation of whatever was established.[898] The King's already choleric disposition was further aggravated by Pope Clement XI's acknowledgement of Archduke Charles of Austria as King of Spain on 15 January 1709 after succumbing to military pressure.[899] A series of decrees followed. On 3 March 1710, Real Cedula was issued ordering Governor Martin de Ursua y Arismendi to immediately expedite the removal of all foreign seminarians and allow only 8 Spanish *becarios* as was originally intended.[900] On 2 May 1710, three Real Cedulas were issued ordering: (1) the *Audiencia de Guadalajara* to reprimand Camacho for permitting, as Archbishop of Manila, the Patriarch of Antioch certain acts of jurisdiction in *Filipinas* that were in violation of the King's spiritual and temporal rights;[901] (2) the *Real Hacienda de Filipinas* to disallow the donation made by Camacho to the seminary from the fruits and income of the Manila Cathedral and to assist the current archbishop and his successors with the amount that were consigned to them;[902] and (3) the *Virey de Nueva España* to monitor the activities of Camacho and other bishops with regard to funding missionaries in China, gather and remit to the *Consejo* Briefs, letters and documents pertaining to Tournon, and investigate and report immediately the amounts, purposes and beneficiaries of money sent by Camacho to China.[903] On 31 December 1712, a Real Cedula was issued thanking Archbishop Francisco de la Cuesta for the application and diligence shown in the erection, planning and regimen of the newly founded Manila seminary and ordering the change of the name to San Felipe.[904] The incident was a glimpse of how the Bourbons would wield power to enforce their regalistic views of the *Patronato*.

The building of the *Real Colegio Seminario de San Clemente* was completely demolished, and in its place on another site rose the *Real Colegio Seminario de San Felipe*. As soon as Abp. Cuesta took possession of the Archdiocese, he instituted changes immediately.[905] The statutes were revised increasing the minimum age of seminarians from eight to twelve years of age and limiting

Table XI
Composition of the Manila Archdiocese Secular Clergy

1760[a]		1786[b]	
Cabildo	12	Cabildo	12
Capellanes de Coro	5	Capellanes de Coro	5
Curia Eclesiatica	4	Sagrario	3
Curas	16	Those assigned in :	
Sacristanes	9		
Co-adjutores de curas	7	Tondo	23
		Cavite	14
		Bulacan	4
		Batangas	5
		Laguna de Bay	5
		Bataan	8
		Pampanga	26
		Mindoro	6
		Zambales	3
Capellanes	19	Chaplains	16
Presbiteros sin empleo	17	Seminary based priests	24
Operarios sin empleo	30		
Diaconos	5	Deacons	9
Sub-diaconos	7	Subdeacons	11
Ordenado menores	9	Minor Orders	6
Ordenado tonsuras	1		
Ordenantes	14	Those without orders	5
		Those in:	
		San Carlos	13
		Santo Tomas	8
		San Jose	3
		San Juan de Letran	23
Total	155	Total	232

[a] Carta de Manuel Antonio Rojo. Manila, 15 julio 1760. Fols. 524r-525v. Cl. *Expediente sobre provisión y visita de doctrinas, 1748.* ES.41091.AGI/23.6.388//FILIPINAS,303,N.5

[b] Coronel, 101-102.

them to *naturales de Filipinas*. The 8 *becas de fundacion* were to be for Spaniards or at least *cuarterones* with no more than 16 *colegiales* in strict compliance with the King's cedula. Admission was opened to *porcionsitas* who paid an annual tuition of 100 pesos. The chair for arts was inaugurated on 6 May 1712 and that of theology on 5 July 1714.[906] These chairs were abolished and seminarians who wished to pursue these degrees were sent to UST. Grammar and other non-degree subjects were retained at *San Felipe*. In as much as *porcionistas* were also accepted in the more established colleges of Manila, it was safe to assume that the latter schools were preferred choices. The *colegiales de letran* among the UST graduates during this period could not be ascertained in view of the *colegiales de san felipe* present among its ranks.

In 1717, the King established the chairs of canons, institutes and laws at *San Felipe* effectively elevating it into a university.[907] The difficulty of sustaining the professors was conveyed to the King by the Audiencia on 10 June 1726. While awaiting for the royal disposition, the Audiencia transferred the chairs to the *Colegio de San Ignacio*. The Dominicans protested the transfer as it effectively qualified the Jesuit *academia* to become a public university of general studies. On 26 July 1730, a Real Cedula was issued suspending the grant of chairs to *Colegio de San Ignacio* by the Manila Audiencia as protested by the *Colegio-Universidad de Santo Tomas*.[908] Three years later, Real Cedula dated 23 October 1733 granted each one of *San Ignacio* and *Santo Tomas* a chair in Canon Law and a chair in Civil Law.[909] The implementation of this decree would technically consider both the Dominican and Jesuit Colleges as full-pledged public universities. Later that year, Dominican Procurator General Salvador de Contreras OP petitioned that Santo Tomas be erected into a general university requesting permission to secure an extension of the bull issued previously by Innocent XI authorizing Santo Tomas to grant degrees in various faculties.[910] Pope Clement XII issued a Bull dated 2 September 1734 granting the extension and included the authority to establish other faculties in the future.[911]

San Felipe continued to operate essentially as a grammar school until it ceased to do so during the British occupation of 1762-1764. It would not be until 1768 that the conciliar seminary reopened in the premises of the *Real Colegio de San Jose* with Spanish *becarios* replaced by native *colegiales* under the care of Piarist religious.[912]

Governor-General Jose de Raon received instructions to implement the expulsion of the Jesuits and the *desamortizacion* (confiscation) of all their assets on 18 May 1767 and implemented them the following day.[913] San Jose was converted into barracks until Abp. Basilio Sancho de Santa Justa y Rufina intervened and secured the governor-general's approval to entrust the college to his care pending the King's action on his petition. In his letter to the King, Santa Justa proposed conversion of the college into a conciliar seminary for the native clergy.[914] He further proposed Santo Tomas to be transferred to the premises of San Ignacio considering that the latter's site was more suitable for a university. Should this be acted upon favorably, he

Plate XLIV

The Native Secular Parish Priest
- *Lozano, Jose Honorato, 1847.* Propiedad del Biblioteca Nacional de España bdh0000025737

further proposed to make the present site of Santo Tomas available for the conciliar seminary in view of the latter's decrepit state.[915]

The Real Audiencia protested the archbishop's petition on 12 July 1769. The King agreed with the Audiencia on 21 March 1771 and reprimanded Santa Justa for employing unlicensed Piarists whose presence and status in the colony were legally unconfirmed, and for violating the original charter of San Jose, which was founded for the education of Spanish boys, and the prohibition to innovate the colleges and secular houses that were previously entrusted to the Jesuits. He was upset by the

> ...spoliation of the Spanish collegiates of their possession of the college of San Joseph and erecting in it what they call a seminary for Indians, since for these and the Sangley mestizos there is the above-mentioned college of San Juan de Letran, and the conciliar seminary was already founded...

He admonished the governor not to

> ... allow the archbishop to meddle with anything pertaining to the college as it is under my royal protection, and consequently, wholly independent of the ecclesiastical ordinary as are the other pious foundations mentioned by the council of Trent. The governor ought not to permit the archbishop to meddle in anything concerning the seminary, as there is also a royal foundation, namely that of San Phelipe, which appears to have been incorporated after the above-mentioned San Joseph.

He resolved

> ...to order and command the present governor and captain-general of those islands, and to charge the said archbishop (as is done by dispatches of this date) that they shall in the future leave things in the condition and state in which they existed before the above-mentioned innovations were made, and that the collegiates must go and take their studies to the university of Santo Tomas of that city.[916]

Carlos III did not however leave the conciliar seminary empty handed. On 3 June 1783, the *Colegio Maximo de San Ignacio* was officially merged with the *Seminario Conciliar de Manila*. San Ignacio's building was perpetually transferred to the seminary and the fate of its church placed under the discretion of the archbishop. The seminary would hence be always under the charge of seculars, free from any intervention by regulars. The hacienda of Mariquina was not however transferred as its income was used to fund the pensions of ex-Jesuits and other court expenses.[917] To augment the seminary's income, the King authorized the Manila Archbishop to utilize the income of San Ignacio's haciendas for the maintenance of the seminarians on 12 March 1784.[918] In view of the King's gracious munificence, the conciliar seminary was renamed *Real Colegio Seminario de San Carlos* after the monarch's patron saint.

The expulsion of the Jesuits changed the landscape of ecclesiastical education in *Filipinas* which persisted until the latter half of the 19th century. The educational innovations introduced by Carlos III in Spain would be transplanted to its colonies in the indies. The *Universidad de Santo Tomas* became the sole public university and the *colegiales* from four *colegios* attended its halls: *españoles* and *criollos* from *Santo Tomas* and *San Jose*, and *indios, mestizo españoles* and *mestizo sangleys* from *San Juan de Letran* and *San Carlos*.

Secularization

Before Camacho took possession of the vacant seat of Manila on 15 September 1697, he was an overstaying guest of the Bishop of Puebla de los Angeles, Manuel Fernandez de Sahagun y Santa Cruz, who was a disciple of Palafox's secularization policy.[919] Sahagun crystallized for Camacho that secularization was the most effective way to enforce his episcopal authorities and the King's royal prerogatives under the *Patronato*.

The influence of Sahagun did not auger well for the five regular religious institutes. It would appear that the prelates of the Manila religious institutes anticipated Camacho to vigorously exact his episcopal authority on them and therefore entered into a secret pact on 5 May 1697 at the Augustinian *Convento de San Pablo*. The pact named as *General de Concordia* (Concordat General) contained 18 articles agreeing to meet and to plan united efforts to address any papal briefs or bulls, royal decrees, or regulations issued by the archbishop and bishops, governor-general or the *real audiencia* with mass resignation as their principal measure against episcopal visitation. It also outlined protocols and observances to be followed in settling differences and in fostering brotherhood in order to ensure perpetual unity, peace, and cooperation among the Augustinians, Franciscans, Jesuits, Dominicans, Recollects and the Brothers of Saint John of God.[920] The concordat would prove to be an effective measure to preserve the status quo.

As soon as Camacho was installed Archbishop of Manila, he immediately conducted *visitas* of the cathedral and its secular parishes. Inspite the opposition of the regulars, he proceeded to conduct *visitas* of their parishes and hospitals. During these forays, the regular clergy invoked obedience to their respective orders' superiors and not to the Ordinary. Camacho excommunicated and replaced the religious concerned with seculars. He unprecedentedly began ordaining *mestizos de español, indios*, and *mestizos de sangley* as secular priests and took initial steps to organize a first Tridentine Seminary after consulting the rector of Letran.

Camacho's actions on enforcing episcopal visitation were approved and supported by the crown. Any further action on the *visita* issue was however held in abeyance while the matter was pending in the courts. The case was eventually elevated to the Congregation of Cardinals in Rome for resolution. In the midst of this and other contentious issues, Camacho's appointment as the new Bishop of Guadalajara was issued in 1703.[921] On 19 January 1705, the Congregation of Cardinals declared regular clerics to be subject to the visitation of the archbishop of Manila and bishops. The implementing brief of Pope Clement XI dated 30 January 1705 contained the following:

> *By apostolic authority and the tenor of these presents, we determine and declare that the right to visit the regulars is within the authority of the archbishop of Manila and the other bishops of the Philippine Islands in matters that concern the healing of souls and the administration of sacraments, and the said regulars cannot resign from the parishes or christian villages mentioned under the penalty of censures and loss of property and other arbitrary penalties…*[922]

The Brief further repealed and rendered all prior rulings and provisions that contravened the Brief's text null and void; including those contained in the constitutions of the religious orders and thus removing a traditional argument to impede episcopal visitation. Felipe V added his *pase regio* and transmitted the Brief with Real Cedula dated 2 September 1705 to the new Archbishop of Manila Francisco de la Cuesta OSH and Governor General Domingo de Zabalburu. The triumphant outcome was however short lived.

The religious orders' petitioned the King to suspend implementation of Pope Clement XI's Brief and to initiate its devolution. The Archbishop and the Governor General withheld implementation of the Brief until the appeal was acted on by the King. The *Consejo de Indias* issued a *consulta* (opinion) dated 6 February 1711 recommending that the Papal Brief should be implemented. However, it cautioned that the imminent abandonment of the parishes and mass resignation of the regular clerics would result in serious consequences. It further highlighted that using their utmost prudence and discretion the Archbishop and suffragan Bishops were better placed to decide whether to implement or suspend the Brief with the crown fully supporting their decision and action. This understanding was referred to as the *Acuerdo de Manila* (Manila Accord).[923] Felipe V agreed and issued a secret decree dated 21 October 1711 authorizing the Archbishop and Bishops to use their discretion in either implementing or suspending the Brief and suggested alternative measures to enforce the *visitas*.[924] Cuesta opted to suspend the Brief and to maintain the status quo. The other Bishops, the Governor General and the Audiencia followed Cuesta's lead.

The succeeding Archbishops and suffragan Bishops would exercise the same policy beyond the next 50 years notwithstanding the apostolic constitutions of Pope Benedict XIV of 6 November 1744 (*Firmandis*), of 24 February 1745 (*Quamvis*) and of 8 November 1751 (*Cum Nuper*) affirming the power of the bishop to conduct *visitas* over regular curates.[925] Meanwhile, Fernando VI ordered the secularization of the *doctrinas* and *curatos* in the archdioceses of Lima, Mexico and Santa Fe on 4 October 1749.[926] This order was extended to all the dioceses in the Indies on 1 February 1753.[927] On that year, the Concordat of Bologna was entered into between Fernando VI and Pope Benedict XIV consolidating the King's control over the Spanish Church under the *Patronato Universal* (Universal Patronage). His royal rights of patronage from then on included the Catholic churches on the Spanish peninsula. On 23 June 1757, Fernando VI modified his

Plate XLV
Patrons of the Native Secular Clergy

Simon de Anda y Salazar

- Artist unknown 1876, Lopez Memorial Museum.

Abp Basilio Sancho de Santa Justa y Rufina Sch P.

- Artist unknown 1766-1787 , The Manila Cathedral.

secularization decree of *doctrinas* by restricting the nomination of a secular cleric only when the *doctrina* was vacant and when the incumbent religious clerics were proficient in the indigenous languages or the indigenes were proficient in Spanish. It was also conceded that every religious order can keep two of the most prosperous curacies in every diocese.[928] The regular clergy in *Filipinas* however continued resolutely to ignore the King's prerogative to secularize parishes and appoint curates under the *patronato*.[929]

In response to the King's inquiry, Dean Miguel de Ezpeleta of the vacant seat of Manila reported on 27 July 1757 that there were 13 regular curacies in the archdiocese that could easily be transferred to secular clerics.[930] These included the parishes of Binondo, Pandacan, Dilao, Sampaloc, Tondo, Malate, Parañaque, Pasig, Santa Cruz, San Miguel, Pagsanjan, Bulacan and Bacolor. By 5 July 1760, Archbishop Antonio Rojo reported to Carlos III the status of the secular clerics of Manila.[931] He indicated that since the time of Camacho the number had doubled but a new problem had emerged. 45 of the 155 secular clerics were unemployed.[932]

It would appear that there were sufficient seculars to take over certain curacies administered by the regular clerics within the archdiocese. The intervening British invasion would however delay whatever secularization measures may had been planned. It would not be until the arrival of Abp. Basilio Sancho de Santa Justa y Rufina SP in 1767 and of Governor-General Simon de Anda y Salazar in 1770 that Carlos III would finally have his way.

End of the Religious Conspiracy

After the death of Fernando VI, Carlos III ascended to the throne and began to make his distinct presence felt. Political observers anticipated that the regalist views of the *patronato* would be rigidly enforced and its major obstacle, the Jesuits, rendered impotent. The Dominican Master General duly instructed the Philippine Dominican Province to adhere and yield to the episcopal authority of the ordinary and the *patronato real* of the King and his vice patron.[933] As such, the Dominicans would be the first party to the *1697 General de Concordia* to withdraw its participation and the first religious institute to comply with the papal bulls on visitation and the dictates of the *patronato real*.[934]

Abp. Basilio Sancho de Santa Justa y Rufina SP took the direct route from *España* to *Filipinas* via the Cape of Good Hope and not through the usual Spain-Vera Cruz-Acapulco-Manila route.[935] One could only surmise that he wanted to arrive in Manila months ahead of the official dispatch bearing the *Pragmatica* (Pragmatic) of Carlos III expelling the Society of Jesus from the Spanish empire. Being adequately briefed about the situation in Manila and the King's confidential plans regarding the Jesuits, his first act was to request the prelates of the five religious institutes on 4 August 1767 to state their positions regarding the bulls of Pope Benedict XIV and the compliance of the regular curates to the real cedulas regarding the visitations of the ordinary. The Dominicans responded with their unequivocal compliance.[936]

The Augustinians, Franciscans and Recollects presented their identical resolution and arguments of maintaining as always the status quo in the archipelago. The Jesuit's reply was surprisingly ambiguous but they would eventually join the ranks of the other three.[937]

Santa Justa began his visitations in January 1768. He visited the secular parishes of his archdiocese and carefully avoided those of the regular clerics. He however visited and was warmly received in the Dominican parishes of Santos Reyes de Parian on 18 March and San Gabriel de Binondo the following day. These were the first visitations of parishes under the care of regular curates ever conducted by the ordinary. The submission of the Dominicans to the visitation prompted Governor General Jose Raon to enforce the *real patronato* on 14 April. The Dominican provincial, P. Fr. Joaquin del Rosario, responded on 15 April by surrendering the Parian, Binondo and the six Bataan parishes to diocesan replacements. Informed the day after, Santa Justa immediately deployed secular curates.[938] The submission of the Dominicans to the vice patron and the archbishop and the measures taken on the Dominican parishes alarmed the other orders.

The expulsion of the Jesuits followed on 19 May with their 15 parishes in the Archdiocese of Manila systematically taken over by seculars.[939] The diocese of Cebu was most affected considering that 62.5% of its *pueblos* were Jesuit parishes. Raon requested the Dominican provincial to deploy the displaced Dominican curates to the south. The Dominicans were sent to minister the towns of Iloilo, Hiniaras, Mandurriao and Molog in the island of Panay and Ilog, Cabancalan, Jimamaylan and Guilgonan in Negros. By 1776, the Bishop of Cebu transferred these ministries to seculars.[940] Governor General Simon de Anda y Salazar arrived in Manila on 15 July 1770 to replace Raon.[941] Anda soon after began to enforce the *patronato real* which Raon abruptly abandoned, and ordered the removal of the Augustinians from their Pampanga and Ilocos parishes for continuing to defy the *visita* and the *patronato*.[942] Seculars took over the Pampanga parishes completely in 1771 while the Dominicans were assigned to the Ilocos parishes of Namacpan, Balanang, Bacnotan, San Fernando. San Juan Evangelista, Bauang, Aringay and Agoo.[943] By then out of the 121 parishes in the Archdiocese of Manila, the secular parishes increased from 16 at the arrival of Santa Justa to 57 at the expense of the religious orders - 15 taken from the Jesuits, 8 from the Dominicans and 18 from the Augustinians.[944] The Augustinian's pleaded their case to the King.

The actions of Anda and Santa Justa were antagonistic to the friars who filed a series of legal cases at the King's court.[945] The deliberations were conducted separately by the Council of the Indies and a five-member Junta headed by the Primate of Toledo, Cardinal F. Antonio Lorenzana. On the matter of *visita*, *patronato real* and secularization, the Council supported the friars' position while the Junta supported the actions of the governor-general and the archbishop. Both however agreed that the manner the Augustinians were expelled from their parishes was not justified and recommended restitution and the return of the parishes to the Augustinians. They likewise agreed that the context of the *1697 General de Concordia* was subversive and scandalous, and should be destroyed. Carlos III acted accordingly by issuing Real Cedula dated 9 November 1774 ordering the restitution of the Augustinian sequestered assets, approving the secularization of the Order's Pampanga parishes and ordering to continue to do the same to parishes throughout the archipelago as they become vacant.[946] On the same date, another Real Cedula was issued annulling the *1697 General de Concordia*, prohibiting its use and ordering the seizure of copies in the conventual archives of Santo Tomas and San Francisco for transmittal to the *Consejo de Indias*.[947]

The King finally had his way with the enforcement of the *visita* and the *patronato real*. The expulsion of the Jesuits and the submission of the Dominicans and Augustinians took its toll on the Franciscans and Recollects who continued obstinately to resist. To accelerate the secularization of the parishes, the crown ceased to issue licenses to transport additional religious personnel from Spain to Filipinas. The Philippine Dominican Province did not receive any new Spanish religious between 1771-1785.[948] During the 15-year ban, the Dominicans had to resort to extraordinary means to address the toll of age, health and mortality.

First Mestizo Sangley Dominicans

The fall of Manila to the British in 1762 precipitated insurrections in various parts of the countryside. The *sangleys* of the Parian and the surrounding areas allied themselves with the invaders and exacted a heavy toll in Spanish lives and property.[949] A group from Guagua even conspired against Simon de Anda y Salazar but suffered a bloody reversal with the plot's timely discovery.[950] At the end of the war in 1764, the British surrendered Manila to Anda who proceeded to impose restrictive measures to guard against treacherous *sangleys*.[951] The Spanish hatred and suspicion for the *sangleys* persisted long after; adversely affecting even the most loyal *mestizo sangleys*. In education, *mestizo sangleys* were consequently discouraged from pursuing higher education. It was under this discriminatory cloud that an application for the *licenciado en filosofia* degree submitted by a *colegial de letran* was rejected in 1773.

The *colegial* was Francisco Mariano de los Santos, a *mestizo de sangley* born in Santa Cruz, Manila in 1754. He was the son of Capitan Julian de los Santos, a noted military man and Letran alumnus. He entered Letran on 14 June 1768 together with his three brothers - Mariano, Manuel and Casimiro. An outstanding student, he became Letran's *decano de colegiales* (senior student), an honor denied to San Vicente Liem de la Paz.[952] He obtained his *bachiller en filosfia* in 1770 and in 1773, he applied for the licentiate degree but was turned down by the university's *claustro* (senate) with no reason given.[953] The *claustro* consisted of the Dominican administrators and the *graduados* (graduates with a licentiate decree and higher). He reapplied later that year and was again rejected but without the Dominicans' opposition this time. With steely determination, he filed a suit against the *graduados* at the Real

Table XII
Ethnic Profile of the Manila Archdiocese Secular Clergy

1760[a]	
Español	67
Indio Tagalo	41
Indio Pampango	12
Mestizo Sangley	18
Mestizo Español	8
Portuguez	5
Mestizo Portuguez	2
Mestizo Japon	1
Indio Yloco	1
Total	155

1782[b]	
Mestizo Sangley	61
Indio Tagalo	57
Indio Pampango	31
Mestizo Español	20
Criollo	15
Unknown	5
Chino	2
Indio Camarino (Bicolano)	2
Indio Ilocano	2
Español Europeo	1
Mestizo Japon	1
Total	197

[a] Carta de Manuel Antonio Rojo. Manila, 15 julio 1760. Fols. 524r-525v. Cl. *Expediente sobre provisión y visita de doctrinas, 1748*. ES.41091.AGI/23.6.388//FILIPINAS,303,N.5

[b] Escoto, Salvador P. and Schumacher, John N. SJ. "Filipino Priests of the Archdiocese of Manil, 1782." *Philippine Studies*, vol. 24, no. 3, (Third Quarter 1976), pp. 326-343. *JSTOR*, JSTOR, www.jstor.org/stable/42632916. The 1782 list did not include the prebends which were usually all Españoles.

Audiencia. The Audiencia queried the grounds for the rejection and the *claustro* replied "for being a *mestizo asiatico*."[954] While waiting for the decision, he earned his *bachiller* in Canon Law in 1775.

Following de los Santos' lead, *a mestizo de sangley* schoolmate, Dionisio Vicente de los Reyes, also applied for *licenciado en filosofia* in 1776. Born in Binondo, de los Reyes completed his *bachiller en filosofia* in 1772 with distinction. Abp. Santa Justa granted him the rare privilege of publishing his thesis just before graduation. He completed his *bachiller en teologia* in 1775. As in de los Santos' case, his application was rejected. The matter was resolved by Anda's interim successor, Pedro Sarrio, who allowed the official admission of the *mestizo de sangley* applicants to the degree in the absence of the *graduados* in 1776. The controversy did not end there. The Audiencia's *oidor*, Emeterio Cacho Calderon de la Barca, brought the case to the attention of the *Consejo de Indias* on 24 December 1776. It would not be until 7 December 1781 when orders were issued to reprimand Barca and to manifest the approval of the action taken by Sarrio.[955]

Both de los Santos and de los Reyes received their *maestro en artes* degree in 1777. Shortly after, they became not only the first *mestizo de sangley* doctors but also the first *naturales de filipinas* to receive doctorate degrees.[956] Their outstanding credentials and the ban on transporting new Spanish Dominicans to the Filipinas opened the door for their admission to the Order. Both received the habit and professed together on 28 April 1778; becoming the first *mestizo de sangley* Dominicans. De los Santos assumed the name of P. Fr. Francisco Borja del Rosario OP and worked in the Dominican missions of Cagayan for 27 years. He became Vicar of Abulug, Fotol and San Juan Nepomuceno (Pamplona) and died receiving the holy sacraments on 17 October 1807 at Abulug. De los Reyes assumed the name of P. Fr. Dionisio de Santo Domingo OP and became a missionary of Ituy and Paniqui. He died in Angadanan in 1780.[957] Aside from the two, there would be only three other *mestizo de sangleys* who would be ordained into the Province of the Most Holy Rosary.[958]

Victims of Propaganda

On 11 December 1776, Carlos III issued a Real Cedula suspending the secularization decree of 9 November 1774 and reinstating the effectivity of Real Cedula dated 23 June 1757.[959] The new decree ordered the return of parishes to their former religious ministers observing the rules of the *patronato real* and *visita eclesiastica*, the devolution of the *mesadas* collected, and the retention of the competent secular clerics in vacated curacies according to the provisions of the 1757 decree.

Santa Justa did not however implement the said ambiguous decree and issued an *acto de obediencia* dated 30 June 1778 (traditional form for *obedesco pero no cumplo*) citing the following reasons: (1) the secularization was carried out with all the laws scrupulously adhered to; (2) as such the current parish priests could not be removed without just cause and due process; (3) in the event that the current parish priests were removed, the Archdiocese would be obligated to assume the burden of sustaining them which it was unable to do so and thus reducing them to mendicancy.[960] Santa Justa's position was supported by the *Promotor Fiscal* on 2 September 1778 and Governor Juan Basco y Vargas on 11 August 1779.[961] Notwithstanding this legal barrier, the implementation of the 11 December 1776 decree would be significantly delayed but not altogether stopped.

Ironically, the gains achieved jointly by Santa Justa and Anda were affected adversely by Anda's own letter to the King before his death. Anda's letter of 3 January 1776 lamented the quality of the indigenous secular priests taking over the parishes and dreaded the future of the native population's Catholic upbringing under their care.[962] The possible motives behind Anda's transformation had been analyzed and dissected comprehensively by Salvador P. Escoto.[963] Whatever his personal motives may actually had been, the issue of the native clergy's competence however was nothing new. It had been the subject of a contentious debate for centuries. The native clergy had its notable detractors and supporters alike. So what could have tilted the precarious balance in its disfavor?

The two sides of the debate could be summarized by two notable churchmen in the mid-18th century: the oppositors represented by P. Fr. Gaspar de San Agustin OSA and the supporters represented by P. Juan Jose Delgado SJ.[964]

P. Fr. Gaspar de San Agustin OSA wrote a letter to a friend on 8 June 1720 disparaging the character of the *indio* by highlighting an array of negative qualities that he claimed to apply to the *indio* racial profile in general.[965] He went on further to decry the consequences if an *indio* was ordained:

> *It does not seem good that I should refrain from touching on a matter which is most worthy of consideration, and that is, that if God because of our sins and theirs should desire to chastise the flourishing Christian communities of these Islands by placing them in the hands of natives ordained to the priesthood (which seems likely to happen very soon), if, I say, God does not provide a remedy for this, what abominations will result from it! because to say that they can change from the said behaviors and bad habits is impossible. Rather their pride will be aggravated with their elevation to so sublime a state; their avarice with the increase opportunity of preying on others; their sloth with their no longer having to work for a living; and their vanity with the adulation that they must needs seek, desiring to be served by those whom in another state of life they would have had to respect and obey; in such wise, that the malediction of Isaias, 24, shall overtake this nation: "It shall be as with the people, so with the priest." for the indio who seeks the holy orders does so not because he has a call to a more perfect state of life, but because of the great and almost infinite advantages which accrue to him along with the new state of life which he chooses. How much better it is to be a Reverend Father than to be a yeoman or a sexton! What a difference between paying a tribute and being paid a stipend! Between being drafted to cut timber (polo) and being waited on hand and foot! Between rowing a galley and being conveyed in one! All of which does not apply to the Spaniard, who by becoming a cleric deprives himself of the opportunity of becoming a mayor, a captain or a general, together with many other comforts of his native land, where his estate has more to offer than the whole nation of indios. Imagine the airs with which such a one will extend his hand to be kissed! What an incubus upon the people shall his father be, and his mother, his sisters, and his female cousins, when they shall become great ladies overnight, while their betters are still pounding rice for their supper! For if the indio is insolent and insufferable with little or no excuse, what will he be when elevated to so high a station? ... What reverence will the indios themselves have for*

such a priest, when they see that he is of their color and race? Especially when they realize that they are equals or betters, perhaps, of one who managed to get himself ordained, when his proper station in life should have been that of a convict or a slave?[966]

P. Juan Jose Delgado SJ wrote *Historia general, sacroprofana, politica y religiosa de las islas del Poniente llamadas Filipinas* which he completed on 6 June 1754. In his description of the archipelago's natives, he included San Agustin's letter and used it as a basis to add his own commentary. In as much as the negative behavior and inclination of the *indios* were comprehensively and passionately covered by San Agustin, Delgado focused on the many positive qualities.[967] Having been exposed to the tremendous diversity of the natives, he went on to criticize San Agustin's letter as a *hyperbolical criticism* that is *unsupported by solid evidence* and that unfairly attributes specific cases to be universally applicable to all the *indio* races.[968] To *uncover the truth, recover the dignity of the indios, and remove the mistrust and ill effects engendered on the readers* of the letter, Delgado eruditely and systematically refuted each of San Agustin's allegations.[969]

On the matter of native clerics, Delgado had the following to say:

I know some seculars in the islands, who although indians, can serve as an example and confusion among the europeans. I shall only bring forward two examples: one, the bachelor Don Eugenio de Santa Cruz, judge-provisor of this bishopric of Santisimo Nombre de Jesus, and calificador of the Holy Office, a full blooded Indian and a native of Pampanga. And inasmuch as the author of this letter confesses that the Pampangos are a different people, I shall name another, namely, the bachelor Don Bartolome Saguinsin, a Tagalog, a cura of Quiapo, outside the walls of Manila, an Indian, and a native of the village of Antipolo. I knew his parents and had friendly relations with them while I was minister in that village. Both men were esteemed for their abilities and venerated for their virtues, in Tagalos and Visayas; leaving the names of many others worthy to be included in this history, living and dead, because brevity exhorts me to do so.

Those reared in any of the four colleges in Manila for the clerical estate are all the sons of chiefs, people of distinction among the Indians themselves and not of the timauà *or of the class of* olipon, *as the Visayan says, or* maharlika *or* alipin, *as the Tagalog calls the slaves and freedmen. The reverend fathers of St Dominic or of the Society [of Jesus] rear these boys and instruct them in virtue and learning; and if they have any of the vices of Indians, these are corrected and suppressed by the teaching and conversation of the fathers. Furthermore, when the most illustrious bishops promote any of these men to holy orders, they do not proceed blindly, ordaining any one whomever to be advanced - but only with great consideration and prudence, and after informing themselves of his birth and his morals, and testing him first before the ministry of souls is entrusted to him; and to say the contrary is to censure the most illustrious prelates, to whom we owe so much veneration and reverence.*[970]

Delgado believed that

> *if children, either boys and girls were taken from Filipinas to Viscaya or to Castilla, the natives [of those countries] would not distinguish them from the Vizcainos, Castilians or mountaineers. For their vices are not due so much to their nature, as to their bad rearing and education; and they are easily instructed both in the evil and in the good.*[971]

Unfortunately, the bad rearing and education he referred to would eventually manifest in the Dominican and Jesuit universities. In 1768, Anda lamented:

> *It is to the interest of the religious orders that there should not be formed and should never be any secular clergy, for so, there being no one to take their places, they may continue in their possession of the curacies, and the King in his long-standing and thoroughly troublesome burden of sending our missionaries at his own expense who when they arrive here are so many more enemies to his interests. In accordance with this policy and with remarkable harmony the two universities [Santo Tomas and San Ignacio] have made it an invariable rule to impart a merely cursory training, in order to spoil in this way even the small number of assistant priests.*[972]

In view of the preceding situation, the Augustinians found it difficult to believe that Abp. Santa Justa was able to source enough qualified and virtuous native secular priests to takeover the vacated Pampanga parishes. Pernicious rumors began to circulate in Manila that *there were no more oarsmen to be found for the coasting vessels, because the archbishop had ordained them all.*[973] The impact of this calumny would continue to reverberate today. As recent as the 1970's, some Philippine secular priests still believed it to be true.[974] This allusion that *indio* clerics were no better than boat rowers echoed Gaspar de San Agustin's scathing criticism. Accusations of inadequacy and immorality would persist. It has since been proven to be untrue. John Larkin attested to the fact that *for a period of nearly eighty years between 1773 and 1854, when the Augustinians returned, only one case hinted that a native priest deviated from his priestly discipline.*[975] Escoto's research also indicated that the indiscriminate mass ordination Abp. Santa Justa was accused of was baseless.[976]

The debate on the native secular priest's competence would continue until the end of Spanish sovereignty. There would always be supporters of the indigenous clerics and their detractors. Unfortunately, the detractors were better organized and had the relentless machinery to lobby the halls of power and to conduct calumnious propaganda. They used both avenues effectively to discredit secularization, the indigenous clergy, and their supporters. Copious disparaging documents were written and incessant repetitive legal pleas filed to bury whatever resistance left. In the end, Anda and Santa Justa wilted to the pressure.

By 1776, Anda was recalled to Spain to serve his remaining term with the *Consejo de Castilla,* while Santa Justa was patiently awaiting action on his request for transfer. Gov. Simon de Anda y Salazar died on 30 October 1776 before receiving his new appointment, while Abp. Basilio de Santa Justa y Rufina died on 12 December 1787 five days before his appointment as Bishop of Granada was approved.[977] Carlos III died on 14 December 1788 and was succeeded by a weak and irresolute son. The secularization of the parishes would continue unabated until Governor General Juan Antonio Martinez assumed office in 1822; opening a new chapter into the ecclesiastical conflicts.

The 19th century ushered in the independence movement among the American colonies. The reaction to the involvement of *naturales* in the wars of independence that followed translated into the reduction of the few native secular parishes in *Filipinas*. The racial issues that traditionally characterized the opposition to native secular clerics evolved into the alarming issue of national security. The sedition card would begin to be played in the friar's propaganda game; making parishes appear vulnerable to the influence of disloyal native priests. The disparagingly accusatory word *filibustero* (subversive) would be used increasingly. The native priests finally came to realize that they had to use countermeasures to neutralize the negative propaganda. A Letran alumnus would assume a leadership role in this venture.

Plate XLVI

CARLOS III, REY DE ESPAÑA
1759 to 1788

Prieto, Tomas Francisco, 1765. Medalla conmemorativa.
Propiedad del Biblioteca Nacional de España bdh0000132426

Chapter XIII

A New World Order

On 20 January 1872, the military personnel of Fort San Felipe in Cavite revolted. Government forces quelled the uprising and executed the perpetrators and accomplices. The incident became a timely pretext to arrest suspected liberal traitors to the Spanish crown. Among those taken into custody were thirteen secular priests. Of this number, ten were deported to Guam and three were found guilty of conspiracy and rebellion and sentenced to death by a controversial court martial. Many believed that they were innocent of the purported charges. Their deaths deeply affected the native intelligentsia and instigated what was to become a reform movement in due course. Philippine national hero, Jose Rizal, dedicated his 1891 book *El Filibusterismo* to the martyred patriots in these words:

> *The Church, by refusing to degrade you, has placed in doubt the crime that has been imputed to you; the Government, by surrounding your trials with mystery and shadows, causes the belief that there was some error, committed in fatal moments; and all the Philippines, by worshipping your memory and calling you martyrs, in no sense recognizes your culpability. In so far, therefor, as your complicity in the Cavite mutiny is not clearly proved, as you may or may not have been patriots, and as you may or may not have cherished sentiments for justice and for liberty, I have the right to dedicate my work to you as victims of the evil which I undertake to combat. And while we await expectantly upon Spain some day to restore your good name and cease to be answerable for your death, let these pages serve as a tardy wreath of dried leaves over your unknown tombs, and let it be understood that every one who without clear proofs attacks your memory stains his hands in your blood!*[978]

Fall of Ancien Regime

Western medieval societies exhibited a common socio-political order. A King would normally rule over his subjects consisting of a hierarchy of three inherited orders: those who prayed, those who fought, and those who labored.[979] A monarchy was deemed to be the ideal political system because religious and biblical precedence supported the King as an institution with its inherent divine rights. Each country would develop its own socio-political systems along these three orders.

The *Ancien Regime* (old order) of France consisted of three estates: clergy as the First Estate, nobility as the Second Estate and commoners as the Third Estate.[980] The United Kingdom, on the other hand, polarized into two: the clergy and nobles constituting the House of Lords and the commoners as the House of Commons.981 Under the old order, the individual was *subservient to the group under strict rules of custom, law and authority. The rights and responsibilities of the individual were determined by his place in a hierarchical social system that place great stress upon acquiesce and conformity.*982 The status quo would only begin to be significantly challenged in the latter part of the seventeenth century. An educated and enterprising middle class emerged and began to challenge absolutist government interventions in their economic affairs and business interests. This challenge would figure significantly in Great Britain's Glorious Revolution of 1688 articulating Classical Liberalism. This political philosophy would consequently result in the United States of America Revolution of 1775 and the French Revolution of 1789.

English philosopher Thomas Hobbes argued in 1651 that the absolute power of the sovereign was ultimately justified by the consent of the governed, who agreed, in a hypothetical social contract theory of government, to obey the sovereign in all matters in exchange for a guarantee of peace and security.983 In 1690, his fellow English philosopher John Locke added that parties to the contract could not reasonably place themselves under the absolute power of a ruler. Absolute power, he argued, is at odds with the point and justification of political authority, which is that it is necessary to protect the person and property of individuals and to guarantee their natural rights to freedom of thought, speech, and worship.984 Justifying the Glorious Revolution of 1688, Locke's treatise gave birth to Classical Liberalism and the beginning of a new world order.

Liberalism signaled the emancipation of the individual from religious conformity and aristocratic privilege, institutionalized competition in the political system, and introduced a laissez-faire market economy. Its form would vary depending on time and circumstance. Each country's liberalism is different and it changes in each generation. The aim of the early liberals was to limit the power of government over the individual while holding it accountable to the governed. This required a system of government which executes the expressed will of a majority of the electorate. The abuse of the majority was likewise addressed through separation of powers and a bill of rights. How these theoretical processes would eventually be implemented became contentious issues over a period of time. The French model would not only introduce radical elements to liberalism. It would also result in the destruction of ancient institutions and in the sanguinary wars between liberal and conservative forces throughout the 19th century.

With a multitude of serious problems besetting France, Louis XVI convened the *1789 Estates General* to establish a constitutional monarchy that would address the crisis. He never anticipated the Third Estate to take control of the proceedings, and to establish itself as the National Constituent Assembly. Among its first acts was the *1789 Declaration of the Rights of Man and the Citizen* initiating the protracted French revolution that would topple

Plate XLVII
THE FRENCH REVOLUTION

- Delacroix, Eugene 1830. La Liberte Guidant le peuple. Musee du Louvre

the monarchy and transform the country's socio-political landscape over the next forty years.

Orientated with the liberal ideas of the times, the French *bourgeoise* rallied behind the principles of liberty, equality and fraternity to address historical injustices against the individual. In the free thought arena, radical ideas would surface from thinking circles known as *sociétés de pensée*. Spawned by radical extremists such as the freemasons, anticlericalism emerged as a dominant force; making it French liberalism's distinct characteristic. Church assets were declared state property and confiscated. The Church was separated from and subordinated to the state under the *1790 Civil Constitution of the Clergy*. Religious orders were suppressed and religion was dechristianized. Wars were subsequently undertaken in defense of the French First Republic; spreading its revolutionary liberal ideas and fervor throughout continental Europe and virtually leaving the Catholic Church in rubbles. The Dominican Order in particular would enter a century of crisis.

At the outbreak of the French Revolution, the Order had fifty-two provinces, many congregations and monasteries, and about 20,000 members.[985] In 1790, the French Assembly suppressed religious orders and many Dominicans were imprisoned, exiled and killed. Hundreds fled from France. These events would be replicated in one country after another as the conquering French armies of the First Republic defeated the European powers in the Wars of the Coalition.

France took possession of the Low Countries and the left bank of the Rhine. To compensate for their lost possessions, German princes confiscated Church property and closed many religious houses under the 1801 Peace of Luneville. By 1825, the Dominican provinces in German states of the former Holy Roman Empire ceased to exist. The victorious French generals closed many religious houses in Northern Italy and the Papal estates. Provinces in the rest of Europe were in varying stages of collapse. It would not be until 1872 when the Order would regain a semblance of normalcy but at a much reduced scale.[986] Pope Pius VI, who vigorously opposed the *Declaration of the Rights of Man and the Citizen* and the *Civil Constitution of the Clergy*, was taken prisoner and transported to Valence, France where he died on 29 August 1799.[987]

Immediately after the execution of Louis XVI on 21 January 1793, Spain joined the First Coalition of European powers in its war against revolutionary France. After a series of French victories, Spain entered into a treaty of peace with France in 1795 and was relegated as the latter's satellite state. The new alliance prompted the British to establish a naval blockade of the peninsula the following year; severing Spain completely from its colonies. The isolation significantly impacted the country. It freed its American colonies to trade with neutral countries such as the United States and consequently made them acutely aware that they could readily exist independently from the motherland. With Spain's principal source of revenues curtailed, additional taxes were imposed and property seized. General discontent was exacerbated when the nobility and clergy were taxed, and municipal and church charity foundation properties were seized and sold for the first time. The period of relative peace enjoyed by Spain under the treaty not only allowed the free flow of French liberal ideas contained in the uncensored *Encyclopedie* of *Denis Diderot* and *Jean le Rond d'Alembert*. It also planted the seeds of turbulent change in the peninsula.[988]

Rise of Spanish Liberalism

In 1808, Emperor of the First French Empire Napoleon Bonaparte ordered the invasion of Spain on the pretext of mediating the rival royal political factions in the country. The royal family was brought to Bayonne, France and in a matter of weeks Carlos IV and Fernando VII abdicated. Napoleon appointed his brother Joseph Bonaparte as the new King of Spain. The unexpected takeover enraged the Spanish people and precipitated the Peninsular War. Although disparaged as a Bonapartist constitution, the 1808 Bayonne Charter was adopted and became the first constitution of Spain

Plate XLVIII
Promulgation of the 1812 Spanish Constitution

- Viniegra, Salvador 1912. Cortes de Cadiz. Museo de las Cortes de Cadiz.

and its domains containing French liberal concepts of government.[989] Among the first measures undertaken by the Bonaparte brothers was the expropriation of ecclesiastical assets. Napoleon ordered the reduction of the number of convents to one-third in 1808 and in the following year his brother ordered the suppression of all religious orders, the confiscation of their assets and the seizure of church jewelry.[990]

Allied with Great Britain and Portugal, Spanish rebel guerrillas would gradually sweep the French forces away from the peninsula by 1814 after initial setbacks in conventional warfare. Interim governing bodies known as *juntas* emerged in the different provinces and colonies reporting to a Supreme Central and Governing Junta of the Kingdom established on 25 September 1808. In defiance of the French usurpation, independence rebellions occurred and interim juntas consequently followed among the American colonies. However, not all the local juntas recognized the legitimacy of the mainland's supreme junta and its successors, and proceeded to govern their respective territories independently. These initial protests in support of the deposed Spanish king would gather momentum and unravel into wars of independence against the motherland.⁹⁹¹ Except for Cuba, Puerto Rico, Filipinas and other Pacific possessions, all of Spanish America would have officially declared independence from Spain by 1825.⁹⁹²

Meanwhile the insurgent *Cortes Generales* (General Courts) convened in Cadiz in 1810 as Spain's first national sovereign assembly. Liberal factions dominated the Cadiz *Cortes* and as such a liberal Spanish Constitution was promulgated on 19 March 1812.⁹⁹³ The 1812 Constitution reduced the power of the Crown, the Catholic Church and the nobility. It established the principles of universal male suffrage, national sovereignty, constitutional monarchy, press freedom, land reform, and free enterprise. It was the most liberal constitution of its time and became the template of emerging liberal governments in Europe and Latin America. Key provisions of the constitution involved the definition of a Spanish national and citizen. Articles 1, 5 and 10 defined nationals as all people born, naturalized or permanently residing for more than ten years in Spanish territories.⁹⁹⁴ Possessing the right to vote, citizens were defined as Spanish nationals whose ancestry originated from Spain or the territories of the Spanish empire as contained in Articles 18 through 22.⁹⁹⁵ The 1812 Constitution effectively transformed the subjects of an absolute monarch into citizens founded on the doctrine of national sovereignty. It further included *casta de indios* as citizens but excluded *casta de negros* who, except for slaves, could opt for naturalization. Widely acclaimed, the liberal changes were not however enthusiastically received by conservatives. After the collapse of the First French Empire in 1814, Fernando VII abolished the constitution, reinstated the old order, returned the privileges and confiscated properties of the Church and arrested many liberal leaders on his return to the throne. Without the 1812 Constitution, the colonial liberal's waning support for the monarchy was completely lost.⁹⁹⁶

The royalists in Spanish America began to regain control of the autonomous governments established by the independence movements. In 1815, Spain sent a large military contingent to reinforce the royalists in Venezuela and to restore its sovereignty in Nueva Granada and Peru. The ensuing wars were no longer simply wars of independence. In as much as the combatants on either side were principally native *americanos*, the conflicts became *de facto* civil wars between liberal and conservative forces.

For the Spanish American, liberalism meant democracy and the end of the *sistema de casta*, slavery and the dominance of the Catholic Church.⁹⁹⁷ On the other hand, conservatives advocated the preservation of an absolute ruler and the *status quo*.⁹⁹⁸ Overseas support for the conservatives was effectively curtailed by the United States Monroe Doctrine since 1823, British intervention, and a military rebellion in Spain. Ultimately, political independence was achieved, but the conflicts between liberals and conservatives in the American continent persisted throughout the 19th century with the balance of power shifting from one end of the political spectrum to the other. Church properties were confiscated in Chile, Argentina, Peru and Colombia with many religious houses closed.⁹⁹⁹

Mexico's *Guerra de Reforma* (War of Reform) ended with the religious orders barely surviving in 1861.[1000] Guatemala suppressed them during its liberal revolution of 1870.[1001] A parallel power struggle transpired in the Spanish mainland sharing an equally sanguine and destructive aftermath.

After Fernando VII's abolition of the 1812 Constitution, a series of minor military revolts led by liberal officers began to erupt in different parts of Spain from 1814 onwards. Led by Rafael del Riego, the *pronunciamiento* (military coup) of 1 January 1820 gained popular support and successfully demanded a complete change of institutions from absolutism to constitutionalism.[1002] By March of the same year, Fernando VII restored the 1812 Constitution. The shifting balance of power would find the King back in control and the constitution suppressed once again in 1823. To assure his daughter's ascendancy to the throne, Fernando VII revoked the Salic law which prohibited royal succession by the female line. His death in 1833 left the Spanish throne to his three year old daughter Isabel II under the Queen Regent Maria Cristina. Carlos, the King's younger brother, would contest the crown with the support of conservatives in a series of clashes known as the Carlist Wars. To protect her daughter, Maria Cristina would rely on the support of the moderate liberals to stay in power. The 1812 Constitution was again restored in 1836. A new constitution would be implemented the following year.[1003] During the 19th century, Spain would have nine constitutions with two not enacted, three Carlists wars, pockets of virtual civil war and anarchy throughout the country, a short-lived republic, a number of notable *coups d'etat* and *de facto* military dictatorships.

Impact on the Spanish Church and Filipinas

The wars with Revolutionary France forced the Spanish government to resort to non-traditional financial resources which over the next 50 years would escalate into an unrestrained suppression of the Church and confiscation of its properties by exponents of radical liberalism.

Beginning with the property sequestration of charitable institutions and disposal of residual Jesuit assets, the measures progressed to the initial imposition of levies to support the war in 1798. By 1806, the *señorios eclesiastico* (ecclesiastical estates) were partially abolished and Papal permission was obtained to sell 1/7 of church properties in return for state bonds. By 1808, the Bonaparte regime introduced the expropriation of ecclesiastical assets, seizure of church jewelry, the suppression of all religious orders and the confiscation of their properties. The 1812 Constitution did not contain measures to reverse the French aftermath. After his return to the throne in 1814, Fernando VII attempted to restore the Church privileges and properties but would be stymied by the constantly changing political realities. In 1820, a royal decree abolished all religious houses that had less than twenty-five members. On 25 October of the same year, a decree was issued prohibiting the communication of the religious provinces with their legitimate heads, suspending the provincial chapters and subjecting the existing religious to their respective Ordinaries. In 1835, an *exclaustracion* (secularization) decree freed religious from their rules and a reign of terror ensued. The religious were beaten and killed and their houses invaded and ransacked. By 1836, the *señorios* were abolished. All monastic lands were declared national property and sold in public auction. In 1836, the Cortes suppressed all the Orders. By 1840, 32 of 62 sees in Spain were vacant.[1004] It was therefore not surprising that the Spanish Catholic Church completely estranged itself from liberalism and supported conservative factions thereafter.

While the Church in Europe was crumbling to the onslaughts of French liberalism and imperialism, the Spanish government pressured Pope Pius IV to divide the Dominican Order into two jurisdictions making the Spanish provinces autonomous in 1804.[1005] Reduced to six years, the office of the Master General would alternate between the Spanish and non-Spanish provinces while a vicar general would concurrently administer the other. In 1825, Pope Leo XII named Joachim Briz OP Master General of the Order. By that time, the Wars of Independence in Spanish America reached its culmination and the Dominican provinces in the new independent states were isolated from him.[1006] Fernando VII had regained power over the *Cortes* providing opportunities to strengthen the only Dominican province unscathed by the turmoil in Spain and in the Americas - the Province of the Holy Rosary in *Filipinas*.

The 1812 Constitution was proclaimed in Manila on 17 April 1813.[1007] The newly acquired Spanish citizenship under the Cadiz constitution precipitated disturbances throughout the archipelago with the natives refusing to pay tribute and to render forced labor. Violent outbursts occurred particularly in Ilocos after news of the constitution's abolition on 4 May 1814 was finally received in 1815.[1008] The resulting anarchy was readily suppressed with the assistance of the friars.[1009] Dominican historian Ferrando attributed the violence as the *indio*'s primal reaction to subversive liberal ideas which more advanced nations were still grappling with.[1010] Under such circumstances, he continued, the liberal principle of equality was considered absolutely absurd and unsustainable.[1011] *Filipinas* would eventually lose its Cortes representation under the Constitution promulgated on 18 June 1837 which decreed that overseas possessions should be governed by special laws.[1012]

Prior to 1822, the Spanish military in *Filipinas* were mostly under the command of *criollo* and *mestizo de español* officers. Influenced by the Wars of Independence in Spanish America, a plot to overthrow the Manila colonial government and declare independence was hatched by Coronel Francisco Bayot. The Bayot clan was one of the distinguished criollo families of *Filipinas* and Francisco headed the King's permanent regiment posted at the *plaza de Manila*.[1013] His sons, Manuel, Jose and Joaquin, were captains of the *mestizo batallon real principe* (Royal Prince Battalion) which carried out the plan to install their father as *director supremo de Filipinas* (Supreme Director) on 17 April 1822.[1014] The plot was however discovered before its execution and Governor Mariano Fernandez de Folgueras had the perpetrators arrested and imprisoned. In his report to Spain, Folgueras recommended the replacement of military officials with those from the Peninsula. His successor, Governor Juan Antonio Martinez arrived with a substantial number of the requested personnel when he assumed his office on 30 October 1822.[1015]

The increase of military officials from Spain stymied the promotion of the *naturales de Filipinas* and were therefor received with resentment. News of secret meetings began to reach the attention of the governor and a planned conspiracy was aborted on 18 February 1823. A number of plotters headed by Luis Rodriguez Varela and Domingo Rojas were implicated and deported to Spain.[1016] The dissatisfaction escalated and affected the *indio* subordinates when other *filipino* officers were reassigned to hardship posts. On the evening of 2 June 1823, 800 *indio* elements of the King's regiment headed by criollo Capitan Andres Novales attempted to take control of Manila; killing lieutenant governor Folgueras among others in the process.[1017] The rebels took possession of the regimental barracks, Palacio Real and the Cabildo before they were subdued. Novales and his co-conspirators were captured and executed.[1018] The racial dissatisfaction in the military would continue to simmer; evincing with the 1843 Tayabas Regiment mutiny led by Sargento Irineo Samaniego, the 1854 Nueva Ecija uprising led by Alferez Jose Cuesta, and the controversial 1872 Cavite Mutiny.

Between 1805 and 1825, the Province of the Holy Rosary received only 32 new religious from Spain to replace 80 who had died.[1019] As in the past, the Province had to rely on non-European Spaniards to fill the need. The Province relied on Letran *colegiales chinos* and *mestizo de sangleys*. One of whom would distinguish himself as the first non-Spanish president of the Santo Domingo Convent.

P. Fr. Juan Evangelista Kang de Santa Maria OP was born in Chanchiu (Zangzhou), in the province of Fo-Kien (Fujian), China. Being a *colegial* of San Juan de Letran, he received the Dominican habit on the 23 June 1837, and professed on the 24 June 1838. He received the first tonsure, the four minor orders and the sub-diaconate some time in September 1838, the diaconate on the 2 December 1838, and the presbytery on the 29 February 1839. By the 1845 Chapter, he was Vicar of San Gabriel de Binondo until he retired sick in the Santo Domingo Convent. On the 6 February 1858, he was named interim Vicar of the house of San Juan del Monte where he was assigned during the Chapter of the following year. On 3 January 1860, he was named the first non-Spanish President of Santo Domingo de Manila, and on 14 November 1862 minister of the Chinese in Binondo. A devout, austere, silent and very charitable religious, he departed ill to his native country. Five days after arriving at Hong Kong on 15 May 1866, he died receiving the Holy Sacraments in the Procurator's House.[1020]

The alarming decline in the number of Spanish Dominicans had to be addressed immediately. As required by article 335 of the constitution, the *Deputacion Provincial* (Provincial Council) of *Filipinas* issued a report dated 23 April 1823 to Madrid regarding the urgent need for European religious to maintain the existing ministries and their extensions. It further highlighted their natural capacity to guaranty public peace and submission of the country's natives. It lamented the poor quality, instruction, and virtues of the native clergy particularly those of the three suffragan dioceses; rendering them incapable of replacing the European religious who above all constituted the true moral force of Filipinos; infinitely superior to all the physical force that could be mustered and irresistible under any sentiment, in whatever foreign invasion as in any seditious movement.[1021] Succeeding governors would echo the clamor for European religious. The superior government was consequently convinced of the political and religious importance of the regular clergy in *Filipinas*, and the necessity to provide and promote personnel increase of each corporation in order to preserve Spanish sovereignty. Ironically in Liberal Spain, the regular clerics were atrociously persecuted, dispossessed of their assets, their convents untimely closed and admission of new young recruits in the different existing institutes rigorously prohibited in order to bring about their ultimate demise.[1022]

Using precedents set during the term of Governor General Rafael Maria de Aguilar, Fernando VII issued on 8 June 1826 a Real Cedula returning to the Augustinians and to other Orders the administration of the *curatos* and *doctrinas* originally under their care that was so declared by Real Cedula of 11 December 1776 notwithstanding the ambiguities of its clauses.[1023] He further halted any further secularization of curacies to be carried out by his vice patron or the diocesan ordinaries without his expressed order. That none of the above determinations shall be executed to the prejudice of the interest and honor of the secular clergy and that they shall not be deprived of any legal rights. By 1829, the Dominican province officially regained the churches of San Gabriel de Binondo, De Los Santos Reyes del Parian and all the Bataan parishes upon the deaths of the lawful incumbent secular curates in order to maintain those possessions in peace, to propagate the Holy Catholic faith, and to conserve the *indios* in absolute obedience and submission.[1024] The return of all original friar parishes was completed by 1870.[1025]

The Dominican Master General Briz providentially moved to secure the King's approval of a *colegio-seminario* in Spain for the Philippine Dominican Province in order to assure the ready number of religious clerics. On 22 May 1827, a *consulta* was submitted by the Superior Council to the King regarding the necessity and convenience to extend everything possible to send religious to the islands of Filipinas in view of the existing scarcity and the need to improve the administration of their curacies, doctrinas and missions, and considering the usefulness of establishing a college in Spain similar to what the Augustinians and Recollects had in Valladolid and Monteagudo respectively, and likewise solicited by the Franciscans.[1026] In December that year, the King issued a Real Cedula authorizing the Master General to found and erect at the expense of the Province of the Holy Rosary a missionary college for the Order to be destined to the same Province.[1027] From the reconstructed ruins of Santo Domingo de Ocaña, a new *colegio-seminario* was inaugurated on 2 May 1830 with P. Fr. Tomas Rosello OP as its first rector.[1028]

The liberals ascended to power during the regency of Queen Maria Cristina. A series of laws began to be enacted by the Cortes to the detriment of the Church. Decrees dated 19 February 1836 and 8 March 1836 were issued ordering the *desamortizacion* (confiscation and sale) of all the assets owned by religious orders and the *exclaustracion* (secularization) of members of their communities.[1029] More than 3,000 religious were expelled from their houses.[1030] Petitions for the Cortes' reconsideration were filed. On the fate of the missionary orders in *Filipinas* and their *colegios-seminarios* in Spain, the decree of 8 March 1836 contained the following articles:

> *Article 1. All the monasteries, convents, colleges, congregations and other houses of male religious communities and institutes, including regular clerics and those of the four military Orders and St John of Jerusalem, existing in the Peninsula, the adjacent Islands and possessions of Spain in Africa shall remain abolished.*
>
> *Article 2. [The following] shall be excepted from the disposition of the preceding article:*
> 1. *The missionary colleges for the Asian provinces of Valladolid, Ocaña and Monteagudo.*
> 2. *The Piarist houses and the convents of the Hospitallers of St John of God, which are actually open.*[1031]

On 26 August 1836, a decree was issued withholding any political changes in *Filipinas* until resolved with finality by the Cortes.[1032] The exceptions continued to be opposed in the Cortes. Gomez Becera summarized the stakes involved during the deliberations on 28 May 1837:

> *What is at hand can be reduced to whether we are to or not to conserve las islas Filipinas, the Marianas and their dependencies. If we are to renounce our possession of them, then we should remove the article in good time, but if we don't, if our intention is to conserve them, its approval is indispensable… to do otherwise you will lose las islas Filipinas, the Marianas and their dependencies where, gentlemen, there is a population of no less than three million inhabitants. And three million inhabitants [that are] 4,000 leagues [away] from the Peninsula. How do you govern them having no more than 6,000 europeans there, which we don't? They can only be conserved in the way they have been conserved until now; for your information, by the influence, by the preponderance that have been adhered and exerted over the natives by the missionaries.*[1033]

The spirit of the epoch viewed the religious institutes as so anachronistic, so absurd and so antithetical that they deserved to be ended. Yet for the sake of conserving a rich overseas possession, their complete demise was held in abeyance. The Asian missionary colleges in Spain were retained as exceptions. Thus, when all other Dominican provinces in Spain ceased to exist, the Philippine province became the lone outpost allowed to preserve the Order's peninsular presence in view of its perceived importance in Filipinas. In 1874, the Province's *Vicariato de España* (Vicarate of Spain) was established and assumed complete responsibility over Ocaña from the Order's Apostolic Commissary.[1034] The success of the first college and the need for more religious personnel would pave the way for the Province's second *colegio-seminario*. With the approval of Isabel II and the support of Avila Bishop Fernando Blanco, the Province acquired the sequestered ancient convent-university of Santo Tomas de Avila. The newly restored college was inaugurated on 1 October 1876.[1035]

The road to normalcy and recovery began after the Vatican entered into the Concordat of 1851 with the Spanish government of Isabel II. It would not be until 1860 when the first house of what was to become the *Provincia Dominicana de España* (Dominican Province of Spain) was reopened at the convent of San Juan Bautista de Corias.[1036] With two other re-opened convents, the restoration of the Province of Spain was officially achieved in 1879.[1037] The Provinces of Betica followed in 1898 and Aragon in 1912. The three Dominican provinces in Spain merged in 2016 to form the *Provincia de Hispania de la Orden de Predicadores.*[1038] The merger of the three Spanish provinces calls for a reassessment of the *Vicariato del Rosario's* relevance with the Mother Province based in Hong Kong and the protocols of collaboration with the new Province of Hispania. Todate the *Vicariato* has 9 Spanish communities under a Vicar Provincial consisting of 4 convents: Santo Tomas (Avila), Nuestra Señora del Rosario (Valladolid), Santisimo Rosario and San Pedro Martir (Madrid) and 5 houses: Santo Domingo (Ocaña), Jesus Obrero (Madrid), San Martin de Porres (Mostotes), San Juan Macias (Caceres), and Santisima Trinidad (Roma).[1039]

The Fall of Secular Parishes

For their continued existence and survival in the 19th century, the friar orders in *Filipinas* were expected to assure the peninsular government that Spanish sovereignty would be conserved and that the submission of the native inhabitants would be maintained. As *de facto* agents of the government, they became complicit to and active participants in all government policy and action. To do otherwise was tantamount to treason. Conversely in due course, enemies of the peninsular friars in *Filipinas* became axiomatically the enemies of the state.[1040] Considering the constant changes in Spain's rulers, opportunities were exploited whenever sympathetic officials were in power. Inaction and delay were resorted to when hostile ones were in place. In so doing, Filipinas was spared from the turmoils and chaos in Spain and the Americas. The price for this relative peace however would eventually manifest its serious consequences.

After Archbishop Santa Justa's 1778 *acto de obediencia* was officially nullified by the 8 June 1826 decree of Fernando VII, a new chapter of the secularization conflicts commenced. All parishes belonging to the religious orders were gradually returned as the incumbent secular curates died. The parish of San Simon in Pampanga was the last secular parish to be returned in 1870. The return of parishes held for over fifty years caused deep resentments within the ranks of the secular priests, and their fortitude was about to be tested further. The symbiotic relationship between the Spanish Church and State moved the peninsular friars in *Filipinas* to explore the extent of their newfound influence and power.

In early 1848, the Franciscans petitioned Narciso Claveria y Zaldua to adjudicate the rich secular parish of Quiapo to them. The Governor General disapproved the petition *for the present*. The Recollects followed shortly. *Comisario Procurador* (Commissary-Procurator) P. Fr. Guillermo Agudo OAR petitioned that secular parishes in Cavite be entrusted to the order because of their proximity to the Recollect's *hacendadas* (plantation estates). The approval dated 9 March 1849 not only granted the parishes of Bacoor, Cavite el Viejo (Kawit) and Silang to the Recollects. It also unexpectedly awarded the parishes of Santa Cruz de Malabon (Tanza), San Francisco de Malabon (General Trias), Naic and Indang to the Dominicans without having to request for them. The secular clergy was outraged by the brazen decision. A Madrid agent was engaged to secure a revocation of the order from higher authorities. His lobby however failed. The peak of indignation reached with the issuance of royal order dated 10 September 1861 granting the Recollects administration of the remaining secular parishes in Cavite as compensation for the Mindanao parishes they lost to the Jesuits. On 20 June the following year, the implementing details of the preceding royal order expanded the coverage of the compensation to include other parishes in the Archdiocese of Manila. Efforts to reverse the orders proved futile. Consequently, the prized secular curacy of Antipolo became a Recollect parish.[1041]

Notwithstanding the losses sustained, the *criollos, mestizos de español, mestizos de sangley* and *indios* which essentially comprised the entire secular clergy found common ground to defend their rights and to counter the encroachments of the religious orders. P. Mariano Gomes de los Angeles, a *mestizo de sangley*, led the Cavite secular curates being Vicar Forane.[1042] His militancy earned him the reputation of being *anti-español*.[1043] P. Pedro Pelaez, a criollo, mobilized the other secular curates within the Archdiocese and coordinated the funding and lobbying activities from Manila.[1044] They drafted a petition in the name of the Cavite clergy for the Queen to revoke the 1849 cedula. In view of the archbishop's misgivings, the petition was not presented to the authorities but was published anonymously instead on 8 May 1850 in the Madrid newspaper *El Clamor Publico* under the title *El Clero Filipino*. It was the first time the secular clergy composed of *naturales* or *hijos del pais* (sons of the country) were collectively referred to as *filipinos*. The writer, P. Pedro Pelaez, consequently assumed leadership of the Filipino clergy's cause until his untimely death on 3 June 1863. His loss left a serious leadership vacuum until the young P. Jose Burgos proved himself worthy to the challenge.[1045]

Plate XLIX

DR. DON JOSE APOLONIO BURGOS
The First Filipino

- *Artist unknown, 1911.* Renacimiento Filipino 14 April 1911.

Chapter XIV

Dr. Don Jose Apolonio Burgos

The New World Order spread rapidly throughout the globe. To insulate the remaining colonies from its revolutionary consequences, the Spanish government undertook measures to address rebellious initiatives undertaken by its educated vassals. In the Antilles, Spain deployed a military contingent of 40,000 peninsular soldiers. In Filipinas where there was a military presence of less than 1,000 *peninsulares*, the government relied principally on the religious friar orders to control the native population and to maintain Spain's domination over the archipelago. The perceived threat emanated from the most educated sector of the native population - the secular priests. Policies and implementing measures to emasculate the secular priests' position of power, prestige and influence were resorted to. The resulting injustice and inequality awakened the awareness of a national identity whose interests were distinct, separate and even contrary to that of the peninsular motherland. In the vanguard of this movement was Doctor Don Jose Apolonio Burgos who would articulate and champion a nationalist cause for the first time.

Colegial de Letran

Burgos was born to Jose Burgos and Florentina Garcia on 9 February 1837 in *Villa Fernandino de Vigan*, Ilocos Sur.[1046] His father, a First Lieutenant of the *Milicias de Ilocos 5 de Linea* (Ilocos Militia 5th in the line of command), was an *Español* and his mother was a *Mestiza de Español*.[1047] He had a sister named Antonia, a *Criolla*.[1048] Four days later, he was christened Jose Apolonio Burgos by the Judge Provisor, acting Vicar General and Parish Priest, P. Don Estanislao Bumatay. The *alcalde mayor* of Ilocos Sur, Don Jose Maria Calderon, stood as his godfather.

A *huerfano de padre* by the age of 10, Burgos moved to Manila to live with his uncle, Juan Antonio Aenlle, who enrolled him in a Dominican *colegio*. His ancestral lineage indicated that he was 7/8 Spanish.[1049] Under Spanish law, a *cuarteron* (quadroon) was considered an *español*. However since he was not a pure *español*, he did not qualify to study at the *Colegio de Santo Tomas* in view of the school's statutes. He was nevertheless accepted as a *becario* of the *Real Colegio de San Juan de Letran* being a poor orphan of a Spanish soldier.[1050] According to the records of Letran, he was admitted on 11 August 1847 as a *colegial* commencing a student life that would last for the next 25 years. Burgos was an *ochavon* (octoroon) born in *Filipinas* and under the *sistema de casta* he was considered a *Criollo* otherwise known as a

Filipino. As such, he could only aspire to become a secular priest should he choose to pursue the Holy Orders.

Burgos completed *latinidad* in March 1852. The completion of the five-year latin grammar course qualified him to pursue the three-year philosophy course. He received his Bachelor in Philosophy degree from *Santo Tomas* in 1855. His mother who wanted him to become a lawyer was disappointed when he decided to become a priest instead.[1051] He pursued a degree in Theology in the next four years. In 1857 while a sophomore Theology student, Burgos worked as an assistant to the cathedral secretary.[1052] He had not yet received the minor orders then. While handling correspondences, he became acquainted with the Vicar Forane of Cavite, P. Mariano Gomes de los Angeles.[1053] On 17 December 1858, Burgos received his minor orders.

1859 and 1860 were eventful years for the promising student. He was conferred the Bachelor of Theology degree on 21 January 1859. Shortly after, he was named *decano* of Letran, the highest honor that could be conferred to a *colegial* of the school. On 15 September 1859, Burgos was named a beneficiary under the *capellania* founded by Dña. Josepha Garcia Monroy, and became a sub-deacon on 17 December 1859.[1054] Having completed all the prerequisites for the Licentiate in Philosophy degree, Burgos formally requested to be admitted for examination. The *releccion* (preliminary examination) transpired on 15 January 1860 and the *noche triste* (main examination) on 16 February 1860.[1055] After successfully passing the *releccion,* an incident occurred in Letran that would altogether influence his future.

The Dominicans appointed a *criollo* who still had to complete his Philosophy baccalaureate as a *mayor*. The four existing *mayores* who possessed superior degrees and pursued advanced studies were offended by the disregard of the school's protocols. Discontented, Cosme Abaya, Criterio Crisologo, Isabelo Marcelino and Mariano Sevilla appealed to the *Padre Presidente* to relieve the newly named *mayor* but were ignored.[1056] Burgos, the *decano,* tried to intervene but was likewise shown the same discourtesy. The *colegiales* agreed among themselves to resist mandates that conflicted with the school's established traditions. On 24 January 1860, eleven protestors accompanied by a throng of *colegiales* confronted and passionately argued their case with the *Padre Presidente*.[1057] The latter imposed his authority that night and provoked a physical confrontation between friars and students. Young students suffered contusions and other serious injuries that by ten in the evening public peace enforcers were called in for assistance. The disorderly conduct of the group was referred to the Judge Provisor and Vicar General of the Archdiocese for proper disciplinary action. While awaiting the verdict, Burgos completed his *noche triste* with a unanimous approval on 16 February 1860 - the first of the three he would undergo during his student life.[1058] Eight days later, the vicar general issued his verdict and sentence.

On 24 February 1860, Sr. D. Francisco Garcia Ortiz, the vicar general, ruled after due investigation that the group of eleven consisting of Jose Burgos,

Plate L
Guardians of the Secular Clergy

Abp Gregorio Meliton Martinez Santa Cruz
1861-1875

- *Artist unknown ca. 1876.* The Manila Cathedral.

Dr. Don Pedro Pablo Pelaez y Sebastian
1812-1863

- *Artist unknown.* Quirino 1973

Gregorio Noblejas, Simon de Jesus, Juan Dilag, Fernando Lugo, Jacinto Zamora, Agaton Estrella, Felix Manguerra, Mariano Sta. Maria, Mariano Sevilla and Melecio Salvidea were punishable for instigating a mob to confront their Superior; demanding the relief of the newly named *mayor* and causing disorder and scandals unbecoming of ordinands. Jose Burgos and Juan Dilag were identified as the principal instigators. He further noted that even assuming the causes alleged by the group of individuals were reasonable, their conduct can never be considered justifiable since their chosen means were unacceptable. He therefore ordered a 2-month reclusion of the eleven at the *Seminario Conciliar de San Carlos* with permission to attend only their respective university classes and religious acts of the Holy Metropolitan Church at the convenient hours and when their assistance were deemed necessary. Burgos and Dilag were further penalized with a six-month suspension from receiving further holy orders. For the public display of disrespect shown to Letran's *Padre Presidente*, all eleven were to apologize publicly. The act was to be entered in the notarial records for general condemnation, at their expense, with a warning that a repeat offense would be dealt with more severely.[1059]

Subjected to the preceding sanctions, Burgos received his Licentiate in Philosophy degree during the investiture ceremonies held on 27 February 1860. It was a very special day. As a *licenciado*, he became a member of the university's *claustro*.[1060] At that time, the *claustro* had among its members the incumbent Capitular Secretary of the Archdiocese, Pedro Pelaez, and other *Criollo* leaders such as Joaquin Pardo de Tavera and Antonio Maria Rigidor with whom he would become closely associated with. The Letran incident had made Burgos a public figure, and fostered general acrimony against the Dominicans. To compensate for the injustice done, Burgos and the four *mayores* were admitted to the *Colegio de Santo Tomas*. The five *criollos* who for one reason or another could not comply with the pure Spanish blood criterion of *Santo Tomas* were suddenly recognized as such. It was a step higher in the *sistema de casta* no matter how contrived it appeared to be. Burgos resigned as *decano* of Letran and was admitted as a *colegial de santo tomas* on 11 August 1860 after passing the *limpieza de sangre* screening protocol and after almost completing his six-month suspension sentence. He was the first *colegial licenciado* to be accepted by the *colegio*. He continued on to receive his diaconate on 22 December 1860 and became eligible for the Licentiate in Theology degree soon after. His involvement in the Letran incident however would closely associate and implicate him with any manifestation of student unrest in the university from then on.

1862 found the cabildo of the Archdiocese of Manila filled with frenzy and anxiety. An order was issued on 6 February to comply with the 21 September 1861 decree of recompensing the Recollects with the remaining secular parishes of Cavite for those to be ceded to the Jesuits in Mindanao. The Manila ecclesiastical cabildo led by vicar capitular Don Pedro Pelaez issued a series of expositions to question the legality of the order. Burgos witnessed the amount of legal work and preparation entailed and realized that the protection and survival of secular parishes rested principally on legal precedents. After being conferred with the Licentiate in Sacred Theology degree on 21 February 1862, Burgos decided to study Canon and Civil Law. The decision meant that he had to delay his priestly ordination for the duration of the three-year course. The church did not allow priests to study civil law while the state required both canon and civil laws to be studied simultaneously. He would not be able to comply with the regulations if he was a priest. His study of law would prove helpful with his appointment as Commissional Judge that year.[1061] By the end of the year, the battle to retain secular parishes became a hopeless cause.

The three years studying law were busy years and the pace would dictate the activities of the young Burgos for the rest of his life. On 3 June 1863, a violent earthquake rocked Manila; destroying many edifices including the Manila Cathedral. Buried dead under its rubbles were Don Ignacio Ponce de Leon and Don Pedro Pelaez who were celebrating the Corpus Christi mass when the disaster struck. Their deaths marked a cross road in Burgos' destiny.

Ponce de Leon was a Prebendary of the Cathedral Chapter and Master of Ceremonies of the University.[1062] Burgos, who was recently named as an interim prebendary, was unanimously elected Master of Ceremonies replacing Ponce de Leon. It was an office that demanded much of his time, but which he carried out faithfully until his death. There were other functions that he would perform for the university from time to time. Among them were as Commissional Judge, Examiner, Grantor of Degrees, Pro-Dean of Theology and Pro-Secretary General. Although a member of the *claustro*, he never had time to be a *catedratico* (professor) considering his scholarly pursuits. He would however accept occasional private tutoring. His future as an academician was virtually assured.

The impact of Pelaez's death was however more profound. It created a leadership vacuum in the secular clergy. A number tried to fill his shoes but proved ineffectual. The vicious black propaganda against the secular clergy carried out by the P. Fr. Guillermo Agudo OAR and P. Fr. Celestino Mayordomo OSA continued unabated in the Madrid newspapers of *El Clamor Publico, La Regeneracion, La Esperanza,* and *La Verdad*. In an article published in *La Verdad* of Madrid, they defamed *filipinos* and the good name of Pelaez with calumny and false accusations of rebellion.[1063] The stain of the aborted 1863 phantom rebellion would be insidiously used as a factual event ten years later.[1064] It was at this juncture that a reply was published in *La America* on 12 September 1864 entitled *A La Nacion*.[1065] The Manifesto was anonymously signed *Los Filipinos*. In time, the authorship would be ascribed to Burgos.[1066] It would appear that the defamation of a respected *criollo* church leader and personal mentor prompted Burgos to write the manifesto and to carry on the interrupted work. The content concerning secularization would appear to be lifted from the works of Pelaez but the approach was entirely different. Jesuit historian Schumacher noted the following:

> *For Pelaez, the major question is the rights of the secular clergy being violated by friars. For Burgos, there is an even more important point - that parishes were being denied to Filipinos because of their race and its alleged inferiority to Europeans. Burgos clearly writes as a Filipino, and if he does not preach disloyalty to Spain - indeed he strongly disclaims it - he is clearly conscious of his nationality, and ready to defend his people. It is not hard to see here the influence of Burgos on later writings of Rizal and Marcelo del Pilar.*[1067]

The date of the original Manifesto was purportedly on 27 June 1864.[1068] It marked the day that Burgos ceased to be a *Criollo* and became a *Filipino* nationalist.

Priest and Nationalist

On 28, 29, 30 September 1864, competitive examinations were held at *San Carlos* seminary for several vacant curacies in the archdiocese. Of the 37 candidates, 22 passed. The government nominated Jose Burgos to the parish of the Manila Cathedral on 26 November 1864 and Jacinto Zamora on 3 December 1864.[1069] Zamora however took possession of the first curacy on 23 December of the same year while Burgos had yet to be ordained priest in order to take possession. His ordination was to take place when he officially completed his course in canon law. He was ordained priest by Archbishop Gregorio Meliton Martinez and in due course took possession of the second curacy of the *Parroquia del Sagrario de San Pedro* in January 1865.[1070] Later that year, he was made *medio racionario* at the cathedral which gave him a seat in the choir and a vote in the chapter.[1071]

It will not be until 12 July 1865 that Burgos formally requested for examination. His school records indicated that canon law was indeed his *forte* garnering *sobresaliente* consistently in all subjects during the three years. His *noche triste* was approved unanimously on 8 February 1866 and earned him the Bachelor of Canon Law degree. The next three years would find Burgos with more responsibilities and more degrees.

On 20 March 1866, Burgos was nominated by the university for the post of *inspector* of Latinity schools in the suburbs of Manila under the new secondary education system to be inaugurated the following school year.[1072] On 2 May, he was named *examinador sinodal* by the Archdiocese.[1073] Burgos was conferred the Doctor of Theology degree on 24 April 1868 and the Licentiate in Canon Law the following 29 October. He was made Secretary of the Archbishop for the latter's diocesan visitations on 24 November and capped the year with his appointment as *promotor fiscal* of the curia on 22 December.[1074] The year ended filled with hopeful expectations that the 1868 Glorious Revolution in Spain would finally bring liberal reforms to *Filipinas*. The arrival of the new liberal governor general was ambivalently awaited.

Governor-General Carlos Maria de la Torre arrived in Manila and took possession of his office on 23 June 1869.[1075] A liberal and active participant in the revolution that toppled the monarchy, he was mindful of the sentiments of the different sectors of society in Filipinas and of the need to be apolitical under the circumstances. On 12 July 1869, a reception organized by the civil governor of Manila was held at the Governor's residence in the Santa Potenciana palace. It was attended by a cross section of Manila's elite society. In attendance were *hijos del país* consisting of some secular and clerical students, lawyers, municipal officials from Santa Cruz, Quiapo and Sampaloc, and a few indios and mestizos of the same suburbs. Peninsular proprietors, businessmen, lawyers and notable public servants, *españoles, filipinos* and even *mestizos* or *indios* of value attended.[1076]

El Porvenir Filipino reported two days later the following names who attended to greet the superior Governor: Sr. D. Joaquin Pardo de Tavera - doctor of laws, member of the Council of Administration and professor of Spanish law at the university; Sr. D. Jose Icaza - alternate magistrate of the royal Audiencia; Jacobo Zobel - proprietor and member of the Ayuntamiento (governing council) of Manila; Ignacio Rocha - businessman; Lorenzo Rocha - artist; Angel Garchitorena - carriage maker; Andres Nieto - property owner; Jose Cañas - landowner; Jose Burgos - doctor of laws and curate of the Manila Cathedral; Vicente Infante - army chaplain and Juan Reyes of the department of finance. Manuel Genato and Maximo Paterno, *mestizo de sangley* businessmen, were included in a later report.[1077] The group was alluded by the newspaper as a Commission of *españoles filipinos*, presumed to represent the country. Another observer referred to the event as the first filipino political manifestation where 5 million *indios* were not represented.[1078] La Torre would eventually deny any exchanges of a political nature transpired and that statements to the contrary were made by his enemies.[1079] Nevertheless, liberal minded Filipinos were seen openly interacting for the first time. These loose and informal associations would eventually earn varying tentative labels. Manuel Artigas would name it *Comite de Reformadores* (Reform Committee), Felipe Buencamino - *Partido Liberal* (Liberal Party), and Rafael Izquierdo - *Club Filipino* or *La Junta*. All tainted with a political flavor.

Among La Torre's first official acts was to address the widespread peace and order problems. After due consultations, he granted amnesty to Casimiro Camerino, leader of the agrarian dissidents from Cavite on 15 August 1869, and commissioned him as colonel of the *batallon de guias* (scouts battalion) composed of 40 from his own band of rebels to be attached to the police forces of the government.[1080] The battalion proved to be an effective force in reducing incidents of brigandage and in improving the security of areas infested with bandits and evil doers.[1081] La Torre's decisive move enhanced his popularity among the liberal-minded *Filipinos* but earned him incessant criticisms from his enemies.

On 21 September, Manila was sworn to the Spanish constitution of 1869. To commemorate the 1868 Revolution, La Torre invited various mestizos from the districts of Santa Cruz, San Miguel, Binondo and Quiapo to a reception in his palace on 26 September. Led by Jose Burgos, Pardo de

Tavera and Maximo Paterno, the group dressed in colorful attires rendered a musical serenade adorned with banners and lanterns and cheered. La Torre's enemies labeled this event as another political manifestation and claimed that ribbons printed with *Viva el pueblo soberano* (Long live the sovereign people), *Viva la libertad* (Long live liberty) or *Viva el general la Torre* (Long live general la Torre) were worn.[1082] La Torre vehemently denied it.[1083]

At this stage, La Torre became well acquainted with the ways of Manila's society. He acerbically described it as follows:

> *In this small society where miseries and gossips abound, just as it lacks self denial and good will, it is prevalent to resort to lies, to calumny, to malediction and to those petty ways that momentarily reveal the elements that makes this society, and all of this by custom, by past time, by what they consider lack of a dignified and elevated object to occupy and distract the spirit. Should it therefore not be surprising that it will continue to do so after September 1868 but in a grander scale and with far worse consequences that would agitate and move your tranquil society?*[1084]

It is in this web of lies that the seeds of destruction would be sown to discredit the liberal-minded Filipinos and to incriminate helpless innocent victims like Burgos. One such occasion presented itself in October 1869 when the students of the university demonstrated their defiance to the established norms.

The liberal ideas espoused by the 1868 Glorious Revolution had caught the imagination of the university students who began to openly interact with other liberal-minded Filipinos during the superior civil government of La Torre. Calling themselves *Juventud Escolar Liberal* (Liberal Student Youth), the group was composed of Gregorio Sanciangco y Gozon, Florentino Villaruel, Gracio Gonzaga, Gregorio Mapa, Ariston Reyes, Bernabe Victorino, Eduardo Munarris, Hermogenes del Rosario, N. Guito, Paciano Rizal, Mariano Alejandrino, Manuel de Leon, Francisco Tison, Domiciano Tison, Ladislaw Dairet, Pablo Luciano, the priests N. Canda, Juan Aniag and Agustin Estrella; and Ramon Soriano, Basilio and Teodorico Teodoro, M. Masigan, N. Vales, Balbino Ventura, Angel Resurreccion, N. Lanco; Fortunato, Potenciano, Victor, Justo and Felipe Buencamino; Sisenando Tecson and Juan Buencamino; with Felipe Buencamino as their leader.[1085] It so happened that sometime 31 January 1869 Felipe Buencamino, Gregorio Sanciangco and Paciano Rizal were admonished by a certain liberal partisan to rid off their Latin text books and to study in Spanish instead because they were all Spaniards.[1086] The following day in the canon law class of P. Fr. Benito Carominas OP, Buencamino recited the lesson in Spanish.[1087] The professor was shocked and dismissed the class early. The incident precipitated a series of events that would divide the university into anti and pro administration factions among the students.

Dominican historian Villaroel relates the incident:

Plate LI
Controversial Governor Generals

Carlos Maria de la Torre y Navacerrada
1869-1870

- Artist unknown 1931. Fulgosio 1931

Rafael Izquierdo y Gutierrez
1871-1873

-Artist unknown 1860-1869. © Biblioteca Nacional de España bdh0000146183

> ...one morning early in October as the students of Canon Law of the University walked into the classroom they were surprised at seeing spread all over the floor copies of an anonymous leaflet, which read:
>
> > **Abajo el si Padre** (Down with the 'Yes, Father")
> > **Abajo el Reverencia** (Down with the Reverence)
> > **Abajo el besamanos** (Down with the hand kissing)
> > **Abajo el tu para nosotros** (Down with the "tu" for us)
>
> For eight successive days, new leaflets were found in the same classroom and in some others. A lampoon was also posted in the so-called "Puente Provisional" near the university. In all cases the tirades ended with a call for academic freedom, but what was more alarming was a new color given to the late manifestos with their allusions to race differences, to slavery and subjugation.
>
> ...The student population responded with counter-manifestoes in the form of letters to the Rector in which they vigorously protested against the vilification of their professors and manifested loyalty to the institution and to the Dominican catedraticos.[1088]

On the urging of the university's rector, La Torre commissioned Dr. Jose de Arrieta to conduct a legal investigation on the matter and to find the authors on 16 October. He had twelve suspects arrested and detained in Bilibid prison two days later. They included Felipe Buencamino, Mariano del Castillo, Lorenzo Salazar, D. Agaton Estrella, Jose and Pedro Mosesgeld Santiago, Francisco Tison, Ladislao Dairit, Mariano Alejandrino, Teodorico and Basilio Teodoro, Ambrosio Robles and Ambrosio Salazar.[1089] Arrieta was Burgos' professor of Civil Law at the university who followed a strict protocol in the investigation. It ended on 7 December without any substantive findings and the suspects were all eventually released. The gossip mill was nevertheless very active and Burgos was rumored as the instigator behind the student unrest when his only role was to tutor Buencamino to catch up for lost time in prison.[1090] There was a seemingly innocuous document found during the investigation that alarmed La Torre however.

The investigation involved parents of suspected students. In a house located in Bulacan, a manifesto on individual rights patterned after the most advanced models used in the Peninsula was found. Whether this manifesto was planted by devious sources or otherwise is another matter altogether. Nevertheless, it proposed or petitioned the removal of the religious Augustinians, Recollects, Franciscans and Dominicans from the islands. That they be deprived from the care of souls, be required to live according to their rule and be replaced by *indio* and *mestizo* clerics in curacies. The controversial statement involved the following means to gain independence: *By replacing the Spanish parish priests with indio and mestizo curates, we can achieve our independence with nothing more than this and with little effort.*[1091] It was the first time that independence was enunciated as a goal and it moved La Torre to action.

La Torre may had been a liberal but a patriot he was first and foremost. On 22 December 1869, he issued a confidential order to the Post Office to hold all letters from Europe and Hong Kong addressed to Jose Gabriel Esquivel, Tomas Fuentes, Manuel Fuentes, Ambrosio Bautista, Agustin Mendoza, Jose Burgos, Juan Adriano, Ignacio Rocha and Joaquin Loyzaga Jr.[1092] The following day a confidential order was issued to the Post Master General making arrangements to examine the letters after the prescribed formalities and to report the results.[1093] The list would be expanded to include [Joaquin] Pardo [de Tavera]; [Mauricio de] Leon; [Enrique] Paraiso; [Jose] Burgos; [Angel] Garchitorena; [D. Jose Guevarra] the parish priest of Quiapo; [D. Agustin Mendoza] of Santa Cruz; [D. Victor Dizon] of Pampanga, where he is the rector of the college; [D. Agaton Estrella] a priest of San Jose; [Jacinto] Zamora; [Lorenzo] Rocha; [Jose Gabriel] Esquivel; [Crisanto de los] Reyes; [Jose and Pio] Basa Brothers.[1094]

The discovery of the alleged broad based plot was disclosed in a Manila newspaper and *La Verdad*. It narrated *the murder and expulsion of friars, of employed and unemployed european spaniards, the mass armament of the country, the proclamation of all the liberties and independence of Filipinas, and other matters in this manner*. *La Discusion* noted that these puerile inventions die quickly once the press is used to discredit them. It further highlighted that the issues were nothing new considering that the issues had been debated and elucidated in the pages of *La Discusion* and that recent agitations were caused by the violent accusations of a friar procurator.[1095] The controversial news report nevertheless elicited varied reactions.

From the emerging confidential dossiers, La Torre reported to the Overseas Minister that *everything, I repeat, leads one to believe that these lawyers and priests are the only ones here who dream of independence of the country.*[1096] By 18 January 1870, La Torre reported:

> *I have intercepted the correspondence of certain persons indicated as suspect by their antecedents, by confidential information given to me, and by public opinion, but have found nothing in the letters which can give reason to proceed against them.*[1097]

Jose Burgos began to write openly under his name to counteract the malicious attacks authored by Franciscan Procurator P. Fr. Joaquin Coria OFM and other detractors in a series of six letters and one memorial, four of which were published in *La Discusion* and one in *La Armonia*.[1098] His first letter was unpublished and contained an exposition addressed to the Captain General dated 14 January 1879 professing the secular clergy's fidelity and loyalty to Spain and denouncing the accusations of which they had been the object. Between 1 March and 12 April 1870, Burgos wrote four letters published in *La Discusion* defending the honor of the Filipino clergy, refuting Coria's self-righteous allegations and disclosing the friars' opposition to proposed parish reforms. Reacting to an anonymous article published in *Altar y Trono*, Burgos wrote his reply to the Editor of *La Armonia* on 6 December 1870 admonishing the article's misguided contents. His last official written work was a memorial of the Filipino clergy dated 14 February 1871 addressed to the Regent of Spain Francisco Serrano and signed by 185 priests and 64 clerics of the Archdiocese of Manila petitioning for the revocation of the 10 September 1861 indemnification decree and for the return of the secular parishes given to the Recollects since then. *Almost all the priests active in the campaign for the rights of the Filipino clergy were priests of Manila who had studied at the Colegio de San Juan de Letran and in the university.*[1099]

D. Jose Burgos' new public persona as a nationalist writer and recognized leader of the Filipinos would attract more notoriety; making him a vulnerable target for malevolent schemers.

Sometime in June 1870, the remains of Simon de Anda y Salazar was to be temporarily transferred from the ruins of the Manila cathedral to the Chapel of the Venerable Third Order of St Francis pending the reconstruction of the former. French observer Edmund Plauchut related the event attended by La Torre and Manila's elite:

> *On the day of the transfer the people, in mourning clothes, gathered as a mass as if directed by secret instructions and went on their way to attend the rites.*
>
> *The funeral cortege left the ruined cathedral, proceeded along the principal streets, and in the midst of the huge crowd entered the church of San Agustin where the blessing was to be sung before the transfer to the Franciscan church. Essences were sprayed and flowers and bouquets strewn over the catafalque along the way. In San Agustin, at the moment when the responsory was to begin, a young priest stepped forth from the group of his fellow priests. He carried a beautiful wreath of laurel and pansies and bowing deferentially as he passed before the esteemed governor-general, he ascended the steps to the bier and lay a long cloth streamer over the shroud, bearing the legend: "The Secular Clergy of Filipinas to Don Simon de Anda y Salazar." Hardly had the young priest come down from the catafalque, pale with emotion, when a student proceeded up the steps and placed a second wreath on the coffin. A group of gobernadorcillos followed him, come to render homage to the persecuted patriot in the name of the pueblos.*
>
> *An inquiry was conducted to find out who was the instigator of the manifestation. Nobody dared to identify him. However, the public rumor was that D. Jose Burgos was responsible.*[1100]

Burgos' confessor, the Jesuit superior P. Pedro Bertran SJ, ominously warned him in early 1870 of the dangers if his writings and the use of radical and anticlerical publications like the *La Discusion* continued:

> *"These matters are purely canonical and ecclesiastical, and hence have their own proper judges and tribunals as you know. To bring them into the public arena and precisely by means of publication of markedly anti religious tendencies, is to distort their nature, and to give them, moreover, in spite of yourself, an importance and a determined political*

color… Give this up; otherwise you will find yourself pushed on to worse steps. Even supposing that you have sufficient strength to turn back, perhaps you may not be able to prevent a hand doubly criminal from writing your name on a banner waved by deluded men and traitors… If you do not cease, I ask you not to call any further at our door".[1101]

Burgos did stop calling on the Jesuits until the eve of his death. His use of the *La Armonia* instead of *La Discusion* later that year may had something to do with his confessor's counsel. On 4 April 1871, Rafael de Izquierdo y Gutierrez became Superior Civil Governor and Captain General of Filipinas.[1102] Twelve days later, Burgos was awarded the Doctorate degree in Canon Law from the university. He continued gaining recognition for his achievements; receiving on 28 August his appointment as magistral canon from the new governor-general.[1103] King Amadeo of Savoy appointed Burgos as Regular Commander of the Order of Isabel the Catholic as early as 5 August 1871 and was given sufficient time to comply with its requirements.[1104] He would not live long enough to receive it.

The Cavite Mutiny

On 22 August 1972, Foreign Secretary Carlos P. Romulo publicly announced that the Spanish government was unable to locate the documents pertaining to the Cavite Mutiny despite an extensive search in the military archives and concluded that they may have been lost during the Spanish Civil War of 1936-1939. The announcement dampened any hopes for a definitive account of the incident or the full disclosure of the underlying evidences for now. With the benefit of hindsight however, one can reconstruct what happened from facts contained in extant documents and first hand accounts. The exercise resulted in crystallizing the revolt's original plan, what actually happened when it was implemented, and the sequence of events that followed after. There is however a note of caution. Certain crucial facts had been based on testimonies from two key witnesses: Francisco Saldua and Bonifacio Octavo whose dubious motives and vexatious circumstances question their reliability.[1105] Nevertheless, the perceived causes of the revolt and its alleged instigators provide interesting insights into the actions taken after. There are two perspectives in this regard - those of Rafael Izquierdo and Antonio Maria Regidor. Based on the succeeding facts, the readers are left to judge for themselves.

The Plan

A secret *Junta* planned a revolt to declare independence from Spain and set it in motion sometime November or December 1871.[1106] The *pronunciamiento* was to be executed by native infantry troops and naval contingents taking control of important military and naval installations in Manila and Cavite and rallying other native military detachments in key provinces throughout the archipelago to join thereafter.[1107] Agitating unrest and soliciting support were to be undertaken clandestinely by word of mouth and handbill distribution.[1108] Sufficient commitments were to be developed and achieved among the native non-commissioned officers of marine and artillery troops with elements from the 1st, 2nd and 7th Regiments enticing them with promotions to colonel or lieutenant colonel.[1109] Preferably while the Spanish naval squadron was away in Jolo, the *pronunciamiento* was to begin in Manila in the early hours after the midnight of a date to be set. Fires were to be set in Tondo so that, while the authorities were occupied with extinguishing them, the artillery regiment and part of the infantry stationed in Manila would take possession of Fort Santiago and signal to those of Cavite by means of canon fire.[1110] All Spaniards were to be killed without failing to except those who would be defenseless or would not resist.[1111] Proclamation of independence would follow. The artillery and marines in Cavite would rise, to be supported by 300 men of the 7th Regiment stationed there commanded by Lt. Col. Horacio Sawa and 500 men of the Scouts Battalion commanded by Casimiro Camerino in Bacoor.[1112]

Actual Operations

The *pronunciamiento* was set to begin in Manila in the early hours after midnight of 20 January 1872. On the night of the 20th, the rebels in Cavite mistook the fireworks from the Sampaloc fiesta for the agreed signal and went to arms between 8:00 and 9:00 in the evening instead.[1113] Sergeant Fernando Lamadrid killed Lt. Nicolas Rodriguez, the commanding officer of Fort San Felipe who refused to surrender, and assumed control.[1114] The rebelling marines and artillerymen entered the barracks of the 7th Regiment in Cavite to combine forces. Sergeant Bonifacio Octavo, the rebel leader of the 7th regiment, was nowhere to be found.[1115] Col. Sawa rallied the regiment and fought the rebels through the night until the regiments of Manila joined them.[1116] All three infantry regiments, in Manila and Cavite, remained loyal to Spain and the rebels retreated to Fort San Felipe until it was overran on 22 January. Three emissaries were sent to Manila to inform the authorities: one by boat and two, Agustin Vasquez and Jose Gomez, by horseback.[1117] The latter two were ambushed and killed by a band of armed natives believed to be Camerino's men who would be impeded from reinforcing the fort by a navy gunboat.[1118]

In response to the news reaching Manila, the 1st and 2nd Regiments arrived at the Cavite *Arsenal* on the 21st under the command of deputy Captain General Felipe Ginoves y Espinar with naval support under the frigate captain General Manuel Carballo. The assault began at 6 in the morning of the 22nd and the fort was taken an hour later.[1119] The fort commander and maid were found dead with his wife wounded.[1120] In the same room was P. Fr. Antonio Rufian OH, a friar of San Juan de Dios.[1121] Two Spanish officers were found among the rebels.[1122] Lieutenant Manuel Montesinos was killed while Lieutenant Vicente Lopez Morquecho attempted suicide and died some time later.[1123] Lamadrid was found suffering from gunpowder burns and was put to death *a cuchillo* (by the blade). Barely three hours after securing the fort, Ginoves telegraphed Izquierdo to arrest *P. Burgos, rector of San Pedro, for the good of the service.*[1124]

The rebels consisted of 38 artillerymen and 54 marines.[1125] Those who did not surrender were bayoneted to death. The remaining 41 were brought to Manila and convicted of treason on 26 January.[1126] The following day, 28 death sentences were commuted to life imprisonment and the remaining 13 were executed by firing squad in front of their peers.[1127] The loyalists suffered 3 deaths and 18 wounded.[1128]

More arrests of military personnel would follow including members of the Scouts Battalion. On 6 February, Casimiro Camerino was found guilty for the deaths of Vasquez and Gomez and was executed the following day by *garrote vil*.[1129] 11 of his men were sentenced to 10 years imprisonment in a *presidio*.[1130] By 28 September, 30 other death sentences meted on rebel soldiers were commuted to life with Sergeant Bonifacio Octavo of the 7th Regiment as the last to be spared.[1131]

The Aftermath

On 19 January, Izquierdo and Carballo both received anonymous letters disclosing a simultaneous revolt in Manila and Cavite planned for the evening of the 20th or the next.[1132] The following were its contents:

> *I make known to you that, as I was informed this very night, in the market here* [Cavite] *and in the walls* [Intramuros] *on Friday or Saturday of this week they will fire a cannon shot in the fort of Manila, the sign of a revolt against the Spaniards. They are taking this occasion since the squadron is not here. The one who is acting as the head of the revolt is the Very Reverend Father Burgos in Manila and in Cavite the artillery sergeants and the corporals of the native marines.*[1133]

Alerted, Izquierdo undertook steps to insure the loyalty of the troops and prepared plans to be executed as soon as events unfolded. A series of civilian arrests were effected a day before the assault of Fort San Felipe. Beginning 21 January, suspected members of the rebel *Junta* and their associates composed of secular priests, lawyers, businessmen and other civilians were imprisoned.

Among the priests were Jose Burgos - cathedral canon and curate of cathedral *sagrario* parish of San Pedro, Jacinto Zamora - first curate of sagrario parish of San Pedro, Mariano Gomes - Vicar Forane of Cavite and curate of Bacoor, Feliciano Gomez, Miguel de Laza - cathedral chaplain, Agustin Mendoza - curate of Santa Cuz, Jose Guevara - curate of Quiapo, Mariano Sevilla - chaplain of the military hospital, Justo Guanzon - coadjutor of the cathedral, Vicente del Rosario - army chaplain, Pedro Dandan, Anacleto Desiderio, and Toribio H. del Pilar. The group of lawyers included Antonio Maria Regidor, Joaquin Pardo de Tavera, Jose Basa, Pedro Carillo, Gervasio Sanchez, and Bartolome Serra. Among the other civilians were Ramon Maurente, Mauricio de Leon, Balbino Mauricio, Pio Basa,

Francisco Saldua, Enrique Paraiso, Maximo Inocencio, Crisanto de los Reyes and a last minute addition Maximo Paterno.[1134]

The court proceedings against the accused civilians were irregularly conducted by a *Consejo de Guerra* (Council of War) presided by Lt. Col. Francisco Moscoso y Lara. Under existing laws, a military tribunal did not have jurisdiction over civilians unless an extraordinary military tribunal had been constituted only after a prior declaration of a state of war.[1135] When the tribunal requested for the background records against the accused, Izquierdo replied citing *confidential reports, anonymous or otherwise ... public talk and also from secret reports ... public notoriety and general opinion* as bases to establish guilt.[1136] Prosecution conducted by Lt. Col. Manuel Boscasa y Perez, needless to say, was based on hearsay and unsupported by creditable evidence. Francisco Saldua was the key eyewitness who confirmed the existence of a separatist *Junta* conspiring to kill all Spaniards and to establish an independent state. He further identified Burgos as president of the *junta directiva* with Gomes, Zamora, Guevara, Regidor, Pardo, Serra and Sanchez as members.[1137] All other corroborating witnesses pointed to Saldua or to the deceased Lamadrid as their source of information.[1138] Incredulously, Saldua incriminated himself as the principal accomplice.

The trials were hurriedly conducted and the accused were not adequately defended. In the case of Burgos, for instance, the defense counsel assigned to him was Dr. Jose de Arrieta, his civil law professor who conducted the 1869 Student Unrest investigation. Regidor described the lawyer's gross mishandling of the case in the following account:

After the routine preliminaries, the reading of a medley of allegations by an infinite number of witnesses, all hearsay and without any specific or direct evidence, the Fiscal Boscasa read his accusation, asking for Gomes, Zamora and Burgos with Saldua the penalty of death by garrote vil; for Paraiso, Reyes and Inocencio, the penalty of 10 years of presidio.

The defense attorneys read their concise statements. The most extraordinary was that of Burgos' counsel; instead of presenting a defense he implored the mercy of the court because, as he said afterwards, it was not possible to plead otherwise, given his own opinion that Burgos had confessed his guilt... Burgos was aghast on hearing his counsel and could not help rising furious and exclaimed to the court: I have neither confessed nor pleaded guilty. That is not my pleading - this gentleman has changed it. I deny all the charges against me, they are all groundless in fact and in law.[1139]

The trials lasted two weeks and a verdict was reached on 15 February. The seven who were tried together were found guilty. Burgos, Gomes, Zamora and Saldua were found guilty of *conspiracy against the constituted authority of the country and of being authors of the military rebellion that broke out in the Fort of Cavite on the night of last 20 January, all this with the sole purpose of separating this archipelago from the mother country, proclaiming in it a republic and thus directly attacking the integrity of the monarchy.* The court condemned

Plate LII
Alumni Casualty and Survivor of the 1872 Cavite Mutiny

B. Don Jacinto Zamora y del Rosario
1835-1872

Dr. Antonio Maria Regidor y Jurado
1845-1910

- Artists unknown 1933. Bazaco 1933.

Burgos, Zamora, Gomes and Saldua to the *penalty of death by the garrote and to ten years imprisonment with the clause of retention for Inocencio and Paraiso and ten years without the clause of retention for Reyes* in the presidio of Cartegena. The court further declared that *this sentence will be made known to His Excellency the Most Reverend Archbishop of the diocese for the degradation of the priests D. Jose Burgos, D. Jacinto Zamora and D. Mariano Gomez.*[1140] The other 21 civilians enumerated herein were sentenced from 6 to 10 years imprisonment in the presidio of Guam, and more than 100 other prisoners were exiled to Paragua (Palawan).[1141]

Abp. Gregorio Meliton Martinez Santa Cruz, in his letter to Izquierdo on 30 January 1872, wrote:

> *... I cannot ignore the character of the lofty, though unmerited, character with which I have been invested and must therefor beg you in the name of religion to mitigate the penalties to the extent that the laws and the maintenance of order and of future tranquility permit, even avoiding, if possible, the shedding of blood. This is what I hope from the noble heart of Your Excellency, whose generous sentiments I cannot but count on. Thus, just as it has been strong and energetic in extinguishing the flame of revolt, after the flame has been put out, it will be kind and merciful with the guilty, reconciling, in your well-known intelligence and prudence, mercy with the demands of justice.*[1142]

The archbishop must had been disappointed to learn that Izquierdo heeded his plea with regard to his fellow freemasons Paraiso, Inocencio and Reyes but not in the case of the three priests and Saldua. He wrote the following letter in response to the degradation of the priests on 15 February 1872:

> *Overwhelmed by the profound sorrow caused by a reading of the sentence accompanying Your Excellency's communication which I have just received, I am compelled to make it known to you with due respect that to proceed with the degradation of the priests D. Jose Burgos, D. Jacinto Zamora and D. Mariano Gomes, condemned to death, I deem it indispensable to have a complete knowledge of the case. I beg that a copy of the record of the proceedings of the Council of War be furnished me, as its perusal would enable me to form a correct opinion essential to cases wherein the severest penalty provided for by Canon Law is imposed. But, Your Excellency, will the devout Filipino people be given the terrifying spectacle of the execution of three priests? If the execution of such a severe sentence had been carried out following the event, when the terrible shock of the treacherous assassinations were still fresh in the public mind, and the extent of the work of the rebels could not be determined, the patriotic desire of preserving the integrity of the Spanish territory, and the instinct of self-preservation, would have hindered heeding the pleas of mercy. But once the insurrection was extinguished, spirits once more serene and peace and order assured, may I not be permitted to implore for a second time of Your Excellency to mitigate the terrible sentence of death? This I hope Your Excellency will do, whose generous heart is more*

attuned to the sentiments of mercy than to the harshness of justice. God save Your Excellency for many years.[1143]

Having already shown his contempt for civil law, Izquierdo ignored the archbishop's request to comply with canon law. He allowed the executions to proceed without the priests being defrocked.

Izquierdo's Perspective

Rafael de Izquierdo viewed the rebellion as a broad conspiracy prepared over a long period of time. 1863 was his starting point referring to the aborted rebellion of D. Pedro Pelaez as alleged by the commissary friars. 1869 became his often quoted year of reckoning. This year was highlighted by the university student unrest marked by the discovery of a dubious document clamoring for independence; triggering the confidential investigation of various suspects. Dossiers were initiated and compiled under La Torre who considered them as a collection of hearsay and public opinion and did not act on them for lack of evidence. Izquierdo, on the otherhand, decided to act on them and the rest is history.

Izquierdo suddenly tendered his resignation and departed for Spain on 8 January 1873. He surrendered the reins of government to the commanding general of the Naval Station, Manuel MacCrohon, in an interim capacity.[1144] As stated in the letter, the reason for this unexpected turn of events was due to his life being in imminent danger.[1145] At the official end of his term of office in December 1872, he submitted a *Memoria* containing an account of the general governance of Filipinas during his term. The following were his insights on the Cavite Mutiny:

The españoles of the country, the mestizos, the secular priests - all of them, which the General La Torre used to say, expected too much from the September revolution and from him being its representative here. They did not expect anything from me. What they longed for was the opportunity to release the cry of rebellion, the voice of death to all the españoles for which they have been working for 2 years in the shadows with such cunning and such guile that it passed the notice of neither authority nor español; having already gained the support of almost the entire army.

Since my arrival to these Islands, I found an administration in disarray by virtue of the continuous changes of personnel and its poor state of condition, with the principle of authority unrecognized and forgotten, with the regular clergy fearful and discontented of Spanish politics, even more so with the conspiracy that has been known in Filipinas already prepared and primed to explode and with almost all the army committed to the rebellion. Combined with the agonizing situation of the Treasury showing an annual deficit in its budget of more than 20 million pesetas and in debt by more than 8 million to the tobacco farmers, one can easily understand the severity of the situation I found the country in.

The military insurrection that erupted in Cavite on 20 January of the current year is the most serious act relative to public order that occurred in these Islands. It had been variably considered as an isolated act without either significance or consequence or as an explosion of sentiments for independence cherished by the Filipino people and consequently like the precursive movement of other events resulting in a brief moment the loss of Filipinas by Spain. Both assessments are nothing farther from the truth. The Cavite insurrection was neither an act without importance for the present and the future, nor is the situation so filled with danger that it is impossible to avert them.

To appreciate duly, it is necessary to examine the causes of the insurrection, the means employed and the goal that they aimed to accomplish.

I had already complained about them somewhat. Notwithstanding the principal character and conditions of the different races that populate the Archipelago, the only ones capable of initiating a conspiracy are naturally the españoles of the country, the mestizos, and between them most specially the secular clergy.

The insane ambition of some and the belief of others that their intellectual superiority over the native race entitles them to own the country and to separate it from the Spanish nation was the sole motive of the conspiracy.

In view of the ideas emanating from 1868 Revolution, the exalted press of Madrid started to propagate the cry of independence launched by the rebels in Cuba. Using freedom as a pretext, the correspondence sustained between the conspirators here and the workers in Spain threaten the national integrity. I ascertained a number of arrangements that were far from good intention. All these contributed to fan the flame of a separatist ideal. The conspiracy began to organize. The Junta Directiva was formed. The newspaper El Eco Filipino was founded in Madrid and was widely circulated with 1500 subscribers here. With an active propaganda, funds were raised and a planned insurrection finally broke out on 20 January. The undertaking was easy and the occasion opportune.

Our domination is sustained solely by moral suasion, and [critical] if this is lost or weakened. We lack the military force in as much as the army is entirely indigenous and consequently a primary enemy in the event of a racial clash. We even lack gunboats which at that time were sailing the waters of Jolo. The españoles are too few in number that resistance would be impossible, and any external assistance would be hopeless in view of the immense distance that separates us from the mother country. To the rebels, the project's success must have appeared to be as sure as it was simple to execute.

They bribed a major part of the army offering native corporals and sergeants promotions to Lieutenant Colonels and Colonels. They promised posts to those who did not belong to the military. They assured liberty to prisoners. And when these elements joined, they launched the rebellion…

The president and two individuals of the Junta were executed, the five remaining were condemned in the Marianas. Those who did not form part of the Junta were exiled to Marianas and other parts.[1146]

Regidor's Perspective

For Antonio Maria Regidor y Jurado, the Cavite Mutiny was an isolated and contained incident contrived by the regular clergy.[1147] Exploiting the widespread discontent, he surmised that the friars set into motion a plan that would underscore their important role in preserving Spain's continuing domination of *Filipinas*, counteract the threats of a fresh wave of *desamortizacion, exclaustracion* and educational reforms mandated after the 1868 Glorious Revolution and simultaneously neutralize their liberal enemies. After obtaining amnesty from his alleged involvement in the mutiny, Regidor wrote a number of articles about the mutiny anonymously or under pseudonyms such as Francisco Engracio Vergara. Unless otherwise cited, the following account is principally from his article published in *Filipinas ante Europa* on 28 February 1900 in Madrid.

> *There are still some who claim that the events of Cavite were part of a separatist movement, directed by various Filipinos of influence in their country. This is utterly false, because its directing authors were all peninsulares as follows: first, the lieutenant Don Jose Montesinos, who was executed by the firing squad; second, the Military Administration Official, 1st class, named [Vicente Lopez] Morquecho, who committed suicide; third, Fray Antonio Rufian, lay brother of San Juan de Dios, who was released upon his testimony that he was in the fort of San Felipe under duress, locked up by the rebels so he would give them confession if that became necessary; and fourth, the Fr. [Juan Cruz] Gomez, Prior of the Recollect convent in Cavite [el Viejo], who according to some, is now the Procurator of the same in Madrid. He was also not harassed; and in his place the most respected elderly curate of Bacoor was hanged, the native cleric don Mariano Gomes.*[1148]

> *The Filipino revolution is traceable* de facto *and* de jure *to the armed protest (of Ilocos) in 1814.*[1149] *It is absolutely untrue that during any time thereafter Filipinas enjoyed peace whether moral or material. The ardor might have intensified or subsided but the struggle persisted without any solution. Let us call to mind the fair number of armed uprisings that took place during the century that is about to close; and it will be seen that the protagonists in this contest always remained the same: the friars absurdly trying to dominate the country and the civilian Filipino resolutely rejecting the autocracy of friar rule.*

> *The Filipinos ultimately triumphed. But because at that time the ruling elements in Spain sided with the friars, the Filipinos could not succeed*

there, with the result that Spain's meaningful participation in the societal life of the Orient came to an end.

Whenever the friars desired more land they inflated their needs in Filipinas, and expanded their influence on the political authorities in Spain. The latter acceded blindly to the friars' tutelage, and allowed inquisitorial excesses and the despotic abuses. The tide of discontent was on the rise, the September revolution gave hope to the liberal-minded Filipinos and even sectors that had been indifferent began to interest themselves in the problem. Drastic action and exemplary punishment thus became necessary: to intimidate one and all, to reenact the period of Oraa and to flood the fields of Filipinas with blood as in Tayabas of 1841 and the regimental mutiny that followed.[1150]

A scheme was hatched and planned, played out in a drama that began on the night of 20 January 1872. The second act was at the gallows erected at the Espaldon. The drama ended with a scene on the beaches of Paragua (Palawan) and another in Guam in the Marianas Islands. The conventual aeropagus was constituted and included Sñres. [Rafael] Castro and [Domingo] Treserra, dominicans; the P. [Mariano] Cuartero, Recollect, much later Bishop of Jaro; the P. [Felix] Huertas, franciscan and the P. [Casimiro] Herrero, agustinian, The agreements were executable and the program was ordained.

The preparations commenced with the election of [Pedro Vilanova] the new Provincial of Santo Domingo, buxom buddy of general Izquierdo, a prominent celebrity in the new political milieu of Spain. The scheme was set on course with Izquierdo's appointment as governor general of Filipinas, bypasssing General Nuvilas who had been appointed before him to the position.

The events in the drama were impelled by the reorganization of the artillery corps. The new organization had one of the two artillery battalions composed of peninsular Spaniards, the other of natives. All officers were peninsulares. That the differences in pay, rations, cots and so forth, would give rise to jealousy, frictions and strife in the barracks was not considered.

Matters heated up with the arrest, relief from all duties and detention in the fort of San Felipe [in Cavite] of the military governor of Fort Santiago [in Manila], Commandant D. Pedro Garde, a general in the artillery corps; the arrest of D. Jose de Azcarraga, D. Jose Ramos and D. Narciso Claveria all captains of peninsular companies, all Filipinos; and the abolition of the office of judge advocate of the corps, where D. Jose del Castillo and D. Antonio Regidor, both Filipinos, the judge advocate and prosecuting attorney, respectively.

Finally, the tension was ignited by the quarter master general Jimeno Agius, who required the workers in the Cavite Arsenal to pay tribute. These workers were all retirees from the navy and had enjoyed exemption from the tribute as their reward for long service with the fleet. The tribute was also arbitrarily imposed on seamen and on the land troopers of the naval infantry; all of them served in Cavite, had no prospects for promotion or reward, but till then had enjoyed exemption from the tribute.

On the otherhand the friar [Juan Cruz] Gomez, prior of the Recollect Convent, in Cavite [el Viejo] was using [Francisco] Saldua and his wife to persuade the arsenal workers not to pay the tribute.[1151] At the same time Gomez used the peninsular lay brother Fray Antonio Rufian of the Order of San Juan de Dios to press the infantry lieutenants Montesinos and Morquecho, both European Spaniards working out disciplinary punishments in the fort of San Felipe, to lead the artillery troops who garrisoned the fort and support the arsenal workers if fighting were to break out.

None of these happened in secret. Colonel Butler, military governor of Cavite, was instructed to implement the weekly payment in the Kanakaw (Cañacao) Arsenal on Saturday the 20th. Each worker's pay was to be deducted by the amount of his tribute including that of his wife and children. Butler protested, reiterated his disagreement, and finally resigned anticipating an unavoidable mutiny that no sufficient forces could stop. If the Arsenal and the artillery troopers united, the surrounding population would be devastated.

One has to take into account that the Rear Admiral D. Manuel MacCrohon, naval commanding general, together with the commanding general of the fleet, disapproved the reform and the tribute which altogether do not represent more than 400 pesos annually to the State. To prevent the conflagration, he met with General Izquierdo with whom quite a lively altercation ensued. Soon after, MacCrohon departed with his squadron for the south of the islands leaving a single gunboat in Manila and Cavite for the disposition of the Manila port captain, D. Manuel Carballo.

Butler warned about the situation of the forces in Cavite, complained about the transfer of the convicted peninsulares Montesinos and Morquecho, and the relief of the Fort San Felipe garrison detachment. His proposal was disregarded and his resignation accepted. Colonel [Fernando] Rojas replaced him and took over in the same morning of the 20th.

The resoluteness of General Izquierdo and the Intendente Jimeno Agius allowed the conflict to transpire as anticipated. At the start of the daily wage payments, the Arsenal workers were outraged at the application of the tribute. They rejected the amounts given to them and declared a strike. When the news reached the fort where the friar Rufian was, the ilongo [Fernando] Lamadrid demanded the surrender of the lieutenant heading the detachment, who reached for his sword. He was shot and left dead by the door of the corps on duty. Lamadrid dressed with the insignias of a lieutenant, and with [Montesinos] and Morquecho divided the command of the forces and began firing at the town.

Naval and artillery troops espoused a common cause. The civilian element was neutral, impassive and indifferent of the battle. Governor Roxas and the regiment under the command of Lt. Col. Sawa used the principal street of the walled city as base until the next day, Sunday 21 January 1872. On that day, the Recollect friars celebrated ostentatiously the feast of the Virgen del Carmen in the Manila church of San Sebastian. It so happens that the Cavite pronunciamiento *occurred between two feasts. When the lights were turned off, the dances, dinners, and the echo of the skyrockets ceased in San Anton (Sampaloc). Later the bells rang, and new skyrockets were launched. Prayers and procession commenced in San Sebastian, a barrio in the outlying district of Quiapo.*

At dawn the first official notice of the pronunciamiento *arrived at Malacañan; and between six and seven one of the river steamers set sail for Cavite bringing troops and the general [Felipe Ginoves y] Espinar, deputy captain general of the islands who once headed the Cuban volunteers that deposed and expelled General [Domingo] Dulce from Cuba. Other smaller steamers followed with more troops.*

The assault of the fort was organized upon arrival in Cavite. By then the gunfire between the fort and the arsenal had ceased. The fort was stormed without minor resistance. All the soldiers inside were executed. The first was sergeant Lamadrid; followed by lieutenant Montesinos. As his turn came, Morquecho grabbed a revolver and discharged a bullet to his temple. He died two or three days later. The others were killed where they stood in the assault. The P. Rufian was freed and shortly departed Filipinas for Spain. Various prisoners confined in vaults and cells remained in detention and sent much later to Paragua (Palawan).

Those of the arsenal were spared from the justice exacted because the marines resisted. A group of the rebels who swam to escape were apprehended and taken on board the gunboat. Another group tried to escape by land but half of them were caught and shot. The rest were brought to Manila where they were executed on the 22nd at 6 in the morning with all the major military rituals conducted to terrify the natives. Those who hid in the arsenal were taken on board the gunboat in the afternoon. The captain general complained about the hand over of prisoners for inclusion in the court martial initiated by the Council of War; prompting the Governor General to order the said transfer. Furthemore the Navy having nominated another Fiscal delayed the issue until the rapid return from the south of Rear Admiral Macrohon who rejected the competence of jurisdiction. General Izquierdo elevated the issue to the Supreme Tribunal of War and Navy which decided in favor of the marines, and much later recommended amnesty.[1152]

The Execution

With the trial concluded, the four condemned to die by *garrote vil* were transferred next morning to the Engineers barracks in Bagumbayan where a chapel was erected. During the next 24 hours, the prisoners were allowed visitors.[1153]

During the whole day of 16 February and until the following dawn, multitudes of people arrived and departed in waves. A number of Burgos' students came to bid their mentor a last farewell. His last counsel to them was recorded and published for posterity by Austin Craig, to wit:

> *Get educated. Use the schools of our country for as much as they can give. Learn from our older men what they know. Read what foreigners have written about the Philippines. Then go abroad.*
>
> *If you can do no better, study in Spain, but preferably study in freer countries. Read what foreigners have written about the Philippines for their writings have not been censored. See the museums of other lands what the ancient Filipinos really were. Be a Filipino always, but an educated Filipino.*
>
> *Heretofore we have had thinkers among us but their thoughts have died with them. Such progress as has been made has been individual and not of the country. I have tried to pass on to you what I received from my teachers. Do you now do the same for those who come after you.*[1154]

By nightfall, Gomes confessed and entrusted his last will and testament to P. Fr. Juan Cruz Gomez OAR who would stay by his side until the end. A Jesuit, P. Magin Ferrando SJ, attended to Burgos and a religious from the Congregation of the Mission to Zamora.[1155]

On the 17th, *indios* from Bulacan, Pampanga, Cavite and Laguna came to see whom they considered their fathers and their beloved martyrs. Most were dressed for mourning and praying. Some 40,000 occupied the space between the gallows and the prison.[1156] An anxious and wary European community joined to witness the spectacle while segregating themselves from the natives.[1157] The proceedings commenced promptly at 7 in the morning with the somber beating of the drums hushing the crowd into a deafening silence. Cordoned by soldiers in their formal uniforms, appeared the four condemned prisoners. Francisco Saldua was attired with the standard hooded white body length tunic which the others refused to wear.[1158] The priests wore black *americanas* and trousers with the customary white clerical collar and bonnet. With hands and feet shackled, each one marched one after the other towards the scaffolds between two priests.[1159]

A carefree Saldua was accompanied by a Franciscan and a Recollect. Appearing to be lost, Zamora was supported by two Jesuits surrounded by friars from different Orders. An Augustinian and a Recollect accompanied the aged Gomes while two Jesuits escorted a tearful Burgos with their heads bowed down in prayer. Burgos wept like a madman and the dazed Zamora was unmindful of what was happening around him. Meanwhile Gomes, whose gaze was alert with brows held high, blessed the *indios* who fell on their knees along his path. All heads were uncovered and all prayed audibly. After ascending the gallows, they were told to kneel as their sentence was read aloud.

Gomes was the first to be called forward. His Recollect confessor counseled him to accept his fate and to commend his soul to God. The septuagenarian replied: *I know that a tree's leaf is not shaken without the will of the Creator. As it is His will that I die under the same circumstance, let it be done.*[1160]

Hearing his name called out, Zamora silently followed the finger pointing towards the seat attached to the fatal post. The ill-fated one surrendered nothing more than his body to the executioner since his soul had withdrawn from the ordeal two days before.[1161]

Burgos was next. As he walked towards the *garrote,* he saw his trial fiscal Manuel Boscaza and serenely told him: *I forgive you all, sir, and God can pardon you all like I do.* He sat peacefully on the stool of death and suddenly rose crying: *But what crime have I committed? Is it possible that I should die like this? My God! Is there no justice on earth?* At that moment, a dozen friars of different Orders surged towards him. The executioner intervened and asked Burgos to take his seat. Obeying tentatively, he stood once again saying: *But I am innocent.* P. Fr. *Benito Corominas* OP, his Dominican canon law professor, replied: *Jesus Christ was likewise innocent.* Hearing these words, he finally acquiesced. Before tightening his neck, the executioner knelt before the condemned. Moved by what transpired, the surrounding multitude unexpectedly imitated his gesture and began to chant the prayer for the dying. He continued: *Padre forgive me for executing you. I do not wish to do it.* Burgos replied: *I forgive you, my son; but I beseech you to do your duty.* The executioner made the sign of the cross and moments later Burgos gasped his last breath.[1162]

The public prayers grew louder and the Europeans became unsettled, panicked and began to run towards the city. There was still one more condemned to be executed but they were frightened at the prospects of an uncontrolled mob. Saldua's tranquility did not abandon him. His eyes however had a far away look searching impatiently for his deliverance. The messenger who was to bring his pardon failed to appear and the executioner ended his hopes forever.

Escorted by peninsular troops, the lifeless bodies were brought to the Paco cemetery by the *Hermandad de la Misericordia* carriage. The *naturales* faithfully followed the cortege but were barred from entering the cemetery's guarded gate. Outside, the *Misericordia* chaplain led the prayer for the dead with the crowd dispersing after. Inside, the soldiers dug a pit and buried the corpses in an unmarked location. Their bodies would never be recovered.[1163]

<u>An Epilogue</u>

The respected Munich newspaper *Allgemeine Zeitung* published the following on 1 October 1892:

Plate LIII

GomBurZa Martyrs
- *Artist unknown 1891.* Original cover of El Filibusterismo

The Cavite revolt was of transcendental importance to Filipinas because to it is due what has been sought in vain by its most noble sons, whose aspirations had not found expression due to the obstacle of antiquated prejudices.

Until that era the Spaniards born in Filipinas, the Spanish mestizos, Chinese mestizos and the natives had been divided by petty racial interests. But the blind rage with which the regime, in aid of the goals of the friars, persecuted everyone known or suspected to be liberal, united the diverse racial groups into a single solid union. The severe and atrocious persecution that followed in the wake of the revolt in Cavite taught the Filipinos the identity of their interests.

The development of contacts with Spain and foreign nations made them compare their country's political condition with that of the European nations and their colonies nearby with the result that, to the educated Filipinos, the burden weighing down upon their country felt heavier and more intolerable than it was in reality.[1164]

Three years earlier on 15 February 1889, the *La Solidaridad* was founded to be the principal organ of the Propaganda Movement aimed to exposing the prevailing abuses and injustices in *Filipinas* and to championing the much needed reforms. Its contributors belonged to the land's best and brightest who joined together to fulfill this mission. Jose Rizal, in his letter of 18 April 1889 to Mariano Ponce and , wrote:

Without 1872, there would not now be a Plaridel, a Jaena, a Sancianco, nor would the brave and generous Filipino colonies exist in Europe. Without 1872 Rizal would now be a Jesuit and instead of writing the Noli me tangere, *would have written the contrary. At the sight of those injustices and cruelties, though still a child, my imagination awoke, and I swore to dedicate myself to avenge one day so many victims. With this idea I have gone on studying, and this can be read in all my works and writings. God will grant me one day to fulfill my promise.*[1165]

Rizal belonged to a generation of *naturales* affected by the events of 1872 and it was the pen of D. Jose Burgos that moved them to be proud of their national identity and to protect it from racist oppressors and detractors. Like Burgos, Rizal served as living testimony that a *natural de Filipinas* is equal to the Peninsular Spaniard. Through the propaganda work, the *naturales* or *hijos del pais* assumed a common cause and identity. Just like what transpired among the secular clergy, the term *Filipino* ceased to refer to *criollos* only and was broadly applied to all.[1166] The influence of Burgos was apparent in the writings of Rizal and Marcelo del Pilar. Notwithstanding the Propaganda Movement's peaceful efforts, Spain continued to be unresponsive to the pleas for justice and change. The Revolution of 1896 became inevitable.

The revolution would uncover fresh facts surrounding the 1872 Cavite Mutiny. The martyrs were held in great esteem by the Katipunan who used the acronym GomBurZa as their secret password. The opportunity of securing information surrounding their deaths transpired when four friars were captured by Aguinaldo's Cavite revolutionaries in 1896. Contained in signed depositions, P. Fr. Antonio Piernavieja OSA on 5 January 1897 and P. Fr. Agapito Echegoyen OAR on 15 January 1897 disclosed a plot to implicate D. Jose Burgos, D. Jacinto Zamora and D. Mariano Gomes to an imminent military revolt in Cavite.[1167] The plot contrived by the four friar provincials involved bribing Izquierdo and distributing money to stir up revolt by a Burgos impostor. Echegoyen further deposed that Saldua was promised a pardon if he testified against the three. Piernavieja identified P. Fr. Claudio de Arceo OAR as the impostor. The friars' statements would tend to support Antonio Regidor's anticlerical version of the 1872 events. The reliability of their testimonies was however tainted by the likelihood of torture and duress. Just like the testimonies of Saldua and Octavo, they need to be approached with prudence and caution. Other questionable historical documents would begin to surface and to enter public awareness by 1941; distorting and embellishing the truth about Burgos and the Cavite Mutiny.

On 17 February 1933 Augusto R. de Luzuriaga published a book entitled *A la memoria de los tres martires del clero filipino, Padres Dr. Jose Apolonio Burgos, Feliciano Gomez y Jacinto Zamora. Leg. 117 - Causa Esp. 1455. Historia veridica de la sagrienta algarada de Cavite (1872) recopilada por su autor D. Francisco de Liñan (1873) con la biografia de algunos, apendice y anedotas, recopilado para su publicacion* (To the memory of the three martyrs of the Filipino clergy, Padres Dr. Jose Apolonio Burgos, Feliciano Gomez y Jacinto Zamora. *Leg. 117 - Causa Esp. 1455.* True History of the Bloody Clash of Cavite (1872) compiled by its author D. Francisco de Liñan with some biographies, appendix and anecdotes, compiled for its publication). This purported eyewitness account contained a prologue by Jose E. Marco who was a known provider of historical manuscripts to the Philippine National Library. The book had a number of subsequent editions and became an often used reference material on the Cavite Mutiny and the martyrs. Variations of the book were also published but the contents of the original Luzuriaga-Marco first edition were essentially retained.[1168]

La Loba Negra (The Black She-wolf) was published in 1938 also by Luzuriaga. The novel was purportedly an unpublished manuscript of Dr. D. Jose Burgos about the widow of the assassinated Governor-General Fernando de Bustamante y Bustillo. The manuscript is part of a collection of 44 known manuscripts attributed to Burgos. Twelve of these were acquired by Luis Maria Araneta.[1169] The most complete list was entitled *Obras Ineditas y Folletos del mismo author Dr. P. Jose Apolonio Burgos. Halladas en el extrangero* (Unedited works and folios of the same author Dr. D. Jose Apolonio Burgos. Found abroad). There was a general unease about the authenticity of the collection principally for two reasons. Burgos' demanding work and study commitments could not possibly afford him the time to produce such a voluminous body of work. The poor quality of Spanish used by the writer do not measure up to the scholarly attainment and dignity of Burgos.[1170] A serious investigation on the reliability of these works would only be undertaken in preparation for the 100th death anniversary of the GomBurZa martyrs slated in 1972.

In a Padre Burgos General Assembly of the Knights of Columbus in 1969, guest speaker Horacio de la Costa SJ admitted that very little reliable information was known about Jose Burgos compared to Rizal, Bonifacio or almost any of our national heroes.[1171] He challenged the Knights to gather and publish by 1972 the extant writings of Burgos in time for the centenary. Acting on this challenge, John N. Schumacher SJ was commissioned to execute the project.[1172] He inventoried and evaluated the current literature on Burgos, exposed the forgeries, identified the genuine writings both anonymous and signed, compiled and published them in a book entitled *Father Jose Burgos: Priest and Nationalist* in time for the 1972 centenary.

In his 1970 exposition *The Authenticity of the Writings Attributed to Father Jose Burgos,* Schumacher comprehensively analyzed the Liñan Manuscript published by Luzuriaga; the extant copies of the *Obras Ineditas* particulary *La Loba Negra* and *Maremagnum,* and exposed them all as forgeries.[1173] He further identified the common origin of these spurious works to Jose E. Marco who was denounced in 1968 by historian William Henry Scott for the fabricated Povedano and Pavon collections which included the Code of Kalantiyaw.[1174]

On the published sources of the Cavite Mutiny, Schumacher wrote a 1972 essay highlighting the reliability of various primary and secondary sources.[1175] He confirmed the existence of three documents written by P. Fr. Agapito Echegoyen OAR, P. Fr. Antonio Piernavieja OSA and P. Fr. Domingo Cardenas OSA who together with an Augustinian *lego* were taken prisoners in 1896. Only Echegoyen's and Piernavieja's documents contained information concerning the 1872 revolt. He confirmed the contents of the documents and highlighted data that only the signors could have known. He even went further to correct the identity of the probable impostor as P. Fr. Claudio del Arco OAR, the parish priest of Santa Cruz, Zambales. He however cautioned that the captives who were initially well treated by Emilio Aguinaldo were tortured and finally executed when they were turned over to the faction of Andres Bonifacio.

When the GomBurZa centenary was celebrated in 1972, it was not done with the same candor in Letran where Burgos spent 13 years of his life as a *colegial*. In fact, Jose Burgos was never given the accolade equal to those given to alumni greats like San Vicente Liem de la Paz OP or President Manuel L. Quezon. I could not help but wonder about this disparity when I was a student there. I surmised that it was a legacy inherited from the Spanish Dominicans. Perhaps acknowledging Burgos was not appropriate for them because it could be construed as disapproving the actions taken by the Spanish government regarding Burgos. Considering that the Spanish Dominicans appeared to be historically complicit with Burgos' execution, it would be in bad taste indeed to celebrate his greatness. The Spanish Dominicans have long since departed, and the Philippine Dominicans are gradually dusting off this legacy of the past.

Jose Apolonio Burgos

The following eulogy in honor of Burgos provides an appropriate ending to this chapter and volume:

> *From the little that we know, I think we can fairly say three things about him. First: he was a priest, loyal to the authority of the Church he served. Second: he was a patriot, loyal to the interests and aspirations of the country of his birth. Third: he was able to integrate in his thought and action, without inconsistency or ambiguity these two things - to be a priest and to be a patriot.*
>
> *There is no evidence, as far as I know, that Burgos was anything but a good priest, dedicated to the duties of the Catholic ministerial priesthood and faithful in fulfilling the obligations imposed by it. The evidence…is, rather, that Burgos was not only a good priest but a zealous priest, zealous for the advancement of religion, zealous above all of justice and specifically for fair and equal treatment of his fellow Filipinos in the priesthood; and, at the same time, loyal to the church of which he was minister… After Burgos, Gomes and Zamora had been sentenced to death, the civil authorities asked the Archbishop to defrock them as a fitting preliminary to their execution as traitors. The Archbishop refused. The significance of this refusal did not escape Rizal -"The Church, by refusing to degrade you, has cast doubt on the crime of which you have been held guilty." Burgos died as he had lived - a priest.*
>
> *He was also a patriot. All the evidence we possess points in this direction also. He may not have been a pure-blooded Filipino; but who among us can claim to be pure-blooded Filipino? Rizal was part Chinese; did that make him any less a Filipino? Patriotism, and nationalism even more, is not a matter of blood but of mind and spirit. Measured by this standard, Burgos was one of the first Filipinos… Burgos was an even earlier Filipino than Rizal. His oft-repeated claim for equality of status for native priests in a colonial Church on the ground that, in God's sight at least, all men are equal, is a pretty clear indication that he had made his own that principle of equality which is at the basis of all national liberation movements.*
>
> *Burgos was then both priest and patriot. He was both* Catolico romano *and* verdadero Filipino. *He was an ordained minister of a universal Church, and at the same time, completely identified with a particular emerging nation and culture. He was a nationalist and, by the same token, a citizen of the world. He was both of these at once, with complete integrity, without any sense of tension or ambiguity.*
>
> *In our present struggle to achieve full consciousness of our national identity, of what it means to be a Filipino and thus make a contribution to the humanization of the world, surely we can derive light and strength from a fuller knowledge of what the first Filipinos were like; what among others, Jose Apolonio Burgos, priest and patriot, was like.*[1176]

Jose Apolonio Burgos

Horatio de la Costa SJ
Rome, 25 November 1971

If there is anyone who deserves to be acknowledged as having fully and faithfully lived up to Letran's motto of Deus Patria Letran, he is unequivocally Doctor Don Jose Apolonio Burgos - *The First Filipino*.

Plate LIV

LETRAN GRAND CROSS
For Jubilarian Alumni

- © Colegio de San Juan de Letran

Sources and References

Books and Ebooks

Aduarte, Diego OP. *Tomo Primero de la Historia de la Provincia del Santo Rosario de Filipinas, Japon y China de la Sagrada Orden de Predicadores.* Zaragosa: Domingo Gascon, Impressor del Santo Hospital Real y General de Nuestra Señora de Gracia, 1693. BDH http://bdh-rd.bne.es/viewer.vm?id=0000188484&page=1

Aguinaldo, Emilio F. *My Memoirs.* Manila: Christina Aguinaldo Suntay, 1967.

Alençon, Ferdinand Philippe Marie d'Orleans, duc d'. *Luçon et Mindanao. Extraits d'un journal de voyage dans l'Extrême Orient. Avec une carte de l'archipel des Philippines.* Paris: Michel Levy Freres, Editeurs,1870. USIT https://quod.lib.umich.edu/p/philamer/ABB1640.0001.001?view=toc

Alzona, Incarnation. *A history of education in the Philippines, 1565-1930.* Manila: University of the Philippines Press, 1932.

Anderson, Gerald H. ed. *Studies in Philippine Church History.* Ithaca and London: Cornell University Press, 1969.

Antequera, Jose Maria. *La Desamortizacion Eclesiastica Considerada en sus Diferentes Aspectos y Relaciones.* Madrid: Imprenta de A. Perez Dubrull, 1885. BDH http://bdh-rd.bne.es/viewer.vm?id=0000064948&page=1

Argensola, Bartolome Leonardo de. *The Discovery and Conquest of the Molucco and Philippine Islands. Containing their History, Ancient and Modern, Natural and Political: Their Description, Product, Religion, Government. Laws, Languages, Customs, Manners, Habits, Shape, and Inclinations of the Natives. With an Account of many other adjacent islands, and several remarkable Voyages through the Streights of Magellan, and in other Parts.* London: 1708. English translation of Spanish original by John Stevens. Internet Archive https://archive.org/details/discoveryandcon00argegoog

Arias, Evaristo Fernandez OP. *Memoria Correspondiente a la Seccion 8.ª Grupos 72 y 73 Exposición General de las Islas Filipinas en Madrid 1887 (Edicion Oficial) Comision Central de Manila.* Manila: Tipografia del Colegio de Santo Tomas, 1887. BDH http://bdh-rd.bne.es/viewer.vm?id=0000077837&page=1

_____. *Memoria Historico-Estadistica sobre la Enseñanza Secundaria y Superior en Filipinas Escrita con Motivo de la Exposition Colonial de Amsterdam por encargo de la Subcomision de estas Islas.* Manila: Est. Tip. de La Oceania Española, 1883. BDH http://bdh-rd.bne.es/viewer.vm?id=0000125079&page=1

Aristotle. *Politics. Translated by Benjamin Jowett.* Kitchener: Batoche Books, 1999 https://socserv2.socsci.mcmaster.ca/econ/ugcm/3ll3/aristotle/Politics.pdf Accessed on 25 October 2017.

Arretxea, Larraitz; Lertxundi, Mikel. *El patronazgo del General Francisco de Echeveste.* Ondare No. 19, 2000. 269-276. Donostia-San Sebastián : Eusko Ikaskuntza, 2000. http://www.eusko-ikaskuntza.org/es/publicaciones/el-patronazgo-del-general-francisco-de-echeveste/art-9392/

Artigas y Cuerva, Manuel. *Los Sucesos de 1872, Reseña Historica Bio-bibliografica. Vol. III de la Serie Glorias Nacionales.* Manila: Imp. de La Vanguardia, 1911. USIT https://quod.lib.umich.edu/p/philamer/APZ3239.0001.001?view=toc

_____. *Historia de Filipinas para uso de los alumnos del Instituto Burgos y otros colegios particulares.* Manila: Imp. La Plarica, 1916. USIT https://quod.lib.umich.edu/p/philamer/APZ3217.0001.001?view=toc

_____. *Galeria de filipinos ilustres: biografias a contar desde las primeros tiempos de la dominaci'on Hispana, de los hijos del pais que en sus respectivas profesiones descollaron o' hayan alcanzado alguń puesto de distinción en sociedad.* Manila: Imp. Casa Editora Renacimiento, 1917. USIT https://quod.lib.umich.edu/p/philamer/ARS3572.0001.001?view=toc

_____. *The Events of 1872, A Historic-Bio-Bibliographical Account. Vol 3 of the National Glories Series. Translation and Notes by O.D. Corpuz.* Diliman, Quezon City: University of the Philippines Press, 1996.

Ashmole, Elias. *The History of the Most Noble Order of the Garter: And the Several Orders of Knighthood Extant in Europe. Containing I. The Antiquity of the Town, Castle, Chapel, and College of Windsor; ... II. The Habits, Ensigns, and Officers of the Order.* London: A. Bell, E. Curll, J. Pemberton, and A. Collins; W. Taylor and J. Baker, 1715. Google Books https://books.google.com.au/books/about/The_History_of_the_Most_Noble_Order_of_t.html?id=e29bAAAAQAAJ&redir_esc=y

Association of Sister Historians of the Order of Preachers (SHOP). *Directory of Dominican Monasteries: A Historical Directory of Communities of Dominican Nuns World-Wide Part 2 Asia.* Fanjeau, 2013. https://shop.op.org/sites/shop.op.org/files/Directory%20of%20Dominican%20Monasteries%20Part%202%20%20Asia_4.pdf Accessed on: 11 July 2015.

Attwater, Donald; John, Catherine Rachel. *The Penguin Dictionary of Saints: Third Edition (Dictionary, Penguin)* Paperback - 1 July 1996.

Bantigue, Pedro. *Provincial Council of Manila, 1771.* Washington: Catholic University, 1957.

Barrantes, Vicente. *Discursos leídos ante la Real Academia de la Historia en la recepción pública del Excmo. Señor D. Vicente Barrantes, el 14 de enero de 1872.* Madrid: Imp. de Julián Peña, 1872. BDH http://bdh-rd.bne.es/viewer.vm?id=0000103734&page=1

Bartlett, Robert. *Why Can the Dead Do Such Great Things? Saints and Worshippers from the Martyrs to the Reformation.* Princeton and Oxford: Princeton University Press, 2013.

Bauzon, Leslie E. *Deficit Government: Mexico and the Philippine Situado, 1606 - 1804.* Tokyo: The Center for East Asian Cultural Studies, 1981

Bazaco, Evergisto OP. *Historia Documentada del Real Colegio de San Juan de Letran.* Manila: Universidad de Santo Tomas, 1933.

_____. *History of education in the Philippines: Spanish period, 1565-1898.* Manila: University of Sto. Tomas Press, 1953.

Beltran, Gonzalo Aguirre. *La Población Negra de Mexico: Estudio Etnohistorico.* Mexico: SRA-CEHAM, 1981.

Benavente, Toribio de OFM. *Historia de los Indios de Nueva España Texto impreso escrita a mediados del siglo XVI.* Barcelona: Herederos de Juan Gili, Editores, 1914. Cervantes Virtual http://www.cervantesvirtual.com/obra/historia-de-los-indios-de-la-nueva-espana/

Berdozido, Pablo Francisco Rodriguez de. *Survey of the Philipinas Islands, 1735.* Ms. in the Museo-Biblioteca de Ultramar, Madrid - BR47:136

Bernard of Clairvaux. *In Praise of the New Knighthood,* in Treatises III, The Works of Bernard of Clairvaux vol. 7, Cistercian Fathers Series 19. Kalamazoo: 1977. pp. 127-167. English translation by Conrad Greenia.

Boisgelin, Louis de. *Ancient and Modern Malta: containing a full and accurate account of the present state of the Islands of Malta and Goza, the History of the Knights of St. John of Jerusalem...* 2 Vols. London: printed for Richard Philips, 1805. Google Books https://books.google.com.au/books?id=8Mp70Rf4c1wC&printsec=frontcover&dq=Boisgelin,+Louis+de.&hl=en&sa=X&ved=0ahUKEwiPpO_996bXAhUIw7wKHbLVD4kQ6AEILDAB#v=onepage&q=Boisgelin%2C%20Louis%20de.&f=false

Bongar, Jacque. *The Speech of Urban II. at the Council of Clermont, 1095. Fulcher of Chartres,* Gesta Dei por Francos. Hanover, 2 v., 1612, v1, p.382f as reproduced in Oliver J. Thatcher, A Source Book for Mediaeval History. Selected Documents

Illustrating the History of Europe in the Middle Age, ed. Oliver J. Thatcher and Edgar Holmes McNeal (New York: Charles Scribner's Sons, 1905).

Bowring, John. *A Visit to the Philippines*. London: Smith, Elder & Co., 1859. USIT https://quod.lib.umich.edu/p/philamer/ARB8045.0001.001?view=toc

Boxer, Charles Ralph. *The Christian Century in Japan: 1549-1650*. Berkley and Los Angeles: University of California Press, 1951

_____. *A note on the triangular trade between Macau, Manila and Nagasaki 1580-1640,* a paper at the 9th Conference of the International Association of Historians of Asia, Manila 21-25 November 1983.

Brown, Stewart J.; Tackett, Timothy. *Cambridge History of Christianity: Volume 7, Enlightenment, Reawakening and Revolution 1660-1815.* Cambridge University Press, 2006.

Bunson, Matthew, Margaret. and Stephen. *John Paul II's Book of Saints.* Indiana: Our Sunday Visitor Publishing, 1999

Buttigieg, Emanuel. *Nobility, Faith and Masculinity: The Hospitaller Knights of Malta, c. 1580-c.1700.* London: Continuum Publishing Corporation, 2011

Buzeta, Manuel OSA and Bravo, Felipe OSA. *Diccionario geografico, estadisco, histórico de las Islas Filipinas.* Madrid. Impr. Jose de la Peña, 1850-51. BDH http://bdh-rd.bne.es/viewer.vm?id=0000007635&page=1

Calderon, Felipe G. *El Colegio de San Jose: Refutacion de las Pretensiones Alegadas en sus Informes por el Sr. Delegado de S.S. y el Sr. Arzobispo de Manila presentada al Comision de los E. U. de America del Norte.* Manila: Tip. Modesto Reyes y Comp[a], 1900. USIT https://quod.lib.umich.edu/p/philamer/AQX2266.0001.001?view=toc

Caluwé, The Reverend Robert de. *Guide Notes on Heraldry of the Sovereign Order of Saint John of Jerusalem Knights Hospitaller* , OSJ ivzw Belgium 2000.

Casas, Bartolome de las OP. *Historia de Indias. Tomo I-V.* Madrid: J. Pueyo, 1927. http://www.gutenberg.org/ebooks/author/9232

_____. *A Brief Account of the Destruction of the Indies.* Project Gutenberg Ebook No. 20321 9 January 2007.

Cavada, Jose de la. *El Contador o Tablas de Reduccion de las pesas y medidas legales de Castilla y demas que están en uso en las Islas Filipinas.* Manila: Amigos del Pais, 1865. BDH http://bdh-rd.bne.es/viewer.vm?id=0000044708&page=1

Cavallini, Giulina & Holland, Caroline. *St. Martin de Porres: Apostle of Charity.* Rockford, IL: Tan Books, 2000, 1979.

Clark, Anthony E. *China's Saints: Catholic Martyrdom During the Qing (1644-1911).* Maryland: Lehigh University Press, 2011.

Cieslik, Hubert SJ. *Blessed Sebastian Kimura (1565-1622).* Retrieved on 16 January 2016 from Francis Britto's *All About Francis Xavier.* http://pweb.cc.sophia.ac.jp/britto/xavier/

Coates, Timothy J. *Convicts and Orphans: Forced and State-sponsored Colonizers in the Portuguese Empire 1550-1775.* Stanford: Stanford University Press, 2001.

Cobo, Juan OP. *Doctrina Cristiana*. Manila: 1593. Wolf 2nd, Edwin ed. *Doctrina Cristiana / The first book printed in the Philippines. Manila, 1593. A Facsimile Copy of the Lessing J. Rosenwald Collection*. Project Gutenberg Ebook #16119 Release Date: June 23, 2005. http://www.gutenberg.org/files/16119/16119-h/16119-h.htm

Cohen, R. *Knights of Malta, 1523-1798.* Project Guttenburg Ebook No.12034 April 15, 2004. http://www.gutenberg.org/cache/epub/12034/pg12034-images.html

Colegio de San Juan de Letran. *Recuerdo del tercer centenario del Colegio de San Juan de Letran 1630-1930*. Manila, 1931.

Colin, Francisco, SJ *Labor Evangelica, Ministerios Apostólicos de los Obreros de la Compañia de Jesus, Fundación, y Progressos de Su Provincia en las Islas Filipinas. Parte Primera IV Libros.* Madrid: Joseph Fernandez de Buendía, 1663. BDH http://bdh-rd.bne.es/viewer.vm?id=0000014692&page=1

Collantes, Domingo OP. *Historia de la Provincia del Santisimo Rosario de Filipinas, China, y Tunquin Orden de Predicadores. Quarta Parte desde el Año de 1700 hasta el de 1765. Libros I y II.* Manila: Colegio y Universidad de Santo Tomas, 1783. BDH http://bdh-rd.bne.es/viewer.vm?id=0000014703&page=1

Colon, Cristobal. *Relaciones y Cartas de Cristobal Colon.* Madrid: Libreria y Casa Editorial Hernando (S.A.), 1927. Biblioteca Digital de Castilla y Leon. http://bibliotecadigital.jcyl.es/es/consulta/registro.cmd?id=18610

Concepcion, Juan de la OAR. *Historia general de Philipinas: conquistas espirituales y temporales de estos españoles dominios, establecimientos progresos, y decadencias.* Manila: 1788. BDH http://bdh-rd.bne.es/viewer.vm?id=0000023184&page=1

Constantino, Renato. *A History of the Philippines: from the Spanish Colonization to the Second World War.* New York and London: Monthly Review Press, 1975.

Cordoba, Martin de OSA. *Jardin de nobles doncellas.* Madrid 1953.

Coronel, Hernando. *Boatmen for Christ: The Early Filipino Priests.* Philippines: Reyes Publishing Inc for Catholic Book Center, 1998.

Corwin, Arthur F. *Spain and the Abolition of Slavery in Cuba, 1817-1886.* Austin and London: Institute of Latin American Studies, University of Texas Press, 1967.

Costa, Horatio de la SJ. *The Jesuits in the Philippines 1581-1768.* Cambridge - Massachusetts: Harvard University Press, 1961.

Cox, Leonard Martin. *The Island of Guam.* Washington: Government Printing Office, 1926. USIT https://quod.lib.umich.edu/p/philamer/AFJ6840.0001.001?view=toc

Craig, Austin. ed. *The Former Philippines thru Foreign Eyes.* 1916. Project Gutenberg Ebook #10770 Release Date: 14 April 2011.

_____. *Gems of Philippine oratory; selections representing fourteen centuries of Philippine thought, carefully compiled from credible sources in substitution for the pre-Spanish writings destroyed by missionary zeal, to supplement the later literature stunted by intolerant religious and political censorship, and as specimens of the untrammeled present-day utterances.* Manila: University of Manila, 1924. USIT https://quod.lib.umich.edu/p/philamer/AHZ9164.0001.001?view=toc

_____. *Lineage, Life and Labors of Jose Rizal, Philippine Patriot - A Study of the Growth of Free Ideas in the Trans-Pacific American Territory.* USIT https://quod.lib.umich.edu/p/philamer/AHZ9295.0001.001?view=toc

Croycroft, Anna. *The Agency of the Orphan: A theoretical inquiry into the imagination behind regressive individuation.* www.agencyoforphan.com/archetypes/ Accessed on 20 June 2015.

Culver, Henry Brundage. *The book of old ships: from Egyptian galleys to clipper ships.* New York: Dover, 1992.

Cushner, Nicholas P. *Documents Illustrating the British Conquest of Manila, 1762-1763.* London, 1971.

Delgado, Juan Jose SJ. *Historia general sacroprofana, politica y religiosa de las islas del Poniente llamadas Filipinas 1751.* Manila: Biblioteca Historica de Filipinas, 1892. Internet Archive https://archive.org/details/aqp5054.0001.001.umich.edu

Diaz, Casimiro OSA. *Conquistas de las islas Filipinas: la temporal, por las armas del señor don Phelipe Segundo el Prudente; y la espiritval, por los religiosos del orden de nuestro padre San Augustin: fvndacion, y progressos de sv provincia del santissimo nombre de Jesus.* Valladolid, L.N. de Gaviria, 1890. BDH http://bdh-rd.bne.es/viewer.vm?id=0000014663&page=1

Doolittle, Justus. *Social Life of the Chinese: A Daguerreotype of Daily Life in China.* London: Sampson Low, Son and Marston, 1868.

Drane, Augusta Theodosia, *The Knights of st. John: with The battle of Lepanto and Siege of Vienna* London: Burns and Lambert 1858. Google Books https://books.google.com.au/books?id=-YVqtglxS18C&printsec=frontcover&dq=Drane,+Augusta+Theodosia,+The+Knights+of+st.+John:+with+The+battle+of+Lepanto+and+Siege+of+Vienna+London:+Burns+and+Lambert+1858.&hl=en&sa=X&ved=0ahUKEwiOmorzg6fXAhVEabwKHaFoAS0Q6AEILzAB#v=onepage&q&f=false

Duby, Georges. *The Three Orders: Feudal Society Imagined.* Chicago: University of Chicago Press, 1981.

Encarnacion, Felix de la, OAR. *Diccionario bisaya-español.* Manila, 1851. BDH http://bdh-rd.bne.es/viewer.vm?id=0000078387&page=1

Engingco, Maria Jesusa OP. *The Congregation of Dominican Sisters of St. Catherine of Siena: Its Missionary Consciousness and Endeavor in the Context of the Church in the Philippines.* Rome: Pontificia Universitas Urbaniana, 2000.

Esperabe Artega, Enrique. *Historia Pragmatica e Interna de la Universidad de Salamanca Tomos I-II.* Salamanca: Izquierdo, 1914. Internet Archive. https://archive.org/details/2historiapragmt01espeuoft

España. *The Political Constitution of the Spanish Monarchy: Promulgated in Cádiz, the nineteenth day of March [1812].* Alicante: Biblioteca Virtual Miguel de Cervantes, 2003. http://www.cervantesvirtual.com/servlet/SirveObras/c1812/12159396448091522976624/index.htm Accessed on 23 July 2017.

Fernandez, Pablo OP. *DOMINICOS DONDE NACE EL SOL: Historia de la Provincia del Santisimo Rosario de Filipinas de la Orden de Predicadores.* Barcelona: Impr. Yuste, 1958.

Fernandez-Morera, Dario. *The Myth of the Andalucian Paradise: Muslims, Christians, and Jews under Islamic Rule.* Wilmington, DE: ISI Books, 2015.

Fernández Sarasola, Ignacio. *La Constitución de Bayona (1808).* Spain: Portal Derecho, S.A. (IUSTEL), 2012. Cervantes Virtual. http://www.cervantesvirtual.com/obra-visor/la-primera-constitucin-espaola---el-estatuto-de-bayona-0/html/ffc6353a-82b1-11df-acc7-002185ce6064_4.html

Ferrando, Juan OP. *Historia de los Pp. Dominicos en las Islas Filipinas y en sus Misiones del Japon, China, Tung-Kin y Formosa, que Comprende los Sucesos Principales de la Historia General de este Archipielago, desde el Descubrimiento y Conquista de estas Islas por las Flotas Españolas hasta el Año de 1840. Tomos I-VI.* Madrid: M. Rivadeneyra, 1870. Hathi Trust https://catalog.hathitrust.org/Record/002240857?type%5B%5D=all&lookfor%5B%5D=ferrando%2C%20juan&ft=

Feuillet, Jean Baptist OP. *The Life of Saint Rose of Lima.* New York: P. J. Kenedy and Sons, 1847. Internet Archive. https://archive.org/details/thelifeofsaintro00hansuoft

Filipiniana Book Guild Editorial Board. *The Colonization and Conquest of the Philippines by Spain: Some Contemporary Source Documents 1559-1577.* Manila: Filipiniana Book Guild, 1965.

Frías y Soto, Hilarión, Niceto de Zamacois, Juan de Dios Arias, José María Rivera, Pantaleón Tovar, Ignacio Ramírez. *Los mexicanos pintados por sí mismos. Tipos y Costumbres Nacionales.* Mexico: Imprenta M. Murgia y Compañía, 1854.

Friis, Herman R. *The Pacific Basin: a history of its geographical exploration.* New York: American Geographical Society, 1967.
Fulgocio, Fernando. *Crónica de las islas Filipinas.* Madrid Rubio, Grilo y Vitturi, 1871. BDH http://bdh-rd.bne.es/viewer.vm?id=0000044970&page=1
Garcia Icazbalceta, Joaquin. *Obras de D. J. García Icazbalceta. 10 Tomos. Opúsculos varios.* Mexico: Imp. de Aguero, 1896 -1899. Cervantes Virtual http://www.cervantesvirtual.com/obra/obras-de-d-j-garcia-icazbalceta-tomo-ii-opusculos-varios-vol-ii/
Giles, Mary E. *The Book of Prayer of Sor Maria of Santo Domingo: A Study and Translation.* Albany: State University of New York Press, 1990.
Gonzales, Jose Maria OP. *Misiones Dominicanas en China 1700-1750. Tomo I-II.* Madrid : Consejo Superior de Investigaciones Cientificas, Instituto Santo Toribio de Mogrovejo, 1952.
_____. *Historia de las Misiones Dominicanas de China. Tomo I-IV.* Madrid: Imprenta, Juan Bravo, 3, 1964.
Gonzalez, Ondina & Premo, Bianca eds. *Raising an Empire: Children in Early Modern Iberia and Colonial Latin America.* Albuquerque: University of New Mexico, 2007.
Grifol y Aliaga, Daniel. *La Instruccion Primaria en Filipinas.* Manila: Tipo-Litografia de Chofre y Cia, 1894. BDH http://bdh-rd.bne.es/viewer.vm?id=0000128139&page=1
Gutierrez y Salazar, Pedro. *Las Procripciones de Sila (remedo de) en Filipinas por el Excmo. Sr. D. Carlos Maria de la Torre Capitan Genral y Gobernador Superior Civil de estas Islas.* Madrid: Imp. Florencio Gamayo, 1870. BDH http://bdh-rd.bne.es/viewer.vm?id=0000129715&page=1
Halili, Maria Christine. *Philippine History.* Manila: Rex Book Store, 2004.
Hazañas y La Rua, Joaquin. *Vasquez de Leca 1573-1649.* Sevilla: Imp. y Lib. de Sobrinos de Izquierdo, 1918. BDH http://bdh-rd.bne.es/viewer.vm?id=0000196621&page=1
Henson, Mariano. *The Province of Pampanga and its Towns.* San Fernando, Pampanga: Standard Mimeograph Service, 1953.
Herrera, Cristobal Perez de. *Discursos de Amparo de los legitimos pobres, y reduccion de los fungidos y de la fundacion y principio de los Albergues de los Reynos y Amparo de la milicia dellos.* Madrid: Luis Sanchez, 1558. BDH http://bdh-rd.bne.es/viewer.vm?id=0000088424&page=1
Hericourt du Vatier, Louis d'. *Les Loix ecclésiastiques de France dans leur ordre naturel, et une analyse des livres du droit canonique, conférez avec les usages de l'Église gallican.* Paris: J. du Nully, 1743. Internet Archive https://archive.org/details/bub_gb_xcXjyiFKzUsC
Herzog, Tamar. *Defining Nations: Immigrants and citizens in Early Modern Spain and Spanish America.* New Haven and London: Yale University Press 2003.
Hinnebusch, William A. OP. *The Dominicans: A Short History.* New York: Alba House, 1975.
Hobbes, Thomas. *Leviathan: reprinted from the edition of 1651.* Oxford: Oxford University Press, 1929. Online Library of Liberty. http://oll.libertyfund.org/titles/hobbes-leviathan-1909-ed
Horn, David and Shepherd, John ed. *Parranda and Parrandera. Popular Music of the World Volume IX: Genres: Caribbean and Latin America.* London: Bloomsbury, 2014.
Huerta, Felix de, OFM. *Estado geografico, topografico, estadistico, historico - religioso, de la Santa y Apostolica Provincia de S. Gregorio Magno, de religiosos menores descalzos de la regular y mas estrecha observancia de N.S.P.S. Francisco, en las Islas Filipinas: Comprende el numero de Religiosos, Conventos, Pueblos, situacion de estos, años de us fundacion, Tributos, Almas, producciones, industrias, cosas y casos especiales de su administracion espiritual, en el Archipelago Filipino, desde su fundacion en el año de 1577 hasta el de 1865.* Binondo: Imp. M. Sanches y C.ª, 1865. BDH http://bdh-rd.bne.es/viewer.vm?id=0000143378&page=1
Iñigo y Miera, Manuel de. *Historia de las Ordenes de Caballeria.* Madrid: 1863. BDH http://bdh-rd.bne.es/viewer.vm?id=0000010683&page=1
Instituto Historico Marina. *Colección de Diarios y Relaciones para la Historia de los Viajes y Descubrimientos 5 Tomos.* Madrid: 1943-1947.

Jagor, Fedor. *Travels in the Philippines. (English Translation)*. London: Chapman and Hall, 1875. Google Books https://books.google.com.au/books/about/Travels_in_the_Philippines.html?id=vnoFAAAAQAAJ&redir_esc=y

Jara, Alvaro; Pinto, Sonia. *Fuentes Para la Historia del Trabajo en El Reino de Chile: Legislación, 1546-1810. 2 Tomos*. Chile: Editorial Andres Bello, 1982, 1983.

Kagan, Richard L., *Students and Society in Early Modern Spain*. Johns Hopkins University Press, 1974 LIBRO http://libro.uca.edu/students/students.htm

Keith, Charles. Catholic Vietnam: A Church from Empire to Nation. Berkley and Los Angeles: University of California Press, 2012

King, Edwin J. *The Rule, Statutes and Customs of the Hospitallers*, Methuen & Co. Ltd, London 1931

King, Georgiana Goddard. *A Brief Account of the Military Order in Spain*. New York: The Hispanic Society of America 1921. Internet Archive https://archive.org/details/briefaccountofmi00kinguoft

Kowner, Rotem. *From White to Yellow: The Japanese in European Racial Thought, 1300-1735*. Montreal and Kingston, London, Ithaca: McGill-Queen's Press, 2014.

Larkin, John. *The Pampangans*. Berkley: University of California Press, 1972.

Le Gentil, Guillaume. *Voyages dans les mers de l'Inde Tome Second*. Paris: De L'Imprimerie 1781. Digitalisierte Sammlungen http://digital.staatsbibliothek-berlin.de/suche/?queryString=aut:Le%20Gentil%20de%20La%20Galaisière,%20Guillaume%20J.

Leclercq, J. and Rochais, H. M., eds., *Liber ad milites Templi de laude novae militiae*, in S. Bernardi Opera, vol. 3. Rome: 1963. English translation by David Carbon.

Leroy, James A. *Philippine Life in Town and Country*. New York and London: G. P. Putnam's Sons, 1905. USIT https://quod.lib.umich.edu/p/philamer/AFJ2156.0001.001?view=toc

_____. *The Philippines, 1860-1898: Some Comment and Bibliographical Notes*. A. H. Clark Company, 1907'. BR52:208-216

Locke, John. *Two Treatises of Civil Government (1689, 1764). The Enhanced Edition*. Online Library of Liberty. http://oll.libertyfund.org/pages/john-locke-two-treatises-1689 Accessed on 16 July 2017.

Lynch, John, ed. *The Spanish American revolutions, 1808-1826: Old and New World origins*. Norman: University of Oklahoma Press, 1994.

Maddicott, John. The Origins of the English Parliament, 924-1327. Oxford: Oxford University Press; 2010.

Mallat, J. *Les Philippines*. Tome Deuxime Paris: Arthus Bertrand, Editeur, 1846. Google Books https://books.google.com.au/books/about/Les_Philippines.html?id=dKdojy6GHccC&redir_esc=y

Manchado Lopez, Marta M. *Conflictos Iglesia-Estado en el Extremo Oriente Ibérico Filipinas (1767-1787)*, Murcia: Universidad, Secretariado de Publicaciones, 1994.

Manning, Susan and France, Peter ed. *Enlightenment and Emancipation*. United States: Associated University Presses, 2006.

Manuel, Esperidion Arsenio; Manuel, Magdalena Avenir. *Dictionary of Philippine biography. 3 Vols*. Manila, 1955, 1970, 1987.

Marin, Catherine, dir. *La Société des Missions Etrangères de Paris: 350 ans a la rencontre de l'Asie 1658-2008*. Paris: Editions Karthala, 2011.

Marin y Morales, Valentin OP. *Ensayo de una sintesis de los Trabajos Realizados por las Corporaciones Religiosas Españolas de Filipinas 2 Tomos*. Manila: Imp. de Sant Tomas, 1901. BDH http://bdh-rd.bne.es/viewer.vm?id=0000015737&page=1

Mas, Sinibaldo de. *Informe sobre el estado de las Islas Filipinas en 1842 escrito por el autor del Aristodemo, del Sistema musical de la lengua castellana, etc. III Tomos*. Madrid, 1843. BDH http://bdh-rd.bne.es/viewer.vm?id=0000040537&page=1

McGonigle, Thomas C., OP and Zagano, Phyllis. *The Dominican Tradition*. Collegeville, Minn.: Liturgical Press, 2006.

Menegon, Eugenio. *Ancestors, Virgins, and Friars: Christianity as a Local Religion in Late Imperial China.* Cambridge, Massachusetts: Harvard University Asia Center, 2009.

Montero y Vidal, Jose. *Historia General de Filipinas desde el Descubrimiento de Dichas Islas Hasta Nuestros Dias en III Tomos.* Madrid: Est. Tip. de la Viuda e Hijos de Tello, 1895. Digitalisierte Sammlungen http://digital.staatsbibliothek-berlin.de/suche?queryString=Montero%20y%20Vidal&fulltext=&junction=&current_page=1&results_on_page=20&sort_on=relevance&sort_direction=desc

Morga, Antonio de. *Sucesos de las Islas Filipinas, 2 vols.* Mexico: Cornelio Adriano Cesar 1609, BR 15 & 16.

Mungello, D.E., ed. *The Chinese Rites Controversy: Its History and Meaning.* Maney - Monumenta Serica, June 30, 1994.

Navarrete, Domingo Fernandez OP. *Tratados Historicos, Politicos, Ethicos, y Religiosos de la Monarchia de China.* Madrid: Imprenta Real, 1676. Google Books. https://books.google.com.au/books?id=V8hKAAAAcAAJ&pg=PA250&lpg=PA250&dq=Navarrete,+Domingo+Fernandez+OP.+Tratados+Historicos,+Politicos,+Ethicos,+y+Religiosos+de+la+Monarchia+de+China.&source=bl&ots=CGpMx88h70&sig=FeolHTvwhgQtAcLdek4Rm5D9tIE&hl=en&sa=X&ved=0ahUKEwjky6Dj96jXAhVHKJQKHetXDBgQ6AEIQjAD#v=onepage&q=Navarrete%2C%20Domingo%20Fernandez%20OP.%20Tratados%20Historicos%2C%20Politicos%2C%20Ethicos%2C%20y%20Religiosos%20de%20la%20Monarchia%20de%20China.&f=false

Navarrete, Martin Fernandez de. *Colección de los viages y descubrimientos que hicieron por mar los españoles desde fines del siglo XV: con varios documentos inéditos concernientes á la historia de la marina castellana y de los establecimientos españoles en Indias, 5 Tomos.,* Madrid: Imprensa Real. v.1 (1825), v. 2 (1825), v. 3 (1829), v. 4 (1837), v. 5 (1837). BDH http://bdh-rd.bne.es/viewer.vm?id=0000052618&page=1

Navarro, Eduardo. *Filipinas: Estudio de algunas asuntos de actualidad.* Madrid: Minuesa de Rios, 1897. BDH http://bdh-rd.bne.es/viewer.vm?id=0000050608&page=1

Neira, Eladio; Ocio, Hilario, and Arnaiz, Gregorio OP. *Misioneros Dominicos en el Extremo Oriente 1836 - 1940. Edicion corregida y actualizada de la obra del P. Hilario Ocio OP.* Life Today Publications. Manila, Filipinas: 2000

Neira, Eladio OP. *Heralds of Christ in the kingdoms of the East: historical reminiscences of the four hundredth anniversary of the foundation of the Dominican Missionary Province of Our Lady of the Holy Rosary (1587-1987).* San Juan City: Corporacion de Padres Dominicos, 2008. [English translation of *Heraldos de Cristo en los reinos del oriente.*]

Nicholson, Helen J. *The Knights Hospitaller.* Woodbridge, UK: The Boydell Press. 2001

Ocio y Viana, Hilario Maria OP. *Reseña Biografica de los Religiosos de la Provincia del Santisimo Rosario de Filipinas desde su fundacion hasta nuestros dias por un religioso de la misma provincia. Partes I y II.* Manila: Real Colegio de Sto. Tomas, 1891. BDH http://bdh-rd.bne.es/viewer.vm?id=0000015763&page=1

_____. *Compendio de la Reseña Biografica de los Religiosos de la Provincia del Santisimo Rosario de Filipinas desde su fundacion hasta nuestros dias por el autor de la misma. Comprende desde 1587 a 1895.* Real Colegio de Sto. Tomas. 1895. USIT https://quod.lib.umich.edu/p/philamer/ARK1148.0001.001?view=toc

Ocio y Viana, Hilario Maria OP, and Neira, Eladio OP. M*isioneros Dominicos en el Extremo Oriente 1587 - 1835. Edicion corregida y actualizada de la obra del P. Hilario Ocio OP.* Manila, Filipinas: Life Today Publications, 2000.

O'Connor, J. B. OP. *Saint Dominic and the Order of Preachers.* New York City: The Holy Name Bureau, 1916. Jacques Maritain Center https://maritain.nd.edu/jmc/etext/dominic.htm

Olmedo, Felix G. *Diego Ramirez Villaescusa 1459-1537.* Madrid, 1944.

Order of Saint Augustine. *Alphabetum Augustinianum, Institutum Historicum Augustinianum.* http://iha.augustinians.net

Orique, David. *Bartolomeo de las Casas: A Brief Outline of His Life and Labor.* www.lascasas.org/manissues.htm#BdeLasCasas: Accessed on 5 July 2015.

Pan, Jose Felipe del. *Ordinances de buen gobierno de Corcuera, Cruzat y Raon.* Manila: 1891, BR50:199.

Pardo de Tavera, Trinidad H. *Una Memoria de Anda y Salazar.* Manila: La Democracia, 1899. BDH http://bdh-rd.bne.es/viewer.vm?id=0000092559&page=1

Patronato de Historia Social del Instituto "Balmes" de Sociologia. *Estudios de Historia Social de Espania Tomos 1- IV.* Madrid: Consejo Superior de Investigations Cientificas, 1949-1960.

Payne, Stanley G. *History of Spain and Portugal Vol. 1 & 2* University of Wisconsin Press, 1973. LIBRO http://libro.uca.edu/payne1/spainport1.htm and http://libro.uca.edu/payne2/spainport2.htm

Pearson, Carol. *Awakening the Heroes Within: Twelve Archetypes To Help Us Find Ourselves and Transform Our World.* Harper Collins, 1991.

Peguero, Juan OP. *Historia en compendio de la Provincia del Santisimo Rosario dos tomos de Historia y otros papeles que tiene dicha Provincia.* Terminada en el Convento de San Juan del Monte en Philipinas a 24 de Deciembre de 1690.

Perez, Elviro, OSA. *Catalogo Bio-Bibliografico de los Religiosos Agustinos de la Provincia del Santísimo Nombre de Jesus de las Islas Filipinas desde su Fundación hasta Nuestros Dias.* Manila: Establecimiento Tipográfico del colegio de Santo Tomas, 1901. BDH http://bdh-rd.bne.es/viewer.vm?id=0000059903&page=1

Perez y Lopez, Antonio Xavier. *Teatro de la Legislacion Universal de España e Indias por Órden Cronologico de sus Cuerpos y Decisiones No Recopiladas; y Alfabetico de sus Titulos y Principales Materias 28 Tomos.* Madrid: Imp. de Don Antonio Espinosa, 1791-1798. BDH http://bdh-rd.bne.es/viewer.vm?id=0000140030&page=1

Pigafeta, Antonio. *Primo viaggio interno al mondo (1519-1522).* Biblioteca Ambrosiana Milan, Italy with pressmark, "L. 103 - Sup." BR33 p. 21 [English Translation].

Pope Alexander IV. *Fratribus militibus Hospitalis S. Johannis Jerosolimitani chlamyde nigra et, in bellis, superinsigniis militaribus utendi facultatem concedit.* 11 August 1259

Pope Anastasius IV. *Christianae fidei religio (reissued).* 1154

Pope Benedict XVI. *Angelus Angelus. 9 November 2008.* Rome www.catholicculture.org/culture/liturgicalyear/calendar/day.cfm?date=2014-11-09. Retrieved on November 19, 2013.

Pope Calixtus II. *Ad hoc nos (Furthermore).* 19 June 1119

Pope Gregory XIII. *Nuper ad Nos.* 25 January 1577

Pope Innocent II. *Ad hoc nos disponente.* 1135

_____. *Christianae fidei religio.* 1137

_____. *Quam amabilis Deo.* 1139-1143

Pope Leo XIII. *In plurimis.* 1888.

Pope Paschal II. *Piae postulatio voluntatis (A Pious Request and Desire).* 15 February 1113. Benevento.

Pope Paul III. *Sublimis Dei.* 1537.

Porter, Whitworth. *A History of the Knights of Malta or the Order of Saint John of Jerusalem.* Revised Edition. London: Longmans, Green & Co. 1883. Google Books https://books.google.com.au/books/about/A_History_of_the_Knights_of_Malta.html?id=HhwNAAAAIAAJ

Provincia del Santisimo Rosario de Filipinas. *Estado General de los Religiosos y Religiosas de la Provincia del Santisimo Rosario del Sagrado Orden de Predicatores de Filipinas en el Año de 1893.* Manila: Real Colegio de Santo Tomas, 1894. BDH http://bdh-rd.bne.es/viewer.vm?id=0000122754&page=1

_____. *Los Dominicos en el Extremo Oriente : provincia del Santísimo Rosario de Filipinas : relaciones publicadas con motivo del séptimo centenario de la confirmación de la Sagrada Orden de Predicadores.* Barcelona: Seix & Barral Herms, 1916. BDH http://bdh-rd.bne.es/viewer.vm?id=0000121921&page=1

_____. *Mapas de las Misiones Dominicanas en Extremo Oriente de la Provincia del Santísimo Rosario de Filipinas.* Madrid, 1924. BDH http://bdh-rd.bne.es/viewer.vm?id=0000048623&page=1

Puebla, Ceferino Pedrosa OP ed. *Witnesses of the Faith in the Orient 2nd edition.* Hongkong: Dominican Province of the Our Lady of the Rosary. 2006. Nominis http://nominis.cef.fr/contenus/witnessesdominicainscanada.pdf

Raymund of Capua OP. *Life of Saint Catharine of Siena.* Translated from the French by the Ladies of the Sacred Heart. New York: P. J. Kenedy & Sons, 1862. Internet Archive. https://archive.org/details/lifeofsaintcatha00raym

Real Academia de la Historia (Spain). *Colección De Documentos Ineditos Relativos Al Descubrimiento: Conquista Y Organización De Las Antiguas Posesiones Españolas De Ultramar. 2. Ser. 25 Tomos.* Madrid: Est. tip. "Sucesores de Rivadeneyra,", 1885 1932.

Reid, Anthony. *Southeast Asia in the Age of Commerce 1450-1680 2 Volumes.* Ann Arbor: Yale University Press, 1988,1993.

Remesal, Antonio de OP. *Historia de la Provincia de S. Vicente de Chyapa y Guatemala de la Orden de nro Glorioso PADRE SANCTO DOMINGO Escrivense Juntamente los principios de las demás Provincias esta Religion de las yndias Occidentales y lo Secular de la Gobernación De Guatemala.* Madrid: 1619. Internet Archive https://archive.org/details/historiadelaprov00reme

Renz, Christopher J. OP, *In this Light which Gives Light - A History of the College of St. Albert the Great.* The Province of the Most Holy Name of Jesus. Oakland: 2009

Repetti, William Charles SJ. *Jesuit education in the Philippine Islands: the College of San Jose of Manila. established August 25, 1601.* Manila: Manila Observatory, 1941.

Retana, Wenceslao E. *Archivo del Bibliófilo Filipino, Recopilacion de Documentos Historicos, Cientificos, Literarios y Politicos y Estudios Bibliograficos Tomo Segundo* Madrid: Viuda de M. Minuesa de los Rios, 1896. Cervantes Virtual https://www.google.com.au/search?biw=1183&bih=751&ei=zEIAWp6gIYKi0QTfi4TIBw&q=Archivo+del+Bibliofilo+Filipino%2C+Recopilacion+de+Documentos+Historicos%2C+Cientificos%2C+Literarios+y+Politicos+y+Estudios+Bibliograficos+Tomo+Segundo+Madrid%3A+Viuda+de+M.+Minuesa+de+los+Rios%2C+1896.+&oq=Archivo+del+Bibliofilo+Filipino%2C+Recopilacion+de+Documentos+Historicos%2C+Cientificos%2C+Literarios+y+Politicos+y+Estudios+Bibliograficos+Tomo+Segundo+Madrid%3A+Viuda+de+M.+Minuesa+de+los+Rios%2C+1896.+&gs_l=psy-ab.3...12244.12244.0.13498.0.0.0.0.0.0.0..0.0....0...1.2.64.psy-ab..0.0.0....0.VfFl9BLi7d8

Ricafort, Mariano. *La reunion de malhechores en cuadrilla en la provincial de Cavite.* Manila, 1828.

Rich, Maria Cruz. *Apuntes Historicos del Beaterio y Colegio de Sta. Catalina.* Manila: University of Santo Tomas, 1939.

Rivas, Manuel de OP. *Idea del Imperio de Annam o de los Reinos Unidos de Tunquin y Cochinchina.* Manila: Imprenta de los Amigos del Pais, 1858. BDH http://bdh-rd.bne.es/viewer.vm?id=0000042887&page=1

Rizal, Jose. *El Filibusterismo*, translated by Leon Maria Guerrero. London and Hong Kong: Longmans, 1965, 93-94.

_____. *El Filibusterismo (Continuacion de Noli me tangere) Novela Filipina.* Gent: Boekdrukkerij F. Meyer-Van Loo, 1891. English version: Derbyshire, Charles. *The Reign of Greed.* Manila: Philippine Education Company, 1912. Project Gutenburg. http://www.gutenberg.org/files/10676/10676-h/10676-h.htm

_____. *Epistolario Rizalino 5 Vol.* Manila; Bureau of Printing, 1930-38. Cervantes Virtual http://www.cervantesvirtual.com/buscador/?q=epistolario+rizalino

Rodriguez, Isacio R. OSA. *Historia de la Provincia agustiniana del Sto. Nombre de Jesus de Filipinas. 20 Tomos.* Manila and Valladolid, 1965-1988.

Rodríguez San Pedro, Joaquín. *Legislacion ultramarina, concordada y anotada Tomo 1-14.* Madrid, 1865-1869. Google Books https://play.google.com/store/books/details/Joaqu%C3%ADn_Rodr%C3%ADguez_San_Pedro_Legislación_ultramarin?id=NT0OAAAAQAAJ

Rosenblat, Angel. *La Población Indigena 1492-1950, La Población Indigena y El Mestizaje en America 2 Vols.* Buenos Aires: Editorial Nova, 1954.

Roth, Dennis Morrow. *The Friar Estates of the Philippines.* Albuquerque: University of New Mexico Press, 1977.

Saco, Jose Antonio. *Historia de Esclavitud desde los Tiempos Mas Remotos Hasta Nuestros Dias. Tomos I- III.* Barcelona: Imprenta de Jaime Jepus, 1875-1877. BDH http://bdh-rd.bne.es/viewer.vm?id=0000045624&page=1

_____. *Historia de la Esclavitud de la Raza Africana en el Nuevo Mundo y en especial en los Países Americo-Hispano Tomo I.* Barcelona: Imprenta de Jaime Jepus, 1879. Internet Archive https://archive.org/details/historiadelaesc00sacogoog

Sadaba del Carmen, Francisco OAR. *Catalogo de los Religiosos Agustinos Recoletos de la Provincia de San Nicolas de Tolentino de Filipinas desde el año 1606 en que llego la primera Mision a Manila, hasta nuestros dias.* Madrid: Imp. del Asilo de Huerfanos del Sagrado Corazon de Jesus, 1906. BDH http://bdh-rd.bne.es/viewer.vm?id=0000147474&page=1

Salazar, Vicente de OP. *Historia de la Provincia de el Santissimo Rosario de Philipinas, China y Tunking, de el Sagrado Orden de Predicadores. Tercera Parte en que se tratan los sucesos de dicha Provincia desde el año 1669 hasta el de 1700.* Manila: Colegio y Universidad de Santo Tomas, 1742. BDH http://bdh-rd.bne.es/viewer.vm?id=0000092770&page=1

Salmoral, Manuel Lucena. *Leyes para esclavos: El ordenamiento jurídico sobre la condicion, tratamiento, defensa y represión de los esclavos en las colonias de la America española.* 2000. Fundacion Ignacio Larramendi. http://www.larramendi.es/catalogo_imagenes/grupo.cmd?path=1000202 Accessed: 15 January 2017.

Salter (Revd.) H. E. *A Cartulary of the Hospital of St. John the Baptist.* Oxford Historical Society. Clarendon Press 1917. Internet Archive https://archive.org/details/cartularyofhosp03salt

San Antonio, Juan Francisco OFM. *Chronicas de la apostolica provincia de S. Gregorio de Religiosos Descalzos de N.S.P.S. Francisco en las Islas Philipinas, China, Japon, &c Parte Primera.* Sampaloc: Imprenta del vso de la propia provincia sita en el Convento de Nra. Señora de Loreto: 1738. BDH http://bdh-rd.bne.es/viewer.vm?id=0000014716&page=1

San Nicolas, Andres de OAR. *Historia general de los religiosos descalsos del orden de San Augustin.* Madrid: 1664 BDH http://bdh-rd.bne.es/viewer.vm?id=0000061709&page=1

San Roman, Miguel Angel. *Luo Wenzao: A Unique Role in the Seventeenth Century Church of China* in Ku Wei-ying, ed. *Missionary Approaches and Linguistics in Mainland China and Taiwan* (Leuven Chinese Studies X) (Leuven 2001).

Santa Catalina, Bernardo de, OP. *Algunos documentos relativo a la Universidad de Manila.* Madrid: 1892. Archivos General de Indias, Sevilla, BR17:155-171.

Santa Cruz, Baltasar de, OP. *Tomo Segundo de la Historia de la Provincia del Santo Rosario de Filipinas, Japon y China de la Sagrada Orden de Predicadores.* Zaragosa: Pascual Bueno, Impressor del Reyno, 1693. BDH http://bdh-rd.bne.es/viewer.vm?id=0000092769&page=1

Santamaria, Alberto OP. *Estudios históricos de la Universidad de Santo Tomas de Manila.* Manila, 1938 from Unitas, vol. XV-XVI, 1936-1938.

Santiago, Luciano P.R. *The Hidden Light: The First Filipino Priests.* Quezon City: Luciano P.R. Santiago and New Day Publishers, 1987.

Santo Domingo, Juan de, OP. *A Brief History of the Foundation of the Beaterio de Santa Catalina.* Translated from the original Spanish by the Congregation of Dominican Sisters of St. Catherine of Siena. Quezon City, 1996.
Sastron, Manuel. *La Insurreccion en Filipinas Tomo I.* Madrid: Imp. de la Viuda de M. Minuesa de los Rios, 1897. USIT https://quod.lib.umich.edu/p/philamer/AFJ2295.0001.001?view=toc
Sauer, Carl Ortwin. *The Early Spanish Main.* Berkeley and Los Angeles: University of California Press, 1966.
Schumacher, John N. SJ, *Father Jose Burgos: Priest and Nationalist.* Manila: Knights of Columbus, 1972.
_____. *Revolutionary Clergy: The Filipino Clergy and the Nationalist Movement, 1850-1903.* Quezon City: Ateneo de Manila University Press,1981.
_____. *Father Jose Burgos: A Documentary History with Spanish Documents and Their Translation.* Quezon City: Ateneo de Manila University Press,1999.
Scott, S. P. & Robert I. Burns, S. *Las Siete Partidas, Volumes 1-5.* Philadelphia: University of Pennsylvania Press, 2012.
Scott, William Henry. *A Critical Study of the Prehispanic Source of Materials for the Study of Philippine History.* Manila: University of Santo Tomas Press, 1968.
_____. *Slavery in the Spanish Philippines.* Manila: De La Salle University Press, 1991.
Seijas, Tatiana. *Asian Slaves in Colonial Mexico: From Chinos to Indians.* New York: Cambridge University Press, 2014
Sheehy. Mary C. *The Dominican Habit.* Ongoing Formation Dominican Laity. March, 1989. Idaho Lay Dominicans http://www.dominicanidaho.org/formation/FORMATION%20LIBRARY/dominican.habit.history.pdf
Spate, Oskar Hermann Khristian. *The Spanish Lake.* Canberra: ANU E Press, 2004.
Taquilla, Jose Barrado, OP. ed. Los Dominicos y el Nuevo Mundo, siglos XIX-XX: actas del Vo Congreso International, Qro., Mexico, 4-8 setiembre 1995. Mexico: Editorial San Esteban, 1997.
[Tamayo, Serapio OP.] *Sobre Una "Reseña Historica de Filipinas."* Manila: Libertas, 1906. Internet Archive https://archive.org/details/sobreunareseah00mani
Thatcher, Oliver J. and McNeal, Edgar Holmes, ed. *A Source Book for Mediaeval History. Selected Documents Illustrating the History of Europe in the Middle Age.* New York: Charles Scribner's Sons, 1905, 513-518. http://oll.libertyfund.org/titles/2277#Thatcher_1508_1507 Accessed on: 19 April 2015.
Tormo Sanz, Leandro. *1872* Translated by Antonio Molina, Manila: Historical Conservation Society, 1973,
Torre, Carlos Maria de la. *Manifesto al Pais sobre los Sucesos de Cavite y Memoria sobre la Administración y Gobierno de las Islas Filipinas.* Madrid: Imp. de Gregorio Hernando, 1872. USIT https://quod.lib.umich.edu/p/philamer/ADT4331.0001.001?view=toc
United States. Bureau of Census. *Census of the Philippine Islands taken under the Direction of the Philippine Commission in the year 1903 in 4 Volumes.* Washington: United States Bureau of the Census, 1905. USIT https://quod.lib.umich.edu/p/philamer/AJB5834.0003.001?view=toc
United States. Bureau of Insular Affairs. *Reports of the Philippine Commission, the Civil Governor, and the Heads of the Executive Departments of the Civil Government of the Philippine Islands (1900-1903).* Washington: Government Printing Office, 1904. USIT https://quod.lib.umich.edu/p/philamer/AEW1480.0001.001?view=toc
_____. *Fourth Annual Report of the Philippine Commission 1903 Part 1 (in three parts).* Washington:Government Printing Office, 1904 Internet Archive. https://archive.org/stream/reportofphilippi00unit#page/144/mode/1up
_____. *Fifth Annual Report of the Philippine Commission 1904 Part 1 (in three parts).* Washington: Government Printing Office, 1905. Internet Archive. https://archive.org/details/acp1475.1904.001.umich.edu
_____. *Seventh Annual Report of the Philippine Commission 1906 Part 2 (in three parts).* Washington: Government Printing Office, 1907. USIT https://quod.lib.umich.edu/p/philamer/ACX1716.1906.002?rgn=main;view=toc

United States. Senate. *Lands Held for Ecclesiastical or Religious Uses in the Philippine Islands, etc.* Document No. 190 56th Congress 2d Session February 25, 1901. Internet Archive. https://archive.org/details/landsheldforeccl00unit

United States. War Department. *Annual Reports of the War Department for the fiscal year ended June 30 1906 Vol VIII Report of the Philippine Commission Part 2.* Washington: Government Printing Office, 1907. Hathi Trust https://babel.hathitrust.org/cgi/pt?id=mdp.35112203989423;view=1up;seq=7

Uriarte, Juan Bautista de. *Manifiesta y resumen historico de la fundacion de la venerable hermandad de la Santa Misericordia.* Manila: 1728, BR28:186-187.

UST Alumni Association Inc. *University of Santo Tomas Alumni Directory 1611-1971.* Manila: University of Santo Tomas, 1972.
    Supplement: 1775-1794. (Typewritten copy courtesy of Fidel Villaroel OP).

Valle, Francisco Navas del; Pastells, Pablo. *Catalogo de los Documentos Relativos a Las Islas Filipinas existentes en el Archivo de Indias de Sevilla (1618-1635) Precidido de Una Historia General de Filipinas por el P. Pablo Pastells SJ X Tomos.* Barcelona: Compañía General de Tabacos de Filipinas, 1918-1934. BDH http://bdh-rd.bne.es/viewer.vm?id=0000191838&page=1

Vassberg, David E. *Land and Society in Golden Age Castile.* Cambridge: Cambridge University Press, 1984. LIBRO http://libro.uca.edu/vassberg/land.htm

Vergara, Francisco Engracio [Regidor, Antonio]. *La Masoneria en Filipinas. Estudio de la actualidad. Apuntes para la historia de la colonizacion española en el siglo XIX.* Paris, 1896. Hathi Trust https://babel.hathitrust.org/cgi/pt?id=miun.adt4863.0001.001;view=1up;seq=3

Vertot, L' Abbe de. *The History of the Knights Hospitallers of St. John of Jerusalem; styled afterwards, The Knights of Rhodes, and at present, The Knights of Malta. 3 Vols.* Edinburgh: printed for Alexander Donaldson 1770. Google Books https://books.google.com.au/books/about/The_History_of_the_Knights_Hospitallers.html?id=acINAAAAQAAJ&redir_esc=y

Vespucci, Amerigo. *The Letters of Amerigo Vespucci and other Documents Illustrative of His Career.* Translated and annotated by Clements R. Markham. London: Hakluyt Society, 1894. Internet Archive https://archive.org/details/lettersofamerigo00vesp

Villaroel, Fidel. *Father Jose Burgos University Student.* Manila: University of Santo Tomas, 1971.
    _____. *Apolinario Mabini, His Birth Date and Student Years.* Manila: National Historical Institute, 1979.

Viana, Francisco Leandro de. *Documentos relativos al estado de las Islas Filipinas. S. XVIII,* 1701-1800 BDH http://bdh-rd.bne.es/viewer.vm?id=0000152097&page=1

Zuñiga, Joaquin Martinez de. *Historia de Las Islas Philipinas Compuesta.* Sampaloc: 1803. BDH http://bdh-rd.bne.es/viewer.vm?id=0000082203&page=1
    _____. *Estadismo de las Islas Filipinas o Mis Viajes por este Pais. 2 Tomos.* Madrid: 1893. BDH http://bdh-rd.bne.es/viewer.vm?id=0000043580&page=1

Warren, James. *The Sulu Zone, 1768-1898: the dynamics of external trade, slavery, and ethnicity in the transformation of a Southeast Asian maritime state.* Singapore: NUS Press, 2007.

Wolf 2nd, Edwin ed. *Doctrina Cristiana / The first book printed in the Philippines. Manila, 1593. A Facsimile Copy of the Lessing J. Rosenwald Collection.* Project Gutenberg Ebook #16119 Release Date: June 23, 2005. http://www.gutenberg.org/files/16119/16119-h/16119-h.htm

Worcester, Dean C. *Slavery and peonage in the Philippine Islands.* Department of Interior, Government of the Philippine Islands. Manila: Bureau of Printing, 1913. USIT https://quod.lib.umich.edu/p/philamer/AHL6699.0001.001?view=toc

Dictionaries and Encyclopedias

Encyclopedia Britannica

Alexandre de Rhodes. Britannica Library, Encyclopædia Britannica, 13 Aug. 2017. library.eb.com.au.rp.nla.gov.au/levels/adults/article/Alexandre-de-Rhodes/63448. Accessed 24 Oct. 2017.

Chinese civil service. Britannica Library, Encyclopædia Britannica, 8 Apr. 2008. library.eb.com.au.rp.nla.gov.au/levels/adults/article/Chinese-civil-service/24152. Accessed: 21 Oct. 2017.

Liberalism. Britannica Library, Encyclopædia Britannica, 15 Jul. 2017. library.eb.com.au.rp.nla.gov.au/levels/adults/article/liberalism/117288. Accessed 16 July 2017.

Slavery. Britannica Library, Encyclopædia Britannica, 25 Mar. 2016. library.eb.com.au.rp.nla.gov.au/levels/adults/article/slavery/109538. Accessed 5 April 2016.

Vietnam. Britannica Library, Encyclopædia Britannica, 3 May. 2017. library.eb.com.au.rp.nla.gov.au/levels/adults/article/Vietnam/111155. Accessed 24 Oct. 2017.

Encyclopedia of the Middle Ages

Vauchez, Andre, ed. *Patronage.* Encyclopedia of the Middle Ages James Clarke & Company, 2005. www.oxfordreference.com Accessed: 31 May 2014. 09:44.

The Catholic Encyclopedia

Barnes, Arthur. *Saint John Lateran*. The Catholic Encyclopedia. Vol. 9. New York: Robert Appleton Company, 1910. www.newadvent.org/cathen/09014b.htm Accessed on: 4 June 2015.

Hanna, Edward. *Purgatory*. The Catholic Encyclopedia. Vol. 12. New York: Robert Appleton Company, 1911. www.newadvent.org/cathen/12575a.htm Accessed on: 19 July 2015.

Loughlin, James. *Pope Clement XI*. The Catholic Encyclopedia. Vol. 4. New York: Robert Appleton Company, 1908. www.newadvent.org/cathen/04029a.htm Accessed on: 19 May 2017.

Thurston, Herbert, and Andrew Shipman. "The Rosary." The Catholic Encyclopedia. Vol. 13. New York: Robert Appleton Company, 1912. 12 Nov. 2017 <http://www.newadvent.org/cathen/13184b.htm>.

The Historical Encyclopedia of World Slavery

Raiswel, Richard. *Eugene IV, Papal bulls of,* The Historical Encyclopedia of World Slavery Vol. 1, Junius P. Rodriguez ed. Santa Barbara, California: ABC-CLIO, 1997.

Online Etymology Dictionary

Seminary | Search Online Etymolgy Dictionary www.etymonline.com http://www.etymonline.com/search?q=seminary Accessed on: 4 June 2015.

Oxford Encyclopedia of the Reformation. Oxford University Press 2005.

Hillebrand, Hans J. *Patronato Real.* www.oxfordreference.com Accessed on: 31 May 2014 09:34.

Medieval Iberia: An Encyclopedia

Literacy. Gerli, E. Michael, ed. *Medieval Iberia: An Encyclopedia.* United States: Taylor & Francis Ltd, 2003, 495-8.

The Stanford Encyclopedia of Philosophy

Rivera, Faviola. *Liberalism in Latin America.* The Stanford Encyclopedia of Philosophy (Spring 2016 Edition), Edward N. Zalta (ed.), https://plato.stanford.edu/archives/spr2016/entries/liberalism-latin-america/ Accessed on 23 July 2017.

Stochastikon GmbH
    Collani, Claudia von. *Biography of Gregorio Luo Wenzao OP, first Chinese Bishop of Nanking*. encyclopedia.stochastikon.com

Journals and Reviews

American Anthropologist
    Bourke, John G. "The Laws of Spain in Their Application to the American Indians." *American Anthropologist*, vol. 7, no. 2, 1894, pp. 193–201. *JSTOR*, JSTOR, www.jstor.org/stable/658541.

The Americas
    Frederick, Jake. "Without Impediment: Crossing Racial Boundaries in Colonial Mexico." *The Americas*, vol. 67, no. 4, 2011, pp. 495–515. *JSTOR*, JSTOR, www.jstor.org/stable/41239107.

Arizona Journal of Hispanic Cultural Studies
    Mariscal, George. "The Role of Spain in Contemporary Race Theory." *Arizona Journal of Hispanic Cultural Studies*, vol. 2, 1998, pp. 7–22. *JSTOR*, JSTOR, www.jstor.org/stable/20641414.

Boletin de la Real Sociedad Economica de Amigos del Pais, Revista Filipina de Ciencias y Artes.
    Moya, Francisco Javier. *Historia de la Real Sociedad Economica Filipina de Amigos del Pais*. Boletin de la Real Sociedad Economica de Amigos del Pais Revista Filipina de Ciencias y Artes. Año I. Numero I. 1 Mayo 1882. Manila: Tipografico de Ramirez y Giraudier, 1882. Digitalisierte Sammlungen http://digital.staatsbibliothek-berlin.de/werkansicht?PPN=PPN749600500&PHYSID=PHYS_0007&DMDID=DMDLOG_0001
    —-. *Historia de la Real Sociedad Economica Filipina de Amigos del Pais*. Boletin de la Real Sociedad Economica de Amigos del Pais Revista Filipina de Ciencias y Artes. Año III. Numero III. 1 Julio 1884. Manila: Imp C. Valdezco, 1884. Digitalisierte Sammlungen http://digital.staatsbibliothek-berlin.de/werkansicht?PPN=PPN74993395X&PHYSID=PHYS_0051&DMDID=DMDLOG_0001 Digitalisierte Sammlungen

The Catholic Historical Review
    Mecham, J. Lloyd. "The Origins of 'Real Patronato De Indias.'" *The Catholic Historical Review*, vol. 14, no. 2, 1928, pp. 205–227. *JSTOR*, JSTOR, www.jstor.org/stable/25012517.
    Shiels, W. Eugene. "Church and State in the First Decade of Mexican Independence." *The Catholic Historical Review*, vol. 28, no. 2, 1942, pp. 206–228. *JSTOR*, JSTOR, www.jstor.org/stable/25014148.

Citizenship Studies
    Herzog, Tamar. *Communities Becoming a Nation: Spain and Spanish America in the Wake of Modernity (and Thereafter)*. Citizenship Studies Vol 11 No, 2 May 2007 151-172. Special Issue: Citizenship Beyond the State. Andrew Girding and Trevor Stack (Eds). Routledge, Taylor and Francis Group. https://www.researchgate.net/profile/Tamar_Herzog/publication/248984176_Communities_Becoming_a_Nation_Spain_and_Spanish_America_in_the_Wake_of_Modernity_and_Thereafter/links/588123a7aca272b7b441742b/Communities-Becoming-a-Nation-Spain-and-Spanish-America-in-the-Wake-of-Modernity-and-Thereafter.pdf

Confluencia
> Routt, Kristin E. "Sanctity or Self-Will? Madre María De San José (1656–1719) and the Ascetic Path to Holiness." *Confluencia*, vol. 22, no. 1, 2006, pp. 42–57. *JSTOR*, JSTOR, www.jstor.org/stable/27923179.

Emeth
> Contreras, Salvador de, OP. *Memorial 1743*. Emeth Vol. 1 No. 1 March, 1963. Manila, Philippines: Colegio de San Juan de Letran, 1963 pp. 38-43.
>
> Valdes, Jose. *Letran College in the 17th Century*. Emeth Vol. 1 No. 1 March, 1963 pp. 30-38. Manila, Philippines: Colegio de San Juan de Letran.

Hispania Sacra
> Álvarez Icaza Longoria, María Teresa. *La reorganización del territorio parroquial de la arquidiócesis de México durante la prelacía de Manuel Rubio y Salinas (1749-1765)*. Hispania Sacra Vol 63, No 128 (2011) pp. 501-518. Instituto de Historia, Consejo Superior de Investigaciones Científicas. http://dx.doi.org/10.3989/hs.2011.v63.i128 Accessed on 21-04-2017 20:08.

The Hispanic American Historical Review
> Poole, Stafford. "Church Law on the Ordination of Indians and Castas in New Spain." *The Hispanic American Historical Review*, vol. 61, no. 4, 1981, pp. 637–650. *JSTOR*, JSTOR, www.jstor.org/stable/2514607.

Journal of the American Academy of Religion
> Flynn, Maureen. "The Spiritual Uses of Pain in Spanish Mysticism." *Journal of the American Academy of Religion*, vol. 64, no. 2, 1996, pp. 257–278. *JSTOR*, JSTOR, www.jstor.org/stable/1466102.

Journal of Asian History
> Escoto, Salvador P. "The Ecclesiastical Controversy of 1767-1776: A Catalyst of Philippine Nationalism." *Journal of Asian History*, vol. 10, no. 2, 1976, pp. 97–133. *JSTOR*, JSTOR, www.jstor.org/stable/41930217.
>
> Simpson, Renate. Higher Education in the Philippines Under the Spanish. Journal of Asian History. *Journal of Asian History*, vol. 14, no. 1, 1980, pp. 1–46. *JSTOR*, JSTOR, www.jstor.org/stable/41930356.

The Journal of Negro History
> Diggs, Irene. "Color in Colonial Spanish America." *The Journal of Negro History*, vol. 38, no. 4, 1953, pp. 403–427. *JSTOR*, JSTOR, www.jstor.org/stable/2715890.
>
> Dusenberry, William H. "Discriminatory Aspects of Legislation in Colonial Mexico." *The Journal of Negro History*, vol. 33, no. 3, 1948, pp. 284–302. *JSTOR*, JSTOR, www.jstor.org/stable/2715477.

Journal de la Societe des americanices
> PIHO, Virve. La Secularizacion de la Parroquias y la Economia Ecclesiastica en la Nueva España. Journal De La Société Des Américanistes, vol. 64, 1977, pp. 81–88. *JSTOR*, JSTOR, www.jstor.org/stable/24603894.

Korean Journal of History of Science
> Jami, Catherine. *Revisiting the Calendar Case (1664-1669): Science, Religion, and Politics in Early Qing Beijing*. Korean Journal of History of Science, 2015, 27 (2), pp. 459-477. HAL-SHS https://halshs.archives-ouvertes.fr/halshs-01222267 Accessed on: 21-12-2015 15:48

Letras Historicas
> Ruiz, Rosa Alicia de la Torre. *Composiciones de tierras en la alcaldia mayor de Sayula, 1692-1754: un estudio de caso sobre el funcionamiento del Juzgado Privativo de Tierras*. Letras Historicas Numero 6, Primavera-verano 2012, pp. 45-69. Centro Universitario de Ciencias Sociales y Humanidades, Universidad de Guadalajara. http://www.revistascientificas.udg.mx/index.php/LH/article/view/2115

Library of Congress Information Bulletin

Herbert, John R. "The Map that Named America - Library Acquires 1507 Waldseemüller Map of the World." *Library of Congress Information Bulletin*. September 2003 Vol. 62, No. 09. The Library of Congress. Washington DC. http://loc.gov/loc/lcib/0309/maps.html Accessed on 27 October 2017.

Mexicon
- Prem, Hanns J., et al. "Reconstructing Central Mexico's Population." *Mexicon*, vol. 15, no. 3, 1993, pp. 50–57. *JSTOR*, JSTOR, www.jstor.org/stable/23760245.

Philippine Quarterly of Culture and Society
- Santiago, Luciano P. R. "The First Filipino Doctors of Ecclesiastical Sciences (1772-1796)." *Philippine Quarterly of Culture and Society*, vol. 12, no. 4, 1984, pp. 257–270. *JSTOR*, JSTOR, www.jstor.org/stable/29791835.
- _____. "To Love and to Suffer: The Development of the Religious Congregations for Women in the Philippines during the Spanish Era (1565-1898). Part I." *Philippine Quarterly of Culture and Society*, vol. 23, no. 2, 1995, pp. 151–195. *JSTOR*, JSTOR, www.jstor.org/stable/29792184.
- _____. "To Love and to Suffer: The Development of the Religious Congregations for Women in the Philippines during the Spanish Era (1565-1898). Part II." *Philippine Quarterly of Culture and Society*, vol. 24, no. 1/2, 1996, pp. 119–179. *JSTOR*, JSTOR, www.jstor.org/stable/29792195.
- _____. "To Love and to Suffer: The Development of the Religious Congregations for Women in the Philippines during the Spanish Era (1565-1898). Part III." *Philippine Quarterly of Culture and Society*, vol. 24, no. 3/4, 1996, pp. 216–254. *JSTOR*, JSTOR, www.jstor.org/stable/29792202.

Philippine Social Sciences and Humanities Review
- Phelan, John Leddy, ed, *The Ordinances issued by the Audiencia of Manila for the Alcaldes Mayores (1642, 1696 and 1739)*. Philippine Social Sciences and Humanities Review Vol. XXIV Nos. 3-4 July-December, 1959, pp. 279-415.

Philippine Studies
- Araneta, Luis Ma. "The Works of Father Jose Burgos." *Philippine Studies*, vol. 7, no. 2, 1959, pp. 187–193. *JSTOR*, JSTOR, www.jstor.org/stable/42719439.
- De La Costa, Horacio de la. "Jesuit Education in the Philippines to 1768." *Philippine Studies*, vol. 4, no. 2, 1956, pp. 127–155. *JSTOR*, JSTOR, www.jstor.org/stable/42719215.
- Escoto, Salvador P. and Schumacher, John N. SJ. "Filipino Priests of the Archdiocese of Manila, 1782." *Philippine Studies*, vol. 24, no. 3, (Third Quarter 1976), pp. 326-343. *JSTOR*, JSTOR, www.jstor.org/stable/42632916.
- Fox, Henry Fredrick. "Primary Education in the Philippines, 1565-1863." *Philippine Studies*, vol. 13, no. 2, 1965, pp. 207–231. *JSTOR*, JSTOR, www.jstor.org/stable/42720593.
- Legarda, Benito. "Two and a Half Centuries of the Galleon Trade." *Philippine Studies*, vol. 3, no. 4, 1955, pp. 345–372. *JSTOR*, JSTOR, www.jstor.org/stable/42719178.
- Palanco, Fernando. "The Tagalog Revolts of 1745 According to Spanish Primary Sources." *Philippine Studies*, vol. 58, no. 1/2, 2010, pp. 45–77. *JSTOR*, JSTOR, www.jstor.org/stable/42632048.
- Quirino, Carlos, and José Burgos. "More Documents on Burgos." *Philippine Studies*, vol. 18, no. 1, 1970, pp. 161–177. *JSTOR*, JSTOR, www.jstor.org/stable/42632001.
- _____. "A Checklist of Documents on Gomburza from the Archdiocesan Archives of Manila." *Philippine Studies*, vol. 21, no. 1/2, 1973, pp. 19–84. *JSTOR*, JSTOR, www.jstor.org/stable/42632208.

Schumacher, John N. SJ. "The Authenticity of the Writings Attributed To Father Jose Burgos." *Philippine Studies*, vol. 18, no. 1, 1970, pp. 3–51. *JSTOR*, JSTOR, www.jstor.org/stable/42631996.

_____. "The Cavite Mutiny: An Essay on the Published Sources." *Philippine Studies*, vol. 20, no. 4, 1972, pp. 603–632. *JSTOR*, JSTOR, www.jstor.org/stable/42634842.

_____."Early Filipino Jesuits: 1593-1930." *Philippine Studies*, vol. 29, no. 3/4, 1981, pp. 271–308. *JSTOR*, JSTOR, www.jstor.org/stable/42635192.

_____."The Early Filipino Clergy: 1698–1762." *Philippine Studies*, vol. 51, no. 1, 2003, pp. 7–62. *JSTOR*, JSTOR, www.jstor.org/stable/42633636.

Religion & Literature

Kieckhefer, Richard. "Today's Shocks, Yesterday's Conventions." *Religion & Literature*, vol. 42, no. 1/2, 2010, pp. 253–278. *JSTOR*, JSTOR, www.jstor.org/stable/23049480.

Revista Latina de Comunicación Social

Calderón, Annie Badilla, Instituto Tecnológico de Costa Rica. *La información y los textos jurídicos de la colonia (II). El poder político Latina*, Revista Latina de Comunicación Social, 13 de enero de 1999. Recuperado el 2 de marzo de 2008 de: http://www.ull.es/publicaciones/latina/a1999c/149badilla2cr.htm

Southwestern Historical Quarterly

Jones, O. Garfield. *Local Government in the Spanish Colonies as Provided by the Recopilación de Leyes de los Reynos de las Indias.* Southwestern Historical Quarterly , Vol. 19, July,1915 - April, 1916. pp. 65-90. The Texas State Historical Association. https://texashistory.unt.edu/ark:/67531/metapth101067/m1/?q=Southwestern%20Historical%20Quarterly%20%2C%20Vol.%2019%2C%20July%2C1915%20-%20April%2C%201916 Accessed on 23-12-2016.

Takwa Revista de Historia

Aguirre, Rodolfo. *El ingreso de los indios al clero secular en el arzobispado de Mexico, 1691-1822.* Takwa Revista de Historia Num. 9 Primavera 2006 pp. 75-108. Centro Universitario de Ciencias Sociales y Humanidades, Universidad de Guadalajara, Mexico. http://148.202.18.157/sitios/publicacionesite/pperiod/takwa/Takwa9/rodolfo_aguirre.pdf Accessed on: 15-11-2016.

The William and Mary Quarterly

Sweet, James H. "The Iberian Roots of American Racist Thought." *The William and Mary Quarterly*, vol. 54, no. 1, 1997, pp. 143–166. *JSTOR*, JSTOR, www.jstor.org/stable/2953315.

Laws

Real Decreto

1863-12-20. *Estableciendo un plan de instruccion primaria en Filipinas.*

Recopilacion de leyes de los reynos de las Indias. Madrid, 1681 - California's Legal Heritage http://calegalheritage.law.berkeley.edu/spanish-law-in-america.html

Tomo I Libro I Titulo VI Ley VII. f. 26. *Que los Clerigos y Religiosos no sean admitidos a Doctrinas, sin saber la lengua general de los Indios, que han de administrar.*

Tomo I Libro I Titulo VII Ley XXX. f. 32. *Que los Prelados ordenen de Sacerdotes a los Mestizos, con informacion de vida y costumbres, y provean, que las Mestizas puedan ser Religiosas, con la misma calidad.*

Tomo I Libro I Titulo XIII Ley IV. f. 55. *Que los Virreyes, Audiencias y Governadores tengan cuidado de que los Doctrineros sepan la lengua de los Indios, o sean removidos.*

Tomo I Libro I Titulo XIII Ley V. f. 55. *Que los Curas dispongan a los Indios en la enseñanza de la lengua Española y en ella la doctrina Christiana.*
Tomo I Libro I Titulo XIV Ley VI. f. 60. *Que a los Religiosos, que por orden de el Rey passaren a las Indias, se les socorra, como se ordena.*
Tomo I Libro I Titulo XV Ley V. f. 76. *Que ningun Religioso pueda tener Doctrina sin saber la lengua de los naturales de ella, y los que passaren de España la aprendan con cuidado, y los Arcobispos y Obispos le tengan de que se execute.*
Tomo I Libro I Titulo XV Ley VI. f. 76. *Que los Religiosos Doctrineros sean examinados por los Prelados Diocesanos en la suficiencia, y lengua de los Indios de sus Doctrinas.*
Tomo I Libro I Titulo XV Ley VIII. f. 77. *Que los Prelados Regulares procuren se guarde lo ordenado para el examen de los Religiosos Doctrineros, y los elijan suficientes.*
Tomo I Libro I Titulo XV Ley XXXIII. f. 82. *Que en las Filipinas se encargue la Doctrina de cada Provincia a una de las Religiones, en caso de nuevas conquistas espirituales y por aora.*
Tomo II Libro VI Titulo I Ley I. f. 188. *Que los Indios sean favorecidos, y amparados por las Justicias Eclesiasticas y Seculares.*
Tomo II Libro VI Titulo I Ley XVIII. f. 190. *Que donde fuere possible se pongan Escuelas de la lengua Castellana, para que la aprendan los Indios.*
Tomo II Libro VI Titulo II Ley V. f. 195. *Que los Indios de Brasil, o demarcacion de Portugal, sean libres en las Indias.*
Tomo II Libro VI Titulo II Ley IX. f. 195. *Que se nombre un Ministro o persona de satisfacion, que conozca de la libertad de los Indios.*
Tomo II Libro VI Titulo II Ley XII. f. 196. *Que dispone sobre la libertad o esclavitud de los Mindanaos.*
Tomo II Libro VI Titulo II Ley XVI. f. 197. *Revalida las ordenes de la libertad de los Indios, y da nueva providencia en los de Chile.*
Tomo II Libro VI Titulo III Ley XXI. f. 200. *Que en Pueblos de Indios no vivan Españoles, Negros, Mestizos, y Mulatos.*
Tomo II Libro VI Titulo III Ley XXII. f. 200 *Que entre los Indios no vivan Españoles, Mestizos, ni Mulatos, aunque hayan comprado tierras en sus Pueblos.*
Tomo II Libro VI Titulo VI Ley VII. f. 218. *Que no se den protectorias a mestizos.*
Tomo II Libro VI Titulo VII Ley VIII. f. 220. *Que se reconozca el derecho de los Caciques, y modere el excesso.*
Tomo II Libro VI Titulo VII Ley XVI. f. 221. *Que los Indios Principales de Filipinas sean bien tratados, y se les encargue el govierno, que solian tener en los otros.*
Tomo II Libro VII Titulo V Ley XIV. f. 287. *Que los mulatos y Zambaigos no traigan armas, y los Mestizos las puedan traer con licencia*
_____. Ley XV. f, 287. *Que los Negros, y Loros; libres, o esclavos no traigan armas.*
_____. Ley XVI. f. 287. *Que loa esclavos, Mestizos y Mulatos de Virreyes, y Ministros no traigan armas, y los de Alguaziles mayores, y otros las puedan traer.*
Tomo II Libro VII Titulo V Ley XXVIII. f. 290. *Que las Negras, y Mulatas horras no traigan oro, seda, mantos, ni perlas.*

Superior Gobierno de Filipinas.
1857-2-6. *Reglamento de Asuntos de Imprenta*. Manila: Imp. Tip. de Santo Tomas, 1857.

Manuscripts

Archdiocesan Archives of Manila

Examenes para Provision de Curatos y Economatos
> 1857-1-23. Burgos, Jose. *Indorsement of the parish priest of Rosario, Cavite to the Vicar Forane (Mariano Gomes de los Angeles) requesting a substitute due to illness.* Examenes para Provision de Curatos y Economatos, 1768-1874.

Officios de Varias Autoridades
> 1860-2-24. Garcia Ortiz, Francisco. *Dictum on Burgos et al.* Oficios de Varias Autoridades, 1860

Officios de Varias Personas
> 1860-2-24. Garcia Ortiz, Francisco. Dictum on *Burgos et al.* Oficios de Varias Personas, 1815-1898.

Testimonios de posesion de curatos
> 1865, January. Pronotario Ramon (last name illegible). *Testimony that Burgos was given "material possession of the curacy of the cathedral between 10 and 11 in the morning in the presence of various priests, Spaniards and some indios in the Sagrario.* Testimonios de posesion de curatos, 1806-1859.

Archives of the University of Santo Tomas, Manila
> 1860-8-7. Burgos, Jose. *Informaciones de Colegiales.* AUST Libros 196, fol. 239.

Archivo del Ayuntamiento (AA)
> 1545-9-2 Sevilla. *Suplica a fundar un orfanato contando razones.* Secc.3, tomo 11, num. 52.

Archivo General de la Nacion, Mexico (AGNM)
> 1749 -10-4 Real Cedula. *Secularizacion de doctrinas y curatos de Lima, Mexico y Santa Fe.* AGNM, Reales Cedulas Originales vol 69 exp. 103 ff.1-11v
>
> 1753-2-1 Real Cedula. *Secularizacion se extiende a todas partes del las indias.* AGNM, Reales Cedulas Originales vol 69 exp. 103 ff.1-11v
>
> 1757-6-23 Real Cedula. *Cambios en las cedulas de secularizacion.* AGNM, Reales Cedulas Originales vol 77

Archivo General de Indias (AGI)
> Consejo de Indias
> > 1573. *Carta de Guido de Lavezaris sobre los esclavos de Filipinas.* ES.41091.AGI/23.6.2//FILIPINAS,6,R.2,N.16 - PARES
> >
> > 1583-6-18 Manila. *Cartas de Domingo de Salazar al Rey.* AGI Filipinas 74, ramo 1.⁰ - PARES
> >
> > 1585-1-26 Alcala de Henares. *Merced de pesos de tepuzque y arroz a jesuitas de Filipinas.* ES.41091.AGI/23.6.829//FILIPINAS,339,L.1,F.315R-315V - PARES
> >
> > 1593-9-20 Manila. *Peticiones del agustino Francisco de Ortega.* ES.41091.AGI/23.6.728//FILIPINAS,79,N.22 - PARES
> >
> > 1598-6-8 Manila. *Relación de Morga de cosas en lo eclesiástico y secular.* ES.41091.AGI/23.6.13//FILIPINAS,18B,R.8,N.91 - PARES
> >
> > 1599-5-21. *Confirmacion de Officio: Jeronimo Guerrero.* ES.41091.AGI/23.13.4.4//SANTA_FE,147,N.11 - PARES
> >
> > 1606/1608. *Caja de Filipinas, Cuentas.* ES.41091.AGI/16.12.14//CONTADURIA,1207 - PARES
> >
> > 1613-12-16. *Petición del jesuita Francisco de Figueroa de limosna de vino y aceite.* ES.41091.AGI/23.6.728//FILIPINAS,79,N.104 - PARES
> >
> > 1622. *Informaciones: Jeronimo Guerrero.* ES.41091.AGI/23.6.425//FILIPINAS,61,N.1 - PARES
> >
> > 1623-7-1. *Peticion de Jeronimo Guerrero de patronazgo real para colegio.* ES.41091.AGI/23.6.848//FILIPINAS,39,N.13 - PARES
> >
> > 1623-7-16 Madrid. *Orden a Fajardo de ayudar al Colegio de niños huérfanos.* ES.41091.AGI/23.6.5//FILIPINAS,7,R.5,N.68 - PARES
> >
> > 1624-5-20. *Peticion de Aumento de prebendas y estipendios para la catedral de Manila.* ES.41091.AGI/23.6.406//FILIPINAS,85,N.57 - PARES
> >
> > 1625-8-3 Manila.. Carta del Cabildo secular de Manila sobre various asuntos. ES.41091.AGI/23.6.6//FILIPINAS,27,N.129 - - PARES

1626-6-19 Madrid. *Orden a Távora de apoyar la obra de niños huérfanos.* ES. 41091.AGI/23.6.474//FILIPINAS,329,L.3,F.91V - PARES

1626-8-1 Manila. *Carta de Juan Jeronimo Guerrero sobre colegio.* ES.41091.AGI/ 23.6.848//FILIPINAS,39,N.52 - PARES

1628-8-4 Manila. *Carta de Niño de Tavora sobre colegios, incendios.* ES. 41091.AGI/23.6.12//FILIPINAS,8,R.1,N.4 - PARES

1629-8-1 Cavite. *Carta de Niño de Távora sobre holandeses e ingleses,* ES. 41091.AGI/23.6.502//FILIPINAS,21,R.3,N.14 - PARES

1630-8-4 Cavite. *Carta de Niño de Tavora sobre comercio con oriente.* ES. 41091.AGI/23.6.12//FILIPINAS,8,R.1,N.10 - PARES

1631-8-19 Madrid. *Respuesta a Tavora sobre asuntos de gobierno.* ES.41091.AGI/ 23.6.474/FILIPNAS,329,L.3,F.195V-197V - PARES

1632-1-27 Madrid. *Orden sobre pasar religiosos a Japon y hospital de Manila.* ES. 41091.AGI/23.6.474//FILIPINAS,329,L.3,F.203R-203V - PARES

1635-2-5 Manila. *Petición del Cabildo secular de Manila sobre no permitir nuevo convento.* ES.41091.AGI/23.6.6//FILIPINAS,27,N.198 - PARES

1635-6-6. *Peticion de Juan Jeronimo Guerrero para Colegio de huerfanos.* ES. 41091.AGI/23.611//FILIPINAS,5,N.452 - PARES

1635-7-10 Madrid. *Orden sobre Colegio de Niños Huérfanos Españoles de Manila.* ES.41091/23.6.1031//FILIPINAS.347,L.1,F.144V-145R - PARES

1635-9-11. *Petición del dominico Mateo de la Villa sobre fundación de convento de Santa Catalina de Siena.* ES.41091.AGI/23.6.654//FILIPINAS,80,N.192 - PARES

1636-1-25. *Titulo de la encomienda de Baratao que tiene 700 tributos, para el Colegio de niños huérfanos de Manila.* AGI 67-6-42 - PARES

1638-11-28. *Confirmación de encomienda al Hospital de Niños Huérfanos.* ES. 41091.AGI/23.6.1031//FILIPINAS,347,L.2,F.82R-84R - PARES

1640-6-18. Corcuera, Sebastian Hurtado. *Mandamiento donde se encarga la administracion de Letran a la Religion de Sto. Domingo, y Provee para el Sustento.* APSR Letran Section Vol. I Doc. 1 leaves 26-32.

1642-7-27 Manila. *Carta del dominico Diego de Santa Maria sobre Colegio de niños huérfanos.* ES.41091.AGI/23.6.406//FILIPINAS,85,N.94 - PARES

1644-2-17 Zaragoza. *Petición de informe sobre cien brazas de tierra.* ES. 41091.AGI/23.6.372//FILIPINAS,340,L.5,F.200R-201R - PARES

1644-12-3. *Peticion del jesuita Baltazar de Lagunilla de confirmacion de mercedes dadas a jesuitas de Manila.* ES.41091.AGI/23.6.406//FILIPINAS,85,N.110 - PARES

1646-2-9 Madrid. *Confirmacion al Colegio y Hospital de San Juan de Letran.* ES. 41091.AGI/23.6.1031//FILIPINAS,347,L.3,F.123V-127V - PARES

1676-3-13 Madrid. *Real Cedula al Virrey de Mexico Cometiendole Que Los Naturales Venidos de Filipinas, Liberados de la Esclavitud, tengan tierras o vivan en barrio separados de la capital.* AGI, Mexico, 1071, lib. 24, flo. 433v. - PARES

1679-6-12 Madrid. *Real Cedula Ordenando el Cumplimiento de la Cedula que Prohibe la Esclavitude de los Indios en Chile y Disponiendo el Traslado de los Liberados al Peru.* AGI, Chile, 167, lib. 6, flo. 30v. - PARES

1680-6-20. *Carta de Viga sobre seminario para indios.* ES.41091.AGI/23.6.10// FILIPINAS,24,R.1,N.5 - PARES

1682 Manila. *Expediente sobre asistencia de colegiales de San Juan de Letran a la catedral.* ES.41091.AGI/23.6.464//FILIPINAS,78,N.15 - PARES

1684-6-22 Manila. Urtado, Escover de et al. *Carta a su Magestad de la Audiencia de Manila respecto a la Cedula de 12 de junio 1679 relacionada con la esclavitud de los Indios.* AGI: Filipinas 67-6-24

1686-5-1 Buen Retiro. *Aviso sobre informe de liberación de esclavos en Filipinas.* ES. 41091.AGI/23.6.1076//FILIPINAS,331,L.8,F.60V-61R - PARES

1687-6-15 San Gabriel. Pardo, Felipe de OP. *Carta sobre becas para indios en Colegio de dominicos..* ES.41091.AGI/23.6.426//FILIPINAS,86,N.59. - PARES
1687-8-1. *Petición de informe sobre niños que ayudan en la Catedral.* ES.41091.AGI/23.6.1076//FILIPINAS.331,L.8.F.240R. - PARES
1690-5-18. *Confirmacion de encomienda de Sangasang, etc.* ES.41091.AGI/23.6.477//FILIPINAS,56,N.5. - PARES
1694-7-14 Manila. *Peticion del dominico Raimundo Berart sobre colegio para indios.* ES.41091.AGI/23.6.426//FILIPINAS,86,N.76. - PARES
1696-8-22. *Petition del dominicano Alonso Sandin sober revolver curator de Tabuco a dominicos y jesuitas.* ES.41091.AGI/23.6.426//FILIPINAS,86,N.81. - PARES
1697-5-13 Madrid. *Carta sobre viaje del arzobispo de Manila a Filipinas.* ES.41091.AGI/23.6.1059//FILIPINAS,332,L.10,F.8R-8V - PARES
1699/1710. *Expediente sobre visita de las doctrinas por los ordinarios.* ES.41091.AGI/23.6.387//FILIPINAS,302,N.1. - PARES
1699-11-9 Madrid. *Memorial de Jaime Mimbela - Expediente sobre visita de las doctrinas por los ordinarios.* ES.41091.AGI/23.6.387//FILIPINAS,302,N.1 - PARES
1702-4-28 Madrid. *Orden sobre sobre fundación de un Seminario en Manila.* ES.41091.AGI/23.61059/FILIPINAS,332,L.10,F.213V-215V - PARES
1703-10-26 Madrid. *Orden de no impedir viaje a Guadalajara al arzobispo Camacho.* ES.41091.AGI/23.6.976//FILIPINAS,341,L.8,F.191R-191V - PARES
1704-6-20 Manila. *Carta de Diego Camacho y Ávila, arzobispo de Manila, sobre no poderse erigir el seminario por falta de medios y que el gobernador no le ha dado copia de los autos.* ES.41091.AGI/23.6.813//FILIPINAS,308,N.4 - PARES
1704-6-22 Manila. *Carta de Domingo de Zabalburu, gobernador de Filipinas, dando cuenta de la falta de medios que hay para la fundación del seminario de que remite testimonio que no está.* ES.41091.AGI/23.6.813//FILIPINAS,308,N.4 - PARES
1707/1708. *Expediente sobre fundación de seminario en Manila.* ES.41091.AGI/23.6.813//FILIPINAS,308,N.4 - PARES
1710-3-3 Madrid. *Orden al gobernador Ursúa sobre Seminario de Manila.* ES.41091.AGI/23.6.1059//FILIPINAS,332,L.11,F.281V-289R - PARES
1710-5-2 Madrid. *Orden de reprender al obispo Camacho por tolerar a Tournon.* ES.41091.AGI/23.6.1059//FILIPINAS,332,L.11,F.334V-341R - PARES
1710-5-2 Madrid. *Orden sobre asignación del arzobispo de Manila.* ES.41091.AGI/23.6.1059//FILIPINAS,332,L.11,F.341V-343R - PARES
1712-12-31 Madrid. *Real Cedula en que se dan las gracias al arzobispo de Manila, por la aplicación y celo que ha manifestado en la erección, planta y régimen del seminario nuevamente fundado en la ciudad de Manila, mandándose que se quite el nombre de San Clemente y se ponga en su lugar el de San Felipe.* ES.41091.AGI/23.6.827//FILIPINAS,290,N.80 - PARES
1714-8-24 El Pardo. *Comunicación sobre la creación de un beaterío en Manila.* ES.41091.AGI/23.6.330//FILIPINAS,333,L.124V-126V - PARES
1716-2-17 Madrid. *Orden sobre fundacion de Beaterio para indias en Manila.* ES.41091.AGI/23.6.551//FILIPINAS,342,L.9,F.22R-24R - PARES
1716-2-17 Madrid. *Aviso al arzobispo sobre fundación de Beaterio para indias.* ES.41091.AGI/23.6.551//FILIPINAS,342,L.9,F.24R-26R - PARES
1716-2-17 Madrid. *Aviso al provincial de dominicos sobre Beaterio para indias.* ES.41091.AGI/23.6.551//FILIPINAS,342,L.9,F.26R-28R - PARES
1718-7-29. *Carta de Bustillo sobre casa de Terceras de Manila.* ES.41091.AGI/23.6.957//FILIPINAS,132,N.13 - PARES
1730-7-26 Cazalla. *Orden de suspender la fundación de Universidad en Manila.* ES.41091.AGI/23.6.330//FILIPINAS,333,L.13,F.63V-67V - PARES

1732-9-18. *Peticion del Dominico Salvador de Contreras de limosna al Colegio de San Juan de Letran.* ES.41091.AGI/23.6.538//FILIPINAS,297,N.120 - PARES

1733-10-23 El Escorial. *Orden de poner ciertas cátedras en Colegios de Manila.* ES. 41091.AGI/23.6.551//FILIPINAS,342,L.10,F.6R-10R - PARES

1733-12-22 Consejo. *Petición del dominico Salvador de Contreras de que el Colegio de Santo Tomás se erija en Universidad.* ES.41091.AGI/23.6.538//FILIPINAS, 297,N.124 - PARES

1734-6-6 Manila. *Carta de Valdes Tamon sobre campana del Beaterio de Santa Catalina.* ES.41091.AGI/23.6.695//FILIPINAS,145,N.6 - PARES

1745-8-14 Manila. *Carta del dominico Bernardo Ustariz sobre beaterio de Santa Catalina de Siena.* ES.41091.AGI/23.6.386//FILIPINAS,299,N,31 - PARES

1748. *Expediente sobre provisión y visita de doctrinas.* ES.41091.AGI/23.6.388// FILIPINAS,303,N.5 - PARES

1750-8-27 Manila. *Carta de Pedro Martinez de Arizala sobre el beaterio de Santa Catalina de Siena.* ES.41091.AGI/23.6.922//FILIPINAS,292,N.31 - PARES

1751-11-7 El Escorial. *Aprobacion de lo dispuesto sobre sublevaciones de indios.* ES. 41091.AGI/23.6.637//FILIPINAS,335,L.16,F.206R-211R - PARES

1757-7-27 Manila. *Carta del Cabildo eclesiástico de Manila: sobre el número de doctrinas de regulares que podrían agregarse al clero.* ES.41091.AGI/23.6.388// FILIPINAS,303,N.5 Fols. 73r-76v - PARES

1762-4-17 Aranjuez. *Orden sobre Beaterio de Santa Catalina de Siena de Manila.* ES.41091.1GI/23.6.637//FILIPINAS,335,L.17,F.194V-199R - PARES

1774-11-9 El Escorial. *Orden de secularizar doctrinas de Filipinas.* ES.41091.AGI/ 23.6.331//FILIPINAS, 336,L.18,F.410R-411V - PARES

1774-11-9 El Escorial. *Anulacion de concordia celebrada en 1697 entre los Ordenes. El Escorial 1774-11-9.* ES.41091.AGI/23.6.331//FILIPINAS,336,L.18,F. 413-416R - PARES

1776-12-11 Madrid. *Orden sobre la secularización de curatos y doctrinas.* ES. 41091.AGI/23.6.124//FILIPINAS,337,L.19,F.148R-153V - PARES

1777-8-5 San Ildefonso. *Orden sobre el Beaterio de Santa Catalina de Siena de Manila.* ES.41091.AGI/23.6.124//FILIPINAS,337,L.19,F.245R-246V - PARES

1779-11-25. *Aviso de lo declarado sobre el beaterío de Santa Catalina.* ES. 41091.AGI/23.6.124//FILIPINAS,337,L.19,F.495R-496R - PARES

1781-12-7 Madrid. *Aviso y orden sobre conflicto en la Universidad de Manila.* ES. 41091.AGI/23.6.124//FILIPINAS,337,L.20,F.94R-106V - PARES

1794-11-15 Madrid. *Peticion de informe sobre extinción de Colegios de Manila.* ES. 41091.AGI/23.6.214//FILIPINAS,338,L.22,F.82V-84V - PARES

1794-11-15 Madrid. *Peticion de informe sobre extinción de Colegios de Manila.* ES. 41091.AGI/23.6.214//FILIPINAS,338,L.22,F.84V-86R - PARES

1781-12-7 Madrid. *Aviso y orden sobre conflicto en la Universidad de Manila.* ES. 41091.AGI/23.6.124//FILIPINAS,337,L.20,F.94R-106V - PARES

1781-12-7 Madrid. *Respuestas sobre conflicto en la Universidad de Manila.* ES. 41091.AGI/23.6.124//FILIPINAS,337,L.20,F.107R-119R - PARES

1783-6-3 Aranjuez. *Agregacion del Colegio de San Ignacio al Seminario Conciliar.* ES.41091.AGI/23.6.124//FILIPINAS,337,L20,F.181V-182V - PARES

1784-3-12 Pardo. *Orden de agregar Colegio de jesuitas de Manila al Seminario.* ES. 41091.AGI/23.6.1234//FILIPINAS,337,L20,F218R-221R - PARES

Ministerio de Hacienda.
 1804/1848. *Real Compañia de Filipinas 1804/1848.* ES.41091.AGI/36.967// ULTRAMAR,640 - PARES

Patronato Real
 1583-6-18. *Cartas de Domingo de Salazar al Rey.* ES.41091.AGI/29.3.5.3// PATRONATO,25,R.8 - PARES

Archivo General de Simancas, Valladolid

1504-10-12 *Testamento de la reina Isabel la Catolica.* Medina del Campo (Valladolid, España). ES.47161.AGS/4.2//PTR,LEG,30,DOC.2.
1576-6-7 Manila. Sande, Francisco de. *Letter to Felipe II.* Simancas - Secular; Audiencia de Filipinas; Cartas y expedientes del gobernador de Filipinas, vistos en el consejo; años 1567 1 1599; esa. 67, caj. 6, leg. 6;6
1585-1636. *Report of Spanish Council.* AGS Secular; Audiencia de Filipinas; consultas originales correspondientes a dicha Audiencia; años 1585 a 1636; est. 67, caj. 6, leg. 1.
1603-12-16 Manila. Benavides, Miguel OP. *Letter to Felipe III.* Simancas: Eclesiastico; cartas y expedientes del arzobispo de Manila vistos en el Consejo; años de 1579 a 1679; est. 68, caj. 1, leg. 32;

Archivo de Museo Naval Madrid
1834 Enero. Becerra, Nicolas OAR. *Carta a Pasqual Enrile.* Ms.1669.

Archivo Histórico Nacional, Madrid (AHN)
1770-1-1 Manila. *Carta de Basilio Sancho de Santa Justa y Santa Rufina, Arzobispo de Filipinas.* AHN, A.18-26-8.
1871-8-25 Manila. Martinez Santa Cruz, Gregorio Meliton. *Letter of the Archbishop to the Regent of Spain Francisco Serrano.* AHN, Ultramar, leg. 2255

Ministerio de Ultramar
1828 11-10, Manila. Ricafort, Mariano. *Letter to the Secretary of State, Grace and Justice.* AHN Ultramar 2140;
1863/1865. *Expediente general de la Instrucción Pública en las islas Filipinas: Plan de Enseñanza primaria de indígenas. Creación y Reglamento de la Escuela Normal de Maestros de Instrucción Primaria de indígenas.1863/1865.* ES. 28079.AHN/2.3.1.16.2.4.4.3//ULTRAMAR,604, Exp.5 - PARES
1863/1872. *Expediente relativo al Plan de Estudios para las Islas Filipinas.* ES. 28079.AHN/2.3.1.16.2.4.4.3//ULTRAMAR,605,Exp.1 - PARES
1871/1873. *Expediente Pesonal de R. Izquierdo, gobernador capitán general.* ES. 28079.AHN/2.3.1.16.5//ULTRAMAR,5222,Exp.37 - PARES
1872-10-12. Izquierdo, Rafael de. *Carta reservada, num. 816, del Gobernadro de Filipinas, Rafael de Izquierdo, al Ministro de Ultramar,* leg. 5216, AHN.

Archivo de la Provincia del Santisimo Rosario de Filipinas (APSR)
1640-6-11 Manila. Guerrero, Juan Geronimo. *Renuncia a favor de la orden.* Recaudos de la posesión que se dio a la orden de nuestro P. Santo Domingo del Colegio de San Juan de Letran, 1640. APSR Letran Section Vol. I Doc. 1 leaves 26-32.
1640-6-18 Manila. Corcuera, Sebastian Hurtado. *Mandamiento donde se encarga la administracion de Letran a la Religion de Sto. Domingo, y Provee para el Sustento.* APSR Letran Section Vol. I Doc. 1 leaves 26-32.
1640-7-12 Manila. Guerrero, Hernando. *Concesion en la persona de H. Fr Diego de Santamaria.* Recaudos de la posesión que se dio a la orden de nuestro P. Santo Domingo del Colegio de San Juan de Letran, 1640. APSR Letran Section Vol. I Doc. 1 leaves 26-32.
1640-7-14 Manila. Gant, Clemente, OP. *Aceptacion de la Orden Dominicana.* Recaudos de la posesión que se dio a la orden de nuestro P. Santo Domingo del Colegio de San Juan de Letran, 1640. APSR Letran Section Vol. I Doc. 1 leaves 26-32.
1653, October. *Document citing Fr. Alonso de Villegas as Administrator of Colegio de Letran de los niños huerfanos.* APSR Seccion de Letran Tomo 3.
1666 Manila. *Capellania de Don Lope Felix de Alcarazo Seccion, 1666.* APSR Letran Section Doc. 4, Fols. 174-175.
1691 Manila. Valdes, Jose OP. *Relacion verdadera de la fundacion del colegio de los niños huerfanos de los Santos Apostoles San Pedro y San Pablo , de San Juan de Letran, de la ciudad de Manila en las Islas Filipinos, sacada fielmente de diversos papeles y escrituras autenticas, que se hallaron en el archivo del Colegio,.* APSR Letran Section Vol I Doc.6 and 7, leaves 161-164;

1732. Contreras, Salvador OP. *Memorial 1732*. APSR Letran Section Vol. I Doc 11-13.
1734. *Venta de la Iglesia de Letran al Beaterio de Santa Catalina* en *1734, 1783*. APSR Letran Section Vol. I Doc 18, fols. 54-55.
1762-10-18. Nien, Pedro. *Letter to P.P. Antonio Loranco and Pedro Feliu.* APSR China Tomo 034 fols. 30-40.

Archivo Servicio Historico Militar
1872-1-23. Lluiz, Luis Roig de. *Diary of Operations.* ASHM *fol .1872-1-1-1-15.*
1872-2-15. Martinez, Gregorio Meliton. *Letter to Gov. Gen. Rafael Izquierdo.* ASHM fol. 4-9-1-14.

National Archives of the Philippines (PNA)
1872-1-25 Cavite, Carballo, Manuel. *Informe sobre el acontecimiento de la insureccion de Cavite en el 20, 21 y 22 de enero.* Cavite 1872 doc. no. 100, Insurgent Records, PNA.
1872-1-30 Manila. Martinez Santa Cruz, Gregorio Meliton. *Letter of the Archbishop to the Gov. Gen. Rafael de Izquierdo.* PNA 1872.
1872-1-31. Izquierdo, Rafael de. *Comunicacion num. 390 del Capitan General dando una completa informacion al Ministro de Ultramar sobre la insureccion de 1872 en Cavite.* Cavite 1872, doc. no. 117, Insurgent Records, PNA.
1872-2-3. Izquierdo, Rafael de. [Letter of Governor-General of the Philippines to the Captain-General of the Philippines] 3 Feb. Sediciones y Rebeliones 1870-1873, PNA.

Varias Provincias, Cavite
1816-1898, Exp. 30, 100-100b.
1816-1898, Exp. 86, 282
1816-1898, Exp. 82

St. Paul's Metropolitan Cathedral, Vigan Ilocos Sur
1837-2-12. Josef Apolonio Burgos. *Libro de Bautismo, Año 1836-1838*, vol.21

University of Illinois
Philippine Manuscripts 1740-1758.

Newspapers and Website Articles

Catholic Online
The Mysteries of the Rosary http://www.catholic.org/prayers/mystery.php Accessed on 12 November 2017.

Catholic Bishops' Conference of Vietnam
History of the Catholic Church in Vietnam. http://cbcvietnam.org/History/history-of-the-catholic-church-in-vietnam.html . Accessed on 1 January 2016.

Diario de Manila
1861-6-4. Edque, Rafael. *Temblor en Manila.*

Dominican Province of St Martin de Porres
2015-11-23. Tran, Hung OP. *St. Vincent Liem OP (Part 1 of 4)*. http://www.opsouth.org/st_vincent-liem-part-1-of-4/ Accessed on: 27 December 2015.
2015-11-24. Tran, Hung OP. *St. Vincent Liem OP (Part 2 of 4)*. http://www.opsouth.org/st_vincent-liem-part-2-of-4/ Accessed on: 27 December 2015.
2015-11-25. Tran, Hung OP. *St. Vincent Liem OP (Part 3 of 4)*. http://www.opsouth.org/st_vincent-liem-part-3-of-4/ Accessed on: 27 December 2015.2015-11-26. Tran, Hung OP. *St. Vincent Liem OP (Part 4 of 4)*. http://www.opsouth.org/st_vincent-liem-part-3-of-4/ Accessed on: 27 December 2015.

Dominicos - Provincia de Hispania.

Quien Somos? https://www.dominicoshispania.org/quienes-somos/ Accessed on 6 August 2014, 12:58pm.

Filipinas ante Europa
1900-2-28 No. 9. [Regidor, Antonio Maria.] *Los Martires de la Patria,* pp. 72-73. BDH http://hemerotecadigital.bne.es/issue.vm?id=0005186875

Florida International University Libraries
Miranda, Salvador. *Braschi, Giovanni Angelo (1717-1799). The Cardinals of the Holy Roman Church.* Florida International University Libraries. http://www2.fiu.edu/~mirandas/bios1773-iii.htm Accessed on 21 July 2017, 12:34.

Joking, JP Viktor
The Patriarchal Cross. http://jpviktorjokinen.deviantart.com/art/The-Patriarchal-Cross-Several-Resolutions-348297810 Accessed on: 1 May 2015,

La America, Madrid
1864-9-12 No.17. [Burgos, Jose] *A La Nacion.* pp. 11-13. BDH http://hemerotecadigital.bne.es/issue.vm?id=0002246396

La Democracia
1901-11-25. Salazar, Hugo. *The Usurpation of Indian lands by friars.*

La Discusion
1870-1-6 Año XV Num 386. *Conspiracion en Manila.* p. 2, col. 1ª BDH http://hemerotecadigital.bne.es/issue.vm?id=0002364174

Orden de Malta España
Historia de la Orden - www.ordendemalta.es Accessed on: 14 April 2015.

Order of Malta:
Names of the Order - www.orderofmalta.int Accessed on: 14 April 2015.

Provincia de España de la Orden de Predicadores
Historia de la Provincia de España. http://dominicos.es/provincia/historia.aspx Accessed on 17 February 2014, 12:03pm.

Revue Des Deux Modes
Plauchut, Edmund. *L'ARCHIPEL DES PHILIPPINES.* Revue Des Deux Modes, juin 1877. http://www.revuedesdeuxmondes.fr/article-revue/iii-lindustrie-le-commerce-la-situation-politique/

Rosademaria
Centro evangelizador y cultural. 13 July 2013. https://rosademaria.wordpress.com https://rosademaria.wordpress.com/2013/07/

Seminario Conciliar de Mexico
Historia. Seminario Conciliar de Mexico http://www.conciliar.mx/el-seminario/historia Accessed on: 1 January 2017 2:15 pm.

Vatican
Agostino Zhao Rong (+ 1815) and 119 Companions, Martyrs In China (+ 1648 – 1930). Vatican. http://www.vatican.va/news_services/liturgy/saints/ns_lit_doc_20001001_zhao-rong-compagni_en.html Accessed on: 20 January 2016:

Lawrence Ruiz, layman Dominic Ibáñez de Erquicia, O.P., James Kyushei Tomonaga, O.P. and 13 companions, Philippines, martyrs in Japan. Vatican. http://www.vatican.va/news_services/liturgy/saints/ns_lit_doc_19871018_ruiz-compagni_en.html Accessed on 20 January 2016.

Martyrs du Vietnam (+1745-1862). Vatican. http://www.vatican.va/news_services/liturgy/saints/ns_lit_doc_19880619_martiri_vietnam_fr.html Accessed on 20 January 2016.

Vicariato del Rosario en España
Dominicos - Vicariato del Rosario en España. http://vicaresp.dominicos.org Accessed on: 6 August 2017, 3:04pm.

Videos

Castor, Helen. *Medieval lives : birth, marriage & death.* Australia: SBS, 2014. DVD

Notes

Abbreviations

AA	Archivo del Ayuntamiento
AAM	Ardiocesan Archives of Manila
AGI	Archivo General de Indias, Sevilla
AGNM	Archivo General de la Nacion, Mexico
AGS	Archivo General de Simancas, Valladolid
AHN	Archivo Histórico Nacional, Madrid
aka	also known as
AM	Archivo Municipal
APD	Archivo Provincial Dominicano de Manila, Filipinas
APSR	Archivo de la Provincia del Santisimo Rosario de Filipinas
ASHM	Archivo Servicio Historico Militar
AUST	Archives of the University of Santo Tomas, Manila
Balmes	Instituto Balmes de Sociologia
B.D.	Bachiller Don
BDCL	Biblioteca Digital de Castilla y Leon
BDH	Biblioteca Digital Hispanica (http://bdh.bne.es)
BE	Biblioteca de El Escorial
BIA	Bureau of Insular Affairs
BNM	Biblioteca Nacional (Madrid)
BR	Emma H. Blair and James A. Robertson, eds. *The Philippine Islands, 1493-1898,* 55 vols. Cleveland: Arthur H. Clark, 1903-1909.
Bro	Brother
CI	Consejo de Indias
CD	Colección de Diarios y Relaciones para la Historia de los Viajes y Descubrimientos 1943-1947
D.	Don
D.D.	Doctor Don
DI	Digital Image
DIU	Coleccion de Documentos Inéditos Relativos al Descubrimiento, Conquista y Organización de las Antiguas Posesiones Españoles de Ultramar Ser. 2 1885-1932
ES	España
FBGEB	Filipiniana Book Guild Editorial Board
fol.	*folleto* (leaf)
Fr.	*Fray* (Frater/Fra/Friar)
H.	*Hermano* (Brother)
H. Fr.	*Hermano Fray* (Brother Friar)
ICM	*Imaculati Cordis Mariae* (Missionary Sisters of the Immaculate Heart of Mary)
L.D.	Licenciado Don
LIBRO	The Library of Iberian Resources Online (http://libro.uca.edu)
M.	*Madre*
M.D., Mtro.D	Maestro Don
MEP	Société des Missions étrangères de Paris
MN	Archivo de Museo Naval Madrid
MU	Museo-Biblioteca de Ultramar Madrid
Ms.	Manuscript
Sor	*Soror* (Sister)
OAR	Order of Agustinian Recollects
OFM	Order of Friars Minors (Disclaced Franciscans)

OH	Hospitaller Order of the Brothers of St. John of God
OP	*Ordo Praedicatorum,* Order of Preachers
OSA	Order of Saint Agustin
P.	*Padre* (Father)
P. Fr.	*Padre Fray* (Father Friar)
PARES	Portal de Archivos Españoles (http://pares.mcu.es)
PEOP	Provincia de España de la Orden de Predicadores
PNA	National Archives of the Philippines Manila
PSRF	Provincia del Santisimo Rosario de Filipinas
RVSVL	Regional Vicariate of St. Vincent Liêm
Sor	*Soror*
SJ	Society of Jesus
TLM	The Letran Mirror
TLN	The Letran News
UILL	University of Indiana, Lilly Library, Bloomington
USWD	United States War Department
USBC	United States Bureau of Census
USIT	United States and Its Territories (https://quod.lib.umich.edu/p/philamer/)
UST	University of Santo Tomas
VPC	Varias Provincias, Cavite (PNA)
VRE	Vicariato del Rosario en España

Chapter One Endnotes

1 Porter, Whitmore. *A History of the Knights of Malta or the Order of Saint John of Jerusalem.* Revised Edition. London: Longmans, Green & Co. 1883, 7-8. Google Books

2 Pope Paschal II. *Piae postulatio voluntatis.* 15 February 1113. Benevento; Porter, 699-700.

3 *Ibid.*

4 Pope Calixtus II. *Ad hoc nos.* 19 June 1119; Nicholson, Helen J. *The Knights Hospitaller.* Woodbridge, UK: The Boydell Press 2001, 6.

5 L' Abbe de Vertot. *The History of the Knights Hospitallers of St. John of Jerusalem; styled afterwards, The Knights of Rhodes, and at present, The Knights of Malta.* Edinburgh: printed for Alexander Donaldson 1770, I: 53-54. Internet Archive - archive.org

6 *Ibid.*

7 Bernard of Clairvaux. *In Praise of the New Knighthood,* in Treatises III, The Works of Bernard of Clairvaux vol. 7, Cistercian Fathers Series 19. Kalamazoo: 1977, 127-167. English translation by Conrad Greenia.

8 Bongar, Jacque. *The Speech of Urban II. at the Council of Clermont, 1095. Fulcher of Chartres,* Gesta Dei por Francos. Hanover, 2 v., 1612, v1, p.382f. as reproduced in Oliver J. Thatcher, A Source Book for Mediaeval History. Selected Documents Illustrating the History of Europe in the Middle Age, ed. Oliver J. Thatcher and Edgar Holmes McNeal (New York: Charles Scribner's Sons, 1905). 513-518. http://oll.libertyfund.org/titles/2277#Thatcher_1508_1507 Accessed on: 19 April 2015.

9 Nicholson, Helen J. *The Knights Hospitaller.* Woodbridge, UK: The Boydell Press. 2001, 16.

10 Pope Innocent II. *Ad hoc nos disponente.* 1135; *Christianae fidei religio.* 1137; *Quam amabilis Deo.* 1139-1143; Nicholson, 6.

11 Porter, 159.

12 *Ibid.*

13 Pope Anastasius IV. *Christianae fidei religio (reissued).* 1154; Nicholson, 7.

14 Boisgelin, Louis de. *Ancient and Modern Malta: containing a full and accurate account of the present state of the Islands of Malta and Goza, the History of the Knights of St. John of Jerusalem... in 2 Vols.* London: printed for Richard Philips, 1805, 2: 211-221. Google Books

15 Sons of noble fathers but mothers of ignoble or plebeian origins were called Knights of Grace. - Vertot 2:115.

16 King, Georgiana Goddard. *A Brief Account of the Military Order in Spain.* New York: The Hispanic Society of America 1921, 6. Internet Archive - archive.org; BR 50 : 93.

17 Boisgelin, 2:222-226.

18 Buttigieg, Emanuel. *Nobility, Faith, and Masculinity: The Hospitaller Knights of Malta, c.1580-c.1700.* London: Continuum Publishing Corporation 2011, 186.

19 Vertot, 1:56.

20 Pope Alexander IV. *Fratribus militibus Hospitalis S. Johannis Jerosolimitani chlamyde nigra et, in bellis, superinsigniis militaribus utendi facultatem concedit.* 11 August 1259; Porter, 705-706.

Notes

21 Ashmole, Elias. *The History of the Most Noble Order of the Garter: And the Several Orders of Knighthood Extant in Europe. Containing I. The Antiquity of the Town, Castle, Chapel, and College of Windsor; ... II. The Habits, Ensigns, and Officers of the Order.* London: A. Bell, E. Curll, J. Pemberton, and A. Collins; W. Taylor and J. Baker, 1715, 23; Joking, JP Viktor. *The Patriarchal Cross.* http://jpviktorjokinen.deviantart.com/art/The-Patriarchal-Cross-Several-Resolutions-348297810 - 1 May 2015; King, Edwin .J. *The Rule, Statutes and Customs of the Hospitallers*, Methuen & Co. Ltd, London 1931 photo-plate opposite, 10. Google Books

22 Salter (Revd.) H. E. (ed.) *A Cartulary of the Hospital of St. John the Baptist.* Oxford Historical Society. Clarendon Press 1917. Vol. III Frontispiece. Internet Archive - archive.org

23 Whitmore, 106-114.

24 Drane, Augusta Theodosia. *The Knights of St. John: with The battle of Lepanto and Siege of Vienna* London: Burns and Lambert 1858, 22-23 Google Books - https://books.google.com.au

25 Whitmore, 375.

26 *Ibid.*, 376-391.

27 Caluwé, The Reverend Robert de. *Guide Notes on Heraldry of the Sovereign Order of Saint John of Jerusalem Knights Hospitaller*, OSJ ivzw Belgium 2000, Illustration 344, 41.

28 Drane, 223-226.

29 Cohen, R. *Knights of Malta, 1523-1798.* Project Guttenburg Ebook No.12034 15 April 2004. pp. 66-81

30 *Ibid.*, 85-92.

31 Iñigo y Miera, Manuel de. *Historia de las Ordenes de Caballeria.* Madrid: 1863, 820-823. BDH

32 Order of Malta: Names of the Order - www.orderofmalta.int Accessed on: 14 April 2015.

33 Antequera, Jose Maria. *La Desamortizacion Eclesiastica Considerada en sus Diferentes Aspectos y Relaciones.* Madrid: Imprenta de A. Perez Dubrull, 1885, 198, 237 BDH

34 Orden de Malta España: Historia de la Orden - www.ordendemalta.es Accessed on: 14 April 2015.

35 Pigafeta, Antonio. *Primo viaggio interno al mondo (1519-1522).* Biblioteca Ambrosiana Milan, Italy with pressmark, "L. 103 - Sup." BR33

36 Navarrete, Martin Fernandez de. *Colección de los viages y descubrimientos que hicieron por mar los españoles desde fines del siglo XV: con varios documentos inéditos concernientes á la historia de la marina castellana y de los establecimientos españoles en Indias, 4 vols.*, Madrid: Imprensa Real. 4:193-439 BDH; (BR2:26).

37 Commanderies comprised the priories, castellany of emposta, bailiwics, demesnes, houses of the members, lands, estates, and all other kind of property belonging to the order. - Boisgelin.

38 Argensola, Bartolome Leonardo de. *The Discovery and Conquest of the Molucco and Philippine Islands.* London: 1708, 129-132, 147,179-261; *Chronological List of the Governors of the Philippines 1565-1899.* Internet Archive - archive.org; BR17:288-289.

39 Cl. *Confirmacion de Oficio: Jeronimo Guerrero 1599-5-21.* ES.41091.AGI/23.13.4.4//SANTA_FE,147,N.11 PARES
The functions of an *Alguacil Mayor* in Spanish colonial administration are similar to that of an English Sheriff who acted as executive officer of the courts and served as chief constable of the town. - Jones, O. Garfield. *Local Government in the Spanish Colonies as Provided by the Recopilación de Leyes de los Reynos de las Indias.* Southwestern Historical Quarterly Vol 19 (July 1915 - April 1916), 77-78.

40 Argensola, 218-219 (BR16 p. 284); Acuña, Pedro Bravo de. *Letter from Acuña to Felipe III. Cavite., 8 July 1605.* Simancas - Secular; Audiencia de Filipinas; cartas y expedientes del gobernador de Filipinas vistos en el Consejo, años de 1600 a 1628, est. 67, caj. 6, leg. 7 (BR14:63); Alcaraz, Andres de. *Letter to Felipe III dated 10 August 1617.* AGI Sevilla Audiencia de Mexico; expedientes sobre el apresto de la armada que salio de Nueva España para las islas Filipinas; años 1612 a 1617; est. 96, caj. 1, leg. 22.(BR18:43); *Report of Spanish Council.* Simancas - Secular; Audiencia de Filipinas; consultas originales correspondientes a dicha Audiencia; años 1585 a 1636; est. 67, caj. 6, leg. 1 (BR22:40).

41 Morga, Antonio de. *Sucesos de las Islas Filipinas Vol. 2.* Mexico: Cornelio Adriano Cesar 1609, BR15&16, BR16:62.

42 Argensola, 258 (BR16 p. 316); San Nicolas, Andres de. *Historia general de los religiosos descalsos del orden de San Augustin.* Madrid: 1664, 396-510; Concepcion, Juan de la. *Historia general de Philipinas: conquistas espirituales y temporales de estos españoles dominios, establecimientos progresos, y decadencias..* Manila: 1788 Tomo 4:189-265, and 5:32-100 BDH (BR21:130-131, 269).

Chapter Two Endnotes

43 Cl. *Peticion de Jeronimo Guerrero de patronazgo real para colegio, 1623-7-1.* ES.41091.AGI/23.6.848// FILIPINAS,39,N.13 PARES Orphanages in Spain were interchangeably known as *hospicio* (hospice), *colegio* (school), or *casa* (house) with the modifier *de huerfano* included in the name. - Gonzales, Ondina E. *et al* ed. *Raising an Empire: Children in Early Modern Iberia and Colonial Latin America.* USA: University of New Mexico, 2007, 46.

44 See chapter one. Guerrero's close association with the *Hermandad de la Santa Misericordia* and the Brothers of the Third Order of St. Francis indicated possible membership in either one and hence the title of Hermano. However, his name never appeared in any of their documented histories. Furthermore, his direct access to the Archbishop and Governor-General indicated the absence of any intermediating superior.

Notes

⁴⁵ Valdes, Jose OP. *Relacion verdadera de la fundacion del colegio de los niños huerfanos de los Santos Apostoles San Pedro y San Pablo , de San Juan de Letran, de la ciudad de Manila en las Islas Filipinos, sacada fielmente de diversos papeles y escrituras autenticas, que se hallaron en el archivo del Colegio, 1691.* APSR Letran Section Vol I Doc. 6 and 7, leaves 161-164; *Letran College in the 17th Century.* Emeth Vol. 1 No. 1 March, 1963. Manila, Philippines: Colegio de San Juan de Letran,1963, 30-38. [English translation]

⁴⁶ Bazaco, Evergisto OP. *Historia Documentada del Real Colegio de San Juan de Letran.* Manila: Universidad de Santo Tomas, 1933, 10.

⁴⁷ Peguero, Juan OP. *Historia en compendio de la Provincia del Santisimo Rosario dos tomos de Historia y otros papeles que tiene dicha Provincia. Terminada en el Convento de San Juan del Monte en Philipinas a 24 de Deciembre de 1690, a*s cited by Artigas y Cuerva, Manuel. *Historia de Filipinas para uso de los alumnos del Instituto Burgos y otros colegios particulares.* Manila: Imp. La Plarica, 1916. USIT

⁴⁸ Cl *1599.*

⁴⁹ Jones, O. Garfield. *Local Government in the Spanish Colonies as Provided by the Recopilación de Leyes de los Reynos de las Indias.* Southwestern Historical Quarterly, Vol. 19, July 1915 - April 1916, 70-73

⁵⁰ *Ibid.*

⁵¹ Uriarte, Juan Bautista de. *Manifiesta y resumen historico de la fundacion de la venerable hermandad de la Santa Misericordia.* Manila: 1728, BR47:39-40; Delgado, Juan J. *Historia general sacroprofana, politica y religiosa de las islas del Poniente llamadas Filipinas. Libro II Parte I.* Manila: 1751 ff. 120-121. Internet Archive-archive.org; BR28:186-187.

⁵² Morales, Pedro Sotelo de. *Declaracion Jurada 19 Julio 1622.* Cl. *Peticion de Jeronimo Guerrero de patronazgo real para colegio, 1623-7-1.* ES.41091.AGI/23.6.848//FILIPINAS,39,N.13 PARES; Mas, Sinibaldo de. *Informe sobre el estado de las Islas Filipinas en 1842 escrito por el autor del Aristodemo, del Sistema musical de la lengua castellana, etc. III Tomos.* Madrid: 1843. 2:12-5 BDH; BR45:251-252.

⁵³ Santa Cruz, Baltasar de OP. *Tomo Segundo de la Historia de la Provincia del Santo Rosario de Filipinas, Japon y China de la Sagrada Orden de Predicadores.* Zaragosa: Pascual Bueno, Impressor del Reyno, 1693, 29-31 BDH; Concepcion, Juan de la OAR. *Historia General de Philipinas, Conquistas Espirituales, Y Temporales de estos Españoles Dominios, establecimientos, Progresos, y Decadencias Tomo VI.* Sampaloc: Conv. de Nra. Sra. de Loreto, 1788, 306 BDH

There was a malpractice of bringing weaponless young lads from Nueva España whose masters draw their pay as regular soldiers in exchange for a meager subsistence. - BR6:181.

⁵⁴ Arceo, Antonio de. *Declaracion Jurada 19 Julio 1622.* Cl. *Peticion de Jeronimo Guerrero de patronazgo real para colegio, 1623-7-1.* ES.41091.AGI/23.6.848//FILIPINAS,39,N.13. PARES
Cl 1623-7-1 PARES; Mas, *op. cit.*

⁵⁵ Santa Cruz, *op. cit;* Concepcion, *op. cit.*

⁵⁶ The term *vecino* in this context is a legal term which means citizen. Please refer to Chapter Ten for a more comprehensive explanation.

⁵⁷ Uriarte. (BR47:23-85)

⁵⁸ *Ibid.*, f. 8. (BR47:38-40)

⁵⁹*Santa Potenciana* was a convent for the shelter of Spanish orphan girls founded as per instructions of Felipe II dated 9 August 1589. The *Misericordia,* which supported the poor Spanish orphan girls in *Santa Potenciana* and other private homes financially, gathered and housed them all in a school they founded in 24 October 1632 named the *Colegio de Santa Isabel.* The latter school was put under the administration of the Daughters of Charity of St Vincent de Paul on 22 July 1862. The 1863 earthquake destroyed many government offices moving these offices to occupy the premises of *Santa Potenciana.* The resulting decline of students forced *Santa Potenciana's* remaining students to transfer to *Santa Isabel.* The two institutions were merged in 1866 with Santa Isabel as the surviving entity.

⁶⁰ *Ibid.*, f. 25. (BR47:65)

⁶¹ Cl. *Carta de Niño de Tavora sobre colegios, incendios 1628-8-4.* ES.41091.AGI/23.6.12//FILIPINAS,8,R.1,N.4 PARES; Tavora, Juan Niño de. *Report of Appointments made by the governor.* 4 August 1628, BR22:223-226.

⁶² Cl 1623-7-1.

⁶³ *Ibid.*

⁶⁴ Bazaco 1933, 67.

⁶⁵ Valle, Francisco Navas del and Pastells, Pablo SJ. *Catalogo de los Documentos Relativos a Las Islas Filipinas existentes en el Archivo de Indias de Sevilla (1618-1635) Precidido de Una Historia General de Filipinas por el P. Pablo Pastells SJ Tomo VII Parte Primera.* Barcelona: Compañía General de Tabacos de Filipinas, 1932, xcii. BDH

66 Other than Letran de Manila, two other schools were named Colegio de San Juan de Letran.- one in the city of Mexico, Nueva España (1529) in charge of the Franciscans, and the other in Hagåtña, Guam (1669) under the Jesuits.

Although already running like a school, Letran de Mexico began officially as an infirmary for indigenous boys on 12 July 1529 on a property set aside for this purpose across the Monastery of San Francisco. By 1533, abandoned mestizo boys began to proliferate the city prompting the *Audiencia* to gather them for their care and education; transforming the hospital into a *de facto* college for mestizos. A series of royal decrees granted financial support to the school under the king's patronage beginning 1548. Felipe II made it available to the general public In 1557. It was known as Colegio de San Juan de Letran since 1567, and became one of Mexico's premier educational institutions. After gaining independence in 1821, sanguine conflicts between the Conservatives and the Liberals characterized the Mexican landscape. Whenever they were in power during a series of Reform Wars, the Liberals curtailed church privileges and confiscated its properties. Letran's stature began to decline until its demolition in 1875 to give way to a new road and housing, - Garcia Icazbalceta, Joaquin. *Obras de D. J. García Icazbalceta. Tomo 2. Opúsculos varios.* Mexico: Imp. de Aguero, 1896. Alicante: Biblioteca Virtual Miguel de Cervantes, 2012., 421-426.

Letran de Guam was founded by Blessed Diego Luis de San Vitores SJ in 1669 for the education of native boys. The school enjoyed the Royal Patronage of Mariana de Austria, Spain's Queen Regent who granted the school a generous endowment. The Recollects took charge of Guam's leading college after the Jesuit expulsion from the Spanish empire in 1768. As a consequence of the Spanish American War, the Recollects surrendered the administration of the school to the US government in 1899. The US navy assumed the island's governance in as much as Guam was groomed to become a naval base. The school became known as "No.1 School" until renamed to Richard P. Cleary School in honor of the first Naval Governor of Guam who resided in the school's premises on his arrival. - Cox, Leonard Martin. *The Island of Guam.* Washington: Government Printing Office, 1926, 26. 60-64; The Guam Recorder August 1934, 93.

67 CI 1623-7-1.

68 CI. *Petición de Aumento de prebendas y estipendios para la catedral de Manila 1624-5-20.* ES.41091.AGI/23.6.406/FILIPINAS,85,N.57 PARES

69 *Ibid.*

70 Uriarte, f.2; BR47:27

71 Santa Cruz, 30.

72 Guerrero, Juan Geronimo. *Carta sobre la utilidad del Colegio de niños huerfanos que ha fundado en Manila y la conveniencia de que estuviera bajo el real patronazgo. Manila 29 de Julio de 1622.* CI. *Peticion de Juan Jeronimo Guerrero para Colegio de huérfanos 1635-6-6* ES.41091.AGI/23.6.11//FILIPINAS,5N,452. PARES

73 This process could be discerned from the dates and sources of the documents discussed here. The approximate year of Letran Manila's foundation was determined by this estimated timetable using the date of the first royal decree (16 July 1623). With the availability of digital archives, more accurate information could now be accessed. It would appear that the process was quicker than expected possibly because of an agent of court and no objections or questions were being raised. Guerrero's letter of 29 July 1622 indicated further that boys leaving the school to become soldiers and priests began in 1619. The school was therefor already existing before then.

74 CI *1628-8-4*; CI. *Peticion del jesuita Baltazar de Lagunilla de confirmacion de mercedes dadas a jesuitas de Manila 1644-12-3* ES.41091.AGI/23.6.406//FILIPINAS,85,N.110 PARES; BR35:173-174

75 CI. *Orden a Fajardo de ayudar al Colegio de niños huérfanos 1623-7-16 Madrid.* ES.41091.AGI/23.6.5/FILIPINAS,7,R.5,N.68 PARES

76 CI. *Carta del Cabildo secular de Manila sobre varios asuntos 1625-8-3 Manila.* ES.41091.AGI/23.6.6/FILIPINAS,27,N.129 PARES

77 CI. *Orden a Tavora de apoyar la obra de niños huérfanos 1626-6-19 Madrid.* ES.41091.AGI/23.6.474/FILIPINAS,329,L.3,F.91V PARES

78 Seminario comes from the Latin word *seminarium* meaning plant nursery or seed plot. - Online Etymology Dictionary. www.etymonline.com Accessed on: 4 June 2015.

79 Costa, Horacio de la SJ. *Jesuit Education in the Philippines to 1768.* Philippine Studies, Vol. 4. No. 2 (1956), 131 JSTOR, JSTOR, www.jstor.org/stable/42719215

80 Barnes, Arthur. *Saint John Lateran.* The Catholic Encyclopedia. Vol. 9. New York: Robert Appleton Company, 1910. http://www.newadvent.org/cathen/09014b.htm. Accessed on: 4 June 2015.

81 Pope Benedict XVI. *Dedication of St. John Lateran. 9 November 2008, Rome.* www.catholicculture.org/culture/liturgicalyear/calendar/day.cfm?date=2014-11-09. Accessed on: 19 November 2013.

82 *Ibid.*

83 A ducado was approximately 1.39 silver pesos.

84 Guerrero, Juan Jeronimo. *Carta sobre colegio y solicitando al rey su amparo para puede continuarse esta obra, 1626-8-1 Manila.* PASADO A FILIPINAS,39,N.52 CI. *Cartas, peticiones y expedientes de personas seculares. 1628/1634.* ES.41091.AGI/23.6.488//FILIPINAS,4 PARES; BR22:108-110.

85 From the vow of the Hospitallers. - Boisgelin See Chapter I.

86 Bauzon, Leslie E. *Deficit Government: Mexico and the Philippine Situado, 1606 - 1804.* Tokyo: The Center for East Asian Cultural Studies, 1981.

87 BR17:290-291.

Notes

[88] Cf. *Carta de Niño de Távora sobre holandeses e ingleses, 1629-8-1 Cavite* ES.41091.AGI/23.6.502//FILIPINAS, 21,R.3,N.14 PARES; BR23:59-60

[89] Cf. *Carta de Niño de Tavora sobre colegios, incendios., 1628-8-4 Manila* ES.41091.AGI/23.6.12/FILIPINAS,8,R. 1,N.4 PARES; BR22:255-268.

[90] *Ibid.*; BR22:225-226, 274-276.

[91] *Ibid.*

[92] Cf. *Respuesta a Tavora sobre asuntos de gobierno 1631-8-19 Madrid.* ES.41091.AGI/23.6.474/FILIPNAS,329,L. 3,F.195V-197V PARES

[93] Cf. *Carta de Niño de Tavora sobre comercio con oriente, 1630-8-4 Cavite.* ES.41091.AGI/23.6.12//FILIPINAS, 8,R.1,N.10 PARES; BR23:107; Concepcion, 307; Bazaco 1933,13.

[94] Cf. *Orden sobre pasar religiosos a Japon y hospital de Manila 1632-1-27 Madrid.* ES.41091.AGI/23.6.474// FILIPINAS,329,L.3,F.203R-203V PARES

[95] Bazaco 1933, 15.

[96] *Ibid.*, 173.

[97] BR17:291.

[98] Diaz, Casimiro OSA. *Conquistas de las islas Filipinas: la temporal, por las armas del señor don Phelipe Segundo el Prudente; y la espiritval, por los religiosos del orden de nuestro padre San Augustin: fvndacion, y progressos de sv provincia del santissimo nombre de Jesus.* Valladolid, L.N. de Gaviria, 1890. pp. 159-200. BDH

[99] The *Capilla Real* was established in 1640 in charge of the Jesuits as chaplains. The *Real Audiencia* and the military celebrated their ecclesiastical functions there. It housed the administrative office of the military hospital and was under a *capellan mayor* and various coadjutors after the Jesuit departure. The edifice began to decay by the end of the18th century and restoration deferred indefinitely. The *Audiencia* opted to use the church of Santa Clara, followed by the former Jesuit church and finally back to its own simple building in 1850 which was by then used to store tobacco beside the Royal warehouses. - Buzeta y Bravo.

Corcuera's *Colegio de San Felipe de Austria* was the first attempt to form an exclusively royal and governmental educational institution in the Philippines. Under the administration of the Jesuits, it was supported with 4000 pesos annually from the royal treasury. The king disapproved the college and the decree of suppression dated 26 November 1645 was executed by the next governor, Diego Fajardo. - Pastells, Pablo.

[100] *Ibid.*; BR25:195-196.

[101] Cf. *1635-6-6*.

[102] Cf. *Orden sobre Colegio de Niños Huerfanos Españoles de Manila 1635-7-10 Madrid.* ES.41091/23.6.1031// FILIPINAS.347,L.1,F.144V-145R PARES

[103] Cf. *Titulo de la encomienda de Baratao que tiene 700 tributos, para el Colegio de niños huérfanos de Manila 1636-1-25.* AGI67-6-42; *Peticion del Dominico Salvador de Contreras de limosna al Colegio de San Juan de Letran 1732-9-18* ES.41091.AGI/23.6.538//FILIPINAS,297,N.120 PARES; Contreras, Salvador de OP. *Memorial 1743* APSR Letran Section Vol. I Doc 11-13 English translation - *Letran College in the 17th Century.* Emeth Vol. 1 No. 1 March, 1963. Manila, Philippines: Colegio de San Juan de Letran,1963, 38-43.

[104] *Ibid.* In different historical accounts, the encomienda found itself in Ilocos, Pangasinan or La Union. All happen to be factual. When Bacnotan was founded in 1599, it was part of Ilocos. In 1785, it became part of Pangasinan. In 1850, It became one of the twelve towns that comprised La Union.

[105] Cf. *Confirmacion de encomienda al Hospital de Niños Huerfanos 1638-11-28 Madrid.* ES.41091.AGI/ 23.6.1031//FILIPINAS,347,L.2,F.82R-84R; *Confirmacion al Colegio y Hospital de San Juan de Letran 1646-2-9 Madrid.* ES.41091.AGI/23.6.1031//FILIPINAS,347,L.3,F.123V-127V PARES

[106] Guerrero, Juan Geronimo. *Renuncia a favor de la Orden Dominicana fechado 11 Junio 1640. Recaudos de la posesión que se dio a la orden de nuestro P. Santo Domingo del Colegio de San Juan de Letran, 1640.* APSR Letran Section Vol. I Doc. 1 leaves 26-32; Bazaco 1933, 21-23. Bazaco's narrative pictured Guerrero pleading for Oquendo to accept the administration of Letran. (1933, 21) The content and tone of Guerrero's *Renuncia* do not support his claim. (1933, 21-23) Furthermore, Letran was already willed to the *Misericordia* and the Third Order of St Francis in 1626, and therefore succession was not a pressing matter for Guerrero. The *Renuncia* was more for the benefit and legal protection of the Dominicans.

[107] Corcuera, Sebastian Hurtado. *Mandamiento donde se encarga la administracion de Letran a la Religion de Sto. Domingo, y Provee para el Sustento 18 Junio 1640* cited by Bazaco 1933, 23-26. APSR Letran Section Vol. I Doc. 1 leaves 26-32. The Bazaco narrative portrayed Corcuera as pleading to the reluctant Dominican superiors to accept the administration of Letran. (1933, 21) Considering Corcuera's despotic profile and his office as Vice Patron, it is strenuous to picture him pleading. He could have readily asked the Jesuits to take over if there were no existing wills.

[108] Guerrero 1640.

[109] This fact does not support Bazaco's narrative that Guerrero professed in *articulo mortis*. Ocio y Viana, Hilario Maria OP. *Compendio de la Reseña Biografica de los Religiosos de la Provincia del Santisimo Rosario de Filipinas desde su fundacion hasta nuestros dias por el autor de la misma. Comprende desde 1587 a 1895.* Real Colegio de Sto. Tomas. 1895. Apendice - Hijos del convento de manila, 36-37; Bazaco 1933, 29.

[110] Guerrero 1640.

[111] Corcuera 1640. A braza is equivalent to 1.671 meters. - Cavada.

[112] Bazaco 1933, 173.

Notes

113 *Ibid.*

114 Guerrero, Hernando. *Concesion en la persona de H. Fr Diego de Santamaria 12 Julio 1640. Recaudos de la posesión que se dio a la orden de nuestro P. Santo Domingo del Colegio de San Juan de Letran, 1640.* APSR Letran Section Vol. I Doc. 1 leaves 26-32; Bazaco 1933, 27-28.

115 Gant, Clemente OP. *Aceptacion de la Orden Dominicana 14 Julio 1640. Recaudos de la posesión que se dio a la orden de nuestro P. Santo Domingo del Colegio de San Juan de Letran, 1640.* APSR Letran Section Vol. I Doc. 1 leaves 26-32; Bazaco 1933, 26-27.

116 Bazaco 1933, 29.

117 CI. *Carta del dominico Diego de Santa Maria sobre Colegio de niños huérfanos 1642-7-27 Manila.* ES.41091.AGI/23.6.406//FILIPINAS,85,N.94 PARES

118 CI. *Petición de informe sobre cien brazas de tierra 1644-2-17 Zaragoza.* ES.41091.AGI/23.6.372//FILIPINAS, 340,L.5,F.200R-201R. PARES

119 CI. *Confirmacion al Colegio y Hospital de San Juan de Letran 1646-2-9 Madrid.* ES.41091.AGI/23.6.1031//FILIPINAS.347,L.3,F.123V-127V PARES

120 Residencia was an institutional device by which superiors in Spain enforced standards and reviewed the performance of subordinates. The procedures were designed to make officers in the colonies sensitive to the wishes of their superiors in Spain. A specially designated *juez de residencia* conducted a public court of inquiry in which he heard all charges of malfeasance against the former incumbent. After receiving the latter's defense, the judge passed sentence and remitted his findings to the Council of the Indies for final review. Heavy fines, confiscation of property, imprisonment, or all three, were customary sentences in cases of misconduct in office. The fact that sentences in the indies were often reversed or altered in Spain does suggest that the original sentences sometime reflected the personal bias of the judges or that the official under investigation was able to bring to bear commanding influence at Court. - Phelan, 291.

121 BR17:291.

Chapter Three Endnotes

122 Bazaco 1933, 50-57. The professed religious brothers, originally known as *Fraters Conversus,* were called *Hermanos de la Obediencia* or *Legos* in the Spanish provinces of the Order. Reliving the spirit of the first Dominican community, the religious brother is currently known as Cooperator Brother and recognized as equals to the ordained Brother Cleric or Brother Deacon as approved in the Order's 2004 Acts of the General Chapter held in Krakow.

123 O'Connor, J. B., OP. *Saint Dominic and the Order of Preachers.* New York City: The Holy Name Bureau, 1916. https://maritain.nd.edu/jmc/etext/dominic.htm

124 Pola, Manuel Gonzales, OP. *Aportacion de la Provincia de Santiago de Mexico a la fundación de la Provincia de Nuestra Señora del Rosario de Filipinas desde la perspectiva del siglo XX.* Taquilla, Jose Barrado, OP. ed. *Los Dominicos y el Nuevo Mundo, siglos XIX-XX: actas del Vo Congreso International, Qro., Mexico, 4-8 septiembre 1995.* Mexico: Editorial San Esteban, 1997, 85-106.

125 Aduarte, Diego, OP. *Tomo Primero de la Historia de la Provincia del Santo Rosario de Filipinas, Japon y China de la Sagrada Orden de Predicadores Libro Primero.* Zaragosa: Domingo Gascon, Impressor del Santo Hospital Real y General de Nuestra Señora de Gracia, 1693, 1-6 BDH; English translation James A. Robertson BR30:115-118.

126 Pola, 102.

127 Aduarte, 6-14; BR30:118-123. The fifteen members of the first Dominican mission of 1578 were: P. Fr. Juan de Castro, Miguel Benavides de Santa Maria, Diego de Soria, Alonso Jimenez, Bernardo Navarro de Santa Catalina, Juan Ormaza de Santo Tomas, Juan Maldonado de San Pedro Martir, Pedro Bolaños, Pedro de Soto, Juan de la Cruz, Juan de Castro (menor), Marcos Soria de San Antonio, Gregorio Ochoa, Domingo de Nieva, and H. Fr. Pedro Rodriguez. - Ocio y Viana 1895, 5-18.

128 BR06:106.

129 Medina, Miguel, OP. *San Jacinto de Mexico entre España y Filipinas.* Taquilla, Jose Barrado, OP. ed. *Los Dominicos y el Nuevo Mundo, siglos XIX-XX: actas del Vo Congreso International, Qro., Mexico, 4-8 septiembre 1995.* Mexico: Editorial San Esteban, 1997, 107.

130 Aduarte,14-27; BR30:124-130

131 *Ibid.,* 29-31; BR30:137-142.

132 P. Fr. Pedro Bolaños OP professed in the Dominican convent of Nuestra Señora del Rosario in Oviedo. At the age of 60, he was Master of Novices in Nuestra Señora de la Peña de Francia in Salamanca when he joined the founders of the Dominican Province of the Holy Rosary. Assigned to the province of Bataan, he founded a mission school which was closed shortly because of his debilitating health. Suffering from recurring extreme stomach pains, he died in Manila during his second stay at the hospital of the Franciscans in 1588. He was the first Dominican to die in the Philippines and was interred in the church of St. Francis. - Ocio y Viana 1895, 12-13; Aduarte, 63-64; BR30:167-170.

133 Aduarte, 114; BR30:250.

Notes

[134] P. Fr. Miguel Benavides de Santa Maria OP was born in 1550 in Carrion de los Condes, Palencia. He professed in the Dominican convent of San Pablo de Valladolid in 1567. He completed his studies at the Colegio de San Gregorio and taught philosophy in various convents. He was a lector of theology in Valladolid when he became one among the founders of the Province. He was the first to minister among the Chinese in the islands and the founder of the Hospital de San Gabriel. Together with the Prior Provincial, he attempted unsuccessfully to establish the first mission in China in 1590. He became Procurador General and accompanied Manila Bishop Fr. Domingo Salazar OP to Spain where he received his appointment as first bishop of Nueva Segovia on 31 August 1595. He was later appointed Archbishop of Manila on 15 April 1602 and died in office on 26 July 1605. He left a behest in his will for the foundation of a college which became the University of Santo Tomas. - Ocio y Viana 1895, 6-8.

[135] Aduarte, 479-481; BR32:97-102.

[136] Santa Catalina, Bernardo de OP. *Algunos documentos relativo a la Universidad de Manila.* Madrid: 1892 pp. 5-20 Archivos General de Indias, Sevilla. English translation by James A. Robertson BR17:155-171.

[137] Aduarte, 481; BR32:101.

[138] The 1906 enactment of the Corporation Law (Act 1459), span off the different Dominican entities from the single personality and ownership structure of the Santo Domingo Convent.

[139] Ocio y Viana 1895, 154.

[140] Seijas, Tatiana. *Asian Slaves in Colonial Mexico: From Chinos to Indians.* New York: Cambridge University Press, 2014. p. 135.

[141] Medina, 110-113.

[142] Seijas, 136

[143] Ocio y Viana 1895, *op. cit.*

[144] Salazar, Vicente de, OP. *Historia de la Provincia de el Santissimo Rosario de Philipinas, China y Tunking, de el Sagrado Orden de Predicadores. Tercera Parte en que se tratan los sucesos de dicha Provincia desde el año 1669 hasta el de 1700.* Manila: Colegio y Universidad de Santo Tomas, 1742, 8 BDH; BR45:209.

[145] Salazar, 8; BR45:209-210.

[146] H. Fr. Martin de Porres OP was born in Lima, Peru in 1579. His father, Don Juan de Porres, was a Spanish hidalgo and his mother, Aña Velasquez, was a freed black slave from Panama. Lima had a diverse population of Spaniards from different social classes, Inca natives, African black slaves and *mulatos* like Martin who belonged to two worlds but would often be seen as an outsider by both groups. He did not see this as a disadvantage but as a call from God to walk in holiness through a life of humble service to one who lived in Lima. He apprenticed as a barber-surgeon to acquire knowledge and skills specially on medicine. At the age of 15, he was received as a tertiary at the Dominican Priory of Santo Domingo and served the community as a *donado* and later as a professed cooperator brother. Martin was involved both in internal ministry to the Dominican community as barber, surgeon, wardrobe-keeper and infirmaries, and in external ministry to the poor and sick of the city. When he died in 1639, people from all walks of life and all classes of society came to honor the humble *mulato* Dominican brother. He was beatified in 1837 and canonized by Pope John XXIII in 1962. He is the patron of social justice and race relations. - McGonigle, Thomas C., OP, 71-74.

[147] Bazaco 1933, 20-21

[148] See Chapter 11. Lavezaris, Guido. *Carta sobre los esclavos de Filipinas, 1573.* ES.41091.AGI/23.6.2// FILIPINAS,6,R.2,N.16 PARES; BR3:286-288.

Slavery was practiced among the indios when the Spanish conquistadors arrived in the Philippines. The colonizers practiced slavery as well until 7 November 1574 when Felipe II prohibited slavery of Filipino indios among the Spaniards. The decree was however generally ignored until 1 May 1686 when indian slavery was totally banned. The 1686 decree was implemented in the Philippines effective 18 August 1692. - Pan, Jose Felipe del. *Ordinances de buen gobierno de Corcuera, Cruzat y Raon.* Manila: 1891, BR50:199.

[149] Garcia Icazbalceta, 423-424.

[150] Salazar, 8; BR45:210

[151] *Ibid.;* BR45:209.

[152] Valdes.

[153] *Ibid.*

[154] Salazar, 9; BR45:212.

[155] Coates, Timothy J. *Convicts and Orphans: Forced and State-sponsored Colonizers in the Portuguese Empire 1550-1775.* Stanford: Stanford University Press, 2001. p. 188.

[156] See AA Sevilla: Secc. 3, tomo 11, no. 52.This is a petition of 2.IX.1545 which lists some reasons for establishing an orphanage in Seville.

[157] Cortes de Valladolid, 1548, pet. 206. See also AA Sevilla: Secc. 3, tomo 12, no. 3 as cited by Kagan, 19.

[158] Gonzalez, O, 51-57.

[159] Pearson, Carol. *Awakening the Heroes Within: Twelve Archetypes To Help Us Find Ourselves and Transform Our World.* Harper Collins, 1991; J. J. Jonas The Twelve Archetypes http://www.uiltexas.org/files/capitalconference/Twelve_Character_Archetypes.pdf

[160] Croycroft, Anna. *The Agency of the Orphan: A theoretical inquiry into the imagination behind regressive individuation.* www.agencyoforphan.com/archetypes/ Accessed on 20 June 2015.

[161] Pearson. *op. cit.*

Notes

162 Croycroft. *op. cit.*

163 Santa Cruz, 30; Concepcion, 309.

164 Bazaco 1933, 50-57.

165 Bazaco 1933, 50. According to Valdes' history of Letran, Guerrero had only three students left. This error continuous to be echoed until this day.

166 The fact that Bazaco himself was aware of the absence of student records prior to 1640 casts his claims of certain Letran alumni prior to that year as dubious.

167 Juan de Pozaleta, Crown Prince of Calonga was admitted at Letran in 1647. - Bazaco 1933, 48. Calonga was a kingdom on the Island of Sanguir (Sangihe Island, North Sulawesi Province, Indonesia) whose monarch sent ambassadors to Manila requesting for missionaries in 1637. The Franciscans established a mission there in 1639 and christianized the kingdoms of Calonga and Tabuca. - Huerta: 684-685.

168 Bazaco 1933, 217.

169 *Ibid.*, 249.

170 *Ibid.*, 232.

171 *Ibid.*, 223.

172 *Ibid.*, 37-41.

173 Salazar, 212

174 Contreras.

175 Santa Cruz, 30-31.

176 Concepcion, 310.

177 Mallat, J. *Les Philippines. Tome Deuxime* Paris: Arthus Bertrand, Editeur, 1846. p. 240 Google Books; BR45:264 English Translation.

178 Bazaco 1933, 67-71.

179 Fernandez, Pablo OP. *Dominicos Donde Nace el Sol - Historia de la Provincia del Santisimo Rosario de Filipinas de la Orden de Predicadores.* Barcelona: Impr. Yuste,1958, 379

180 Schumacher, John N. SJ, *The Early Filipino Clergy: 1698-1762.* Philippine Studies, Vol. 51, No. 1 (2003), 12. JSTOR, JSTOR, www.jstor.org/stable/42635192.

181 *Ibid.*, 31, 173-174.

182 Bazaco 1933, 31, 177.

183 *Ibid.*, 31.

184 Santa Cruz, 30.

185 Fayol, Joseph. *Affairs in Filipinas 1644-47,* BR35:222-223.

186 *Ibid.*

187 BR35:199-208; BR45:141-150; Santa Cruz,168-172;

188 Founded by the Society of Jesus, *Colegio de San Jose* obtained its licenses of the oridinary and of the secular government on 25 August 1601. 13 sons of the principal citizens of Manila became its inaugural students of letters. Estevan Rodriguez de Figueroa, Adelantado of Mindanao, willed to the *colegio* a substantial bequest which gave it a new legal status as an *obra pia* on 28 February 1610. It was the benefactor's wish that a school for the study of first letters and for the rearing of ministers of the holy gospel of well born Spaniards be established. *San Jose* obtained the right to grant university degrees by virtue of Pope Gregory XV's Brief dated 9 July 1621. Felipe V honored the *colegio* with the title Royal *ad honorem* on 3 May 1722. With the expulsion of the Jesuits in 1768, *San Jose* continued as a secondary institution administered by the diocesan clergy of Manila after failed attempts to convert it into a conciliar seminary initially. On 29 October 1875, the *colegio* was constituted as the faculty of medicine and pharmacy of the University of Santo Tomas under the Dominicans. With the establishment of American sovereignty in the Philippines in 1899, the Supreme Court deemed *San Jose* as an ecclesiastic *obra pia* and surrendered the *colegio* to the Archdiocese to carry out its original purpose as a seminary on 8 December 1909. The seminary was turned over to the Jesuits in 1915 and remains under their administration to this day. - Repetti

189 *Ibid.,* 35-37; BR45:150-152.

190 *Ibid.*

191 Santa Cruz, 30.

192 Fayol, BR35:227-250.

193 Santa Cruz, 102.

194 BR35:249-250.

195 Bazaco 1933, 223-224, 235, 252-253.

196 P. Fr. Juan de los Angeles OP made his profession in the Dominican convent at Zafra, Badajoz in 1626, and came to the Philippines in 1635. He was sent to Formosa and remained there until its capture by the Dutch. Returning to Manila in 1643, he labored many years, sometimes among the natives, but mainly in high offices of his order - among them, as prior of his convent, and as provincial of Filipinas; he was also rector of Santo Tomas college, and for many years president of San Juan de Letran college. He died in Manila in 1682, aged eighty years. - Ocio y Viana 1895, 155.

Notes

197 Salazar, 10; BR45:213-214.

198 Bazaco 1933, 51-57.

199 *Ibid.*

200 *Ibid.*, 243-244.

201 *Ibid.*, 224.

202 Bishop Luo was the Dominican Order's third Chinese priest. The first was P. Fr. Dionisio de la Cruz of the Province of San Antonio del Nuevo Reino de Granada: born in 1510; died 1630 in Caracas. The second was P. Fr. Antonio de Santa Maria, mestizo portugues-sangley who received his habit around 1589 in Macao. - Gonzales, Jose Maria OP 1964, 543-544.

203 Adults studying their first letters at a late age were not uncommon in Letran. Another student, Pedro de Lugo, was admitted at the age of 20 in 1654. Depending on meritorious circumstances, certain cases were entertained. - Bazaco 1933.

204 *Ibid.*, 231; Ocio y Viana 1895, Apendice - Hijos del convento de Manila, 29-31.

205 *Ibid.*, 167; Mallat, 241; BR45:265. A piastre is a Spanish coin of eight reales which dates back from the reign of Ferdinand and Isabela. It is practically the same as the peso or piece of 8 reales. - BR28:195.

206 Buzeta, 226.

207 Bazaco 1933, 48.

208 Santa Cruz, 30.

209 Bazaco 1933, 48-49.

210 *Document citing Fr. Alonso de Villegas as Administrator of Colegio de Letran de los niños huerfanos, 1653 October.* APSR Seccion de Letran Tomo 3 as referenced by Bazaco 1933, 49.

211 Ocio y Viana 1895, 154.

Chapter Four Endnotes

212 Bazaco *1933,* 67-68. This arrangement ended in 1826.

213 *Ibid.*

214 Cl. *Expediente sobre asistencia de colegiales de San Juan de Letran a la catedral. Manila, 1682.* ES.41091.AGI/23.6.464//FILIPINAS,78,N.15 PARES

215 San Antonio, Juan Francisco. *Chronicas de la Apostolica Provincia de S. Gregorio de Religiosos Descalsos de N. S. P. S. Francisco en las Islas Philippines, China, Japon, & c.* Manila: 1738, 205-206 BDH; BR28:139-140.

216 Shiels, W. Eugene. *Church and State in the First Decade of Mexican Independence*. The Catholic Historical Review, Vol. 28 No. 2 (Jul., 1942), 206-228. JSTOR, JSTOR, www.jstor.org/stable/25014148.

Pase Regio (*placet regi* - royal assent) was the assumed prerogative of the Spanish Monarch to take previous cognizance of, with a view to confirming papal edicts or briefs, or such as were issued by other foreign ecclesiastics or by the superiors of religious Orders, before they could be valid in Spanish dominion.

217 Vauchez, Andre, ed. *Patronage.* Encyclopedia of the Middle Ages. James Clarke & Company, 2005. www.oxfordreference.com Accessed: 31 May 2014. 09:44.

218 Hillebrand, Hans J. *Patronato Real.* The Oxford Encyclopedia of the Reformation. Oxford University Press 2005. www.oxfordreference.com Accessed: 31 May 2014 09:34.

219 Mecham, J. Lloyd. *The Origins of "Real Patronato de Indias".* The Catholic Historical Review, Vol. 14 No. 2 (Jul., 1928) pp. 205-227. JSTOR, JSTOR, www.jstor.org/stable/25012517.

220 Hillebrand.

221 The Christian settlements evolved into three stages - *mision, doctrina* and *curato. A mision* was the stage when the settlement was composed mostly of heathens. A *doctrina* was the stage when the settlement was composed principally of Christian converts. A *curato* was the stage when the people of an established town were fully indoctrinated in faith, acculturated in religious observances and administered under formal episcopal protocols.

The *diezmo* involved one-tenth of essentially agricultural produce which was used principally to fund ecclesiastical expenses. It was mainly imposed among the Spaniards in the Philippines since they had the largest landholdings. What was implemented among the general Philippine population however was the annual *bandala,* wherein the government exacts for its own use a quantity and quality of agriculture produce from each town.

The *repartimiento* was also known as *polo* in the Philippines and *mita* in Peru.

222 Cl. *Memorial de Jaime Mimbela. Madrid 9 Noviembre 1699.* - *Expediente sobre visita de las doctrinas por los ordinarios. 1699/1710* ES.41091.AGI/23.6.387//FILIPINAS,302,N.1 PARES; BR42:69-112. Dominican Raimond Berart claims that he wrote this memorial. - Ocio y Viana 1891.

Notes

²²³ Fr. Bartolome de las Casas was born in Sevilla, Spain in 1484. He obtained two degrees in canon law, a *bachillerato* at Salamanca and a *licenciatura* at Valladolid. He travelled to the island of *Española* in 1502 and witnessed the tragic atrocities and massacre of indians on the island. Returning to Spain, he was ordained a deacon in 1506 and a priest in 1507. He returned to *Española* in 1510 and was influenced by Dominican Fr. Antonio Montesino who delivered his famous speech denouncing the encomienda system of forced labor as a mortal sin in behalf of the *indios* on 21 December 1511. It will not be until 1514 that Las Casas started to preach his own provocative sermons and embarked on numerous reform attempts. He returned to Spain in 1515 and was given the title of "Protector of the Indians" by the regent, Cardinal Ximenez de Cisneros. He entered the Dominican Order in 1522 at the age of 36. Through principally his efforts, Pope Paul III's landmark Bull, *Sublimes Deus*, often called the Magna Carta of Indian Rights was issued in 1537. This was followed by the New Laws of 1542 of Holy Roman Emperor Charles V abolishing slavery and the encomienda system, which was however later withdrawn due to political and economic expediency. He wrote a number of monumental works but his most widely read was the *Brevissima Relacion de la Destruccion de las Indias* in 1552. Las Casas died in Madrid in July 1566. - Orique, David.

²²⁴ Casas, Bartolome de las. *A Brief Account of the Destruction of the Indies*. Project Gutenberg Ebook No.20321 9 January 2007 www.gutenberg.org/ebooks/20321 Accessed: 28 June 2015.

²²⁵ Fr. Domingo Salazar was born in the villa of Labastida, Rioja around 1512. He studied at the University of Salamanca before receiving the Dominican habit on 16 November 1546 in the convent of San Esteban. He moved to the Dominican Province of Santiago in Mexico as professor of theology. Because of his desire to minister among the *indios*, he was posted to the missions in Guaja as prior and in Florida where he witnessed cruelties inflicted on the natives as a pioneering missionary. Returning to Mexico, he became vicar provincial and the first Consult of the Holy Office. After 30 years in Mexico, he was sent to Spain to advocate the cause of the *indios* and was unexpectedly appointed by Felipe II as the first bishop of Fllipinas in 1579. In Manila, he erected the cathedral of the new bishopric under the advocacy of the Immaculate Conception on 21 December 1581 and convoked the First Synod of Manila. In view of conflicts with Governor General Gomez Peres Dasmariñas, he departed for Spain in 1591 to make his case with the king. He was made Archbishop of Manila and the Metropolitan of three suffragan bishops but died before then on 4 December 1594. - Ocio y Viana 1891, 36-48.

²²⁶ Aduarte, 173-178; BR31:39-47.

²²⁷ *Ibid.*, 282-285; BR31:221-223.

²²⁸ *Ibid.*

²²⁹ *Ibid.*, 94-102; BR30:215-234.

²³⁰ *Ibid.*, 107-112; BR30:246-249.

²³¹ Delgado, Jose Garcia. *Martyrs of Japan*. Puebla, Ceferino Pedrosa ed. Witnesses of the Faith in the Orient 2nd edition Hongkong: Dominican Province of the Our Lady of the Rosary. 2006, 8-18. Nominis http://nominis.cef.fr/contenus/witnessesdominicainscanada.pdf

²³² There was a proposal made to invade China as early as 1576 using the Philippines as the staging point, but was deemed untimely by Felipe II. In 1586, a more comprehensive invasion plan was forwarded to him, but was not acted on.

²³³ *Ibid.*, 285; BR31:223.

²³⁴ Bartlett, Robert. *Why Can the Dead Do Such Great Things? Saints and Worshippers from the Martyrs to the Reformation*. Princeton and Oxford: Princeton University Press, 2013, 183.

²³⁵ Mallat, 389.

²³⁶ US War Department, Bureau of Insular Affairs. *Reports of the Philippine Commission, the Civil Governor, and the Heads of the Executive Departments of the Civil Government of the Philippine Islands (1900-1903)*. Washington: Government Printing Office, 1904, 39, 48. USIT

²³⁷ The friars were exempt from trials for offenses, except the most heinous, in the ordinary civil courts of the islands under the Spanish rule, and were entitled to a hearing before an ecclesiastical court. Even in the expected cases, trials must first be had in the latter tribunal.

²³⁸ Cl. *Relación de Morga de cosas en lo eclesiástico y secular. 1598-6-8 Manila.* ES.41091.AGI/23.6.13// FILIPINAS,18B,R.8,N.91 PARES; BR10:80-81; Santiago, Luciano P.R. *To Love and to Suffer: The Development of the Religious Congregations for Women in the Philippines during the Spanish Era 91565-1898*. Philippine Quarterly of Culture and Society, Vol. 24, No. 1/2, Special Issue: Advances in Visayan Prehistory (March/June 1996), 133. JSTOR, JSTOR, www.jstor.org/stable/29792195.

²³⁹ Pardo de Tavera, Trinidad H. *Una Memoria de Anda y Salazar*. Manila: La Democracia, 1899, 28-30 BDH; BR50:169-172.

²⁴⁰ *Recopilacion de leyes de los reynos de las Indias. Madrid, 1681* Bk. 6 Tit. 3 Law 21; Bk. 6 Tit. 3 Law 22.

²⁴¹ Pardo de Tavera, 35-36; BR50:178-179.

²⁴² *Ibid.*,16; BR50:150

²⁴³ US Senate. *Lands Held for Ecclesiastical or Religious Uses in the Philippine Islands, etc.* U.S. Senate Document No. 190 56th Congress 2d Session February 25, 1901, 38. Internet Archive - archive.org

²⁴⁴ *Ibid.*, 22-30.

²⁴⁵ Le Gentil, Guillaume. *Voyages dans les mers de l'Inde Tome Second*. Paris: De L'Imprimerie 1781, 183. Digitalisierte Sammlungen; BR28:210.

²⁴⁶ Recopilacion 1681, Bk. 1 Tit. 15 Law 33; BR28:69.

Notes

247 San Antonio, 205, 224; BR28:140, 159-160.

248 Thurston, Herbert, and Andrew Shipman. "The Rosary." The Catholic Encyclopedia. Vol. 13. New York: Robert Appleton Company, 1912. 12 Nov. 2017 <http://www.newadvent.org/cathen/13184b.htm>. The complete rosary is composed of 20 decades divided into the five Joyful Mysteries, the five Luminous Mysteries, the five Sorrowful Mysteries, and the five Glorious Mysteries. Catholic Online http://www.catholic.org/prayers/mystery.php

249 Ibid.

250 Navarrete, Domingo Fernandez. *Tratados Historicos, Politicos, Ethicos, y Religiosos de la Monarchia de China.* Madrid: Imprenta Real, 1676, 323 Google Books; BR38:53-54.

251 Bazaco 1933, 32

252 Ibid.

253 Villaroel, Fidel OP. *Father Jose Burgos University Student.* Manila: University of Santo Tomas, 1971, 9.

254 Ibid., 34.

255 Ibid.

256 Ibid.

257 Ibid., 35

258 *Aparato funebre y Real pyra de honor, que erigio la piedad, y consagro el dolor de la muy insigne, y siempre leal ciudad de manila a las memorias del serenissimo Principe de España Don Balthassar Carlos, que este en gloria. (Funerales en honra del Principe Baltasar Carlos)* Manila: S. Pinpin, 1649 Retana, W.E. *Archivo del Bibliofilo Filipino, Recopilacion de Documentos Historicos, Cientificos, Literarios y Politicos y Estudios Bibliograficos Tomo Segundo* Madrid: Viuda de M. Minuesa de los Rios, 1896 Cervantes Virtual; BR36:25-43

259 According to Santa Cruz (31) and Salazar (10), the property of Maria Ramirez Pinto was purchased by the province. Bazaco's history, however, states that the lady's property was willed to Letran as a *capellania* without any cited reference. In as much as no such *capellania* had been found in the APSR archives, we are adopting Santa Cruz's and Salazar's version of the narrative.

260 Salazar, 11; BR45:215

Chapter Five Endnotes

261 *Fabrica* (Latin, Italian, and Spanish; French, *fabrique*): a technical term in church administration usage. The ordinary and common meaning is the material building or edifice, which (technically) includes repairs, improvements, changes, etc., as well as the necessary expense for caretakers of it, as watchmen, beadles, sweepers, etc.; these people are paid from the funds of the *fabrica* - which might be rendered as "building-fund," except that its ecclesiastical usage *fabrica* usually presupposes that the building is already reared, while the English phrase "building-fund" includes the idea of constructing it. (Yet in Latin, Italian, and Spanish the term *fabrica* is also used to include money for the erection of the church edifice, in cases where it has not yet been built; where it has been completed and paid for, *fabrica* is restricted to the meaning first given above, the "keep" of the building.)

Thus usually the term has a material sense only; but sometimes (though not commonly) *fabrica* is taken, as in the present text, in a spiritual sense, and implies the support or maintenance (*honoraria*) of the churchmen, the ministers attached to the building, as well as the maintenance of divine worship, as required by ritual. *Fabrica* then refers to affairs of the soul or spirit, the spiritual upbuilding or edifice of the faithful. By extension, the same term is sometimes used to mean the board of church wardens who administer the property. In the Philippines the church property (save that belonging to the religious corporations) was in the hands of the bishop as sole trustee and administrator, a power which he might delegate to his provisor or vicar. - BR47:130.

262 Recopilacion 1681, Bk. I Tit. 14 Law 6.

263 Viana, Francisco Leandro de. *Demostraciones de lo que contribuyen a S.M. los naturales de las Islas Filipinas.* Manila 1766-07-10 Escritos al Marqués de Grimaldo. S. XVIII (h.123r-138v) BDH; BR50:80-81.

264 Cl. *Peticiones del agustino Francisco de Ortega 1593-9-20 Manila.* ES.41091.AGI/23.6.728//FILIPINAS,79,N. 22 PARES; BR9:106-107; Berdozido, Pablo Francisco Rodriguez de. *Survey of the Philipinas 1742.* MS. in the Museo-Biblioteca de Ultramar, Madrid - press mark, "24-4a.-I.735, BR47:136. Tepuzque is a corruption of the native Mexican word, *teputzli,* meaning compensation.

265 Cl. *Merced de pesos de tepuzque y arroz a jesuitas de Filipinas 1585-1-26 Alcala de Henares.* ES.41091.AGI/ 23.6.829//FILIPINAS,339,L.1,F.315R-315V. PARES

266 Cl 1593-9-20. op.cit; BR9:107.

267 Cl. *Petición del jesuita Francisco de Figueroa de limosna de vino y aceite 1613-12-16.* ES.41091.AGI/ 23.6.728//FILIPINAS,79,N.104 PARES; BR9:107. An arroba is liquid weight equivalent to 11.502 kilos.

268 Berdozido, op.cit.; BR47:136.

269 Ibid.

270 Cl. *Caja de Filipinas, Cuentas 1606/1608.* ES.41091.AGI/16.12.14//CONTADURIA,1207 PARES; BR14:243-269

271 Gutierrez, Manuel et al. *The Friar Memorial of 1898* Manila 21 April 1898, BR52:274.

272 Ibid., 151.

273 Ibid., 152.

Notes

274 Nozaleda, Bernardino V., OP. *Testimony of Archbishop of Manila.* U.S. Senate. Document No. 190 56th Congress 2d Session February 25, 1901, 65. Internet Archive - archive.org

275 Viana, Francisco Leandro. *Documentos relativos al estado de las Islas Filipinas [Manuscrito].* Siglo XVIII (h. 123r-138v) BDH; BR50:87-91

276 BR48:261.

277 Hanna, Edward. *Purgatory.* The Catholic Encyclopedia. Vol. 12. New York: Robert Appleton Company, 1911. www.newadvent.org/cathen/12575a.htm Accessed on 19 July 2015.

278 *Ibid.*

279 Castor, Helen. *Medieval lives : birth, marriage & death.* Australia: SBS, 2014.

280 Repetti, William Charles, SJ. *Jesuit education in the Philippine Islands: the College of San Jose of Manila. established August 25, 1601.* Manila: Manila Observatory, 1941.

281 US Senate 1901, 67-69.

282 *Ibid.*

283 Legarda, Benito Jr. *Two and a Half Centuries of the Galleon Trade.* Philippine Studies Vol. 3, No. 4 (1995) p. 363. JSTOR, JSTOR, www.jstor.org/stable/42632048

284 Bazaco 1953, 173-178.

285 *Ibid.,* 108-110; *Capellania de Don Lope Felix de Alcarazo Seccion, 1666.* APSR Letran Section Vol 1. Doc. 4, Fols. 174-175.

286 *Ibid.*, 59-66.

287 *Ibid.*, 110-112.

288 *Ibid.*, 112-122.

289 A relocation survey conducted in 1904 by government engineers revealed a shortage of 1193 hectares. The actual net area was 916 hectares. See USWD. *Annual Reports of the War Department for the fiscal year ended June 30 1906 Vol VIII Report of the Philippine Commission Part 2.* Washington: Government Printing Office, 1907, 134. Hathi Trust

290 APSR, Consejos Provinciales, tomo 2, folio 5.

291 USWD-BIA. *Fifth Annual Report of the Philippine Commission 1904 Part 1 (in three parts).* Washington: Government Printing Office, 1905, 805-808. Internet Archive - archive.org

292 USWD-BIA. *Fourth Annual Report of the Philippine Commission 1903 Part 1 (in three parts).* Washington: Government Printing Office, 1904, 202. Internet Archive - archive.org

293 USWD-BIA 1904,1:808-812. Both estates were in the name of the College of Santo Tomas. A relocation survey conducted in 1904 by government engineers revealed a shortage of 80 hectares, 10 ares, and 15 centuries for Biñan and a considerable excess for Santa Rosa by 820 hectares. (USWD 1907,134)

294 *Ibid.*

295 *Ibid.*,1:797-804. A part of the Lolomboy Estate was owned by the College of Santo Tomas and other by the Beaterio de Santa Catalina. Adjusted hectarage revealed additional 789 hectares for Lolomboy. (USWD 1907, op. cit.)

296 *Ibid.*, 804-805. Adjusted hectarage for Santa Maria de Pandi revealed a reduction of 1,727 hectares (USWD 1907, op. cit.)

297 Roth, Dennis Morrow. *The Friar Estates of the Philippines.* Albuquerque: University of New Mexico Press, 1977, 28.

298 *Desamortizacion* is the act of setting free any lands (mainly religious) to enable other persons to acquire such lands.

299 *Ibid.*, 791-795. A *censo* was a contract involving an annual payment. The *censo al guitar* was essentially a mortgage on property in which the principal was redeemable. The *censo enfitéutico* was quitrent or agricultural lease that usually was long term, staying with families over generations. - Vassberg, 205-6.

A *dacion en pago* entails the surrender of a mortgaged property to the lender, and in exchange the lender fully discharges all mortgage debt and future liability. The lender also renounces pursuing the debt against any other assets the debtor may hold in the home country or elsewhere. - Spanish Civil Code.

300 *Composicion*, a technical meaning as applied to lands, may be defined as a method by which the State enabled an individual, who held lands without legal title thereto, to convert his mere possession into a perfect right of property by virtue of compliance with the requirements of law. *Composicion* was made in the nature of a compact or compromise between the State and the individual who was illegally holding lands in excess of those to which he was legally entitled and, by virtue of this compliance with the law, the State conferred on him a good title to the lands that he had formerly held under a mere claim of title. BR52:296.

301 Ruiz, Rosa Alicia de la Torre. *Composiciones de tierras en la alcaide mayor de Sayula, 1692-1754: un estudio de caso sobre el funcionamiento del Juzgado Privativo de Tierras.* Letras Historias Numero 6, Primavera-verano 2012, 45-69.

302 Diaz, Casimiro, OSA. *Conquistas de las Islas Filipinas: la temporal por las armas de nuestros Católicos Reyes de España, y la espiritual por los religiosos de la Órden de San Agustín ... Parte segunda que a beneficio de los materiales que dejó recopilados el M.R.P. Fr. Gaspar de San Agustín, autor de la primera parte* Valladolid: L. N. de Gaviria, 1890, 440-444 BDH: BR42:271-273, 303-306.

303 Salazar, 674-682.

Notes

304 *Ibid.*, 681-682.

305 USWD-BIA 1904., 791-815.

306 *Ibid.*, 797. One quiñon is approximately 3 hectares. - Cavada.

307 Palanco, Fernando Aguado. *The Tagalog Revolts of 1745 According to Spanish Primary Sources.* Philippine Studies Vol. 58 nos. 1 & 2 (2010): 45-77 *JSTOR*, JSTOR, www.jstor.org/stable/42632048.

308 The excessive discrepancy in land area could only be attributed to bribery. The following instructions found in the Augustinian manual for priests supports the casualness of this occurrence: *"The order should try to have selected an oidor sympathetic to us or one of our members. He should be approached by one of the religious with whom he is most friendly and asked not to reject the commission if it is given to him... Ask the Governor-General to appoint this oidor... When the day arrives to begin the survey, escort the oidor and lodge him in the monastery where he be suitably entertained. The oidor's salary for such work is twelve pesos a day and when he arrives, he should be given the same amount by the procurator who should tell him that the prior would be happy if he were to accept a purse of money. In this way he admits his good will. Sometimes an oidor is reluctant to accept the money, but he can be given various gifts which may equal half the value of the money... This only serves to begin the case. Another amount of money may have to be given when the proper time arrives."* - UILL, Philippine MSS. 1740-1758, folios 205-207.

309 BIA 1904, 809.

310 Palanco, 58.

311 *Ibid.*, 60-62.

312 *Ibid.*, 63-65

313 The Visayan word *tulisan* or *tolisan* had the exact connotation of the Spanish *bandolero* meaning bandit. It first appeared in Encarnacion's *Diccionario bisaya-español* (Manila, 1851).

314 BIA 1904, 809.

315 Cl. *Aprobacion de lo dispuesto sobre sublevaciones de indios 1751-11-7 El Escorial.* ES.41091.AGI/23.6.637// FILIPINAS,335,L.16,F.206R-211R PARES; Salazar, Hugo. *The Usurpation of Indian lands by friars.* La Democracia 25 November 1901 BR48:27-36.

316 *Ibid.*

317 Palanco, 62-63.

318 Cushner, Nicholas P. *Documents Illustrating the British Conquest of Manila, 1762-1763.* London, 1971, 167-8.

319 Collantes, 638; Ocio y Viana 1895, 422-423, 440.

320 Ricafort, Mariano. *La reunion de malhechores en cuadrilla en la provincial de Cavite.* Manila,1828.

321 Ocio y Viana 1895, 585.

322 BIA 1904, I:454.

323 Manuel, Esperidion Arsenio and Manuel, Magdalena Avenir. *Dictionary of Philippine biography. 3 Vol.* Manila, 1955, 1970, 1987) I, 197.

324 Ricafort. *op. cit.*

325 Ricafort, Mariano. *Letter to the Secretary of State, Grace and Justice, Manila, 10 November 1828.* AHN Ultramar 2140; *Letter to the Secretary of State, Grace and Justice, Manila, 13 November 1828.* AHN Ultramar 2140.

326 PNA, VPC, 1816-1898, Exp. 30, 100-100b.

327 Becerra, Nicolas OAR. *Carta a Pasqual Enrile, Imus, Enero, 1834.* MN, Ms. 1669

328 PNA, VPC, 1816-1898, Exp. 86, 282. See also PNA, VPC, 1816-1898, Exp. 82.

329 Calderon, Felipe. *Observations about the Hacienda de Imus. Manila, 19 November 1900.* United States. Senate. Document No. 190 56th Congress 2d Session February 25, 1901, 246-7; Sadaba del Carmen, Francisco OAR. *Catalogo de los Religiosos Agustinos Recoletos de la Provincia de San Nicolas de Tolentino de Filipinas desde el año 1606 en que llego la primera Mision a Manila, hasta nuestros dias.* Madrid: Imp. del Asilo de Huerfanos del Sagrado Corazon de Jesus, 1906, 385-6. BDH

330 La Torre, Carlos Maria. *Manifesto al Pais sobre los Sucesos de Cavite y Memoria sobre la Administracion y Gobierno de la Islas Filipinas.* Madrid: Imp. Gregorio Hernando, 1872, xiii; Montero y Vidal, Jose. *Historia General de Filipinas desde el Descubrimiento de Dichas Islas Hasta Nuestros Dias.* Madrid: Est. Tip. de la Viuda e Hijos de Tello, 1895. *Tomo III,* 506. USIT

331 La Torre, *op. cit.*

332 Montero y Vidal, Jose. *Historia General de Filipinas desde el Descubrimiento de Dichas Islas Hasta Nuestros Dias en III Tomos.* Madrid: Est. Tip. de la Viuda e Hijos de Tello, 1895, 3:584. Digitalisierte Sammlungen

333 US-Senate, 242-255.

334 Provincia del Santisimo Rosario de Filipinas. *Estado General de los Religiosos y Religiosas de la Provincia del Santisimo Rosario del Sagrado Orden de Predicatores de Filipinas en el Año de 1893.* Manila: Real Colegio de Santo Tomas, 1894. p. 44. BDH

335 U.S. War Department, Bureau of Insular Affairs, *4th Annual Report of the Philippine Commission 1903 (in three parts).* Washington: Government Printing Office, 1904. Part 1: 202-203. Internet Archive - archive.org

336 Craig, Austin. *Lineage, Life and Labors of Jose Rizal, Philippine Patriot - A Study of the Growth of Free Ideas in the Trans-Pacific American Territory.* Project Gutenberg Ebook#6867 Release Date; June 18, 2004, 67-78.

Notes

337 [Tamayo, Serapio, OP]. *Sobre Una "Reseña Historica de Filipinas."* Manila: Libertas, 1906, 195. Internet Archive - archive.org

Chapter Six Endnotes

338 Radcliffe, Timothy, OP.*Acts of Elective General Chapter of Order of Preachers Mexico. July 1 to 31, 1992.* Rome: Curia Generalitia at Santa Sabina, 1992. *http://www.op.org/sites/www.op.org/files/public/documents/fichier/mexico1992.pdf*

339 McGonigle, xvii-xviii.

340 Engingco, Maria Jesusa. *The Congregation of Dominican Sisters of St. Catherine of Siena: Its Missionary Consciousness and Endeavor in the Context of the Church in the Philippines.* Rome: Pontificia Universitas Urbaniana, 2000, 5-26.

341 Concepcion, 1-17.

342 Fayol. BR35:244-249.

343 Buzeta, 218-219.

344 Cl. *Petición del dominico Mateo de la Villa sobre fundación de convento de Santa Catalina de Siena. 1635-9-11.* ES.41091.AGI/23.6.654//FILIPINAS,80,N.192 PARES*;* Salazar, 639-640.

345 Cl. *Petición del Cabildo secular de Manila sobre no permitir nuevo convento 1635-2-5 Manila.* ES.41091.AGI/23.6.6//FILIPINAS,27,N.198 PARES

346 Cl 1635-9-11, *op. cit.*

347 Salazar, 640.

348 The presence of Dominican nuns in the Philippines would not materialize until after the Philippine Dominican Province was established 1971. Two such convents were founded in 1977.

The Monastery of Our Lady of the Rosary in Cainta, Rizal was founded by the Dominican Monastery at Summit New Jersey, USA. On 10 January 1975, the Summit chapter voted in favor of a new foundation with agreeing to train Filipino women in the Dominican monastic contemplative life and admitted Sor Maria Aurea of the Nativity (Perez) O.P. as its first Filipina on 20 October 1975. Headed by Mother Marie Rosario, five nuns including Sor Maria Aurea left Summit on 4 August 1977 and arrived in the Philippines. Cardinal Jaime Sin gave the nuns a piece of land for perpetual use in Cainta where the monastery can now be found.

The Queen of Angels Monastery in Bocaue, Bulacan was founded when six Filipino nuns arrived in the Philippines in 1977 after a year of training in Dominican monastic life in Los Angeles USA. The Filipina nuns belonged originally to the Dominican Congregation of Saint Catherine of Siena who asked permission from their superior to live in a two story house in Bocaue according to the rule of the cloistered nuns, with the possibility of eventually founding a Dominican Monastery in the Philippines. At the suggestion of the Master General, they went to the Monastery of the Angels in Los Angeles to complete their formation. Three other nuns from the mother chapter arrived later and the monastery was completed in 1982.-*Association of Sister Historians of the Order of Preachers.*

349 Santiago, Luciano P. R. *To Love and to Suffer: The Development of the Religious Congregations for Women in the Philippines during the Spanish Era (1565-1898). Part I.* Philippine Quarterly of Culture and Society. Vol. 23, No. 2 (July 1995), 151-195. *JSTOR,* JSTOR, www.jstor.org/stable/29792184.

350 The Dominican religious habit consists of a white tunic with a belt, a scapular, hood (*capuce*), and an outer garment, a black *cappa* to cover all. The scapular is the only part of the Dominican habit that is blessed. - Sheehy, Mary C, 4-5.

351 *Ibid.,* 7-8.

352 Cavallini, Giulina & Holland, Caroline. *St. Martin de Porres: Apostle of Charity.* Rockford, IL: Tan Books, 2000, 1979.

353 McGonigle, 71-73.

354 Giles, Mary E. *The Book of Prayer of Sor Maria of Santo Domingo: A Study and Translation.* Albany: State University of New York Press, 1990, 2.

355 Santiago, *op. cit.*

356 Santo Domingo, Juan de OP. *A Brief History of the Foundation of the Beaterio de Santa Catalina.* Translated from the original Spanish by the Congregation of Dominican Sisters of St. Catherine of Siena . Quezon City, 1996, 4.

357 Routt, Kristin E. *Sanctity or Self-Will? Madre Maria de San Jose (1656-1719) and the Ascetic Path to Holiness.* Confluencia, Vol. 22, No. 1 (Fall 2006), pp. 42-57. *JSTOR,* JSTOR, www.jstor.org/stable/27923179.

358 Raymund of Capua. *Life of Saint Catharine of Sienna.* Translated from the French by the Ladies of the Sacred Heart. New York: P. J. Kenedy & Sons, 1862. Internet Archive - archive.org

359 Flynn, Maureen. *The Spiritual Uses of Pain in Spanish Mysticism.* Journal of the American Academy of Religion. Vol. 64. No. 2 (Summer, 1996), pp. 257-278. *JSTOR,* JSTOR, www.jstor.org/stable/1466102.

360 *Ibid.*

361 Kieckhefer, Richard. *Today's Shocks, Yesterday's Conventions.* Religion & Literature, Vol. 42, No. 1/2, "Something Fearful": Medievalist Scholars on the Religious Turn (spring-summer 2010) pp. 253-278. *JSTOR,* JSTOR, www.jstor.org/stable/23049480.

Notes

362 [Feuillegt, Jean Baptist OP.] *The Life of Saint Rose of Lima.* New York: P. J. Kenedy and Sons, 1847. Internet Archive - archive.org

363 Routt, *op. cit.*

364 Salazar, 641.

365 *Ibid.,* 600-606.

366 Santo Domingo, 38. Salazar's version (642) of the same story presented Antonia de Jesus y Esguerra as the person with the moment of grace and attributed her to be founder of the beaterio. Zuñiga (1893,1:230) also referred to Sor Antonia as its founder. Collante's version (270) referred to Madre Sor Francisca. Considering that Santo Domingo was the party involved in the dialogue, his version prevails.

P. Fray Juan de Santo Domingo OP was born in 1640 near Calatayud, and professed in the convent of Ocaña 22 October 1661. He went to the Philippines in 1666, his first two years being occupied in duties in Manila. Assigned to the province of Pangasinan, he labored there for eighteen years, and exercised various duties. In 1682 he was transferred to the Manila convent. He was a founder of the Beaterio de Santa Catalina de Sena, and ordained its rules on 26 July 1696 while provincial. During his term as provincial he also organized the tertiary branch of his order. After his term as provincial he was appointed vicar of the *beatas* and president of the college of San Juan de Letran. In 1702, he was again elected prior of the Manila convent, and because of the death of the provincial exercised the duties of that office, to which he was regularly elected again in 1706. At the end of the second term, he again took up his duties as head of the beaterio and college. Besides the above posts and offices he was also Commissary of the Holy Office and definitor in the Chapters of 1682 and 1716. His died in Manila on 15 January 1726. - Ocio y Viana 1891 2:26-34.

367 Salazar, 642-643.

368 *Ibid;* Ferrando, Juan OP. *Historia de los Pp. Dominicos en las Islas Filipinas y en sus Misiones del Japon, China, Tung-Kin y Formosa, que Comprende los Sucesos Principales de la Historia General de este Archipielago, desde el Descubrimiento y Conquista de estas Islas por las Flotas Españolas hasta el Año de 1840.* Madrid: M. Rivadeneyra, 1870, 3:616-662. Hathi Trust

369 Salazar, 615

370 *Ibid.,* 660.

371 The phrase *of Spanish blood* included Spaniards, *mestizas,* and *cuarteronas* (quadroons). In view of this restriction, Sor Sebastiana Santa Maria, the *india terciera,* would have not qualified had she been alive.

372 In view of historical circumstances, the solemn vows were changed to simple vows. The changes were prompted by a landmark decision on the case involving the 12 July 1731 petition of Sor Cecilia de Hita y Salazar to nullify her vows in order to marry Don Francisco Figueroa. The Archbishop of Manila ruled that her vows were null and void and allowed the marriage in as much as Santa Catalina was prohibited by His Majesty from being a convent and therefore the perpetual solemn vows could not be valid. The Dominicans appealed the ruling to the Archbishop of Mexico who ruled the couple's subsequent marriage as valid and the vows annulled. The Sor Cecilia affair moved the *Consejo de Indias* to order the cessation of the *Beaterio* at the eventual death of all the remaining *beatas*. The Dominicans were able to secure the revocation of this order. - Zuñiga 1803, 563-565.

The vow of poverty was eventually construed as *"poverty of the spirit"* or *"voluntary poverty."* This appeared to be a concession extended to the rich *beatas* who might like to make bequests to their family of origin before they died. - Santiago 1996a, 128.

373 In as much as opposition from Santa Clara was most certainly anticipated. This oversight appeared to be intentional and used precedents in Spain to justify the move as an internal matter within the Order. The Beaterio could had been a calculated attempt to introduce the Second Order under the guise of the Third Order.

374 *Ibid.,* 650-658.

375 Collantes, 1:244-245.

376 Cl. *Comunicación sobre la creación de un beaterío en Manila. 1714-8-24 El Pardo.* ES.41091.AGI/23.6.330// FILIPINAS,333,L.124V-126V. PARES

377 Cl. *Orden sobre fundacion de Beaterio para indias en Manila. 1716-2-17 Madrid.* ES.41091.AGI/23.6.551// FILIPINAS,342,L.9,F.22R-24R. PARES

378 Cl. *Aviso al arzobispo sobre fundación de Beaterio para indias. 1716-2-17 Madrid.* ES.41091.AGI/23.6.551// FILIPINAS,342,L.9,F.24R-26R PARES; *Aviso al provincial de dominicos sobre Beaterio para indias. 1716-2-17 Madrid.* ES.41091.AGI/23.6.551//FILIPINAS,342,L.9,F.26R-28R. PARES

379 Cl. *Carta del dominico Bernardo Ustariz sobre beaterio de Santa Catalina de Siena 1745-8-14 Manila.* ES. 41091.AGI/23.6.386//FILIPINAS,299,N,31 PARES

380 Cl. *Carta de Bustillo sobre casa de Terceras de Manila. 1718-7-29.* ES.41091.AGI/23.6.957//FILIPINAS,132,N. 13. PARES

381 Cl. *Carta de Valdes Tamon sobre campana del Beaterio de Santa Catalina. 1734-6-6 Manila.* ES.41091.AGI/ 23.6.695//FILIPINAS,145,N.6 PARES

382 Cl. *Aviso de lo declarado sobre el beaterío de Santa Catalina 1779-11-25.* ES.41091.AGI/23.6.124//FILIPINAS, 337,L.19,F.495R-496R PARES; *Orden sobre el Beaterio de Santa Catalina de Siena de Manila 1777-8-5 San Ildefonso.* ES.41091.AGI/23.6.124//FILIPINAS,337,L.19,F.245R-246V PARES; *Orden sobre Beaterio de Santa Catalina de Siena de Manila 1762-4-17 Aranjuez.* ES.41091.1GI/23.6.637//FILIPINAS,335,L.17,F.194V-199R PARES; *Carta de Pedro Martinez de Arizala sobre el beaterio de Santa Catalina de Siena 1750-8-27 Manila.* ES. 41091.AGI/23.6.922//FILIPINAS,292,N.31 PARES

383 Collantes, 1:267-71.

384 Santo Domingo, 91-93

385 *Ibid*.

386 *Ibid*.

387 Bazaco 1933, 76-80.

388 *Ibid.*, 91. P. Fr. Juan Arrechedera OP was born in Leon, capital of Caracas (Venezuela). He professed in the Dominican Province of Santa Cruz de Indias, and moved to Santo Domingo de Mejico. He was master of students at the Colegio de Porta-coeli and Doctor of the University when he arrived in the Philippines. He occupied various positions: Presidente of the Hospital de San Gabriel and Colegio de San Juan de Letran, Definitor, Commissary of the Holy Office, Provincial, Rector and Chancellor of the University of Santo Tomas, Bishop of Nueva Segovia and Governor General of the Philippines for five years. He died on 12 November 1751 and was interred in the Santo Domingo church.

389 Horn, David and Shepherd, John ed. *Parranda and Parrandera*. Popular Music of the World Volume IX: Genres: Caribbean and Latin America. London: Bloomsbury, 2014, 590-591.

390 There is a mistaken notion that the *misa de gallo* was introduced in the Philippines by the *obra pia de misas de aguinaldo* established 1n 1743 by Doña Maria Magdalena Fernandez y Guevara, the widow of General Don Juan Domingo Henebra. Other than the earlier observance of the Novena to Our Lady of Aranzazu, the said *obra pia* was never implemented because the intended funding did not materialize. - Bazaco 1933, 102. APSR. Section de Letran Tomo I, Doc. 14, fols. 1-4.

391 *Ibid.*, 90-91.

392 Francisco de Echeveste was born to Capitan Geronimo de Echeveste and Maria Ana de Abalia on 20 November 1683 in Usurbil, Gipuzkoa. A professional soldier, he arrived in Nueva España as General of His Majesty's Galleons and from there traversed the Pacific Ocean to reach the Philippines and Tonkin (North Vietnam). Retiring from military service, he founded a commercial enterprise in Mexico, known as *Casa Echeveste*, to trade with the Orient. He served as consul and prior of the *Real Tribunal del Consulado* (a kind of chamber of commerce). He was actively involved with the *Confradia de Nuestra Señora de Aranzazu*, a confraternity founded in 1681 by Basques in Mexico, where he served as board director and rector in 1740. He died a bachelor in Mexico on 20 October 1753 leaving behind a number of foundations which benefited from his generous patronage. They include among others the following landmarks: *Colegio de la Vizcainas* and the church of the *Colegio de la Enseñanza* in Mexico; and the tower of the church of *San Salvador de Usurbil* and the hermitage of *San Francisco de Asis in Aginanga* in Gipuzkoa. - Arretxea, Larraitz.

393 From its approval by Pope Benedict IV in 1749, it took 23 years for the Confraternity to be organized. The delays could be attributed to two factors: (1) the inaction on the part of the Manila Archbishops in view of the Dominican's resistance to submit to episcopal visitation, and (2) the intervening 1762 British invasion of Manila which took the Dominicans 20 years to recover from their losses (Collantes), It was only after the Dominicans submitted to episcopal oversight that the Confraternity's documents were processed. The Dominicans were the first friar order to submit to the *Real Vice Patron* and the Archbishop in 1767 (Ferrando,5:79) and cooperated fully with the Metropolitan Archbishop Basilio Sancho de Santa Justa y Rufina in all his directives thereafter (Escoto). The stricter enforcement of the Patronato Real towards the end of the century led to a discordant relationship with the secular authorities and a general disinterest in the Confraternity. Among the many issues that emerged was the proposed closure of San Juan de Letran and San Jose petitioned unsuccessfully on 6 July 1793 by the *real audiencia* on the rationale that Santo Tomas alone was sufficient for the islands' population. (Cl *Peticion de informe sobre extinction de Colegios de Manila. 1794-11-15 Madrid.* ES.41091.AGI/23.6.214//FILIPINAS,338,L. 22,F.82V-84V); ES.41091.AGI/23.6.214//FILIPINAS,338,L.22,F.84V-86R - PARES

394 The statue of Our Lady was donated by Francisco de Echeveste in 1732.

395 *Ibid.*, 91-106.

396 *Ibid.*, 67.

397 APSR. *Venta de la Iglesia de Letran al Beaterio de Santa Catalina en 1734, 1783*. Seccion de San Juan de Letran Tomo 1, Doc. 18, fols. 54-55; Ocio y Viana 1891, 2: 28.

398 Bazaco 1933, 72.

399 Edaque, Rafael. *Temblor en Manila*. Diario de Manila, 6 June 1863. English translation, Earthquake in Manila made for the "Sydney Herald" and published in Hawke's Bay Herald, Volume 6, Issue 418, 9 September 1863. National Library of New Zealand http://paperspast.natlib.govt.nz/cgi-bin/paperspast?a=d&d=HBH18630909.2.14

400 Bazaco 1933, 80-89.

401 *Ibid*.

402 Colegio de San Juan de Letran. *Recuerdo del tercer centenario del Colegio de San Juan de Letran 1630-1930* Manila: 1931, 568-569; Fernandez, Pablo. p. 562.;

403 Santiago, Luciano P. R. *To Love and to Suffer: The Development of the Religious Congregations for Women in the Philippines during the Spanish Era (1565-1898). Part 3*. Philippine Quarterly of Culture and Society. Vol. 24, No. 3/4 SPECIAL ISSUE: THE PHILIPPINE REVOLUTION OF 1896 (Sept/December 1996), 216-254. JSTOR, JSTOR, www.jstor.org/stable/29792202.

404 Rich, Maria Cruz. *Apuntes Historicos del Beaterio y Colegio de Sta. Catalina*. Manila: University of Santo Tomas, 1939, 16-18.

Notes

⁴⁰⁵ Provincia del Santisimo Rosario de Filipinas. *Los Dominicos en el Extremo Oriente : provincia del Santísimo Rosario de Filipinas : relaciones publicadas con motivo del séptimo centenario de la confirmación de la Sagrada Orden de Predicadores.* Barcelona: Seix & Barral Herms, 1916, 94-97, 100-101. BDH

⁴⁰⁶ Provincia del Santisimo Rosario de Filipinas. *Estado General de Los Religiosos y Religiosas en el Año de 1893.* Manila: Colegio de Santo Tomas, 1894, 14. BDH

⁴⁰⁷ Madre Filomena de la Soledad (1873-1955) was the former Filomena Medalle of Cebu, Cebu. Her father, Don Francisco Jose Medalle was an influential Spanish mestizo and her mother, Doña Vlcenta Ramas, was a Filipino. She professed her vows in 1891. Her two younger sisters, Sor Remedios and Sor Francisca, entered the Congregation of the Daughters of Charity. Madre Filemona became the first Filipino prioress (1933-1937) as well as the first Filipino vicaress general (1943-55) of the congregation.

Madre Catalina de la Visitacion (1868-1940) was the former Vicenta Osmeña of Cebu, Cebu. She was the only surviving child of Don Tomas Osmeña, a *mestizo sangley* business magnate and Doña Agustina Rafols, a Spanish mestiza. It was on the basis of her mother's background that she was admitted as a choir sister in 1891 although legally she was classified as a *mestiza sangley* like her father. President Sergio Osmeña was her first cousin. Although she did not work in the missions, she kept an ardent interest in them. In 1917, she founded the *Colegio de Santa Catalina de Matsuyama* in Shikoku, Japan by donating its entire edifice. She became the second Filipino prioress of the *Beaterio* (1937-40). - Santiago 1996b, 222-223.

⁴⁰⁸ Rich, 18, 44.

⁴⁰⁹ *Ibid,* 16-21.

⁴¹⁰ Salazar, 644.

Chapter Seven Endnotes

⁴¹¹ Payne, Stanley G. *History of Spain and Portugal Vol. 1 & 2* University of Wisconsin Press, 1973, 1:305. LIBRO

⁴¹² Kagan, Richard L., *Students and Society in Early Modern Spain.* Johns Hopkins University Press, 1974, 9, 31. LIBRO

⁴¹³ *Ibid.*, 63.

⁴¹⁴ Costa, Horacio de la, SJ. *Jesuit Education in the Philippines to 1768.* Philippine Studies, Vol. 4 No. 2 (1956), 141-143. JSTOR, JSTOR, www.jstor.org/stable/42719215.

⁴¹⁵ See AA Sevilla: Secc. 3, tomo 11, no. 52. This is a petition of 2.IX.1545 which lists some reasons for establishing an orphanage in Seville.

⁴¹⁶ Hericourt du Vatier, Louis d'. *Les Loix ecclésiastiques de France dans leur ordre naturel, et une analyse des livres du droit canonique, conférez avec les usages de l'Église gallican* .Paris: J. du Nully, 1743. chap. 1 art. xxx, 14. Internet Archive - archive.org. In the Middle Ages, the "age of discretion" appears to have come somewhat later. The Council of Beziers in 1246, for example, fixed it at seven, while the synodal statutes of Tournai in 1346 placed it around ten, "*cirecter decennium*". - Kagan

⁴¹⁷ BE: Ms. L.I.13, "*Advertencias sobre el remedio que se podria poner para que los maestros de escuelas saquen con brevedad los muchachos en ellos buenos lectores y escribanos y contadores,*" folio 264, cites the complaints of schoolmasters during the 1580's "who say that one of the reasons they cannot teach the boys well is that some of the fathers order them not to whip [their sons], and if they do it, the fathers immediately remove their boys from the schools." For arguments on leniency toward children in the sixteenth century, see Felix G. Olmedo, *Diego Ramirez Villaescusa 1459-1537* (Madrid, 1944), xxiii. - Kagan

⁴¹⁸ Hazañas y La Rua, Joaquin. *Vasquez de Leca 1573-1649*, Sevilla: Imp. y Lib. de Sobrinos de Izquierdo, 1918. 15-16. BDH In the home of Mateo Vasquez's nephew, Agustinillo, aged five, there be a room of "arms" and another of "letters" to see to which the boy was most inclined. It was soon noted by the boy's step-father that the child would be more inclined to the profession of arms than to study. - Kagan

⁴¹⁹ Herrera, Cristobal Perez de. *Discourse de Amparo de los Legitimos Pobres.* Madrid: Luis Sanchez, 1558, 88-94. BDH Herrera recommended that at the age of eight poor boys be given jobs and girls be sent to find work as servants.

⁴²⁰ See Hazañas, chap. 2, for decisions made by Mateo Vasquez regarding the schooling and future careers of his nephews. Curiously, young Agustinillo, aged six, who only a year earlier had demonstrated a preference for a room of "arms" and his distaste for "letters" by the tears he shed in school, was ordered into the household of the Archbishop of Zaragoza and launched onto an ecclesiastical career. - Kagan

⁴²¹ AM Toledo: Registro Ms., "Colegio de los Niños de la Doctrina." The statutes expressly stated that its incoming wards "have to be between the ages of seven and ten since the latter is the latest at which good doctrines and customs can be imprinted." - Kagan

⁴²² See Hericourt, chap. V, art. Ii, 78. In Spain, Hernando de Salazar, "Tratado que se dio el Rey el año 1643 sobre materias de gobierno y hacienda," BNM: Ms. 2375, folio 234v, claimed the age of fourteen for boys was "that of puberty." Antonio Xavier Perez y Lopez, *Theatro de la Legislacion Universal de España e Indias* por Orden Cronologico ... Madrid: Imp. de Don Antonio Espinosa, 1797, 20:91 noted that in traditional Spanish law boys under fourteen and girls under twelve could not be accused of incest. Presumably, the law rested upon the premise that children below these ages were sexually immature. - Kagan

⁴²³ Kagan, 9-10.

Notes

[424] Esperabe Artega, Enrique. *Historia Pragmatica e Interna de la Universidad de Salamanca.Tomo I* Salamanca: Izquierdo, 1914, 631. Internet Archive - archive.org

[425] O'Connor.

[426] Renz, Christopher J OP., *In this Light which Gives Light - A History of the College of St. Albert the Great.* The Province of the Most Holy Name of Jesus. Oakland: 2009, 39-45.

[427] Universities of Granada, Lerida, Santiago de Compostela, Toledo and Valencia. - Kagan, 51.

[428] Kagan, 51-53.

[429] The *Ratio Studiorum* of 1599, the elaborate and detailed plan of studies formulated and developed by St. Ignatius Loyola and his successors, was practiced by the Society of Jesus world-wide and became a standard emulated by other educational institutions.

[430] Kagan. *op. cit.*

[431] Recopilacion 1681, Bk. 6 Tit. 1 Law 18.

[432] *Ibid.,* Bk. I Tit. 6 Law 30.

[433] *Ibid.,* Bk. I Tit.13 Law 4.

[434] *Ibid.,* Bk. I Tit. 13 Law 5.

[435] Fox, Henry Fredrick. Primary Education in the Philippines, 1565-1863. Philippine Studies, Vol. 13, No. 2 (April 1965) pp. 207-231. *JSTOR*, JSTOR, www.jstor.org/stable/42720593. The Augustinians were the first to formally require the teaching of Spanish to school boys during their Tenth Provincial Chapter in the Philippines held on 9 May 1596. - Navarro, 137.

[436] In a 1581 meeting of the religious prelates with Bishop Domingo Salazar, it was decided to use the indigenous languages to spread the gospel; adopting Plasencia's works using the Tagalog language. - San Antonio.

[437] San Antonio, 1:532.

[438] The Augustinians credited P. Fr. Agustin de Albuquerque OSA as the writer of their *Arte* (Navarro), but documents would indicate that P. Fr. Juan de Quiñones OSA was the more likely author of the manuscript. (Wolf) The work of P. Fr. Juan de Plasencia was also benefited from the contributions of Franciscans Miguel de Talavera OFM and Juan de Oliver OFM; giving rise to a template that became known as the "Talavera-Plasencia-Oliver Text." (Wolf) Edwin Wolf 2nd provided a comprehensive historical overview of the personalities involved and the circumstances surrounding the development of the first printed book in the Philippines in his introductory essay to the *Doctrina Cristiana / The first book printed in the Philippines. Manila, 1593. A Facsimile Copy of the Lessing J. Rosenwald Collection.*

[439] San Antonio, 1:533, 563-565; 2:134, 531.

[440] A Chinese edition of the *Doctrina Cristiana* written by P. Fr. Juan de Cobo OP was also published in 1583. P. Fr. Juan de Cobo OP was born in Alcazar de San Juan, Ciudad Real, Spain. He professed his vows in 1563 at the Dominican Convent of Ocaña. He studied at the Santo Tomas de Alcala de Henares and became master of students at Santo Tomas de Avila. He arrived in the Philippines in 1588 and was immediately assigned to the Chinese ministry where he mastered the language. He moved later to the convent's faculty of theology. In view of his gift for languages, he was sent as ambassador to Japan by the governor general in 1592. After successfully concluding his commission, his returning ship sank off the coast of Formosa where he died. - Ocio y Viana 1895, 18-20.

[441] Tagalog used to be written with the Baybayin alphabet whose origins could be traced to the Pallava script, one of the southern indian scripts derived from Brami.

[442] The Tagalog edition of the 1583 xylographic book was based on the Talavera-Plasencia-Oliver Text and possibly edited by Dominicans Domingo de Nieva, Juan de San Pedro Martir and Juan de la Cruz. - Wolf.

[443] San Antonio, 2:12; Marin y Morales, Valentin OP. *Sintesis de los Trabajos Realizados por las Corporaciones Religiosas Españolas de Filipinas Tomo II.* Manila: Imp. de Sant Tomas, 1901, 577. BDH

[444] *Ibid.*

[445] *Ibid.,* 14.

[446] Gerli, E. Michael, ed. *Medieval Iberia: An Encyclopedia.* United States: Taylor & Francis Ltd, 2003, 496.

[447] Wolf 2nd, Edwin ed. *Doctrina Cristiana / The first book printed in the Philippines. Manila, 1593. A Facsimile Copy of the Lessing J. Rosenwald Collection.* Project Gutenberg Ebook #16119 Release Date: June 23, 2005. *Toksohan* is a Tagalog word which literally means mutual teasing. It is typical of Plasencia's usage of the *juego* to transform the serious question-and-answer segment of the catechism into a kind of game.

[448] Barrantes, Vicente. *Discursos leídos ante la Real Academia de la Historia en la recepción pública del Excmo. Señor D. Vicente Barrantes, el 14 de enero de 1872.* Madrid: Impr. de Julián Peña, 1872, 68-70. BDH It was noted by Barrantes that the technique used by Plasencia in the 16th century was known as the Madras or Lancaster system developed by Andrew Bell between 1780-1790 for a school established by the East India Company. The "cord" kissed by the students referred to the cord worn by the Franciscans around the waist.

[449] San Antonio, 2:134.

[450] Costa 1956, 127-155.

[451] The *Colegio de Manila* was renamed *Colegio de San Ignacio* after St. Ignatius of Loyola, the founder of the Society of Jesus, was canonized in 1622.

[452] *Ibid.*

[453] Aduarte, 63-64.

Notes

454 Cobo, *op. cit.*

455 Bazaco 1933, 54.

456 *Ibid.*, 227, 249.

457 CI 1623-7-1.

458 Valdes, *op cit.*

459 Navarro, Eduardo OSA. *Filipinas: Estudio de algunas asuntos de actualidad.* Madrid: Minuesa de Rios, 1897, 136. BDH; San Antonio, 1:457.

460 Delgado, 226-227.

461 Delgado, *op. cit.*

462 Costa 1956. *op. cit.*

463 Aduarte, 479-481; Collantes,1; List of Provincial Priors No. 3.

464 Ferrando,1:589; Arias, Evaristo Fernandez OP. *Memoria Historico-Estadisca sobre la Enseñanza Segundaria y Superior en Filipinas escrita con motivo de la Exposición Colonial de Amsterdam por encargo de la subcomisión de estas islas (Edicion Official)*. Establecimiento Tipografico de la Oceania Española. Manila: 1883, 7. BDH

465 *Ibid.*

466 The rector of Santo Tomas filed a petition with the Real Audiencia to restrain the rector of San Ignacio from conferring university degrees by virtue of Pope Innocent X's Brief of 20 November 1645. The Audiencia ruled in favor of Santo Tomas but was overturned by the Consejo de Indias on 12 August 1652 and reaffirmed by decree on 25 November 1652 ruling that "until a university of general studies shall be established in the city of Manila, both the said colleges of San Ignacio and Santo Tomas may make use of the power to confer degrees and may actually confer them on those who shall have studied and taken courses in the faculties of arts, philosophy and theology in the said colleges or in each of them." - Costa.

467 As an *obra pia*, *Colegio de Santo Tomas* was under the Department of Justice and Ecclesiastical Affairs. The *Universidad de Santo Tomas* was under the Department of Public Instruction, Public Works, etc. - Bazaco 1953,157-158.

468 Bazaco, Evergisto, OP. *History of education in the Philippines: Spanish period, 1565-1898.* Manila: University of Sto. Tomas Press, 1953,157-158.

469 Arias 1883, 12.

470 Schumacher, John N., SJ. *The Early Filipino Clergy: 1698-1762.* Philippine Studies, Vol. 51, No. 1 (2003), pp. 7-62. JSTOR, JSTOR, www.jstor.org/stable/42633636, 12.

471 Arias, Evaristo Fernandez, OP.. *Memoria Correspondiente a la Seccion 8.ª Grupos 72 y 73 Exposición General de las Islas Filipinas en Madrid 1887 (Edicion Oficial) Comision Central de Manila.* Tipografia del Colegio de Santo Tomas. Manila,1887, 66 BDH; Del Rosario, Antonio. *Education under the Spanish Rule.* Census of the Philippine Islands taken under the direction of the Philippine Commission in the year 1903 Vol. 3. United States Bureau of the Census. Washington: 1905, 597. USIT

472 *Ibid.*, 8; USBC 1905, 3:623.

473 Payne, 2:356-358.

474 Manning, Susan and France, Peter ed. *Enlightenment and Emancipation.* United States: Associated University Presses, 2006, 106-107.

475 *Ibid.*, 366, 368-369.

476 Arias 1883, 10.

477 *Ibid.*, 19.

478 Bazaco 1933, 192-200.

479 Arias 1883, 10.

480 *Ibid.*

481 Bazaco 1933. *op. cit.*

482 O'Connor.

483 Gonzalez, Jose Ramon, OP. *Memoria sobre el Real Colegio de S. Juan de Letran de Manila formada por el Presidente del mismo, y remitida por el Gobernador Superior civil en cumplimiento de la Real orden de 26 Julio de 1861.* Legislacion ultramarina, concordada y anotada ... v.4. Rodríguez San Pedro, Joaquín. Madrid 1865, 4:249-250. Google Books

484 *Ordenanzas de buen gobierno,* Ordenanza No. 52 de Ovando (October 19,1752). It is to be noted that the Ordenanza No.93 de Raon repeats the foregoing Ovando directive. - Pan

485 Bantigue, Pedro. *Provincial Council of Manila, 1771.* Washington: Catholic University, 1957, 96-98. Although Carlos III and Rome did not approve its decrees, the recommendations on primary education merely formalized what to some extent were already being practiced in the parishes.

486 Originally known as the *Real Tribunal de Consulado,* the *Tribunal* was established to promote and oversee commercial activities in 1772. It was replaced by the *Tribunal de Comercio* by virtue of Real Cedula of 26 July 1852 which ordained the observance of the new Code of Commerce in the Philippines effective 15 July 1855. The *Real Sociedad Economica Filipina de Amigos del Pais* was created by royal order dated 27 August 1780 to promote the development of the colony's agriculture, industry, arts and commerce. - Buzeta, 254.

487 Moya, Francisco Javier. *Historia de la Real Sociedad Economica Filipina de Amigos del Pais*. Boletin de la Real Sociedad Economica de Amigos del Pais Revista Filipina de Ciencias y Artes. Año I. Numero I. 1 Mayo 1882 Manila: Imp. de C. Valdezco, 1882, 16. Digitalisierte Sammlungen

488 Ministerio de Hacienda. *Real Compañia de Filipinas 1804/1848*. ES.41091.AGI/36.967//ULTRAMAR,640. PARES The first English commercial house was allowed to be established in 1809. (Montero 2:394) The extinguishment of the *Real Compañia de Filipinas* on 6 September 1834 by the *Ministerio de Hacienda* opened Manila to free trade soon after. By 1858, there were seven English, three American, two French, two Swiss and one German commercial establishments in Manila. (Bowring, 301)

489 Moya. *Boletin* Año III No. 3 Manila 1 Julio 1884, 48; Montero y Vidal, Jose. *Historia General de Filipinas desde el Discubrimiento de Dichas Islas hasta Nuestros Dias Tomo III*. Madrid: Est. Tip. dela Viuda y Hijos de Tello, 1895, 317-8. Digitalisierte Sammlungen The *Escuela de Dibujo* was closed and was revived on 14 November 1849 as *Escuela de Dibujo y Pintura*. By Royal Decree of 11 August 1893, the school was reformed into a professional school of arts and crafts, and a school of fine arts and renamed as *Escuela Superior de Pintura, Escultura y Grabado* by Superior Decree of 1 December 1893. The *Escuela de Botanica y Agricultura* became the *Escuela de Agricultura de Manila* in 1889. See BR45:282-283,315-318.

490 Moya. *Boletin Año I. Numero I. op. cit.*

491 The Sociedad did not operate between 1797-1818.

492 Leroy, James A. *The Philippines, 1860-1898: Some Comment and Bibliographical Notes*. A. H. Clark Company, 1907 BR52:208-216.

493 Villaroel, Fidel. Father Jose Burgos University Student. Manila: University of Santo Tomas, 1971, 5-11.

494 Ministerio de Ultramar. *Expediente general de la Instrucción Pública en las islas Filipinas: Plan de Enseñanza primaria de indígenas. Creación y Reglamento de la Escuela Normal de Maestros de Instrucción Primaria de indígenas.1863/1865*. ES.28079.AHN/2.3.1.16.2.4.4.3//ULTRAMAR,604,Exp.5 PARES

495 Grifol y Aliaga, Daniel. *La Instruccion Primaria en Filipinas*. Manila: Tipo-Litografia de Chofre y Cia, 1894, 1-7, 56, 117-128, BDH

496 The *de termino* category in boy schools were either second class or first class. Girl schools had only one class of *de termino*. The first class primary schools were located only in Manila. - Article 5 of Royal Decree of 20 December 1863.

497 Bazaco 1933, 260; Fernandez, 379.

498 Arias 1883, 14

499 *Ibid.*, 10.

500 Ministerio de Ultramar. *Expediente relativo al Plan de Estudios para las Islas Filipinas 1863 /1872* ES. 28079.AHN/2.3.1.16.2.4.4.3//ULTRAMAR,605,Exp.1 PARES; Marin, 1:416-423;

501 Arias 1887, 68.

502 Arias 1883, 49.

503 Arias 1887, 33-34.

504 *Ibid.* Cuadro No. 5.B.

505 *Ibid.*, 66-68.

506 Aguinaldo, Emilio F. *My Memoirs*. Manila: Christina Aguinaldo Suntay, 1967, 9-11.

507 Arias 1887, 99.

508 Villaroel, Fidel. *Apolinario Mabini, His Birth Date and Student Years*. Manila : National Historical Institute, 1979, 14-23.

509 UST Alumni Association Inc. *University of Santo Tomas Alumni Directory 1611-1971*. Manila: University of Santo Tomas. 1972, 24C-27c

510 *Ibid.*, 33c-35c.

511 *Ibid.*, 31c-32c.

512 Santamaria, Alberto OP. *Estudios históricos de la Universidad de Santo Tomas de Manila*. Manila, 1938, 109. from Unitas, vol. XV-XVI, 1936-1938.

513 Simpson, Renate. *Higher Education in the Philippines Under the Spanish*. Journal of Asian History, Vol. 14, No. 1 (1980), 16 *JSTOR*, JSTOR, www.jstor.org/stable/41930356.

514 Montero y Vidal, 3:485-491, 542-556.

515 To keep Colegio de Santo Tomas alive, the fifth year of General Studies and the Studies of Application in Letran were to be taken at Colegio de Santo Tomas as an annex to the university. This was why the student population of these courses in Letran and Santo Tomas were always reported together in official documents. Ironically, the official graduate roster of Letran during this period could be found in Santo Tomas and not in Letran. Ateneo, on the other hand, offered the complete five year General Studies and Studies of Application entirely on its own.

516 Arias 1887, 6-10.

517 *Ibid.*, 54-55.

518 This regulation was instituted in the Moret decrees but was not changed in subsequent amendments.

519 AUST, Folletos, 93. as cited by Simpson.

520 Leroy, James A. *Philippine Life in Town and Country*. Ann Arbor, Michigan: University of Michigan Library, 2005, 205-206. USIT

Notes

[521] Superior Gobierno de Filipinas. *Reglamento de Asuntos de Imprenta 16 Febrero 1857*. Manila: Imp. Tip. de Santo Tomas, 1857.

[522] Rizal, Jose. *El Filibusterismo*, translated by Leon Maria Guerrero. London and Hong Kong: Longmans, 1965, 93-94.

[523] Rosario, Tomas G. del. *Education under the Spanish Rule*. Census of the Philippine Islands taken under the Direction of the Philippine Commission in the year 1903 Vol. III. Washington: United States Bureau of the Census, 1905, 3:632-633. USIT Tomas Guillermo T. del Rosario (10 February 1857 - 4 July 1913) earned his Licentiate in Civil Law at the University of Santo Tomas in 1886. He served as justice of the peace, fiscal and judge of the First Instance of Manila between 1888 and 1896. He was exiled to Ceuta for his involvement in the 1896 Philippine revolution. Upon his return from exile, he became a delegate to the Malolos Congress in 1898. He was elected Governor of the province of Bataan 1904-1906 and representative of the Philippine Assembly 1909-1912. - National Historical Institute marker Balanga City, 2007

[524] Mas, Sinibaldo de. *Informe sobre el estado de las Islas Filipinas en 1842 escrito por el autor del Aristodemo, del Sistema musical de la lengua castellana, etc.* Madrid: 1843, 3:8. BDH

[525] Mallat. J. *Les Philippines*. Tome Deuxime Paris: Arthus Bertrand, Editeur, 1846, 239-253. Google Books.

[526] Bowring, John. *A Visit to the Philippines*. London: Smith, Elder & Co., 1859,18-19 USIT; Alençon, Ferdinand Philippe Marie d'Orleans, duc d'. *Luçon et Mindanao. Extraits d'un journal de voyage dans l'Extrême Orient. Avec une carte de l'archipel des Philippines*. Paris: Michel Levy Freres, Editeurs,1870, 216-217 USIT; Marin, 148-152.

Chapter Eight Endnotes

[527] Jagor, Fedor. *Travels in the Philippines. (English Translation)*. London: Chapman and Hall, 1975, 366-367. . Google Books

[528] Bartlett, Robert. *Why Can the Dead Do Such Great Things? Saints and Worshippers from the Martyrs to the Reformation*. Princeton and Oxford: Princeton University Press, 2013, 183.

[529] Puebla, 169.

[530] Boxer, Charles Ralph. *The Christian Century in Japan: 1549-1650*. Berkley and Los Angeles: University of California Press, 1951, 308-328.

[531] *Ibid.,* 10-11.

[532] Colin, Francisco, SJ *Labor Evangelica, Ministerios Apostólicos de los Obreros de la Compañía de Jesus, Fundación, y Progressos de Su Provincia en las Islas Filipinas. Parte Primera*. Madrid: Joseph Fernandez de Buendía, 1663, 704-795. BDH

[533] Schumacher, John N. SJ. *Early Filipino Jesuits: 1593-1930*. Philippine Studies, Vol. 29, No. 3/4 (Third and Fourth Quarter 1981), pp., 274, 279 *JSTOR*, JSTOR, www.jstor.org/stable/42635192. Unlike the Spanish Jesuits in the Philippines, it would appear that the Portuguese Jesuits were able to secure approval from their superior to establish a novitiate in Usuki, Japan in 1581 and a college in Funai (Bungo) in 1583. The first Japanese Jesuit priests, Blessed Sebastiao Kimura SJ and Luis Niabara SJ, were admitted into the Society of Jesus in 1585 and ordained in 1601. - *Cieslik.* Zheng Weixin SJ, the first Chinese Jesuit priest, was ordained in 1664, ten years after Luo Wenzao OP. - Kowner.

[534] Puebla, 65-67, 80-82. *Ana-tsurushi* involved bodily suspension in a pit or hole. The victim was tightly bound around the body as high as the breast (one hand being left free to signal recantation). From gallows, the head was then hanged downwards into a pit which usually contained excreta and other filth. The victim is then lowered until his knees were at level of the pit's top. The forehead was lightly slashed with a knife in order to vent the blood. Some of the stronger martyrs lived more than a week in this position, but the majority did not survive more than a day or two. - Boxer.

[535] *Ibid.,* 95-96.

[536] Boxer, 362-376.

[537] Bazaco 1933, 51. In his *Historia Documentada,* Bazaco claimed 6 Japanese martyrs to be alumni of Letran. Of this number, only three Dominican martyrs cited in this book were recorded to had been in the Philippines prior to 1640. As Bazaco himself previously noted, there were no records concerning Letran students prior to 1640. Considering that no Dominican convent was yet established in Japan at that time, these 6 martyrs together with other Japanese were in Ocio y Viana's list of the Sons of Santo Domingo Convent.

[538] The Treaty of Amity and Commerce between the United State and Japan was signed on 29 July 1858.

[539] Gonzales, Jose Maria. *Historia de las Misiones Dominicanas de China 1632-1700 Tomo I*. Madrid: Imprenta, Juan Bravo, 3, 1964, 33-48

[540] Menegon, Eugenio. *Ancestors, Virgins, and Friars: Christianity as a Local Religion in Late Imperial China*. Cambridge, Massachusetts: Harvard University Asia Center, 2009, 18-32.

In a descending order, the four occupations under the Confucian class system were: the scholar-official or *literado,* farmers, artisans and merchants. A civil service examination system called the *Keju* was conducted in Imperial China to select candidates for the imperial bureaucracy. There were three levels of *literado* degrees with sub-levels each: Shengyuan (Xucai), Juren, and Jinshi. - Encyclopedia Britannica

[541] Puebla, 10-11.

[542] Gonzales 1964, 1:251-256.

543 A comprehensive treatment of the controversy could be found in Mungello, D.E., ed. *The Chinese Rites Controversy: Its History and Meaning.* Maney - Monumenta Serica, June 30, 1994.

544 After over two centuries of conflicts and sufferings caused by the Chinese Rites Ban, the *Propaganda Fide* (now called the Congregation for the Evangelization of Peoples) issued the instruction *Plane Compertum Est* on 8 December 1939 during the reign of Pope Pius XII. The instruction recognized the civil characteristics of the Chinese Rites and allowed Catholics to show respect to the images or tablets of Confucius and their ancestors. In view of these pronouncements, the Chinese Rites oath prescribed by Pope Benedict XIV had become superfluous. Spawned by the reforms of the Second Vatican Council, Pope Paul VI recognized a culturally pluralistic world and the need to spread the message of Christianity beyond the limits of a Euro-Roman cultural understanding in his encyclical *Evangelic Nuntiandi* on 8 December 1975. Fifteen years later in his encyclical *Redemptoris Missio*, Pope John Paul II urged the *intimate transformation of authentic cultural values through their integration in Christianity and the insertion of Christianity in the various human cultures* using the term inculturation.

545 For an excellent concise contemporary account of the issues surrounding the Calendar Case, refer to Jami, Catherine. *Revisiting the Calendar Case (1664-1669): Science, Religion, and Politics in Early Qing Beijing.* Korean Journal of History of Science, 2015, 27 (2), pp. 459-477. HAL-SHS https://halshs.archives-ouvertes.fr/halshs-01222267

546 Santa Cruz, 447. Gregorio Lo Lopez OP (Lo Vuen-taso, Lo Chai, Lo A, Luo Wenzao) was born in 1615 in Luojiaxiang, Fuan, Fujian to humble and honest gentile parents. His father was Li Zhu and his mother belonged to the Liu family. He raised ducks as a young man until he was baptized by Franciscan missionaries in 1634. P. Fr. Antonio de Santa Maria Caballero OFM christened him Gregorio Lo after the Franciscan Philippine Province of San Gregorio. He left behind his family and became a *dojico* of the Franciscans; serving them throughout the China mission. Santa Maria petitioned to accept Gregorio into the Order but was rejected. He was encouraged to pursue his vocation with the Dominicans who worked closely with the Franciscans in Fuan. He studied his first Spanish letters in Santo Domingo Convent where Letran was housed after the San Andres earthquake in 1645. He continued his philosophy studies at Santo Tomas where his Spanish surname of Lopez was adopted for the registry. He received his Dominican habit on 1 January 1650 and professed on 7 March 1651. After being ordained a priest in 1654, he worked as a missionary in China and distinguished himself during the persecutions of 1665-1671. In recognition of his exceptional pastoral work, he was consecrated titular Bishop of Basilitanus, Vicar Apostolic of Nanjing and Administrator of seven other provinces of China in Guangzhou on 8 April 1685. He struck a delicate balance among the many controversial issues facing China's Christians. He died in Nanjing on 28 February 1690 after receiving the sacred sacraments. - Ocio y Viana 1895; Gonzales 1964₁, Santa Cruz, San Roman, Collani,

Dojico (Japanese: dojuku) was a word originated from the Japanese Mission and used to refer to young male native catechists/seminarians who assisted the missionary priests. While a *dojico* is essentially itinerant, a Dominican *donado* is attached to a convent. - Menegon.

547 Ibid., 279-280. San Roman, Miguel Angel. *Lou Wenzao: A Unique Role in the Seventeenth Century Church of China*; Ku Wei-ying, ed. Missionary Approaches and Linguistics in Mainland China and Taiwan. Leuven Chinese Studies X. Belgium: Leuven University Press, Ferdinand Verbiest Foundation, K.U. Leuven, 2001. pp.133-152.

548 *Ibid.*, 435.

549 Gonzales 1964, 1:525-526.

550 San Roman, *op cit.*

551 *Ibid.*, 527-543.

552 Stewart J. Brown; Timothy Tackett. Cambridge History of Christianity: Volume 7, Enlightenment, Reawakening and Revolution 1660-1815. Cambridge University Press, 2006, 463.

553 Gonzales 1964, 2:262-263.

554 Marin, Catherine, dir. La Société des Missions Etrangères de Paris: 350 ans a la rencontre de l'Asie 1658-2008. Paris: Editions Karthala, 2011, 18-21.

555 Bazaco 1933., 124-128.

556 *Ibid.*, 128-130; Collantes, 556-558.

557 Gonzales 1964, 2:297-298; Bazaco 1933, 134-135, 140-141.

558 Ocio y Viana 1895, *appendice* 43-46.

559 Menegon, Eugenio. *Ancestors, Virgins, and Friars: Christianity as a Local Religion in Late Imperial China.* Cambridge, Massachusetts: Harvard University Asia Center, 2009, 183-4

560 Gonzalez 1964, 2:448.

561 Bazaco 1933, 134.

562 *Ibid.*, 135.

563 Ocio y Viana 1895, *appendice* 70; Gonzales 1964, 1:509-511.

564 Gonzales 1964, 2:244-246, 251-253.

565 *Xiucai* or *Shengyuan* is equivalent to a bachelor's degree with examinations held on the local-prefecture level.

566 Gonzales 1952, 503,505.

567 *Ibid.*, 252. See footnote no. 40. In view of the extreme cold, banishment to the empire's frontiers meant a slow death.

568 ., 510. The legal tortures and punishments practiced in China at that time were divided into the superior and the inferior class. According to a descending order of severity, the superior class included: beheading, strangulation, banishment beyond the frontiers of the Empire, banishment 3000 li from home, banishment 1000 li for 3 years, or to another place (commutable to a fine). The inferior class included: wearing the cangue (a square collar made of boards and is locked upon the neck), beating, squeezing the fingers, squeezing the ankles, and imprisonment. Unauthorized tortures always accompanied imprisonment in order to extort money or extract information or confession and included: fastening on a bedstead, frame of the flowery eyebrow, monkey grasping a peach, standing in a cage, smoking the head in a tube, a shirt made of iron wire, hot water snake, whip of hooks, kneeling on chains or bits of crockery, different forms of bondage while suspended in the air, and other resourceful methods of inflicting pain. - Doolittle, Justus, 268-279.

569 Ocio y Viana 1895, *appendice* 43-46, 70; Gonzales 1964,1:447-448.

570 Gonzales 1964, 2:448-455.

571 *Ibid.*, 455-456.

572 *Ibid.*, 456-462.

573 *Ibid.*, 423.

574 *Ibid.*, 424. See footnote no. 9.

575 *Ibid.*, 442.

576 *Ibid.*, 424-426, 427.

577 *Ibid.*, 424.

578 *Ibid.*, 422, 466-467.

579 Gonzales 1952, 501, 505.

580 *Ibid.*

581 Puebla, 170.

582 Ocio y Viana 1895. *Apendice,* 46.

583 Neira, Eladio et al. *Misioneros Dominicos en el Extremo Oriente 1836 - 1940. Edicion corregida y actualizada de la obra del P. Hilario Ocio OP.* Life Today Publications. Manila, Filipinas: 2000, 553.

584 Puebla, *op cit.*

585 Ocio y Viana 1895. *op cit.*

586 Clark, Anthony E. *Chinas's Saints: Catholic Martyrdom During the Qing (1644-1911).* Maryland: Lehigh University Press, 2011, 59-88.

587 Ocio y Viana 1895, 70.

588 Gonzales 1964. 2:502-503.

589 *Ibid.*, 507.

590 Ferrando, 5:16-17.

591 *Ibid.*, 502.

592 *Ibid.*, 503. See footnotes.

593 *Ibid.*, 541-543

594 *Ibid.*, 427, 442.

595 Menegon, 343.

596 Gonzales 1964, 2:474.

597 Nien (Yan), Pedro. *Letter to PP. Antonio Loranco and Pedro Feliu dated 18 October 1762.* APSR China Tomo 034 fols. 30-40

598 Ferrando, 5:17. The *Bull Omnimoda* of Pope Adrian VI granted to the Religious in missions apostolic powers and faculties as belonged to the Apostolic See.

599 P. Fr. Domingo Pablo Yan OP accused Terradillos and Pallas for what happened to his cousin, Pedro Yan, and the resulting schism to the *Propaganda Fide* and the authorities in Rome. See Gonzales 1964, 2:486-487 footnotes.

600 Accusations of sexual misconduct against the five schismatic Dominicans were publicly investigated by Terradillos and Pallas to discredit them. This backfired when Bishop Pallas' own sexual indiscretions were exposed by P. Fr. Pablo Domingo Yan OP. Although a recurring issue since the Chinese mission's inception, sexual proclivity did not appear to affect the local parishioners' high regard for their priests. - Menegon.

601 Menegon, 343-344.

602 Gonzales 1964, 2:546

603 *Ibid.*, 534.

604 *Ibid.*, 534, 550.

605 The four Letran alumni were: PP. Fr Esteban del Rosario OP (1749), Benito Han de San Vicente OP (1762), Felix Uan del Rosario OP (1762) and Joaquin de Santa Rosa OP (1762). The fifth Chinese Dominican was P. Fr. Pablo Domingo Nien (Yan) who was educated at the French seminary in Siam. - Ocio y Viana 1895, Gonzalez 1964$_2$, Bazaco 1933.

606 Ocio y Viana 1895, 427-428.

607 *Ibid.*, 410-412.

608 *Ibid. appendice,* 70-71, 82.

Notes

609 *Ibid. appendice,* 70.
610 Puebla, 145.
611 Ocio y Viana1895, Appendice, 46.
612 Bazaco 1933, 238-239.
613 Fernandez, 229-233.
614 Puebla, 169.
615 Neira 2000, 253.

Chapter Nine Endnotes

616 The saint is also known as Vicent Diem The Nguyen, Vinh Sơn Lê Quang Liêm, Vincent Liem Le Duang, Vicente de la Paz, Vicente Liem de la Paz. In the official saints roster of the Vatican, the saint is named as Vincenzo NGUYEN THE DIEM. The name used personally by the saint in his written works was Vicente de la Paz. According to Bazaco, the acts of the beatification process honored the martyr with the honorific title of *Thien-Khan,* a high Vietnamese noble rank. - Bazaco 1933, 203.

617 Bunson, Mathew and Margaret. *John Pauls II's Book of Saints.* Indiana: Our Sunday Visitor, 1999, 2007, 162-163.

618 Ocio y Viana 1895. Appendices, 119. P. Fr. Jose Chen OP appears in Ocio's list, and his year of profession was in 1777. As noted by Bazaco, Chien was a catechist when he baptized Liem.

619 *Vietnam. Britannica Library,* Encyclopædia Britannica, 3 May 2017. library.eb.com.au.rp.nla.gov.au/levels/adults/article/Vietnam/111155. Accessed 24 Oct. 2017.

620 Gonzalez 1964, 1:557-578.

621 Rivas, Manuel de OP. *Idea del Imperio de Annam o de los Reinos Unidos de Tunquin y Cochinchina.* Manila: Imprenta de los Amigos del Pais, 1858, 154. BDH

622 "Alexandre de Rhodes." *Britannica Library,* Encyclopædia Britannica, 13 Aug. 2017. library.eb.com.au.rp.nla.gov.au/levels/adults/article/Alexandre-de-Rhodes/63448. Accessed 24 Oct. 2017.

623 *Ibid.*

624 Marin, C., 15-16.

625 *Ibid.,* 17.

626 Rivas, 156-157.

627 *Ibid.,* 157.

628 Provincia del Santisimo Rosario de Filipinas. *Mapas de las Misiones Dominicanas en Extremo Oriente de la Provincia del Santisimo Rosario de Filipinas.* Madrid, 1924, 51-54. BDH

629 Puebla, 176-177.

630 Keith, Charles. Catholic Vietnam: A Church from Empire to Nation. Berkley and Los Angeles: University of California Press, 2012, 24.

631 Bazaco 1933, 204. This priest was also known as P. Fr. Espinosa Huy OP (RVSVL). However, neither names appeared in Ocio's roster.

632 *Ibid.,* 204-207.

633 Bazaco admitted this constraint in his *Historia (*1933, 205). The pretentious title of "Valedictorian of Valedictorians" alternatively conferred on Liem did not officially exist and appeared tainted with condescending sarcasm.

634 Ocio y Viana 1895, Appendice, 47.

635 *Ibid.,* 48-49.

636 *Ibid.,* 47.

637 *Ibid.,* 71.

638 *Ibid.,* 47-48.

639 Bazaco 1933, 207-208, Ferrando, 5:170-171.

640 Catholic Bishops' Conference of Vietnam. *History of the Catholic Church in Vietnam.* http://cbcvietnam.org/History/history-of-the-catholic-church-in-vietnam.html . Accessed on 1 January 2016.

641 *Ibid.*

642 Puebla, 217-219; 220-222.

643 Luong Dong, Thain Binh (Attwater); Lu-Ducong (Ferrando); Cu-Duong (Bazaco); Co Dau (Tran); Co Duo (RVSVL).

644 Hung Yen (Puebla); Pho Hien (Attwater); Ke Bic (Bazaco); Xich Bich, Dou Hoi (RVSVL).

645 Hie-nam (Bazaco); Kien Nam (RVSVL)

Notes

646 Regional Vicariate of St. Vincent Liêm, O.P. *St. Vincent Liem.* http://www.vinhsonliem.net/stvsl.html Accessed on 30 December 2016. RVSVL's narrative is based on the following sources written in Vietnamese: *Giáo Hội Công Giáo Ở Việt Nam*, Vol. I, Veritas, Calgary, Canada, 1998, 2nd edition, by a professor of history; *Dòng Máu Anh Hùng*, Vol. I, Fr. Vũ Thành, U.S., 1987; *Lịch Sử Giáo Hội Công Giáo*, Fr. Bùi Đức Sinh, O.P., Chân Lý, Saigon, 1972.

647 Bazaco 1933, 211.

648 RVSVL, *op cit.*

649 Bazaco 1933, 213-214; Ferrando, 5:175-180.

650 Phan Sinh, a Vietnamese Catholic layman, was executed for his faith between 1630-31. However, there was no official warrant issued and was thus unrecorded. Liem was the first Vietnamese religious martyr - RVSVL.

651 Bazaco 1933, 207.

652 Ferrando, 5:448-449.

653 Ocio y Viana 1895, Appendice, 101.

654 Bazaco mistakenly claimed that Vietnamese Dominican martyr saints San Vicente Yen OP and San Domingo Tuoc OP were Letran alumni (1933, 225, 254). They both professed in Tonkin in 1808 and 1812 respectively. - Ocio y Viana 1895, Appendices, 93, 120.

655 Ocio y Viana 1895, Appendice, 122.

656 Ferrando, 5:449-450.

657 Ocio y Viana 1895, Appendice, 122.

658 Ferrando, 5:549, 620.

659 *Ibid.*, 465-466

660 Puebla, 187-188

661 *Ibid.*, 269-270.

662 *Ibid.*, 179; Bunson, 56.

663 Bazaco 1933, 215.

664 Bunson, 55.

665 Puebla, 215.

666 Bunson, *op. cit.*

667 Puebla, 269-270.

668 Blessed Eugenio Sanz-Orozco Mortar was born in Manila, Philippines on 5 September 1880. He studied at the Ateneo de Manila, Colegio de San Juan de Letran and Colegio de Santo Tomas. In 1896, he left for Spain to pursue further studies. He joined the Order of Friars Minor Capuchins and took the name of Jose Maria de Manila shortly after. He took his simple vows on 4 October 1905 and his solemn vows on 18 October 1908 in Lecaroz, Navarra. He was ordained priest on 30 November 1910. During the Spanish Civil War in 1936-1939, he was imprisoned by anti-Catholic factions and executed on 17 August 1936 at the gardens of the Cartel de la Montaña because of his Roman Catholic faith. He was beatified by Pope Francis together with 521 other companions on 13 October 2013 in a Holy Mass presided over by the prefect of the Congregation of the Causes of Saints, Angelo Cardinal Amaro SDB. He is the third Filipino to be beatified.

Blessed Jesús Villaverde Andrés OP was born in San Miguel de Dueñas,. León, Spain on 4 October 1877. He entered the Dominican Novitiate at Ocaña and made his profession on 4 June 1895. He was ordained in Avila on 26 June, 1903. His priestly life was marked by the constant movement and activity as professor and as superior. He taught at Letran College of Manila (1905-1910); and was assigned in the Convent of Valencia. He returned to the Philippines in 1916, taught Theology and was Dean at the University of Santo Tomás of Manila. He was the Prior of the Community of Rosaryville in New Orleans, USA (1921-1924); Rector of the aforementioned Letran College (1924-1927); Prior of Santo Tomás de Ávila in 1934. He was a member of the community of Madrid when it was assaulted. When he was detained on 15 October 1936, he confessed that he was a religious and was ready to die for Christ. He was brought to the checa of Fomento in Madrid and was executed the following day, 16 October. On 28 October 2007, he was among the group of 498 martyrs of Spanish Civil War that were beatified by Pope Benedict XVI in a Holy Mass presided over by the prefect of the Congregation of the Causes of Saints, Cardinal José Saraiva Martins.

Blessed Antonio Varona Ortega OP born in Zumel, Burgos, Spain on 16 January 1901. He entered the Apostolic School of La Mejorada (Valladolid) in 1913 and professed in Ávila on 9 September 1918. After his solemn profession on 18 January 1922, he was sent to the Convent of Rosaryville, New Orleans, USA and he completed his theological studies at the Dominican House of Studies in Washington (1922-1924). At the same time, he attended some post graduate courses in Pedagogy at the Catholic University of America (1924-1926). On 13 June 1926, he was ordained by the Archbishop of New Orleans. He arrived in the Philippines in 1926 and taught at the Letran College of Manila where he was the Athletics Moderator. He returned sick with tuberculosis to Spain in 1933 and was assigned to the Convent of Santo Tomás de Ávila. Between 1934-1936, he transferred from one institution after another unable to recuperate. Together with Blessed José Luis Palacio, he was executed on 25 July 1936 beside the Algodor train station with outstretched hands blessing in the name of the Lord. He was beatified with 497 other companions by Pope Benedict XVI in a Holy Mass presided over by the prefect of the Congregation of the Causes of Saints, Cardinal José Saraiva Martins on 28 October 2007.

669 Pope John Paul II canonized 120 martyrs of China on 1 October 2000. The first six were Dominicans who were martyred prior to the Schism of Fuan. - Vatican.va

Notes

670 Ferrando, 5:179.

Chapter Ten Endnotes

671 Mariscal, George. *The Role of Spain in Contemporary RaceTheory.* Arizona Journal of Hispanic Cultural Studies, Vol. 2 (1998), pp. 7-22. *JSTOR*, JSTOR, www.jstor.org/stable/20641414.

672 *Slavery. Britannica Library*, Encyclopædia Britannica, 25 Mar. 2016. library.eb.com.au.rp.nla.gov.au/levels/adults/article/slavery/109538. Accessed 5 April 2016.

673 Aristotle. *Politics.* Translated by Benjamin Jowett. Kitchener: Batoche Books, 1999, 9. https://socserv2.socsci.mcmaster.ca/econ/ugcm/3ll3/aristotle/Politics.pdf Accessed on 25 October 2017.

674 Scott, S. P. & Robert I. Burns, S..*Las Siete Partidas, Volume 4: Family, Commerce, and the Sea: The Worlds of Women and Merchants (Partidas IV and V).* Philadelphia: University of Pennsylvania Press, 2012, Partida 4, tit. 21, ley 6.

675 Saco, Jose Antonio. *Historia de Esclavitud desde los Tiempos Mas Remotos Hasta Nuestros Dias. Tomo III.* Barcelona: Imprenta de Jaime Jepus, 1877, 176-177. BDH

676 *Ibid.*, 184.

677 *Ibid.*, 186.

678 *Ibid.*, 192.

679 Sweet, James H. *The Iberian Roots of American Racist Thought.* The William and Mary Quarterly, Third Series, Vol. 54, No. 1 (Jan., 1997), pp. 143-166. JSTOR, JSTOR, www.jstor.org/stable/2953315.

680 *Ibid.*, 155.

681 *Ibid.*, 166.

682 Martin de Cordoba. *Jardin de nobles doncellas.* Madrid 1953.

683 Raiswel, Richard. *Eugene IV, Papal bulls of,* The Historical Encyclopedia of World Slavery Vol. 1, Junius P. Rodriguez ed. Santa Barbara, California: ABC-CLIO, 1997, 260-261.

684 Fernandez-Morera, Dario. *The Myth of the Andalucian Paradise: Muslims, Christians, and Jews under Islamic Rule.* Wilmington, DE: ISI Books, 2015.

685 The work of Antonio Dominguez Ortiz entitled *Los Conversos de Origen Judio después de la Expulsion* contains a comprehensive documented historical account of Spanish Jews before and after the expulsion. It can be found in the *Estudios de Historia Social de Espania Tomo III* Patronato de Historia Social del Instituto "Balmes" de Sociologia (Balmes), Madrid: Consejo Superior de Investigaciones Cientificas,1955, 224-431.

686 The work of Antonio Dominguez Ortiz entitled *La Esclavitud en Castilla durante la Edad Moderna* contains a comprehensive documented Modern Age history of slavery in Spain including accounts of captive Muslims before and after their expulsion. It can be found in the *Estudios de Historia Social de Espania Tomo II.* Balmes. Madrid: Consejo Superior de Investigaciones Cientificas, 1952, 367-428.

687 Balmes 1952, op. cit.

688 Pope Sixtus IV, Papal Bull *Exigit Sinceras Devotionis Affectus, 1 November 1478* granting the Spanish monarchs Fernando II and Isabel exclusive authority to name the inquisitors in their kingdoms.

689 "Spanish Inquisition." *Britannica Library*, Encyclopædia Britannica, 29 May. 2015. library.eb.com.au.rp.nla.gov.au/levels/adults/article/Spanish-Inquisition/624066. Accessed 27 Oct. 2017.

690 Prof. Tamar Herzog's works provide comprehensive understanding of and insights into the citizenship laws of an evolving Spanish nation and their impact on Spanish America. Information on this section of the chapter is largely based on her works.

691 Herzog, Tamar. *Communities Becoming a Nation: Spain and Spanish America in the Wake of Modernity (and Thereafter).* Citizenship Studies Vol 11 No, 2 May 2007 151-172. Special Issue: Citizenship Beyond the State. Andrew Girding and Trevor Stack (Eds). Routledge, Taylor and Francis Group

692 *Ibid.*

693 Herzog, Tamar. *Defining Nations: Immigrants and citizens in Early Modern Spain and Spanish America.* New Haven and London: Yale University Press 2003, 53-54.

694 Colon, Cristobal. *Relaciones y Cartas de Cristobal Colon.* Madrid: Libreria y Casa Editorial Hernando (S.A.), 1927, 24-25. BDCL Unless otherwise cited, the Columbus narrative in this chapter is based on the information found in this book.

695 Navarrete M, 1:283.

696 Vespucci, Amerigo. *The Letters of Amerigo Vespucci and other Documents Illustrative of His Career.* Translated and annotated by Clements R. Markham. London: Hakluyt Society, 1894. Internet Archive - archive.org.

697 Herbert, John R. *The Map that Named America - Library Acquires 1507 Waldseemüller Map of the World.* Library of Congress Information Bulletin. September 2003 Vol. 62, No. 09. The Library of Congress. Washington DC. http://loc.gov/loc/lcib/0309/maps.html Accessed on 27 October 2017.

698 The work of Konetzke, Richard entitled *La esclavitud de loas indios como elemento en la estructuracion social de Hispanoamerica* contains a comprehensive documented history of slavery in Spanish America. It can be found in the *Studios de Historia Social de Espania Tomo I* Balmes. Madrid: Consejo Superior de Investigaciones Cientificas, 1949.

Notes

[699] Navarrete M, 1:274-275.

[700] *Ibid.*,1: 460-463.

[701] AGS. *Testamento de la reina Isabel la Catolica.* Valladolid, 1504-10-12 Medina del Campo (Valladolid, España) ES.47161.AGS/4.2//PTR,LEG,30,DOC.2 PARES; Recopilacion 1681, Bk. 6 Tit. 10 Law 1; Bourke, John. *The Laws of Spain in Their Application to the American Indians.* American Anthropologist, Vol. 7, No. 2 (Apr., 1894), pp. 193-201. JSTOR, JSTOR, www.jstor.org/stable/658541. English translation by John Bourke.

[702] Balmes 1949, 1:457. The *Islas y Tierra Firme de Indias* was known as the Spanish Main in the English world. - Sauer.

[703] Islands that cannot produce commercial quantities of precious metals or other marketable commodities were considered *inutil* or useless and thus the native inhabitants became the only tradable commodity as slaves or domestics.

[704] *Ibid.*, 1:458.

[705] Heredia, Vicente de. *El P. Matias de Paz, O.P. y su tratado "De domingo regué Hispaniae super Indos",* Ciencia Tomista, tomo XL, 1929 as cited by Konetzke in Balmes 1949 1:461-462.

[706] Palacios Rubios, Juan Lopez de. *Tractus insularum maris Oceani et de Indis in servituten non redigendis* as cited by Konetzke in Balmes 1949, 1:461.

[707] Balmes 1949, *op. cit.*

[708] The full text of the Requerimiento can be found in Casas, Bartolome de las. *Historia de Indias. Vol. 2.* Madrid: J. Pueyo, 1927, 2:578-580.

[709] Calderón, Annie Badilla, Instituto Tecnológico de Costa Rica, "La información y los textos jurídicos de la colonia (II). El poder político Latina," *Revista Latina de Comunicación Social* 13 de enero de 1999. Recuperado el 2 de marzo de 2008 de: http://www.ull.es/publicaciones/latina/a1999c/149badilla2cr.htm

[710] Casas, Bartolome de las OP. *A Brief Account of the Destruction of the Indies.* Project Gutenberg Ebook No. 20321 9 January 2007.

[711] Benavente, Toribio de OFM. *Historia de los Indios de Nueva España Texto impreso escrita a mediados del siglo XVI.* Barcelona: Herederos de Juan Gili, Editores, 1914, 13-19. Cervantes Virtual

[712] *Ibid.*

[713] Prem, Hanns J., Dyckerhoff and Feldweg, Helmut. *Reconstructing Central Mexico's Population.* Mexicon, Vol. 15. No. 3 (May 1993) pp. 50-57. JSTOR, JSTOR, www.jstor.org/stable/23760245.

[714] Balmes 1949, 1:463-467.

[715] Balmes 1949, *op cit.*

[716] The *just war* clause would eventually allow enslavement of belligerent *Indio* tribes such as the *Chichimecas* of Northern Mexico, *Caribes* of the Antilles, *Moros* of the Philippines, and *Araucanos* of Chile.

[717] Corwin, Arthur F. *Spain and the Abolition of Slavery in Cuba, 1817-1886.* Austin and London: Institute of Latin American Studies, University of Texas Press, 1967, 311.

[718] Pope Leo XIII. *In plurimis.* 1888.

[719] Rosenblat, Angel. *La Población Indigena 1492-1950, La Población Indigena y El Mestizaje en America Vol I.* Buenos Aires: Editorial Nova, 1954, 1:175.

[720] *Ibid.*, 143.

[721] Rosenblat, Angel. *El Mestizaje y Las Castas Coloniales, La Población Indigena y El Mestizaje en America Vol II.* Buenos Aires: Editorial Nova, 1954. 2:66.

[722] *Ibid.*

[723] Saco, Jose Antonio. *Historia de la Esclavitud de la Raza Africana en el Nuevo Mundo y en especial en los Países Americo-Hispano Tomo I.* Barcelona: Imprenta de Jaime Jepus, 1879, 1:113. Internet Archive - archive.org

[724] *Ibid.*, 1:114.

[725] *Ibid.*

[726] *Ibid.* The Zapotecas were the pre-columbian indigenes of the Valley of Oaxaca in Mesoamerica.

[727] Pope Clement XI ordained that baptized *cuarterones* (quadroons) and *ochavones* (octoroons) should be considered as white. - Rosenblat, 2:180

[728] Seijas, Tatiana. *Asian Slaves in Colonial Mexico: From Chinos to Indians.* New York: Cambridge University Press, 2014, 266.

[729] Scott, William Henry. *Slavery in the Spanish Philippines.* Manila: De La Salle University Press, 1991, 61.

[730] Frederick, Jake. *Without Impediment: Crossing Racial Boundaries in Colonial Mexico.* The Americas, Vol. 67, No. 4 (April 2011) p, 497. JSTOR, JSTOR, www.jstor.org/stable/41239107.

[731] Beltran, Gonzalo Aguirre. *La Población Negra de Mexico: Estudio Etnohistorico.* Mexico: SRA-CEHAM, 1981. p. 153-154.

[732] Rosenblat, 2:134.

[733] Rosenblat, 2:187.

734 The articles of William H. Dusenberry and Irene Diggs provide comprehensive summaries of the laws and observances on racial segregation, prohibition and discrimination under the *sistema de castas*.

Dusenberry, William H. *Discriminatory Aspects of Legislation in Colonial Mexico*. The Journal of Negro History Vol. 33 No. 3 (Jul.1948) pp. 284-302. *JSTOR*, JSTOR, www.jstor.org/stable/2715477.

Diggs, Irene. *Color in Colonial Spanish America*. The Journal of Negro History, Vol. 38 No. 4 (Oct., 1953) pp. 403-427.*JSTOR*, JSTOR, www.jstor.org/stable/2715890.

735 Recopliacion Bk, 6, Tit. 3, Law 21.

736 Recopliacion Bk. 6, Tit. 3, Law 22.

737 Rosenblat, 2:137.

738 *Ibid.*

739 Rosenblat, 2:134.

740 Rosenblat, 2:136.

741 Recopilacion, Bk. 7, Tit. 5, Law 28.

742 Recopilacion, Bk. 7, Tit. 5, Laws 14-16.

743 Recopilacion, Bk. VI Tit. VI, Ley 7.

744 Diggs, 415-6.

745 Rosenblat, 2:134.

746 Rosenblat, 2:269.

747 Remesal, Antonio de OP. *Historia de la Provincial de S. Vicente de Chyapa y Guatemala de la Orden de nro Glorioso PADRE SANCTO DOMINGO Escrivense Juntamente los principios de las demás Provincias esta Religion de las yndias Occidentales y lo Secular de la Gobernación De Guatemala.* Madrid: 1619, 564. Internet Archive - archive.org.

748 Garcia Icazbalceta, 2:421-426.

749 *Ibid.*

750 Aguirre, Rodolfo. *El ingreso de los indios al clero secular en el arzobispado de Mexico, 1691-1822*. Takwa Revista de Historia Num. 9 Primavera 2006 pp. 75-108. Centro Universitario de Ciencias Sociales y Humanidades, Universidad de Guadalajara, Mexico, 75. http://148.202.18.157/sitios/publicacionesite/pperiod/takwa/Takwa9/rodolfo_aguirre.pdf

751 Poole, Stafford. *Church Law on the Ordination of Indians and Castas in New Spain*. The Hispanic American Historical Review, Vol. 61, No. 4 (Nov., 1981), pp. 637-650. *JSTOR*, JSTOR, www.jstor.org/stable/2514607 Stafford Poole's article provides comprehensive information on the subject matter. It includes the nuances behind the different latin translations of the Third Mexican Council of 1585 and interesting insights as to the motives behind the restrictions and changes in interpretations.

752 The minor orders include porter, lector, exorcist and acolyte. The minor vows were not considered permanent or irrevocable and if indians or mestizos proved unsuitable, they could return to their former way of life. - Poole, 639.

753 *Ibid., 639*

754 *Ibid., 641*

755 *Ibid., 642*

756 Recopilacion: Bk 1, Tit. 7 Law 7.

757 Poole, 643.

758 *Ibid., 643-644.*

759 Carlos II was considered to be incapable of conceiving these controversial decrees because of his physical, emotional and mental disabilities as a result of the Spanish Habsburg's extreme inbreeding. It was generally accepted that his mother, the Queen Regent Mariana of Austria, was the principal mover and influence.

760 A.N., A.C.G., v. 718, fs. 387-388; A.N., A.R.A., v. 3.117, f. 82; A.A.S., lib. LXXXIV, p. 602; Lizana, C.D.H.A.A.S., t. III, pp. 532-536 as cited in Jara, Alvaro; Pinto, Sonia. *Fuentes Para la Historia del Trabajo en El Reino de Chile: Legislación, 1546-1810. Tomo i.* Chile: Editorial Andres Bello, 1982, 378-380.

761 *Ibid.*

762 Poole, 641.

763 Jara, *op cit.*

764 AGN, Reales Cedulas originales 27, exp. 11, de 26 de marzo de 1697 as cited by Aguirre,83.

765 Seminario Conciliar de Mexico. *Historia*. http://www.conciliar.mx/el-seminario/historia Accessed 1 January 2017 2:15 pm.

766 *Ibid.*

767 Aguirre, 84.

Chapter Eleven Endnotes

768 Spate, Oskar Hermann Khristian. *The Spanish Lake*. Canberra: ANU E Press, 2004, 87-100.

Notes

769 Philip II. *Letter to Luis de Velasco. Valladolid 24 September 1559.* AGI 1-1-1/23; DIU 2:94-97; CD 5:139-140 as cited in Filipiniana Book Guild Editorial Board. *The Colonization and Conquest of the Philippines by Spain: Some Contemporary Source Documents 1559-1577.* Manila: Filipiniana Book Guild, 1965, 1-3.

770 Royal Audiencia of Nueva España (RANE). *Instruction to Miguel Lopez de Legazpi.* AGI 1-1-1/23; DIU 2:145-200; CD 5:147-171 as cited by FBGEB, 11- 40.

771 Rodriguez, Esteban. *Legazpi's Voyage of Discovery and Conquest of the Philippines (1564-1565).* AGI 1-1-1/23; DIU 2:373-427; CD 5:15-39 as cited in FBGEB, 41-73.

772 *Ibid.*

773 In an undated letter to Felipe II, Urdaneta reminded the King that the Philippines was within the Portuguese side of the demarcation line defined by the Treaty of Zaragoza. DIU:109-113; CD5:144-145 as cited in FBGEB, 7-10.

774 FBGEB, 20.

775 *Ibid.,* 24-32.

776 *Ibid.,*11-12. A *patache* is a type of vessel with two masts, very light and shallow, a sort of cross between a brig and a schooner, which originally was a war ship being intended for surveillance and inspection of the coasts and ports. - Culver.

777 Friis, Herman R. *The Pacific Basin: a history of its geographical exploration.* New York: American Geographical Society, 1967. 123.

778 EBFBG, 53-73, 100.

779 *Ibid.,* 108, 152. Espinosa, Rodrigo de. *Deroterro de la navegación de las islas del Poniente para la Nueva España 1565.* CD, 5:121-135.

780 The lost ship *San Lucas* commanded by Alonso de Arellano returned to the port Navidad on 8 August 1675, two months earlier than the *San Pedro,* but was not given official recognition because of the dubious circumstances of its voyage. - DIU 3:1-76.

781 Rada, Martin de, OSA. *Letter to the Marquis de Falces. Cebu: 8 July 1569.* AGI 68-1-37; BR 34:223-228; as cited by FBGEB, 149-152.

782 Scott W., 49-50.

783 Goiti, Martin de et al. *Memoria de lo que se embio a pedir a su magestad de merced franquezas e libertades por los capitanes conquistadores oficiales que al presente en esta jornada e nuevo descubrimiento le sirven en las yslas filipinas gobernador miguel lopez de legazpi.* (1566?). DIU, 2:322-323.

784 Ibid., 324.

785 Felipe II. *Letter to Miguel Lopez de Legazpi. The Escorial 16 November 1568.* AGI 105-2-11; BR 34:235-255; FBGEB,187-189.

786 By 1581, Felipe II became King of Portugal. Although he respected the territorial jurisdiction of Portugal, the ensuing relations between Spain and Portugal led to friendly trade and lax accommodations in territorial integrity.

787 Herrera, Diego de, OSA. *Letter to Philip II Mexico 16 January 1570.* AGI 2-2-2/24; BR 3:69-72; FBGEB, 157-159.

788 *Ibid.*

789 Recopilacion Bk. 6, Tit. 2 Law 12.

790 Seijas, 116-122.

791 Lavezaris, Guido. *Slavery among the natives.* BR 3:286-288.

792 Recopilacion Bk 6, Tit. 2, Law 9

793 Recopilacion Bk 6, Tit. 7 recognizes the nobility or *Cacicazgo* of native chiefs and conserves their titles, succession, rights, jurisdiction and income. The *Cacicazgo* was officially extended to *Indio Principales de Filipinas* in 1594 under Law 16.

794 Salazar, Domingo OP. *Council Regarding Slaves.* BR 34:325-331.

795 *Ibid.*

796 BR 6:193.

797 Colin, Francisco SJ. *Labor Evangelica, Ministerios Apostolicos de los Obreros de la Compañía de Jesus, fundación, y progresos de su Provincia en la Isla Filipinas Libro 2,* Madrid: Joseph Fernandez de Buendía, 1663, 2:248-249

798 Salazar, Domingo de, OP. *Cartas al Rey 1583-6-18,* ES.41091.AGI/29.3.5.3//PATRONATO,25,R.8

799 Recopilacion Bk 6, Tit. 2 Law 5 - 7 July 1550.

800 Reid, Anthony. *Southeast Asia in the Age of Commerce 1450-1680 Vol. 1.* Ann Arbor: Yale University Press, 1988, 1:122.

801 The *moros* were reinstated under the just war provisions by Felipe III on 29 May 1620. The öld" muslim law under Recopilacion Bk. 6, Tit. 2 Law 12 was likewise reinstated on the same date.

802 Felipe II. *Instructions to Gomez Perez Dasmariñas. San Lorenzo 9 August 1589.* BR 7:171.

803 The right of *caciques* to maintain slaves among their subjects is recognized by Spanish Law if done by legitimate title, voluntary surrender, established ancestry of slaves, non-payment of debts and other traditionally accepted practices. See Recopilacion Bk. 6 Tit. 7 Law 8.

Notes

804 Seijas, 100.

805 Scott W, 18-35.

806 Baeza, Pedro de. *Memorial y discurso 5 April 1608* cited in C.R. Boxer's *A note on the triangular trade between Macau, Manila and Nagasaki 1580-1640,* a paper at the 9th Conference of the International Association of Historians of Asia, Manila 21-25 November 1983.

807 Garcia Serrano, Miguel, OSA. *Letter to Felipe III 25 July 1621*. cited in Rodriguez, Isacio R. OSA. *Historia de la Provincia agustiniana del Sto. Nombre de Jesus de Filipinas*. Manila and Valladolid, 1965-1987. 18:66-67.

808 Archives of the Archdiocese of Manila (AAM): LGE (1620-28), doc. 173 as cited by Scott W. under note 65 p. 73.

809 Archivos de los Padres agustinos de Filipinos: *Libro Provincial*°., fols. 17, 18; *Libro de Gobierno II*, fol. 147 as cited by Scott W. under note 34 p. 69.

810 Albuquerque, Agustin de. *5 June 1575*. Rodriguez I, 14:245.

811 Salmoral, Manuel Lucena. *Leyes para esclavos: El ordenamiento jurídico sobre la condicion, tratamiento, defensa y represión de los esclavos en las colonias de la America española*. 2000, 40. http://www.larramendi.es/catalogo_imagenes/grupo.cmd?path=1000202 Accessed: 15 January 2017.

812 Seijas, 139-142.

813 *Ibid*.

814 *Ibid*.

815 Carlos II. *Real Cedula al Virrey de Mexico Cometiendole Que Los Naturales Venidos de Filipinas, Liberados de la Esclavitud, tengan tierras o vivan en barrio separados de la capital. Madrid, 13 marzo 1676*. AGI, Mexico, 1071, lib. 24, flo. 433v.; Balmes 2:626.

816 Seijas, 229.

817 Carlos II. *Real Cedula Ordenando el Cumplimiento de la Cedula que Prohibe la Esclavitude de los Indios en Chile y Disponiendo el Traslado de los Liberados al Peru. Madrid, 12 junio 1679*. AGI, Chile, 167, lib. 6, flo. 30v.: Balmes 2:675-678, extractada en AHN, Codices, 686, flo. 248v. On the same day, another Real Cedula was issued applying the preceding cedula as a general law in all the *Indias*. Recopilacion Libro 6, tit. 2, ley 16.

818 CI. *Aviso sobre informe de liberación de esclavos en Filipinas. Buen Retiro 1 mayo 1686*. ES.41091.AGI/23.6.1076//FILIPINAS,331,L.8,F.60V-61R PARES

819 Pan, BR50:199.

820 Warren, James. *The Sulu Zone, 1768-1898: the dynamics of external trade, slavery, and ethnicity in the transformation of a Southeast Asian maritime state*. Singapore: NUS Press,2007, 208

821 *Ibid.*, 196.

822 *Ibid.*, 197.

823 Garcia Serrano, *op. cit.*

824 Benavides, Miguel OP. *Letter to Felipe III. Manila,16 December 1603*. Simancas: Eclesiastico; cartas y expedientes del arzobispo de Manila vistos en el Consejo; años de 1579 a 1679; est. 68, caj. 1, leg. 32; BR12:150; Bobadilla, Diego SJ. *Relation of the Filipinas Islands, 1640*. BR29:305.

825 Garcia Serrano, Miguel OSA. *Letter to Felipe IV, Manila, 25 July 1626*. BR22:86.

826 Ventura del Arco MSS (Ayer Library) Tomo ii, 401-419; BR36:264-265.

827 *Ibid*.

828 *Ibid*.

829 BR6:172; BR7:157.

830 Oripon (Olipon) is the equivalent Visayan term for Alipin. Scott's book, *Slavery in Spanish Philippines*, contains a fairly recent rendition of the history of Philippine slavery with fresh contemporary insights. Traditional accounts can be found in P. Fr. Juan de Plasencia OFM's *Customs of Tagalogs, Nagcarlan 21 October 1599* (BR7:173-185), and Antonio de Morga's *Events in the Filipinas Islands, Mexico 1609* (BR16:162-163).

831 Sande, Francisco de. *Letter to Felipe II. Manila 7 June 1576*. Simancas - Secular; Audiencia de Filipinas; Cartas y expedientes del gobernador de Filipinas, vistos en el consejo; años 1567 1 1599; esa. 67, caj. 6, leg. 6; 6 BR4:50. The manuscript circa 1590 called the Boxer Codex contains a colored illustration (folio 204) of a China man and lady with the label Sangley on top together with Hokkien characters *siong lay*.

832 Great numbers of Sangleys were either killed or deported during the sangley insurrections of 1603, 1639-40, 1662, 1686, and 1762-64.

833 See Pan's *Ordinances de buen gobierno*.

834 *Relation of the Voyage to Luzon June 1570*. BR 3:101; *Conquest of the Island of Luzon. Manila 20 April 1572*. BR 3:167-168

835 Salazar, Domingo de OP. *Letter to Felipe II regarding the Chinese and the Parian. Manila 24 June 1590*. BR7:223, 231-232, 237.

836 Seijas, 266.

837 *Ibid*.

838 *Ibid*.

Notes

[839] Urtado, Escover de *et al. Carta a su Magestad de la Audiencia de Manila respecto a la Cedula de 12 de junio 1679 relacionada con la esclavitud de los Indios. Manila, 22 de junio 1684.* AGI: Filipinas 67-6-24.

[840] Seijas, *op. cit.*

[841] Worcester, Dean C. *Slavery and peonage in the Philippine Islands.* Department of Interior, Government of the Philippine Islands. Manila: Bureau of Printing, 1913, 6, 14, 48,7, 51, 12, 5, 23, 20, 6,42, 16, 46, 16, 46. USIT

[842] *Ibid.,* 108-116.

[843] The Philippine Organic Act of 1902 was enacted by the US Congress on 1 July 1902 temporarily providing for a civil government of the Philippine Islands and for other purposes. It provided that "neither slavery nor involuntary servitude except as punishment of crime whereof the parties have been duly convicted shall exist in the said Islands." The Supreme Court of the Philippine Islands in the case of the US vs. Cabanag (Vol. VIII, p.64, Phil. Repts.), decided on 16 March 1907 that "there is no law applicable here either of the United States or of the Archipelago punishing slavery as a crime. In order to remedy this condition, the Philippine Commission in its exclusive legislative jurisdiction over all that part of the Philippine Islands inhabited by Moros or other non-Christian tribes (Mountain Province, Nueva Vizcaya and Agusan) passed Act No. 2071, and as a branch of the Philippine Legislature has in four successive sessions passed an act prohibiting and penalizing slavery, involuntary servitude, peonage, or the sale of human beings over the rest of the Archipelago. During each of the said sessions however, the Philippine Assembly failed to concur in the passage of such Act. The Philippine Legislative Assembly refused to recognize the existence of slavery in the Christian parts of the Archipelago for fear that to do so would project and reinforce the country's image of a largely primitive people being led by a few oligarchs, and therefor not ready for independence. - Worcester. The Philippine Legislature would finally amend the Penal Code after the Philippine Autonomy Act (Jones Law) was enacted and a promise of independence was within reach.

Chapter Twelve Endnotes

[844] Costa 1956, 130.

[845] *Ibid.*

[846] *Ibid.*

[847] Juxtaposed with Seijas' origin table of chino slaves (Seijas, 267), Bazaco's 1655 origin table of Letran students (Bazaco, 51-2) exhibited parallel similarities.

[848] Anonymous. *Papel, sin fecha, que una persona celosa del servicio de Dios, dio al señor presidente sobre diferentes puntos tocantes a Filipinas. Consejo, 7 de abril de 1677.* Among documents found with *Carta de Viga sobre seminario para indios 1680-6-20* ES.41091.AGI/23.6.10//FILIPINAS,24,R.1,N.5 PARES

[849] *Ibid.* It is more likely that the *sacerdotes* referred to were those ordained in the minor orders as practiced in Mexico in the early 16th century. This was perhaps resorted to by Bishop Juan Lopez OP in view of the dire lack of priests in his diocese.

Archbishop Juan Lopez Galvan OP - He was born in Martin-Muñoz de las Posadas, in the province of Segovia, diocese of Avila on 21 April 1613. Having taken the habit at San Esteban de Salamanca, he professed on 15 December 1634 at the age of 20. He was an intern of the San Gregorio de Valladolid when he volunteered for the Province of the Most Holy Rosary. He taught Philosophy and Theology and then became Master of Students and Regent of Studies in the College-University of Manila. Nominated as Procurator General in the Courts of Madrid and Rome, and General Chapter definitor, he was honored by the Order with the degree of Master in Sacred Theology, and by the King with the bishopry of Cebu. Receiving the bulls of the Holy Seat on 23 April 1663, he was consecrated in Mechoacan on 4 January 1665. On 31 August of the same year, he took possession of his church which he governed zealously and vigilantly until 21 August 1672 when he was transferred to Manila to head the archdiocese having just been nominated Prelate and Pastor. On 22 February 1674, he died in Manila at 61 years of age after receiving the Holy Sacraments. He was buried at the Santo Domingo Church. - Ocio 1895, 167-168.

[850] Archbishop P. Fr. Felipe Fernandez de Pardo OP - Born to noble parents in Valladolid on 7 February 1611, he took the habit in the Convent of San Pablo on 5 March 1626, and professed there on 7 March 1627. He expounded Philosophy in Santa Maria la Real de Trianos, and in his own covent after where he was also honored with the position of Master of Students. Arriving in the Philippines, he first learned Tagalog very well. He was later assigned to the Colegio de Santo Tomas where he was a Lector in Theology, Rector and Regent of Studies. He became Prior of the Santo Domingo Convent, Vicar Provincial of the Province, twice a Definitor, Provincial and Commissary of the Holy Office. Named Archbishop of Manila earlier, he was consecrated on 28 October 1681 to primarily attend to the reported improprieties in the cathedral chapter and his diocese. Being a controversial figure, passionate or ignorant writers bitterly criticized his keen interest to perform his pastoral office by exceeding the bounds of propriety. After defending ecclesiastical immunity at a cost of severe penalties, he died on 31 December 1689 at 78 years of age. His body was laid to rest in the presbytery of the Santo Domingo Church on the 5 January 1690. - Ocio 1895, 172-174.

[851] *Copia del real cedula de 22 de agosto de 1678 (sic por 1677) al arzobispo de Manila, encargando procurar que se den estudios a los indios mas inclinados para ello, haciendo entrar a algunos niños en los colegios seminarios que hubiere, y no habiéndolos procurar su fundación, disponiendo en el interim su entrada en los colegios de Santo Domingo y de la Compañía de Jesus, para promoverlos tras su instrucción al orden sacro.* Among documents found with *Carta de Viga sobre seminario para indios 1680-6-20* ES.41091.AGI/23.6.10//FILIPINAS, 24,R.1,N.5 PARES

[852] Ventura del Arco MSS. (Ayer library) iii, 9-10. BR45:182-183. At about the same time, a letter written by Diego Antonio de Viga, Fiscal of the Real Audiencia de Manila, opposed the Junta's position, justified and supported the establishment of a *colegio de indios* for 50 scholars in preparation for the Holy Orders with a supporting income of 3000 pesos under the supervision of the Audiencia. - Viga, Diego Antonio. *Carta sobre seminario para indios. 1680-6-20*. ES.41091.AGI/23.6.10//FILIPINAS,24,R.1,N.5 PARES; See Anderson, 82-84.

[853] Pardo, Felipe de OP. *Carta sobre becas para indios en Colegio de dominicos. San Gabriel 1687-6-15*. ES. 41091.AGI/23.6.426//FILIPINAS,86,N.59. PARES

[854] *Ibid.*

[855] *Ibid.* - Pardo's *colegio de indios* proposal was actually a small part of a more elaborate plan to elevate the Colegio de Santo Tomas from an academy to a public university of general studies. The plan consisted of establishing the Chairs of Canon Law, Civil Law and Medicine in Santo Tomas in order to be acknowledged as a university. As was admitted in his last will and testament of 5 August 1689, Pardo was the prime mover of securing the approvals of Pope Innocent XI and Carlos II for the three Chairs and the consequent university status. To be able to financially support the Chairs and the 6 scholars from Letran, he bequeathed 13,000 pesos for their financial support. Mindful that the amount was inadequate, he requested the King to grant Santo Tomas the encomienda of Tabuco with 2,000 tributes. In preparation for this eventuality, Pardo transferred the secular curacy of Tabuco to the charge of the Dominicans and Jesuits.

[856] Cummins, James S. *Archbishop Felipe Pardo's "Last Will"*. Anderson, Gerald H. ed. *Studies in Philippine Church History*. Ithaca and London: Cornell University Press, 1969, 105-112. The transcript of the complete document found in the article is taken from the copy written into the minutes of the MS "Libro de consejos de province ...1621..."(fols. 18v-19r) in the Archive of Santo Domingo Priory, Quezon City - Cummins.

[857] Ocio 1891, I:478.

[858] *Informe del fiscal del Consejo sobre los antecedentes*. Document found together with *Peticion del dominico Raimundo Berart sobre colegio para indios. Manila 1694-7-14*. ES.41091.AGI/23.6.426//FILIPINAS,86,N.76 PARES It was noted that the Province was hesitant to accept the responsibility of sustaining the proposed Professorial Chairs considering the uncertain nature of the bequest's income as experienced by the failed *obras pias* of the late Governor Manuel de Leon - Ocio 1891, I:478.

[859] *Copia autentica del escrito presentado por el rector del Colegio de Santo Tomas de Manila fray Jose Vila, dominico, con los instrumentos de la ultima voluntad del arzobispo fray Felipe Pardo para la fundación de unas cátedras de Canones, Leyes y Medicina en dicho Colegio; y legado de 13,000 pesos que dicho arzobispo dejo para la dotación de dichas cátedras. Manila, 5 julio de 1691*. Document found together with *Peticion del dominico Raimundo Berart sobre colegio para indios. Manila 1694-7-14*. ES.41091.AGI/23.6.426//FILIPINAS,86,N.76. PARES

[860] *Ibid.*

[861] *Ibid.*

[862] Cl. *Petición de informe sobre niños que ayudan en la Catedral. 1687-8-1*. ES.41091.AGI/23.6.1076//FILIPINAS.331,L.8.F.240R. PARES

[863] Bazaco 1933:68-71. Bazaco attributed the declaration to an incident regarding fraternities and confraternities struggling to gain a preferred position over the Letran collegians in a public function. The incident was the apparent cause. There were however other underlying reasons. In view of the recent awareness and anticipation of the upcoming developments of Pardo's bequest, the Religious and the Episcopal Authorities would appear to consider Letran students as deserving of certain ecclesiastic entitlements in public functions.

[864] P. Fr. Raimundo Berart OP - Born in the Villa of Figueras, province and diocese of Gerona, he was a Doctor of Canon and Civil Laws. At the age of 20, he was Regent of Canon Law at the University of Lerida when he obtained the habit of the Order at Santa Catalina Virgen y Martir in Barcelona. He professed there on 19 April 1671. Arriving in the Philippines, he learned Tagalog and became the minister of the *indios* at the Santo Domingo Convent and was assigned at the *Colegio de Santo Tomas*. He became Vice-Rector and shortly after Rector and Chancellor of the *Universidad de Santo Tomas* in 1686 and 1688. Causing negative reactions, his appointment as personal arbitration advisor of Archbishop Pardo earned him the license to appear in Madrid, where he was summoned by virtue of a Real Cedula of His Majesty addressed effectively to the Governor of the Islands. In the Provincial Chapter of 1696, he was nominated Definitor to General Chapter and served many years after as Procurator of Madrid. He died in the Convent of Atocha on 13 April 1713. - Ocio 1895: 243-244.

[865] Cl. *Confirmacion de encomienda de Sangasang, etc. 1690-5-18*. ES.41091.AGI/23.6.477//FILIPINAS,56,N.5 PARES.; Cl. *Petition del dominico Alonso Sandin sobre devolver curato de Tabuco a dominicos y jesuitas. 1696-8-22*. ES.41091.AGI/23.6.426//FILIPINAS,86,N.81 PARES. The curacy of Tabuco was assigned by Pardo to the Dominicans and Jesuits, but he died before the transfer was approved. The *Cabildo Eclesiatico* expelled the religious and reinstituted the secular benefice. The Dominicans countered that the curacy had remained vacant and the Pardo alternative was the viable option to administer the souls of the locality. The Dominicans lost the appeal. The Tabuco encomienda encompassed the present day Cabuyao, and the areas known today as Calamba, Biñan and Santa Rosa.

[866] Santiago, Luciano P.R. *The Hidden Light: The First Filipino Priests*. Quezon City: Luciano P.R. Santiago and New Day Publishers, 1987, 81.

Notes

867 On 26 July 1730, a Real Cedula was issued suspending the grant of Chairs to Colegio de San Ignacio by the Manila Audiencia as protested by the Colegio-Universidad de Santo Tomas. Three years later, Real Cedula dated 23 October 1733 granted each one of San Ignacio and Santo Tomas a chair in Canon Law and a chair in Civil Law. Later that year, Dominican Procurator General Salvador de Contreras OP petitioned that Santo Tomas be erected into a general university requesting permission to secure an extension of the bull Issued by Innocent XI authorizing Santo Tomas to grant degrees in various faculties. A brief from Pope Clement XII dated 11 September 1734 attesting that the bull of extension had been dispatched. (ES.41091.AGI/23.6.330//FILIPINAS,333,L.13,F.63V-67V; AGI/23.6.551//FILIPINAS,342,L.10,F.6R-10R; AGI/23.6.538//FILIPINAS,297,N.124 PARES)

868 Santiago 1987, 34, 74-76. The determination of non-Spanish recipients of university degrees or the Holy Orders is hampered in most cases by the use of Spanish names and surnames. Only when an indigenous or Chinese surname were found in the baptismal or other personal records could the person concerned be verifiably ascertained as non-spanish *naturales*. Considering these constraints, Francisco Baluyot was identified as the first *indio* cleric and Joseph de Ocampo as the first *mestizo sangley* cleric. Baluyot's educational background was not however determined.

869 *Ibid*.

870 PIHO, Virve. *La Secularizacion de la Parroquias y la Economia Ecclesiastica en la Nueva España*. Journal de la Societe des americanices, Vol. 64 (1977), pp. 81-88. JSTOR, JSTOR, www.jstor.org/stable/24603894.

871 Recopilacion. Bk. 1 Tit. 15 Laws 5, 6, and 8.

872 PIHO, 84.

873 *Ibid*.

874 Anderson, 44-64.

875 *Visita* is an inspection trip and investigation of a province or an audiencia district conducted by a high official whose primary purpose was to root out abuses or to initiate reforms. - Phelan 1959.

876 Don Diego Camacho y Avila was born to Dr. Miguel Sanchez Sevillano and Maria Vaca y Avila in the city of Badajos, Extremadura on 12 November 1652. The second of three children, he studied his first letters under a family cleric and consequently entered the *Seminario de San Anton* for his initial ecclesiastical studies. He obtained a *beca* from the *Colegio Mayor de Cuenca de la Universidad de Salamanca* where he studied the arts and theology between 1679-1682 and earned the title of Doctor. He became a professor of philosophy and theology at the Salamanca University. He returned to Badajoz and was elected magistral canon of its cathedral in 1683. On 19 April 1694, he was nominated to the vacant seat of the Archdiocese of Manila which he accepted on 14 May of the same year. Pope Innocent XI approved his appointment on 29 September 1695. Camacho was consecrated Archbishop of Manila on 19 August 1696 by Bishop Manuel Fernandez de Santa Cruz y Sahagun in the cathedral of Puebla de los Angeles. He arrived in Manila and took possession of his seat on 15 September 1697.

Many controversies transpired during his term as Archbishop of Manila. The four major ones included the visitation of the hospitals; the visitation of the parishes of regular curates; the *composicion* of the friar estates and the collection of the *diezmos*. The visitation of the hospitals was resolved with the surrender of the hospital records to representatives of the *vice patron* while the ecclesiastical matters were held in abeyance until the parish visitation issue was resolved. The visitation of the parishes was decided in favor of the ordinary by the Brief of Clement XI, but its implementation was suspended by Camacho's successor, Archbishop Francisco de la Cuesta. The *composicion* was settled extrajudicially in the friar's favor while the collection of the *diezmo* on the friar estates was enforced to benefit the King and the archdiocese.

Camacho's significant accomplishments included the ordination of the first non-spanish secular priests and the foundation of the first conciliar seminary in the Philippines. His papal appointment as Bishop of Guadalajara was signed on 4 January 1704. The *Real Colegio Seminario de San Clemente,* which he founded, violated the King's prerogatives under the *Patronato Real* and was ordered demolished and rebuilt under the patronage of *San Felipe*. Camacho died on 19 October 1712 in Guadalajara amidst the reprimand and investigations conducted in this regard. - Merino.

877 Santiago 1987, 34. There are no records to ascertain the educational background of Baluyut.

878 The narrative on the first non-Spanish priests of UST was based entirely on Santiago's book.

879 Santiago researched the Archives of the Archdiocese of Manila extensively. Schumacher (2003:48) questioned the reliability of the source: UST Alumni Association Inc. University of Santo Tomas Alumni Directory 1611-1971. University of Santo Tomas. Manila: 1972. The information contained therein were culled from the records of the university and prepared by respected historian P. Fr. Fidel Villaroel OP. The UST Alumni Association Inc. merely published the information. According to Santiago, an additional list was prepared by Villaroel and had not been included in any published material as of that date. - Santiago 1984, 269.

880 The native clerics were addressed by the highest degree they completed: Maestro Don, Mro. or M.D.; Bachiller Don, Br. or B.D. and so on.

881 Santiago 1987, 74-76.

882 *Ibid.*, 80-81.

883 *Ibid.*, 87-89.

884 *Ibid.*, 73-145.

885 San Antonio, 206; English translation BR28:140

Notes

886 Razón individual de la clerecía del arzobispado de Manila con distinción de personas, empleo, congrua, idioma, edad y raza o nación. Manila, 4 de julio de 1760. Gran formato: 410x310mm. Fols. 553r-553v. *1748 - Expediente sobre provisión y visita de doctrinas.* ES.41091.AGI/23.6.388//FILIPINAS,303,N.5 PARES

887 Testimonio de la lista original que contiene los clérigos del obispado de Nueva Segovia. Manila, 14 de julio de 1760. Fols. 527r-529v. ES.41091.AGI/23.6.388//FILIPINAS,303,N.5 PARES

888 Cl. *Carta de Miguel de Ezpeleta, obispo de Cebú, gobernador de Filipinas, informando del estado de los curatos seculares y regulares de su obispado, párrocos que las administran, número de personas de cada curato y destrozos de los enemigos moros, en respuesta a la carta de 24 de diciembre de 1756 de Manuel Quintano Bonifaz, obispo de Farsalia. Manila, 5 de julio de 1761.* Fols. 631r-642v. *1748 - Expediente sobre provisión y visita de doctrinas.* ES.41091.AGI/23.6.388//FILIPINAS,303,N.5 PARES

889 Cl. *Carta de Isidoro [de Arévalo], obispo de Nueva Cáceres, informando sobre la administración espiritual del obispado a cargo principalmente de regulares y el modo de poner en orden aquellas provincias. Nueva Cáceres, 2 de junio de 1751.* Fols. 64r-72v. *1748 - Expediente sobre provisión y visita de doctrinas.* ES.41091.AGI/23.6.388//FILIPINAS,303,N.5 PARES

890 Coronel, Hernando. *Boatmen for Christ: The Early Filipino Priests.* Philippines: Reyes Publishing Inc for Catholic Book Center, 1998, 101-102.

891 Cl. *Orden sobre sobre fundación de un Seminario en Manila.* Madrid, 1702-4-28. ES.41091.AGI/23.61059/FILIPINAS,332,L.10,F.213V-215V PARES

892 Cl. *Carta de Diego Camacho y Ávila, arzobispo de Manila, sobre no poderse erigir el seminario por falta de medios y que el gobernador no le ha dado copia de los autos.* Manila, 20 de junio de 1704. ES.41091.AGI/23.6.813//FILIPINAS,308,N.4 PARES

893 Cl. *Carta de Domingo de Zabalburu, gobernador de Filipinas, dando cuenta de la falta de medios que hay para la fundación del seminario de que remite testimonio que no está.* Manila, 22 de junio de 1704. ES.41091.AGI/23.6.813//FILIPINAS,308,N.4 PARES

894 The narrative on the first conciliar seminary was based principally on the documents contained in Cl. *Expediente sobre fundación de seminario en Manila. 1707/1708.* ES.41091.AGI/23.6.813//FILIPINAS,308,N.4 PARES

895 Coronel, 48-49.

896 Cl. *Carta de Domingo de Zabalburu sobre haberse iniciado la fábrica del seminario gracias a las limosnas conseguidas por el Abad [Sidoti], erigido conforme a los estatutos que dejó el arzobispo antes de pasar a la sede de Guadalajara remitiendo testimonio para que se vean.* Manila, 22 de junio de 1707. *1707 / 1708 Expediente sobre fundación de seminario en Manila.* ES.41091.AGI/23.6.813//FILIPINAS,308,N.4 PARES

897 Breve de Clemente XI al rey Felipe V, exhortándole a la fundación de un Seminario en la ciudad de Manila, para cuyo fin había instado al cardenal Turnon, patriarca de Antioquía, de acuerdo con el arzobispo de aquella ciudad Diego Camacho y Avila. Roma, 15 de octubre de 1707. En MP-BULAS_BREVES,543.*1707 / 1708 Expediente sobre fundación de seminario en Manila.* ES.41091.AGI/23.6.813//FILIPINAS,308,N.4 PARES

898 Cl. *Real decreto al duque de Atrisco para que el Consejo expida las órdenes convenientes de represión al gobernador, Audiencia y obispo de Guadalajara por lo ejecutado respecto al seminario y de revocación de lo que han establecido.* Buen Retiro, 15 agosto 1708. Expediente sobre fundación de seminario en Manila. *1707 / 1708 Expediente sobre fundación de seminario en Manila.* ES.41091.AGI/23.6.813//FILIPINAS,308,N.4 PARES

899 Loughlin, James. *Pope Clement XI.* The Catholic Encyclopedia. Vol. 4. New York: Robert Appleton Company, 1908. www.newadvent.org/cathen/04029a.htm Accessed on: 19 May 2017. The Pope acknowledged Felipe V as king of Spain in 1701. His change of heart caused considerable strain on his relationship with the Spanish church.

900 Cl. *Orden al gobernador Ursúa sobre Seminario de Manila.* Madrid 3 marzo 1710. ES.41091.AGI/23.6.1059//FILIPINAS,332,L.11,F.281V-289R PARES

901 Cl. *Orden de reprender al obispo Camacho por tolerar a Tournon.* Madrid 2 mayo 1710. ES.41091.AGI/23.6.1059//FILIPINAS,332,L.11,F.334V-341R PARES

902 Cl. *Orden sobre asignación del arzobispo de Manila.* Madrid 2 mayo 1710. ES.41091.AGI/23.6.1059//FILIPINAS,332,L.11,F.341V-343R PARES

903 Cl. *Orden de vigilar e investigar a los obispos de Nueva España.* Madrid 2 mayo 1710. ES.41091.AGI/23.6.1059//FILIPINAS,332,L.11,F.348V-351V PARES

904 Cl. *Real Cedula en que se dan las gracias al arzobispo de Manila, por la aplicación y celo que ha manifestado en la erección, planta y régimen del seminario nuevamente fundado en la ciudad de Manila, mandándose que se quite el nombre de San Clemente y se ponga en su lugar el de San Felipe.* Madrid 31 diciembre 1712. ES.41091.AGI/23.6.827//FILIPINAS,290,N.80 PARES

905 Coronel: 59-60.

906 San Antonio,19; BR28:121

907 *Ibid.* BR28:122-123.

908 Cl. *Orden de suspender la fundación de Universidad en Manila.* Cazalla 1730-7-26. ES.41091.AGI/23.6.330//FILIPINAS,333,L.13,F.63V-67V PARES

909 Cl. *Orden de poner ciertas cátedras en Colegios de Manila.* El Escorial 1733-10-23. ES.41091.AGI/23.6.551//FILIPINAS,342,L.10,F.6R-10R PARES

910 Cl. *Petición del dominico Salvador de Contreras de que el Colegio de Santo Tomás se erija en Universidad.* Probable 1733-12-22. ES.41091.AGI/23.6.538//FILIPINAS,297,N.124 PARES

Notes

911 Ferrando, 4:364. The chairs granted to both the Dominican and Jesuit universities were closely monitored by the *Audiencia* and reported regularly in compliance with the Real Cedula dated 26 July 1734. After the Jesuits were expelled in 1768, only the chairs at Santo Tomas were faithfully reported with the last one rendered on 21 June 1795.

912 *Carta de Basilio Sancho de Santa Justa y Santa Rufina, Arzobispo de Filipinas.* Manila 1 January 1770. Archivo Historico Nacional, Madrid A.18-26-8; BR45:123-124.

913 Montero y Vidal, 2:187-216. A native of Navarra, Field Marshall Jose Raon arrived in Manila on 6 July 1765 with his term ending in July 1770. His term of office was marked by the revision of Arrandia's ordinances, conflicts with the regular clergy, the 1768 expulsion of the jesuits and his collusion with them, and the 1769 expulsion of the sangleys. He died on 4 January 1773 while in *residencia*. - BR17:298.

914 Santa Justa. *op. cit.*

915 *Ibid.*

916 Calderon, Felipe. *Colegio de San Jose,* appendix, document no. 3, pp. ix-xiii; Nozaleda OP. *Colegio de San Jose,* appendix, document no. 3, pp. xv-xix; BR45:125-130. USIT

917 Cl. *Agregacion del Colegio de San Ignacio al Seminario Conciliar.* Aranjuez, 3 June 1783. ES.41091.AGI/23.6.124//FILIPINAS,337,L20,F.181V-182V PARES

918 Cl. *Orden de agregar Colegio de jesuitas de Manila al Seminario.* Pardo, 12 Marzo 1784, ES.41091.AGI/23.6.1234//FILIPINAS,337,L20,F218R-221R. PARES

919 Cl. *Carta sobre viaje del arzobispo de Manila a Filipinas. Madrid 1697-5-13.* - ES.41091.AGI/23.6.1059//FILIPINAS,332,L.10,F.8R-8V PARES

920 Camacho uncovered and exposed the pact three years later in his letter dated 28 June 1702 containing a copy of the seditious document. A copy of the letter and pact can be found among the documents in Cl. *Expediente sobre visita de las doctrinas por los ordinarios 1699/1710.* ES.41091.AGI/23.6.387//FILIPINAS,302,N.1 PARES. This book's narrative of the visita controversy is based on the preceding *Expediente* together with Cl. *Expediente sobre provisión y visita de doctrinas 1748.* ES.41091.AGI/23.6.388//FILIPINAS,303,N.5 PARES

921 Cl. *Orden de no impedir viaje a Guadalajara al arzobispo Camacho. Madrid 1703-10-26.* ES.41091.AGI/23.6.976//FILIPINAS,341,L.8,F.191R-191V PARES

922 Cl. *Traducción al castellano del breve de Clemente XI de 30 de enero de 1705. Madrid, 23 de abril de 1705. Fols. 610R-612V. 1699 / 1710 - Expediente sobre visita de las doctrinas por los ordinarios.* ES.41091.AGI/23.6.387//FILIPINAS,302,N.1 PARES

923 Cl. *Consulta del Consejo de Indias acerca de la suspensión del breve sobre la visita de las doctrinas por los ordinarios. Madrid, 6 febrero 1711. Fols. 21r-59v Expediente sobre provisión y visita de doctrinas 1748.* ES.41091.AGI/23.6.388//FILIPINAS,303,N.5 PARES

924 Cl. *Real decreto al conde de Frigiliana sobre los religiosos doctrineros de Filipinas. Almenar, 21 de octubre de 1711. Fols. 60r-63v 1748 - Expediente sobre provisión y visita de doctrinas.* ES.41091.AGI/23.6.388//FILIPINAS,303,N.5 PARES

The suspension of the Papal Brief only applied within the jurisdiction of the *Patronato Real*. The missions of the 5 religious provinces outside *Filipinas* were subject to the Brief.

925 A good account of the problems entailed in enforcing *visitas* are contained in Cl. *Rojo, Manuel Antonio. Carta de arzobispo de Manila sobre las dificultades que hacen inexigibles la cédula de 20 de septiembre de 1757 como consta en los autos que remite, y la de 14 de febrero de 1703. Manila, 5 de julio de 1760. Fols. 98r-115v. Con duplicado. Fols. 116r-123v.* - *Expediente sobre provisión y visita de doctrinas.* ES.41091.AGI/23.6.388//FILIPINAS,303,N.5 PARES

926 AGNM, Reales Cedulas Originales vol 69 exp. 103 ff.1-11v

927 AGNM, Reales Cedulas Originales vol 73 exp. 13 ff. 35-38v

928 AGNM, Reales Cedulas Originales vol 77.

929 The impact of Fernando VI's secularization decrees on the Archdiocese of Mexico is discussed in María Teresa Álvarez Icaza Longoria's *La reorganización del territorio parroquial de la arquidiócesis de México durante la prelacía de Manuel Rubio y Salinas (1749-1765).* Hispania Sacra Vol 63, No 128 (2011) pp. 501-518. Instituto de Historia, Consejo Superior de Investigaciones Cientificas.

930 Cl. *Carta del Cabildo eclesiástico de Manila: sobre el número de doctrinas de regulares que podrían agregarse al clero. Manila, 27 de julio de 1757. Fols. 73r-76v - Expediente sobre provisión y visita de doctrinas.* ES.41091.AGI/23.6.388//FILIPINAS,303,N.5 PARES

931 Cl. *Carta de Manuel Antonio Rojo, arzobispo de Manila, sobre las dificultades que hacen inexigibles la cédula de 20 de setiembre de 1757 como consta en los autos que remite, y la de 14 de febrero de 1703. Manila, 5 de julio de 1760. Fols. 98r-115v. Con duplicado. Fols. 116r-123v.* - *Expediente sobre provisión y visita de doctrinas.* ES.41091.AGI/23.6.388//FILIPINAS,303,N.5 PARES

932 Cl. *Razón individual de la clerecía del arzobispado de Manila con distinción de personas, empleo, congrua, idioma, edad y raza o nación. Manila, 4 de julio de 1760. Fols. 201r-206v. Con duplicado. Fols. 207r-212r. Gran formato: 400x310 - Expediente sobre provisión y visita de doctrinas.* ES.41091.AGI/23.6.388//FILIPINAS,303,N.5 PARES

Notes

⁹³³ Ferrando 5:37,79. Dominican Master General Juan Tomas de Boxadors did not tolerate any transgression of his edicts. Three Dominicans were recalled to Spain for supporting a Jesuit's homily delivered on 9 and 10 of March 1764 attacking certain government officials for corruption. Known as the Francisco Javier Puch SJ affair, PP. Fr. Joaquin del Rosario OP, Cristobal Ausina OP and Santiago de la Portilla OP were subjected to disciplinary action with del Rosario removed as provincial before the expiry of his term. The measure was viewed as an overreaction on Boxadors' part considering that the province was the only religious institute that cooperated fully with the Archbishop and the Governor General.

⁹³⁴ The first order to yield was actually the Hospitaller Order of the Brothers of Saint John of God during the hospital visitations conducted by Abp. Diego Camacho y Avila. The other orders did not consider this as a serious breach as the hospitallers were not curates.

⁹³⁵ Don Basilio Sancho de Santa Justa y Rufina was born on 17 September 1728 in Villanueva del Rebollar, Teruel. He was baptized with the name of Tomas which was changed to Basilio when he entered the *Escuelas Pias*. He completed his primary education in his birth town and was sent to Zaragoza to continue his studies in latin grammar and rhetorics. He was vested with the Piarist habit on 15 December 1743 and professed on 18 February 1745 at the Colegio de Peralta de la Sal. He was sent to Daroca to study philosophy and upon completion proceeded to Zaragoza to complete theology and be ordained a priest. He taught philosophy and rhetorics in Daroca and theology in Valencia. He became provincial secretary of the Order, his first official duty. He rapidly ascended the Order's hierarchy becoming the Procurator General of the Province of Aragon in the King's court in 1762. On 25 February 1764, he was appointed royal preacher, and within the same week, theologian and censor of the Holy Office, and adviser of the *infante* Felipe Duke of Parma and brother of the King. He became an adviser of Carlos III and the Count of Campomanes on delicate matters. In December 1765, Carlos III proposed his appointment as archbishop of Manila and Pope Clement XIII recommended it on 14 April 1766. He was consecrated on 18 August 1776 at the *Iglesia de la Merced de Madrid* by the Archbishop of Toledo, Cardinal Don Luis de Cordova, with the Count of Aranda assisting. He took possession of his seat on 23 July 1767. His significant achievements included the enforcement of the episcopal visitation and royal patronage, reopening of the conciliar seminary which had ceased to operate since the British invasion, the secularizations of the Dominican, Jesuit and Augustinian parishes in the Archdiocese of Manila, standardization of church fees and the celebration of the First Council of Manila. He was promoted as Archbishop of Granada on 17 December 1787 but died five days earlier on 12 December 1787 in Manila. - Manchado.

⁹³⁶ Ferrando 5:141.

⁹³⁷ Manchado Lopez, Marta M. *Conflictos Iglesia-Estado en el Extremo Oriente Ibérico Filipinas (1767-1787)*, Murcia: Universidad, Secretariado de Publicaciones, 1994, 36.

⁹³⁸ *Ibid.*, 89-103.

⁹³⁹ Escoto, Salvador P. *The Ecclesiastical Controversy of 1767-1776: A Catalyst of Philippine Nationalism*. Journal of Asian History, Vol. 10, No. 2 (1976) pp. 97-133. JSTOR, JSTOR, www.jstor.org/stable/41930217

⁹⁴⁰ Ferrando 5:43.

⁹⁴¹ Simon de Anda y Salazar was born on 28 October 1701 in Subija. Having served as an *oidor*, he was appointed by the Real Audiencia as lieutenant of the governor and captain-general. During the Seven Year War British invasion of Manila, he left Manila on 4 October 1762 to establish the capital in Bacolor, Pampanga, and proclaimed himself *ad interim* governor. The imprisoned Manila Archbishop Manuel Rojo ceded the archipelago to the British who maintained him as governor until his death on 30 January 1764. Between 1762 and 1764, Anda had to deal with the insurrections of the *indios* and *sangleys* in the provinces. At the end of the Seven Year War, negotiations started in 1763 with the British surrendering Manila to Anda in April 1764. He was replaced by the new governor, Francisco Javier de la Torre; returning to Spain where he was well received and made a councillor of Castilla. He directed a letter to the King dated 12 April 1768 complaining of certain disorders in the Philippines; highlighting a number against friars. He returned to Manila as governor in July 1770 and proceeded against his predecessor, Juan Raon, among others; roused opposition of the regulars; reformed the army, and engaged in other public works. During his term, troubles with Moros continued. He opposed the King's order of 9 November 1774 to secularize curacies held by regulars, which led to its repeal on 11 December 1776. His rule was characterized by his energy, foresight, honesty, and conflicts with the regulars. He died on 30 October 1776, at seventy-six years of age. - BR17:297-298,

⁹⁴² Anda charged the Augustinians with seditious activities using as evidence a copy of the Concordat General found among the documents left by the Jesuits. - Escoto:106.

⁹⁴³ *Ibid.*, 82.

⁹⁴⁴ *Ibid.*, 129.

⁹⁴⁵ All other aspects of the complex issues are discussed in Escoto 1976.

⁹⁴⁶ Cl. *Orden de secularizar doctrinas de Filipinas. El Escorial 1774-11-9.* ES.41091.AGI/23.6.331//FILIPINAS, 336,L.18,F.410R-411V. PARES

⁹⁴⁷ Cl. *Anulacion de concordia celebrada en 1697 entre los Ordenes. El Escorial 1774-11-9.* ES.41091.AGI/23.6.331//FILIPINAS,336,L.18,F.413-416R. PARES

⁹⁴⁸ Ferrando 5:293.

Notes

⁹⁴⁹ During the British blockade, the Santo Domingo Convent, Colegio de Santo Tomas and San Juan de Letran became hostels, lodgings and houses of refuge where food was available for all the *vecinos* of Manila and, at the cost of the Dominican province, all necessities were provided to all kinds of people whether poor or rich, military or civilian as was publicly and evidently known throughout the city. Troops consisting of *Indios* from Batanes, 1500 from Pangasinan and 200 students and colegiales from Santo Tomas were maintained, clothed and housed by the Province. After the city capitulated, the war against the British and their sangley and indio supporters continued in the provinces. The Dominican Province provided funds, all the harvested grain and cattle of its estates, and the use of its galleys to Simon de Anda's troops while suffering and containing the insurrections in Cagayan and Pangasinan. - Ferrando 4:698-701.

⁹⁵⁰ BR49:147-149.

⁹⁵¹ Ferrando 4:696.

⁹⁵² Bazaco 1933, 231.

⁹⁵³ All information regarding degrees conferred by UST were sourced from UST Alumni Association (USTAA), *UST Graduate Listing 1611-1971*. Manila: UST, 1972; and *1775-1794 Supplement* (typewritten copy courtesy of Fr. Fidel Villaroel OP) as cited in Santiago, Luciano P.R. *The First Filipino Doctors of Ecclesiastical Sciences (1772-1796)* Philippine Quarterly of Culture and Society, Vol. 12 No. 4 (December 1984) ,pp. 257-270 JSTOR, JSTOR, www.jstor.org/stable/29791835.

⁹⁵⁴ Cl. *Aviso y orden sobre conflicto en la Universidad de Manila. Madrid 7 diciembre 1781.* ES.41091.AGI/ 23.6.124//FILIPINAS,337,L.20,F.94R-106V PARES

⁹⁵⁵ Cl. *Aviso y orden sobre conflicto en la Universidad de Manila. Madrid 7 diciembre 1781.* ES.41091.AGI/ 23.6.124//FILIPINAS,337,L.20,F.94R-106V; *Respuestas sobre conflicto en la Universidad de Manila. Madrid 7 diciembre 1781.* ES.41091.AGI/23.6.124//FILIPINAS,337,L.20,F.107R-119R. PARES

⁹⁵⁶ Schumacher 1981, 276; Santiago 1984, 261.

⁹⁵⁷ Ocio y Viana 1895. *Apendice,* 16, 25.

⁹⁵⁸ P. Fr. Domingo Canuto Caulas OP in 1816, P. Fr. Domingo del Rosario OP (Balbino Lozano) in 1841 and P. Fr. Jose de Santa Teresa (Santiago de Victoria) in 1846. - Ocio y Viana 1895.

⁹⁵⁹ Cl. *Orden sobre la secularización de curatos y doctrinas. Madrid,11 diciembre 1776.* ES.41091.AGI/23.6.124// FILIPINAS,337,L.19,F.148R-153V.PARES

⁹⁶⁰ Manchado, 216-218.

⁹⁶¹ *Ibid.*

⁹⁶² *Anda to the King, 3 January 1776,* AGI Ultramar leg. 691 as cited by Escoto, 122.

⁹⁶³ Escoto, 121-124

⁹⁶⁴ Gaspar de San Agustin OSA was born in Corte de Madrid on 5 July 1650. At the age of 17, he professed in the *convento de San Felipe el Real.* He had a gift for languages, fine arts, philosophy, history with a superior intelligence, prodigious memory and privileged ingenuity that distinguished him in everything. He had such a tremendous energy not only to devote in the study of his chosen fields but also to administer the towns of Leyte, and assume the duties of *Procurador General* (1680-1686), *Secretario de Provincia* (1686-1689), *prior de Lipa* (1689), Parañaque (1693,1708,1719), Pasig (1695,1716), Malate (1698,1710), Tondo (1699,1706,1710), Tambobong (1702,1707,1711) *Definidor Provincial* (1689,1710), *Visitador Provincial* and *Comisario del Santo Oficio (*1704). The catalog of his 18 written works attest to his scholarly merits. Among his noted works included *Conquista de Filipinas* and *Compendia de la Arte de la lengua tagala,* After a long and difficult illness spent in isolation, he died in the *convento de San Pablo o*n 8 August 1724. - *Institutum Historicum Augustinianum*; Elviro Perez OSA,133-136.

Juan Jose Delgado SJ was born in Cadiz on 23 June 1697. He entered the Society of Jesus on 15 May 1714. Departing from Spain for the Philippines in 1718, he was assigned in Samar where he assumed various responsibilities with *Superior de la Residencia de Palapag* among them. He was an *operario* of Taytay and Antipolo, and lived many years in Cebu. He became the minister of the *doctrinas* in Palompon and Poro, Rector of Guiguan, Rector and Superior of Carigara in Leyte. He spent some time in the missions of Inabangan and Talibon in Bohol. He had traveled extensively throughout the archipelago collecting immense and exceptional information and knowledge about it. He began writing his monumental work, *Historia General Sacro-profana, Politica y Natural de las Islas del Poniente, llamadas Filipinas,* in Guinguan in 1751 and completed it in between his busy schedule as Rector and Superior three years later. He died in Carigara, Leyte on 24 March 1755. A copy of his manuscript was found in the archives of Loyola and was published for the first time by the *Biblioteca Historica Filipina* in 1892. - *Historia General* prologo: ix-xiv; Costa 1961, 611.

⁹⁶⁵ Mas, 1:63-132. BR40:183-279. The letter must had been widely circulated and commonplace for Mas to reproduce the letter 118 years later. Mas equally prejudiced commentary further exacerbated the letter's contents.

⁹⁶⁶ Mas 3:33-34 (*Politica Interior).* English translation by Horatio de la Costa SJ - Anderson:86,88. Mas described the letter as dated 8 June 1725 and was sourced more likely from the Navarro copy of the manuscript. The actual date is 8 June 1720. - BR40:279. Santiago introduced a fresh context to this letter when he referred to Abp. Francisco de la Cuesta's definitive and consistent policy of appointing native priests as full-fledged pastors of parishes in the archdiocese. In a pivotal document dated 29 May 1721, Cuesta announced the roll of nominees for the vacant curacy of Rosario, Batangas. A native secular priest, BD Agustin Baluyot, was consequently chosen over Spanish candidates to replace the curate of what had been an Augustinian parish. It was Gaspar de San Agustin's dreaded event that had come to pass. Santiago 1987, 63-67.

967 Delgado, Juan Jose SJ. *Historia general, sacroprofana, politica y religiosa de las islas del Poniente llamadas Filipinas 1751*. Manila: Biblioteca Historica de Filipinas, 1892, 300-302 Internet Archive - archive.org; BR40:291-295. Never published by the Jesuit Philippine Province, Delgado's superiors could have suppressed his work in view of the *1697 General de Concordia*. His work remained unpublished for over 140 years.

968 *Ibid.*, 38-39: BR40:283-285. Delgado quotes P. Pedro Murillo Velarde SJ: *There is no fixed rule by which to construe the Indians; for each one needs a new syntax, all being anomalous.*

969 *Ibid.*, 303-322.

970 *Ibid.*, 293-94 English translation by James Alexander Robertson BR40:278-279

971 *Ibid.*, 299; BR40:289

972 Pardo de Tavera, T. H.*Una memoria de Anda y Salazar 1768*. Manila: Imprenta La Democracia, 1899; BR50:139-140. English translation by Horacio de la Costa - Andersen, 93.

973 Buzeta, 2: 279. English translation by Horatio de la Costa - Andersen, 95.

974 Escoto, 133. See footnote.

975 Larkin, John. *The Pampangans*. Berkley:University of California Press, 1972, 59.

976 Escoto,124-130.

977 Manchado, 225.

Chapter Thirteen Endnotes

978 Rizal, Jose. *El Filibusterismo (Continuacion de Noli me tangere) Novela Filipina*. Gent: Boekdrukkerij F. Meyer-Van Loo, 1891. English version by Derbyshire, Charles. *The Reign of Greed*. Manila: Philippine Education Company, 1912. Project Gutenburg

979 Duby, Georges.*The Three Orders: Feudal Society Imagined. Part 1*. Chicago: University of Chicago Press, 1981.

980 *Ancien régime*. Britannica Library, Encyclopædia Britannica, 21 Feb. 2009. library.eb.com.au.rp.nla.gov.au/levels/adults/article/ancien-r%C3%A9gime/471746. Accessed 26 February 2017

981 Maddicott, John. The Origins of the English Parliament, 924-1327. Oxford: Oxford University Press; 2010.

982 *Liberalism. Britannica Library*, Encyclopædia Britannica, 15 Jul. 2017. library.eb.com.au.rp.nla.gov.au/levels/adults/article/liberalism/117288. Accessed 16 July 2017.

983 Hobbes, Thomas. *Leviathan: reprinted from the edition of 1651*. Oxford: Oxford University Press, 1929.

984 Locke, John. *Two Treatises of Civil Government (1689, 1764). The Enhanced Edition* Online Library of Liberty. http://oll.libertyfund.org/pages/john-locke-two-treatises-1689 Accessed on 16 July 2017.

985 Hinnebusch, William A. OP. *The Dominicans: A Short History*. New York: Alba House, 1975, 151-163.

986 *Ibid*.

987 Miranda, Salvador. *Braschi, Giovanni Angelo (1717-1799). The Cardinals of the Holy Roman Church*. Florida International University Libraries. http://www2.fiu.edu/~mirandas/bios1773-iii.htm Accessed on 21 July 2017, 12:34.

988 Payne, 2:418.

989 Fernández Sarasola, Ignacio. *La Constitución de Bayona (1808)*. Spain: Portal Derecho, S.A. (IUSTEL), 2012.

990 Antequera, 163.

991 Lynch, John, ed. *The Spanish American revolutions, 1808-1826: Old and New World origins*. Norman: University of Oklahoma Press, 1994.

992 Payne, 2:428-429.

993 España. *The Political Constitution of the Spanish Monarchy: Promulgated in Cádiz, the nineteenth day of March [1812]*. Alicante: Biblioteca Virtual Miguel de Cervantes, 2003. http://www.cervantesvirtual.com/servlet/SirveObras/c1812/12159396448091522976624/index.htm Accessed on 23 July 2017.

994 *Ibid*.

995 *Ibid*.

996 Payne, *op. clt*.

997 Rivera, Faviola. *Liberalism in Latin America*. The Stanford Encyclopedia of Philosophy (Spring 2016 Edition), Edward N. Zalta (ed.), https://plato.stanford.edu/archives/spr2016/entries/liberalism-latin-america/ Accessed on 23 July 2017.

998 *Ibid*.

999 Hinnebusch, 153.

1000 *Ibid*.

1001 *Ibid*.

1002 The Spanish concept of *coup d'etat* involved a pronouncement of a small group of disgruntled military officers in the hope of soliciting and inciting a broader base of support. If the *pronunciamiento* evokes popular support, the handover of sovereign authority is assured. Otherwise, it becomes an unsuccessful petty revolt destined for oblivion.

1003 Payne, 2:436-437.

1004 *Ibid.*

1005 Ferrando, 5:386-388.

1006 Heinbusch, 152-153.

1007 Montero y Vidal, 2:408.

1008 *Ibid.*, 422-427.

1009 Mas, 1:58-64.

1010 Ferrando, 5:443-444.

1011 *Ibid.*

1012 Montero y Vidal, 2:572-573.

1013 Artigas y Cuerva, Manuel. *Galeria de filipinos ilustres: biografias a contar desde las primeros tiempos de la dominaci'on Hispana, de los hijos del pais que en sus respectivas profesiones descollaron o̕ hayan alcanzado alguń puesto de distinción en sociedad.* Manila: Imp. Casa Editora Renacimiento, 1917, 325-327. USIT

1014 *Ibid.* Halili, Maria Christine *Philippine History* Manila: Rex Book Store, 2004, 122.

1015 Montero y Vidal, 2:466-467.

1016 *Ibid.*

1017 *Ibid.*, 469.

1018 *Ibid.*, 475.

1019 Ferrando, 5: 499.

1020 Ocio y Viana 1895. *Apendice - Hijos del convento de Manila* 54-55.

1021 Ferrando, 5:500-501.

1022 *Ibid.* 5:502

1023 *Ibid.* 5:522-526

1024 *Ibid.* 5:533

1025 Martinez, Gregorio Meliton. *Letter to the Regent of Spain Francisco Serrano.* Manila, 31 December 1870. Schumacher, John N. SJ *Father Jose Burgos: A Documentary History with Spanish Documents and Their Translation.* Quezon City: Ateneo de Manila University Press, 1999, 210-211.

1026 Ferrando 5:529-530; PSRF 1916, 174-180. The Augustinians founded their *colegio-seminario* in Valladolid in 1759, the Recollects in Monteagudo in 1824, 4the Jesuits in Loyola in 1852, and the Franciscans in Aranjuez in 1853.

1027 *Ibid.*, 5:535

1028 *Ibid.*, 5:538

1029 Antequera, 486-492

1030 *Ibid.*, 185.

1031 *Ibid.*, 487.

1032 Montero y Vidal 2:570.

1033 Antequera, 192.

1034 Vicariato del Rosario en España (VRE). *Dominicos - Vicariato del Rosario en España.* http://vicaresp.dominicos.org Accessed on: 6 August 2017, 3:04pm.

1035 PSRF 1916, 181-187

1036 Provincia de España de la Orden de Predicadores (PEOP). *Historia de la Provincia de España.* http://dominicos.es/provincia/historia.aspx Accessed on 17 February 2014, 12:03pm.

1037 *Ibid.*

1038 Dominicos - Provincia de Hispania. *Quien Somos?* https://www.dominicoshispania.org/quienes-somos/ Accessed on 6 August 2014, 12:58pm.

1039 VRE., *op cit.*

1040 Torre, Carlos Maria de la. *Memoria sobre la Administración y Gobierno de las Islas Filipinas.* Madrid: Imp. de Gregorio Hernando, 1872. p. 22 found in *Manifesto al Pais sobre los Sucesos de Cavite y Memoria sobre la Administración y Gobierno de las Islas Filipinas.* Madrid: Imp. de Gregorio Hernando, 1872. USIT

1041 Martinez Santa Cruz, Gregorio Meliton. *Letter of the Archbishop to the Regent of Spain Francisco Serrano. Manila, 25 August 1871.* AHN, Ultramar, leg. 2255; Schumacher 1999,193-213.

Notes

1042 BD Mariano Gomes de los Angeles was born in Santa Cruz, Manila on 2 August 1799 to Alejandro Francisco Gomes and Martina Custodio. Of Malay and Chinese descent, he graduated with a Bachelor of Philosophy degree from the *Colegio de San Jose* in 1815. He continued his education at the *Universidad de Santo Tomas* where he earned the degrees in Bachelor of Canon Law in 1818 and Bachelor of Sacred Theology in 1823. He was appointed president of the *Seminario Conciliar de San Carlos* on 1 August 1822 being the most senior scholar of the seminary. On 22 August 1822, Gomes was formally given the title of sacristan of the cathedral parish serving concurrent positions as chaplain and seminary president. He was ordained priest on 21 September 1822 after securing dispensation for his young age and received his license to celebrate mass on 5 October 1822.

He became proprietary parish priest of Bacoor on 24 May 1824 and took possession on 2 June 1824. He became acting Vicar Forane of Cavite on 12 May 1844 and received his regular appointment on 23 September 1846. During his term as Parish Priest of Bacoor and Vicar Forane of Cavite, Gomes figured in a number of events that attested to his leadership, courage and militancy. He mediated and secured on 22 June 1828 the surrender and pardon of peasant dissidents led by Luis de los Santos, otherwise known as Luis Parang; ending the 1822 agrarian uprisings that started in Imus, Cavite. He championed the cause of the native secular priests and led a futile attempt to reverse the turnover of Cavite secular parishes to the Recollects and Dominicans that began in 1849. His parish of Bacoor was the last secular parish to be taken over. He was convicted of conspiracy, rebellion and treason by a Spanish military court in a controversial trial and was executed by *garrote vil* in Bagumbayan on 17 February 1872 at the age of 72.

1043 Martinez Santa Cruz, Gregorio Meliton. *Letter of the Archbishop to the Gov. Gen. Rafael de Izquierdo. Manila, 30 January 1872.* PNA 1872; Schumacher 1999, 262-267.

1044 Pedro Pablo Pelaez was born in Pagsanjan, Laguna on 29 June 1812. His parents were Jose Pelaez Rubio, a native of the Principado de Asturias, Spain and *alcalde mayor* of the Province, and Doña Josefa Sebastian Gomez Lozada, a *criolla* of Manila. Orphaned at a young age, Pelaez, a criollo, moved to Manila to study at the *Colegio de Santo Tomas* where he enjoyed a scholarship and became an outstanding student. He received his degrees in Bachelor of Arts (1829), Bachelor of Theology (1833), Licentiate in Theology (1836) and Doctor of Theology (1844). He served in various capacities in the academe: as teacher to the *colegiales* of the *Colegio de Santo Tomas*; assistant to the chairs of the different faculties of *Universidad de Santo Tomas* (1833-1836); full philosophy professor of the *Real Colegio de San Jose*; as examiner for the major and minor levels of the Faculty of Theology; university cojudge for two years; substitute for the chairs of philosophy and theology. A member of the *claustro*, he maintained his intimate ties with the University all his life; serving as member of the faculty between 1836 and 1862.

He was ordained priest in 1837 by the Archbishop of Manila Jose Segue and subsequently followed a career in the ecclesiastical cabildo of the archdiocese. He performed various functions such as administrator of the cathedral revenues, trial cojudge, or secretary. He received the appointment of interim canonjia magistral (magisterial canon, March 1839); subdelegate judge of the Manila diocese (July 1839); acting canonjia magistral (1847); medio racionero (assistant cathedral prebend, 1854); Synod examiner for the archbishop (1848-1863), penitenciario (confessor of the cathedral, 1858); comisario de cruzadas (commissary of crusades); visitador and the commissions as appointed by the government or assigned by the city. From 1845-1850 and 1855-1861, Pelaez was the secretary capitular of Archbishop Jose Aranguren and upon the latter's death became vicar capitular of the vacant seat in 1861-1862. The last position he occupied was as treasurer of the cathedral 1862-1863.

Between 1849 and 1863, Pelaez was involved in the protest against a series of arbitrary takeover of secular parishes by religious orders. Under his leadership, the secular clergy of the archdiocese was mobilized and measures were undertaken to have the pertinent decrees revoked. A Madrid agent was engaged to lobby for the revocation. Simultaneously a propaganda effort was launched to muster support and to neutralize a counter move undertaken by the friar orders. The expositions contained in El Clero Filipino, Breves Apuntes sobre la Cuestion de Curatos en Filipinas and Documentos Importantes para la Cuestion Pendiente sobre la Provision de Curatos en Filipinas were published citing the legal basis for the revocations and highlighting the unjust and unequal treatment of the loyal secular clergy collectively referred to as Filipinos. The authorship of these works could only be attributed to Pelaez. The Filipino clerics lost their champion on 3 June 1863 when the cathedral ceiling fell upon Pelaez among others during a vicious earthquake to hit Manila. Pelaez was the principal spokesman of the Filipino clergy and purveyor of proto-nationalist consciousness.

1045 Schumacher, John N. SJ, *Revolutionary Clergy: The Filipino Clergy and the Nationalist Movement, 1850-1903.* Quezon City: Ateneo de Manila University Press,1981, 1-12.

Chapter Fourteen Endnotes

1046 *Libro de Bautismo, Año 1836-1838*, vol.21, in St. Paul's Metropolitan Cathedral, Vigan Ilocos Sur. A facsimile of the baptismal certificate can be found in Schumacher 1999:298 (Appendix).

1047 *Informaciones de Colegiales.* AUST Libros 196, fol. 239. Transcription found in Villaroel 1971, Appendix 37.

1048 Antonia was the mother of Manuel Jerez Burgos whose baptismal certificate classified her as española natural. - Villaroel 1971, 1-2.

1049 Schumacher 1999, 44-45 footnotes.

1050 Villaroel, Fidel OP. *Father Jose Burgos: University Student.* Manila:University of Santo Tomas, 1971. The details about the student life of Jose Burgos had been largely based on this book.

Notes

1051 Artigas y Cuerva, Manuel. *Galeria de filipinos ilustres: biografias a contar desde las primeros tiempos de la dominaci'on Hispana, de los hijos del pais que en sus respectivas profesiones descollaron o hayan alcanzado alguń puesto de distinción en sociedad.* Manila: Imp. Casa Editora Renacimiento, 1917, 513-514. USIT

1052 Quirino, Carlos *A Checklist of Documents on Gomburza from the Archdiocesan Archives of Manila.* Philippine Studies, Vol. 21, No. 1/2 (First and Second Quarters 1973), 26. *JSTOR*, JSTOR, www.jstor.org/stable/42632208.

1053 AAM. *Examenes para Provision de Curatos y Economatos,* 1768-1874.

1054 Quirino, *op cit.* Burgos would later decline the *capellania*.

1055 *Noche triste* or Woeful Night was the name given to describe the ordeal a candidate of licentiate and higher degrees had to undergo on the eve of the main examination conducted the following morning. A procedure was prescribed and followed in Santo Tomas. See Villaroel 1971, 30-31.

1056 Unless otherwise cited, the narrative on the Letran incident was lifted from the account in the *Filipinas ante Europa No.9, 28 February 1900* pp. 72-73. It is generally believed that the article, *Los Martires de la Patria,* was written by Antonio Maria Regidor. Certain unsupported facts were altered to be consistent with established documentary evidence.

1057 AAM. *Burgos et al Dictum. Manila, 24 February 1860.* Oficios de Varias Personas, 1815-1898, under Oficios de Varias Autoridades, 1860; Quirino 1973, 66, 74-75.

1058 Villaroel 1971, 31-32

1059 AAM, *op.cit.*

1060 The *Claustro* was a body composed of all the Doctors, Masters and Licentiates graduated by or incorporated to the University. It had supreme powers to judge and make decisions on a number of important matters pertaining to the academic life as specified by the Statutes, and to update the Statutes themselves in conformity with new government legislation on educational matters. The Claustro during those times would roughly correspond to our modern Academic Senate, Council of Regents, Economic Council and Faculty staff put together. - Villaroel 1971:51.

1061 A Commissional Judge was one of two elected annually that are empowered to demand from the student his baptismal certificate and to summon three witnesses who could testify about the student and his family strictly adhering to the questionnaire supplied by the statutes concerning the informative process of the *limpieza de sangre.* The findings of the two judges were then passed to the Fiscal Promoter for a verdict on the matter and for recommendation to the Rector. Villaroel 1971:81-82.

1062 As per the university statutes, a Master of Ceremonies attends all public acts, competitive examinations, *relecciones*, graduations of Licentiates, Masters and Doctors, all the celebrations of the University, the funeral services of Doctors, and public literary acts. And in all these occasions, he arranges the placings of the graduates, of all the distinguished guests and never permitting non-University graduates to take seats assigned to Doctors, strictly observing the statutes. As a sign of distinction, the Master of Ceremonies carried a baton in his hand, with the upper end set in gold or silver showing the coat of arms of the University. - Villaroel 1971:53

1063 [Burgos, Jose] *A La Nacion.* La America No. 17 Madrid, 12 Setiembre 1864, 11-13 BDH

1064 Please note Izquierdo's reference to the planned rebellion of 1863 aborted by the death of Pelaez as one of his justifications of an ongoing conspiracy.

1065 [Burgos 1864], *op cit.*

1066 Schumacher 1999, 20-21.

1067 *Ibid.*, 21-22.

1068 *Ibid.,* 104-105.

1069 Jacinto Zamora was born in Pandacan, Manila on 14 August 1835 to Venancio Zamora and Hilaria del Rosario. A Spanish mestizo, he studied at the Real Colegio de San Juan de Letran and was a year ahead of Jose Burgos. He completed his Bachelor of Canon Law degree in 1858 and Bachelor of Civil Law in 1859 at the University of Santo Tomas. He received his first tonsure on 7 June 1859 and admitted into the minor orders on 23 September 1859. He was ordained priest in January 1862 and was assigned to Pateros. He was subsequently named coadjutor of Lipa on 5 December 1862. On 1 June 1864, Zamora was named acting curate of Mariquina parish. He took possession of the first curacy of the cathedral parish on 23 December 1865. He was among those accused to be a member of the rebel junta responsible for the Cavite mutiny and was executed together with D. Jose Burgos and D. Mariano Gomes on 17 February 1872. It was generally believed that he was an unfortunate victim of mistaken identity.

1070 AAM. *Testimonios de posesion de curatos, 1806-1859.* (The entry date was January _ 1865.) Burgos officially completed his course in canon law on 31 January 1865 - Villaroel 1971, 64.

1071 The cathedral chapter had five members called dignities whose president was the Dean or Provost. After them came the three canons (five in 1885) with the titles of Penitentiary, Doctoral and Magistral; and lastly six beneficiaries called *racioneros.* - Villaroel 1971, 88.

1072 The Latinity Inspector had the duty to visit the schools under his jurisdiction, to inspect the conditions of the buildings, examine the enrollment registers, the methods of teaching, the schedule of classes, particularly the quality of religious instruction, and report about the state and condition of each school to the government. - Villaroel 1971, 68.

1073 The *Examinador Sinodal* was one of a number designated to examine applicants for parishes in the archdiocese.

Notes

1074 As an ecclesiastical attorney, the *Promotor Fiscal* or attorney general passes legal opinion on scores of cases submitted to the chapter.

1075 Carlos Maria de la Torre y Navacerrada was Superior Civil Governor and Captain General of the Philippines from 23 June 1869 to 4 April 1871. A native of Cuenca, he was lieutenant general actively involved in the 1868 Glorious Revolution that toppled the government of Isabel II of Spain. Among his noted achievements included the improvement of the peace and order situation with the establishment of the Guardia Civil and a Battalion of Scouts, creation of an administrative civil service corps, revival of commercial code provisions of founding and organizing stock companies, regulating the mining sector, liberalizing the status of foreigners and abolishing the guard of halberdiers and the caning of deserters. He had failed to implement the educational reforms, secularization of religious and the confiscation of church properties using his *cumplase* discretion on the basis that the laws in Spain did not apply to the Philippine situation. He was criticized and maligned by both liberals and conservatives for failing to live up to either expectations.

1076 Gutierrez y Salazar, Pedro. *Las Procripciones de Sila (remedo de) en Filipinas por el Excmo. Sr. D. Carlos Maria de la Torre Capitan Genral y Gobernador Superior Civil de estas Islas*. Madrid: Imp. Florencio Gamayo, 1870, 9. BDH

1077 *El Porvenir Filipino No. 148*, 14 July 1869. Seccion Gacetilla plana 3ª, columna 4ª. as cited by Gutierrez y Salazar, 12 and Monterro y Vidal, 503.

1078 Gutierrez y Salazar, 8, 13.

1079 La Torre 1872 vii. Two of La Torre's critics were Pedro Gutierrez y Salazar and Jose Montero y Vidal. La Torre dismissed Gutierrez y Salazar from his posts as executive director of the board of the Misericordia and of the Colegio de Santa Isabel in view of irregularities and abuses. Montero y Vidal used Gutierrez y Salazar as his principal source to disparage La Torre,

1080 *Ibid., xiii.*

1081 *Ibid.*

1082 Montero y Vidal, 3:510-511; Gutierrez y Salazar, 54-55.

1083 La Torre 1872, 10

1084 *Ibid.*, 6.

1085 Artigas y Cuerva, Manuel. *The Events of 1872, A Historic-Bio-Bibliographical Account. Vol 3 of the National Glories Series. Translation and Notes by O.D. Corpuz*. Diliman, Quezon City: University of the Philippines Press, 1996, 28.

1086 *Ibid.*, 157. Artigas claimed that it was Antonio Regidor who chided the students. However, Regidor was not in the Philippines in 1869. He was in Spain. See Artigas 1996, 168.

1087 *Ibid.*

1088 Villaroel 1971, 98-99.

1089 *Ibid.*, 103.

1090 *Ibid.*, 105.

1091 Gutierrez y Salazar, 83-84.

1092 La Torre, Carlos Maria de. *Confidential Letter to the General Administration of the Post Office of the Philippines Manila, 22 December 1869*. Schumacher 1999, 108-109.

1093 La Torre, Carlos Maria de. *Confidential Letter to the Postmaster-General of the Philippines. Manila, 23 December 1869*. Schumacher 1999, 110-111.

1094 True copy of Letter to the Postmaster-General, 1869. Schumacher 1999, 110-111.

1095 *La Discusion Año XV Num 386, 6 enero 1870. p. 2. col. 1.* P. Fr. Joaquin Coria OFM authored controversial articles that were published in *La Discusion* in 1869.

1096 La Torre, Carlos Maria de. *Confidential Letter No. 167 to the Overseas Minister. Manila, 4 January 1870* Schumacher 1999, 114-115.

1097 La Torre, Carlos Maria de. *Confidential Letter No. 179 to the Overseas Minister. Manila, 18 January 1870.* Schumacher 1999, 118-119.

1098 These seven letters and one memorial are found in Schumacher 1999.

1099 Schumacher 1999, 219.

1100 Plauchut, Edmund. *L'ARCHIPEL DES PHILIPPINES*. Revue Des Deux Modes, juin 1877 p. 915; Artigas 1996, 71-72.

1101 Schumacher 1999, 292-293.

1102 Rafael de Izquierdo y Gutierrez was Superior Civil Governor and Captain General of Filipinas from 4 April 1871 to 8 January 1873. A native of Santander, he was a lieutenant general actively involved in the 1868 Glorious Revolution that toppled the government of Queen Isabel II of Spain. His short term of office was marked by the opening of the steamship line and telegraph lines, the establishment of an additional regiment of the Guardia Civil and the abolition of the Battalion of Scouts, the suppression of the 1872 Cavite and Zamboanga insurrections, the disbandment of the artillery corps and its replacement by a complete european regiment, the controversial court martial of civilians implicated in the insurrections, the virtual emasculation of the Filipino secular clergy and liberals, the compromised educational reform, and the further entrenchment of friar orders' hold on power. He resigned because of ill-health.

1103 *Ibid.*, 240-243.

1104 Tormo Sanz, Leandro. *1872* Translated by Antonio Molina, Manila: Historical Conservation Society, 1973, 50.

1105 Francisco Saldua was a soldier who served in the native artillery battalion. Assigned in Cavite, he was assistant to First Lieutenant Faustino Villabrille. There he met his prospective wife who was under the protection of P. Fr. Juan Cruz Gomez OAR, the curate of the Cavite Viejo parish since 16 December 1861. On his wedding day, he received a dowry that was enough for him to retire from the service. He became a contractor to the Cavite Arsenal supplying firewood. He involved himself in gambling and converted his house into an establishment while carrying on as a model auxilliary to his two patrons, the Lieutenant and the Recoleto. Saldua was transporting a cargo of firewood from Mariveles to Cañacao when he and his wife were detained and brought to Bilibid prison. There he was visited by his protector, P. Fr. Juan Cruz Gomez OAR. By then, the Recoleto was the Secretary of the Province. During the trial, Saldua incredulously incriminated himself as the immediate instigator of the revolt and on his word implicated Burgos and Zamora. Never having met Burgos, rebel witnesses traced their awareness of Burgos' alleged role in the revolt to Saldua. When he was collected for the gallows, neither he nor his wife were upset. They were confident that a pardon was forthcoming. P. Fr. Juan Cruz Gomez OAR was present on the scaffold as D. Mariano Gomes' confessor and successor to the Bacoor curacy. The Recoleto's reassuring presence faded when Saldua realized that he was deceived. He was executed by *garrote vil* on 17 February 1872 in Bagumbayan. - Regidor 1900, 68, 75; Montero y Vidal 3: 585;

Bonifacio Octavo y Samson was a mestizo de sangley native of Imus, Cavite. He was implicated by the Spanish colonial authorities as one of the leaders of the 1872 Cavite mutiny. He was a second sergeant of the Seventh Infantry Regiment when he was tried for complicity in the rebellion. Octavo testified that he was to lead the rebels of his regiment but deserted instead in the early afternoon of 20 January and took refuge in the mountains and barrios of Bataan until his capture in September. He was tried by the Spanish military court for 10 days. He confessed that in November or December 1871, a marine infantry corporal, Pedro Manonson, showed him a paper exhorting all the native troops to rebel against the Spaniards. In the afternoon of October 1871, he met a certain sergeant Madrid, a clerk in the Cavite Arsenal, Vicente Generoso, Francisco Saldua, an unnamed artillery corporal, another corporal of the marine infantry, a retired sergeant, and many more in Manonson's house on the main street of Cavite. Generoso presented to the group a piece of paper which listed an estimate of forces ready for the rebellion. Octavo said that Saldua told the group that the forces were for Fathers Burgos, Gomes, Zamora, and Guevarra and other leaders who would direct the rebellion. Octavo's death sentence meted on 29 February 1872 was commuted to 10 years imprisonment in Cartagena, Spain on 28 September of the same year. He was also ordered chained for life. - Tormo Sanz, 73-90.

1106 Octavo, Bonifacio. *Testimonio del proceso del sargento Bonifacio Octavo.* Tormo Sanz, 76-79,154-55, 158.

1107 *Ibid.,* 87, 165; Izquierdo, Rafael de. 1872a. Comunicacion num. 390 del Capitan General dando una completa informacion al Ministro de Ultramar sobre la insureccion de 1872 en Cavite, 31 Jan. Cavite 1872, doc. no. 117, Insurgent Records Cavite, PNA

1108 Izquierdo, Rafael de. 1872c. Carta reservada, num. 816, del Gobernardo de Filipinas, Rafael de Izquierdo, al Ministro de Ultramar, 12 Oct., leg. 5216, AHN.

1109 Izquierdo 1872a, 53-54; Tormo Sanz, 77, 82, 87, 156, 160, 165

1110 Izquierdo 1872a, 23-24; Tormo Sanz, 82, 161.

1111 Tormo Sanz, 83, 85, 161, 163.

1112 Izquierdo 1872a, 54-55.

1113 Montero y Vidal 3:573

1114 Izquierdo 1872a, 21.

1115 Tormo Sanz, 77, 79, 82, 86, 155,158, 161, 164.

1116 *Ibid.* 4-13; Carballo, Manuel. 1872. Informe sobre el acontecimiento de la insureccion de Cavite en el 20, 21 y 22 de enero, Cavite, 25 Jan. 1872. doc. no. 100, Insurgent Records Cavite, PNA, 6-8.

1117 Montero y Vidal 3:575.

1118 Izquierdo 1872c, 54-56; Carballo 1872, 11-12.

1119 *Ibid.,* 18-20.

1120 *Ibid.,* 21

1121 *Ibid.* Reported earlier as a lay brother, Antonio Rufian was actually a priest.

1122 *Ibid.* Izquierdo did not mention any names and avoided referring to any peninsular Spanish involvement in *pronunciamiento.*

1123 Vergara, Francisco Engracio [Regidor, Antonio]. *La masoneria en Filipinas estudio de actualidad apuntes para la historia de la colonizacion española en el siglo xix.* Paris: 1896. pp. 14-15; Artigas 1990, 165-166. Francisco Engracio Vergara was a pseudonym used by Antonio Regidor.

1124 Schumacher 1999:256-257. Ginoves may had been informed by the widow of the fort commander that Burgos was implicated by Lamadrid as the leader.

1125 Izquierdo 1872a, 5, 9.

1126 Montero y Vidal 3:580.

1127 *Ibid.,* 581.

1128 Lluiz, Luis Roig de. *Diary of Operations 23 January 1872.* ASHM fol. 1872-1-1-1-15 as cited by Quirino 1970,

1129 Montero y Vidal 3:584

1130 Artigas 1996, 107.

1131 Montero y Vidal 3:583-584, 588-589; Artigas 1996, 149.

1132 Izquierdo 1872a, 58-59; Carballo 1872, 2-5.

1133 BNM. ms 13.288; Tormo Sanz, 70.

1134 Montero y Vidal 3:579; Artigas 1996, 79, 107.

1135 Law of 17 April 1821 in conformity with royal decree of 23 January 1866. Under Article 27 of the 1 February 1869 decree amending and consolidating the jurisdiction of military tribunals provides, verbatim: "The military tribunals organized in Cuba under the authority granted by the royal order of 25 February 1867 are hereby abolished. These tribunals were not organized in Filipinas. See Artigas 1996, 170-171.

1136 Izquierdo 1872b [Letter of Governor-General of the Philippines to the Captain-General of the Philippines] 3 Feb. Sediciones y Rebeliones 1870-1873, PNA; Artigas 1996, 151-153.

1137 Not knowing the members of the Junta personally, Bonifacio Octavo corroborated established facts and claimed that Saldua was his source of information - Izquierdo 1872c.

1138 Artigas 1996, 85-88,156.

1139 [Regidor, Antonio 1900]. *A los martires de la Patria, Burgos, Gomez y Zamora.* Filipinas ante Europa, Año II Madrid 28 Febrero 1900 Num. 9 p. 70 BDH; Artigas 1996, 90.

1140 Cernudo, Tomas G. *Attestation of the Sentence of the Priests Jose Burgos, Jacinto Zamora, Mariano Gomez, and the Laymen Maximo Inocencio, Crisante de los Reyes, Francisco Zaldua and Enrique Paraiso. Manila 18 February 1872.* Schumacher 1999, 268-275.

1141 All the exiles would eventually obtain their amnesty by 1875 because the contentious jurisdictional issue [caused by the appeal raised by Regidor and company] had come to an end and if the trial contained irregularities in the proceedings or errors in the ruling, it must take into consideration that the exceptional circumstances in Manila where and when the events transpired were of a political nature. - Regidor 1900, 76-77. Note: Had capital punishment not been meted on Burgos, Gomes, Zamora and Saldua, they would had similarly been granted amnesty.

1142 Martinez, Gregorio Meliton. *Letter to Gov. Gen. Rafael Izquierdo. Manila 30 January 1872.* Schumacher 1996, 262-267.

1143 Martinez, Gregorio Meliton. *Letter to Gov. Gen. Rafael Izquierdo. Manila 15 February 1872.* ASHM fol. 4-9-1-14. Quirino, Carlos and Burgos, Jose. *More Documents on Burgos.* Philippine Studies, Vol. 18. No. 1 (January 1970), 172-174 JSTOR, JSTOR, www.jstor.org/stable/42632001; Tormo Sanz, 93-94, 171.

1144 Ultramar. *Expediente Pesonal de R. Izquierdo, gobernador capitán general 1871/1873.* ES.28079.AHN/2.3.1.16.5//ULTRAMAR,5222,Exp.37 PARES

1145 *Ibid.*

1146 Izquierdo, Rafael. *Memoria sobre la gobernacion General de Filipinas por. D. Rafael Izquierdo al cesar en el mando en el mes de Diciembre de 1872.* Expte. p. de R. Izquierdo, gobernador capitán general. ES.28079.AHN/2.3.1.16.5//ULTRAMAR,5222,Exp.37

1147 Antonio Maria Regidor y Jurado was born to a Spanish couple on 16 April 1845. He finished his *primera* and *segunda enseñaza* at the Colegio de San Juan de Letran. At the University of Santo Tomas, he completed his Bachelor of Philosophy degree in 1863, Bachelor of Laws in 1867 and Doctor of Civil Law in 1871. He left for Spain in 1869 where he studied his Doctorate in Canon Laws at the Universidad Central de Madrid. Returning to the Philippines 1870, he worked for the colonial government under different capacities: Secretary to the Provincial Audiencia, Fiscal of the Artillery and Engineering Corps, President of Public Instruction, Secretary of the Committee on training Filipinos for civil service, Head of the Statistics Board of Quiapo, and Chief Inspector of Municipal Schools. During his term as Chief Inspector of Municipal Schools, he secured the royal decree that allowed Filipinos from any social status to enter in public schools. In 1871, Regidor joined the University of Santo Tomas faculty of Law and its *claustro*.

He was an active Filipino liberal closely associated with D. Jose Burgos, and his brother, Manuel, acted as Burgos' legal agent in Madrid. He was among those implicated and arrested for the Cavite Mutiny and was sentenced to six years imprisonment in Guam. Through his brother's legal representation in Madrid, he was able to secure his pardon in April 1876. He married Julia Stanton, an Irish lady, and had since settled in Stanford Hills, London with a lucrative legal practice. Using the pen names like Luis Rances and Engracio Vergara, he was an active contributor to *La Solidaridad, La Igualdad, La Discusion, El Imparcial, El Porvenir, El Liberal, El Pais, La Bandera Española and Filipinas Ante Europa.* He wrote *La Masoneria en Filipinas* and co-authored Commercial Progress in the Philippines. On 10 August 1898, he became member of the subcommittee of the Executive Board of the Hong Kong Revolutionary Junta. Pursuant to President Emilio Aguinaldo's Diplomatic Missions decree of 23 November 1898, he became a member of the Agoncillo missions that presented the case of the Philippines before the United States Congress. He died on 28 December 1910 in Nice, France.

1148 Vergara [Regidor 1896], 14-15.

1149 The Ilocos revolt of 1814 referred to the violence that ensued over the non-implementation of the 1812 Spanish constitution.

1150 The term of Governor General Marcelino de Oraa Lecumberri was marked by two sanguine incidents. On 1 November 1841, hundreds of Apolinario de la Cruz's outlawed *Confradia de San Jose* followers were massacred in Tayabas. De la Cruz, also known as Hermano Pule, was executed by firing squad and his body quartered three days later. In retaliation for the Tayabas massacre, the Tayabas Regiment stationed in Manila revolted under the leadership of Sergeant Irineo Samaniego. The mutiny was suppressed and the conspirators executed.

Notes

[1151] P. Fr. Juan Cruz Gomez del Sagrado Corazon de Jesus OAR was born in Bribiesca (Burgos) on 24 November 1835, he professed on 4 June 1854 and was ordained on 25 November 1858. From the Convento de San Sebastian he was named missionary of Balabac on 19 June 1859. After studying Tagalog in Las Piñas, he was given charge of Cavite Viejo on 16 December 1862, Carmona in 1862 and Taytay in 1866. He was elected Subprior and Master of Novices of Manila In 1870 and Secretary of the Province in 1871. He became parish priest of Bacoor in March 1872 until 1894 except for the three-year period of 1882-85 when he served as Provincial of the Order. In 1894, he was elected Commissary, Vicar Provincial and Procurator General of the Province in Madrid while holding the positions of Prior vocal of Imus (1873), Definidor (1876) and Prior vocal of Romblon (1879). He was re-elected Commissary in 1897 and served until 1902 when he was named Procurator General of the Order in Madrid. - Sadaba, 492-493.

[1152] Regidor 1900, 75-76.

[1153] Montero y Vidal 3:586. The dates and facts contained in the execution narrative are based on Montero's account unless otherwise cited. Details contained in the accounts of Plauchut and *Filipinas Ante Europa* that did not conflict with Montero's were incorporated and modified to maintain consistency.

[1154] Craig, Austin. *Gems of Philippine oratory; selections representing fourteen centuries of Philippine thought, carefully compiled from credible sources in substitution for the pre-Spanish writings destroyed by missionary zeal, to supplement the later literature stunted by intolerant religious and political censorship, and as specimens of the untrammeled present-day utterances.* Manila: University of Manila, 1924, 30. USIT

[1155] Montero y Vidal 3:585; Schumacher 1996, 293.

[1156] Plauchut, Edmund. *L'ARCHIPEL DES PHILIPPINES.* Revue Des Deux Modes, juin 1877, 921-923. http://www.revuedesdeuxmondes.fr/article-revue/iii-lindustrie-le-commerce-la-situation-politique/

[1157] Regidor 1900, 67.

[1158] *Ibid*, 68. Regidor referred to Francisco Saldua as Miguel Zaldua.

[1159] *Ibid*.

[1160] Plauchut, *op cit*.

[1161] *Ibid*.

[1162] *Ibid*.

[1163] Regidor 1900, *op.cit*. During the 126th death anniversary of the GomBurZa martyrs on 17 February 1998, a historical marker was unveiled on the site where bones believed to be those of the martyrs were unearthed a month earlier. They were found under a latrine. The bones have not been authenticated to this date.

[1164] *Allgemeine Zeitung* No. 273 1 October 1892 as quoted by Artigas 1996, 75.

[1165] Rizal, Jose. *Carta a Mariano Ponce y Compañeros de La Solidaridad 18 April 1889. Epistolario Rizalino 5 Vol.* Manila; Bureau of Printing, 1930-38, 2:166. Cervantes Virtual.

[1166] Constantino, Renato. *A History of the Philippines: from the Spanish Colonization to the Second World War.* New York and London: Monthly Review Press, 1975. p. 148.

[1167] Transcripts of the depositions are found in Artigas' *Los Sucesos de 1872*.

[1168] Schumacher, John N. SJ. *The Authenticity of the Writings Attributed to Father Jose Burgos.* Philippine Studies, Vol. 18, No. 1 (January 1970) pp. 3-51. JSTOR, JSTOR, www.jstor.org/stable/42631996.

[1169] Araneta, Luis Ma. *The Works of Father Jose Burgos.* Philippine Studies, Vol. 7, No. 2 (April 1959) pp. 187-193. JSTOR, JSTOR, www.jstor.org/stable/42719439.

[1170] Schumacher 1970, *op cit*.

[1171] Schumacher, John N. SJ, *Father Jose Burgos: Priest and Nationalist.* Manila: Knights of Columbus, 1972. p. ix

[1172] Schumacher 1991, x.

[1173] Schumacher 1970, *op. cit.*

[1174] Scott, William Henry. *A Critical Study of the Prehispanic Source of Materials for the Study of Philippine History.* Manila: University of Santo Tomas Press, 1968, 104-136.

[1175] Schumacher, John N. SJ. *The Cavite Mutiny: An Essay on the Published Sources.* Philippine Studies, Vol. 20, No. 4 (1972) pp. 603-632. JSTOR, JSTOR, www.jstor.org/stable/42634842.

[1176] Schumacher 1972: xi-xiii.

INDEX

A
abad , 365
Abad Santos, Pedro, xx
Abad, Bernardino, 94–95
Abad, Casimiro, 94
Abaya, Cosme, 274
Abellafuertes, Alonso, 81
abid, 185
Academia, 46, 122, 130, 244
Academia de Dibujo y Pintura, 147
Academia Nautica, 137, 147
Acuerdo de Manila, 248
Adriano, Juan, 283
Aduana, Luis de, 31, 48
Aduarte, Diego, xv, 55, 305
Aenlle, Juan Antonio, 273
Agius, Jimeno, 294–295
Agrarian Revolts of 1745, 82–86, 102
Agrarian Unrest of 1822, 86–88, 279, 371
Aguado, Fernando Polanco, 82
Aguas, Diego de, 49
Agudo, Guillermo, 271, 277
Aguiar y Seixas, Francisco, 207
Aguilar, Jeronimo de, 199
Aguinaldo, Emilio, xx, 145, 301–302, 305, 351, 375
Aguinaldo, Misa de, 113, 115, 347
Ahi al-Kitab, 187
Al-Andalus, 187
Alaguero, Benito, 86
Albornoz, Sebastian de, 48
alcaiceria, 223
Alcarazo, Diego de, 48
Alcarazo, Juan de, 48, 74
Alcarazo, Lope Felix de, 48, 73–75
Alejandrino, Mariano, 280, 282
alguacil mayor, 11, 14, 24, 333
alipin (oripon), 224, 256, 361
Alonso, Diego, 41
ana-tsurushi, 154, 352
Anahuac, 197
Ancien Regime, 259
Angeles, Juan de los, 48, 66, 78, 339

Angeles, Miguel de los, 157
Aniag, Juan, 280
Anunciacion, Domingo de la, 34
Apellaniz, Valentin, 96
Araneta, Luis Maria, 301, 321
Aranjuez, 370
Arceo, Antonio de, 13
Archbishops of Manila
Aranguren, Jose, 371
Arizala, Pedro de la Santisima Trinidad Martinez de, 160
Benavides de Santa Maria, Miguel de, 35, 54–56, 337–338
Camacho y Avila, Diego, 81, 110, 238–240, 242, 247, 250, 364, 366–367
Cuesta, Francisco de la, 239, 242, 248, 364, 368
Garcia Serrano, Miguel, 17, 115, 223
Guerrero, Hernando, 26, 28–29, 64, 115
Lopez Galvan, Juan, 228, 362
Martinez Santa Cruz, Gregorio Meliton, 290
Nozaleda, Bernardino, 143
Pardo, Felipe Fernandez de, 228–235, 362–363
Rojo, Antonio, 240–241, 250
Salazar, Domingo, 34–35, 54, 124, 127, 218, 236, 338, 341, 349
Santa Justa y Rufina, Basilio Sancho de, 115, 238, 240, 244, 246, 250–251, 253–254, 257–258, 270, 347, 367
Arco (Arceo), Claudio del,, 301–302
Arellano, Joaquin, 92
Arevalo, Isidro, 240
Arias, Evaristo Fernandez, 132, 144, 305
Aristotle, 122, 129–130, 184, 186, 305
Arjona, Juan de, 172

Arrieta, Jose de, 282, 288
Artigas, Manuel, 279, 305–306
Ateneo Municipal, 147–148, 351
Ausina, Cristobal, 367
Austria, Juan de, 10
Ayala y Herrera, Adelardo Lopez de, 147
Azcarraga, Jose de, 294

B
Balthasar Carlos, 65
Baluyut, Francisco, 238, 364
Baratao (Bacnotan), 28–30
Barca, Emeterio Cacho Calderon de la, 254
Barrantes, Vicente, 126, 306
Barreda, Santiago, 160
Barredo Valdes, Jeronimo de, 81
Basa, Jose, 283, 287
Basa, Pio, 283, 287
Batallon de Guias (Scouts Battalion), 88, 279
Battle of Lepanto, 10, 46
Bautista, Ambrosio, 283
Bayonne Charter, 262
Bayot, Francisco, 266
Bazaco, Evergisto, xv, 14, 73, 114, 168, 306, 336, 342, 347, 352, 355–356, 362
beata, 106–110, 113, 117–119, 343–344
Beaterio
residence, xvi, 103–104, 107–110, 112–113, 116, 118–120, 343, 346, 348
street, 45, 66, 75, 103
beca
bursary, 17, 45, 230, 240, 242, 244, 364
tippet, 44, 66, 142
Becera, Gomez, 269
Becerra, Nicolas, 88, 90, 92–93
Berart, Raimundo, 234, 340, 363
Berdozido, Pablo Francisco Rodriguez de, 70, 306
Bertran, Pedro, 284
Betanzos, Domingo de, 34

Biron Sagrado Corazon de Jesus, Pascuala, 119
Blancas de San Jose, Francisco, 128
Blanco, Fernando, 270
Bobadilla, Francisco de, 192
Bolaños, Pedro, 35, 128, 337
Bonaparte, Joseph, 262–263, 265
Bonaparte, Napoleon, 10, 262–263
Bonifacio, Andres, 301–302
Boxadors, Juan Tomas de, 367
Bravo de Acuña, Tomas, 11, 17
braza, 29, 83–84, 336
British Invasion of 1762, 86, 102, 240, 244, 250, 252, 347, 367–368
Briz, Joachim, 266, 268
Buencamino, Felipe, 279–280, 282
Buencamino, Fortunato, 280
Buencamino, Juan, 280
Buencamino, Justo, 280
Buencamino, Potenciano, 280
Buencamino, Victor, 280
Bull Omnimoda, 166, 354
Bumatay, Estanislao, 273
Burgos, Florentina Garcia de, 273
Burgos, Jose, 273
Burgos, Jose Apolonio
   Anda demonstration, 284
   Cavite Mutiny, 285–296
   execution, 297–298
   legacy, 298–300, 303–304
   Letran alumnus, 273–274, 276
   post-controversies, 300–302
   priest and nationalist, 276–278, 283–284, 303
   student unrest, 280, 282, 284
Butler, 295

C

Cabezas, Protacio, 239
cabildo ecclesiastico, 17–18, 65–66, 182, 234, 243, 276, 358, 363, 371
cabildo secular, 13, 20, 65–66, 182, 197–198, 267
cacique (principal), xx, 49, 83, 88, 192, 197–199, 204–205, 207, 214–215, 217, 220, 224–225, 228, 360
Calderon y Henriquez, Pedro, 83–84, 86, 88
Calderon, Felipe, 88, 307
Calderon, Jose Maria, 273
Calendar Case, 156
Camerino, Casimiro, 88, 279, 286–287
Cañas, Jose, 279
Canda, N., 280
Canduela, Juan, 173
capellania, 69, 72–75, 78, 80, 101, 238, 274, 342, 372
Capilla Real, 26, 28–29, 48, 51, 336
Capitulacion de Santa Fe, 192
Carballo, Manuel, 285–286, 294
Carbonel, Matias, 91
Cardenas, Domingo, 302
Cardenas, Francisco de, 78
caribe, 193–194, 353
Carillo, Pedro, 286
Carlist Wars, 265
Carominas, Benito, 280
Carpena Diaz, Roque, 179
Carvallo, Geronimo, 232
Casas, Bartolome de las, 54, 192, 196–197, 307, 341, 358
Casas, Pedro de las, 192
Castañedo, Domingo, 161, 164
Castillo, Gabriel Gomez del, 73
Castillo, Jose del, 294
Castillo, Mariano del, 282
Castillo, Sebastian, 116
castizo, 199, 201
Castro, Juan de, 34, 55, 337
Castro, Juan de (menor), 337
Castro, Rafael, 294
Caulas, Domingo Canuto, 368
censo, 72–73, 80, 343
Cevicos, Juan, 18, 20
Chaves, Pedro de, 104
Chien, Jose, 170, 355
Chiesa, Bernardino della, 157
Chinos
   Asians, 36, 198–201, 216, 218, 220–222, 224–225, 228, 362
   Chinese nationals, 223, 226, 253, 267
Chrisostomo, Juan, 34
cilicia, 107
Cisneros, Francisco Jimenez de, 197

Cistercian, 2
claustro, 252–253, 276–277, 371–372, 375
Club Filipino, 279
Cobo, Juan de, 55, 124, 307, 349
Cobrizos, 186, 198–200
Cocchi, Angelo, 154
Colombo, Bartolomeo, 192
Colombo, Cristoforo (Christopher Columbus), 191–193
Colombo, Diego, 192
Colonial Education
   primary, 121–128, 136, 138, 143
   secondary, 122–123, 129, 131–136, 139–141, 144–146
   tertiary, 121, 133, 147–151
Comite de Reformadores, 279
composicion, 81–82, 84, 343, 364
compradores, 226
Comyn, Tomas de, 225
Concordat of Bologna, 247
Confraternity of the Rosary, 172
Congregacion de Religiosas de la Tercer Orden de Santo Domingo, 119
Congregation of Dominican Sisters of Saint Catherine of Siena, 104, 119–120, 345
Consejo de Indias, 18, 20, 36, 56, 242, 247, 251–252, 257, 345–346
Constantine the Great, 21
Constitution of 1812, 263–266
Constitution of 1837, 266
Constitution of 1869, 278
consulta, 247, 268
Contreras, Salvador de, 244, 358
conversos
   cristianos nuevos, 187
   marano, 187–188
   morisco, 187, 199, 201
Cordoba, Martin Alfonso de, 147
Cordoba, Pedro de, 186
Coria, Joaquin, 282
Coronado, Domingo, 156
Cortes Generales, 9, 264, 266, 269
Cortes, Hernan, 197, 199

Costa, Horacio de la, 127, 129, 302–304, 308
Cotolendi, Ignace, 172
Craig, Austin, 297
criollo
   Americano, 200, 203, 205, 226, 264
   Filipino, 36, 137, 142, 147, 221, 225–226, 267–268, 271, 273, 276–279, 282–283, 289–293, 337
Crisologo, Criterio, 273
crusade, 1–2, 234, 236, 364
Cruz, Apolinario de la, 367
Cruz, Dionisio de la, 338
Cruz, Juan de la, 172, 336, 346
Cruz, Monica de la, 78
Cruz, Pedro de la, 78
Cruz, Roque de la, 75
cuarenta vacas de santo tomas, 78
Cuartero, Mariano, 293
cuarteron, 199, 201, 244, 272, 343, 354
Cuesta, Jose, 267
cumplase (Acto de Obediencia), 58, 252, 365

D
dacion en pago, 80, 341
Dairit (Dairet), Ladislao, 279–280
Dandan, Pedro, 286
decano, 62, 173, 251, 273–274
Delgado, Agustin, 41
Delgado, Juan Jose, 254–256, 308, 361–362
desamortizacion, 80, 244, 269, 292, 341
Desiderio, Anacleto, 286
Dhimma, 187
diezmo, 52, 72, 236, 339, 358
Dilag, Juan, 274
Dizon, Victor, 282
dojico, 349
Dominican Sisters of the Most Holy Rosary of the Philippines, 120
donado, 106, 220, 337, 349
Drake, Francis, 10
Dutch War of Independence, 46

E
Echague, Francisco Muñoz de, 29

Echegoyen, Agapito, 301–302
Echeveste, Francisco, 114, 344
encomienda, 16, 22–23, 25–26, 28–30, 39, 52, 61, 106, 214, 230–231, 234, 335, 339, 357–358
epidemic, 193, 197, 199
Escaño y Cordoba, Juan de, 110
Escosura, 93
escribano, 25, 33, 100
Escuela de Botanica y Agricultura, 137, 347
Escuela de Comercio, 137, 147
Escuela de Dibujo, 137, 347
escuela de gramatica, 121, 128
escuela de niños, 124, 126–128
escuela de primeras letras, 121, 128
escuela de segunda enseñanza, 143
escuelas patrioticas, 137
Espiritu Santo, Francisca del (Francisca de Fuentes), 108–110, 112–113, 120, 343
Esquivel, Jose Gabriel, 282
Estrella, Agaton, 274, 280, 282
Estrella, Agustin, 279
estudios generales, 121
estudios particulares, 121
examinador sinodal, 277, 365
exclaustracion, 265, 269, 292

F
fabrica, 69–70, 340
fanega, 69
Feliu, Pedro, 161, 163–167
Feng Shiming, Juan, (Juan Bautista Fung de Santa Maria), ii, xviii, 158–162, 164, 167–168, 175, 178, 180
Fernandez Carvallo, Geronimo, 232–234
Fernandez, Maximo, 179
Fernandez, Pablo, xv, 168, 309
Ferrando, Juan, xv, 163, 178, 182, 266, 309, 344, 361
Ferrando, Magin, 297
Ferrara, Pablo Constable de, 34
Figueroa, Esteban Rodriguez de, 226, 338
Filibusterismo, El, 148, 259
Filipino, xiii, xviii–xxii, 118–119, 148, 150–151, 297, 299–301, 303–304, 343, 345, 352, 364, 366–367

forasteros, 225
Fraternal Order of Knights, 50
French Revolution, 260–262
Friar Estates, 69, 78–82, 85, 358
Fuente, Luis de, 75
Fuentes, Manuel, 282
Fuentes, Tomas, 282
fuero eclesiastico, 81

G
gachupines, 200, 203
Galamino, Agustin, 36
Galdeano, Andres, 94–95
galleon, 46, 73, 114, 211, 218, 344
Galleon Trade, 16, 25, 69, 72, 137, 199, 215, 218, 224
Gant, Clemente, 29, 44, 75
Garchitorena, Angel, 217, 220
Garcia Monroy, Josepha, 273
Garcia Ortiz, Francisco, 273
Garde, Pedro, 293
Garrido, Juan, 199
Genato, Manuel, 278
General de Concordia, 246, 248, 250–251, 362
Giam Kiong, 161
Ginoves y Espinar, Felipe, 285, 296, 366
Glorious Revolution, 1688, 260
Glorious Revolution, 1868, 147, 277–279, 291–292, 365–366
GomBurZa, 301–302
Gomes de los Angeles, Mariano, 86, 271, 273, 286, 288–289, 292, 297–298, 301, 303, 363, 365–367
Gomez Becera, 269
Gomez del Castillo, Gabriel, 73
Gomez, Feliciano, 286, 301
Gomez, Jose, 285–286
Gomez, Juan, 75
Gomez, Juan Cruz, 292, 294, 297, 366–367
Gonsales, Francisco, 75
Gonzaga, Gracio, 279
Gonzales de Pulgar, Juan, 83
Gonzales, Andres, 82
Governor-Generals
   Aguilar, Rafael Maria de,, 268
   Anda y Salazar, Simon de, 86, 115, 248, 250–254, 256–257, 282–283, 361

Arechederra, Juan de, 113, 115
Basco y Vargas, Jose, 137, 253
Bravo de Acuña, Pedro, 10, 12, 17
Bustamante y Bustillo, Fernando de, 301
Claveria y Zaldua, Narciso, 271
Corcuera, Sebastian Hurtado de, 26–30, 46, 51, 335–336
Cuesta, Francisco de la, 239, 242, 247, 358, 361–362
Ezpeleta, Miguel de, 240–241, 248
Fajardo Chacon, Diego, 30, 46, 335
Fajardo de Tenza, Alonso, 18, 20
Folgueras, Mariano Fernandez de, 266
Izquierdo y Gutierrez, Rafael de, 147, 168, 278, 284, 286–287, 289–294, 296, 301, 365–366
Lavezaris, Guido, 210, 216–217
Legazpi, Miguel Lopez de, 69, 207, 210, 212–213, 215–216, 224
Leon, Manuel de, 357
Martinez, Juan Antonio, 257, 267
Oraa Lecumberri, Marcelino de, 293, 367
Ovando, Jose de, 136
Perez de Dasmariñas, Gomez, 218, 339
Perez de Dasmariñas, Luis, 224
Raon, Jose de, 244, 250, 361
Ricafort Palacin y Abarca, Mariano, 86, 314
Rojo, Antonio, 240–241, 243, 248, 253, 360–361
Silva, Fernando de, 20, 22–23, 25
Tavora, Juan Niño de, 21, 25–26
Torre, Carlos Maria de la, 87, 277–283, 290, 316, 365
Torre, Francisco Javier de la, 361
Torre, Gaspar de la, 83
Ursua y Arismendi, Martin de, 242
Zabalburu, Domingo, 240, 242, 247
graduados, 251
gremios, 202
Guanches, 186, 191
Guanzon, Justo, 286
Guardia Civil, 87, 365–366
Guerrero, Gonzalo, 199
Guerrero, Juan Geronimo, ii, xiv, xvii–xviii, xx, 9–10, 12–25, 28–30, 38–39, 73, 75, 106, 115, 128, 333–334, 336
Guevarra, Jose, 281, 366
Guito, N., 279
Guzman, Petronila de, 78

H
Han de San Vicente, Benito, 350
Hao Lang Dao, 172, 176
Hawkins, William, 10
Hermano Compañero, 41
Hermosa (Formosa), 26, 153, 338, 346
Herrera, Diego de, 214
Herrero, Casimiro, 293
Herrero, Juan, 96, 98, 100
Herzog, Tamar, 190, 310, 319, 353
hijos del pais, xviii, xxi, 225–226, 271, 278, 300
Hita y Salazar, Cecilia, 344
Hobbes, Thomas, 260, 310
Hospital Real, 30
House of God, 172
Houy (Huy), Espinosa, 172, 351
Huertas, Felix, 293
Huy, Juan, 173, 175
Huy, Vicente, 158, 161, 163, 166–167
Huyen, Jose, 173
Huyen, Pablo, 173, 175

I
Icaza, Jose, 278
Iglesia y España, Pedro de la, 86
ilustrado, xix, 226
Infante, Vicente, 278
Inocencio, Maximo, 288–289
inquisition, 188, 198
Instituto Filipino, 147
Isla, Juan de la, 211
Islas del Poniente, 31, 209–210, 255
Izquierdo, Javier Gonzalez, 168

J
Jagor, Fedor, 152, 311
Jesuit Expulsion, 46, 130, 133, 244–245, 250–251, 334, 338
Jesus Maria, Antonia de (Antonia Esguerra), 108–109, 112, 343
Jesus, Simon de, 272
jihad, 2
Jimenez, Alonso, 336
Jubera de la Concepcion, Alonso, 88
Junta Apostolica 1539, 206
Junta de Burgos, 194
Junta de Tondo, 218
Junta General de Manila 1586, 34–35, 218, 220
Justinian Code, 184
Juventud Escoral Liberal, 279
Juzgado Primativo de Tierras, 81

K
Kang de Santa Maria, Juan Evangelista, 267
Kangxi Emperor, 157
Katipunan, 300
Kengsun de Ocampo, Joseph, 235, 238–239
Knights
　Alcantara, 10, 26
　Calatrava, 10, 25, 81
　Santiago, 10
　Templar, 2
Knights Hospitallers of St John
　birth, 1–2
　classes, 2
　colors, 5, 8
　crosses, 6–8
　Filipinas, 9–12
　fortresses, 8
　Grand Masters, 1–2, 8, 10–11
　Grand Priories, 2
　investiture, 2, 4

names, 1–2, 8–9

L

La Junta, 278
ladina, 108
Lady of Aranzazu, xix, 113–116, 177, 344
Lady of the Holy Rosary, 46, 61, 115
Lamadrid, Fernando, 285, 288, 294, 296, 366
Lamco, Domingo, 101
Lanco, N., 279
Las Siete Partidas, 184
Laterani Family, 21
latinidad, 122, 134, 143, 146, 273
Laza, Miguel de, 286
Learte, Jose M., 95–96, 99
Leon, Manuel de, 279
Leon, Mauricio de, 282, 286
Leonardo, Felipe, 156
Leverastigui, Justo Claudio, 13
Leyenda Negra (Black Legend), 183
Leyes de Burgos, 196
Liberalism, Classical, 260
limpieza de sangre, xx, 187–188, 200, 205, 207, 228, 274, 364
linaje maculado, 207
Ling de San Bernardo, Tomas, 179
Liongson y Alonso, Francisco, xii–xiii
Liongson y Ocampo, Francisco, xii–xiii
Liongson y Tongio, Francisco, xii, 146
Liongson y Tongio, Pedro, 146
Liongson, Dominique, ii
literado, 154, 158, 166, 349
Loaisa, Garcia Jofre de, 10, 210
Lobo, Jose, 58
Locke, John, 260, 311
Lolomboy Estate, 75, 80, 82–83, 85, 118, 341
Lopez Morquecho, Vicente, 285, 293–294, 296
Lopez, Hernando, 41
Lopez, Tomas, 48
Loranco, Antonio, 161, 163–167
Lorenzana, F. Antonio, 250
Louis XVI, 260, 262
Loyola, 361, 363
Loyzaga, Joaquin Jr, 282
Lozano, Balbino, 296
Luciano, Pablo, 361
Lugo, Fernando, 274
Luo Wenzao, Gregorio (Gregorio Lo Lopez), 49, 156–157, 160, 338, 348–349
Luo, Simon, 158, 161–163
Luzuriaga, Augusto R. de, 301–302
Luzuriaga, Nicolas, 75

M

Mabini, Apolinario, 146
MacCrohon, Manuel, 290, 294
Magalhães, Fernão de (Ferdinand Magellan), 9, 31, 209
Magdalena, Bernabe de, 160
Mah-jun, Pablo, 41
Maharlika, 223, 255
Malabanan, Valerio, 146
Malabon Estate, 80, 85–86
Malanday y Lingahan Estate, 80, 85
Maldonado de San Pedro Martir, Juan, 336
mamluks, 185
Mañago, Juan, 238
Manguerra, Felix, 274
Manila Provincial Council of 1771, 123, 136, 347
Mapa, Gregorio, 279
Mar del Sur, 209
maravides, 188
Marcelino, Isabelo, 273
Marco, Jose E., 301–302
Maria Cristina, 265, 269
Marquez, Gaudencio, 94

Martyrs
  beatified, 162, 179, 337
    Sanz-Orozco Mortar, Eugenio, 180–181, 352
    Verona Ortega, Antonio, 180–181, 352
    Villaverde Andres, Jesus, 180–181, 352
  canonized, 107, 162, 168, 170, 175, 179, 337, 346, 352
    Alcober Figuera, Juan, 160
    Alonso Liciniana, Mateo, 176
    Capillas, Francisco Fernandez de, 154
    Castañeda, Jacinto de, 174, 176, 178
    Cruz, Vicente de la (Luis Shiwosuka), 154
    Delgado, Clemente Ignacio, 179
    Diaz del Rincon, Francisco, 160
    Federich, Francisco Gil de, 176
    Liem de la Paz, Vicente, xiv, xviii, xxi, 115, 153, 169–173, 175–180, 251, 302, 351
    Navarrete, Alfonso de, 154
    Royo Perez, Joaquin, 158, 160
    San Jacinto, Tomas de (Hioji Rokasayemon Nishi), 154
    Santa Maria, Jacob de (Kyusei Gorobioye Tomonaga), 154
    Sanz e Jorda, Pedro Martir, 160
    Serrano Frias, Francisco, 160–161, 164
Masigan, M., 279
Maurente, Ramon, 286
Mauricio, Balbino, 286
Mayor del colegio, 62, 273–274
Mayordomo, Celestino, 276
Mendoza, Agustin, 281–282, 286
Mendoza, Diego de, 10
Mendoza, Felipe de, 128
MEP, 156–157, 172, 331
Mercado Rizal, Francisco, 101
Mercado, Francisco, 101
Mercado, Jose del, 47
mesada ecleciastica, 235, 252
mestizo
  de español, xxi, 24, 39, 129, 142, 205, 223, 225–228, 230–231, 240, 246, 253, 266, 271, 300, 334, 345, 365
  de sangley, xviii, xxi, 45, 84, 86, 129, 224–226, 235, 238, 240–241,

245–246, 251–253, 267, 271, 278, 300, 345, 358, 366
Mexican Provincial Council 1566, First, 206
Mexican Provincial Council 1585, Third, 206
Miao, Pedro, 158, 161, 163, 165–167
Minh Mang, 179
misa cantada de aguinaldo, 113, 115, 344
Misericordia (Hermandad de la Santa Misericordia de Manila), 14, 16–18, 22, 25, 65–66, 72–73, 110, 231–232, 298, 300–301, 333–334, 336, 365
Monarchs of Spain
  Bourbon, 28, 43, 121, 132, 136, 147, 190, 240, 242
    Alfonso XII, 10, 147
    Carlos III, 46, 115, 123, 132, 246–247, 250, 252, 254, 258, 350, 367
    Carlos IV, 10, 262
    Felipe V, 28, 132, 157, 240, 242, 248, 339, 365
    Fernando VI, 115, 248, 250, 262
    Fernando VII, 264–266, 268, 270, 366
    Isabel II, 10, 116, 143, 265, 270, 373
  Habsburg, 28, 43, 121–122, 132, 136, 147, 190, 207, 240, 242, 359
    Carlos I (Charles V Holy Roman Empire), 8, 52, 123, 197–198, 210, 339
    Carlos II, 46, 81, 200, 207, 222, 228, 234–235, 238, 240, 354, 356–357, 359, 363
    Felipe II, 16, 52, 54, 56, 60, 70, 81, 104, 123, 170, 188, 205–207, 209, 212–215, 217–218, 220, 334–335, 338, 341,

360
    Felipe III, 123, 361
    Felipe IV, 22, 25, 46, 123
  Ivrea, 184
    Alfonso X, 184
  Savoy, 285
    Amadeo I, 147, 285
  Trastamara, 52, 186, 191, 193–194, 353, 357
    Fernando V (Fernando II Aragon), 52, 193–194, 357
    Isabel I, 52, 186, 191, 193–194, 353
Monastery of our Lady of the Rosary, 120, 345
Monroe Doctrine, 264
Monteagudo, 99, 268–269, 370
Montesinos, Antonio de, 54, 194, 341
Montesinos, Manuel (Jose), 286, 293, 295–296
Morales, Augustina de, 17, 25, 106
Morales, Geronimo de, 75
Morales, Juan Bautista de, 154
Morales, Ruis de, 17, 25
Moreno de Garcia, Maria, 75, 80
Moret, Segismundo, 146–147, 351
Moro, 26, 212–215, 217–218, 220, 223–225, 228, 358, 360, 362, 367
Moroto, Miguel de, 31
Moscoso y Lara, Francisco, 288
Mosesgeld Santiago, Jose, 282
Mosesgeld Santiago, Pedro, 282
Motte, Pierre Lambert de la, 156
mulato, 58, 191, 199, 201–204, 206, 338
Munarris, Eduardo, 280

N
Narvaez, Panfilo, 199
naturales, xix, xxii, 188, 190–191, 199, 207–208, 226–227, 238–239, 241, 244, 254, 258, 267, 271, 298, 300, 364
Navarrete, Domingo Fernandez, 61, 156, 312
Navarrete, Pedro de, 17, 25–26, 106

Naveda, Clemencia de, 108–109
Neira, Eladio, xv, 168, 312
Nien (Yan), Pablo Domingo, 173, 350
Nieto, Andres, 279
Nieto, Antonio, 234
Nieva, Domingo de, 337, 349
Noblejas, Gregorio, 274
noche triste, 273, 277, 364
Novales, Andres, 267
Nuvilas, 294

O
O'Connor, J.B., 134, 312
obras pias, 14, 45, 69, 72–73, 75, 78, 80, 101, 130, 363
ochavón, 273, 358
Ochoa, Gregorio, 337
Ocio y Viana, Hilario, xv, 162, 168, 174
Octavo, Bonifacio, 285–287, 301, 374–375
Olipon, 256, 361
Oquendo, Sebastian de, 28–29, 41, 44, 336
Order of Preachers
  crisis, 265–266
  foundation, 31
  orders, 104, 106–107
  protectors of the indios, 54, 194–197, 202, 341
  Province of Santa Cruz de Indias, 346
  Province of Santiago, 31, 34
  Province of the Most Holy Rosary, 34–36, 46, 48, 78–80, 102, 104, 107, 110, 118–119, 128, 130, 132–136, 144–148, 153–154, 156, 161–162, 164, 168, 172, 176, 178–180, 221, 230–234, 244, 250, 252, 254, 267–271
  Province St Vincent of Chiapa and Guatemala, 205
  Provincia de Hispania, 270
Order of the Poor Knights of Christ and the Temple of Jerusalem, 2
Orion Estate, 78, 80, 82
Ormaza de Santo Tomas, Juan, 337
orphans (huerfanos), xiv–xv,

13–14, 17–18, 20–21, 24, 26, 29, 38–41, 45, 48, 61, 73, 115, 128, 137, 142, 229–231, 239, 273, 333
Ortiz, Francisco, 38
Ozaeta y Oro, Juan de, 81–82

P
Padre Presidente, 62, 274
Palacios Rubios, Juan de, 194
Palafox y Mendoza, Juan de, 236
Palensuela, Tomas de, 31
Pallas, Francisco, 163–168, 354
Pallu, François, 156, 172
Paraiso, Enrique, 283, 288, 290
pardo, 204
Pardo de Tavera, Joaquin, 276, 279, 287
Parian, 11, 26, 29–30, 35–36, 39, 46, 48, 55, 66, 73–75, 109, 116, 223, 251–252, 268
parrandero, 113
Partido Liberal, 279
pasadiso, 112–113, 118
Pasantia, 133
pase regio, 34, 51, 115, 235, 248, 340
Paso, 142
Pasolo e Isla Estate, 80
Paterno, Maximo, 279–280, 288
Patronato Real, xxi, 51–52, 58, 60–61, 68, 198, 227, 235–236, 242, 247–248, 250–252, 254, 347, 364, 366
Patronato Universal, 248
Patronazgo Real, 17, 26, 28, 31, 45
Pavon Collection, 302
Paz, Fernando de la, 34
Paz, Matias de, 194
Peguero, Juan, 14, 313
Pelaez, Pedro Pablo, 271, 273–278, 291, 371–372
peninsulares, 205, 273, 293–295
pensionista noble, 40
Philippine Republic, First, 145
piao, 157
Piernavieja, Antonio, 301–302
Pigafetta, Antonio, 10
Pilar, Marcelo del, 278, 300
Pilar, Toribio H. del, 287
Pinel, Pedro, 45, 73
Pinto, Maria Ramirez, 66, 75, 342
Plasencia, Juan de, 124, 126–128, 349, 361
Plauchut, Edmund, 284, 376
polo, 84, 86, 222, 224, 255, 340
Polo, Marco, 191
Ponce de Leon, Ignacio, 277
Ponce de Leon, Juan, 192
Popes
Adrian VI, 52, 354
Alexander IV, 8
Alexander VI, 52, 193, 198
Anastasius IV, 2
Benedict XI, 185
Benedict XIV, 115, 156, 164, 248, 250, 347, 353
Benedict XVI, 21, 356
Calixtus II, 1
Clement IX, 157
Clement V, 185
Clement VII, 8
Clement X, 107
Clement XI, 156–157, 242, 248, 354, 358, 365
Clement XII, 130, 244, 358, 364
Clement XIII, 367
Eugene IV, 186
Francis, 356
Gregory XIII, 34, 206
Gregory XV, 129, 170, 339
Honorius III, 31
Innocent II, 2
Innocent VII, 52
Innocent X, 46, 130, 350
Innocent XI, 234, 244, 347, 363–364
John Paul II, 162, 170, 180, 349, 352, 356
John XXIII, 338
Julius III, 128
Leo XII, 266
Leo XIII, 162, 180
Martin V, 185
Nicolas V, 187
Paschal II, 1
Paul III, 197, 341
Paul V, 36, 130
Paul VI, 353
Pius IV, 129, 266
Pius V, 54
Pius VI, 262
Pius X, 180
Pius XII, 353
Urban II, 2
Urban VIII, 130, 170
Zachary, 185
Portilla, Santiago de la, 367
Povedano Collection, 302
Pozaleta, Juan de, 41, 339
Pragmatica, 250
Prat, Ramon, 227
probanza, 188, 205, 207
proceso, 164, 178–179
promotor fiscal, 254, 278, 373
pronunciamiento, 265, 285–286, 296, 369, 374
Propaganda Fide, 156, 166, 168, 170, 179, 353–354
Protector of the Indians, 54, 197, 202, 341
proveedor (purveyor), 16, 18
Puch, Francisco Javier, 367
Puebla Pedrosa, Ceferino, 168
purgatory, 72, 78, 116, 126

Q
Qianlong, 158
Queen of Angels Monastery, 120, 345
Quezon, Manuel, xiv, xx, xxiii, 302
Quianlong, 158
Quiñones, Juan de, 124, 349
quinta, 29

R
Rada, Martin de, 212
Ramos, Jose, 294
Real Audiencia, 18, 26, 81, 182, 210, 222, 246, 273, 336, 347, 350, 363, 367
Real Colegio, xv, 28, 173, 180, 242, 244, 246, 273, 364, 371–372
Real Sociedad Economica Filipina de Amigos del Pais, 137, 350
Reconquista, 51, 58, 184, 191, 194
reduccion, 52, 58, 213
Regidor, Antonio Maria, 285, 288, 293–296, 301, 372–373, 375–376
Regio Vicariato Indiano, 52
releccion, 274, 372
repartimiento, 52, 192, 213, 340
republica, 198

Requerimiento, 196–197, 358
rescatado, 220
residencia, 30, 337, 366
Resurreccion, Angel, 280
Reyes, Ariston, 280
Reyes, Crisanto de los, 283, 288, 290
Reyes, Dionisio Vicente de los, 253–254
Reyes, Juan, 279
Ribera y Guzman, Nicolas de, 28
Ringmann, Matthias, 192
Rizal, Jose, 259, 278, 300, 302–303, 314
Rizal, Paciano, 280
Robles, Ambrosio, 282
Robles, Antonio, 115
Rocha, Ignacio, 279, 283
Rocha, Lorenzo, 279, 283
Rodriguez Varela, Luis, 267
Rodriguez, Cristobal, 115
Rodriguez, Lorenzo, 168
Rodriguez, Nicolas, 286
Rodriguez, Pedro, 337
Rojas, Domingo, 267
Rojas, Fernando, 295
Romero, Gonzalo, 18
Romulo, Carlos P., 285
Rosario, Claudio Diaz del, 88
Rosario, Domingo del, 368
Rosario, Esteban del, 354, 368
Rosario, Felix Uan del, 354
Rosario, Francisco Borja del, 254
Rosario, Francisco del, 157
Rosario, Hermogenes del, 280
Rosario, Joaquin del, 251, 367
Rosario, Maria del, 158
Rosario, Tomas Guillermo del, 150–151, 352
Rosario, Vicente del, 287
Rosary, 61, 64, 110, 126, 128, 230, 342
Rosello, Tomas, 269
Royo, Guillermo, 93
Rufian, Antonio, 286, 293, 295–296, 374
Rule of St Augustine, 1–2, 31, 44
Rule of St Benedict, 2

S
Saavedra Ceron, Alvaro de, 209
Sagrada Familia, Colegio-Asilo de la, 119
Sagrado Corazon de Jesus, Ana del, 119
Sagrario, 243, 278, 287
Saguinsin, Bartolome, 256
Sahagun y Santa Cruz, Manuel Fernandez de, 247, 364
Saint John Lateran, Basilica, 21
Saint John Lateran, Convent, 169
Saints
   Albert the Great, 123
   Alcantara, Pedro de, 107
   Aquino, Tomas, 113, 123, 130, 132, 134
   Avila, Teresa de, 107
   Clairvaux, Bernard of, 2
   Cruz, Juan de la, 107
   Guzman, Dominic, 31, 60–61, 65, 75, 112, 134, 158, 228, 256
   John the Baptist, xiv, 1, 5, 13, 21, 99, 160
   John the Evangelist, 21
   Lima, Rosa de, 107
   Porres, Martin de, 38, 106, 180, 338
   Sena, Catalina de, 107
Sakoku Edict, 154
Sala, Tomas, 179
Salazar, Ambrosio, 282
Salazar, Lorenzo, 282
Salazar, Pedro de Augusto, 73
Salazar, Vicente, xv, 38, 40, 44, 68, 109, 342, 346
Saldua, Francisco, 285, 288, 290, 295, 297–298, 301, 374–376
Salic Law, 265
Salvatierra, Cristobal de, 54
Salvidea, Melecio, 276
Salzedo, Mariana de, 108–109
Samaniego, Irineo, 267, 375
San Agustin, Gaspar de, 255–257, 368
San Antonio, Juan Francisco de, 124, 239, 315
San Carlos, Colegio Seminario de, 243, 246–247, 276, 278, 371
San Clemente, Colegio Seminario de, 242, 364

San Felipe de Austria, Colegio, 26, 28, 335
San Felipe, Colegio Seminario de, 242, 244, 364
San Felipe, Fort, 259, 286–287, 293–295
San Francisco de Malabon Estate, 80, 86, 271
San Gabriel de Binondo, 232, 251, 267–268
San Gabriel, Baluarte de, 66, 116, 120
San Gabriel, Hospital de, 36, 55, 338, 347
San Ignacio, Colegio Maximo de, 46, 127, 129, 227, 244, 246, 257, 349–350, 364
San Isidro de Biñan Estate, 80, 82, 84–85, 102, 343, 363
San Jacinto, Colegio de, 119
San Jacinto, Hospicio de, 36, 221–222, 228
San Jose, Colegio de, 17, 36, 44, 61, 65–66, 81, 128–129, 147, 227, 243–244, 246–247, 283, 339, 347, 371
San Jose, Confradia de, 367, 375
San Juan Bautista de Calamba Estate, 80, 85, 102, 358, 363
San Juan de Letran, Colegio de Guam, 335
San Juan de Letran, Colegio de Manila
   alumni, 18, 23–24, 41, 48–49, 73–75, 128, 156–167, 173–174, 176, 178–180, 230–235, 238–239, 243, 247, 252–254, 267, 273–274, 276–285, 287–290, 297–299, 303–304
   colors, xiv, 44
   cross, xiv, 7, 9
   early supporters, 14, 16–18, 24–28, 63, 75, 78
   locations, 45–46, 48, 66, 76–77
   motto, 24, 67, 304
   names, xiv–xv, 13, 21–22, 28–29, 39
   petitions, 17–20, 22–24, 246
   uniforms, 14, 44–45, 64, 132, 143

San Juan de Letran, Colegio de Mexico, 18, 205, 335
San Juan de Letran, Iglesia de, 112–113, 115–118
San Juan de Letran, sea vessels, 211
San Miguel, Manuel de, 90
San Miguel, Mariano de, 90
San Pedro, Domingo de, 156
Sanchez, Alfonso, 34, 54
Sanchez, Gervasio, 287–288
Sanciangco y Gozon Gregorio, 280, 300
Sanctos Reyes, Iglesia de, 36, 251, 268
Sangley, 11, 17, 26, 35–36, 38–39, 41, 48, 55, 61, 75, 84, 86, 102, 109, 223–226, 231, 238, 252, 361, 366–368
Sanlucas, Teodoro de, 73
Santa Catalina de Matsuyama, Colegio de, 348
Santa Catalina de Sena, Beaterio y Colegio de, xvi, 103–104, 107–113, 116, 118–120, 343, 346, 348
Santa Catalina, Bernardo Navarro de, 338
Santa Clara, Monasterio de, 81, 104, 106, 110, 112, 116, 336, 346
Santa Cruz de Malabon Estate, 80, 86, 271
Santa Cruz de Tlatelolco, Colegio de, 205–206
Santa Cruz, Baltasar de, xv, 275, 342
Santa Cruz, Eugenio de, 256
Santa Cruz, Seminario de, 179
Santa Infancia, Asilo de, 119
Santa Isabel, Colegio de, 16–17, 334, 373
Santa Maria ad Latinos, 1
Santa Maria Caballero, Antonio de, 353
Santa Maria de Pandi Estate, 80, 83, 85–86, 343
Santa Maria, Antonio, 340
Santa Maria, Diego de, ii, xiv, xvi, xix, xxi, 28–29, 31–36, 38–41, 44, 48–50, 128, 180, 227
Santa Maria, Juan de, 108
Santa Maria, Mariano, 276

Santa Maria, Sebastiana de, 108–109, 346
Santa Mesa, 16–17, 73
Santa Potenciana, Seminario de, 16–17, 110, 279, 334
Santa Rosa Estate, 80, 85, 343, 363
Santa Rosa, Blas de, 238–239
Santa Rosa, Joaquin, 354
Santa Rosa, Juan de, 173
Santa Teresa, Jose de, 368
Santiago, 90, 92
Santiago, Francisco de, 89
Santiago, Luciano P. R., 238, 315, 321, 346, 364, 368
Santisimo Rosario de Madrid, Beaterio y Colegio del, 119
Santísimo Rosario, Colegio de, 119
Santo Domingo de Ocaña, 268, 270, 346, 349, 356
Santo Domingo, Convento de, xv, 28–29, 35–36, 38, 41, 46, 61, 66, 70, 74–75, 108–109, 116, 118, 130, 158, 161, 174–175, 267, 294, 338, 347, 352–353, 357–358, 362–363, 368
Santo Domingo, Dionisio, 253–254
Santo Domingo, Dominican Republic, 192
Santo Domingo, Iglesia de, 29, 35, 64, 109, 116, 344, 362
Santo Domingo, Juan de, 108–109, 112–113, 116, 316, 345–346, 362
Santo Domingo, Juan de, 179
Santo Tomas de Avila, 211, 270, 349, 356
Santo Tomas, Colegio-Universidad de, xv–xvi, xxii, 17, 20, 35–36, 38, 41, 44–46, 48–49, 61, 66, 70, 78, 80–82, 84, 103, 113, 118, 128, 130, 132–134, 142, 144–147, 150, 154, 157, 164, 173, 228–232, 235, 238–239, 243–244, 246–247, 252, 257, 273–274, 276, 338–339, 343, 347, 350–353, 356, 362–364, 366, 368, 371–372, 375

Santos, Francisco Mariano de los, 252–253
Santos, Luis de los (Luis Parang), 86, 371
Santos, Matias de los, 157
Sawa, Horacio, 286, 296
Schism of Fuan, 162–168, 174, 182, 354
Schumacher, John, 277, 302, 364
Scott, William Henry, 302
Secular clergy, xix–xx, xxii, 41, 48, 54, 56, 58, 61, 65, 67, 81, 103, 157, 170, 172, 182, 205, 220, 227, 229, 231, 234–236, 238–240, 243, 245–248, 250–254, 257–259, 266, 268–271, 273–274, 276–278, 283–284, 287, 291–292, 300, 363–364, 367–368, 371, 373
sei-chai (xucai), 158, 353
seminario, 16, 21, 24–26, 39, 121, 179, 207, 242, 246, 269–270, 276, 335, 364
seminario de indios, 21, 35, 127
señorios eclesiastico, 265
Sentencia Estatuto, 188
Serra, Bartolome, 287–288
Serrano, Francisco, 146, 284
Serrano, Francisco de, 157
Sevilla, Mariano, 274, 276, 287
shahid, 2
Sidoti, Gianbattista, 240, 242
Sierra y Osorio, Juan de, 81–82
Silva, Geronimo de, 11
Silvestre, Juan (Juan Upay), 86
simbang gabi, 113
sistema de castas, 198–204, 223, 225–226, 264, 273, 276
situado, 25
Slavery, 54, 183–187, 191–198, 200, 207, 209, 212–223
Soledad, Filomena de la, 119, 348
Soria de San Antonio, Marcos, 337
Soria, Diego de, 337
Soriano, Ramon, 280
Sotelo de Morales, Pedro, 13
Soto, Felipe de, 75
Soto, Pedro de, 337

Sotomayor, Juan Infante de, 78
students
    agraciado, 142
    artista, 133
    becario, 45, 230, 232, 235, 240, 242, 244, 273
    canonista, 142
    capista, 61, 141, 220
    colegiales, ii, xv, 45, 51, 62, 64, 66, 132, 142, 230, 235, 238, 240, 244, 246–247, 252, 267, 273–274, 276, 302, 368, 371
    cuartista, 142
    esculapio, 142
    externo, 45, 142
    famulo, 61, 142
    filosofo, 142
    fisico, 142
    gramático, 133, 142
    interno, 45
    legista, 142
    librero, v
    logico, 142
    manteista, 230–231, 235
    metafisico, 142
    minimista, 142
    moralista, 142
    oficios mecanico, 49
    oracionista, 142
    porcionista, 45, 230, 235, 244
    portero, 49, 142
    pupilo, 142
    quintista, 142
    sacristan, 49, 142
    temporista, 142
    teologo, 133, 142
Sultan Suleiman the Magnificent, 8
superior eclesiastico, 17–18
superior secular, 18

T
tanores, 225
Tecson, Sisenando, 280
Tenochtitlan, 197
Teodoro, Teodorico, 280
tepuzque, 69, 342
Tercer Orden de San Francisco, 14, 17, 22, 25, 72, 284, 334, 336
Terradillos, Diego, 161, 164–166, 168, 354
Theisling, Ludwig, 119
Thenorio, Bartolome, 45
Thi Kong, Juan, 173
Thieng, Pedro Martir, 173
Tierra Firme, 192–193, 353
timawa (timaua), 224, 256
Tison, Domiciano, 280
Tison, Francisco, 280, 282
Tokugawa Ieyasu Expulsion Edict 1614, 154
Tonkin Pamphlet, 174
Toro, Pasolo e Isla Estate, 80, 85
Torquemada, Tomas de, 189
Torre, Bernardo de la, 211
Torres, Diego de, 74–75
Torres, Juan de, 31, 75
Tournon, Charles Thomas Maillard de, 240, 242
Treaty of Tordesillas, 52, 210
Treaty of Zaragoza, 210, 214, 360
Treserra, Domingo, 294
Tribunal de Comercio (del Consulado), 137, 347, 350
Trinh Cuong, 176
Trinh Sam, 176

U
Uan del Rosario, Felix, 354
Universalis Cosmographia, 192
Universidad de Filipinas, 147
Urdaneta, Andres, 53, 210, 212, 355, 360
Uriarte, Juan Bautista, 16, 78

V
Valderrama, Juan Saavedra de, 13
Valdes, Jose, xiv–xv, xxi, 13, 232, 234, 339
Vales, N., 280
Valin, Felipe, 86
vandala (bandala), 86, 340
Varela, Jose, 93–95
vasallos, 190
Vasquez, Agustin, 286–287
vecinos, 14, 17, 25, 30, 46, 69, 101, 190–191, 204, 218, 220, 223–224, 368
Ventura, Balbino, 280
Vera, Ana de, 104
Vergara, Francisco Engracio, 293, 374–375
Vespucci, Amerigo, 192

vicar forane, 86, 239, 271, 274, 287, 371
vice patrons, 25–30, 58, 60, 147, 251, 268, 336, 347, 364
Victoria, 11
Victoria, Santiago de, 368
Victorino, Bernabe, 280
Vilanova, Pedro, 294
villa, 58, 114, 207, 223, 272
Villa, Mateo de, 36
Villabrille, Faustino, 374
Villafama, Ursula de, 74
Villalobos, Ruy Lopez de, 209–211
villancico, 113
Villaroel, Fidel, 62, 107, 137, 280, 364
Villaruel, Florentino, 280
Villas, Francisco, 93–95
Villegas, Alonso de, 50
Villegas, Juan, 58–60
Villiers l'Isle-Adam, Philippe de, 9, 11
visita (visitation), 58, 235–236, 247–248, 250–252, 254, 278, 347, 364, 367
Visitacion, Catalina de la, 119, 348
Vries, Maarten Gerritz, 46

W
Waldseemuller, Martin, 192

Y
Yan, Agustin, 161
Yan, Antonio, 158, 161
Yan, Pedro, 158, 160–167, 354
Yang Guanxian, 156
Yongzheng, 158
Yucatan, 197, 199

Z
Zaldierna de Mariaca, Pedro, 70
zambo, 199–204
Zamora, Jacinto, ii, 180, 276, 278, 283, 287–290, 297–298, 301, 303, 372, 374–375
Zamora, Jeronimo de, 39
Zapotecas, 199
Zarate, Pedro de, 75
Zobel, Jacobo, 279
Zubiri, Manuel, 93

www.ingramcontent.com/pod-product-compliance
Lightning Source LLC
Chambersburg PA
CBHW060302010526
44108CB00042B/2612